D1157390

HARCOURT BRACE & COMPANY
1919–
1994
SEVENTY-FIVE YEARS

THE FLOWER AND THE NETTLE

Books by Anne Morrow Lindbergh

North to the Orient

Listen! The Wind

The Wave of the Future

The Steep Ascent

Gift from the Sea

The Unicorn

Dearly Beloved

Earth Shine

Bring Me a Unicorn

Hour of Gold, Hour of Lead

Locked Rooms and Open Doors

The Flower and the Nettle

War Within and Without

THE FLOWER
AND THE NETTLE

Diaries
and Letters
of
Anne Morrow Lindbergh

1936-1939

A Harvest Book
A Helen and Kurt Wolff Book
Harcourt Brace & Company
San Diego   New York   London

Requests for permission to make copies of any part of the
work should be mailed to: Permissions Department,
Harcourt Brace & Company, 6277 Sea Harbor Drive,
Orlando, Florida 32887-6777.

W. B. Yeats's lines on page 545 are from "Coole Park, 1929"
from *The Collected Poems* and are reprinted by permission of
Macmillan Publishing Co., Inc., M. B. Yeats, Miss Anne
Yeats, and Macmillan of London and Basingstoke, copyright
1933 by Macmillan Publishing Co., Inc., renewed 1961 by
Bertha Georgie Yeats.

Library of Congress Cataloging-in-Publication Data
Lindbergh, Anne Morrow, 1906–
The flower and the nettle.
Continuation of the author's Locked rooms and open doors.
"A Helen and Kurt Wolff book."
Includes index.
1. Lindbergh, Anne Morrow, 1906–   —Diaries.
2. Lindbergh, Anne Morrow, 1906–   —Correspondence.
I. Title.
PS3523.I516Z516   1976   818'.5'209[B]   75-25708

ISBN 0-15-631942-X

Printed in the United States of America

First Harvest edition 1994

A B C D E

Editorial Note

The diary and letter material in this book has been cut for repetition and corrected for readability. Since this is a personal rather than a historical record, the footnotes were kept, in general, contemporary with the diary and purposely brief, confined to information essential to understanding the text.

The following abbreviations have been used throughout:

D.W.M.—Dwight W. Morrow

E.C.M.—Elizabeth Cutter Morrow

E.R.M.M.—Elisabeth Reeve Morrow Morgan

C.C.M.M.—Constance Cutter Morrow Morgan

E.L.L.L.—Evangeline Lodge Land Lindbergh

A.M.L.—Anne Morrow Lindbergh

C.A.L.—Charles A. Lindbergh

ILLUSTRATIONS

Illustrations

Charles Lindbergh and Jon, Christmas, 1936

Anne Lindbergh, Jon, Thor, and Skean, 1937

Segesta, Sicily

Airport at Raipur, India

Udaipur, India

Charles Lindbergh with Jon, spring, 1937

Anne Lindbergh with Jon and Skean

Long Barn, spring, 1937

Charles Lindbergh with Jon

Anne Lindbergh and Land, June, 1937

Anne Lindbergh with Land and Thor

Long Barn, summer, 1937

Anne Lindbergh with Land and Jon, 1937

Long Barn, summer, 1937

Jon in his peat igloo

Constance Morrow Morgan, June, 1937

Charles Lindbergh with Jon, fall, 1937

The Lindberghs at Prien airport, 1937

Baroness Cramer-Klett, Charles Lindbergh,
Major and Frau Braun, Prien, 1937

Charles Lindbergh with Frau Braun

Between pages 512 and 513

Portrait of Charles Lindbergh by Robert Brackman, 1938

Approach to Illiec at low tide

Work on Illiec grounds

Entering Illiec

Illiec, house and chapel

Mrs. Dwight Morrow with Land, 1938

Mrs. Dwight Morrow, Anne Lindbergh, Land, Thor, and Skean

Illustrations

INTRODUCTION

The Flower

The earlier volumes of my Diaries and Letters cover my youth
within a sheltered and closely knit family in the once small town
of Englewood, New Jersey. Although Englewood was our home,
we shuttled back and forth to a New York City apartment for
the work week when my father became a partner of J.P. Morgan
& Co. During my last year at Smith College (1927–1928) my
father was appointed Ambassador to Mexico. For Christmas vacation, those of us left behind in school journeyed to Mexico City to
join the family. Here I met—in awe and tongue-tied shyness—
Charles Lindbergh, who had made the first solo flight over the
Atlantic the spring before and was invited to Mexico City by my
father as part of a "goodwill" flight to Central and South America
in his single-engined plane, *The Spirit of St. Louis*.

Less than a year later, I was overwhelmed when he telephoned
me in New Jersey and, following a week or two of flying jaunts,
asked me to marry him. Our wedding, which we succeeded in
keeping a private family occasion, was on May 27, 1929 and was
swiftly followed by a continuation of my husband's flying career.
I accompanied him on survey flights across the continent, not yet
spanned by commercial air routes, for T.A.T. (later T.W.A.),
then around the Caribbean, inaugurating Pan American's pioneering air-mail service, and in the following years we flew across
Canada and Alaska, to study routes "north to the Orient," and
later across Greenland and Iceland, around the North Atlantic,
investigating possible air terminals for Pan American's first trans-
Atlantic commercial air service.

The early years of our marriage were not all golden adventure. Both of us very private individuals, we were thrown into the glare of publicity and were pursued by newspaper reporters and a public curious for every detail of our private lives. We could not walk the streets, go into restaurants together, or shop like normal people. Experiencing a kind of publicity hitherto known only by royal families, Presidents, or movie stars, we had none of the official protection of public figures. We tried unsuccessfully to separate our private lives from our public flying lives and started to make our home in the country near Princeton, New Jersey.

The climax of our struggle to live as ordinary citizens came when our first baby was kidnapped from our newly built house on March 1st, 1932. After months of fruitless negotiation and search, his dead body was found several miles from our place. The "hour of gold" was suddenly turned into an "hour of lead." Our second son, Jon, was born in August of the same year in my mother's house in New Jersey where we had retreated for security and privacy, but we continued to be hounded by publicity and curiosity seekers, and even by letters threatening our new baby. The pressures mounted in the succeeding three years during the arrest and trial of Bruno Hauptmann, who was convicted in 1935 of the kidnapping and murder of the baby. In an attempt to find a normal life for our new son and ourselves, we left the country in December of that year in carefully guarded secrecy, for an indefinite stay in England.

Volume IV starts after our arrival in Liverpool, where we visited first in Wales with the generous welcoming family of Aubrey Morgan, husband of my older sister, Elisabeth, who had died of pneumonia the year before. The new year 1936 begins with our attempts to find a base of our own abroad.

Our search for peace and privacy was at last successful. The years in Europe gave us private happiness as we had never experienced it before. We had two remarkable homes. The first one, Long Barn, an old and rambling reconstructed barn and cottage, belonged to Harold Nicolson and his wife, Victoria (Vita) Sackville-West, near Sevenoaks, Kent. Here, in the terraced garden and rolling countryside, our son Jon could play freely without a guard; I could work at a new book about our flights around the North Atlantic (*Listen, the Wind*) and my husband could continue the scientific study and research he had started with Dr. Carrel of the Rockefeller Institute in New York City. To this idyllic spot I brought home our third son, Land, born in London on May 12, 1937. With Long Barn as a secure base, we were free to travel about Europe, to Paris, to Italy, to India.

Eventually we moved to France into our second remarkable place, a wild rocky island off the coast of Brittany near Ile St. Gildas, owned by the Carrels. In this beautiful and isolated setting my husband could pursue his discussions and experiments on tissue culture and the perfusion of organs, while I worked, happily and energetically, to bring up a family in a turreted stone house, built in the last century, which had neither heat, plumbing, nor electricity. (The "simple" life that many men extol, I learned that first summer, is extremely complicated for women.)

I am deeply grateful to the British and the French for this interim of private peace and happiness. To them I owe among the happiest years of my life. I emerged from my "locked rooms" into the freedom of personality and strength that happiness in personal life brings. But the expansion was not only in personal life—the harmonious home, the second book, the third child—but also into the outer environment.

The environment of England and France in the pre-war years of 1936 and 1937, although outwardly peaceful, stimulating, and sympathetic to us, was under the surface, as we discovered, uncertain and troubled, overshadowed by the threat of the most terrible war the world was to experience. We soon began to be aware of the rumblings of the storm. The civil war in Spain had already erupted in 1936, and by 1938, with the rising Nazi power in Germany, it became obvious that private peace and happiness were threatened not only for everyone in Europe but that—even if one were protected from the direct threat—in some mysterious rule of inter-relation, private peace and happiness were not enough. The pre-war years in Europe were those in which I began to learn this hard lesson.

The Nettle

I have come to a difficult point in the project of publishing my diaries and letters, one which I anticipated when I started the work and even discussed in an early introduction. When one decides to leave a record of one's life there are several choices open: a biography, an autobiography, or the untouched diaries and letters. There are advantages and disadvantages to any road taken. A biography or autobiography is shorter, better expressed, clearer for reader and writer alike. If done by the subject herself, the account can be written in maturity with all the advantages of a lifetime of technical experience, skillful approach, and wise hindsight. Errors in judgment and awkward blunders can be omitted, slurred over, smoothed out until the image which is left is more complimentary to the writer and more popular with the reader. The temptation is great and often unconscious to somewhat falsify and touch up the original picture. One historical figure reputedly refused to write his memoirs because, as he remarked tersely, "I have nothing to hide."

It would have been easier, and far kinder to myself and my husband, if I had written a condensed, softened, and retouched autobiography, omitting what I disliked, adding later knowledge, creating, in fact, the desired pleasant image I wanted to remain in the minds of my readers and posterity.

But in my life I have become sickened with images. Fame always creates images around its victims or heroes. "Fame," as Rilke once said, "is the sum of the misunderstanding that gathers around a new name." We have been the victims—not entirely blamelessly—of images, over-sugary and bitterly sour, for almost fifty years. In these volumes, I wanted above all to dispel the images, both good and bad, to give our lives as they were—or, at least, as they seemed to me *then,* not now in retrospect.

In this context I think of an acutely perceptive conversation from a novel of Max Frisch.[1] At some point in the story the wife says to the husband, "You've made an image of me . . . a complete and final image . . . not for nothing does it say in the Commandments 'Thou shalt not make unto thee any image' . . . Every image is a sin." This remark seems to me profoundly true. It is not only those in the limelight who are trapped by images. Even in daily life we enclose those nearest to us in images we find convenient. Husbands compress wives into the desired pattern ("It's not like you to do this"). Wives pin down husbands ("That's a husband's job"). We dress our children in images almost as soon as they are born. And, unfortunately, children learn early to fasten images onto their parents, often with the unconscious and grateful acquiescence of their elders. The roles into which we lock the sexes are images that are useful for society. And we all know those tragic images that are focussed onto entire nations or races. The Nazis threw false images on the Jews; East Africans, on the Hindus; and many members of the white race, inside and outside of America, still see the black race through distorted images.

There are also images made of whole periods of history, especially times of conflict when deep emotions are aroused and idealistic hopes or fears distort the realities and paint an oversimplified picture for posterity. The pre-war years in Europe fall into such a period and my diaries may bring to light some forgotten aspects of that troubled era.

For the post-war generation, however, it is necessary first to give a factual outline of the historical events preceding and following our entrance into the Old World in 1936. Hitler had been in power for three years as Chancellor of Germany's Weimar Republic. He had already started his strategic program for the "regeneration" of Germany. In May of 1933 he launched his world campaign diplomatically with a much publicized "Peace Speech," which quoted the Versailles peacemakers' own slogans of "self-determination" and a "just peace" to defend his case for a rebuilt Germany. His latest and most critical biographer, Joachim Fest, analyzes the effect of this speech in the following words: "So great was the general gratification at Hitler's moderation that no one detected the warning contained within his speech. Along with the London *Times* many influential voices throughout the world supported Hitler's demand that Germany be treated on a footing of equality with the other powers."[2]

Having prepared his ground psychologically, Hitler then withdrew from the League of Nations and the Disarmament Conference. In June of 1934, he consolidated his power by the "blood purge" of Röhm's Storm Troopers. His next step in March of 1935 was to hold a plebiscite in the Saarland, then administered by the League of Nations. The result of this plebiscite showed the region to be overwhelmingly in favor of reincorporation within the German Reich. On the strength of this success, Hitler repudiated the arms provision of the Treaty of Versailles and reintroduced conscription in Germany. In the same year Mussolini, who had been promised by secret treaties (the Hoare-Laval Agreements) economic control in Abyssinia, having failed to obtain satisfaction through the League, invaded Abyssinia and quickly overcame Haile Selassie's African warriors; Addis Ababa fell in 1936.

In response, the League of Nations, led by Great Britain, enforced economic sanctions against Italy, a move which had no effect on the campaign but diplomatically led to the Rome-Berlin Axis Agreement of 1936. When France was about to conclude a countering agreement in the Franco-Soviet Pact of 1936, Hitler denounced the pact as a violation of the Treaty of Locarno, and, in retaliation, German troops reoccupied the demilitarized Rhineland. This startling move was accompanied by pledges of good behavior and offers of alliances for twenty-five years between Germany and most of her neighbors.

"The occupation," to quote a contemporary British diary, "made a tremendous sensation in England, but it was soon clear that the great majority were averse to taking any counterstep which might involve the risk of war."[3] "The Paris government," according to Fest, "did consider a military counterblow . . . but shrank from general mobilization in view of the prevailing pacifist mood. . . . The British," he adds, "thought that the Germans were merely returning 'to their own back garden.' "[4] Most historians agree that the occupation of the Rhineland was the last opportunity to say "No" to the dictator without provoking general war.

The years from March 1936 to March 1938, according to the war historian J. W. Wheeler-Bennett (now Sir John Wheeler-Bennett), "were the 'respectable years' of the Nazi Revolution, and Hitler took full advantage of them. He indulged in no more outbursts of international violence but confined himself to activities of diplomacy."[5] The European nations were reassured by Hitler's repeated denials that the Nazis had any plans for territorial conquests. Respect for other nationalities was still the declared principle of Nazism. Foreign diplomats flocked to Berlin and admired the Socialist programs of National Socialism; the reduction of unemployment, the establishment and extension of the Labor Service, where boys of all classes worked together in the reclaiming of swamps and wetlands, reforestation, building *autobahns,* and regulating streams. They inspected institutions to provide labor with new housing, vacation travel, sports festivals, and training courses.

Many diplomats had interviews with Hitler, among them Anthony Eden, John Simon, Mussolini, André François-Poncet, Lloyd George, Thomas Jones, a former member of his Secretariat, and the historian, Arnold Toynbee. Thomas Jones reports Toynbee's impressions, which corroborated his own, in his diary of March 8, 1936: "I went this morning for a walk with Toynbee—[who] has just returned from a visit to Germany where he lectured at Bonn, Berlin, and Hamburg. He had an interview with Hitler which lasted 1¾ hours. He is convinced of his sincerity in desiring peace in Europe and close friendship with England."[6]

There were other countering voices of warning, particularly in the United States, where the first wave of Jewish refugees had arrived with stories of repression and the tightening of anti-Semitic measures. Abraham Flexner was outspoken in admonishing his friend Thomas Jones not to trust Hitler. There were also courageous opposing voices in England who warned of the growing strength of Germany's military machine, especially her air power. Winston Churchill was a staunch leader of dissent. Nevile Henderson, as British Ambassador in Berlin, consistently argued for rearmament as a back-up to the peace policy to which he was committed by Baldwin as well as Chamberlain. Roy Fedden (chief engineer of the Bristol Aeroplane Co. Ltd., 1920–1942), urged the government to pursue a really vigorous rearmament program.[7] But on the whole the warnings fell on deaf ears.

C.A.L. was one of this company of early-warning signalers. He did not initiate his exploratory trips around Europe, but was called into them in 1936 by a request from Colonel (then Major) Truman Smith, Military Attaché in Berlin, who was unable to obtain the detailed information he needed for U.S. Intelligence, particularly about the tremendous expansion of Germany's Air Force. In essence, C.A.L. reported that Germany's strength in military aviation was greater than that of all other European countries combined, and that the U.S. was the only country in the world capable of competing with Germany in aviation.[8]

Only the most inexperienced or else biassed observer would credit the stories bandied about in newspapers or thundered by politicians in Washington that C.A.L. was jockeying around Europe on his own, accepting invitations from Göring, being flattered and brainwashed by the Nazis to their point of view. On the contrary, every one of C.A.L.'s trips to Germany, France, Russia, and Czechoslovakia was not only "cleared" by the U.S. embassies in Europe, but also in most cases engineered by them in order to get air intelligence that was desperately needed and difficult to obtain any other way. We made three trips to Germany in 1936, 1937, and 1938 for U.S. Intelligence. C.A.L. made two trips to Berlin in 1938 and early 1939 at the request of the French government in order to sound out the Germans on a plan proposed by the French Air Minister to purchase German engines for French planes.

In Germany C.A.L. never met Hitler and he met Göring only three or four times, always at large formal occasions, never alone. (The facts belie the rumors of friendship.) His talks were with World War I ace, Ernst Udet, and with Erhard Milch (formerly head of Lufthansa Civil Airline and later Inspector-General of the Luftwaffe and State Secretary).

There is no doubt that Göring did "use" C.A.L. to show off his air production, anticipating that stories of its strength would spread abroad and delay opposition to Hitler's aggressive program. But a double game was being played at the same time by U.S. Intelligence. Even the notorious dinner in Berlin given by U.S. Ambassador Hugh Wilson, where Göring unexpectedly presented a medal to C.A.L., was part of a diplomatic maneuver.

"The American Ambassador," to quote Colonel Smith's Intelligence Report, "was most anxious at this time [October 1938] to establish friendly personal relations with Göring. This he had not yet been able to do, because of Foreign Minister Ribbentrop's jealousy of his own prerogatives, especially that of himself handling all diplomatic matters with foreign embassies. Mr. Wilson saw in a visit by Lindbergh the chance to entertain Göring in the American Embassy without Ribbentrop's presence. The Ambassador further informed the military attaché that he hoped to obtain, at such a dinner, Göring's support for certain measures especially desired by the State Department concerning the easing of the financial plight of the large number of Jews who were being forced to emigrate from Germany in a penniless condition. Mr. Wilson felt that Göring was about the only leader in the Nazi government who might be won over to favor such a humanitarian measure."[9]

In the words of the diary of the Attaché's wife, "the dinner therefore had a very serious purpose, and Charles was to be the bait."

The civil decoration was presented to C.A.L. "for his services to the aviation of the world and particularly for his historic 1927 solo flight across the Atlantic." The presentation was not mentioned before the dinner to any American, including Ambassador Wilson or C.A.L. It was a complete surprise. Under the circumstances, as Ambassador Wilson later wrote to C.A.L., there was no alternative to accepting the medal at that time. It would have torpedoed the purpose of the dinner and put an end to any further Intelligence investigations by C.A.L. Needless to say, he never wore the medal and it was sent to be stored with all his other 1927 medals in the Jefferson Memorial Museum in St. Louis. Germany was the only European power which had not awarded him a decoration at that time. In the heat of pre-war emotions— and even to this day—C.A.L. has been accused of accepting a medal from Göring as though it were a deliberate act of approval of the Nazi regime, or even a reward for services rendered to them, when, in fact, it was an unforeseen incident that took place in the course of his duties while carrying out a planned mission for U.S. Intelligence.

This is not to deny that we were indeed newcomers to the European scene. We had never visited Germany before (except for my own visit as a child) and we had visited Russia only once briefly. We could not speak or read German or Russian, and in the capitals we visited we met chiefly members of the Diplomatic Corps and Air Force officers of the country. Air Force personnel are much the same all over the world and usually of very high dedication and valor, which we felt to be the case in both Russia and Germany. In those days, a kind of international brotherhood of airmen existed much as it exists today among astronauts. In official circles foreign affairs were not mentioned by the German air officers.

In diplomatic circles, however, it was rumored that Milch was partly Jewish, and it was well known that Göring waived the anti-Semitic restrictions when he wanted able men or women in whatever field. This fact is commented upon by J. W. Wheeler-Bennett. "Certain outstanding non-Aryan officers were advised to transfer to the Air Force, where the powerful influence of Hermann Göring, who never took his anti-Semitism seriously when a case of technical ability was involved, afforded a safer protection than the Army."[10]

Our naïveté, however, if such it was, should be placed in the context of the time. The atmosphere we moved through in the embassies of Europe was pervaded by one aim: the achievement of peace by negotiation. As Bruce Lockhart wrote in 1938: "I met no minister, no public man who did not believe that the key to European peace was to be found in an Anglo-German understanding."[11] The same theme is repeated in François-Poncet's account: "The Democratic peoples no less than their governments entertained feelings which stand as a keystone to the whole period: a basic pacifism, an aversion to permitting Europe to plunge into a general war. They were inclined to believe that peace was worth safeguarding even at the price of sacrifices, however painful."[12]

And in J. W. Wheeler-Bennett's study, *Munich, Prologue to Tragedy,* he describes the English point of view on foreign policy both within the government and in the public mind. "Mr. Chamberlain honestly believed that some sort of agreement could be worked out with Germany and with Italy for the peaceful solution of Europe's problems. Himself essentially a businessman, he could not conceive how any problem could possibly be settled by a recourse to arms. nor could his mentality envisage that any other leader in Europe, either Democratic or Totalitarian, could think otherwise. There was a naïveté in this approach which, in looking back across the years, is startling. It must, however, be remembered that in 1937 Mr. Chamberlain's attitude to peace and war was very representative of the national reaction of Britain."[13]

This was the point of view that was proposed and urged, among others, by Ambassador Joseph Kennedy in London, by Ambassador Hugh Wilson in Berlin, by Chargé d'Affaires Alexander

Kirk in Moscow, and by Ambassador William Bullitt in Paris. The letters of William Bullitt to President Roosevelt from 1936 through 1939 are constantly pleading this cause—evidently with some success in Washington. "I am more convinced every day that the only chance of preserving peace in Europe lies in the possibility that the French and the Germans may reach some basis of understanding. The new element which has created this possibility is that the bombing plane has been developed to such a pitch of efficiency. . . . There is beginning to be a general realization, therefore, that war will mean such horrible suffering that it will end in general revolution, and that the only winners will be Stalin & Co."[14]

It must be said at this juncture that my point of view and my husband's were not identical. His viewpoint was primarily technical. He was interested in the facts and he saw them clearly. In the field of technical aviation in which he was put to work he was not naïve. By nature and by training he was fitted for the job he was asked to do and that he willingly accepted without thought of personal loss or gain. He was astonished and impressed by the rapid growth of German air power, but he also saw its danger. True to his basic nature, wherever there was danger he wanted to get closer to it, to face it, measure it, and, if possible, prepare to combat it. It was as a "trouble-shooter" that he became of such value to the airlines which he served all his life. His role was to detect the danger points and try to circumvent them. Even in early air pioneering, this was his method in approaching storms. If we got a bad weather report, his response was invariably, "We'll go and see what it looks like—we can always turn back." I am sure it was this characteristic attitude that led him to consider spending the winter of 1938/39 in Germany. He knew without a doubt that Germany was the danger point of Europe. He wanted to get as close as possible to the danger, to assess it accurately, and to warn others of its potential.

We did not, of course, carry out this proposal. On November 7, 1938, a young Polish Jew, grief-crazed over the fate of his deported parents, shot a German Secretary in the Paris Embassy. Using this incident as a pretext, on November 9th and 10th the Nazis carried out an infamous planned pogrom against the Jews, burning Jewish synagogues and systematically sacking and destroying Jewish shops all over Germany. C.A.L.'s immediate response was to telephone the Military Attaché in Berlin, whose wife recorded in her diary: "He would not take a house in Berlin, in a country that committed such outrages—he was vehement."

If my husband's point of view was chiefly technical and practical, mine was quite the opposite, largely emotional and far more trusting. In one of the reviews of an earlier book of mine, I remember being called, with some justification, "a confused pacifist." My basic feelings of pacifism were bred in my youth, a youth immersed in the hopeful post-World War I atmosphere of belief in "a war to end all wars." The talk I heard around the family table in my school years was full of enthusiasm for Woodrow Wilson's Fourteen Points: "The right of self-determination" for nations, "a new order of World Peace." In that halcyon period we believed that negotiations within the League of Nations would be the means of avoiding wars in the future by "open covenants, openly arrived at." My father wrote a small study of the past attempts of nations to negotiate their problems (Dwight W. Morrow, *The Society of Free States*). In my teens, Erich Maria Remarque's *All Quiet on the Western Front* made an indelible impression on me and convinced me that war was the ultimate evil.

It is only now, looking back, that I can see how widespread across a whole generation in Europe was the general horror and rejection of war, along with the hope and faith in cooperation and open discussion. In England a basic pacifism, combined with some guilt over the patently unfair clauses of the Versailles Treaty, was buttressed by the attitude of Labor, strongly anti-war and opposed to the rising budget for rearmament which would rob workers of benefits.

In France, pacifism was not guilt-induced but visceral. Within living memory, the French had suffered two wars and occupation by Germany. One can understand why they recoiled at facing a third assault. J. W. Wheeler-Bennett reports that "with the exception of the extreme left, France was pacifist with varying degrees of sincerity and interest. In the debate on Munich, the only party to vote against the government was the Communist Party."[15]

These diaries reflect the opinions which were current in the embassies of Europe in the pre-war years. The German "line" was openly given me by General Milch on our first trip to Germany in July 1936—a "line" which I believed credulously at the time, and possibly Milch did also. "Always France has been our enemy. We have been brought up to hate France and France to hate us. But Hitler is the first to say that there must be an end to this. We do not hate France any longer. We do not want to fight France. We do not want to conquer people. Germany is overpopulated. We want unpopulated land."

The implication of his argument was that the Germans would turn east, to the open spaces of Russia. This theory of German intentions was widely circulated in England, and editorials were written stating that the only way to stop the dictators was to play them off against each other. This course, it was argued, was only a broader application of the balance of power policy that England had practiced for years on the European scene. The democracies, it was advanced, should now apply it to the fascist countries. In France, as Ambassador Bullitt expressed in his letters to President Roosevelt, the argument was: "If war should begin, the result would be such a devastation of Europe that it would make small difference which side should emerge the ostensible victor. I am more convinced than ever that we should attempt to stay out and be ready to reconstruct whatever may be left of European civilization."[16]

There was no doubt that I was influenced by the prevailing arguments in diplomatic circles. With my natural pacifist tendencies overlaid with visions of a war-devastated Europe, according to C.A.L.'s technical estimates, I came to feel that there was nothing worse than "the blind, stupid, terrible chaos of war." I learned slowly—more slowly than most people—that there were worse things. The degradation and horror that was uncovered at Auschwitz, Buchenwald, and Dachau was worse than war. But at the time these diaries were written those man-made infernos were unknown to us. One heard rumors of internment camps which from time to time kept political dissenters in custody, but little was revealed about them. They were not yet camps for mass extermination such as Camp Dora that so appalled my husband when he saw it at the end of the war that he wrote in his *Wartime Journals*: "Here was a place where men and life and death had reached the lowest form of degradation. How could any reward in national progress even faintly justify the establishment and operation of such a place?"[17]

At the time these diaries were written the majority of people in Europe, public and private, statesmen and men in the streets, still hoped for and believed in the possibility of avoiding war. In the United States, too, the desire to avoid war was powerful and nearly decisive at many points. (As late as December 19, 1941, a bill extending military service passed the House by only one vote.) In hindsight, it is easy to call all of us who had such hopes naïve—if not "appeasers" or "Nazi sympathizers." Understandably, we were the scapegoats for a generation of failed hopes for peace. Scapegoats and villains are irresistible images on whom to unload frustrated hopes and bitter recrimination.

Ultimately, it is the task of the historian to sort out and unmask the images of another epoch. I am not a historian and the record in this present volume is of value only as it reflects the atmosphere of Europe in the pre-war years—an atmosphere which largely evaporated in the fiery furnace of the war that followed. The thoughts, feelings, and actions of many men and women of that time may be better understood in my picture of the past as it seemed then.

The diaries, although not history, fall under the heading of history's raw material. We met and talked to people who made history; we did not make it ourselves. Nor did we meet the main protagonists of the drama: Churchill, Hitler, Mussolini, or Stalin. It is even questionable how much influence my husband had on events of the time. He came closest to it when he visited Germany in 1936 and was one of the first to witness and report to U.S. Intelligence the tremendous rise in German air power. His reports were listened to in American and French official circles, less so in those of the British—an experience that was duplicated for other, later, observers in 1938 and 1939. A notable example was the American airplane manufacturer, J. B. "Dutch" Kindelberger, who, after a guided tour of Germany in 1938, reported to the opposition leader, Churchill, through mutual friends, his staggering impression of the Luftwaffe. Churchill, who was convinced by the account, relayed the picture to Sir Kingsley Wood, then Minister for Air, who reportedly brushed it aside with the comment: "We've heard all that sort of thing before."[18]

As readers of his *Wartime Journals* will remember, my husband admired the British but was baffled by their blindness in regard to the growth of German air power and distressed at their unpreparedness in the threat of major war. He felt in sympathy with the French, who seemed awake to the danger of Germany, but he was shocked by their apathy—almost paralysis—in the face of that danger.

The diaries on the whole, then, are the personal history of two young Americans in the beauty and complexity of the European scene. We, in common with the most experienced diplomats, were facing an era of unprecedented change in world politics. Some of our impressions were mistaken. It took time to appreciate the warm hearts and staunch loyalty of the British underneath their shyness and reserve. We felt quick sympathy for the French but were disturbed by their conflicting reactions. We did not perceive the full horror of the Nazi regime. There were, in fact, in our European years a goodly number of flowers, but also many nettles.

1. Max Frisch, *I'm Not Stiller* (New York: Alfred A. Knopf, Vintage Books, 1958), p. 132.
2. Joachim C. Fest, *Hitler* (New York: Harcourt Brace Jovanovich, 1973), p. 436.
3. Thomas Jones, *A Diary With Letters, 1931–1950* (London: Oxford University Press, 1954), p. 195.
4. Fest, *op. cit.,* p. 498.
5. J. W. Wheeler-Bennett, *The Nemesis of Power—The German Army in Politics 1918–1945* (New York: Macmillan Co., 1953), p. 354.
6. Jones, *op. cit.,* p. 181.
7. *Ibid,* p. 422.
8. Charles A. Lindbergh, *The Wartime Journals of Charles A. Lindbergh* (New York: Harcourt Brace Jovanovich, 1970), p. 73.
9. *Air Intelligence Activities,* Office of the Military Attaché, American Embassy, Berlin, Germany, August 1935–April 1939, p. 91.
10. Wheeler-Bennett, *op. cit.,* p. 342.
11. R. H. Bruce Lockhart, *Guns or Butter* (Boston: Little, Brown and Co., 1938), p. 420.
12. André François-Poncet, *The Fateful Years—Memoirs of a French Ambassador in Berlin 1931–1938* (New York: Harcourt Brace and Company, 1949), p. 254.
13. J. W. Wheeler-Bennett, *Munich—Prologue to Tragedy* (New York: Macmillan Co., 1948), p. 268.
14. Orville H. Bullitt, ed., *For the President—Personal and Secret Correspondence Between Franklin D. Roosevelt and William C. Bullitt* (Boston: Houghton Mifflin Co., 1972), p. 200.
15. Wheeler-Bennett, *Munich,* p. 191.
16. Bullitt, *op. cit.,* p. 283.
17. Lindbergh, *op. cit.,* p. 995.
18. Andrew Boyle, *Poor, Dear Brendan: The Quest for Brendan Bracken* (London: Hutchinson and Co., 1974), pp. 219–20.

1936

Dear M.

I am sitting in the little old nursery of Aubrey's[1] home. Jon is sitting at the same table eating his supper happily. We are here for the present and perhaps two weeks or so more. For C. does not want to look around for a house until things are completely quieted down (the American press will be the only pressure).

So far everything has gone well. The trip was rough but Jon was very good all the way. One afternoon and evening of a storm he was seasick but otherwise he ate and slept well, and as it was mild we were up on deck every day. There was a small kitten on board which delighted him.

It was quiet and a nice boat and crew—the captain was Scandinavian, which may account for his steadiness and quiet dependability.

There was not much trouble at Liverpool, after running the gauntlet of photographers going down the gangplank. And then we motored very quietly here.

I am still rather dazed about this whole trip. I cannot quite believe we are here and it is hard to look into the future. The speed with which we left (although C. has talked of it for over a year, generally) has cut us off from everything we were doing and planning in America and leaves me feeling very confused. I do think we did the right thing and even temporarily in this quiet garden I feel the difference. No fear of the press trespassing on the grounds, or eavesdropping. No fear at night putting Jon up to bed and then running up to see if he is all right. Is there a

[1] Aubrey Niel Morgan, A. M. L.'s brother-in-law.

dog there? etc. We have been bothered very little and seem to be left quietly alone here, both by people and press.

As for the future I cannot tell. I think when everything dies down we will try to rent a little house in the country, get a nurse and settle down for a few months. C. says there is much studying he would like to do; there are people interested in the same work he was doing at home, here in England and also perhaps in Sweden and France. When we left, although our plans were completely free and indefinite, we said vaguely to ourselves that it was "for six months." I don't know how long it will be or if we will be here or in Sweden or somewhere else this summer. But if we have a home somewhere, I wish you would begin to think about coming over to visit us. We will be sure to be living very quietly and I do hope we have some kind of temporary home of our own.

I cannot write any more of our plans for I know nothing. C. is well and quite happy, I think—at least the tension has dropped from him. He has been studying mathematics (at which I marvel!) ever since we left, plunging ahead through calculus.

Today I left Jon with him and went to take a nap. When I came back in half an hour C. had taught Jon the beginning of "Dan McGrew":

> "A bunch of boys were whooping it up
> In the Mamaloot saloon
> The kid that handles the music box
> Was hitting a jag-time tune
> Yippee!"
> [ROBERT W. SERVICE]

The "yippee" was shrill and high and evidently *very* much enjoyed—both by father and son. I think he will stay an American!

P.S. Mother and Con are in London, on their way to Italy. We do not expect to see them at all until they come back. They are going to visit Amey Aldrich[1] in Rome.

[1] Amey Aldrich, college friend of E. C. M., was staying with her brother Chester Aldrich, Director of the American Academy in Rome 1935–1940.

DIARY   *Friday, January 10th*

Yesterday Mother and Con got in. Aubrey has gone to Southampton to meet them, also Charlie Whigham[1] and Harold Nicolson.[2] Then they went to London. I long to see them and talk and laugh and feel the complete understanding, humor, delight in talking over things and that blooming of the person that is *you*, from being in the sun of such understanding. I feel homesick for it even though I just left them two weeks ago, because the changes have been so great that it seems like a year and also because I feel such a stranger here.

Also I am foolishly envious—Mother and Con, gay at the Grenfells',[3] with all the warmth of a homecoming, tasting the inheritance of Daddy. Shopping in the glitter and shine of London streets, going to the Berkeley and theater with Aubrey, and talking, quick family jokes. Going to the Chinese exhibit, feeling the excitement of London, men's talk about the war, the Disarmament Conference, the hope of peace. Talk about books. I am hungry for it and the sparkle that comes to you when you are in it, relishing the family quality, each a foil for the others.

Yesterday it was a pang of longing I couldn't do anything with. Today, though, is better. I have found some balance. I sang all morning—Jon and I out in the "summer house," while the rain poured around us. It was a great release for feelings: the rain and wind, the shine of wet leaves, and the moon (last night) sailing suddenly through thin bright clouds in a sky surprisingly calm and clear and high. Really putting yourself into the essence of things around you—being absorbed in them—suddenly turns you inside out and dissolves foolish longings and envy.

And then Jon—so funny. I, in exasperation at supper: *"Jon,* either you eat your apple . . ." (Waiting for a threat, I pause.) Jon, wickedly, "or I don't," reducing me to tears of laughter.

---

[1] Partner of Morgan, Grenfell & Co., London.

[2] English career diplomat, biographer, and critic. Friend of the Morrows and author of *Dwight Morrow,* a biography of A. M. L.'s father.

[3] Edward C. Grenfell (Lord St. Just), head of Morgan, Grenfell & Co., London, and his wife, Florrie, friends of the Morrows.

I am so soaked in Jon—it is like becoming a child. Today looking at a shot pigeon, fallen on the step, his neck curved and his beak meeting a little splotch of bright red blood on the stone, I felt, with Jon, instinctive horror and attraction.

Mrs. Morgan[1] talking to me about servants for my house. She is so sound and sensible. Then that sudden shock running up against "But you must think of the dignity of your house. You must keep up your position, you must remember he is Colonel Lindbergh's son and Mrs. Dwight Morrow's grandson. You must have just as good a nurse as the Duchess of York"! to which I could say nothing but only think, *"There*—there she is," as one might say of C.'s leap up the stairs, "There—there he is." And then again, Oh, if *only* I could talk to Elisabeth. What fun to talk to Elisabeth.

At night Aubrey back and letters from Mother and Con.

Brynderwen, Llandaff, January 12th

Darling Con—

You seem so tantalizingly near—I hate not seeing you, and there is so much to say. I have not been able to write because Jon has been so absorbing. It is not that all does not go well or that I am tired out. Everything has gone beautifully. It is far easier than taking care of him at home, when I was always exhausted. No—I am appalled and delighted by the efficiency of me as a nurse! Only it is strange. It is so absorbing mentally, emotionally, etc., that it is impossible to read, write, diary or letters—think even—about anything but Jon.

I long to be with you in London, though of course it is best to stay here quietly, nor do I feel much like meeting Morgan, Grenfell and Co. in full regalia at this moment—I feel very governessy. I find I can't talk about anything at meals (the only time I see people, really). I have that governessy silence and the bright grateful perky look when anyone asks me, "And how did Master

[1] Mrs. Jack Morgan, mother of Aubrey Morgan.

Jon eat his lunch?" Also I am beginning to look like one, too, that flat-footed look, and the way I put my hat on, as if I didn't care who saw it. And my nose is always red and shiny (climate?). You see, it really seems more important to get him out on time than to put powder on my face. And I haven't seen a lipstick since I left New York! There doesn't seem to be any use putting lipstick on with my hair the way it is, and my skirts too long (the old tweed round-the-North-Atlantic one got soaked by "the wave" and now hangs about my ankles).

I always wondered why governesses did not get marvelously well educated and read tomes of history in their hours of waiting and watching with nothing to do. Now I understand. It is impossible to apply the mind to anything but light novels or magazines. It isn't the time—you *have* the time if you manage well and are halfway efficient. It is the mood. I do not mind much. I miss more not having the time to myself—long stretches of time *alone* to think or write letters, or even a diary; not having *that,* is difficult and the only thing I really miss. It is like having a source of strength cut off from you.

P.S. Aubrey has just taken me out to a china place. C. put the baby to bed! Very exhilarating. I took off my flat shoes and put on some lipstick. Hurrah!

DIARY   *Sunday, January 12th*

The pigeon is still there on the step, his head tucked around to meet his breast and the splotch of blood under his beak, but today his pearl wings are completely silvered over with cold dew, like a flower held under water.

Aubrey takes him away. Jon is still fascinated: "Where is that bird that ate the Brussels sprouts?" (I explained that he had been eating in the garden and therefore was shot.) "They buried him, Jon, in the ground." Much later he asks, "What is in the ground?" "Oh—roots and flowers and bulbs and worms." Jon adds (sinisterly!), "And one bird."

The sense I am getting gradually of the different family

strands; likes and dislikes, loyalties, jokes, etc. (If only I could talk it over with Elisabeth!) "If you ask me, I call it sheer lack of breeding." (Puss puss!) Strange remark, too—one would never say that in America. It is again, "Oh, but you must keep up your dignity, your position." I don't think much of my dignity or my position exteriorly. Interiorly yes, very decidedly, but not exteriorly.

Monday, January 13th

The routine of Jon is sometimes irritating: his incessant questions, talking, demand for attention. His indomitable energy; but mostly the impossibility of ever shaking free of him—physically or mentally—the constant interruptions of his demand for attention. I can't even sing or think—he resents it as something that (rightly so) takes my attention away from him.

The desire to be alone getting to be a mania. I am very seldom alone, though, as when I leave Jon (nap) I find C. in the study; naturally, he wants to be alone too.

At night, the time peters out in family conversations which I like—especially with Margaret.[1] She is very honest, perceptive, and sensitive and has a wonderful sense of proportion and marvelous humor—that is enough to live for; humor like that is a string through the whole of life. We sit in the upstairs sitting room and gossip.

I do not talk to her about myself. Neither does she talk to me about herself, but there is understanding enough in little things to make something very firm.

The hours outside in the garden—sinking into the feeling of the garden, the hedges and brick walls, the stone borders. The formal garden beds in front—intricate to roll a hoop through. The kitchen gardens to the back, behind hedges, rows of Brussels sprouts, a robin on the top of one, and large glass bells covering young plants cloudily. The greenhouse; the newly spaded garden; a spade stuck in the ground and the tangle and mystery

[1] Margaret Morgan, sister of Aubrey Morgan.

through the thick hedge into the next field. The warm still part of the walled garden with fruit trees pinned to the wall and tiny little birds rustling under the shrubs.

The different spheres, or realms, for each place are like different countries—like childhood—for playing. Under the chestnut tree, the dark corner of the hedge, leaves all black and moldy to poke in for old chestnuts. Jon wedged into the tree (by C.) looking for chestnuts up there. The big square lawn in the middle for ball or airplane (Gerald's) or rolling hoops or throwing things for the dogs. The damp dark overhanging pines and dark passages underneath quite dry, for looking for pine cones. The vegetable garden to run around—C. timing me and Jon.

There is the skyline too, which I watch morning and afternoon—the tall line of pines a boundary to the west through which you see the sun set and from which all those sudden rain squalls come—against the dark of which you can see the light strings of rain.

Sometimes I become Jon and feel with him the excitement of finding a hollow "house" completely covered by the overhanging branches of pine or under high bushes. Only the flicker of light and specks of grass seen through the leaves—but no one can see you! Safe, hidden, covered . . . delicious childhood feeling. Everything quiet, even those flickering leaves, spying on you, keeping the secret with you, in league with you.

Sometimes I walk up and down for hours and think out why there is so little understanding between generations, should a woman be satisfied to be "just a mother" and wife, etc.! While Jon picks up acorns.

Sometimes I fight pangs of envy and depression by trying to put myself *into* the oak branches against the sky, or the smooth effortless glide of sea gulls, or the exciting beating of wings of other birds, or clouds—the whole sky racing by the still pines. Those days when the sky is so much more compelling than the ground. (I think one develops a sky sense from flying.)

One lovely still clear day—sunny. Mad with joy, I raced around the garden with a hoop, took my coat off, unbuttoned my collar to get the sun. One could sit in it, one felt warm inside but chilled slightly on the outside, like coming in from a sail. So terribly happy just from the day—like spring. If only I could keep it as armor. Encased in this day I could meet anything, anyone; I felt completely self-assured and yet unself-conscious, as though the day and I were one.

Monday, the King [George V]—and Elsie [Whateley][1]—(died).

Tuesday morning, January 21st

Jon: "Where did Monday go?"

A. M. L.: "It went down with the sun."

Jon, looking out the window at the sun: "Did it come up with the sun too?"

Depressed all morning. The trouble is that kind of depression can only be fought with those wells of resource of yourself, those things in you that are essentially and most intensely you, that you care about the most. And I cannot even think about them now. There is no time, no space, no quiet. Nothing to encourage me, and everything seems to say to me: Give it up; you can never—and you know it—write anything more than a travelogue. Everything points that way—the general British attitude about wives and family. The wives around me, and now I read a book in which I find: "To bring a child into the world and lead him and guide him with her mother's wisdom into manhood is enough work for any human being in a sane-minded society." "There are talented women, as there are talented men, but their number is actually less than democracy would have us believe." "I feel confident that her soup will still be better than her poetry and that her real masterpiece will be her chubby-faced boy. The ideal woman remains for me the wise, gentle, and firm Mother"!

I did not feel like the "wise, gentle, and firm Mother" today! I

[1] The Whateleys were the English couple who took care of the Lindberghs' house in Hopewell.

was very irritable and then cross at myself for being irritable. Jon's talk interrupted my thoughts *all* day and I was trying to think *out* of the gloom.

Today the wind has roared through the pines "hissing to Leeward like a ton of Spray."

Thursday, January 23rd

The Morgans leave—Margaret at the last moment with two Mexican hats she was going to carry unwrapped, but Mrs. Morgan insists on a paper parcel! So like Mother. Aubrey leaves for London and "the party." I sit outside watching Jon and looking at the stilled house and wondering why it is that a house suddenly changes appearance after its family leaves. It looks empty and darker and sucked out. I look up at Mrs. Morgan's windows with the curtains flapping gently around the sill and try to say with conviction, "She's just gone to town"—but it's no use. The curtains and the shadowy windows and the whole house answer back with stony conviction; "Oh no, she's gone . . . the house will all be put away . . . they've gone."

Saturday, January 25th

Last night the family came. Going to bed, Con told me her secret (Con's engagement to Aubrey). I had foreseen it, but I had not expected it so quickly. I felt, Yes, it is right—right for her, right for him. It is wonderful—perfect. And yet a jolt to my whole picture of life at the moment. I lay awake all night trying to make it fit in my mind. At times it did focus and I tried to remember how I managed that gigantic effort so I could help Mother.

Sunday, January 26th

C. was lovely to me last night and understood everything, I think. I felt closer to him than perhaps for a long time—as though it were a permanent step closer. I felt very tired but as though I could start over again, we could start over again and be very happy in a home of our own at last.

> "If thou canst get but thither,
>   There grows the flower of Peace,
> The Rose that cannot wither,
>   Thy fortress, and thy ease."
>   [HENRY VAUGHAN]

I told him all about last winter and summer and how dreadfully I had felt. ("But why didn't you *tell* me—why didn't you ask me to take you away?") In laying it all out and admitting it and in his understanding and also his giving me the other picture—the picture of a successful me that he sees—I felt such solidity and strength.

And also he asked, what did I want, where should we go, what should we do?

I didn't want anything except to have a home—quietly, anywhere, a home with him and Jon.

Monday 27th

To London, and the sense in the train of suddenly being allied to the past—those very realest yous that you only realize in odd suspended bits of time like waiting in strange houses and riding on trains and long days on boats. When one is disconnected from all one's strings and conventions, taken out of all ruts and at last the free person that is you comes out. I remembered long train rides back to college, when I summed up what I had done during vacations, what I meant to do the next term. Then those independent trips in the short period between college and marriage, when I felt young, confident, attractive, and powerful, setting out to do anything I wanted. They were only trips to Boston, but on my own.

Then the long trips to Mexico and all the pain and indecision and heady excitement about C. But mostly I remembered the heady excitement of that independent feeling, stepping out onto the cold damp pavements in stations, feeling crisp and trim, feeling: See—I am an independent young woman, traveling by herself. I could go anywhere, I might be anyone. I had a leap of return to this feeling.

Then London: the damp, the cabs, the misty lights, the toots, the sudden quiet, mistily treed squares, lovely old houses. The arches and entrances into the parks, the great glittery stream of traffic, familiar turns in the park, on Piccadilly, the ride in the car to the hotel, and my dropping luxuriously into a sense of being sixteen again in London with my family, my father, under the great cloak of his strength and welcomeness and the sense that life was moving along interestingly and I could sit under it and take what I wanted. Sit quietly and shyly behind the "family" feeling and watch and enjoy. The sense of the romance of London, too, I felt returning. And these memories strengthened me. This isn't new and hostile, this city. It has memories for me too, so it belongs a little to me and welcomes me and comes around me protectively, helping me to meet strangers and strange situations.

The Ritz: carnations, gilt door handles, satin curtains, mirrors, and the telephone . . . and the sense that anyone may drop in at any moment.

London, Tuesday the 28th (*King's funeral*)
A strange day, personally and otherwise. In the first place, the terrific excitement of the City the night before. Those black and purple banners marking the route of the procession, men tearing up islands in the street in preparation. The draped shop windows, the flags at half-mast, everyone in black on the street. The billboards in the station being painted black, stands being put up, streets being blocked off with wooden gates, and at night, the unrest in the streets, the sound of feet, people selling programs. The crowds were forming (C. said) at three in the morning on both sides of the street. It was quite dark and rainy. We looked out of our window onto a big canvas tent covering some stands.

Across the park was a big canvas tent for first aid. All down the street in the windows and on balconies were seats for people (also in a store-front window I passed last night rows of gilt chairs—I couldn't imagine what for at first).

By the time we had breakfast the crowds below us were jammed into two lines on either side of the street, held in by brown lines of police. Crowds inside were moving loosely up and down the streets; almost no cars. Then gradually the police moved this shifting center crowd out, a mounted police pushing at the rear. Very slowly they dispersed, still odd people walking down the center. A man in a top hat and full dress carrying a child pig-a-back, the red leggings poking through under his arms. Also men carrying stretchers, brown rolled-up tentlike, also occasional officials with high plumed casques, with bearskins on their heads. (Some plumed officials riding in a swell open car, plumes flying, bumping along incongruously!)

The sense—looking at the crowd—that every other person had on a brown khaki mackintosh. The men who climbed trees in the park. People peering through the windows of the Underground station. The moment when someone decided to climb up on top. The scramble, the ease with which people got up, broke over it. Then the tall helmeted bobbies gradually getting them down again—no hurry, no force, very polite. The last to go was a photographer. He went down a ladder while the bobby held his packages and camera and handed them down after him one by one. You could almost hear him say, "And here's your hat!" A big loudspeaker going in the tent below us, describing the start of ceremonies. The minute guns begin to boom.

Then the parade. The bands in the distance, the different regiments. The purple banners fluttering. It seemed very quiet—just that slow-moving line of men in somber colors and the muffled drums (covered in black) and the music at a distance.

The sound of pipers—unmistakable and rather eerie—in the distance and then, with a startling suddenness, below us around the corner those even lines of sailors, white collars all in line and the white ropes, taut like a woven pattern. Con gasped, "It's the gun carriage!" They pulled evenly that little bare gun carriage—the coffin, terribly small, covered in the rich gold of the flag. On top, those familiar unbelievable signs of the throne: the orb, the crown, the scepter, and a crown of roses. The tiny and yet terrifically powerful sight of that coffin, wrapped in the standard, fastened your attention, your emotions, in a strange way.

I could hardly look at the people following and had to quickly remember afterward when it was almost too late. The standard, flapping down, so it was not conspicuous, the King [Edward VIII] in naval uniform, walking jerkily (it must be he, for he is walking alone, small and pathetic). The Queen's coach and the red cloaks of the footmen behind and then that line of gorgeous coaches stretching up Piccadilly, over the tops of the park trees. The gold and the red cloaks and the plumed attendants and the distant sound of the band ahead and (when you remembered) the dull sound of the minute gun punctuating it.

Later, when it was over, we watched the crowds break through the lines like water through a sieve and move unevenly down. When it rained umbrellas popped up on top like hundreds of mushrooms and seemed carried down the street on top of the moving mass, as though floating on a stream.

Then we went down and heard the service at Windsor. That beautiful march (the Dead March in *Saul*—Handel) and "Alone . . . in a coach . . . the Queen" and the reading of the King's "styles"—once for the dead King, and then right after for the present King.

Then the "silence" in the streets at 1:30—terribly impressive. The growing crowd on the corner . . . the gradual slowing up of traffic . . . stopping . . . the gradual stopping of all noise. Men jumped out of taxis and stood with bared heads at attention. A man walking with two women stopped dead, took off his hat. And the gun going off and then no noise or movement at all. Only natural things, like birds wheeling in the sky and papers blowing in the street. It was so strange, like one of those fairy stories with sleep catching everyone where they stood, for a thousand years, or the world turned to stone. And again one had the impression that the City was transformed to "Country" at the moment. The sky became more important and seemed to come down in the streets. Birds were the actors in that world and the wind blowing about bits of paper in the street. One knew what kind of day it was in the country or what that corner had been like before it was a city block.

And all of it out of true feeling for one man who had known sublimely how to fill the place he was meant to fill in the world and in his life.

No—of course, that is not all. It is much much more: it is the continuity of history, of intensely national history. The continuity of all kinds of traditional beliefs, ideals, standards, characteristics—a strong pride and sense of them and their permanence.

It was a strange day, too, for I had looked ahead to it with such dread. The impact with London—all those people, and being "Mother's little girl, Daddy's little daughter, C.'s little wife"—and yet the strange person that is I and how to reconcile them. How to act "naturally"—when I didn't feel secure enough to know *what* to act natural *to*. That kind of "humility shyness" that has grown to such proportions from living unsuccessfully so long in someone else's home, someone else's atmosphere, with someone else's friends, in someone else's work, in someone else's past.

The kind of shyness that develops from it can be terrible. It can freeze your face and tongue and paralyze the muscles in your jaw, paralyze your limbs too, so you can't walk into a room or speak or even smile.

Everything was stacked to make a high-grade shyness-agony day—no chance at air, exercise, and the calmness of being outside with trees (which is strengthening)—and one of those occasions when unexpected people drop in on you at the same time, so you have to adjust to all kinds, different stages in your life, different emotions, different memories.

If only they could come one at a time instead of all at once in a mob, but I came in with a plate of cookies in my hand and Mrs. Grenfell kissed me! Mrs. Grenfell kissed me as though I were Elisabeth. Spontaneously—sweetly—gaily. You can never tell people how wonderful they are at times like that, for they would not understand: how they dispelled terror, how they took you in, how they strengthened you and made you yourself by some perfectly careless, natural gesture.

Going down the hall we met Harold Nicolson with top hat, morning coat, etc. One is at a great advantage meeting people unexpectedly, especially if they are carrying top hats at the end of a long passage! I didn't feel shy at all, but just a little amused.

Still, to get through that day without any paralysis was wonderful.

Aubrey talked to me and I felt quite happy about it all [his engagement to Con]—the pictures are both there now, focused. I have Elisabeth too.

Wednesday 29th

To the Chinese exhibit. Terribly excited by it, feeling as I always do with things like this, or music: nothing matters. Age doesn't matter, loneliness doesn't matter—there is always always this. "You are the answer merciful to hear." Feeling, too, this is *my* world—feeling intensely possessive about it. That intensely possessive, tenacious quality we all have—and dislike, or clash with, in the *other* person!

Back to Cardiff.

Monday, February 3rd

C. and I drive to Cambridge. A wonderful feeling of freedom setting out, a young married feeling, that we can stop anywhere, that we will not be followed or noticed. We are just two people in a car, not to be disguised, not to think every time a car passes: Did they know us? Not to have to consider before going in to eat somewhere: "No, there are too many people here, we will be recognized"—not to hide your face in a handkerchief when you stop at a gas station, to avoid the inevitable stare, giggle, curiosity, and comment, which had got to be like a rub on a sore place. To be free from consciousness of self—a strange newspaper self, at that.

Very beautiful country. Climbing through those narrow crooked little towns of gray stone, peering down through them to green valleys. Finally, when we got to Cambridge, dark, cold, very flat, I was quite disappointed. I cannot see the trees. Only rows and rows of ugly modern houses show from the road.

University Arms. Thank God for hot-water bottles.

Tuesday, February 4th

C. wants to drive around the country before contacting anyone. We drive for *hours*. Only Grantchester has any charming houses. When you get to the country, there are only thatch-roofed farms —no in between, no lovely old house. I have a headache from peering at signs and the long drive yesterday.

Wednesday, February 5th

We stay on and drive to Madeley, very charming, and Ditton and Shelford, to look over places suggested by Miss Chase[1] and Mrs. B. Nothing tangible. Then C. goes in to Rutter's agency. Nothing available: no houses in country except big estates, and those not available except to buy; no house for rent except attached ones; no short rents *at all*—a year the shortest.

We go back, have tea, and talk it over. C. very discouraged, walks up and down that cold hotel room and thinks it over. The difficulty really is in ourselves. That is, we have no absolutely fixed factor; everything is uncertain. C. is not *sure* that Cambridge is the place where he can best work. I am not *sure* that Cambridge offers any particular advantage, except school for Jon. We had hoped that the "sureness" of a beautiful old house in the

---

[1] Mary Ellen Chase, writer and teacher at Smith College, temporarily in Cambridge.

country would settle it all for us and make us decide. But we do not want to buy—not "sure" enough—and there aren't any beautiful old places anyway, only ugly places to rent.

C. says he has never never in his life got anything that was really worthwhile without this period (of indecision and impassibility) beforehand. I say it is like the period of depression before writing. It is something not to be avoided but to be gone through. It lies *on* the road. There are no bypasses. You must go through it.

We are rather together in gloom tonight. It is not really as bad as those awful glooms alone and you know there is no one to go to.

Thursday, February 6th

To Rutter's again. Go to see unfurnished houses. Lockhampton: very nice house and grounds, but too near—*in* Cambridge and too large and too expensive. Also a dreadful temporary house which looks like "a semi-detached villa," right on a bus line but with a garden and protected. The house is hideous, Victorian, stuffed with bric-a-brac and sepia photographs of Michelangelos and pale watercolors of the Scottish Highlands. One bathroom, no heat, a tiny stove. C. discouraged by the house and furniture. I think a lot could be moved out and we *could* live there—better than a hotel.

We start off for Wales, then change our mind and go to London to look first around London. I very pleased as I really would prefer, I think, being near London. I don't know why, though. No one there really means anything in my life—no one in England. But the streets at least are familiar and give me a sense of security, stretching back into other parts of my life.

Besides, there is the Chinese exhibit, and Margaret Morgan, and I could go to exhibitions and music, and the shops on Bond Street, and the young romantic sense that anything may be around the corner—out of that mist off the pavements what face might not appear!

Anyway, going to London, even for the night, is exciting. I sing all the way down.

Mother is there alone. Great fun.

Tuesday, February 11th

Mother's broken tooth delays sailing.

Con and I talk very late but it is such a help and I feel so much closer to her. She has now entered the same phase of life as I, when marriage and all its problems are the most important thing.

Wednesday, February 12th

Interview a nurse, Katharine W. I like her very much.

Mother and Con go—awful. C., Aubrey, and I back to Wales. Jon with very rosy cheeks in bed; mail.

[February 13th]

Mother darling—

I couldn't talk last night. I never can when I want to, and it is so difficult not to cry. We seem always to be having these heart-tearing good-bys in our family. But if it is dreadful to say good-by it is also wonderful to meet again and talk over everything and share and laugh and understand each other's situations as no one else can!

I do want to say over and over: please please come as soon as you can. It will be such a joy—to me, but also to C. Really, Mother, he will be so proud and so happy to have you come to *our* home. It will be lovely as those first few Sundays in Hopewell. Can you remember our pride and delight—C.'s pride and delight—in having people see and love his home?

So don't feel "No, I must leave them alone." It won't be like that, and besides, you have your own friends and life here in England, so there are several reasons for coming. And Jon, who has a real and direct relationship with you, not through me at all—a special "Daddy Bee" relationship. And there are letters we can write. Thank God we all can! I shall miss you terribly but I couldn't say so, but we shall be closer when we are both happier and more settled. It isn't really time or space that separates people but states of mind. We never were separated from Elisabeth, were we? And never will be, really. I can only repeat her "Come for just a little time"!

DIARY   *Thursday, February 13th*
C. and I to start back in the morning to Cambridge to look at an unfurnished house in the country to rent. Although large, it sounds old and nice and right location, between Cambridge and London.

Wash *all* my stockings and repack.

Friday, February 14th—St. Valentine's
To Cambridge—Aubrey with us. We go to Rutter's and then to Thriplow. Enormous, ugly, and has large lugubrious pine trees around it. The country is flat and near an airfield! We don't even look in but turn around discouraged. To Layston Park: red brick house on a hill, back from road, adequate—a good size and good grounds but not very appealing (I don't say this to C.). No nice trees, no heat, one bathroom. It is adequate in size, location, looks, grounds, etc.—quite possible. But not a house that could absorb you so you are happy to live in and with it. Not a house, or grounds, that go halfway to meet you and take you in.

However, I prepare to take it in my mind. It could be made much nicer. Aubrey is encouraging. C. says it is practical and just where he wants it. Feel reasonably happy about it.

We decide to go to London and look at the two or three possible furnished houses there. The lists look dry and theoretical. I cannot believe that we can get a nice house through that cut-and-dried method.

To London—*Washington Hotel.*

Saturday, February 15th
Fog, out to Chesham. The best place—Lye Green House—is not open but we walk around it. It is very charming, secluded, nice-looking house, *lovely* garden, a few old trees, and beautifully

protected. I hardly dare say how much I like it, because I think it would satisfy me much better than C. It looks comfortable and easily run. We could put Jon right out in the garden and let him loose in perfect safety. A goldfish pond and a pigeon roost would make him ecstatic. It has (oh, miracle) central heating, electric light, and three bathrooms! Besides a guest cottage with a bath! Don't dare say too much or press it as it sounds too perfect. In fact, I find objections: not near Cambridge, "twenty-eight miles from nowhere." Not country enough—no fields (we can't see in the mist what the country is like). All in order not to sway C. As I would like it so much.

But he is charmed by it too. We could perhaps get it on a short lease while he finds out about his work plans. He doesn't want to be tied to anything till he is sure and tells me later he felt about *Layston Park* as I did but didn't want to discourage me as it was the most possible place!

Go back to London, very encouraged.

Sunday, February 16th

A long Sunday. Fog and dark. C. and I walk the streets and drive around. Everything is shut up, dead and deserted. Try to go to the Zoo (C.'s monkeys!), shut up. Burlington House, closed. Streets empty. Go to the British Museum—walk miles. A few things stand out: those waves of horsemen in the Pan-Athenaic procession. The gravestone of a woman taking off her bracelet (Ephesus). The windblown woman C. found, her thin veil-like skirt blown against her. You can see the flesh underneath—wonderful transparency of stone. The head of Euripides (very Presbyterian—sense of sin, etc.).

Then out to look for something to eat. Dark streets, everything shut. We finally eat in a tea place, walk home, learning the streets. The sense of security it gives you.

Monday 17th

Wait around all day for phone messages. Can we see inside of the Chesham house? Long delays, long calls; yes, but not till tomor-

row morning. Walk around interminably, looking for paper,
books, meals.

Tuesday 18th

Inside of Chesham is very charming. I can see us there. The man
is evidently surprised we want to rent—thought we wanted to
buy.

C. considers calling Harold Nicolson about his house to have
something else "lined up" if this falls through. We *must* get
something and are feeling desperate. We *must* move from Brynderwen. I worry about Mrs. Morgan and the servants.

Wednesday 19th

Lye Green won't rent, only sell. We must start all over again—go
home, move to hotel, etc.; very discouraged. C. calls Harold
Nicolson off and on all evening; no answer—it's so hard to reach
people.

Thursday 20th

A very happy day—one of those days when everything combines
to release you. Suddenly you seem free and light. How easy to be
happy, how easy life seems, how easy to combine all the different
emotions inside you. And walking through the day like that with
confidence, everything opens as it should. Everything answers
you, because you have no fear, like a child smiling at strangers in
a streetcar. They can't resist and smile back. Was it the attitude
that changed the day, or was it the combination of things?

First C. called Harold Nicolson in the morning and got him!
(That alone, after this hide-and-seek business we strike everywhere in England, was enough to encourage us.) No—the house
was still free! Yes—he could see us. Could we have lunch with
him today? C. and I both had a great lift of heart—here was
something rolling! I went out and bought toys for Jon and a
pretty blouse. Then in a taxi to the Houses of Parliament. Harold
Nicolson twinkling and bustling, showing us around. The old
part . . . the new part . . . where Guy Fawkes was killed . . .

"Where we vote" . . . "Where I sit"! etc., etc. (and having quite a good time doing it).

Also he was in some difficulty as he had asked someone "just come back from Abyssinia—I think you'll find him quite interesting"—for lunch, and *then* us and then to have someone else, a woman, for us—Miss Megan Lloyd George. And he was doing his best (which is very good) to swing us all. Poor Abyssinia didn't have a chance to talk to H. N. or about his subject as he was next to me. C. talked to him, though. H. N. divided his time talking about how-to-keep-your-constituents with Miss M. Lloyd George and "house" with me. It was a *little* confused but very nice. I liked Miss Lloyd George very much. They are so quick and perceptive and sensitive, the Welsh, and such expressive faces, and spontaneous, thank God.

I felt stimulated and happy and gay. H. N. was nice about the house. It was hard, though, to get anything concrete about it. He said vaguely and sweetly that it was a very "happy" house. They had been so happy there and he felt those things carried over. Also, when I said I didn't like a house you have to make an effort about—a house you had to go more than halfway to meet—he said, "Well, this house just comes out and jumps all over you like a spaniel."

I was discouraging: Was it near the road? Was it protected? Could people set up cameras in your front window? Wasn't Sevenoaks awfully built up? It was a dreadful drive down there, etc. He gave very cautious answers, not too encouraging, and I was prepared for it to be quite the wrong thing and tried to prepare him. (I *think* he *wants* to rent it to us—or to anyone. I don't think he's just being nice; hope not.)

Then to Sevenoaks. Arrived with card: "Long Barn, Weald, Sevenoaks." All the way down we kept saying gloomily and angrily, as though to prepare ourselves, "I don't call *this* 'country'!" and "I don't call *this* a little town." "He said it *wasn't* suburbia," and, at various houses on the road, large, ugly, and unprotected, "There it is!"

Finally we asked for "Long Barn" and were told "Over the brow of the hill" and then we both said, "There it is!" Low and crouching to the hill, on a corner. There were no houses either in front or behind it, screened from the road by low feathery trees. A gate, a little court, and the sense of an old rambling house fitting the side of the hill.

It was suddenly very quiet as we stepped out and opened the gate. There were lots of birds singing. We tiptoed around to the back and found the two arms of the low house made a court and then looking down the hill—over gardens to fields and hills and farms—all quiet, all country, all still. It was evening and very peaceful and C. and I laughed—for joy, really, such a house! I had an incredible feeling of peace and security—the low house backed up to a hill, its arms around you. Security at your back and there in front of you that great sweep of freedom—complete country, fields and hills, escape. Lye Green had *security* but not *escape*. C.'s face after we had walked around to the back! He was completely decided from that moment. It was an overwhelming feeling of "At last, here it is—of course. It was here all the time waiting for us."

Then we went and looked up the gardener and saw the inside. Crooked, rambling, tipsy floors and slanting walls. Nice things in it, though, nice colors: warm zinnia colors of tapestries. But the arrangement of rooms! Upstairs, no hall—all rooms leading out of each other, but hundreds of little staircases, ladder-steep and spiral. I found myself laughing and laughing, for joy and relief and amusement at the place. I thought perhaps C. would think it too big, but a nod from him and a few words, "Of course there's no question about it—it'll do!" Then we walked around the garden again and found a tennis court and a pool and some lovely trees. And the first star, which I wished on: Oh God, may something good come of this! And then we both said: C.: "My, I would have been sore if we'd taken Lye Green and then we'd seen this!" and I: "Thank God the man at Lye Green didn't take our offer!"

We drove home extraordinarily happy and glowing. I sang all the way home in the car. We both felt released. I told C. it was like the feeling in a plane, after fighting through fog and rain and clouds, suddenly coming out into "unlimited" sunshine and vision and space and the sky spreading free and clear ahead of you. He felt it too. He said it was *by far* the best place. He didn't care how far away it was. He didn't care about any of my objections (it would please me so easily; all the disadvantages are his—distance from Cambridge, wrong side of London, etc.).

I was so grateful to Harold Nicolson for not overstating it, for not pressing it, for saying so little. (Only the garden, her garden, did he let himself be unguarded about: "It really is a *lovely* garden (shyly). It is quite a show place.") For leaving it around carelessly, where we could find it. Perhaps it was accidental on his part, but it does fall in with my theory that the only way you can help people is accidentally by leaving things around where people can find them—crumbs to the birds, again. And I wanted to wire H. N. or write him how lovely the house was and how grateful I was to him and how happy we were. And then I realized of course that I couldn't do that. You can't ever *thank* people. It would be out of proportion and a burden. You can't ever explain just why at that moment what they did was so marvelous. It must always be unsaid, only—oh, God, there is so much left unsaid in life.

C. and I laughed too on the way home, a strange repetition of theme of coming down, only in a gayer tone, repeating things H. N. had said: "He said you went over the hill and left suburbia behind." "He said there was a lovely view." "He said it was a happy house." "He said this house comes out and jumps all over you like a spaniel!" C. laughed. "It does, too!"

Friday 21st

C. calls Harold Nicolson. I gather from the conversation that he is pleased but still offers objections (as I do when I want something, to make sure I am getting it honestly). "Is it screened enough from the road? I know of a house in Oxford . . . are you sure you don't want to look at that first?" etc. C.: "We like it so much we don't want to look at anything else." Then he calls her and she calls me. She was nice and easy and practical. How long did we want it for? Could she help with servants? She knew of a man. I, giggling, "You see—I don't believe that would do, because, you see . . . we hate butlers" (Silly, Anne!) "???" over the telephone. "I said I don't think we'll have a butler." C. and I took turns at the telephone.

Now I've got all this cook-furniture business to get through, an awful period until we get back—if we ever do—the promise of joy of that first evening:

> "If thou canst get but thither,
>   There grows the flower of Peace,
>   The Rose that cannot wither,
>   Thy fortress, and thy ease."

Tuesday, February 25th

Leave Brynderwen 5:20. Sleep at Cotswold Gateway Hotel.

Wednesday

Arrive London.

Thursday

Lunch at the Italian Embassy. *Why* did we go! Stopping at the curb in a taxi the doors fling open—six butlers behind. The cardboard plaque of where to sit; hundreds of people (at least twenty!).

Beautifully dressed women standing in front of the fire (no, one doesn't take off one's coat, one boils until one sits down at table), lipstick, pearls, satin, and Persian lamb—and me in my little black dress! Nothing between me and the world but one lovely pin and Elisabeth's watch (she'd like it protecting me). *Courage, mon amie!* Keep your head high. It helps to stand well (if only I'd worn brighter lipstick!). The sherry is a help, and that man with glasses who knows H. N. and who talks about

Gertrude Stein and D. H. Lawrence. Beautiful things in the house; waves of people, gushing. Pond's cream Americans. "Ah, charmed—charmed." Everyone seems to know everyone else.

Everyone there seems to live near Sevenoaks. And then the women upstairs. "I'd love to see you again, but really we are so unsettled right now that . . ." "Well, thank you, but I really don't think we'll be here . . ." (Oh drat, drat, why did we get into this!) "I'll drop you a note anyway." "I live near Sevenoaks and when my grandchildren come down and visit me we'll have to have a party." I knew there was a snag to that lovely place. If only we hadn't met all those people we could have lived oblivious. Out the door and into a taxi and then—explosions.

I went to the Chinese exhibition to cool off. But it has spoiled the fresh, untouched, lovely, hidden picture of our house. I feel uncertain and unhappy about it: we will be besieged by people. Now we have started just the kind of thing we dislike most. Pure society.

C. and I both felt caught and laughed about it together afterward. But how were we to know? We thought it would be very small and informal. C. even called up to try and find out beforehand.

Tuesday, March 3rd

To Long Barn to meet Mrs. Nicolson.[1] I was a little panicky but she came out (bending under the low door) in riding trousers and a kind of velvet doublet and seemed very nice and natural and easy. We sat down in the long room and discussed servants and tradesmen and contracts, etc. (C. mostly, there.) I felt her respect for him. It is curious, but I do feel it when someone of her caliber likes C. It is like metal meeting metal, almost as though I could hear it ring! I felt like a child, though, terribly young and pale, as if she had lived so much more than I and suffered much more and learned much more. I do not feel that way with most women, I feel older, usually. Then, too, I felt curiously feminine,

---

[1] The novelist and poet Vita Sackville-West.

terribly frivolous and feminine, and half the time as if she weren't a woman at all.

It was a day, too, that dropped things into our lap which had bothered us for long. The couple: the man drives, the woman willing and helpful. We decide to take them. We can move in—now!

Long Barn, Weald, March 6th

We pack up after breakfast, fill the back seat, Miss W. [the nurse] to go by train. Stop on way to buy some flowers from a flower wagon: two dozen purple tulips, two dozen narcissi, and some anemones; such a nice old man. "You don't want to give me all that." I sing the German song that only comes when I feel gay. I woke up singing it. Jon notices every flag, even the red ones on the road. He is very happy. Long Barn—a reporter behind us. We hurry in; no pressure once inside the gates. Jon looks out the window and sees the yellow crocuses, and Mrs. Donovan has put flowers in the dining room. The tulips are lovely in the sitting room. Jon says, "Flowers for me! I am very pleased."

We walk outside. Jon finds two white feathers from the white pigeons and an acorn tree and throws stones in the pool! Also, his spade and gardening things come and Mr. Hook[1] gives him a plot to dig.

C. and I explore the house, look at the books, climb into the attic rooms, move furniture, get very dusty, open drawers, find lots of old junk, unsuccessful portraits (mostly of H. N.), empty suitcases with *Lord Carnock* printed on them, broken lamp shades, old palm-leaf fans, etc.

I have a strange feeling, going around the rooms, that it is Elisabeth's house, that I am getting it ready for a visit from her. I plan, "This room for Mother, this for Con, this for Aubrey," as though I *were* E., seeing it with her eyes. E. would put crackers in jars on the bedside tables.

C. and I sit opposite each other in the dining room at the oak table, feeling very happy, "playing house" or "playing married,"

[1] The Nicolsons' gardener and caretaker of Long Barn.

and then in the little sitting room, with the tulips against the green curtains, and a fire and coffee. Our own home. We are terribly happy.

We plan to move into the old part of the house tomorrow.

Saturday, moving furniture all day! C. and I take the old slanting room. We move (1) a chiffonier to hold clothes, (2) a cupboard to hold papers for C. And into Jon's room a bed, a bureau, two little cupboards for toys.

Sunday is such a lovely spring day. Miss W. goes to church. Jon and I go out with the tools and do a little digging, climb up the hill and find primroses and acorns, also down to the pool. Betty, the couple's little girl, follows us with a hoop. It is so delicious. The white pigeons fluttering over us, the hills clearing down the valley. I have found a line of elms across the valley to watch against the sky.

We have breakfast and lunch all together, Jon sitting up on pillows and eating very nicely. Jon says so expressively when the chicken comes on, "Poor chicken—he was boiled."

I cannot write, though. I am frantically moving furniture. In the evening I go out and sit on the steps. It is so beautiful and calm and still and the birds singing. I am reminded strangely of Hopewell—of all we hoped to find there—and also of those strange suspended days of hope in the middle of those awful weeks, days when it was warm and like spring and I said, It is going to be all right. It *can't* be so terrible in beauty like this. It was the feeling that I had then of hope and life pounding back into you when you got *some* good word. (Like lack of pain after pain—a *positive* stream.) So I felt, sitting there, relief and peace and joy in living—a *positive* stream flowing back into me.

> "It cannot be
> That I am he
> On whom Thy tempests fell all night."
> [GEORGE HERBERT]

Monday. A lovely walk with Jon down a path in the woods. (It does remind me of those spring days in Hopewell, looking for signs of spring on that little path behind the house, living passionately in the present, because I had to. Now I want to, as it is so lovely. And now I have Jon.) The buds of primroses, violet leaves, new green on twigs, pussy willows (we pick some), and lovely moss. Jon loves it too and holds my hand (wants to!). After lunch we meet Miss H.[1] She is very nice and young and anxious to please, but oh, such a stranger. How sick I am of strangers. Both of them (Miss W. and Miss H.) for dinner. Miss W. is intelligent and natural. She is perceptive and understanding and so easy to live with.

Long argument with Charles about France's position at the present moment[2] and what the hope was of solution, both of us getting very heated and intense about it, as though it were a personal thing. C. arguing that from her own standpoint France's big mistake was at the time of the war not to crush Germany *completely,* while she was at it, because, once entered on a war (which he agrees is horrible and to be avoided if possible), you should make it effective. Otherwise, why go in, why spill all that blood? Germany, for France's own good, should, he argues, have been completely incapacitated for a century or else not humiliated at all. The middle course led to this present impasse. He argues, If I were a Frenchman I certainly would feel . . . well, after all we won the war. War is war, and we *won* it, and those were the conditions we imposed, and that's that.

I argue that by incapacitating a country you only sow seeds of militarism and humiliation and war feeling. That it is only a temporary cure—safety for a generation—but after that, worse danger than ever. He says no, because after a generation, feeling would not be so bitter, would be glossed over. I don't know. He

[1] Secretary to the Lindberghs.

[2] On March 7th, on the pretext of the Franco-Soviet Pact, German troops occupy the Rhineland, Hitler proposing at the same time a nonaggression pact with France.

says if France has her choice of attacking and crushing a comparatively weak Germany now or of waiting until Germany has equal strength and a line of forts just like hers on a zone newly militarized equal to hers, wouldn't it be the best thing she could do (from a Frenchman's standpoint) to attack Germany and crush her now rather than wait?

By *why* must she crush her *at all?* I argue, why isn't there more security in pacts, in alliances in which each is equal, in defensive alliances too? She isn't going to sink or swim on that line of forts. The alliances like the Soviet one give her much greater strength. (And are far more fickle, C. argues.) Why must Germany be kept down and kept therefore militant and humiliated and bitter and hungry—and perpetuate a gnawing grievance? C.'s answer is, I think, that according to the French after all they won the war. They won it for something. The war would have been fought for nothing if they permit Germany again to build the military machine she had in 1914, if they can't keep Germany down.[1]

But must it *always* always go on that way? Because there *was* a war once, must everything be based on that? Forever? I feel very bitter and disillusioned and hurt about it, as though I were arguing for something terribly personal to me. As perhaps we are—for we come again to C.'s thesis (that I hate so much) that everything is built and rests on Force. All nations are built on it and stand on it, and that nothing can last without—at least in the background—physical force. I recognize that he is right but I feel still bitter and rebellious about it. Isn't there something that is not contained in that creed?

Monday

A delicious spring day. Jon and I go out on the terrace and look to see what has come up. The scilla and the peach blossoms are

---

[1] The point C. A. L. was making is now almost universally agreed upon by most historians. The reoccupation of the Rhineland was the last moment Hitler could have been stopped by France and England with a minimum of bloodshed.

out. Then I leave Jon playing outside and go in. We find a baby pigeon that has fallen out of the nest. The mother is pecking at it to make it fly. C. picks it up and says it is in good shape and we put it in a cage. It is badly pecked: no feathers on its head. Jon is very excited. It takes water off C.'s finger but won't eat.

The feeling of it in my hands quivering and alive reminds me of when you feel a child stirring in you—fifth or sixth month. At teatime we have it in the living room; it walks about uncertainly pecking at the carpet.

C. to Jon at mealtime (Jon puffs so over his food); "Jon, try to make as *little* noise as you can when you eat."

Jon then gives a very little squeak with each mouthful!

Long Barn, Weald, Sevenoaks, March 17th

Mother darling—

It is almost impossible to realize that you left over a month ago and this is my first letter, except the one sent by Aubrey. I cannot quite understand it. It is because things have catapulted along ever since you left. Finding this house, going back to Wales, moving to London, a temporary nurse, the permanent nurse, arrangements about moving in, getting a couple, moving in and the first week's general moving of furniture, and because you seem so frightfully far away and mail seems so uncertain to reach you. It is like sending something off into the blue.[1]

We moved out of Brynderwen—at last—exactly a week after Aubrey. I have felt very worried at overstaying so long.

Then to London for a week, to get cooks, etc., and see Winston.[2] Miss W. arrived about this time and has been so careful and intelligent. It is wonderful to get someone who is both good with Jon and yet sensitive, understanding, tactful, intelligent to live with. She took the train down here so as not to overcrowd us. She loved the place, and spoke about the smell of burning leaves and the quiet! She has taken over a good deal of seeing that the house goes—meals for Jon—and she helps with the beds (her

[1] Mrs. Morrow, Constance, and Aubrey Morgan were on a trip to China.
[2] A maid E. R. M. M. had had in Wales.

own suggestion!). She sees that rooms are ready when an extra person comes down, goes to the village and shops for ironing boards, hangers, sewing silk, etc. She leaves Jon alone a lot—while watching him—loves the country and is teaching Jon to watch for plants and birds. But her humor is the best. This house is terribly higgledy-piggledy: lamps don't fit plugs and doors don't lock and toilet chains seldom function when pulled. You have to coax them. One day she came to me and said, "You know I must tell you something that happened today. It seemed so exactly like this house." She had asked Donovan (the handyman-butler) to fix a clock in her room to which the key was lost. She found him working on it with a key which evidently turned it. "Oh, you found the key, did you?" "Oh no," he said. "This is the key to the radiator"!

Winston has been very sweet. She came by train alone that first day and looked rather wispy and frightened. I found out that the reporters, getting word of this house and our taking it, had writ-ten a long story in the *Express,* describing the house and saying how old it was and that it was *haunted*! Caxton[1] was born here, and in the room in which he was born, on dark nights you could "hear" his "press" going! Winston came up to me very wide-eyed and timid and giggling a little said, "My, this *is* an old-fashioned house. It's worse than Tynewydd!"[2] Then when I took her to her room she said she hoped we weren't too far away and "I read in the papers . . . And . . . one room, they said . . . ?" I had to tell her that I had a letter from Mrs. Nicolson that morning saying she had *never* heard of the story (although Caxton *was* born there, supposedly) and ending up amusingly by saying she hoped we would live there happily, "untroubled by callers or Caxton"!

It is such a funny house, very rambling, as it was made from two or three tiny cottages pushed up together and then a long barn pushed up to that—crooked passages, brick walks, rickety

---

[1] William Caxton, 1422?–1491, first English printer.

[2] Former home of Elisabeth and Aubrey Morgan in Wales.

staircases, etc. It is not very warm despite the central heating and it is *terribly* drafty—lots of cracks in the walls, in the windows, and the floors are all uneven so that it is like walking on shipboard. Every piece of furniture in our room is set up on a prop of a different height and the walls lean so that you think you can push them over.

Jon is so happy here. He runs about all day and I do not worry about him. He climbs fences and picks "lying-down" crocuses and pigeon's feathers (there is a roost of white pigeons over one of the eaves), and digs in the garden, rolls his hoop up and down the steps, collects acorns, throws stones in the pool, and chases the cat. It has been lovely spring weather the last week, quite warm and delicious. There are a few peach blossoms out on the wall of the house and hyacinths showing blue through the green. Jon loves the word *hyacinth* and says over and over, "How high is a hyacinth" and "The hyacinths grow higher and higher."

C. is getting in touch with the Pasteur Institute and may go to Paris, for which this situation is good. Jon still insists that "Daddy Bee is on her way here." "She isn't going home—she's coming *here*." Also, "When she comes *then* what will I do?" "Go into her room." "And will she have the checkers?" Dear Mother, I do so *long* to have you here. It is so beautiful and peaceful and you will love it.

DIARY   March *21st, 22nd, 23rd*
                   Porto Praia [a section in *Listen! the Wind*]
Jon interrupting me from time to time by coming to the study window, blowing through the pane, passing feathers and flowers through when I open the widow. And an apple on a plate! He runs about the garden after Hook and Hammond [the gardeners] in his red rubber boots and blue-topped snowsuit.

Daffodils are coming out, and a flowering tree against the wall of the house and the pink and blue hyacinths. We go out in the car with Jon one evening and stop by a field of sheep and lambs. C. makes two of them come to him. Jon tells about it later at table, much to the amusement of Miss W. and H. "And Father baaed at them."

Tuesday, March 23rd

A lovely still day—sunny.

Jon gets scolded by his father for throwing stones in the pond. He is told he is not to go near the pools or roads without his father or mother or Miss W. Later in the morning when I go out he greets me gaily and asks me to take a walk with him. We go through the woods and find the first violets—the woods are sprinkled with primroses—and up the field to the two muddy pools where Jon throws sticks. Then I say I must go down and work.

"Because you want to do *what?*"

A.: "Oh, write letters and things."

Jon: "And when there isn't any more clean paper left *then* what will Mother and Father have to do?"

A.: "What, Jon?"

J.: "They'll have to play with Jon."

Write Con. C. and I walk across the fields in the evening and find a rabbit and bring it back to Jon and put it on his bed. Jon is first dazzled by the light, then opens his eyes and looks at this furry animal right next to his pillow. He does not move but slowly a broad smile comes over his face—incredulous and hushed delight. Then in a whisper, "What is it—a mouse?" (He cannot see the ears as C. holds it.) Then C. lets him stroke it, which he does very gently. Then we take it and let it run away in the garden.

A lovely new moon tonight "with the old moon in her arms" and later *all* the stars. We go out on the grass and count them.

Long Barn, Weald, Sevenoaks, March 23rd

Darling Con—

It is that zero hour in the afternoon and I cannot work. (C. comes in every once in a while and looks to see what I am doing and says either with satisfaction "Constructive work!" or with restraint *"Whom* are you writing to?" or *"Letters* again?" So it gives me the fidgets and is one reason I haven't written sooner or oftener.) This morning I got the third batch of letters from you and Mother, from Singapore, about Kandy (which has always sounded so romantic!).

I am amused at the impression you got from the cable that we had found a lovely house *but* were temporarily in H. N.'s. I wonder when it will dawn gradually that the "enchanting house" *is* H. N.'s. I have written all details to Mother (to Shanghai). You say, what overcame the objections of expense, too large, wrong direction, etc.? It is one of those inexplicable things that has to do with moods—vague ideas and prejudices.

It wasn't the price exactly that was too high—that is, we could afford it. It was much more the fact that H. N. has become a kind of family "connection" now, I think, that made C. shy off looking here in the beginning. Also the feeling that as H. N. had lived in Englewood he had an inflated idea of what we wanted and could afford. Also the general English idea of servants. H. N. spoke of four being necessary (and unfortunately used the phrase "a person like Banks[1] more or less in the dining room") whereas the former tenant ran it on weekends on two and we are doing beautifully with three. The place "sounded" very large on paper and has a good many rooms but it gives you the *impression* of being "cottage." Lastly and mainly: the place was so enchanting, gave us such a feeling of peace and security and freedom, that all other considerations were swept away.

For the first week or two I couldn't feel at home here. It was too beautiful and I woke up each morning feeling detached and weekendy—like a guest. A delicious feeling of newness and delight and surprise at the beauty of it. I had to walk out onto the terrace in back and just look at it, the peach blossoms on the old gray walls, the white pigeons over the lawns, the crocuses in pots, and the rolling fields and hills, green below us.

[1] The Morrows' butler in Englewood.

Also the personalities of the house disturbed me. All H. N.'s books in the little study—I kept looking up at them and fitting them with him, with curiosity and humor! *International Law*—yes, but also *English Table Glass. Byron's Life and Letters*—yes, but also *The Film Till Now. The American Commonwealth* but also Thurber's *Is Sex Necessary? Home Life of the Greeks* and also *Salome, the Wandering Jewess, The Study of Psychic Science*, and *How to Speak Russian, Ten Sermons of Donne*, and *Letters of Henry Adams*. Lots of French novels and poetry and also *Effective After-Dinner Speaking* . . . etc. I could go on forever: books on Persia, Greece, Chinese ceramics, Italian Renaissance painting, and how to keep chimneys from smoking (I understand the last, as with each different wind a different chimney smokes!).

Her personality rubbed mostly in the pictures—thousands of pictures of Knole all over the house, in the halls, bedrooms, bathrooms, etc. They are very nice and appropriate but very much a personality. The pictures as a whole seem to suggest her: portraits and old oil paintings of scenes in big houses, the kind of richly tapestried and candle-lit house that she might have gone through as a courtier (like *Orlando*) in a former reincarnation, dressed in velvet trousers and doublet. She has given the house all its dignity, color, traditional sense, etc. (I may be just making this up—it's pure guesswork.)

The house is not what is called "in good order"—that is, every drawer you open and every cupboard is stuffed with old tapestries, now moth-eaten, just rolled up and stuck away, old pictures, albums, shoes, inkpots, broken vases, broken shelves, broken lamp shades, empty cigarette boxes, etc. Also—much more shocking to me—open a bureau drawer and you find curled-up photographs of Ben and Nigel sitting in a window, or "Mitya" in pompadour, very beautiful at nineteen, old photographs, old letters, a whole chest full of letters in the front hall—"The Hon. Mrs. Nicolson," "The Hon. Harold Nicolson," tied up in ribbons. Also the attic, where it is understandable (where C. of course explored the first night looking for a ghost!), old brief cases marked "Lord Carnock," broken children's chairs. . . .

Some of the things are funny: scrawled across a fireplace, dimly in chalk, "Nigel is a nasty fellow," and in Jon's room faint arrows and marks on the beams "to London→" "←to Hell to Heaven→" Also, in H. N.'s neat handwriting on the bathroom wall a careful list of weights during three or four years. In the guest room, on the walls, a huge collection of people's heights: "Ben at three" but also "Stephen Spender in bare feet"—"Sibyl Colefax in what she calls moderate heels," etc. It gives you an uncanny feeling that they are all there in the room with you!

The house is beautifully furnished—all antiques. They are not in good condition (as apparently nothing in an old English house is, what with the damp, etc.). There are worms in the furniture and I am a little worried about it, as it is too good to be neglected. It must be dreadful to rent a house with nice things in it. It has leaked in over some of the lovely paintings and paint has curled off.

Yesterday I moved furniture all day—*again*. We moved a great deal the first week. This is the "no, I-think-it-would-be-better-*there*" phase. The pendulum swinging back (direct inheritance from E. C. M.). Donovan said long-sufferingly (under a large chiffonier) the first week, "I notice it is always the *women* who suggest moving furniture!" However, yesterday he seemed to have got quite in the spirit of it and really enjoyed it.

This is a long letter but such fun to write! Partly because now I have the house and having one is so heavenly again. Planning to make it nicer and feeling pride in it is such a strange pleasant joy—planning for guests, planning for your appreciation, Mother's, Aubrey's, etc.! The right color candles for the dining room, new reading lamps, places to write. Also because we have seen no one since we arrived. We talked desperately to Mrs. Nicolson (who was very understanding) about not wanting to make or receive calls, so we have been untroubled.

Until now I have hardly missed people, except to talk, like this, for the happiness of this house is so absorbing. Also I have got out my diaries and pictures and have started working on "Bathurst,"[1] with what success I don't know yet—I am very rusty and it is hard to work when fixing a house is so absorbing and so easy to see results in. I am just getting so I can disregard the Nicolsons' books, pictures, etc. I have put up my own books and pictures in one corner of the study and that helps. And anyway Bathurst is very absorbing—absorbing enough to satisfy me completely and make me feel stronger spiritually. The house, a physical resource and sense of security, and Bathurst, a spiritual one—and Jon and spring, relaxation! I am perfectly happy—only I would like to talk with you.

C. is very happy here. He has found some sympathetic people in the Pasteur Institute (Paris) and has bought a row of books on "Big Game in Africa," "Alone in the Sleeping Sickness Country" (!), "Congorilla," etc. Also has located a secretary and keeps her busy all day catching up on mail. We walk across the fields for miles each evening. Jon is at every meal. C. goes two or three times a week to London to talk to people about tsetse flies, yellow fever, and apes. I am glad he has found people interested in these subjects but I pray (selfishly) that we do not go off too soon to Africa as I am so perfectly happy here!

Long Barn, Weald, Sevenoaks, Kent, March 25th

Dwight darling—

You were terribly nice to write me about the *Petrouchka,* which was a happy guess anyhow, and influenced by what I like. It is funny, in London, the first week or so, C. and I went to a Communist movie—a *frightful* one—called the battleship *Potemkin.* All about how the officers of the old regime made the poor sailors eat wormy meat and flayed them when they complained, and finally were going to shoot them but someone shouted, "Brothers, would you shoot your own brothers?" and so there

---

[1] A section of *Listen! the Wind.*

was a meeting and a Russian Revolution and the Tsar's troops shot down lots of little babies and trampled unheeding on their hands, etc. But all through this glorious modern war film they were playing old Russian music—at least *Petrouchka,* which certainly is not Communist!

No one here is nearly as excited as people at home were about the chance of war,[1] although things looked pretty frightening before Eden got the Germans to send a representative here. And they do not look too bright now, with France saying she won't negotiate until she gets her terms for temporary security. And Germany refusing to negotiate except on terms of unequivocal equality. That is, refusing to admit that she has been a treaty-breaker when all the evidence is against her.

The feeling here, from the newspapers, is quite strongly pro-German: if only the Germans would be a little tactful and less rude and not keep socking people in the jaw every time they get ready to like her.

The newspapers, on foreign affairs (or home affairs as they happen to be now), are terribly good and interesting—much more so than at home. But I get no home news at all, presidential or otherwise. The English just aren't interested. Thank you for sending late news. C. was interested too.

DIARY   *Friday*

To London. A day that carries last night's dream around with it, clinging to it, faint and indescribable but definitely there, like the smell of burning leaves through an autumn day or a wind from the sea when you are far away from it. I dreamt of Elisabeth so vividly. In all my dreams of her there is a dreadful feeling of ominous impending disaster. The knowledge that she has died, has just gone to sleep for a little while—but it is a very light sleep. I am almost afraid of waking it. She is going to be operated on for appendicitis. She treats it gaily and lightly but I am terrified

---

[1] The reference is to Hitler's reoccupation of the Rhineland, March 7, 1936, in breach of the Versailles Peace Treaty.

and think to myself, "She has just gotten through *this* (what is *this*—I don't ask myself) and now the appendix. I am terrified. She will never get through it." And I touch her wrist very lightly. In that touch I had Elisabeth so vividly, so heart-breakingly, and the possibility of losing her—her frailty and her dearness.

And all day long I carry it with me.

Sunday

Take care of Jon. It is raining but stops enough for us to go out. Jon works with clay all morning, very interested. It is lovely outside and I feel so happy, watching the sky and the way the rain beads around the outside of lupine leaves, so they look like stars.

Jon is a "hungry old wolf" and eats me up. "And then what would you do?" "Then I wouldn't be able to eat." "Except things I'd slide down to you."

[London], April 21st

A rainy night after the theater outside in the street packing up the car. The doorman of the hotel is carrying the bags out. Margaret [Morgan] and I stand in the rain by the curb holding up our skirts from the puddles. Gerald[1] picks up the large doorman's umbrella from under the door where it was left and holds it over us. It is enormous and covers all of us. Gerald looks very funny under it. The wind is blowing and G. says he hopes that he doesn't lose his balance and be carried off—sailing off way up in the air. "You know," says Gerald: " 'Man last seen going over Piccadilly Circus . . .' " Margaret and I shake with delicious laughter. It is so funny: we standing in the puddle with our skirts held up; the doorman wet and ducking as he pokes the bags into the car; Gerald lighthearted with the umbrella. I was touched and delighted. It was perfect for the night, for the occasion, and for Gerald.

[1] Gerald Morgan, younger brother of Aubrey Morgan.

And suddenly I saw that in that humor, in that sentence, in that manifestation of G. was some essence, something very very G. For that quality someone would fall in love with him—not that she would realize that—oh no. He would say, like that, carelessly, " 'Man last seen floating over Piccadilly Circus'!" and she would say, "Oh, Gerald!" and think, smiling to herself, "How *like* Gerald that is! How *like* him!" And be in love with him for saying so.

For that is being in love, seeing in every little act of a person the manifestation of them, the essence of them. It is being able to say all the time about everything they do, "How *like* him." It is being able to accept everything they do or say because it is "like them." I went on thinking about it all the way down in the car—a dreadful ride in the rain, a dark night, blurred lights, a narrow road, and C. going like mad (or so it seemed to me in the back seat, trying not to look, trying not to feel, trying to accept it).

But why *do* you? It isn't necessary, I said to myself. If you are really frightened you can just say, "Charles, do you mind going a little slower?" And he will stop. Why don't you speak? Because it is *he,* that's all, going like this, fast, concentrated, tearing ahead relentlessly through the storm, making good time, not letting anything stop him, sure, skillful, efficient, and enjoying fighting something (unconsciously perhaps—because of course he probably does not think of it as difficult; an ordinary ride home in the rain). An essence of C. is in this fast ride home, as an essence of Gerald is in " 'Man last seen floating over Piccadilly Circus.' " As an essence of Margaret is in quietly holding on to the seat in front of her, as an essence of me is in that sudden cringe of fear, going around a corner, and yet holding it in. Then I thought, No, the essence of me is in sitting here holding all those people in my mind.

It was such a strange ride. I felt it was my whole life, rushing ahead like that in the darkness with C., too fast, too blind, only for that faith in C., always that faith in C. being the thing to hold on to.

———

C. says it was a very conservative ride. He wasn't even trying to hurry or make time! I suppose that is true, as he is really conservative. It is all in me—that fear, that picture—as it so often is.

April 23rd–26th

To Paris and Claire Fontaine [the country house of the du Noüys]—the du Noüys[1] and Mme Carrel.

Mme Carrel is my idea of a very wonderful woman. For she is womanly. That is, she is the kind of person on whose shoulders one could cry and yet one would not do it lightly or for no reason, because she is so strong and courageous and hard in the way a man is hard because he understands and has met the hard things in life. One would not go to her and cry on her shoulder except for the big things, because she would make you feel ashamed if you went for a little thing.

She has a woman's emotion, quick intuition and understanding, and yet a man's breadth of mind, breadth of view, clarity of vision, impersonality of attitude (the scientific attitude).

I feel very proud of C. He is like sunlight to them. They turn to him, his practicalness, his vision, his simplicity, his clarity.

I feel, too: Who am I to say No, I want my own life, No, I want my own work, No, I will not go to Africa because I want to finish a book. Of what value would that book be? A personal account of hashed-over dead experiences. Of what value, next to the vision, the new ways that C. can give, and I by keeping him happy, by doing what he wants? And yet, he does not want that. He wants me to have my own life—to write.

[1] Pierre Lecomte du Noüy, French biophysicist, writer, and philosopher, friend of and co-worker with Dr. Carrel in front-line hospital in World War I.

The French point of view on the Italian campaign [in Abyssinia]: "Marvelously worked out!" On Eden: "Very dangerous person in the hands of . . ."

On Hitler: "Why doesn't he suppress *Mein Kampf?*" (I can understand their point of view there.) On the Masons, on the League: "Great Britain's tool . . . no sanctions against Germany, against Japan, against the South American countries . . . just Italy, where it is to Great Britain's interest." It makes me gasp a little and rather (surprisingly) angry and protective.

Also the terrific picture you get of the internal mess of French politics, intrigue, corruption, distrust, suspicion, and gossip.

The fun of driving through France with C. Like "playing married." Can I convince the innkeepers that we want supper, a room, etc., with my bad French and my timidity? But it seems to work!

Poplar trees dividing in rows ahead of us, as though we were in a boat and the keel were cutting a path through the water.

Mont-Saint-Michel: "There it is!"—fairylike and atmospheric across the fields, in the evening sun.

Then down close to it, rising in cliffs, with that slightly hunch-backed look to one side of it. There are very few cars. It is quiet. We climb up on the ramparts. We find a steep footpath around the back. We crawl over it, dusty and slipping, hanging on to the weeds, under a door in a stone wall, to a chapel on the beach below us. Out beyond the flats the sea, and the wind blowing hard in our faces. C. climbs up higher. I sit on a rock and look down over the steep green hill, over the chapel, with the blessing figure on top, over the sea, the wind making smooth patches on it and the sand. I sit a long time, it is almost dark, and feel as if I owned the island!

Then down to the inn—Poulard, where Elisabeth and Daddy and Mother and I stayed. A late and delicious meal and to bed. But C. goes out on the walls, and then comes back for me. I am tired and do not want to go, but he is right. It is too beautiful, very quiet, no one on the ramparts or on the steps. We climb up and up, looking down over steep roofs shining below us in the moonlight. The half-moon behind the spire and Michael!

Tuesday, April 28th

We walk around the island on sand and mud and rocks, then up through the *abbaye*. But the best of it was the morning's walk, or at least sitting again where I sat last night looking out over the chapel, over the sands. Such a beautiful color, not pearl, not putty, not white, not cream—a warm pearly-pinky sand color, translucent, smooth with patches of opalescent blue water. Then back to the town, and I suddenly realized that part of the beauty of the town was in the repetition of the color of the sands and the water. The stones repeat that warm pinkish-putty color of the sand, and the slate roofs repeat the blue patches of the water, reflecting sky. There were lilacs in bloom, too, and yellow wall-flowers growing in the cracks in the walls.

This has been a wonderful visit. C. has loved it. We have caught it unaware, quiet and still, and as it might have been.

Then a long, long drive, trying to find a place for the night. It is foggy. The coast towns are shut for the winter. We go from one place to another—all shut—getting nearer and nearer to Boulogne. We find ourselves just outside at about 4:30, with day breaking! We have driven all night. It is absurd. I feel very tired and for no reason. How like us it is—terribly funny! We get to a hotel in Wimereux at five and sleep till two.

Take the 5:35 boat to Folkestone, arriving Long Barn about twelve.

Thursday, April 30th

There are one or two pink tulips showing along the walk and buds in green sheaths—that lovely pale green with white in it. The poplars are golden with little leaves. There are two beds of orange and white tulips out on the warm side of the house. The daffodils are gone in the front. The oak trees down in the field are misted with a pinky brown. The elms in the field beyond a little blurred. The cherry trees behind the tennis court are white, and an espaliered tree is white at the gate. The bed on the terrace is lovely with wallflowers, yellow and brown and almost a wine color.

Also there is one pink clematis on the wall outside our window.

I cannot work; the woods are full of "bluebells," wild hyacinths that Jon picks, and violets. We go down to the brook, Jon and I. He throws sticks in the water while I lie back and look straight up at the sky through the thinly leaved bushes. I love lying flat on the earth and looking straight up, face to face with the sky—you feel like an open flower.

Jon is a tiger in the "long grass" (in the uncut grass around a little tree). Jon is a mother kangaroo! "But you have no baby!" Then he is a father kangaroo. "What do kangaroos do when they get shot?" "We don't shoot them." "What do you do when you want a kangaroo rug?"

Jon says he wants a baby and is going to buy one. "You can't buy one, Jon." "If I found one without a mother then I could have it!"

Letter from Mrs. Nicolson says something nice about Jon and makes me happy.

Talk with C. about my working and my feeling about his work and flying, and my general shaken feeling and fear about life and everything. Feeling that there are great pits on either side of this lovely path one happens to be on in ignorant bliss for a few seconds. That very near to the surface of this lovely glaze of a safe peaceful normal life lies the terrible, the unbearable. Scratch the surface and it is there. I think this general feeling of insecurity explains my fear and timidity of many things. He is very helpful and kind and says I will get it back again—the feeling of security. He says he wants me to write more than anything.

If I can now—O Lord!

Sunday

I thought today looking out of my window at Jon, in red rubber boots and blue jacket, swinging around a tree to make himself dizzy and then rolling downhill on the grass (I was in the middle of impatience—a feeling of pressure at so little done, so much to do, so little time, so many interruptions, and such imperfections at the best), that Jon was the only "perfect" thing in life, that is, in him there was no past and no future, no sense of impatience or wanting to change anything, no sense of time rushing away or standing still. Just Jon and complete satisfaction in that "All losses are restored and sorrows end." When I look at him I am satisfied. I do not long for other things. I do not look back, or forward—simply *Here* and *Now*. Why chastise myself for work not done or people I long for? That is enough. "Whose looks could all my bitter thoughts assuage."

Jon, after the trip to London, questions the stone lions in Trafalgar Square.

"Were they always stone lions, or were they once *real* lions?"

Miss W. explains carefully that they were always stone—how a man cut them out of a block of stone, etc. Jon listens carefully and then says quietly, "Dan has a stone lion that was once a real lion."

May 12th

Up to London to meet the King. The Scanlons'[1] "tea." All very amusing, especially my ten-year-old black silk suit that I took up the night before. I did the coat and pinned the skirt. Then Miss W. and I corrected it. That suit—Elisabeth's many trips abroad in it—with that gay ruffly blouse that was so expensive. I tried to get one like it yesterday, a cheap one, though. Pressing it, trying it on—yes, it'll *do*.

We set out with clean white gloves that shed white all over my

[1] Colonel Martin F. Scanlon, assistant Military Attaché for Air in the U. S. Embassy in London, 1936–41.

newly brushed bag and coat (also Elisabeth's old one that I borrowed from her on our trip three years ago and wore all over Paris and two winters after). And the *new* blouse and the *new* hat, which did look nice, and sticking-plaster on the button that was chipped off, to make it look white where it had broken off black.

We arrive. No tea (I knew I should have had some at the hotel). That beautiful American, in a fur coat and pearls, with her eye on the door. She lives only three months with her husband in England in order to miss the double income tax! It never has occurred to her that anything else might be more important. She spends a month in the "Season" and a month in Scotland for the shooting and perhaps one at Christmas! He can spend six with her at Miami! The rest of the time she travels to avoid the tax.

Everyone calls everyone else "Darling." There are white lilies everywhere and a table spread with drinks and hors d'oeuvres. They all shake hands, to my surprise—oh, they're all Americans, then. We talk about English central heating and the difficulty of finding a house and vaguely "His Majesty." At least, I don't, but they do. "Hasn't come yet . . . said to have it early . . . has to get . . . by dark . . . just a quiet informal little talk . . . my *dear* Mrs. Lindbergh." And how odd it is to go to the theaters in broad daylight, and weekending and a "shoot" in Scotland, and how to get real hot dogs in Soho (very good hot dogs, and some pineapple juice), and Mrs.—, who was afraid to take another for fear the King might come in in the middle of it.

I felt very expressionless with the women, as that purely conventional social type always makes me feel. I feel like standing quite still and staring at them quietly until they are all raveled out. It must ravel out somewhere—except that it's rather pathetic when it does. I want to shake them and find something real, something *"them"* inside. No matter what it is, it must be better than the veneer which is nothing—worse than nothing. A denial of life. But the men are different. There is almost always *some-*

thing to touch, something real to strike on in a man. He usually answers you if you strike it. I feel I've failed when I don't strike it a little in everyone I meet. That's why the women annoy me: I feel frustrated. Also the English in general are harder to strike something in.

But that nice man looking for a house for his wife and seven-weeks baby. He was social too, of course, but only from position, not by nature. He said some nice things. About the Russians turning the corner when they allowed fairy stories to be told, and about Woolley, who discovered Ur, talking about the bricks he uncovered—many of them were "broken treaties"!

Yes, one could talk to him—though I didn't, really. And of course he was socially correct at all times—everyone there was "socially correct." Even I was correctly dressed (except for the pink blouse). That was a help, really. Yes, I look well. Yes, I am properly dressed. Yes, I am well disguised—no one knows what's inside. That this is all a fake—that I'm in a ten-year-old suit and never have my nails manicured (except yesterday). Until I talk—then I can't bear to put on the clothes of conventional talk. It's so dull. What's the use of being all dressed up and meeting people if you can't meet them, mentally, somewhere, on something real?

Then the King. We see them through the window. Mrs. Simpson and the King. Everyone stands up—a hush—a flurry. He is small and quick and wiry. He comes in quickly, bending almost from modesty, as though he'd be less conspicuous that way. It gives you a feeling of warmth as though he were going out of his way to make people feel comfortable. He comes around the room shaking hands. His face is drawn, lean, and terribly sad—not old, exactly. He has all the appearance of youth, really—even his face is rather wistful and young like a boy's, only it has hardened. That boy's face drawn tight into the responsibilities of age. Very sad to look at. One feels either he is prematurely old for his looks or else still nostalgically young for his age.

Everyone curtsies. I try and do a half one.

Mrs. Simpson beautifully dressed with the poise and ease of

knowing that whatever she does is right and that she is the person in the room that people will turn to, make excuses for, copy, play up to. All she has to do is to play her role and everyone else will follow the cues. But I rather like her. She at least is honest and playing her own part, not someone else's. She is one of the few authentic characters in a social world—one of those who *start* fashions, not one of those who follow them. Besides, there is a vital energy to her: "sun in her bones," as she said of Americans. She is not beautiful and yet vital and real to watch. Her vitality invests her movements with charm or a kind of beauty. I like watching her.

The King talks to C., to the men. The Beautiful American is flabbergasted. She stands watching helplessly. She looks a child. Suddenly, I feel quite sorry for her. She looks across at me wistfully, almost as though she envied me, for being able to go on talking to Mrs. Scanlon, to the men.

The lull. He is coming over to me—oh God. Yes, he is crossing the room, being polite, going the rounds. First a few minutes with him, then a few minutes with her. Don't look—yes, it is inevitable. "Are you enjoying the country? I don't know where that is, exactly . . . I know Harold Nicolson. Yes—yes," abrupt polite questions shot out and then hardly waiting for my answers (which he can't hear because I get shy and low-voiced because I am embarrassed). (Does one or does one not say Your Majesty? I *can't* say it. It will slow up the conversation too much. Does one or does one not say "You"? Does one start a sentence or must one only answer?) These doubts act as a brake on me: I speak lower and lower. He bends toward me looking away from me—that good ear! And then answers his own questions for me. "Have you done any flying yourself . . . No, not lately, no. I can't call myself a flier . . . You have to keep at it all the time . . . Can't say I like it so very much—but it is so convenient getting around."

"But," I find myself blurting out, "that's the *best* way to look at flying—to make it useful . . ." And about aviation, a cause in

U.S.: "Yes, yes—of course, of course." And then his saying it wasn't the best way of seeing the country—a car better. I said I agreed but C. didn't, and why—my long elaborate explanation of what cows look like to C. at great height. The King bends his ear and looks even further away—thinks it is supposed to be funny—is smiling very kindly.

Then finally it eases off and he breaks away for a drink in the next room. Whee—that's over! Why was I so shy? He is very kind, quick and perceptive, and terribly terribly wound up so that all his actions are jerky and trigger speed.

Then he sits and talks with C. about aviation, about planes, gliding. C. is real, anyway. And they both seem at ease—more or less—with the Beautiful American relaxing between them. And once in a while the King laughs: "The last time I saw you was at Albert Hall!" I would like to listen too to C. and the King, but it's no use. The Englishman on my left is slowly going on and on. Whenever I turn toward the group he pulls me back.

Though gradually the outer group's conversation trails off, leaving only one large group all looking at C. and the King. Then I see Mrs. Simpson fumbling for the little inside ribbon of her coat—such a slight gesture—might not be seen. But the King sees it and rises immediately (or was she acting from some signal from him that I didn't see?).

And we all rise. Too bad, for just then I felt it was getting informal. Everyone sitting in a ring, the men squatted on the floor and the King laughing at some American slang expression. And I feeling, Why, he's like V. a little, those squizzled-up eyes, that quizzical look, one eyebrow raised, the twinkle, the quick response, the nervousness. Only he can never let go. He is still a boy. And all the people in this room (only C., the youngest, is really mature—C. and I), only they don't quite dare let go. And that's what he wants. He wants the after-the-party-kitchen-life one has in America. He is still that age, too. Perhaps that's why he likes Americans.

But Mrs. Simpson is fingering the ribbon of her coat. He rises bolt upright. We all rise bolt upright. We stiffen, we bow. The handshakes, the turnings one to the other, the curtsies. Thank you, I said—wrong again! I can't remember the "Sir."

The aftertalk. Mrs. Scanlon: "After *all*, I *do* think *aside* from being a King, he is *so* charming as a *person*. Don't you think so?" Such a conventional question that I feel, as usual, I have no answer to it. And only smile. Besides, I don't feel like discussing the King just after he's left the room.

He's much bigger than all those people too—only young. Why was he there? It reminded me of Mexico and meeting Charles. The stiffness, the impossibility of being natural, and a real person trying to fit the mold of a hopelessly conventional life.

May 13th–14th

Jon on the swing. His father turns him around and around and then lets him spin, Jon hanging on tight and loving it. "Merry-go-round."

"A darn fast one," says C.

"A darn fast one," repeats Jon.

At night I go in to Jon and he is lying awake twisting his pillowcase into a tight spiral.

"There, that'll do," says Jon (imitating C.) spinning it round. "A *darn* fast one, a darn fast one."

Saturday, May 16th

I have sat out two evenings now on the stone steps after supper while C. teaches Miss W. to drive. It is so beautiful and still, looking across the fields. The elms no longer show clearly their outlines. They are blurred with leaves and the oaks are full and round and have lost the pinky brown look and the field is lush and yellow dotted. The hedge is a wavy carpet of leaves.

I walk very slowly down the brick walk, past the pale pink tulips next to the velvety dark blue iris (a lovely combination). Then I sit on the steps and look at the pale blue iris on the next terrace, clear and watery blue, like puddles in the evening reflecting the sky. I look at the sheathed buds of the iris at my feet too. You can see the pale blue through the mauve gray sheath. It pleases me to see it and excites me with a kind of pleasure—like seeing through the tissue paper of a present you are about to open as a child.

I look up at the poplars and at the house, red brown, now covered with vines, the pink clematis trailing below our window. A blackbird sitting on the roof. Jon's closed curtains, musty brown and blue through the windows.

I am very quiet and a thrush comes back to the lawn in front of me—triumph!

The cuckoos are going, and some trains in the distance.

I think I must keep this place in my mind always, part of the web of me, even when we leave it—a mark of permanent peace and beauty. As people are marks too in your life even when they are not there, or you have them no longer—permanent values.

I think how small this place would be looked down at from the air—how small to hold so much happiness, such worlds of happiness.

I think I have not been very conscious lately, not eager to exchange things with people, not discovering things about life and wanting to write them down. Not alive and growing the way I felt last year (even in unhappiness). Am I too happy, or is it the writing—sitting all morning at the desk, soaked in Porto Praia, trying to make them live and talk *inevitably?*

Perhaps writing is a kind of blind period, walking through the long grass, and periods of awareness come afterwards or before, or instead of.

Besides, when I walk on this brick walk in the evening, counting the different flowers that have come out one by one, thinking it is all mine—this and the house and the sense of Jon and C. with me safely—then I think writing is not important. Nothing is important except this.

When I go in to Jon at night he puts his arms around my neck and pulls me down, so I can't get away. He said tonight, "This is much nicer than a tree"! (putting his arms around a tree).

"*Why,* Jon?"

"There aren't any squiggles on it."

I dreamt about Elisabeth very vividly again. We were lying on a big bed, she on my right. I felt again that old feeling of my being young and coming to her for advice, for strength. She was talking to me about my life—how I must plan and arrange and accept. It was all terribly important and vital what she was saying, but now I cannot remember what she said. I was feeling it with such intensity—the wisdom of what she was saying—and feeling, too, I must keep this, I must remember, with always that sense of impending disaster. She would not always be there, she would not be there long. (I was apparently making her a visit and I must go—go back to my own life.) I couldn't take one day more—not one, even though I knew how precious the days were, that I might never have another chance like this again. I felt cruelly hurt by the inevitability of my having to leave her to go back to my life. And I cried out—right in the middle of what she was saying—cried out from the pain of the thought. And she scolded me, in a matter-of-fact, sensible way, for my self-pity. "Nonsense, Anne, you've got to take it—there's no use crying about it. It's your life. You've got to accept it and manage it . . ." and I thought about all she had accepted in her life, and felt ashamed.

She was funny too. I told her something funny, about Long Barn I think, and she understood and laughed as no one else could have. And I thought, How lucky I am to have this, this wonderful understanding, this wonderful click of humor with Elisabeth. How precious and rare it is.

And then I woke up, but the sense of Elisabeth was so strong. I looked to C. half expecting it to be Elisabeth.

And then I realized, Oh no, I am not young and coming to her for advice. I am old and without her. I am much much older than the little sister in that dream, because she has died and I am left. I am the old one, now. But if I could only remember what she said. That was wisdom. That was what I needed. Then, too, I had a feeling of security in having tapped that spring of memory.

"Nothing is lost." It was all there curled up inside of me, vivid and alive, if only I could reach it.

Donovan gets the message from the King's secretary—a message from "His Majesty." D., absolutely unconvinced, thinks it a press gag. He says in his most "come-off now" manner, "His Majesty of *what!*" The polite dignified voice at the other end. "His Majesty, the King." D. is completely flabbergasted and takes the message, "for dinner—Wednesday week." We accept, of course, but D. is still unconvinced (though we have soared in his estimation: he is a little awed). Later during supper he recovers his equanimity and says, "I've been thinking about that invitation and I wonder if it's a genuine invitation. Why isn't it a written invitation?" He thinks someone is playing a joke on us!

Working on Porto Praia. Sometimes it seems to go inevitably— that is, what the *people do*. I am awkward about translating it into words—technique. There is the first difficulty of making it actual in your mind, to feel that it proceeds *inevitably* and that you are not moving the wires. Then after you feel sure it is real and running on its own, there is the difficulty of getting it to flow clearly in words, so it isn't muddy through wrong syllables and wrong words and hazy sentences.

Long Barn, Weald, Sevenoaks, May 21st

Dear Corliss,[1]

You ask me about dedicating the anthology to Elisabeth, and I again felt rather unhappy about it although it is a little difficult to analyze.

I am sure that when you first mentioned it, sometime last winter or spring, I told you then how I felt. I think I said, and still feel, that an anthology about Death is hard to associate with

---

[1] Corliss Lamont, teacher of philosophy and author, a long-time friend of A. M. L.

Elisabeth. I feel somehow that she is much more vitally connected with life than with death, as she was more a person of Spring than of Autumn. (It had nothing to do with age. It would always have been so, no matter to what age she had lived.) I therefore feel that the essential preocccupation of the book is not *Hers,* not really *Her,* and therefore it seems somehow wrong to have it dedicated to her from that standpoint.

But Elisabeth's death? One can argue. Isn't that a strong enough connection? In my mind it isn't, really. I feel that a book of poems about Death, dedicated to Elisabeth, rather than being a commemoration of Elisabeth, is a commemoration of her death, or even of one's personal grief at her death. That I feel is not fair to Elisabeth. Nor do I think it is fair to your anthology. It is *not* a temple around personal grief. It is a much bigger work than that and I think, although perhaps greatly spurred on by your feelings at Elisabeth's death, it is an outgrowth of very fundamental general beliefs of yours. An expression of certain principles and beliefs which you have worked out during your life.

On the other hand, of course, there is always the perfectly justifiable and understandable feeling of wanting to lay down at the feet of the people you admire and love, work which you have put your heart into. This feeling I very strongly respect and sympathize with.

You ask me about the "acknowledgments" in the preface. Really, Corliss, it is terribly nice of you to think of putting me there, though I must say I felt a little surprised. *What* did I do? Except have some very nice afternoons when I had the pleasure of saying "Yes, that's a wonderful anthology. Do you know *this* one?" or "Yes, I *love* that poem, have you seen that one?" I should feel honestly out of place in a list of people to whom you acknowledge gratitude in your work.

As to "Fame" (answering your little discourse!), of course I feel too, as any person who has lived at all must feel, that it is nothing to be either excited or impressed by. On the other hand, it is not to be disregarded in its consequences. (As it is not my personal "fame," I can talk about it dispassionately.) And it is just silly to say you can go ahead as if it weren't there. One's name changes. It no longer symbolizes the person you are in everyday life. It covers another figure—a strange newspaper figure created by other people's minds and tongues. When people see it, it calls up strange and different images than one might expect.

On the other hand I do thank you very much for writing me about it, and I am genuinely pleased that you should think I have helped you at all with the book.

Which brings me at last to the book. I am glad it has materialized so well—that it is actually finished and coming out.

As for the Greek epitaph, it is one of my favorite favorites. The whole Greek attitude on Death (and Life, as far as that goes) is so very helpful. Mrs. Hand[1] and I were talking about it before I left. She sent me a photo of a Greek gravestone in which a woman is gently, quietly taking off her rings. It is such a beautiful conception—to accept death as gently, as naturally, as quietly as that.

Charles, Jon, and I are so very happy in this lovely old house and garden, I did not know one could so completely drop out of the world, as one can in the English country. People read the papers, but they do not seem to worry as much over here, even though they are nearer to world catastrophes. There is far less talk and excitement about war than there was at home. One reads about it, but one talks about a new variety of saxifrage for the alpine garden, or about the *Queen Mary!*

DIARY   *May 24th*

C. and I motor to see Rosamond Lehmann[2] Philipps for Sunday lunch. A lovely day: red and white hawthorn out along the roads, and lilacs, and all the chestnut candles. R. and her two sisters. I am fascinated watching them. She is very aware and sensitive and yet I feel that living life as an art is more important to her than writing it. Life is the art—or living, rather—and that

[1] Wife of Judge Learned Hand.

[2] English novelist.

is what draws me to her. It is a difficult art, too—even though she is happy.

May 25th and 26th

Janey[1] here for two nights. Such a joy—first just laughing at the English. "Have you stumbled on sea kale yet?" and "That bird-seedy stuff they put on top of salad?" and "Now I understand why cuckoo stands for insanity."

It was wonderful, for I could work all morning and then just go out in the sun and laugh with her—such nice humor and understanding.

And then talking Rilke at night. How dull my mind has grown. It was wonderful to sharpen it against her awareness.

Carrel's[2] book too—making my mind stretch and feeling that I have not been using it enough. No wonder I can't write.

May 27th

Up to London for the King's dinner. Tea at the Washington. C. arrives; the unpacking, the panic; the white violets look very shoddy. Suppose they all wear long white gloves. I am not enough dressed—should be full evening. Feel very shy, young—from the country.

The huge rumbly car taking us in broad daylight down Piccadilly; a goldfish bowl feeling, asking the bobby the way to St. James's, York House. The expectant look on the butlers' faces. Do I or do I not leave my coat here? I do. "Colonel and Mrs. Lindbergh." There are only men in the room—no, there are women around the fire. Yes, they are in black. The King comes out, shakes hands, takes us around. He gives you a feeling immediately of trying to make you at home. A kind of generous going

[1] Jane Bannard Greene, friend of Constance and co-translator with M. D. Herter Norton of *Letters of Rainer Maria Rilke*.

[2] Alexis Carrel, French surgeon and biologist, awarded 1912 Nobel Prize for physiology and medicine, friend of C. A. L., who constructed a perfusion pump used by Carrel to keep organs alive outside of the body. Author of *Man, the Unknown*.

out to meet people, very surprising in an Englishman—a *positive* kindness instead of their usual negative kind.

Introductions; I am paralyzed with shyness—the kind that freezes your face. But the introductions cover it, and his extreme kindness. The room is beautiful, with flowers like modern paintings and beautiful old portraits. The women do not talk well as they are watching the people come in. Lady Duff Cooper as extraordinarily beautiful as she was seven years ago in Nassau. And I—how much has happened to me since then, the month before our engagement was announced, when Elisabeth and I sat at the table in that little beach house and watched her exquisite in pale pink and Daddy made jokes about it afterward.

Somebody tells me where I sit at dinner. The King takes Mrs. Baldwin in. Mrs. Simpson extremely smart in black linen with white lace around the tiers of ruffles in back. She is a very vivid person, with that strange, quick, arresting, and twisted little face. I think it looks hard and tortured as though she had endured a good deal of pain.

The King makes a great effort. At first it is dreadful. His clipped nervous questions fall against my soft and timorous shyness and there is no return. It is like tennis, with a good player on the other side: hard serves coming across and your returns too soft to get back.

Then somehow it breaks on something—Gambia, I think, or our buying a Ford—and I laugh and feel so relieved to break through that stiffness, and so grateful. And then I am talking too much and not very well. Nothing I said mattered, so there is no point putting it down: aviation and Bathurst and Charles and women flying, and men getting into politics in England, and the selling policy in England and America. It isn't that that mattered. For it wasn't contact exactly—only *I* was getting something, impressions in strange flashes. His getting out at San Vicente in a burning sun and climbing up the volcano like mad for exercise, and the people thinking him crazy. And, "You're surprised that I know that? I know quite a lot!" with a twinkle. And the Scottish band that came out to meet him at Duluth: "As a matter of fact I wrote that tune . . . we were on a yacht off Majorca, in the Balearic Islands, and I . . . so we called it 'Majorca.' " The glance across the table. His explaining all the people at the table, very kindly helping me to get started talking with the man on my left! The Scottish bagpipes before the end—like fairy music, I think always: something strange and weird and sad and fey about it. I was transfixed by it as I always am and thought, It doesn't matter that I'm shy and can't express things. This is lovely—right now—this. I don't have to talk. Perhaps it may please him if people are just happy, naturally happy, around him.

He is extraordinarily aware (for a man) of people. Perhaps he doesn't analyze them or think about them but he is sensitive to them. He sees and notices little things, rather like our sensitivity to people watching us, knowing immediately when people have recognized us. Perhaps his life in the limelight has taught him that.

Trying to catch C.'s eye across the table. He is talking to Mrs. Simpson, who has her eye on us—sympathetically but awarely.

Her barely perceptible gesture or flick of the brow that it is time for us to leave the room. He rises; he tries to make it easy for people by saying what they are going to do.

I had forgotten about that curtsy when leaving the room! Do a half one. Then out with the women, discussing flower arrangements and how tired one gets going out to dinner every night and how one must tell a few lies in London otherwise one should be completely exhausted! (Do they ever consider that one might have something more exciting to do than "going out"!)

Those two women: "I've just read your book, Mrs. Lindbergh," then turning to the Beauty beside her, *"She's* written a *book!"* They both look at me with astonished curiosity. "Has *she* written a *book?"* Incredulous, as though to say, "She has a pet chimpanzee," or "She hangs by her teeth in the circus"! I feel like Alice in Wonderland. Somehow this demands an explanation:

"It's just a book about our trip, you see." "Oh," said the Beauty, somewhat relieved and comprehending. This is not so strange. "Oh, a sort of a diary, I suppose." "Well, not exactly—I wrote it two or three years later." Vague confusion on the part of the ladies. Then (ah—the explanation!): "Did you write it yourself or did someone help you with it?" "No," I laugh out loud, "oh no, I wrote it myself." "Well . . . well, all yourself." Complete mystification, and I feeling, But it's child's play, these people, absolute child's play. It's too ridiculous, they have nothing to talk about. They can't say anything except the same thing over and over. And feeling years older than they and more secure in spite of my social shyness.

The movies. Poor Mr. Baldwin, who wanted to go home. Poor Mrs. B. trying to be tactful yet firm. One real moment when Mr. B. spoke about Daddy. One intelligent (and beautiful) woman on Russia.

Downstairs again, sitting around. Lemonade (for me) and sandwiches; portraits.

I got a feeling, though, of great admiration for the King, and great sympathy. He seemed to be trying so hard (and succeeding) to fill that set mold and yet in a way to break it—at least to make something living inside of it.

The feeling I had all the time of his trying to live that sentence of his in his [Coronation] speech: "I am that same man."

The struggle of any human being trying to fit into his mold and make it living is to me thrilling to watch. It is the thing about Daddy's life, about Elisabeth's, and of this man's. It is, too, I think the fundamental problem in art: "The leaping hare caught in the rectangular panel." But then, too, there seemed to be a very human struggle going on, like that dream in the play where the man is surrounded by invisible people and he tries so hard to touch one. It seemed to me that he was making such an effort to make people at home, to make them act naturally, to move naturally, to talk naturally, to "sit down"—a gigantic effort. Why? Not entirely his inherent kindness and a kind of pity for awkward and shy people, but also, I felt, in a kind of nightmare effort to break through—to break through the form to "people natural" and himself natural. He does it, of course, with Mrs. Simpson and with others perhaps.

It was the only way I could explain so much effort for *those* people. (Though of course I only talked to a few and some of them *must* be intelligent. A party like that isn't the best chance in the world to show intelligence.)

C. and I have talked it over and have decided that they were intelligent people—some of them—but so bored by the routine of their society life that they don't bother to break through, but hide behind a perfectly conventional front of "Do you enjoy racing?" "Do you play golf?" etc.

Also, as C. says, a great many of the most able people are not interested in people as such. They are only interested in talking to people who can give them something on their special subject. To them all social contacts are meaningless and they use the conventional manner too.

However, this makes the King even more remarkable—that he should not use the conventional front, or at least that he should use it but invest it with reality.

He seemed quite American in that effort to break through (I can't believe that was all training and politeness. It wasn't done in the English manner). I think he is the most "human" Englishman I've met. I wish so much I could have broken through even in a superficial way—anything for naturalness, for realness, especially as I felt such genuine admiration and sympathy. But it is again like writing: knowing what is needed, *know*ing it with absolute certainty, and then failure in expression, in technique of expression.

C. must have helped, though. There is no lag between his perceptions and his actions. His feelings *are,* and wear the clothes of, sincerity.

I feel that he has a great deal of understanding and sympathy for C. and a kind of curiosity—being drawn to a person who has by accident been put into very much the same situation in certain ways that he was born to.

A late drive home. The chestnut trees are out. It is our wedding night.

We drive to Sandwich Bay to the Grenfells'. A good deal of traffic, and raining. We come on a holdup in the road outside of Canterbury—a man lying on the ground, thrown from his motorcycle, a small crowd of people around. C. draws up in front, gets out his first-aid kit, and goes back to see if he can do anything. I have a feeling of great confidence and relief. The man doesn't know, but now someone is coming who will know what is wrong, who will take hold. Gradually all those lesser people, who know nothing and who are bothering him, will fade away—only C. will be left taking care of him.

I stood by the car, waiting if C. should call me, and watched, only I did not want to look at the man, though he was too badly dazed to mind. C. apparently did take things in hand, lifted his leg out of the gutter (compound fracture), getting the man in the bus to direct traffic and keep cars out of way; saw that an ambulance had been sent for; got out his first-aid kit and put gauze on the place bleeding. He tried to lift the man out of the road but an artery started flowing, so he simply lifted the leg up and put his hat under it. He got another man to cover him with a mackintosh, and got a cigarette lighted for him. He told the man that his leg was broken but that the bleeding had stopped and he'd be all right.

We stayed until they got him into an ambulance. The ambulance people didn't know a thing and did everything C. told them. The friend was very grateful and asked C. if he thought he could get out of the hospital all right that night!

Then we drove on. C. says it's the worst compound fracture he's ever seen—that he'd never have the full use of his leg again and perhaps would lose it.

———

C. pacing up and down the room at Florrie's [Florrie Grenfell, Lady St. Just] at night, thinking about the man and what one

Anne Lindbergh with Jon, Brynderwen, Wales, January, 1936

*Jon Lindbergh,
Brynderwen,
January, 1936*

Funeral of King George V, London, January 28, 1936

Long Barn, Weald, Sevenoaks, early spring, 1936

Long Barn, front entrance

Long Barn, dining room

Long Barn, long room

Long Barn, bedroom

Charles Lindbergh with Jon, Long Barn, 1936

Anne Linabergh with Thor in Kent countryside, 1936

Anne Lindbergh in the study, Long Barn, 1936

Jon at Long Barn, spring, 1936

The Lindberghs with the German Crown Prince,
Eitel Friedrich von Hohenzollern, July, 1936

could do about a fracture like that out in the "sticks" with no doctor or hospital near.

Weekend at Florrie's

The first feeling of surprise: Why, she isn't pretty after all and I'd remembered her as pretty. And then by the end of the weekend falling so in love with her again that I thought she *was* pretty— enchanting— fawnlike and fragile. That little curly head and her slanting eyebrows, her tilted chin, her eyes curling up when she smiled. Her stoop, her awkward wide stance, her hunched shoulders, half-sitting on the fire screen with a long cigarette holder. The jerky toss of her kilt as she walks. The feeling that Florrie is incorrigibly young, little girl, and likes to be teased. Everyone seems younger than me, except a few rare people. Lord St. Just didn't. It was fun talking to him. I felt a little like Elisabeth.

He is very charming. I am proud of C., always so alive and well informed—interesting and vital to everyone he talks to.

Thursday

That man at Porto Praia; still leaning over the table because I can't think of the right gesture to put with his words, "He said I was black. He said I was 'nègre'. . . ." I finally get the man out of the chair! But do not get packed (until late at night), or write Mother, or finish *Man, the Unknown,* or write Lady St. Just.

Friday

Up early and drive to Folkestone, very cold, wet, and blowy. A short trip across, quickly through the customs. As there is a strike on, can we get gas? In Folkestone C. got some cans of baked beans, fruit salad, and a loaf of bread, butter and crackers.

We stop at a charming little inn near Montreuil, in La Madeleine, *La Grenouillère.* It is very quiet. A little low farmhouse, pink shutters, honeysuckle over the roof, pigeons in the court, sparrows sunning themselves in a nest of gravel. They show us but do not ask us to sign their *livre d'or,* so we do. The woman is so happy: *"Je suis très fière,"* holding the book to herself. The man is English and says mildly, "Don't come here on a holiday for there are crowds of people."

A long drive through the rain: fields of poppy, cornflower, daisy, yellow clover, and pink gorse. We stop and get out, C. saying it was the loveliest field he had ever seen.

Everything is very dead. It is like driving through a sleeping world—those wet fields, those shut-up blank plaster-walled French towns. Is it the rain or the strike, or just sleepy French towns? Or that I feel so far away from those black-shawled peasants. The great gulf between us seems more unbridgeable than in England.

We get gas without trouble on the little country roads.

Claire Fontaine

The pleasure at feeling: they really are pleased to see us! [The du Noüys]

That lovely stream, slow-flowing and smooth. First I look at the iris bending over its dark depths, yellow iris growing out of the side of the bank, and think, How lovely the iris against that dark background. Then gradually I see beyond the iris—the trees, the sky, the world mirrored in the stream below, and think, How could I have noticed the iris on the surface with those depths, that world opening out below. And I thought, This is like polyphony to people who understand music.

Mme Carrel hurrying me along the path to see the nest of the little *poule d'eau* in the middle of the stream.

Mme Carrel, an incredibly strong, beautiful person.

"Oh, you were far beyond all fame. You were unnotable; you had gently taken in your beauty as we take in a festal flag on the gray morning of a working day, and desired nothing, only a long work—which is not done: in spite of all, not done."

Dr. Carrel, so compact, alert, trigger-pulled. Terrific force, under control. It is stimulating and rather (to me) scaring. I feel shy and stumbling and *wasteful*—wasteful of speech, time, energy, mind, etc. The lack of waste is like C.

I talk to Mme C. I tell her that I want to be part of C.'s work—new work—*personally* but that I know I cannot enter it technically. She says, "But it is very fortunate that you do not want . . ." I think she is rather relieved, and so am I, to have stated my position. "Besides," she said, "you have other interests." Have I, I wonder? Over here I feel that I have no interests that weigh against the *importance* of C. and what he can do in the world. And yet for us, between us, it is necessary for me to have my own interests.

Driving back through the war country. It is still horrible beyond words—after twenty years. Everything you look at reminding you of the terror and destruction. The worst was walking over Côte 108 between Rheims and Arras. Pitted and repitted by shells, mines, etc. Not one piece of ground left untouched—great craters and pits in which nothing grew. And over the hills a little gorse and cornflower waving inconsequently—with barbed wire and pieces of shells, shrapnel, bones, boots, helmets, broken fragments of planes. It was horrible, and the cuckoos going in the distance. Lots of unexploded shells. We drove through a lot more, C. getting out to look at trenches, I refusing to at last and then realizing weakly that it was sheer cowardice, not wanting to look at it, avoiding it and the thought that it may all be again, and for no reason, for no purpose.

And the crosses—fields of them, crops of them—and that statue to the Basques, from the "Hautes Pyrénées" to die there. Vimy Ridge and the Canadians.

It was a great relief to get into England and not see the signs, reminding you of it every second.

Thursday

Mrs. Lamont[1] for tea, very gay and pretty, full of a dinner at Sibyl Colefax's, meeting the King, talking to Gandhi about sanctions (!), Walter de la Mare about dreams, Lady Astor about Roosevelt, Winston Churchill, etc., etc., etc.—in high form. She

[1] Wife of Thomas Lamont, old family friend, partner of J. P. Morgan & Co.

talked to C. the whole time with zest on everything from the English telephone system to Mrs. Simpson.

She wanted to know what *we* did at *our* dinner with the King, and remarked (with a slight pang, I thought) how close Harold Nicolson seemed to him!

Sunday

Janey[1] for lunch and thunderstorms. Miss H. arrives—with mother and sister. Jon has a cold, in bed. We worry about "was-is." I change the whole of Porto Praia into the past tense and then back into the present. I get jittery with so many people. "Miss W., how will you have coffee? Miss H., you take sugar? Miss S., do you want cream?" And Janey calmly goes on doing counterpoint, the angel. And over the radio suddenly, *"Wachet Auf."* I am transfixed—only this matters—only this.

Monday

We go to see Thor and Skean [the dogs in quarantine in England], all ruffled and excited; Skean very fat and happy.

Thunderstorms burst. The Donovans are leaving. Oh dear, I hate the fuss.

Tuesday

The Embassy dinner. The fun of looking well-dressed and of feeling pretty. I feel like Elisabeth tonight, confident. C. very good-looking. The fun of talking with intelligent young people, though on the whole I think it is more interesting and enjoyable talking to older men than to younger men. Younger men don't want *you* to be intelligent. They prefer to have you dumb—but not *too* dumb to realize how intelligent *they* are. They want to be reassured, they are still justifying themselves. They are not talking to you but always to some imagined figure in the back of their minds that they want to impress. ("If X. could only have heard *that!*")

With older men, you must always be as intelligent as you

[1] See note p. 59.

possibly can. They don't want as much, and no longer care (since they have some confidence and assurance) for your flattery or your admiration. They don't need it. Clear of those fogs and mists (besides those of watching a stylish or pretty or smart woman for merely exterior charms), they are free and interested to look at you and what you have to say.

That strange discussion and my sitting watching, with my mind on one side and my sympathy on the other. I knew *so* well what was going to happen. I knew that the intelligent, quick, successful, aggressive, virile American lawyer would beat the slightly fuzzy, out-of-contact-with-the-world, charming, sensitive, perceptive, finely tuned artist. I knew it from the beginning—he didn't have a chance.

I wanted to say, Don't do it—don't *try* to argue with him. It's no use. He'll beat you to the ground. He'll ask you what you mean by Communism. Do you mean Bolshevism, Marxism? Do you mean equal reward for all? And you will stumble around bravely and say you mean "Liberalism" and "Individualism." *"Individualism"*—and then you will be lost. It's no use.

Oh dear, how dreadfully *right* the successful always are. Are there other standards? "They have their reward"? But not in arguments.

June 19, 1936

Darling Mother—

I got a very Englewood letter from you this morning, also one from Con. You do sound so rushed—happy but so awfully rushed. All those people—and the problems of Uncle Jay.[1]

Our local news is a little petty: our *whole* household is leaving! Not only Winston (who won't carry down Miss W.'s scrapbasket etc.). She leaves, though, thank goodness, of her own accord for a more permanent position. But also the Donovans, who go back to Mr. Bernstein, who offers them more and also a more permanent position. I am sorry as I like her very much and she is so willing and helpful—and also because she likes us and is the kind

---

[1] General Jay J. Morrow, brother of Dwight W. Morrow.

of a person who *cares* about whom she works for and gets attached to them. She was crying when she spoke to me.

"If it weren't for Betty (her little girl of seven) I'd never leave you—even if it were only temporary, I'd stay. I've never been so happy anywhere, but we've got to think of Betty."

So we are changing from the bottom to top. However, Miss W. is taking things over well. She is going to the agency and seeing people first, so there will be no Winston trouble again.

The Donovans leave the day Mrs. Lindbergh arrives—tum tee tum tum tum tee!

DIARY   *June 20th, to Paris*

Very thrilling watching the French coast appear and thinking, It is just like discovering truths in life. Sometimes you see them on the horizon, a low shallow line, a long way off, that broadens and deepens slowly. But sometimes it is like this and just comes on you full-grown out of the haze. Suddenly—cliffs!

The excitement of the days with the Carrels. On tiptoe all the time, I feel.

The morning with a clairvoyant [Dr. Carrel was investigating]. He makes a mistake and then loses confidence, under the penetrating clear burning light of Dr. Carrel's critical observation. Then he does everything wrong. I feel so sorry for him. Mme Carrel comforts him.

Dinner at the Club: faded glories and impending thunderstorms in that closed garden, and people running in panic with their wineglasses up the steps into the dining room. Dr. Carrel says, "They live like that—in fear."

Then that long drive to Rouen, in the dark, and I on edge the whole way, watching maps—so afraid I will get off the road and lose the way and Dr. Carrel's time.

June 22nd

To Château de Clères. A beautiful Garden of Eden, a park-zoo [run by Jean Delacourt, a friend of Dr. Carrel's] with pink fla-

mingoes walking delicately over the lawns under the blue
larkspur and canterbury bells. Brittle-legged antelopes and deer
leaping across a hill and kangaroos staring at us with their
scared rabbity faces. And gibbons swinging, turning, dropping,
crouching in the trees, much more graceful than any animals I
have ever seen—like slow-motion pictures.

June 24th

Jon comes in while I unpack and helps me carry my shoes into
the cupboard—with delight! "I'm helping you, aren't I?"

He asks me about dying. "Does everyone die?" "Yes, everyone
dies someday." Jon (rather worried), "I don't want to die." Then
I take him on my lap and try to explain to him about flowers
fading and going back into the ground and leaves dropping off
the trees and people getting old and tired. I try to explain that it
is a long time off, that I'm not worrying about it and I will die
before him so he has even longer to live. It is a long long way off
and he will be tired and old and not mind.

Jon: "Who will fade first—you or Father?"

He doesn't like it that trees will live longer than he but is
comforted that he lives longer than flowers. He realizes, though,
that sometimes things die before they should. He remembers that
bird at Brynderwen.

Jon does "bucking bronchos" and "landing bursts" on the bed
before going to bed. A "landing burst" is a leap on his stomach.
He did several of these up and down the bed one night. I said,
"Now that's the last one," and he did some more. So I picked
him up by force and tucked him into bed. Jon, very cross, threw a
pillow at me and said in irritation, "You're naughty—you're very
naughty." "No," I said, "Jon, you were naughty, because I said
only one more and you went right on doing them. Now I am
going straight out—no more playing." Jon was quiet till I reached
the door, then a little sharp malicious voice: "What do warlocks
do—*eat* people?!"

Porto Praia not done. I analyzed, one morning when I was
too flustered to think well about writing, that I was writing

badly and that I must stop until I was calm again. Looking ahead at a scene there is usually some point of light, or importance. Not big, not clear, not analyzed, but a point that catches light, that catches your mind. You don't know what it is, what it will mean, what it will do, but you know that if you approach it right it will do something. It will open into something you never dreamed of when you saw it as a point of light, like those miraculous Japanese flowers in water—scraps of paper into flower bushes. Or like peepholes opening to one's eye long views over distant landscapes.

Only you must *not* slur over them. Treat them with quiet, with time, with respect. Never try to write them down just as bright points, just as scraps of paper or as peepholes. That is bad writing, lazy writing, or, at least, unimportant writing. If you pass over them you will pass over the only thing that really matters in your writing. The rest of it is just shell, just support for those moments of vision.

And when you are tired, crowded, rushed, they simply remain closed. It takes so much time, patience, and complete *openness* to your subject—receptivity.

July 4th

Mary Hand[1] here for the night and day. Wonderful talks about everything: the English, feminism, how to best adapt one's child for this world, marriage, women and careers. Terribly stimulating and exciting. It is very clarifying to talk to someone sensitive and aware, who has thought about the same problems that you have.

I felt a great many things clearly after she left, sitting out in the garden tonight—not necessarily things I had talked to her about but things that grew out of it:

That the most ordinary everyday living is as delicate, as breathtaking, as difficult, takes as terrific physical and mental control and effort, as walking a tightrope.

[1] Daughter of Judge Learned Hand, later Mrs. Norris Darrell.

That marriage is the most interesting, difficult, and important thing in life.

That everything that I am trying to live and be and do is nothing if I cannot somehow give it to Jon.

That living is a more important art than any other one. That writing is only important in that it gives me the balance required to live life as an art. Something more, too, intangible, difficult to analyze. It is important to me not because I think I can write great things and give them to the world, but because it happens to be the lens of me, clarifying me, enabling me to see things and to think, and to concentrate what's in me and therefore to live better.

To compete with "writers" or "artists," to work at their intensity, speed, level, etc., is impossible—and not for me. I must have my own measure.

That the people who are most important in one's life, and the people who make life worth living, can be quite different and do not conflict. There is love and there is understanding.

How can I give to Jon? I must spend much more time with him and thinking it out.

C. has done most. *Example:* all that work on the ladder and the swing and the trapeze rope, teaching him control, quickness, alertness, combativeness, caution, and adaptability.

Today, Jon—grinning all over—showed me how he climbed up a ladder (over C.'s height) and caught the rope, twisted his feet around it, and came down hand over hand. Also climbing up the $\bigvee$ loose loop rope (tied like a swing both ends) and hung by his knees, then got up and held the ropes.

Long Barn, Weald, Sevenoaks, July 9th

Mother darling—

It is a very rainy day. Mrs. Lindbergh and Jon are racing autogiros on the floor in the Long Barn room. And all the fires are going. The dim smoky smell of the house reminds me of North Haven (I have North Haven clothes on, too!). And a picture of

Leadbetter's Island before me, propped up against the letter box.

Mrs. Lindbergh arrived without any trouble or fuss on Monday. C. and I motored down to Southampton to meet her, staying the night in a quiet little hotel in Winchester. We walked into the green peaceful close under those wonderful trees the next morning. How lovely and gray and English Winchester is!

Last Sunday Mrs. Morgan, Margaret, and Gerald came from Gerald's school for tea. Mrs. Morgan was such a delight to take around, noticing everything, appreciating everything, pointing out lovely pieces, saying what could be done here and what there. "Anyone who wanted to, could repiece that with new silk"! etc. Also all over the garden, noticing how the different roses grew.

We talked a lot of you: "How your mother would love it," "How Elisabeth would love it!"

Our summer is completely gone, except for two weeks, now to the 22nd, when we leave for Germany. We come back about the 1st, go off again the 8th to Copenhagen. Back the 15th and then perhaps Brittany.

I think it would be just silly to say, "No, Charles, I do not want to go to Paris, or Copenhagen, or Germany, or Brittany, or Africa, because I am finishing a book"—just plain silly and arty and cut off from life. It isn't a sense of duty, either, though I have some of that, but rather the feeling that I don't want to cut myself off from being a part of the big things in C.'s life. And that if I did, some flow or growth would stop and that there would not be much point in being married.

At the same time I can't give up writing because that contributes to the "flow" in marriage too, at least for me.

What a long North Haven fire-misty afternoon letter. It must amuse you to have me write you about marriage, as you are a supreme example. But perhaps that is why I do it.

DIARY   *July 18th*

A lovely day after weeks of rain, cold, and a cold wind: greenbottle days endlessly the same—blowing, gray, cold. After weeks of slightly upset household (did the Donovans leave two weeks ago?), the new couple: "This is meant to be rice pudding." "No, Harrison, not that cup." Miss W. racing back and forth to kitchen telling them how to set the table, how to make the coffee, how to tidy the shelves, etc. Mrs. Hook slaving away at her work, their work, never complaining. And screamingly funny, too. Harrison to C., who is teaching him about the car: "You must excuse me Sarr, but I only catch about every other word you're saying"! Little Donald—fat, bow-legged, pale, chewy, sitting on his pot under the icebox, having his face washed with the dishcloths! Raspberries rotting in the larder. No, we don't have coffee after tea, too! Helping ourselves to every meal, clearing off the dirty dishes; not enough dishes, knives, forks, spoons; glasses broken. "No, Harrison, *not* that cup." C. carving: "Mother, what kind of meat do you want?" "Oh, any kind at all—just *anything.*" The steak overdone, the apples undercooked. Two hot-water bottles in Mrs. Lindbergh's bed. "Where's Jon?" Careful, careful now, Anne—it's all right, all right. ("It takes all the running you can do to stay where you are.") *"Where's* Jon?" "No, Harrison, *not* that cup."

And sitting in the little room, unable to work, Jon running autogiro races up above me, Donald mewing at the windows, and the wind blowing, gray and troubled, as though to spite me. "You can't beat me—I'm just making it as bad a day as I can."

And I feeling, But this is my summer, my two weeks of quiet at home, my two weeks to work—and I can't work. What a hothouse flower I am, not to be able to work. It's silly. You have to have conditions just perfect. Running off to London in desperation (everyone else comes too!) and trying to find shoes: "No, Madam, we have no wide sizes." And hats: "Yes, it will look just as nice as the other when it's done, Madam." (I look *just* like an Englishwoman—dowdy, dowdy: that whoops-up brim over the ear, and a printed silk dress.) "Well, you *are* hard to fit, Madam. Our smallest size is thirty-six." "Nothing at all, Madam."

And then today the sunshine and a lovely wind from the sea, from the south—cool, fresh, but not really cold, like cool water on a hot day, delicious, soothing. C. and I went out and walked up the fields onto the hills. You wanted to lift up your arms and sail gently on it like swimming in the evening off Falaise[1] after a hot day. The still bay, and no effort—just strike out deliciously, cutting the water with cool arms.

But I wanted to get out and walk. It doesn't suit this garden, this pleasant English garden, the roses blowing away, the poplars bending uncertainly, the maple leaves flapping. But out on the hills it was lovely.

It is the kind of day when one can't look at the earth, but one is bent back, forced to look up at the changing face of the sky—big white clouds blowing loosely by. One feels, the real drama, the real life today, is up there. This is just imitation down here in the trees and the grass. Up there is this day as it should be, free and unrestricted.

It made me feel free and unrestricted too. The wind against my ears, roaring like distant bowling, and the soft deep sigh going on outside me, in the trees, the grass, everywhere.

To be part of it, to let it go through your hair, arms, clothes, was delicious. I could understand then why C. likes storms, going through them, being part of them. I must try and remember, when I am next frightened in the air, that he feels as secure, as happy as I, then.

One gets so cramped in ordinary living.

July 19th

Fixing the flowers all morning, getting tired, loving it, feeling domestic and extravagant. Going out with my big basket and my scissors, for I want the house to look lovely. They[2] won't notice it. It's always that way. They probably won't even come in the house, or go hurriedly through the rooms talking, getting

[1] The Guggenheim estate on Long Island.

[2] The Nicolsons were coming to tea.

through the rooms, getting *through* the call. Not seeing that I've put amethyst sweet peas and pink and white stock so carefully in that amethyst glass bowl, to catch the eye and link up with the amethyst and pink bottles in the hall window. And calendulas and snapdragon, to catch the colors of the old painted box in the hall (lovely fruity colors) and the big heavy old-fashioned pink roses in the old silver baskets in the dining room, like old prints. Or the blackberry sprays; the whitish undersides of the leaves and the unopened buds are just the color of the Cézanne greens, and the faint dusty pink, bringing out the hills. They were dreadfully hard to pick. My hands were scratched from them, and so much time spent. Why—*why* do it? No one will notice except Miss W. and perhaps Miss H. Though that is enough. To have anyone notice is wonderful. (Mrs. Lindbergh did.)

I don't know why I must do it. I want the house to look lovely—to glow. I want it not to look shabby and neglected ("It looked *so* much better when we were here"). Even if they don't notice, flowers pervade the atmosphere, like a very delicate perfume, or like a woman's voice. You think, Why is that woman so utterly lovely, and it comes almost as a shock, from its very inconspicuousness, its perfection, it is her *voice*. That is the way I want flowers to help the house.

Besides, it is like giving something, to make things lovely; to give without any reward, or any notice, has a special quality of its own. It is like presents made for older people when you were a child. So much went into them—dreams and prayers and hours of knotted fingers and frozen effort and there . . . only a dirty piece of knotted string came out of it. But you knew, even if they didn't, that you were giving them something worthy of them.

There is something of worship in it—or prayer—that laying down of an offering at someone's feet and then going away quickly.

Besides, it is better for them not to know that you did it, because then you would burden them with the demand for gratitude or appreciation. The nicest gifts are those left, nameless and quiet, unburdened with love, or vanity, or the desire for attention.

So much for the blackberry blossoms. What an afternoon. First all the Nicolsons—she in a huge floppy hat. Mrs. St. Aubyn[1] quiet, watching, quick, in gray; H. N. with a slightly faded carnation in his buttonhole; the boys, limp, tall, quiet, bored—very nice. All ducking into the little living room, shaking hands. I, embarrassed, cringing (what *happens* to me!), apologetic. All ducking out again, through the house (no, no one noticed the flowers) into the long room. Jon, coming down; Mrs. Lindbergh. Introductions (Mrs. St. Aubyn's name wouldn't come until late): "Miss Sackville-West" (she likes to be introduced that way) "two other Mr. Nicolsons" (that sounds funny too). All stand around embarrassed. Mrs. L., calmly and clearly (slightly embarrassed and trying to be helpful): "Will you two gentlemen come down with Jon and me and see the rabbit?" Somewhat startled silence and embarrassment. Ben's face gets that soft baby pink. C. and I giggle a little. Of course they would go—Eton and Balliol! How wonderful, how marvelous. "Come down with me and see the rabbit."

Anyway, we all went out, Mrs. N. to see the garden. I cling to Mrs. St. Aubyn. She is an angel. C. has Mrs. Nicolson. Yes, *that's* all right. Mrs. St. Aubyn and I gossiping about servants, couples, babies. Still, it's better than paralysis. Then H. N. coming up, polite, questioning, "Is that your mother-in-law? I think I'll go down and talk to her . . ."

"Do—she's very shy." Then as an afterthought I called out after him, "She's been to Turkey!"

Mrs. St. A.: "Will she play tricks on him?"

A.: *"Tricks?* Why?" (We're all going ga-ga here!)

Mrs. St. A.: "Well, you said she was tricky."

A.: *"Tricky!* I said she'd been to *Turkey."*

Mrs. St. A.: "Oh, I thought it was a little odd . . ."

A.: "Turkey—no, Turkey." (Really, this is all dotty.) I explain to C. He laughs—the darling.

Then we wander down and see Jon do the trapeze work and

[1] Gwen St. Aubyn, sister of Harold Nicolson.

spinning. It's all pretty grizzly. I am worried about the effect the people may have on him. But he hangs on just as before and loves it. Everyone else is dizzy. H. N. on Mother (he always gives me the impression that he alone understands her and that I am a rather heartless, unseeing daughter): "I think she's rather lonely. . . . She said she might come over." "I'm afraid we're going to be away." (Do you think I *like* being away? Don't you realize I'm *dying* to have her here?)

Then tea. It is terribly strong and there is no slop basin and the boys won't touch the cake until it's cut. C. and H. N. stand in the door and talk Germany. I want to listen. C. said he'd bring me into it but he can't, across the tea things and the sofa and the table and the lamps—too far to jump. I try to talk to the boys. I like them, but it is hard work. I am just giddy and American and chatty and expose myself too much, talking about family and living with family and family occasions. Nigel is kind and tries to help me out like his father, very politely asking me questions.

Then Mrs. Nicolson: "I see your book is still selling—I get the *Herald Tribune* Books." "Yes. It doesn't mean a thing, though. It hasn't sold at all over here, you know." "I know," she said, with an expression of sympathy and no comment. There is a pause and I try to pass it off lightly, and talk about the publishers' comforting me. An Englishman reading American books, etc. They listen politely, smile a little, and say nothing. Of *course*— America looks to England for literature.

Well, try again. "I bought your book and took it to France as a present, and I got back a long and enthusiastic letter about it.".

"That was very kind of you." She looked young and pleased.

Mrs. N. and the books: "Why, you seem to have too many— why, I had no idea" (despite C.'s letter and telephone call!!). "Would you like us to take them away? Here, Nigel, these are *your* books. You can take them right now."

Nigel looks doubtfully at the books—an *enormous* pile. There are *five* people in their car! Where did she think he'd put them?

"Well, here's one, anyway, that Ben would like even if you don't."

"All right, I give it to you, Ben."

And then "We must go." Trooping through the house again. "You must come to Sissinghurst." "Yes, we'd love to, when Mother comes." "We must see you when you get back from Germany." (Of course he'll want to talk to C.)

July 20th–21st

My navy crepe dress and coat have run at the cleaners, are being redyed and will not be ready for Germany. The dotted wool suit has come back too shrunk for me to get into. The navy shantung has come and looks very dowdy and British. The coat too short. I am very discouraged; too late to get anything new. There is nothing to be done about it. Miss W. says, "Anyway, the Germans dress terribly."

At night C. reads me a speech[1] he might give in Germany—at least we thought he might make it into a speech, if they ask him to speak. It has vision, depth, thought, challenge in it. I get terribly excited—it is so important. It should be said, and he can say it. Besides, it is allied to the most important things in life—in my life—all those passionate arguments we have had about "Force" ruling the world—different kinds of force. The arguments about France and Germany—Athens and Sparta, Italy and England.

And by this speech he points the way—the responsibility.

I would go to Germany just to hear it.

Wednesday, July 22nd

Leave for Germany.[2] Up early. Harrison has breakfast ready. A lovely day—"not even a little puffy cloud."

[1] See note, p. 87.

[2] C. A. L. was going to Berlin at the request of the U. S. Military Attaché, Lieutenant Colonel Truman Smith, who was dissatisfied with the meager air intelligence he was able to obtain through normal channels. He hoped Lindbergh would be able to investigate more thoroughly German technical aviation development and obtain information on the growth of the Luftwaffe desired by the Intelligence section of the U. S. War Department.

Drive off to airport at Penshurst. So strange, quiet, and English. The hanger big and empty except for our little gray low-wing monoplane.[1] No sound except lots of birds twittering in the eaves. The long feathery grass heavy with dew, little bits burning red, green, blue in the sun. The oast-house at the end of the field, the sheep.

Suddenly stiffening to my old role. "There's no radio in here?" "Oh no, no radio." "It looks awfully small." "Well, it *is* small—we have to refuel at Cologne. Nice plane, though."

Pushing on the wing to roll plane out. Miss H. getting her little bare sandaled feet wet in the long grass.

We get in. "All set?" "All right." Cotton in the ears. Look at the time. We get off easily, leaving the sheep and the oast-house behind, and hedges, fields, tennis courts, and gardens, neat little gardens. How tiny—how sweet. How perfect England is—and asleep, fast asleep.

We make several landings, bump along the ground. The engine stops; try and start it—no use—over and over. Float stuck; try again, man tries—nothing. C. goes to telephone Miles Aircraft. I sit and wait. The sun is well up, the grass drying, the sheep wandering over the field. I read the *Times* for a long, long time. How much of flying is like this, always: sitting on a field, the grass waving, the sun shining, nothing happening . . . waiting.

He comes back. We try again—it starts!

We get off and head for Lympne. We fly over our house—so tiny, small, and unprotected; green squares of terraces, embroidered with French-knot roses, figures running out, Jon doing a war dance and waving a large towel.

Off to Lympne; a quiet field, all grass, lovely, untouched. "Cut off your engine—you'll be here some time." We get out and go into Customs and sign papers. No one around, very nice and casual Aviation Country-club boys.

Winds aloft? Weather? What octane gas?

[1] A plane rented in England for the trip to Germany while the Lindbergh plane was being built by Miles Aircraft.

They will check us out over Channel (the *Channel,* I think, what's that? No one ever checks us out over *anything*).

Two radio men come out for autographs.

No signals on field, no lights for take-off? Oh no, no one else there, lovely green expanse—asleep.

Off we go over the Channel. C. is very happy about the plane, delighted, boyish, and gay. "There's the dock we left from— there's Boulogne." We skirt the coast of Belgium, narrow fields laid every which way like a spilled box of matches. Canals raked by barges leaving lines of ripples. Local storms. The sky is the same all over the world, no matter how the earth below changes.

The cathedrals center every town, pulling all the houses toward them, like the center of a flower—or the sun.

Following the maps by canals, towns, railroads.

The regular forests of Germany, and bigger fields.

Cologne, and the cathedral pierced by light, in the center. We land—nice landing. A strange octagonal stone tower, looking very German and anchor-blocky to me.

German faces, a few officers. No crowd. The army biplane. We get out. Clicking of heels, the salute. Shake hands. Captain [Theodore] Koenig.[1] Cameras. Everyone is in uniform; lots of clicking of heels. "Yah." Clipped speech. They hardly notice me; very few women.

We have lunch in the station. No, thank you—no Moselle. Some official from Cologne with us.

German boys come up, click heels, raise hands in *"Heil Hitler"* like one man, ask for autographs, bow, go out.

Maps on the wall. The map includes the Polish Corridor and the Alsace-Lorraine territory, only in a lighter blue.

A large bunch of roses. "Very beautiful . . . thank you so much."

Captain Koenig says the weather is soupy over the mountains. We may have to detour. He gives us a map.

We start off. C. swings the propeller. I am at the switch.

[1] Assistant Military Attaché for Air with the U. S. Embassy in Berlin.

The Army plane goes like mad and it's hard to keep up in this plane at the speed we said. (He said he'd go about 120 but he goes about 140.) We try to follow maps. Rolling country, wind and rain. C. doesn't detour. We lose the Army plane. C. says "Soup! This is good night flying for passengers!" Over the Harz Mountains (Bad Harzburg). More towns, flat fields, forests.

Potsdam and the lakes and tiny sails. The palace. Berlin ahead, lots of green and lots of water. The field: Junkers planes all out in lines, men signaling (the Signal Corps is out for a practice, C. thinks). He lands away from them. He was meant to land between them! Sorry. . . .

Lots of officers come up, clicking of heels, salutes, bows, hand-kissing. Cameras behind. No crowd, but a line of officers and people. They come up, shake hands, more salutes. The back line of people comes up: "Your friends—your countrymen." The quick separation from C. (Ah, yes—subservience of women in Germany!) He goes off with the officers in an open car. Cheers etc. We drive behind quietly, Mrs. Smith,[1] her daughter, and I, in a closed car. I feel suddenly that C. is being whisked off and that I will never see him again while we are in Germany.

First impressions driving in: the newness of things, streets, buildings, houses. The neatness, order, trimness, cleanliness (very different from French roads). The activity, lots of people on streets, middle-class, dowdy, but in good condition and nice clothes. No sense of poverty. Lots of bicycles and cars. The sense of festivity, flags hung out, the Nazi flag, red with a swastika on it, *everywhere,* and the Olympic flag, five rings on white. Avenues hung with flags, islands of tall standards, flags of the world. Lots of building going up along the roads. Where the Olympic judges will stay, where the teams, etc. The entrance to the Stadium. The new pseudo-Greek statues of runners along the route (named jocularly by the Berliners "The last four taxpayers leave Berlin").

[1] Wife of Lieutenant Colonel Truman Smith, U. S. Military Attaché in Berlin 1935–39 (see note p. 80).

Crossing bridges, canals, and lakes, lots of little sailboats. Coming in to Berlin, heavy ugly statues on old bridges.

Beautiful park, like a forest, but better kept. No one is walking off the paths. Rather ugly heavy buildings, ornate, clumsy, and gingerbready, all built of Anchor blocks. The Brandenburger Tor, the Unter den Linden. Famous names—impressive, yes, but not beautiful, decidedly not beautiful.

We go to the Smiths' apartment. It is cool and lovely. We drive out around the city, down the Unter den Linden very busy and strung with flags. It is newly painted and shining clean and decked with flags and looks as if it had all grown up overnight. The impression is intensified because no old trees. Two lines of young slips of trees planted. Also the flags, posters, hemlock, wreaths, etc., going up for the Olympic Games give it the impression of a world's fair. Big heavy ornate old buildings which might have looked quite impressive under a coating of respectable grime look garish and dreadful, coated with fresh custard paint.

Lots of uniforms on the street. We drive by the Göring Air Ministry, a beautiful new building, starkly modern, simple concrete, and yet magnificent, huge, impressive—very strange set in the middle of the old heavy bric-a-brac buildings. Drive by Hitler's house, a black-uniformed guard at the gate—nothing elaborate—and Göring's opera house, with window boxes full of flowers. Boy Scouts in the streets, black shorts and brown shirts on bicycles, tanned and strong-looking—Hitler Jungen.

We go home and talk; very interesting. Colonel Smith is alive, questioning, and talks well. She is observant, intelligent, and amusing.

Thursday

To the Air Club for lunch. A crowd lining the street. The sound of drums, music. What is it—a parade? Oh no, the guard is changing. What guard? The Air Ministry guard. Is it something special today? Oh no, it happens every day—the clomp clomp of feet, the helmets, the goose step. We go in. It is palatial—arches and arches, steps and steps, all decorated in modern style, marble, grays and buffs, very luxurious. Officers and much clicking of heels, raising of arms (*"Heil Hitler!"*), salutes and hand kissing.

Upstairs, meeting people. Udet,[1] birdlike, quick and humorous, on gliders. The von Gronaus,[2] Thea Rasche,[3] many officers. We go in to lunch, a long table decorated with white porcelain figures. A beautiful modern map on the wall of world flights. General Milch[4] is on my left. Very German-looking, stocky, ruddy, round-faced, fair, but an intelligent and forceful face—quick intense blue eyes. His eyes when he looked at you were childlike and earnest, but his mouth, compact, disciplined, and firm. We talked a little about aviation, starting with a remark on "this beautiful club." He said it was due to Göring's being head of Air Ministry as well as Finance. I said that it was quite right that aviation should have the best as it was so terribly important in the modern world and the nations who did not realize it would fall behind. We talked about England [General Milch]: "She is just now beginning . . ." (Come now—a good word for England.) "But my husband feels (a glance across the table) that in certain fields they are far ahead—for instance, our plane . . ." (Quick now—pass the conversation across the table. General Milch will like that better and also C. C. bends forward eagerly and they talk across the flowers.) I talk to the lovely-looking Mrs. Dieckhoff,[5] across from me. So there *are* lovely-looking German women!

Also to a very German-looking officer on my right. Very diffi-

[1] Ernst Udet, a leading World War I German ace. He became chief of the Technical Bureau of the German Air Force, and was promoted to General. He developed the dive-bombing techniques used by the Germans in World War II.

[2] Hans Wolfgang von Gronau, president of the German Aero-Club 1934–38.

[3] First German woman pilot after World War I.

[4] General Erhard Milch, originally in Lufthansa civil airline, Inspector General of the Luftwaffe and state Secretary of the Air Ministry.

[5] Wife of Hans Dieckhoff, the German Ambassador to the United States.

cult. He does not speak much English and I no German. Then to General Milch again. He talks about the international feeling among fliers—how even during the war the English and Germans, after combat, could talk and laugh together. Not the French: they could not drop enmity, but the English could. (You were not invading England, I did not say.) I did say, however, more as a feeler than anything else, "But the English have always felt close to you—in character, in race, in temperament." "You think so?" His eyes sharpened for a second as he looked quickly at me. It was one of those glances that are like a crack of light, letting one see through to a vista beyond. He showed, in that glance, pleasure, eagerness, hope, vulnerability, held under check behind that quick taken-by-surprise "You think so?" He can't make conversation about it. They are so eager for it. That sense of vulnerability . . .

Very difficult conversation with a high-rank officer on my right. Finally, in desperation, I admire the porcelain figures on the table (something one can *point* to!). It is German work—yes? Beams, smiles. Ah, yes. He lifts up the large white porcelain stag, turns it over. Then a wave of delight creeps over his face. (Oh God, I think, he's going to give it to me!) I look across the table at C. He is oblivious. I try to talk about something else. But the officer puts it in front of me. He starts to speak, sputters, turns to woman on right and speaks in German. She smiles and repeats, "In remembrance of . . . the happy occasion, etc." I protest and try to look pleased, say it's very nice, absurd, mustn't do it, etc. No use. He waves his hands. He puts the stag nearer. He explodes with delighted laughter and exclamations and then sits back, satisfied.

The toast to C. (It is short and his speech is long, but it must be given.)

C. getting up. His face compressed and serious. He starts well, informally without the paper. Then goes on reading, but very earnestly. (Lord, how serious it is, how grim—too grim for this occasion? No, it *must* be said, it's all right.) The faces are very serious, thoughtful, still. (I don't believe half of them understand it or its implications.) But Milch turns to me afterward with his serious thoughtful eyes and says, "That is a very good speech." He has integrity and sincerity in his face.[1]

Through the club, decorated by Göring himself, beautifully done in soft modern colors and simple lines. A huge picture of Hitler and of Göring in a big military cloak with all the medals.

The German wives, scurrying down the passages, awed, rabbity, giggling a little. "We are never allowed in here—only today."

This raising of the arms business adds to the complications of life. It is done so often and takes so much room.

In the afternoon to the Lufthansa air terminal at Tempelhof. Big, bustling, efficient, like a huge railroad station. Crowds of people. The Junkers planes out in rows. The sense of great activity in the terminal, ticket offices, maps on walls, schedules, timetables, offices, turnstiles, bureaus, etc., all humming with life. People coming and going with bags, like the Grand Central, like a futuristic dream of air travel.

Tea in a room overlooking the field. People staring in at us through the great glass windows and photographing us. C. cannot eat. The sense of *crowds* of people around all the time.

We are to be taken up in one of the big Lufthansa planes (eight years old), enormous. Prince Louis Ferdinand (in Lufthansa uniform) and I in the very front observation cockpit in the nose (right out over the world, like a glider). Cameras. He is thin, tall, dark, narrow-featured, smiles whenever you look at him and bends alertly to kiss the hand and talks with a strong American Middle West accent. He is quick, observant, sophisticated with a kind of loose American pleasantness. No formality at all. He gets out the map and points things out to me. "Pots-

---

[1] This speech issued a note of warning to aviators: "Aviation has brought a revolutionary change to a world already staggering from changes. It is our responsibility to make sure that in doing so, we do not destroy the very things we wish to protect." It was not commented on editorially in Germany, as it was considered counter to Hitler's expansionist and bellicose policies.

dam, where my father lives. The little palace where I was born—
and Sans Souci, there, built by Frederick the Great . . ." Over
Berlin, "The Imperial Palace (then with a shrug and a twinkle in
his eye), the *former* Imperial Palace." It is very strange, especially
through the roar of the airplane. Up in the front of the plane, the
Lufthansa uniform, the Detroit accent, the American smile, "You
jus' met the King—King Edward. He is nize—yez? Vairy
charming—yez?"

He is loose-gestured, too, in a strange way. I cannot believe
who he is.

I am quite nervous because I am never in transport planes and
do not feel at home. Yet at one moment, in a bank, I feel, This is
all right, Charles is at the controls. Prince Louis looks back and
laughs and says, Yes, he is. A pursuit plane jazzes us. We feel the
bump. We land very easily. Pictures, people, handshakes, and
desultory conversation. Who is a reporter and who not? Whom
have I met before?

Finally scurrying along passages with Prince Louis and then
out.

Friday, July 24th

We go out, Mrs. Smith, Katchen, her daughter of thirteen, and
I. Unter den Linden: more flags up, more wreaths around lampposts, more posters of the cities of Germany, more people. There
is a crowd in front of the little temple that holds the Unknown
Soldier. Why? Oh, someone is laying a wreath, probably.

We work around the crowd. No, we can't cross the street until
the policeman turns. Even if the street is empty. You can be
arrested for it. We get across and walk along with the crowds.
No poor people, no well-dressed people—except for an occasional
American. A lot of informally dressed people out for a country
fair, a kind of "unbuttoned" bourgeois air. I think they are very
unattractive, untidy, perspiring, heavy, and yet not evil-looking.
Not poor, not unhappy. A very contented healthy country-fair
crowd.

That pasty baby in the baby carriage with pale blue eyes and one ear bent under, staring up at the hot sky. I think the small children look pasty and anemic.

The shops are shining, smart, full, bustling. Everyone is busy. The German men knock you right off the street, long-legged, black-shirted Hitler Jungen, some children in gay peasanty blouses, one or two very pretty German girls in peasant dresses, much the most becoming costume they can wear. Full skirt, tight bodice, and flowered shirtwaist.

Suddenly drums, music, marching. What is it? The guards changing. What guards? Oh well, these look like the marine guards. All the sidewalks begin to march with them. It is hard to make your way in the opposite direction. We cross the street and start back, marching with the crowd, men, women, and children. Is this something unusual? Oh no, only on Saturdays and holidays (and during the Olympics) they have a band.

Also there is still a crowd around the Unknown Soldier's grave. Two soldiers stand on either side of the entrance, familiar helmet, feet spread apart, bayonet over shoulder. The wide stance, so unlike the leaden-soldier British and American stance, gives a peculiar impression of rough forcefulness—defiant. Go by me if you dare!

In the afternoon to the Reichsportsfeld. The Stadium, buildings, fields ready for the Olympics. They are all mammoth, modern, simple, beautifully done—"the Hitler style," marble, stone, concrete. To be used permanently for all sport for Berlin afterward. They are set beautifully in their surroundings; everything, the grass, the trees, the flower beds, pools. There is no spot around the corner where the debris is hidden, no trace of plaster of Paris. We see the college to train athletic teachers, among pine trees—those tall white Japanesy ones left inside the court, perfect against the modern buildings. Natural surfaces are used in decorating as much as possible: lovely woods, rough-spun woolens, simple useful furniture.

I am quite tired by this time, walking around with officers, much saluting and shaking hands and hand-kissing. Also photography at every step, and looking up at blazing bigness everywhere. I keep thinking of Carrel's book: Of what use is it? Is the emphasis correct? Is the spiritual and mental up to this? Or will it breed a race of tall soft-headed athletes?

Tea at Mrs. Dodd's[1]—*so* diplomatic—and Mrs. Dodd, the patient, slightly vague all-suffering Ambassador's wife. I feel as if she were very weary and it were just a little bit too much for her.

Ely Culbertson [contract bridge expert and writer] (I had no idea who he is!) and my agreeing that bridge is a waste of time! And then, "My father loved bridge." Bright look of expectation. "Did he really?" "Oh yes, only he hated all the conventions." (Look of blurred discomfort on the faces around me.) "He said he played by common sense." (Realize definitely that something is wrong; try to laugh openly and frankly!)

The glowing sunburned face of Frau von Gronau. The childlike sweet smile of von Gronau. The beaming good nature of Thea Rasche (yes, really quite beautiful though she is fat, good will and kindliness and patient humor beaming from her). General Milch starched and rosy and a little stiff in a corner of the porch.

Drive to the Air Clubhouse on the Wannsee—lake near Potsdam. Mr. Mayer[2] takes me. It is rather fun, a great relief to talk quietly and freely. One of those realer moments in a week of unreality, like finding yourself again, and stability. About China, and the philosophy in *My Country and My People*,[3] about the Greeks' acceptance of life. About the French. Can't you get it in a virile nation, that philosophy, that acceptance, that balance, that civilized attitude? The contrasts in the Germans . . .

And then we drive up to the entrance of the club; *hundreds* of

---

[1] Wife of Dr. William E. Dodd, U. S. Ambassador, former university professor, historian, and pacifist.

[2] Ferdinand Mayer, U. S. Counselor and experienced career diplomat, acting as Chargé d'Affaires in Ambassador Dodd's absence.

[3] By the Chinese-American writer Lin Yutang.

cars. Someone taking tickets at the gate—as many people as that! I hate the unreal person I become at these things.

The club a big house, gingerbready. Set terraces of flowers going down to lawns and the lake. Tables under lovely old trees. Lots of people floating about, a faint band, and photographers with sinister black boxes hopping furtively about. Well, this will be an evening! Introductions, salutes, handshakes, hand-kissing, and polite conversation: "And how do you like Berlin? And how long are you staying? This is your first visit?"—"It is so wonderful to find this lovely spot so near Berlin,", over and over again.

I sit down between two fat, rather oldish, bristly Germans. Conversation is heavy. The Olympics. "You are fond of the arts?" "Richard Strauss, my friend, says it's a sacrilege to play the Ninth Symphony at the opening night." (Quite right, I think, it is.)

More food, heavy cake, and wine. Photographers waiting behind trees to watch us eat and snap us. We do not eat. C. tight-lipped, angry. Mosquitoes. The lights go on, lighting up the undersides of leaves, the terraces, the house on the hill. It looks like a stage. And the music going.

A voice at my elbow, soft, thick, German: "Mrs. Lindbergh, do you remember me? Carl von Bauer. I met you at President Olds' house in Amherst." A young face, earnest and polite. "Of course!" I get up very pleased. Note from the past: those stuffy Thanksgiving days (because I overate and was plump). Lovely, birdlike, direct Mrs. Olds, playing the piano like a puritan! Dear Professor Olds[1] watching, brisk, shy, quick, twinkling at Daddy. How terribly kind they were to me, how thrilling it was to get away from college into that bric-a-brac, New England professor's house. Those hearty dinners and the "nice" Amherst boys coming in afterward. Polite sweet round-faced Mr. von Bauer bowing . . .

I had a flood of warm feeling. "Will you dance?" He is bowing

[1] Professor George Olds, friend of D. W. M., later President of Amherst College.

just as stiffly. I smile. "I'm sorry—I don't dance" (not with these photographers here!). "But you used to dance, at Professor Olds'." "Yes, I used to dance . . ." I laugh and feel very sentimental. The band is playing gently: "And when I grow too old to dreeeeam . . ."

Mr. von Bauer, bowing, "Perhaps you would like to see the gardens . . ." I get up, beaming apologetically on the two old gentlemen. "You will excuse me?" Everyone else has left the table, to dance or walk. We walk under the lighted trees, slowly, talking of Amherst, of Professor Olds. "And have you heard from . . . ? And what has happened to . . . ?" Not eagerly, just gently and sentimentally to the distant music. (How Dwight would laugh!) "And you—what are you doing?"

"I am married, I live in the country, I have three children." (Beams on his round pink face!) But he's so young—I can't understand it. Why is everyone else so young? He takes me up to see the garden from the roof. We walk sedately, I in my high heels. He sighs. "Ach—I knew you as Anne Morrow then. You were in your first year—so? Are you still interested in ze youth movements?" (Heavens! Was I ever interested in ze youth movements?)

We wander down, always to the music, sedately (it is so funny) and I find C. and the Smiths and Mr. Mayer and Mrs. Henry[1] and introduce Mr. von B. He talks to C. about sailing. He is a babe. I am giggling. He waits on the outside of the group, hurt, polite, wistful. "Perhaps I could see you again—no? You also? You are so busy, I had hoped . . . perhaps one night I could show you Berlin." I thank him very warmly, but I am firm. I seem to have vague recollections of a very sweet nice but insistent young man at Amherst.

Saturday, July 25th

Out to Potsdam, a trip on the Wannsee and lakes around Berlin in a motorboat. The Smiths, Mrs. Henry, the Duttons (Naval

[1] Wife of General Guy V. Henry, in charge of the U. S. Army mounted Olympic team.

Attaché), the Koenigs, a German Admiral and his wife and daughter and the daughter's husband. It rains the whole time. They put the curtains up and down and keep saying, "Such dreadful weather—if only it had been fine. It is so beautiful. We had planned . . ." They are chagrined. It is rather cold. We all say we are not cold—not at all. C. goes up front and talks to the Captain.

We go by Potsdam. It is rather lovely going in and out of the canals, under bridges, gardens coming down to the water.

I have a very good time, in my raincoat and bandanna, absorbing history from Major Smith (the kingdom of Lothair and the division of races in Germany, the old role of Germany), thinking that the rain and the shores are like Maine, watching the very pretty German girls on board. But I think most of the people are cold. I like the old Admiral. He was in command of a fleet on the North Sea during the war. He is an aristocrat, intelligent and a little stern.

Then we drive off to Rangsdorf to the Air Club, outside of Berlin on a small field (smaller than Tempelhof), a beautiful new building again in modern style. I begin to realize the difference between the *old* Army and the new—the sharp line between them: on one side, aristocracy, manners, tradition, sophistication, weariness. On the other, strength, energy, crudeness (sometimes), natural insight, ability—youth.

Von Gronau is in neither category, to my mind, although really a "new" man. But by temperament, I mean, he is *hors de combat,* one of those adventurers (of the best kind), scientists, explorers, who remain perpetually young, childish, and alone—on the outside, uninterested in politics or social movements. Set down in them, they are helpless, lose their power. They should be left free, pioneering in the North. He talked about Greenland quite beautifully—how you could "hear the silence right through the sound of the engine"! You could see *that* was the real life for him and that he wanted to go back.

Then General Milch came in, rosy, bright-eyed, smiling, bowing stiffly. He sits down next to me. It is easy to talk to him. We talk about the club. He tells me it was done by the same man who did the Air Club in town and of course all under General Göring's direction. "The club," explains General Milch, looking at me earnestly with his round blue eyes, "he has no money to build such a one hisself." Ah, no—that is very plain. "The club he has no money." They never have, but somebody has. Where does it all come from? I do not ask.

Some wine? Some cigarettes? No, thank you. Yes, I do smoke, but not much. "You are very wise." He bends that sweet and earnest look on me again. "You take very little of wine, of smoke. You do not put such on your lips (he rubs his finger over his firm mouth) or on your cheeks. That we like very much, we admire very much. We find Americans they are not like that always. . . ."

I make some banal remark about New York not being the whole of America, and talk a little about the West, and Charles coming from the West, and his life. And then for some reason—I do not know how it gets started—we are talking about Germany, its unity, or lack of unity, until now. And I am bending forward and General Milch is talking earnestly and intensely about the history of Germany: the early pushing down of tribes; the Franks, a Germanic tribe. How (with some humor) Charlemagne is claimed as the first King by both Germany and France. The kingdom of Lothair. I do not interrupt—I want him to go on. Always there has been fighting; every thirty (?) years that ground has been fought over and has changed hands. Hitler is the first man who has had the courage to say there must be an end to this.

So much blood spilled on this line. Always France has been our enemy. We have been brought up to hate France and France to hate us. But Hitler is the first to say that there must be an end to this. We do not hate France any longer. We do not want to fight France. We do not want to conquer people. Germany is over-populated (he gave me the figures for Germany compared to the United States, France, Russia). "And your population is increasing?" "Every year" (he gives me the figures—eyes very wide open). "France is already overpopulated—not as much as Germany, but still it is very high. We want unpopulated land. . . ." He gave figures on France's population: so many people to the square kilometer. Germany, so many; Russia, only one, to the . . . and in parts far less, even—"and that, we feel, is not fair."

He spoke about France still hating them, still the enemy, and Hitler feeling if only there were a strong man in France to whom he could talk, then he could make peace, "but there is no such one."

I say nothing. I am silenced by the number of conflicting thoughts arising from the implications of his words.

Then the men and women separate in true German fashion. I struggle to find out something about Rilke from some German women. They are not very interested. They say he is a little "degenerate."

Finally we get up to leave and join the men. Udet is drawing caricatures. General Milch shows me all the drawings Udet made in his (General Milch's) little memo book. I keep forgetting about the humor of the Germans. It comes as a surprise every time, next to their earnestness and thoroughness and seriousness and sentimentality; and yet, there it is—a sharp quick sense of the ridiculous. It is quite strong in Milch, anyway.

Major Smith did not turn up at the dinner. He caught cold sitting in the rain in his Palm Beach suit on the boat. That was rather stupid of me—not to realize he was sitting there getting wet, talking.

Sunday, July 26th

We go out with the Smiths in the car down Unter den Linden to see the crowds, the marching, etc. A whole big block or several blocks are cut off because there are parades or demonstrations going on. We get out and walk. Flags hide the buildings and line the streets. Sound of bands in distance; looking down closed streets, you can see boys or young men massing, with flags. A public building with a balcony draped for a speech. All kinds of uniforms in the streets. S.A. in brown, S.S. in black—Hitler's special shock troops (one is always guarding his entrance). Also Hitler Jugend—boy scouts and B.D.M. girl scouts. The boys wear black corduroy shorts and brown shirts. The girls wear quite long black skirts (Hitler likes modesty in women!). The crowds are awe-struck. *"Wunderbar!"* It is a great show.

Out to Potsdam to see the palaces. The Germans are open-car mad. They rush to put down the top so you can get the fresh air at every opportunity. *Ach! Natürlich!* I am blown to bits the whole time—squint-eyed and chewing ends of hair.

There are a great many German sightseers—the fat, unbuttoned, loose-coated, unhatted variety—wandering around the gardens.

Koepelle[1] turns around in a courtly manner to me and says with a gentle beaming smile, "And all the papers they speak of ze faithful companion of Oberst Leendbairgh" (the pet Pomeranian!).

The big palaces are terrific, like Versailles or Russia. (Frederick the Great built one to show he was not broke after the wars.) Used by Kaiser! How? How could he have filled them? Impossible.

Walking down allées—the damp shady patted-down paths with the smell of linden leaves, smell of childhood. Germany of course, parks and Elisabeth[2] and naughty boys throwing sand in our eyes and running away. So *that*'s the smell—that's what it was!

The Kaiserin's tomb. They certainly go in for tombs: dim light, marble statues, pine trees, and wreaths!

Back to the car. The chauffeur has disappeared. Koepelle leaps into the car. *"Ach!* It is dreadful, it is shocking! It is too much!" He is angry—but not angry for himself, a kind of propriety

[1] A civilian aide assigned to the Lindberghs during their visit to Berlin.
[2] Reference is to a summer the Morrows spent in Germany when A. M. L. was a child.

anger: "It is an outrage"—that kind of anger. It is not going according to plan. He draws himself up in pride. The chauffeur is not here; we will not wait. He leaps into the front seat and starts the car brusquely. (I am sure the poor man is just around the corner—why all this fuss? I am quite shocked. Mild, courtly, sweet, smiling little Koepelle stiffens into a superior tyrannical officer: Off with his head!)

Finally he comes up running. There is no scene but I tremble for him afterward.

We drive to the Garrison Church, where the King's Guard went to church, where Frederick the Great is buried, where Napoleon put a wreath in honor of a greater general than he, and where Hitler took his oath. Very interesting—where else did a King's Guard get a church to themselves? The old S.S.? Always the emphasis on the armed man being the aristocrat, the superior person.

The church is quite simple and nice on the outside. Victorian inside, rather ugly. Bach's bench. (I *can't* place Bach in all this. That clear, perfect, pure, spiritual world.)

July 28th. Lunch with General Göring
The drive down through traffic to the heart of the city. The guards, the long entrance, up carpeted steps. People running down, doors open. We get out—salutes, officers, vague officials and butlers, up the steps into a long hall. A group of people and a woman in long green velvet with corn-yellow hair, her pin a diamond swastika set in emeralds, gracious and queenly, Mrs. Göring shaking hands. Then doors open. General Göring blazoned in a white coat, with gold braid, good-looking, young, colossal—an inflated Alcibiades—shakes hands. Flurry in the group. Silence—everyone turned to him. He shakes my hand without looking at me—at least only with veiled eyes, and then, as he turned to the next person, looked back.

The dining room: a huge room with glass mirrors, roses, china, candlesticks on the table.

She watching across table. His questions—not to me at all.

An inscrutable face, unflatterable, untouchable.

"I designed it." (Of course—no comment.)

Questions about C. and his flight: What C. did in England, his work as scientist, the new pump? Why doesn't he work here? There are better scientists.

He is brought an important paper and gets up.

On Bayreuth and the opera—why did we not go?

C. must come to the Party Day in Nuremberg—why not?

The wine—yes, it is the best . . . whispers—1911.

Radio operator? Flier? On round-the-world trip? [He asks about my part on the flights.]

We go through long large high halls, beautifully hung with old tapestries lit with lights (like pictures). A feeling of great richness, all the royal colors of the tapestries standing out. The backdrops extraordinarily rich and gorgeous, but no scattered furniture in the large rooms, empty as a stage—a very big stage, too. I felt very small and out of the picture. Beautiful single pieces of furniture, works of art on them, one piece of sculpture. Pictures, set like gems in the big rooms.

Cases of silver, porcelain, old paintings, on way out to a modern porch of plain wood. The garden, a pool beyond, and flowers. The Air Ministry behind.

The (pet) lion sprawling over Göring on the couch. A box is rushed in—"the water closet." Frau G. pets it. He calls it away. The same performance. Then the dribbles on the uniform. I see and say nothing. Someone laughs. Göring leaps up and throws him away. Frau G. acts as though she had discovered it and laughs. All laugh. He explains, "Just like a child," and mock-scolds the lion. The interpreter going on at my elbow.

Will we see the trophies? All go out into the "office," a long drawing room, lined with books, scarlet and gold, tapestries at both ends, and beautiful old wood carving. Madonnas are set around the walls, a mammoth desk at the end, a mammoth chair. We look at the Madonnas, at pictures, at trophies. Göring comes back changed into a pongee suit, whiffs of eau de Cologne, and a diamond pin. He shows off the Madonnas, pictures, trophies, and a sword. He brandishes it and gives it to C. to test [which C. A. L. avoided]. Madonnas for me: "From a church in Augsburg" . . . "from Greece" . . . "from Nuremberg," Hitler's painting.

"Is the Colonel a hunting man?" We go to see Göring's heads and birds. More handshakes—a beam, this time—long trek back through the rooms.

Saturday, August 1st

Write in morning.

C. to see Messerschmitt.[1]

We drive out to the Stadium. The S.A. and S.S. are guarding the streets. At the Stadium, a huge crowd. Hitler's arrival—a child comes out and presents flowers.

The march of nations—Austria, France, Hungary, Italy—the salute, dipping the flag. Cheers from crowd.

The runner comes in with the flame. . . .

The march out.

Sunday, August 2nd

Leave at 2:35 from Staaken for Copenhagan; clouds.

Arrive Copenhagen 5:07. To Commander Dam's[2] for supper.

Monday, August 3rd [Copenhagen]

Walk in garden. Write Jon and Mother.

In to the Carlsbad Biological Institute[3] for lunch with Mr. and Mrs. Fischer.[4] C. asks questions on certain methods of handling tissue culture.

---

[1] German aircraft designer and manufacturer.

[2] Commander Dam, liaison officer to the Lindberghs on their Atlantic air-route survey flight in 1933. See *Locked Rooms and Open Doors,* pp. 62–109.

[3] C. A. L. was going to Copenhagen to attend a meeting of the cytologists' congress, to which he and the Carrels had been invited.

[4] Head of the Carlsbad Biological Institute.

Supper at night with Commander Dam. C. still working at Institute.

With the Dams, Copenhagen, August 5th, 1936

Mother darling—

I have had ten days in Berlin—bursting to talk about it and none of my family at hand and Charles now absorbed in what the papers call "his heart" ("Lindbergh and his heart"!). The feeling that one was right in the center of the volcano of Europe—watching, hearing, listening—talking like mad about it with people aware and interested. To be suddenly dropped on the other side of a question you had been looking at all winter through the Gothic windows of the London *Times*.

The shock of it, too, after the pictures given at home and in England, by the papers—the strictly puritanical view at home that dictatorships are of necessity wrong, evil, unstable, and no good can come of them, combined with our funny-paper view of Hitler as a clown.

The English newspaper attitude to Germany as a rude, badly brought-up, obstinate, difficult, but not very formidable bad boy. The French, of course, do not underestimate the strength of Germany, but are not quite aware of the direction in which it is pointed. (Or perhaps they *are* aware, and the rest of us are being fooled.)

Anyway, there is no question of the power, unity, and purposefulness of Germany. It is terrific. I have never in my life been so conscious of such a *directed* force. It is thrilling when seen manifested in the energy, pride, and morale of the people—especially the young people.

But also terrifying in its very unity—a weapon made by one man but also to be used by one man. Hitler, I am beginning to feel, is like an inspired religious leader, and as such fanatical—a visionary who really wants the best for his country.

It is true that we saw only the best, as we did in Russia, and there is no comparison between the two—Germany is so far on top. Of course it did not go down as low, although I think no one at home or in England realizes how near to Communism Germany came, and how it has really been through a revolution.

In spite of the excesses, it does look as though there had been less waste in Germany than in Russia and the results are certainly better. They have not cut off their past or distorted it as much as the Russians have.

There are great big blurred uncomfortable patches of dislike in my mind about them: their treatment of the Jews, their brute-force manner, their stupidity, their rudeness, their regimentation. Things which I hate so much that I hardly know whether the efficiency, unity, spirit that comes out of it can be worth it.

And yet there they are, a strong, united, physical, and spiritual force to be reckoned with—a spirit of hope, pride, and self-sacrifice. We haven't got it—or France or England. It bothers me that it seems to be gotten that way—not by democracy. It bothers me, too, that people look at it simply as a repetition in history and say that it is Germany before the war—same Prussian spirit, same military attitude, same aims, etc. I suppose it is the same spirit, the same characteristics, the same force; but I keep feeling that it could be directed, it could be a force for good in the world, if only it could be looked at, acknowledged, turned in the right direction, whereas if it is ignored, insulted, trampled on, or falls into the wrong hands, it could be a horribly destructive force. I feel as if England were the only hope. They say that Hitler worships England. They want England as a friend, and peace with France, but they will *have* to expand somewhere. The colonies or Russia—by war or peace. They say they don't want to fight France. France is overpopulated too. They want *un*populated land. "People—and no space!" is the motto set up over the big map of Germany in the big "All Germany" propaganda exhibit in Berlin. No wonder Russia is worried!

The big propaganda exhibit was terribly interesting. Naturally, as propaganda, I cannot help comparing it to Russian propaganda. In the first place, it was not destructive (I know destructive propaganda *does* go on—about the Jews, Communists, etc.) but in the exhibit there was none (that I saw), none about other nations, about their own past regimes, except to show in one room the headlines of old newspapers (fall of governments, fall of value of money, percentage of unemployed, etc.) the time Hitler came in. The rest of the exhibit showed what the Hitler regime had done—was doing—in health, eugenics, labor conditions, economic conditions, public works, etc. I did not pay much attention to *what* they said because that is naturally propaganda. I could judge the methods of propaganda—of teaching—which are extremely clever and able. Each thing to be shown is first written in words on the walls (usually Hitler's words), then shown in photographic murals and also in graphs, statistics, in plastic art—a small model of a farm, or a railway (an electric train running through it!) or of road systems. People are taught one thing in four or five different mediums.

It was an exhibit 1, to show what the Hitler regime had done, was doing, etc., and 2, to encourage a feeling of national pride, unity, strength. There were large rooms devoted to different parts of Germany, showing a little of their history, their architecture, their art, their science, their products, their own special qualities: art, religion, history, commerce, science, literature, nothing was left out (except always the Jews, and Jewish names and works). Goethe's carriage, the Gutenberg press, things of Luther's, the Nuremberg Madonna, the medieval churches and the modern dirigibles. It was all German—all Germany.

Hôtel Angleterre [*Copenhagen*], *August 11th*

Mother darling—

This must go off, as I have been writing this for days. I held it, first thinking we were going back to England before the conference but the time was so short we stayed right on. It is so very odd to find myself in a cytologists' congress! "And you, Mrs. Lindbergh, are you also interested in tissue culture?"

Except for the Carrels (he always seems so very vital, and everything he touches) there is a slightly musty beardy atmosphere about it (chiefly, I suppose, due to my ignorance!).

Charles was so pleased by what you wrote about the speech [in Germany].[1] I was terribly thrilled by the speech. You know the feeling, "Yes, you *must* say it. It is terribly important, and only you can say it. It is the kind of thing you were *made* to say." Also, we had not seen the *Times* editorial and thank you so much for it.

I was so glad to get your cable. I hardly dare breathe but everything seems to be working out perfectly. We go home on the 15th for a bare week, take Mrs. Lindbergh to the boat on the 22nd, leave for Brittany on the 23rd, arrive the night of the 24th, stay a week, leave on the 1st (?), and arrive at Long Barn on the 2nd, I *hope*. Which should be, I think, when you arrive. I hope terribly I get there first. I want so much to welcome you, to fix the house with flowers and *see* you come in. However, it really is too wonderful to think you can be there in the free-est month in the summer, and even if we are not there before you, Miss W. will have everything ready. I *hope* to have changed the household again before you arrive but if it isn't possible I hope you won't mind a week of the heaviest cooking and most clumsy service you ever had. They are honest and willing, but we practically serve ourselves. There is a room for Emily or Isabel, if you bring her, but it has, I am afraid, *no* conveniences at all.

This must go off. I will send it to Englewood, hoping to catch you. It will be so wonderful to see you—a quiet time with you and Jon. (I have not seen Jon all summer, I feel!) I hope the roses will be in their second blooming and that we have some sun.

DIARY   *Monday, August 24th*

Spend Sunday night in a small hotel south of Caen, Condé-sur-Noireau. Motor all day to arrive at Tréguier at six. The Carrels

[1] See p. 87. The speech was favorably commented on in United States newspapers but did not please German official opinion. Colonel Hanesse of the Air Ministry, who was in charge of C. A. L.'s program in Germany, warned the U. S. Military Attaché, "But no more speeches."

are there in front of the cathedral. We drive to Port Blanc, on the coast, where we are to leave for the island. Over a hill and below us, tall white pines, green fields sloping to the sea. And out to sea, on all sides down the coast, a fantastic line of rocks rising in strange wild shapes, and rocky islands. It is almost 7:30, and there is a slight haze on the horizon. You do not see the rocks too clearly, just their fantastic forms, and not much beyond them. They are the end of the world.

Île Saint-Gildas lies in the midst of them, low, rocky, a clump of green pines against a great fortresslike rock with a white cone [marker] on top, some roofs huddled together, and a green field.

We change cars in a garage, run across a road, across a field of artichokes, over a wall to the pier. (Mme Carrel has it all planned so that we will not see anyone. No one will know we are here.) Then into their little motorboat. Mme Carrel takes the rudder, manages the engine with Pierre, the shock-headed barefooted (espadrilles) Breton boatman.

We come to a beach piled up with many large round stones, almost a breakwater. (It is too low tide to get into the harbor, which in high tide goes right up to the steps of the wall around their farm and house.)

We walk across a low-tide mud flat. Behind a wall are the roofs of farm buildings, gray stone, ivy-covered, a kind of yellowing moss on the tiled roofs. To the left (against which the houses and the big pines are huddled) is a great rock, like a citadel, half ivy covered.

We climb up the steps to the wall and gate. In the stone gatepost is a niche, a pottery Breton St. Anne and the Virgin (as a girl) and a bowl of flowers and a fernlike leaf. It is covered by a little glass door. We open the gate and step down into a farm courtyard. We are enclosed. A line of low cypresses shuts out the sea. The dusty courtyard is in front of us, the farm buildings around it, cows being milked in the shadowy stalls. We open a gate to the right, back of the yard, and we are in a second walled garden. An ivy-covered stone house, with low green-shuttered windows, faces a walled garden; paths, a big fuchsia bush, a few trees, grass, and over the wall at the end, partly hidden by cypress again, the rocks, water, and the coast of the mainland. We feel completely enclosed, protected.

Into the house: gray flagstones, and beautiful old French provincial furniture, lovely carved wood, cupboards, chairs, dressers. Quimper plates on the walls, a few soft dahlia-colored long-haired rugs (ragged like their dogs' coats), lovely reproductions of oil paintings on the walls. A wooden Madonna and next to her a pewter pitcher full of white daisies. I feel warmed and welcomed by the beauty of it all.

After supper at a small refectory table we go out and walk. They have a big walled garden on the other side of the house, long and spacious and bordered by a high wall with pine trees showing over the top. A long sandy path stretches the length of it, rose trees on each side, vegetables growing in most of the garden and flowers bordering them, fruit trees against the high walls. It is intensely peaceful, self-contained, at rest—like the garden of a monastery.

Outside the gate and down a tree-sheltered road, you are out of the safety and enclosed feeling. You are immediately in the world of bare tidal flats and rocks, rising like strange figures around you, heather-covered slopes, and a few sparse fields.

Tuesday, 25th

We walk over the island in the morning. It is a beautiful day, sunny, cloudless, warm, with a slight haze at a distance. This has the strange effect of softening everything, making it all a little unreal. The colors are softened too and seem always to follow the same pattern. The soft gray-green of the pines, the soft gray of the rocks, with green ivy covering or half covering them, the soft blue of the sea and the sky, a gray-white horse on a soft green field. This softness gives a dreamlike impression of the place, as though it had all just risen up out of the sea. The impression is intensified as one walks, because the island for the most part is quite low and out of this comparatively flat land rise these gigantic rocks and rock piles, strange, twisted, fantastic, against the hazy horizon. Unless you are on a hill you do not even see the sea beyond. These strange shapes look active and not static, as if they had just pushed up out of the sea or as if, when your back was turned, they would change their positions like the child's game of statues.

Sometimes looking across at those rocks in the sea, I would be reminded of icebergs in the north—the fantastic forms of floating ice, pushed up, frozen; and sometimes, looking across the dry deserted tide beds, at their (in some lights) reddish stone towers, I think of the rock formations in the desert.

Heather, sun, a sea wind, and your skirt flapping, delicious. I sink into it, unable to talk, or even think much, filled up with it. Mme Carrel and I walk, C. and Dr. Carrel walk behind slowly, talking.

We go home and sit and talk in *"le bois du coeur,"*[1] behind the garden. The ideas in Dr. Carrel's paper, "L'Amélioration de la race humaine," a science of man . . . an institute of man. What is needed, what could be done—practically, immediately? What would interest people?

Saturday, August 29th

We go out after supper and walk. There are still a few streaks of light left behind the western rocks, but the moon is coming up. It is low tide. The moon flickers in the little pools left in the mud flats, in the wavelike ripples that still hold a little water. The rocks loom up dark and solid; at first they are clear silhouettes against the clear, far, evening light, the outline of their black contours against the sky seems intense and trembling. Then, as the light fades and the moon comes out, their shapes are vague, pervaded with moonlight as the landscape is, and seem to merge with the unreality of the world.

The field is wet with dew and slowly gets quite bright as we

[1] Named for a heart-shaped stone in the wall.

walk across it. One becomes aware with delight that the whole world is bathed in this soft milky mist—the fields, the great piles of rocks, the gentle hill of heather, the strange bare stretches of low-tide pebbles and flats, the fantastic shapes of rocks rising at intervals, everywhere on the horizon and on the glimpses of the mirror-still sea.

The stars have come out, sharp points of light above, in contrast to the softly glowing moon. They are comfortingly the same in an alien world: the Dipper, Arcturus. Hold on to Arcturus. Looking across the rough mud flats, softly lit by the moon, and the unearthly shapes of the piled-up stones as far as one could see a bare desolate landscape—it was, as Dr. Carrel said, the world before man. It was like the world first made—*still,* after cataclysm (to me, for the rocks look cataclysmic), untouched, unknown—or like the mountains of the moon.

We stand by the fence and look across at the landscape and the stars beyond. Suddenly a very bright star—yes, a star—shooting; but it is going *up*—up the sky! I touch C. We all look. It tears up the sky—a long streak—then out. Everything is as new, as fantastic, as completely reversed as that: the island, the rocks, the ideas discussed, the conceptions, plans, beliefs—all new, strange, and cataclysmic to me and yet apparently true, real.

Sunday, August 30th

I sat on top of the big rock near Saint-Gildas Rock and looked out over the sea—so soft and still and warm in the sun. So still that all sounds came to me, the farmyard behind, but also Pierre far below on the low-tide pebbles, crunching on the pebbles, splashing through the water. Also, cars on the mainland and small boats fishing off on the water and the calls of children, and the stamping of some animal in the yard, and birds and small crackings in the pine trees below me. But the view itself did not bring anything to me or suggest anything. I felt it should, somehow, that there was something in it for me.

Then I went down lower and sat on a ledge in some ferns and

heather where I was just at the height to see under the tops of the pines, out between the reddish brown trunks, over covered walls and fields to the rocks and the sea, everything seen through and framed by the trunks of the pines. I wondered why it was so much more beautiful than the view on top, and decided it was that wonderful combination of "the near and the far." Sun on the pine needles and also sun on the sea far beyond. And I thought about frames and how important they were. They were direction and emphasis and a lens. And I wondered if that is not what women are meant to be—the near, framing the far.

Tuesday, September 1st

In a way this week has seemed to be one to emphasize our differences. A thing which, as a matter of fact, I approve of. But it is very strange. There seem to be strong lines drawn unconsciously and divisions made unintentionally. The near and the far again. It isn't just science and those technical talks which divide me from them, but everything. Colonel Lindbergh is "deep deep violet"[1]; Mrs. Lindbergh "pale pale blue." Colonel L. is "very sensitive" (to touch); Mrs. Lindbergh feels nothing. Colonel L. sees into the infra-red; Mrs. Lindbergh does not. Those who have good digestion; those who have not! Those who have unusual powers; those who have not. Those whose bringing up was good; those whose early training was poor. ("You have only to bring up your child exactly as your husband was brought up.") The shy and the bold. The strong and the weak. The adventurous and the conservative. The courageous and the fearful. It is not really what is said, at least nothing pointedly said, but only my own conscience looking at them, taking their standards. Seeing their strength, power, health, courage, adventurousness, ability—and the ordeals they have been through—and thinking, Could I go through that? Could I measure up to that?

And seeing C. race ahead, way way ahead, into "the far"—new

[1] Reference is to the "auras" Mme Carrel said she saw emanating from her guests.

fields, new ideas, new countries, new schemes. Can I follow? "There are no classes in life for beginners; it is always the most difficult thing that is asked of one first."

Last night we went out and walked again in the moonlight—full moon. It was again unearthly, cold, grown to vast proportions in the dim light. The rocks were lines of mountains. The stretches of mud flats, great wastes; the trickle of receding tide silver ahead of us, a river seen at great distance from the air at night. C. went off and climbed the heather hill, Dr. Carrel, too, and I felt: I must learn to be alone in this desolate world and to love it. I felt I must keep this landscape in my mind. If I can keep it, if I can absorb it, if I can love it, I will learn to understand better the landscape of C.'s mind. And I went off alone and sat for a long time and became happy and felt not afraid. And just as I got to that state C. whistled for me to come to him among the rocks!

September, Long Barn, Weald, Sevenoaks

Darling Con—

What a wonderful letter. I have read and reread it about "the twisted-thread kind of life a woman always seems to have"—so wonderfully put. I keep saying, She must *act,* she must *write,* if she can say things like that. And always with more finality, Oh, she must *marry.*

It is strange that you should write it and put in words what I have been thinking about for so long this year. I have finally come around this year to realizing that for me the twisted-thread kind of life is and must be my special talent. But in order to do it well I must also somewhat specialize. I must write, not because I feel I have anything to give ("Hurrah!"), not because being an artist comes first (it doesn't), not because it matters to anyone else what I say (that has no bearing on it at all), but simply because the "thread" will not be strong without that strand. It is quite selfish of me. Writing is taking, then, and not giving. I must do it—without it I should not be able to breathe or talk or walk at all smoothly. So you see I don't really think that the specialized life—or a little specialization—spoils you for the "twisted-thread" life. I think it helps.

"Twisted-thread" life of course spoils you for specialized life, in a certain sense. I don't really believe that a woman who makes a real success of the twisted-thread life can ever equal a man in technical ability in specialized lines. She can never again summon up that concentration, that ruthlessness, that narrowness that it inevitably takes—should take. She cannot get such concrete results. She has got to be content with a different kind of result—not a tangible one, not one you can weigh. But perhaps one that is bigger, broader, more general, more intangible—but nevertheless a whole.

If you could put it down at all I think it would be something like a "sphere of influence." Something wheel-like, with the essence of you at the center, reaching out on all sides in various directions. Of course there must be a concentrated core, a hub at the center that is specialized, in order to hold all those diverse spokes together. And each person must find her own specialized core. But she must never fool herself into thinking that the core is the whole. It is just there so that the wheel can go round—to keep the whole going.

DIARY   *October 3rd*

A long and silent month—really a very successful one—but busy, absorbed in fitting in layers of different portions of living. Mother and Con here; but I must not neglect the writing. I must protect myself against "It's no use, you can't work when anyone is here." I must work *better* than before. Just to prove something, to save something. Mother is absorbed and happy with Jon, clipping roses in the garden. Wonderful, just as I imagined her—a basket and scissors and that old black wool suit and hat, clipping quietly and neatly—and Jon gay and quick running after her. "Let's be the gardeners, Jon!" "Yes, let's be the gardeners—but let's be the gardeners having a holiday!"

The Grenfells come and C. talks to him and I love it too. And the Nicolsons come—*en famille,* as usual—and it is just like every other time. (It was nice at Sissinghurst, though—talking Germany.) It was alive and real, only H. N. looked so old and tired and fallen together and altogether weary, even of talking politics. Why do people get like that? It isn't age. It's something else—a lack of core or inner fire to keep you warm. *She* has it. I was very conscious of it. She was well and serene and glowing, and he, just troubled and restless and weary. I felt the kindest thing to do was to go away quickly and let him get those things done he had on his mind.

Not much time with Con, though, and it was hard to meet her—to feel really conscious of the preciousness of our moments together. Just a little, about the life of women. The feeling: she is no longer single, really, in spirit. Those infinitesimal double worries which bind you so much more than the big ones that are only your own—which are connected with someone you love and therefore become unbearably heavy. Because it is all really just that one big burden of loving someone.

And all the time that hidden suspended secret inside: Is it true? Will I have another child? I mustn't do too much, I mustn't take chances. . . .

October 9th

I have been rather sick, and though it is miserable and delays the writing, because it is only possible—and not always then—to write a little in the morning, it has its compensations and has thrown me into books with an intensity, because it is the only thing that distracts me. And also because of not sleeping very well, into those long dream-arguments with imaginary people at night that are sometimes valuable in showing you where you are.

November 3rd

More apathy and feeling not very well and wondering why I do not get more done. I feel fairly well in the morning but everything is slowed up, letters not written, work not done. C. is very good about it—much less impatient than I am. I think he gives me the benefit of the doubt too often. I feel it is not all due to the sickness but somewhat my general apathy and laziness creeping up on me in a weak moment. But I am happy—really happy underneath, and sometimes on top so thrillingly, when the sickness gives me a chance. For there are good days. Those lovely golden slightly misty days ("Season of mists and mellow fruitfulness") when Jon and I go out and pick blackberries, or look for mushrooms, or just leaves and berries to put in the house.

And that lovely day that was warm and I felt so well, walking along the street in London and suddenly realizing how happy I was—how lucky I was. Charles loves me and I'm going to have another baby!

And then a few mornings when the writing went well.

And the morning, lovely sunny and still, when I looked out of the window onto the court below and saw a sparrow bathing in the pool left in the bricks by the rain of the night before, and feeling suddenly: Oh God, how I love this house!

The birds nesting in the eaves, in the rose vines, on the walls, and fearlessly pecking worms on the lawns outside seems to me so very perfect—the last step in its openness and quietness and peace. That it should be so open, so gentle, kind and quiet, that even the birds should come to it seems to indicate to me that it has reached a state of grace above other houses. Like the birds coming to St. Francis.

Saturday, November 21st

The last few weeks have been full of people. Very stimulating, but usually exhausting afterward. A lot of very bad damp, dark, wet weather, depressingly the same. You put on the lights when you get up to do your hair and have them on to read, from two on; out around the garden in rubber boots (come now, Anne, it's good for you!). Less sickness but a lot of eye strain. (The lights are *so* bad.)

The du Noüys, rather an effort for me because of sickness, but very nice and stimulating. Then a lovely weekend with Rosamond Philipps [Lehmann] and her husband. I am so happy to be with people like that that I talk like mad, too much; all those long night conversations that have been pent up—all come out.

She said some lovely things: "Women are *reflective*, men, *affective*." And the two symbols—the sea and the wind. We talk about Rilke and feminists! C. enjoys it too, and talks well.

Their quiet, grave, sensitive little boy. Jon looks tough and rosy next to him.

The Trippes[1] coming down for the night, and that party in town at the Dorchester. Fun talking, until twelve, when I got *terribly* tired and wilted. And everyone else dancing and I minding that I couldn't—minding awfully that I should have to say no, when I love it so.

Fun to hear C. with Americans again, talking aviation shop, like the old days, and American slang: "You know the Lockheed used to land like a bat out of hell."

Simply exhausted by 2 A.M., when we got up to leave.

Back to Long Barn at 3:15!

I like Betty. She manages a difficult life well—in the middle of New York. The hardest kind of modern American businessman's life. And she manages it cheerfully, happily, and remains normal, unlacquered, unhardened, natural, with American humor, American understanding and sympathy, and American good sportsmanship. Really, she is remarkable, does the social end, the business trips, the strange contacts, the New York life, the family, marriage, and remains *genuine,* through all the conventionality of it. Of course, he is remarkable too. But he is a kind of genius, following his own bent. He is typically U. S. A. too, in the best sense, and so is she. If there are people like that there, our country is not so badly off.

Last night, C. away, I got out all Elisabeth's letters (I had brought with me) and got into bed and read them all. I have

[1] Juan Trippe, World War I naval pilot, airline pioneer, organizer and President of Pan American Airways, later chairman of the board. Betty Trippe, his wife. Both old friends of the Lindberghs.

been dreading it in a way, and yet saving it. Afraid of the loss it would make me face, longing for that warm glow of her presence, but dreading the shock and the cold afterward. I have not dared read them with people around, afraid I would cry.

It was a shock but different from what I expected. I expected much more. There was really so little of her there. It was like looking at old photographs. There was more of her in the look of her handwriting, agile, nervous, quick, delicate, and precise—like her hands.

But not in her letters, not in what she said. She *didn't* talk in the letters, that was the blow. The letters were not much more (and that is enough) than the deft swift press of her hand. In talking she was direct, intuitive, daring. In talk she towered—"summer lightning." Writing was too slow for her, too cramped, too self-conscious. Her letters were never self-conscious, but somehow her genius is not in them.

For me the reality of Elisabeth is not there—I found that tonight. It is not in the letters. It is not even in memories . . . very much. But in something undefined in me, in Con, and in Dwight in flashes, something that goes along with me and has—this is the shock—*grown with me*. The Elisabeth I carry around with me every day is much much older than the Elisabeth of those letters. It is she *in me* growing old along with me. Is that possible?

It has something to do with my belief that if you have a person, understand them or perceive them really and deeply at any one instant in their lives, you have them for ever: what they were like as a child, what they will believe in when they are old. It is again in a different dimension the symbol of the crystal: if you could break it up into its component parts, right down to the molecules, each portion would have the same shape—crystalline.

It is only saying *in another dimension* that the essence of a person is as much to be seen in a little act as in a big act. *Everything* is a manifestation of them, of the essence of them, if only you have the intensity of perception to see it—

Perhaps all that I am trying to say is in that paragraph of Rilke's—at least a breath of the same thing.

"We, local and ephemeral as we are, are not for one moment contented in the world of time nor confined within it; we keep on crossing over and over to our predecessors, to our descent, and to those who apparently come after us. In that greatest 'open' world all *are*, one cannot say 'contemporary,' for it is the very discontinuance of time that makes them all *be*. Transitoriness is everywhere plunging into a deep being. And therefore all the forms of the here and now are not merely to be used in a time-limited way, but, so far as we can, instated into those superior significances in which we share."[1]

Christmas 1936, Long Barn

This is the first Christmas we have had as a family—our own little family together in a house of our own.

Christmas Day was Friday. On Wednesday morning Jon, Miss W., and I went in to Sevenoaks to get decorations for the tree, a live one that Hook had got.

Jon is very interested in the tree and finds a small oak branch which he sticks in mud in a box and brings to my study window. Isn't it a nice tree and can he hang things on it? I think it would make a nice bird's Christmas tree and that we could hang food on it. We could put it out on the old table on the terrace. Jon, however, wants to have his tree inside, but likes the idea of a bird's tree, too. So we go out for a walk to find some. We stick two branches, one of hawthorn, with berries on it, in the cracks in the old table and then spread bird-seed and crumbs underneath, and old "Cracker-jack." Several birds come the first afternoon. Jon can see them from his window. Sparrows, robins, and starlings. We put Jon's "tree" in a flower holder and during his nap-time he makes paper chains to hang on it.

[1] Extract from Rainer Maria Rilke's letter of November 13, 1925, to his Polish translator, Witold von Hulewicz, on the meaning of the *Duino Elegies*.

Hook has picked a huge armful of holly from the bushes around the place. There is a big holly tree next to a large oak in the center of the field above the house. He also has brought in pots of blue iris he has forced in the greenhouse and several pots of hyacinths and tulips.

We have put the blue iris in the long room, where they catch the color of the Venetian blue glass and the greens and blues in the tapestries; one bowl of hyacinths on the stool by the fireplace in the big room (I get a whiff of spring each time I go past into the study) and one in the "Italian room," or little in-between hall, with the amethyst-colored bottles. Another pink hyacinth in the sitting room in the sunny window. The pots of tulips, one red, one yellow, on either side of the mirror in the front hall.

Thursday

After lunch we decide where to put the tree. We set it up by itself against the tapestry. It looks lovely against the background of woven trees and riders.

Miss W. decorates the house with holly, putting big sprays in the stone urn at one end of the big room. The glossy leaves and red berries brighten the room and look beautiful between the Venetian blue glass vases. As we work we listen to the carol service broadcast from King's College Chapel, Cambridge.

At 3:30, Jon calls that he wants to come in and help to put things on the tree (very muddy in his overalls). He and I pin Christmas paper around the base of the tree, Jon telling me where it needs a pin. We start with tinsel, Jon taking one end and I the other. We drape the tree, Jon dancing around every once in a while with excitement. Then we get the paper chains he had been making and we put them on. They are gay and bright and give more color to the tree. Jon picks out the balls to hang and where to hang them and holds them while I tie them on.

We have tea in the long room with the fire lit. Jon and C. are closeted in the study and come out later with a long paper chain made with paper painted by Jon and punched together by C.

I find we have nothing for the top of the tree. I take the rather large painted wooden angel (rosy cheeks, red and gold wings, holly painted on her white skirt) that I was going to use as a candlestick in the dining room, and tie her with a bright red ribbon sash to the point. She stands quite securely and crowns the tree. The bright Viennese colors, red and white and green, seem to fit the rather simple decorations on the tree, the kindergarten colored paper chains. I am childishly pleased at the accidental *rightness* of it.

Jon comes in (from the study) and notices her immediately. "What have you put on top?" He smiles at her, very pleased too.

C. discovers the balloons, blows them up, ties them on Thor and Skean, who romp around and inevitably explode them.

I do the centerpiece. First a mirror mat in the center of the table. On this, the kneeling pewter Madonna. And on either end a little pine-tree candlestick. The pine trees have red stands and red candles on top and their feathery "branches" and pine cones are sprinkled with a silvery snow-powder. Around the edge of the mat a border of holly. It is done in a hurry but comes out as I planned and surprisingly looks very well. Down to supper late, in a red hostess coat. (Have also found we have *just* four bright red candles to put in our regular pewter candlesticks, on the four corners of the scene.)

C. said it was the most beautiful centerpiece he had ever seen! I was terribly touched and specially pleased. It made me happy all evening. He seldom says as much.

I remember that Jon has no stocking hung up. Remembering our ceremony of marching downstairs with our stockings, I feel I've cheated him and run downstairs with a long wool one I pin to a chair by the tree.

To bed quite tired from decorating the house and running up and downstairs.

A package comes in the last mail in Mother's handwriting: Christmas Eve!

It is a heavenly day, still and bright, the sun shining in the window. I go in to Jon, who crawls out of bed and jumps up and down on the mattress.

Before going down to breakfast, I lean out of the window, the sunny window that looks down over the flower beds, where I first saw crocuses last year and then hyacinth and then heliotrope and then zinnias! The little bare apple tree where Jon has climbed so much, the oak tree and the pool, with the marshy places where the birds used to bathe all summer, and then across to the fields. There are no flowers now, only little slips of stock Hook has put in, in readiness for spring. But it was fresh and sunny, dazzling and drying, the wet earth and red stones of the brick walk glistening and smelling like spring, below me. And the memory of the year warming my heart. I thought of last year, sitting on the bed in my cabin on the boat, very tired and wondering what was ahead of us. We have been so happy in this house. I was grateful, leaning out of the window in the sun, that we were here together, Jon, C., and I in this lovely house, happy and secure. I thought, too, of the times I have felt I could never really be happy again.

> "It cannot be
> That I am he
> On whom Thy tempests fell all night."

And yet, one does not forget, one keeps those things inside, a living part of one, not the sorrow exactly, or memory, but something else that has taken seed and grown from both, and is there, indescribably a part of you forever. I never thought I could be happy again without Elisabeth. But it isn't "without Elisabeth." I know I haven't her. I haven't forgotten or overlooked the loss, but something is there permanently, grown both from the realization of her and the loss of her. "He bore transplanting into common ground."

After breakfast Jon goes out, and I show C. the bow and

arrows I have for Jon. They are pretty deadly, we agree. But C. thinks if Jon is taught to use them as he might be taught to use a gun and has a sense of responsibility about them, and only uses them when we are there, he can have them. He takes them downstairs to give Jon. When I catch up with them, C. is going out to the lawn, carrying them, and Jon running after along the brick walk, jumping up and down, galloping with excitement. We go onto the lawn (I only in a sweater and skirt, it is so warm and sunny) and C. shoots the arrows into the air, straight up, dazzling and dizzy into the blue air. They come down plunk, straight up in the lawn. Jon chases them. Then they go down on the bigger lawn and shoot. It is a great success. Finally C. and Jon go off together into the big field we usually walk in, to learn to shoot.

Jon comes in to undo his presents quite early. It is getting misty and dark. We have tea in the big room by the fire. Jon has now discovered his gun (a little toy cannon) in his stocking, to his great joy (I think he likes it better than anything else), and shoots paper cannonballs.

Jon goes up to bed carrying his gun. (And I was the person who swore never to give a child of mine anything that suggested war!)

One's own presents are private and special and nice to gloat over quietly and alone, after all the excitement is over. They are testaments to people's understanding and love, and one likes to linger over their different and comforting quality.

One slips into that luxury of being someone else for a moment, one's old self, not married, not mother, not the person who has tried to make Christmas run well, ordered meals, arranged presents, etc. No, someone quite irresponsible and young, a young girl, loved and spoiled, lapped around in undeserved love, undeserved luxuries and gifts.

1937

Dear Mary,[1]

This is not really a thank-you letter—though it is that, too, for your perfect presents. It is so rare that one feels *both* touched that the person remembered you and took that much time and trouble *and* also delighted by the fitness of the present.

We do thank you. I know it takes time, thought, and energy to get presents, besides other things. The most important almost seems the spending or dispensing of one's concentrated energy, or power of concentration. I think that is the heaviest toll on women anyway. The waste or leakage in that part of one's budget seems terrific. It is such a necessary and such a hidden expenditure. It isn't time. One can budget time all right, though even that is difficult. But I find myself always saying, "Where did it go to—the spark with which I was going to write that chapter or that letter?"

I had to answer this letter immediately, and on the train, because you touched a subject that I have been fighting over in my own mind for years. I know so exactly how you feel about the work at Columbia, and you are honest enough to admit that it isn't "really important," "everything can and does interfere with it."

My writing, Mary—I *haven't* worked steadily at it. I let spring and the joy in this house interrupt me last year, and trips to France and Germany and Denmark with Charles last summer (I

[1] Mary Landenberger Scandrett, wife of Richard Scandrett, cousin of A. M. L.

wanted to go on the trips), and then this fall, feeling sick, having another baby. And now we are going away again! And I look at my amateurishness in disgust: "Not really getting down to the job." And I'm thirty—it's time I did "get down to" something, "too old" to be "promising." Yes, I know all that feeling so well.

Isn't it possible for a woman to be a woman and yet produce something tangible besides children, something that stands up in a man's world? In other words, is it possible to live up to women's standards and men's standards at the same time? Is it possible to make them the same? (As the feminists do.)

I have finally, through many stages, come round to the conclusion that for me, it isn't. Because, really, deep down in my heart, I don't honestly want to be a "woman writer" any more than I once wanted to be a "woman aviator" (perhaps this is "sour grapes"!). It involves sacrificing things I am not prepared to sacrifice. Not that I do not believe in women writers and fliers and doctors, etc. Not that I don't believe they can equal men—if they care to—in some fields (the feminists have proved to us that they can) but because I think in doing so they sacrifice just those advantages and qualities that are truly feminine. I do not mean simply the "children, home, and fireside" most people talk about in those endless arguments of "career vs. home-life" for women. For a lot of women do succeed in combining the two. But I think they do it (if successfully) at the price of a pigeonholed life—a man's life. Because in order to compete with men they must concentrate their energies into a narrow line. And I think in doing that they deny themselves the special attributes and qualities of women.

I don't think women should try to be straight lines. I think they should be circles. (Does this sound incoherent?) I think they should be rounded and receptive and sensitive in all directions. I think they should be perceptive and aware and open to many currents and calls and—yes—even distractions. So that they are as a kind of background (not *back*ground—*ground*) of much

knowledge, wisdom, culture, sympathy, tolerance—to men. Great
reservoirs of spiritual, emotional, and mental strength. I think
their lives, functions, etc., fit them to be this. And the women
who compete in men's fields sacrifice these peculiarly feminine
aptitudes in order to get "straight-line" results.

I think part of our depression (or *mine,* rather, for you did not
sound depressed—only a little humorously wistful) and discouragement now come from still judging our lives today by our
standards of ten years ago. I, anyway, had very definite and material standards. I did not want to be simply "somebody's wife." I
wanted my own work and, to some degree, life. I wanted tangible
results from my work—just as tangible as I had in college. I
wanted A's on my themes, or at least B's, but I wanted the mark
plain so I could see it. I wanted a professional mark, too, one that
anyone would be proud of, something good and thick and heavy
that one could weigh.

I am beginning to think that women (most) should never
work for results that can be weighed, or even for marks on
themes. I think they must be content, or wise enough, to work
for something much bigger and much more intangible, something that includes husbands and children and homes and background and character—and work too. But the work is only part
of it, only a spoke in the wheel without which, perhaps, the
wheel won't go round as well, but not an end in itself, not a
"straight-line" objective. Our grandmothers, I think, left that
"room of one's own" spoke out of the wheel (they couldn't help
it, really) and our mothers (I am speaking of the generation of
feminists) forgot about the "circle" and wanted and (in some
ways) proved that they could be "straight lines." And now we
have somehow got to do both. We have got to have our own
work in order to feed or illumine or fire that bigger thing we are
creating. Something that we can't see, that isn't tangible, that gets
no reward, that we must continue to work at and believe in even
though perhaps the people around us don't. (Especially men;
men will go right on wanting tangible results from us because, of

course, those are the terms they deal in—and should—those are the things they work for. "Women," a friend of mine said, "are reflective; men, affective.")

Oddly enough, you know, I feel that out of this new rounded life one is going to get "tangible" results from women, too, but only as by-products and not in *quantity*. But I feel that out of a truly feminine life some very great art might spring: something far more startling than anything we have seen from women yet—not much, but pure gold. A little of it has come already: Virginia Woolf writing about Mrs. Ramsay in *To the Lighthouse;* Vita Sackville-West in *All Passion Spent;* the thread about marriage that runs through Rebecca West's *Thinking Reed;* some of Rosamond Lehmann's writing. There must be more, but I haven't read much lately. And in the other worlds of art and accomplishments. But never "professional" in the sense that men's accomplishments are professional.

I am comforted somewhat in the loss of this much-longed-for "professional" stamp by a quotation I read the other day of Maurice Baring's[1]: . . . the following fragment of conversation occurs between Willmott, an actor-manager, and Giles, a critic and man-of-letters. They are discussing Rostand.

"Willmott says: 'He's an amateur. He's never written professionally for his bread, but only for pleasure.'

'But in that sense,' said Giles, 'God is an amateur.' "

But you, Mary, do not need to be comforted because you have been "professional." It must give one a great feeling of confidence—but also a discouragingly high standard to measure by. The part-time effort a married woman can give must seem very feeble in comparison.

But I am not sure that we were not gathering strength in those years of adjustment. (And how well you describe that appalling gulf, so narrow but so deep, between those years when we were "too young" and now at thirty, when we are "too old" to begin something big.) "The growth of personality," Carrel says, "in-

[1] *Have You Anything to Declare?*, anthology by Maurice Baring.

volves a constant trimming of oneself." Those years "when the iron sizzled" were years of trimming and of acquiring strength within our limitations. "Every man (again Carrel) is a fluid that becomes solid . . . a personality that is being created." And the "limitations" do it, I am beginning to think, although it is hard to accept. That, I think, is the hard thing about thirty, facing your limitations. I once heard a discussion between a man of about fifty and a girl about our age (of some talent). She said that the most terrible moment in life was when one came up against the walls of one's self. And he said that although it was a difficult moment, once you had recognized them, life was much better and easier after that. I am hoping so—hoping that one gains a kind of strength within the walls. Perhaps they aren't "walls" at all, but the sides of a frame which can hold great distances and vistas of perspective.

If you were here I know I should not get away with this argument as easily as this. I can imagine your saying mildly, "It must be very easy to be the 'rounded woman' in England where trains are so slow and life so quiet that one has time to write a twenty-page letter in January!" As a matter of fact, this has taken two train trips and a finish-off at home. And I am now going off flying for a month, with what might have become a book only a third begun, and my complete household having "given notice" and my Christmas letters still unwritten, which doesn't speak too well for the "rounded woman"!

Long Barn, Weald, Sevenoaks, January 15th

Mother darling,

This is really to tell you before it gets too "cold" what a heavenly evening we had at Lady Astor's.[1] It was rather an effort—a three or so hour drive and back the next day—and the tension of "Can I scrape up enough clothes, scarves, etc. to look presentable for an afternoon and evening?" and "Will it be a *huge* house, full of

[1] Nancy Langhorne Astor, wife of Waldorf Astor, 2nd Viscount. She was the first woman to sit in Parliament. Old friends of the Morrow family.

smart people?" But it was only her "family" (relations, etc., mostly young people). We got there after dark and Lord Astor welcomed us by the big fireplace (I had never met him before. He is *so* nice) and then she came in, gay and spontaneous and natural as always. She put us in "My best bedroom" because it had the lovely view, out over the lawns between those high elms to the bluff and the glimpse of the river, and because she said you had had it.

I loved talking to Lord Astor at dinner. He is so kind and quick and sensitive and sympathetic, and not "English" at all. But the best was after dinner. Lady Astor took me by the arm into the little library, after showing me that beautiful big green drawing room "where your father sat and talked way into the night with Smuts."[1] I could see all your and Elisabeth's letters come to life. James Stephens[2] reading his poetry and Daddy stopping to listen. Then she took me into the little library with the enchanting portraits of children (Dutch?), sitting in front of a fire looking up at two fall flowering mimosa trees in the corner. She sat and talked to me about Elisabeth. Not exactly reminiscing, nor sentimentally, but laughing and joking. "Every man at the conference[3] was in love with her," and, "That disgustin' evenin' dress with no back"!

Then in the morning that lovely view. C. walked to the [World War I soldiers] garden cemetery with Lord Astor. The place is so beautiful and really grand, with the grandeur of true dignity, worth, and pride. I felt the justification of big places like Knole, of the servants all working happily with a real pride in taking part on the place. Knole, alive—what Knole used to be. And yet justified in a modern way, too, because they are both in public service and reach so many people, officially and nonoffi-

[1] Jan Christian Smuts, South African statesman.

[2] Irish poet and novelist.

[3] Reference is to the 1930 Naval Conference in London. D. W. M. served on the United States Delegation.

cially. C. loved it all too—was terribly impressed—and I was proud of him, listening to him talk to Lord Astor on Germany.

Long Barn, Weald, Sevenoaks, Friday, January 22nd

Darling Mother,

What a beautiful poem! It has just come in the mail this morning. I did not read it at the breakfast table but waited till I could get alone. (One of those pouring-with-rain, all-in-the-house days when the only place one can read a letter alone is in the bathroom!) How can you write like that and yet do so many other things besides? It isn't the time exactly, but one is put into another mood, or another person, by details and a busy life—and then I can't keep that place inside of me *still* enough to get writing from. It is all agitated by thoughts about clearing the toys out of Katharine's[1] cupboard to make room for her clothes, or calling Harrods to get some dark brown sherry for Uncle Jay,[1] or the persistence of my mind on shopping[2]—how to economize in weight, size, color, convenience, etc. "If I have an inner lining put in that coat I can do with *one* coat instead of two." "Get a white scarf for the front of *both* suits," etc.

If I had one quiet day I could finish Part I of the "book." I have not touched it since Christmas—shopping and letters and being tired at night, and not being able to shut off my "efficient" planning mind from my contemplative mind. How *do* you do both at the same time?

As you see, we have been delayed by last things on the plane, in general, and expect to get off next week early. We will only be gone six weeks at the most, getting back here the last week in March, at the latest. We have had inoculations, etc., and I saw Dr. H. [obstetrician] last week. He is very pleased, everything progresses well. He said be back surely four weeks ahead, but I am allowing six anyway. (All of April and two weeks in May.)

[1] The Lindberghs were expecting a visit from Anne's uncle, General J. J. Morrow, and cousin Katharine McIlvaine Leighton.

[2] The Lindberghs were planning a flying trip to India.

C. must be in India the first week in March, possibly the first two. I shall go with him, if I can. Although I've left it entirely open, planning to go back from Egypt, or sooner, if the trip seems too much. C. says we might go through Italy coming or going and stop for a few days in Rome with Amey![1]

I have bought some dowdy but practical maternity wash silks from a motherly place called "Treasure Cot." (Their idea is *yards* of material and not a single line of the body defined!) And one expensive navy angora suit made to measure and wrap, at a very good place with an intelligent woman at the head. It is well designed and cut and will last me all the trip and looks smart. The woman likes simple nonfussy lines and has a *good* tailor. I fell into her arms with relief after battling with the usual British saleswoman who insists that she knows better than you what you want.

I am so glad we have not missed Uncle Jay and Katharine. I was a little worried about them, as our whole household has just moved out again—even the unconventional maid! But Mr. and Mrs. Hook have moved up here for the time being, and we have located an extra person who comes in to help. Also Uncle Jay is so contented and Katharine has been so thoughtful and helpful making her bed, helping to clear the dishes, that she is a real asset in the house. Miss H. has been frightfully busy with Charles on all the last papers (income tax, etc.). But that office is left entirely undisturbed and C. is not put out of his routine by the extra people, as it is important he not be. He has had a hundred things on his hands. (The room is strewn with boots, rubber boat, tent, cans, etc.—as usual before a trip, all emergency equipment—giving tidy Mrs. Hook the horrors and Thor a deep depression!).

We (except C., of course!) play a kind of anagram game in the evenings. It is quite fun except that it cuts out a large chunk of letter-writing time. Uncle Jay has seemed in good spirits. He and C. laughing over train and telephone service in England. Uncle Jay says they had better trains in America before he was born

[1] Amey Aldrich, see note p. 4.

than the one they traveled up on from Plymouth. C. has enjoyed him very much, and I am terribly glad we have had this time with him.

I have had such joy from Jon lately: lots of walks together, and when I come back from town he runs to meet me, and when I don't come he says to Miss W., *"Why* couldn't Mother come home on the early train?" I shall miss him frightfully.

Has Aubrey heard the latest "crisis"[1] story—Welsh, supposedly. I got it from Lady Astor.

Two Welsh women in the market: "What is it that's happened to our King?"

"Oh, it's a woman he's got into trouble and he's blamin' the Prime Minister for it," which, for all characters considered, has elements of humor in it!

DIARY   *January 31st*

Late in the afternoon—evening, really, for Jon was in bed—we left Long Barn. I whistled to Jon from my room, packing, as I do every night after he goes to bed. Thinking how little he cared really about our going, and how hard it was for me to leave him. Once we got off in the car (in the pouring rain—Uncle Jay went out and held an umbrella over us) it was easier; that awful "leaving" lump left my chest. Dinner on the way and the night in an inn outside Dorking to be near the airport for an early start next morning.[2]

February 1st

Wake early in the dark, breakfast, and off to the airport. A "good" sky, overcast but clearing—a wind. Took off Reading at 8:06. About 8:30 we circled Long Barn (already miles, days,

---

[1] Reference is to the "Parliamentary Crisis" aroused by Edward VIII when he announced his intention to marry Mrs. Wallis Simpson.

[2] The Lindberghs were flying to India in their Miles Mohawk monoplane, stopping in Rome en route.

away). A white flutter from Jon's window, then figures running out, Jon dancing up and down waving a white handkerchief. Then off to Lympne. Landed 8:49. Customs not open. C. telephoned the day before and found they opened at 9:00. Not quite nine. We wait and wait. "He has had a spot of trouble with his car." At about 9:45 he arrives, very apologetic, and gets us through quickly. A long take-off, heavy tanks, over the trees into an overcast sky. The Channel, circling the lighthouse, out over France, overcast, occasional clear skies, not very cold. No fog and very little rain. Over the coal areas and the war country, the zigzag light brown lines of old trenches in the dark brown fields, the pitted dumps where there had been a forest. The flooded rivers, Laon and Rheims. Then a long time over thin overcast, a sea of clouds.

We are coming up into the hills; we are getting near the Alps. Up green slopes, climbing now, patches clear and snow-capped mountains on the horizon, blue, distant. The hills are very green, cottages red-roofed, pine trees. It must be Switzerland (then he *is* going across the Alps and not around). Climbing over high hills, mountains, a blue lake below us. Gained Neuchâtel—we're as far as that! Lake Geneva—a corner of it pointed out.

We are still in that layer of shifting white clouds and there ahead of us, towering into the clear sunshine and dazzling blue, a wall shot up dizzyingly high. *There* are the Alps, so giantlike, pure, and unearthly they seemed, so austere and far above us that I felt humble. How can we ever climb to them, surpass them? How arrogant—how flippantly arrogant of us—to think we could.

Then we climbed and climbed, gained more height, more confidence, breathed more easily. Yes, we could perhaps do it, we were up to their shoulders, up in the dazzling upper world, a lake shimmering far below the clouds. Now we set off across them, in among them, round their heads, over their sides, the engine puttering out clearly in those cold heights. It was cold, icy against my face, but it would not take long. Hannibal took his elephants over these—looking down on those glassy slopes. Think of it! I write it down for C.

In the gullies below huts are snow-roofed. We follow a railroad line. There is a pass. We go over a cut in the mountains. Now surely (although we are still among peaks) we will start to go down; we have passed the crest. We will follow the pass down, into Italy.

We follow a valley, not green, but snowless and many-roofed. A railroad, a river. The railroad peters out; the roofs peter out. C. turns the plane, looks at his maps and looks out at the valley, circles, shakes his head. We head back in the other direction. I feel discouraged. C. shouts back that he was following wrong valley. Where, I think, is the right one? Peaks and clouds all around us.

"This is a hell of a place to get lost!" I try to shout. We are now below the peaks. We start to climb to regain altitude. Up into the cold air, up over a sea of even white billows with the whiter peaks pushing up through. Going *over* it, then? I suppose we'll pick up the pass on the other side. It is very cold. I take off my fur gloves (silk and wool ones still on) to get out something. My hands are numb and then burn terribly—too cold. I stick them inside of my suit. Gradually the pain goes. But we must be going down now.

Gradually we leave the peaks behind. Nothing but the sea of clouds ahead, smooth, shadowed, and gray, for there is no sun on them. There is another layer of clouds above us with occasional breaks through to the sky—a pale sky. What would he do now if the engine cut? Stall through, blind? On a mountain? No parachutes. I thought we weren't going to do this kind of flying.

I wonder how long the mountains take to flatten out into Italy? Is Italy flat, though? The "hill towns" of Italy. It must be flat around Rome—the marshes. We are going down all the time anyway. It is getting warmer. I can take my hands out. But no change in the sea of cloud. The sky is just the same, overcast, dull, streaked now and then with a lighter patch—which is not very blue. How late is it? Where is the sun? I study the sky for some change. A small light streak on the horizon. Perhaps when we get to that patch of sky it will be clear below too. Perhaps we will come out onto Italy, beautiful sunny Italy, warm and clear. But how far away that clear streak is. We do not seem to get any nearer to it.

Suddenly I think I see through the haze the cold blue of a lake, obscured by mist. A lake! I look on my map. Lake Maggiore, Lake Como—near Milan, then, we would be!

No, it is not lake. It is sky—a streak of sky, pale blue. But surely *those* are hills—they are dark. They don't move. I keep my eyes on them, trying to watch a certain bump and pin it down. But it changes almost imperceptibly. I give it up.

The lake episode has made me realize that I am afraid. I am trembling, with cold, too. Perhaps he would say it wasn't anything to worry about. Perhaps I could just tap his shoulder. But then, if he *is* in a tight spot, it won't help any if he sees how afraid I am. No, I mustn't ask him. But I could write a note. So I scribble, "Where do you think we are—over the Mediterranean?"

He smiles, shakes his head, and shouts, "We aren't over the Mediterranean." He doesn't know where we are and he is worried. We are "in it." But I feel a little less afraid, stronger, more keyed up and not alone. Well, we are in it. See if I can find some land, perhaps I can see something he doesn't. Finally I think I have a line of mountains to our left. They seem to stay the same. I scribble, "That *must* be land there—it stays the same."

He looks sharply at it but does not alter his course. We go on straight ahead. Some of my mountains melt. *They* weren't real, either!

There is still that patch, that streak of clear sky ahead, far ahead on the horizon—a slit in the overcast, translucent blue, pale and gold tinged, idyllic like those blue landscapes that stretch away in back of the Italian Madonnas. Is that world waiting for us? And have we time to get there? The pale gold-tinged streak has the gentleness and pallor of evening about it. But it is only about 4:00—surely we have time? But I had forgotten about losing an hour, going east.

What are we going to do? Behind us the sea of cloud stretches just as far, just as monotonous. And we can't go back. It is uphill all the way.

He is turning his course, out to the right, away from my imaginary line of Apennines, out toward the sea. He circles a slightly darker spot. Is there land below? No, I can see nothing. He means to go down through—*blind!*

My God—is it as bad as that? Go down *blind* through the stuff, circle down, stall into what? Sea? Mountains? Crash before you see?

There is nothing else to do then. The other alternatives are worse. This is the last chance. I look to see that maps are fast in the ship. I put them away. I fasten my belt. I sit ready. He puts on his goggles and pushes down the hatch so he can see. He turns around to me. Briefly, "Got your belt on?" I nod. Yes, that means be prepared for anything. Very likely death—never been so near it before. What are the chances? I weigh them gravely. Yes, there is a chance. There may be a ceiling. There may be time to pull out—anyway to make some kind of landing.

And on the other side, the chance of the plane getting out of control—more likely to hook a wing in the side of a mountain. A sound of cracking and it will all be over.

Yes, death was down there, but I could face it. I do not know why, for I am an awful coward about everything and this is terrible to look back on. But at the time I had enough strength for it.

We start turning. The flaps are out, a quiver of sensation as we go under. There is no turning back. We must go through it now. Nothing to do but wait. Down in the mist, darkly. The mist covers us up, closes over our heads, shuts out the sky. Submerged now, floating, turning, like a maple seed falling to earth on a still autumn day—so softly falling to death. It is quiet, the engine throttled down. I feel calm. We are together; I am glad we are together. I do not mind dying. I am glad for our life. It has been a wonderful life. I am sorry to leave Jon, but I think we have given him a good start. I am glad for this year we have all had together.

Down, down into the darkness, but so gently. I never thought meeting death would be so quiet and so gentle. Slow, strange descent into the underworld.

But while accepting, sinking into this featherlike descent, somehow I was watching every second with every inch of concentration, watching the spin of the low wing for what it would show. It would be death or escape and life for us both.

Before I could see anything off that low wing, I was aware, out of the side of my eye, of my husband's head moving up and down, nodding with assurance, with relief, with, "Yes, yes, that's all right, then, as I thought, a ceiling." I could read all that in his slow assured nod. Then, a second later, off the wing, I saw what it was that made him nod. First, just a slightly different texture to the mist below. The sea, then quickly the coast on our left, steep green, volcanic hills dotted with towns.

It was suddenly warm and damp and solid and real. Quite subdued in light, dusky. Above us hung that gray curtain we had just come through. It was right down on the hilltops. We were quite a comfortable distance offshore, but there was a volcanic island ahead of us. Suppose . . . but I did not stop to think, now it did not matter. Now we were down, part of the earth again, alive, warm, breathing—part of this earth, covered with little towns, houses, ports, and ships.

It was a dream we had waked to—so different was this world, so new to us, tangible, precious, green—to us reborn. C. turned around now and smiled at me and said ruefully, "And after all my promises!"[1]

We came down off the coast of Genoa and flew to Pisa. It was getting dark. Here the curtain petered off, clear sky above. So it

[1] This episode was expanded into a book by A. M. L., *The Steep Ascent,* published 1944.

was there after all, if we had gone on. We could have gained it, that strip of sky. I pointed it out to C. He turned and shouted, "I didn't dare wait for it—getting dark." No, we couldn't have waited on the chance and then had to come down through in the dark.

We landed at Pisa, almost dark, too tired to go on to Rome. Miraculously warm, it seemed, soft air, good to breathe, good to walk and be alive. A long wait at the airport, officials talking. But what did it matter? Then through dark narrow streets full of people, new and different, to the hotel on a river. Old bridges, old towers, reflections in the water. Bells ringing, bicycles, street stalls.

A delicious supper (ordinary world of hotels, guides, waiters, hotel managers, who had no conception that we had come back from the dead). And then baths and bed and talking it over, "Not very good for your emotional epidermis!" And finding out that the gyro had stopped functioning just as he started down through the stuff (I didn't know that) just when he needed it most. And that he had had a confirmed belief (with nothing to go on but those hidden perceptions underneath) that there *was* a ceiling under the stuff. And then again a kind of intuition and experience that made him choose just that spot to come down through; it had a slightly different texture—thinner.

Pisa, February 2nd

The next morning we woke to the sound of many bells and brilliant sunshine, and after breakfast took a car to the Leaning Tower. Over old bridges, through narrow streets, honking shrilly, past stalls selling fruit and flowers to the square, where three beautiful buildings are set in white-daisied lawns of green: a cathedral, a small round domed chapel, and the tower, all brilliant in a soft-colored marble that was sometimes white, sometimes creamy, and sometimes pinkish.

There in the brilliant sunshine we got out and walked. It was very quiet, sunny, and peaceful. Only a few people strolling back and forth across the daisied green. A man stretched out asleep on the grass, a mother with her child. The sun, the stillness, the soft perfection of the old marble buildings was delicious. We could not get over the color, the warmth, the soft air, the mellow beauty. After an English winter—to wake up in this. It was overpowering.

Then we walked slowly up the Leaning Tower, stopping at each balcony to rest (C. taking care of me) and sit in the sun and look out between the soft white pillars over the lawn, over the old red walls, over brown roofs and pink houses, closed gardens with vines on the walls, and fig trees, a square of cloisters, and then towers and roofs, to the green plain and beyond, very blue and translucent, the mountains we had come over yesterday. And above a pale blue sky, scattered with small soft cherubs' wings, like the ones in Italian paintings.

Below us, across the street, out of an old warm-brown stone building (a church or monastic college perhaps) filed a procession of men in black robes that fluttered gently. Each man carried a long white taper. They walked two by two across a path, across the green into the cathedral.

After lunch (and soft Italian wine), we pack up and go to the field and set out for Rome. We leave a clear dazzling sky and fly into some rain and come onto Rome, covered by an evening mist just about sunset. Land at Littoria in the curve of a twilight-lit river below a hill on which are those tall green cypress trees. Quite a crowd of people, hundreds of monkey photographers jumping about as we walk. No one knows what to do. "Can't we get in the hangar?" We walk up a big ramp into the hangar. The photographers all come too. Then, a tall nice-looking man, an American, Captain White,[1] takes us into an office, people jammed out by glass doors. Some Embassy people, polite remarks, we get in a car and go to their home. They are very kind; a bathroom, tea, telephones.

[1] Captain Thomas D. White, U. S. Air Attaché in Rome, became a general in 1942, and Air Force Chief of Staff in 1957.

Amey, yes, we will come out to supper. We drive to a hotel. A modern Rome, lights, shops, wide streets, brilliant. A large hotel, from the steps of which smart Italian women in black, silver fox, and pearls are just coming from a reception. We go in wearing our flying clothes and carrying our clothing rolls! A rush to dress for dinner. The little suit, the mussed hat. Then in a taxi to Villa Aurelia.[1] A long drive, out of the lighted smart streets into little narrow ones, and up a steep hill, winding, past a great fountain and in a gate. Through a garden and palms. A big house, a marble hall, up an elevator. Amey and Chester and the gay rooms full of flowers. Bowls of mimosa, iris, narcissus. Chintz-covered sofas on each side of the fireplace, lamps, pictures, magazines, books, and Tinker[2] sitting up on a corner of the sofa sticking out his tongue. All just like Amey at home, and I too happy to talk very much. They want us to stay. We decide to move out tomorrow.

Wednesday, February 3rd

C. to make calls on Italian aviation officials. I, to settle the bill, pack, etc. Never done it before, feel stupid to be so helpless. C. always does it. Absurd. I can—very easy. I get everything off and done and into the taxi with several baskets of violets—Roman violets—which smell delicious. Very happy to go to Amey's. The brilliant sunshine, the fountains, the flower stalls, the fruit stands are all dazzling to me. Villa Aurelia is very quiet. There are narcissus and mimosa in our room. The view out over Rome. The flowering tree out the window, the deep green umbrella pine. Amey's dear old "Eleanora" (a Juliet's nurse). I just get settled when C. arrives and we have a quiet lunch on the porch in hot hot sunshine. Amey and Chester arrive, after a wedding.

Out in the afternoon to see the old Roman Forum, Palatine hill, and the triumphal arches, where Cicero spoke, the cobble-

---

[1] Official residence of the director of the American Academy in Rome.

[2] Amey Aldrich's West Highland white terrier.

stoned road the Emperors rode down. The color of the pillars, standing against the deep green cypress trees on the Palatine hill. The Colosseum (like Germany and the Olympic Games, the same spirit too—how like the Romans).

The Pantheon . . .

Driving around the new broad avenues of Rome, we see big plaques on the wall, showing what the Roman Empire was, what it dwindled to, and what it has gained under Mussolini.

I like best the orange-pinky color of the old buildings, the glimpses of deep green cypress and pine down a street, the fountains and their sound, unexpectedly everywhere, and the flower stalls.

At night, a quiet supper and C. discussing Italy, Germany, and dictatorships versus democracy with Amey and Chester.

Drop to sleep early.

Thursday, February 4th, C.'s birthday

Drive out to Tivoli (reporters as we leave) to see Hadrian's Villa. A heavenly day, soft sunshine and soft color. The old walls of a ruined villa, and cool cypress trees (silver-barked), and silver-leaved olives with little blue iris growing wild. I like Hadrian's "island" in the very center, where he turned the bridge and no one could cross the moat.

Although in ruins, the quality of the place remained because of trees and sun and being apart (not like the Forum in the center of Rome). One understood why it was the "country place" of Hadrian and what peace had lain there.

Villa d'Este: fountains upon fountains terraced down a steep hill of shady cypresses, dazzling to look down on, and yet when you walked about the shaded paths with their old stone walls and statues the fountains did not seem showy and brilliant like Versailles or at most palaces. They are hidden and, although all around you, not obvious. Simply part of the coolness, shade, and music of the place. The sight of water always in your eyes, like shade. The sound of it in your ears, like music. I will keep it for my cool dream.

Quiet lunch in the sun.

I drop asleep early after supper, and sleep late. Eleanora comes in with a breakfast tray each morning, yellow china and her *"Buon giorno."* And I eat in bed, looking out at the big umbrella pine. It is delicious.

Friday, February 5th

Two cars of reporters follow us. We go through the Doria Gardens to escape. The Vatican City, sense of tremendous size, history, riches, power, etc. Nothing moves me except that lovely corridor of maps and the little Fra Angelico chapel, still and sainted with a halo round it, like that monk's figure on the far wall. And the Michelangelo ceiling—the hand of Adam. (The touch of the divine in everything is like that, even when it is simply understanding—or love.)

The Academy "boys" for lunch and Alexander Kirk[1] (C. to see Balbo[2]).

Saturday, February 6th

C. to the field. Amey and I to the Keats-Shelley house at the foot of the Spanish Steps. Just as it was, a very quiet musty old place, with prints and books and a nice soft-voiced girl taking care of it. Keats's drawing of a Grecian urn, the little vined porch off the back, looking up at the flights of steps. The flower stalls at the foot, freesia, stock, narcissus. I thought of Elisabeth. I have thought of her so much on this trip—someone with whom to share Italy, as we two shared our first luscious impressions of Mexico. Someone with a more childlike superficial delight than

[1] American career diplomat, Chargé d'Affaires in U. S. S. R. in 1938, in Germany 1939, later American Ambassador in Egypt and in Italy.
[2] Italo Balbo, 1896–1940, Italian aviator and statesman, commanded mass transatlantic flights to Brazil (1929) and U. S. (summer 1933). Made Air Marshal 1933.

C., to whom everything was not quite new (because of a similar education and background) as with C., but also someone to whom everything was not old, as with Amey and Chester, who know so much and have seen so much. She would be the perfect person, to whom the flowering fruit trees would be as wonderful as an old temple or gate, and yet to whom would come the pleasure of finding what was familiar and old. The Keats house would have meant so much to her, but also the little Italian children dressed up in carnival costumes, sticking out their tongues to make you notice them, standing in a shabby door or back alley.

Monday, February 8th

Leave Rome. An overcast sky, fly over Roman aqueduct ruins. A strange feeling flying over ruins cropping up out of the earth, under another civilization's layer of buildings or farms—discarded and bare, the bones of another civilization.

Still overcast and lowering at Naples. Can just see the outline of Capri. Vesuvius' head under the clouds. Herculaneum and Pompeii are brown bones, open graves in the center of modern settlements.

Very rough, storm clouds. As we round the toe and approach Sicily, the skies clear, though a strong head wind. Skies very soft and blue. The Strait of Messina and Etna's white cap over the hills in the distance. Crinkly bare hills coming down steeply to the deep blue water.

The mountains get a more and more intense blue, unreal and fairylike. Sometimes a wide band of bright blue edges the beaches, like a morning-glory petal, before the sea becomes that darker purplish blue. It is all soft, dreamy, unreal (not like the hard northern mountains), even to the slow white sails below us. I keep thinking of "I have seen old ships like swans asleep" and try to remember the line about the ship that was "so old . . . one watched in vain to see the mast burst open with a rose."

A fantastic conception, but, yes, it could happen here.

As we approached Palermo, we could see a long arm of volcanic peaks, a great blue bay, and the city itself, white and green, spreading like a hand through gaps in the volcanic hills to the sea.

The field lies on the side of hills at the back of the town. It was frightfully rough, I was shaken from one side to another. I hate wind. The wind and storm clouds rolling right down over the mountains and across the field. The plane bucked and kicked taking the turns. I was frightened, but C. laughed and said it was perfectly all right, and we landed easily cross-field. Only one photographer jumping round and a little reporter taking our address carefully off the plane. Air Force men—very quiet. Drive through the streets at break-neck speed, honking shrilly, past children and donkey carts to the Villa Igeia, facing the harbor and that long line of irregular volcanic mountains, all topsy-turvy, one behind another like clouds. They seemed to be changing their color and shape too, like clouds, in the evening light, now amethyst, now pink, now deep blue. It is very beautiful and quiet. We take a walk in the garden along the waterfront and decide to stay a day and take a car and motor to Segesta.

Tuesday, February 9th

Such a lovely day—a perfect day, snatched. ("He who kisses the joy as it flies . . .")

After a quiet breakfast, we start out with maps. Through the streets of Palermo, not having the slightest idea what road to get on and without a word of Italian! Also we find we do not know how to work the *reverse*. We get in a back street and C. practices and finds out. I say "Monreale" to some of the women and we get on the right road and start climbing steeply, past those two-wheeled donkey carts, very gaily painted and carved underneath. They look like old Italian primitives—rich blues, reds, golds. The scenes are of lives of saints, of Christ, Crusaders' battles, and sometimes ballet dancers! They carry great loads of vegetables (cauliflower) going to market.

We do not stop but push slowly through the crowded cobbled

streets past little open shops, the doors hung with wares, food, meat, or baskets, pots, and pans. Lots of men in the streets, strolling back and forth. It is like pushing through lily pads in a boat, C. says. We get through, up and up, over the mountains. It gets bare and rough with volcanic stone, cactus and olive trees growing up the sides of the hills at first and then nothing but rough grass and volcanic stone. We are up in the rain and the clouds. Then start twisting down.

Finally we see the temple of Segesta, perfect and by itself, far off on the top of a hill, against other hills. We stop below and buy lunch from the lodge, a loaf of bread, some cheese, some slices of sausage (fruit we brought with us), crackers and *vino del paese*. There is no one about. We eat it quietly in the car, delicious meal. (It is quite cold and windy.)

Then we climb up alone to the temple. There is nothing around it, no marks, no signs, no ropes—nothing but the temple, perfect on all sides and open to the sky. It is set on a green hill, with a great bluff or mountain behind it, gray-green, with the pinkish-brownish volcanic stone showing through, the same stone that the temple was built of. The floor of the temple is green grass, covered with little white daisies and sweet alyssum, and as we walked up the massive steps, a flock of blackbirds blew gustily through the open sides between the great pillars, up through the open roof to the sky. There were two Sicilian women with shawls over their heads and a child walking over the daisied grass—no one else.

The pillars were utterly simple, made out of massive blocks of volcanic stone. No ornament (except underneath on the corner of the ends, a leaf?) but the whole did not give you a feeling of massiveness, but of grace and delicacy. Looking out through the pillars, across the valley, down the hills, over olive trees and a winding road, across to a great blufflike mountain. Below it, the roofs of a town and a tiny blue corner, an arm of the sea!

Of course, it would catch that glimpse of the sea, being Greek.

It was quite perfect and holy, though I do not know to what god it was built. It is still holy ground.

Then we started, in the rain, to climb up the next hill to see the theater. A long, slow climb between rocks and little pink flowers growing everywhere stiffly out of spearlike leaves. Looking back every stop to see the temple on that green hill below us. And as we climbed, the temple grew more beautiful to look down on. Its color, now in rain and now in sunshine, was sometimes gray-white and sometimes pinky brown and sometimes a tawny gold. Alone, perfect, delicate against the rough mountain, streaked with granite, as though to show what man could make out of the elements around him, what civilization could make out of nature, pure spirit flowering out of rock. "The rock whence it was hewn . . ."

Finally we rounded the hill in the wind, past tumble-down rocks, once quarried there, walked a little even stretch, and came quite suddenly on the back wall of the small amphitheater, and an entrance into it. And through the entrance opened up a view of the whole valley below, the great mountainous bluff opposite, the little town at its feet, and the glistening blue (in sunshine now) arm of the sea.

It was breath-taking. C. said only under his breath, "They *would* build it just here!"

State Hotel, Jodhpur, Rajputana, February 21st

Mother darling,

We have gone rather fast from Cairo, although the days have not been hard. But I usually go straight to bed after supper when we get in and there is no time even write in a diary.

It has been a terribly different trip from any of the others. Traveling along air routes, we have been along the Imperial Airways or Dutch KLM routes almost all the way since Cairo, which makes landing facilities, comfort on the ground, and accessibility to civilization much easier.

That has been the big difference on this trip, really—to travel over such *old* country from the point of view of civilization, so much history underneath us. To fly over the bones of other civilizations, Roman aqueducts, Greek temples, and even along the north shores of Africa, here and there along the coast, between the brown desert and the blue Mediterranean, half buried in sand, Roman baths, Roman theaters. At Tunis we flew over the site of Carthage. At Tripoli, where we stayed with Marshal Balbo, there was an old Roman triumphal arch knee-deep in the new concrete city and quite a big Roman town excavated nearby. Our first port in Egypt was by a small natural harbor where Antony and Cleopatra were supposed to have beached. It was brilliant, jeweled, scarab-blue. Egypt from the air was thrilling. That great land of green plains between the brown deserts, and those curved scimitarlike sails, white on the thin blue canals. And the pyramids, sand-colored, looking out over the desert, marking a line between the desert and the green stretch of the Nile. Seen from the air, they are extraordinarily impressive, because, of course, they are geographic and geographic things look best from the air. All the riffraff of hotels, telegraph lines, train tracks, camel stands etc. look like insignificant bits of gravel at their feet, unpermanent, temporary, and unimportant next to their eternal massive magnificence.

From the ground Egypt is pretty touristy. Huge hotels, French cooking, tours, ladies in silk skirts riding decorated camels, holding on to new sun helmets as the dusty wind blows. We were there in a duststorm that they said was "*very* rare." They extolled the health and climate of the place, in a tone that sounded very Californian.

Then on across Palestine, which I thought would be shocking somehow, after one's Biblical and childlike impressions. Perhaps it would be from the ground. But from the air it was very satisfying to come on the fertile fields in the south and pleasant hills after the desert and the flat monotonous Nile country. You could understand why it looked a land "flowing with milk and honey" to the Israelites. We flew only over farming or sheep country, no commercial towns. Even the bare stony hills were comforting and friendly after all our desert flying. I imagine it is much the same as it was, grazing country with some cultivation, and even Bethlehem from the air was amazingly satisfying. From that height you could not see whether the buildings were modern or not, but only the collection of their walls and roofs, clay-mud-colored, clinging to the side of a crescent hill, in the middle of bare stony hills, up which you could still imagine—and see—donkeys plodding.

Jerusalem looks pretty modern, though not a modern city in a Western sense. There is still an old wall. And both of them, far away in those barren hills, look from the air quite distant and untouched, part of another world. I was terribly glad to have seen them. Then down from the hills over Jericho (nothing but a tiny collection of houses), with its back to the hills and facing the dry breathless valley of the Dead Sea. (It is 1293 feet below sea level.) I wondered from which direction Gideon attacked with trumpets!

Over the desert we followed a pipeline, famous to aviators, with a road, air "fields" along it to Baghdad—which we never got to because of a sandstorm. Then over the Tigris-Euphrates Valley (still in the dust), flat and parched in spite of the great rivers and dusty palm groves. I was very disappointed, expecting to see a "fertile basin," "the cradle of civilization," etc. We flew over the excavated ruins of Babylon, great walls up to their necks in sand. Then down the Persian Gulf, the dust behind us at last, great walls of mountains on one side and "Persian blue" sea on the other. Gradually the mountains dried out into bones of mountains, ashen colored, and deserts and we came to India, Karachi, and the Indus River. (Didn't Alexander's empire reach to the Indus? It seemed so utterly incredible. How *could* he have conquered and ruled what we have covered since we left Sicily!)

Yesterday from the borders of India (Gwadar) to Jodhpur (associated in my mind vaguely with polo, sun helmets, Kipling, "rupees," etc.). After C. checks the plane, at a very good base, we will do a little sightseeing, going on tomorrow perhaps to Agra or Udaipur, where I intend to stay for a few days. C. may go to Bombay, pick up Sir Francis Younghusband,[1] take

[1] British soldier, explorer, and author; led the British expedition into the forbidden city of Lhasa in 1904.

him to Calcutta, and then come back for me. C. has seen a little of Sir Francis in England (you remember, he was the first man into Lhasa)—a grand old man. They live at Westerham, twenty minutes from us. Sir F. is here for a conference of all faiths and C. thinks it a great opportunity to be in India at the same time because Sir Francis knows India and Indians so well.

I have felt well and it has been really an easy trip, stopping each night at a clean, comfortable place. Only I dream of Jon every night. It seems so far back to him. You do not seem so far, for I know your thought can bridge it, but Jon's cannot.

Calcutta, March 8th

Mother darling—

India has been quite absorbing and everything has gone well, but I somehow can't get the energy to write, even a diary, only post-cards to Jon. It isn't just the warm damp of Calcutta. It is something about the weight of India that is oppressive. Did you feel it? The weight seems too great to carry even in one's imagination. The size, the complexity, the diversity, the masses of people, the terrific poverty, the dirt, the smells: incense and food frying, and cows and cow dung, and mango trees in flower and pavements sluiced to cool them, drying in the heat, and dust and people—those bundles of rags lying on the sidewalk that you think are piles of refuse and you find they are people, sleeping.

And the complexity of it as a whole—trying to understand the layers upon layers of history, races and cultures, laid on top of one another; religions, social customs, layered and subdivided and intertwined so that one is appalled trying to grasp it. The classes, the types, the great range between the educated woman-politician and the monk in rags and barefoot (we met and talked to both of these with equal interest).

Then the problems—the combination of miseries, poverty, tangles, mistakes, wrongs that look impossible to work out, at least without the weight of centuries to come. (It all seems to me typified in the weight, the ornamentation, symbolism, of the intricate, overcarved architecture of the temples and shrines.)

And that thin hard lacquer of the English on top, also impossible to understand and baffling in a strange way. And the oppressively soft cotton-wool atmosphere of the servant class, pressing in on you on all sides—hundreds of poor, servile, fawning animal-like people, trying to do every possible service for you—unfold your napkin, ring for the elevator, sell you things, fix your corns, be your personal servants. They lie outside the tourists' doors who have engaged them, like dogs, sleeping, squatting on the concrete, sometimes cleaning a shoe—all for a few cents.

Of course, there have been the educated high-class (you have to use some such term) Indians who are so stimulating to talk to, extraordinarily aware, sensitive, quick, responsive, and at the same time profound—not that superficial sensitivity. It is more than a sympathetic or aesthetic sensitivity, rather a deeply philosophical and spiritual one. I feel very drawn to them.

The ones we have seen are for the most part very bitter about the English, whose attitude (if not treatment) still seems to be that described in *A Passage to India* by Forster. I can quite understand the bitterness, although the British have undoubtedly given them the peace and order which has allowed them to be free enough to be proud of themselves and eager for a new India. They are of course bitter against the "superior" British rule[1] with its incredibly snobbish, insular manner.

Sir Francis Younghusband, whom we met here (by prearrangement in England), is not a bit like that. He is a very remarkable man. It is through him that we have been able to meet Indians. (The other English for the most part seldom meet them socially, except of course the Princes, Rajahs, Maharanis, etc., at garden parties.) He was born here. His father helped put down the border troubles of early India, and he himself headed the first English expedition into Tibet—a diplomatic mission sent by Curzon to make Tibet friendly to the English rule in India. I

[1] India at this time was still under British rule.

gather there was some stiff fighting but it turned out to be friendly in the end and they have never had any trouble since.

He has a remarkable faculty—although a dry, practical soldier, and quite English and shy—for reaching people on their own level, for touching them and, if not understanding them, making them trust and love him. He had to talk separately with and win over the confidence of every lama (Tibet is ruled by a large body of monks, or lamas, a religious hierarchy, I gather). He said he always talked to them alone and let each one give his story first, say everything he had to say and could say or object to or complain of. Then he would present his case, and he had the advantage of knowing the hardest obstacles and also getting some understanding of his man. It reminded me of Daddy, and I told him so. He seemed quite pleased. "Oh, Mr. Morrow—he did that too, did he?" Sir Francis is a much older man (over eighty, I think, now). He does not say much when he is pleased, you have to guess it from the twinkle in his eye.

Sir Francis is here as head of a World Fellowship of Religions, an idea that is his main interest now, understanding between religions of the world. The conference in India is an anniversary of a great Hindu saint. We have only gone to a few meetings.

The effort of keeping a straight face at C., sitting up in the front row of a religious conference facing a large sugary picture of Ramakrishna[1] decked with flowers. Banners all around the walls: "Religion is the highest expression of man"—"Blessed is he who is free from thoughts of I-Am," with crowds of barefoot Indian monks, holy men, students, and a few stray, wispy people from Pasadena, London, Boston, following an Indian swami in an orange turban, is simply too stifling to meet. I nearly died of the incongruity the first day. Also C.'s alarm watch went off in the middle of a prayer! But there was so much rustling of programs, shuffling and whispering, cooing of pigeons nesting in the ceiling, bicycle bells outside, etc., that no one was really disturbed by it, except me! C. has a great kick out of it. The aviation people

[1] Hindu yogi and mystic, 1834–1886, revered by Hindus as a holy man.

are seriously worried: "You'd better drop this religion stuff, you know!"

I am afraid we have been rather a disappointment to Sir Francis that we have not gone to more meetings. I think in England there was more exchange of thought. Although the idea in itself seems very idealistic, once you have said that all religions should try to understand and appreciate and get something from each other, there doesn't seem to me much else you can do about it in a "world" way, except in a small way getting those people who are vitally interested to exchange ideas, much as scholars or students do.

The meetings here have been vague muddles, for the most part, of proselytizing, praising one's own religion, or technical, theoretical papers read badly by obscure monks or ladies (large ladies) in chiffon, talking about love with arms outstretched, and a few people like Tagore[1] and Mrs. Naidu,[2] who gave inspiring talks. She is a poet (her things have been translated into English) and a violent nationalist, deep in the revival of India. (Rather like Yeats and Ireland.) I do not know how much wisdom or profundity of understanding there is in her politics (the English have had to put her in prison several times!), but there is a great profundity and understanding in her poetry and in her as a person—"*intelligence du coeur.*" She is very vigorous, capable, and enthusiastic and makes the best speech I have heard a woman or man make for a long time. (I'm sure she could easily stir a crowd to revolution, or anything!) *Far* the best speaker (though not the most intellectual) of the conference. But I liked her for none of this really but for her understanding and courage.

We have met (Indian) lawyers, doctors, teachers, dancers, and of course (in the smaller places) British officials who have been incredibly nice to us. There is quite a different attitude here than

[1] Rabindranath Tagore, 1861–1941, poet, playwright, lecturer, awarded the Nobel Prize for literature (1913).

[2] Sarojini Naidu, Hindu poet and reformer, first woman President (1925) of the Indian National Congress.

in England toward the stranger (of one's own race), and the extent of kindness, spontaneous welcome, and taking you in has quite overpowered me—English hospitality as warm as anything in our West! Perhaps the most enthusiastic, spontaneous, "American" English go to the colonies, or perhaps it is just environment.

I have missed Jon frightfully, for we have had so much together this winter, Jon really talking to me and sharing things with me in a grown-up way, on walks together and talks and plays at night.

Anyway, we are going home very soon now, waiting for a spare part for our engine, due today or tomorrow, and then we set out slowly back across India and following somewhat our course out, but perhaps going on the north side of the Mediterranean. It is more direct.

The Great Eastern Hotel Ltd., Calcutta, March 12th

Mother darling,

It was such a joy to get your letter and feel in touch again. I feel far away here and long to get back. I can do so little now. I do not enjoy sightseeing in my state and Calcutta is a rather depressing place. We have been delayed because C. sent to London for a spare part of the engine. We expect it tomorrow and then will pick up our plane and slowly start back. Calcutta, Delhi, Jodhpur, Karachi, and up the Persian Gulf, following the regular lines, only we do not expect to go through Egypt but north through Athens. I don't know where I will be on March 17th [E. R. M. M.'s birthday], probably in Jodhpur or Delhi, but I shall think of you in Mexico, in the garden. What a lovely place to be, having, I hope, peace and time to think.

This must not be a long letter as I must go to bed. Tomorrow night we will be on the train (we left the plane in Nagpur, central India. C. found the weak part there, on the ground).

I think your Englewood–New York life sounds too awful, really. There is something wrong about it. But it is always that way when you are living for other people and cannot explain. I feel it so often in marriage: "But *why, why* do you do this or that?" And you cannot explain the inner pressures that weight the balance quite differently from the way it looks to the outside.

Yes, I should like some of the baby clothes. I remember Elisabeth and me going up to the attic before the first baby secretly to look at the baby things. Absolutely unbelievable they looked, and a baby so unreal, until Elisabeth picked up a cake of baby soap in among the clothes and we both sniffed at it together in a kind of ecstasy—umistakably, vividly, and miraculously "baby"! Then I really believed that one was coming. It is just as unreal now and I cannot imagine having two children, or another baby, in Long Barn.

I want you at Long Barn at least part of the time. The week of Uncle Jay, however, was unaccountably exhausting. I felt in a kind of despair, "I can never have guests again—we all become too irritable." But of course that is exaggeration. C., though, feels very firmly that the house must not be upset at that time. It must be quiet and peaceful for the good of both the baby and everyone during the weeks just preceding and following the event.

Calcutta, March 16th

Darling Con—

I had just sent off a letter to Mother when I got yours. I have written her the difficulties. The exhaustion after Uncle Jay (though I am awfully happy about it now) and our consequent desperate feeling that we "could never have a guest again"— though, of course (and I told her that), that is not strictly true.

Personally I feel that the *mechanics* of the thing will work out all right, but I have a slightly uneasy feeling that it is really not that at all, but a fundamental difficulty underneath. That C. really dislikes so much (to a sensitive point) any *fuss* about anything, any fuss about a baby or a wedding or a coronation, and *we* are all rather inclined to mildly *like* one! However, that must be worked out little by little as we go along and the mechanics being guided will help some. Anyway, your wedding will not bother him, so don't worry about that. In fact, he feels most sympathetic! He said your letter sounded as though you were having quite a winter yourself.

I can just see you entertaining Morgans, friends of Dwight, friends of the family, rushing back and forth to New York, time for Aubrey, work, clothes for the wedding, etc., etc. And then getting a thesis done before coming abroad!

This seems incredibly unreal—both the baby and your wedding. Will this spring be one of those crowded times when I don't get a chance to talk to you at all? One must spend all one's time on plans and feel perpetually as one does in the car on the way from Englewood to New York: something behind, something ahead, nothing in the middle (except the George Washington Bridge!).

Well, there will be time later—much better nicer time. How wonderful that C. and you and Aubrey and C. and Aubrey and I, and you and I, get on so well—just like Elisabeth. It does make for a security ahead.

I have bought you a sari (does this sound like one of those odd prickly metal-embroidered wrappers aunts-on-tour bring back?). Just a long strip of silk, the borders printed in paisley, that you can have made into an evening dress or negligee.

Long Barn, Weald, Sevenoaks, Sunday, April 11th

Mother darling,

Both Con's wedding and a nice visit from you seem more important to me than the Coronation.[1] Also your degree seems more important. I think it is lovely especially that it was voted by the Faculty. I can see President Neilson twinkling, but I wish I could see you very small and cunning on the platform bowing your

[1] Following the abdication of Edward VIII (1936), George VI was to be crowned on May 12, 1937.

head for the hood (do you get a new one?) and hear what he has to say. But that is impossible.

I hope it will be possible to be at Con's wedding—that is, I hope of course that it is over here. But I shall understand if things get so complicated that they get it over with quickly at home. I feel so happy about it and anxious for it to be settled. One does not usually feel that way about people one loves being married. One feels one is losing them. But with this I feel that it leads to closer understanding and more security and permanence in the personal relationships in all our lives (though in this life one ought never to boast or even speak about "security" or "permanence"). I am very anxious for that new life we are all going to have together and for the happiness I think it is going to bring everyone. So that the wedding in itself does not seem important compared with that big thing that is coming slowly and normally afterward.

As for the baby—yes, of course that does seem important more than anything else—naturally—to me! But the actual moment of its birth does not seem so important. That is, I don't think being here at its arrival should change everyone's plans. I shall be in a nursing home with, I gather, rigid British rules as to my conduct and hours of visitors.

I don't believe you ever feel the baby is yours until you get it home in your own house with your own things. And that is what I look forward to, rather unbelievingly: to having the baby snugly upstairs in the middle guest room and Jon and I and my family going in softly to look at it, sleeping in a Moses basket on top of an old table! And Thor sniffing underneath and Skean standing up on his hind legs to see what is making that funny noise.

As for the Coronation, it no longer even counts in my mind. There are going to be such crowds of people here that London will be worse than a world's fair—not really London at all. All normal London life will be thrown out of kilter.

Really, what a bad time to choose to have a baby!

This is all "plans." I shall have to write you again about the bliss of being at home (how I understood your letter describing the house at Englewood full of flowers, when you got back). It is soft sunny April weather here, the aubretia blue again over the walls and daffodils along the borders, and thrushes and blackbirds singing every morning, and primroses along the wood path and the peach blossoms pink on the tennis-court wall. Jon and I have been out almost all day today, choosing a bed for his "garden," looking for his trowel (Hammond thinks it is in the swimming pool!), choosing seeds in Hook's woodshed.

Also a general spring cleaning, looking for more room and (finally) cleaning out the bureaus, chests, boxes etc. that had Mrs. Nicolson's things left in them. We are moving furniture. You know, "that little white bureau from the cottage will be just right in the bathroom for a baby's things." "That long narrow white table will be useful for bath things." "This big chest with open shelves splendid for blankets, towels, drapes, etc." It is such fun to do.

Long Barn, Weald, Sevenoaks, April 17th

Mother darling,

I have just got your cable about Uncle Jay and sent one back, and I have thought about you all day. I know it has been hard for you. It is not that one did not expect Uncle Jay to die, perhaps soon, and it is not that it didn't happen in the best possible way. He had not been ill or relapsed into one of those depressed periods again. He was still happy and his confidence set up by the memory of the trip.

But one may still feel all that and yet one can't help but feel inexpressibly saddened. Although Uncle Jay was *not a bit* like Daddy, you must feel that it is a link with your past life gone, and have a double sadness in losing Uncle Jay and in losing that link. Although I feel it is an illusory link, really. That is, that Uncle Jay, ill and broken, changed from what he was, was infinitely sadder than his death and more of a link gone. And to have him go, more like his old self than he had been for years, is better.

But then it is so hard, going through it again, the details, the telegrams, the family, the funeral. The service in that old house, now cleaned and unnaturally tidy, when it was always so *full* of Uncle Jay and tobacco and ashes and papers.

And there does not seem any way to oppose the sadness of those inevitable things except perhaps, as I felt this morning (thinking about a shrunken Morrow family), looking out of my study window and seeing Jon in his ragged red raincoat, thumping along with a wheelbarrow, his inevitably Morrow nose and Morrow twinkle showing up under his red sou'wester hat! He must have been thinking about you too, tonight, for he said, for no apparent reason, "If it's summer pretty soon, will Daddy Bee be coming pretty soon?" I said you would—in May. And I have told him (in dead secret) about the baby coming in May. Then he said (with a delighted secret smile!), "Won't Daddy Bee be surprised!" He is worried lest you come before he has any vegetables grown. It has been so wet we haven't been able to plant them yet.

P.S. Sunday night, April 18th

It is so strange. I have stuck in my letter case about seven letters from Uncle Jay, written after his visit, crammed and overflowing with love, praise, gratitude, exuberant affection, that I didn't deserve and seems out of all proportion. Why? And what return did he get? I suppose the only answer or justice is or will be, in my loving some nephew or great-grandchild in the future, the same way. The laws of loving people seem only compensated in some distant way like the tides or shifting of sands. Or it is perhaps said best in that quotation of Rilke's. That is really how I feel and felt about Uncle Jay.

"Ask no advice from them and count upon no understanding; but believe in a love that is being preserved for you like an inheritance and trust that in this love there is a strength and a blessing, beyond which you do not have to move in order to go very far indeed!"[1]

TO E. L. L. L.   *Long Barn, Weald, Sevenoaks, May 5th*
Dear M.

I have just had such a very understanding letter from you which you wrote after getting one of mine written just before we left on the trip. You said, "I do not know why. I feel you were very tired when you wrote that letter." And saying something very nice about not wanting to add any difficulties to my life.

I *was* awfully tired then. It was a very difficult time because Uncle Jay and Katharine Leighton (my cousin) were here on an unexpected visit. And we had no regular people helping in the house, and all the time trying to get ready to go off. And yet I am so grateful for every effort we made, for since his visit here Uncle Jay died, about three weeks ago—perhaps you saw in the papers.

He loved just watching Jon, or playing with him. I wrote you, didn't I, how he played your blackboard spelling game by the hour with him, saying (much to his mother's surprise!) that he was the "most intelligent youngster" he had ever seen.

I am so grateful that we could give him any happiness and to know that we did; the difficulties do not matter now. And I like to remember him happy and full of fun and humor as he was here. He was such a wonderful old soldier.

Though that letter was a "tired" one because of the circumstances, it is not an effort to write to you, and I love doing it. I feel that you will enjoy as much as I do all those little things about Jon, that I can almost not say to anyone else, in case they think me silly about him, or anyway a bore. And it is a joy to share them and to know you appreciate them.

I do not like the thought of going to London for the baby but it seems to be the best idea. We are moving up (C. and I) on the

[1] From *Letters to a Young Poet,* translated by M. D. Herter Norton, p. 39, Norton, 1934.

16th because the doctor thinks I should be near the hospital after that and not trust to coming when things start, as it is rather a long drive.

I want you to think about another visit here. You know how easy it is now and you are still very vivid to Jon, and I shall be anxious to show you the new baby and to see what Jon thinks of it. This must go in the mail tonight to catch the *Europa*.

Long Barn, Weald, Sevenoaks, May 3rd

Dear Grandma,

Thank you so much for writing to me. I know it is hard to write in bed—twice as hard as at a desk. You seem to be pushing against gravity the whole time. I do appreciate your taking that strength to write me. I will be very happy to have something from you for the new baby, although I have still some lovely baby things you gave me before, that Mother is bringing over.

The time has gone quickly this time. I have been very well and the trip made the days go fast. When we were in Calcutta I meant to write you for I had a letter from the leper hospital in Allahabad saying that we must stop in Allahabad and see them because you had been knitting scarves for them for thirty years. It doesn't matter how far I travel—Japan, China, Korea, India—you have got there before me with scarves or missionary work! We flew over Allahabad on our way back but did not have time to stop so I could not tell the head of the hospital that, under my grandmother's influence, I also as a child knitted some very nubbly shortish scarves with odd bits of wool, purple and yellow, on the back porch at Quissett!

It was lovely to be home again. Jon is tall and sturdy and well. He is out in the garden all day in rubber boots with a wheelbarrow. His father has got him some tools and we have planted a little garden. It has been a wet spring.

But the last week has been lovely. The cuckoo goes incessantly and the nightingale every night. The woods are full of primroses and what the English call "bluebells"—a flower with a little blue bell, like a wild hyacinth. Jon and Charles and I and the dogs go for walks over the fields—I with a trowel and basket—and sometimes we bring back a wild orchid to plant in a "wild-flower bed" that Jon has. But most of the time I just sit in the sun or walk slowly around the paths, cutting a few tulips and narcissi, feeling very happy to be at home in the garden and to have Jon and Charles and to be having another baby.

DIARY   *Thursday, May 20th—The London Clinic*
A week ago last night my third little boy was born. To go back to before then in my mind is like spanning a great chasm. It was really only a few hours, and yet hours of such intense feeling, both physically and emotionally, that I feel, as I did the other times, reborn. One's mind has been asleep for six months. (The first three months it is still alive, but painfully so. The last six months all the sharpness of it, as the sharpness of all feelings, is absorbed into the process of making a baby. One is self-centered in a way, and yet the sharp pointed flame of you *yourself* is lost, blurred, absorbed.) Suddenly it leaps to life again, racing ahead, making up for lost time, day and night. To think, to write, to talk, to contact people again!

It brings such extreme happiness, this having a child, the nine months before, and even those last terrible hours. This time, though, it was not nearly as bad, and I was not as frightened and felt I could control myself more.

Two uncomfortable days and nights at Long Barn. Pain and wondering if it meant anything and wondering if we should go up early to the hospital (the room at the hotel was not free until the sixteenth). The traffic problem: it would not be possible to go up after 11 P.M. Coronation Eve, and not at all for twenty-four hours after.

Finally about 10:30 we decide to go on the chance and steal away in the quiet of the night, with Thor looking mournful. Such a strange drive up, through those decorated streets, flags, people out walking in a holiday mood, all thinking about the

Coronation—and I thinking about my baby. It was an extraordinarily happy drive, though: the gay streets, the lights thrown up on the dark leaves and chestnut candles out, as they were the night of our wedding. I felt very happy and very close to C., as though we were going down the same road together, wondering how far down that road he could go with me.

Bad traffic across Oxford Street, pains, and I worried about getting there. Pretty girls without hats running down the streets, sitting on top of cars, flinging remarks at passers-by. Oxford Street is blocked off, filled with pedestrians, people already forming in line to see the procession.

A long traffic jam at Portman Place and Wigmore Street. C.: "I have something better than a pass, I have my wife, who is going to have a baby."

Then the hospital. The quiet, and a night and a day of slight irregular pains. Waiting, and the shouting crowds at a distance, the radios in the street, the flags from the roofs.

Then from six o'clock on the pains regular and increasing. I was reading *The Years* [by Virginia Woolf] in between counting the breaths—that long hill one climbs, now at the top, now down. The sense that C. and I were together, not separated by nurses and doctors. The sense that this pain I could control, and welcomed. Dr. Holland casually coming in at 10:10. That strange voice counting breaths painfully, that wasn't mine at all. The feeling that they (the hospital and nurses) were underestimating my progress.

"Now will you believe me!" The chloroform and back in that strange world I remembered from the other times. Here I am again. The sense of endless time passing. Coming back. "I thought it was all over." The sense that I could not get the mask quickly enough. The sense that people were handling me about rather clumsily—lifting me, turning me. Again that terrific pain that one thinks is a mistake. There must be something wrong—it can't be allowed to go on. Then eternities of blissful unconsciousness (of a few seconds). Finding Charles's eyes among the masked faces. And then that new sensation—colossal and frightening—of birth itself. (I have had that now, anyway.)

And then after aeons of unconsciousness (several minutes?) coming to. And seeing faces again, finding C.'s face again among the white caps. A baby crying. "Yes, *your* baby." "It's all over." "All over?" "A boy." "A boy?" "A little boy." "Perhaps she'd like to see him." (Dr. H. very kind.) Bringing him over. "Grandma Morrow's nose—just like the others." And I was very happy. It was all over. "It was a bit of a rush. . . ." Was it? It had seemed years. But it was still Coronation night, 11:45—three quarters of an hour since the first bad pains. The window was open and up through it came sounds of people shouting on their way home. A Coronation baby, after all! Only three quarters of an hour. A year seemed to separate me from three quarters of an hour ago. So arbitrary is time.

And then feeling very weak. Pain, but no more struggling—it was over. "Yes, it's not bad." But how weak I feel. Thank goodness, I don't have to do anything more. They give me something for the pain. "Isn't it splendid—it's all over. You might have been a fortnight more" (waiting). "He's two years late," I manage to sigh. "Yes, but how wonderful to have him now!" The doctor's voice through the dark and numbness: "Yes, wonderful." And then gradually coming out of the numbness to the peaceful dark of my room. Coming to, happily, and that night of wakefulness—ecstatic wakefulness, floating on waves of happiness. When I hear the baby cry next door, everything is startled to a new, more acute consciousness of happiness—almost painful—beating in me.

And then lying perfectly happy—awake, aware, my mind racing ahead all night long; feeling alive again, feeling sharp again after months of numbness. I thought of the year and our happiness, our married happiness in England. Perhaps I hadn't accomplished very much but I had been so happy in Charles and Jon. Yes—this had been living. This was life itself, and I realized it thankfully, for once. How much of one's life one is thinking, "After this is over, then I can start living. . . ." The way one looks at spring and thinks, "Tomorrow it will be spring," "It is almost spring," or "Now spring is over," but never does one catch that instant—spring itself. One evening before I left for the hospital I *did,* though. After supper I walked out and the garden was softly mistily green, nothing very much out but all the greens were just fresh, and the fruit trees in the bottom terrace, soft pinks against the greens, so fresh and soft—melting the evening was, and I called C. out. This—*this* is spring, I felt—this instant! It will never be so perfect again. I must go out in it. C. must see it. Perhaps he will mind being interrupted? No, he didn't, and he came out and felt it, too.

That is the way this year has been in my life. This, *this* is life, happiness, married happiness. I wished C. had been there to tell him, and wondered how I could wait till morning.

Then I put myself to thinking of all the places where this child had been—such a nice thought game. Coming back from those far places in time and space to the baby *there—now*—in the next room. Over the Alps, the sunshine of Pisa, the Greek temple at Segesta; over the deserts of Arabia; across the blue Persian Gulf, the burning desert heat of India, the walls of a Crusaders' city at Rhodes, the Mediterranean, the Turkish mountains, prickly and blue on the coast, the Aegean Sea, Cape Sounion, beautiful hill pushing out to sea, and, through the white columns, the sea, the Greek islands, and white sails coming home to port.

Then a succession of pleasant white days in the hospital—clean sheets, cool emotions. One is protected even from one's own emotions, somehow, and one's own conscience.

Then the day Jon came up. The gentle knock at the door, it opens . . . a pause, and Jon in his brown overalls walking in slowly, quietly, and a little awe-struck, wide-eyed.

"Jon!" I put out my hand to him, "I didn't know you were coming, it was a surprise—a surprise for Mother!" This pleased him. "You didn't know I was coming—it was a surprise." Smiling with pleasure and taking my hand.

Then they wheeled the crib in. Jon, very quiet, tiptoed over to it and just looked and smiled, very much impressed. Then it was wheeled back. "What do you think of him, Jon?" Jon, in his agreeable, anxious-to-please voice, "I think very well of him." "What is the first thing you are anxious to do with him when he gets to Long Barn?" Hesitation—then in a rush and a little perplexed, "Do you think he could pick up very little sticks?" (Rather a comedown from the logs of wood Jon expected a little "brother" to help him carry!)

Then we had a large tea. The door to the nursery was left open, and every once in a while Jon would tiptoe in to look at the crib and then come back, smiling and quiet.

We asked him what color his eyes were. Jon couldn't tell because he was asleep, but kept running in to see. "He opened his eyes but he shut them again so quickly that I couldn't tell."

Than, looking at me, "He isn't there any more." *"Who,* Jon?" "My brother."

My brother. It was so thrilling, opening up the past and the future, as though I had waited a lifetime for it, waited and waited for my boy to say, "My brother." The first baby, and the morning after Jon's birth, Emily sticking her head in and saying in a choking broken English voice, "If only he could see his little broder."

And then so many years when I wondered if Jon would ever have a little brother and then finally, like a strange repetition of a dream, "My brother."

It sounded prophetic, too, like the beginning of a new line of history, personal history, a new relationship for Jon, something I would never share but that he alone had: "My brother." It was new now, but it would become familiar, unconscious, old, unnoticeable, part of life, a long life that was to come and would continue after I wasn't any more. I tried to snatch some of it from the future—from time. In the laboratory, on an expedition. "My brother and I . . ." "My brother's wife . . ." "My brother's children," "My brother says," "My brother thinks the war in

Tanganyika . . ." "That's my brother's field, you know." On and on, "My brother," forever now.

Long Barn, Weald, Sevenoaks, June 17th
(Yesterday was your wedding day)

Mother darling,

This letter will get to you, I suppose, sometime between Con's and Dwight's weddings.[1] It seems quite unreal. And almost as though I shouldn't write about everyday things at such a time. But still I want to write you.

Florrie came down today. It was one of those abnormally cold summer days. Florrie had on a warm suit and warm topcoat. It rained spasmodically. Why is it when one has guests that it is always on that day that the piano tuner (who comes once in six months) turns up (a rainy day, too!), and you cannot quite send him away, and the flowers you have arranged on the piano have to be moved and the one presentable room is disarranged, and Thor is definitely uneasy (a strange man at the piano, a strange woman coming in a car)!

Also, on that day the plumbing by the terrace (main) door, which has leaked for months, has to be fixed. You walk in from the dining room and find the hall abnormally dark, the door to the terrace closed, a large blow-torch burning in the corner and a man with overalls and a tool kit on his knees!

Florrie didn't mind. C. had a nice talk with her about Scotland and then she saw the babies (both) and Jon's "eight-year-old wheelbarrow" and helped to cut roses, showing Jon which to cut. And then talked in the study with me. She talked about Con and Aubrey—how lovely she thought it was—and about Elisabeth and how we all talked of her and kept her living among us. She talked of second marriages, how it did not ever mean the first was "forgotten," and then she gave an example. She said it made her so angry when people said to her that she had "forgotten" her

[1] Constance Morrow was marrying Aubrey Morgan; Margot Loines, a friend of Constance, was marrying Dwight Morrow.

old friends—people of childhood times, or people she had not seen for fifteen years or so. "You haven't forgotten them," she said. "When I see them I can talk with them again, but my life has moved into a different channel."

It was so simple, but a great comfort to me (not about Elisabeth but of other people you don't see any more but who occupy the same original place in your mind). The truth of it was all in that simple statement: "My life has moved into a different channel." That is why it is hard to keep in touch with people at home, and hard to write letters at times. It is not disloyalty or forgetfulness, but the *small* things in life you no longer have in common, and the *small* things are what make up letters and everyday conversation—and the "channel" of your life—to a great extent. You can't keep up a running commentary on only the *big* things in your life.

Long Barn, Weald, Sevenoaks, June 16th

Dear Margot—

I cannot tell you how happy your letter made me—how heartening it was to touch you again. I have not written, partly, I am afraid, because England, babies, home life, and health have settled down on me in a rather soporific way. And partly, too, because I did not know quite what was happening to you and remembering my own pre-engagement, or premarriage time, I thought it was better not to say anything. Not that one doubts one's love, but I don't believe any serious person has ever gotten married without wondering rather tremulously about their capacity for making a success out of the serious business of marriage itself—if you look at it that way—as more important than anything else. If you look at it the way you and I and all of us do.

I can't say anything about you except that I am so glad you are getting married—partly, yes, because I feel one doesn't begin to live until then. But partly, too, I have the strange feeling (and about Con, too) of happiness that you have arrived "here" too. As though it were a location in space, being married.

But it is a selfish happiness. I am glad that Con and Margot are "here too" because I think what you discover and think and make of marriage will be so valuable. It will help me too. As though in marriage all the time it was an unknown language, like an enigma in science or history that one was working on. It gives you the most wonderful satisfaction when you piece out a little bit yourself and you value the little bits you see other people piece and feel it all adds to the general sum. It is strange, in a way, to talk like this to you, because I feel that you have done so much piecing already without ever being married. I felt that the first time I met you. "How did she get as far as that, without being married?" I thought. Which only proves that some people can learn by intuition and imagination and sensitivity and don't have to be taught by the trial-and-error, hit-or-miss methods.

Long Barn, Weald, Sevenoaks, morning, June 22nd

Mother darling,

This is such a beautiful day. I have thought of all of you since early this morning. (I know it is five hours earlier in Maine, and that you aren't up yet or perhaps not even arrived. Still, one's thoughts go through a strange transmutation too, traveling over the ocean, and may get there at the right time after all.) I sat up in bed feeding the baby, looking out over the garden, which was still and fresh and glistening, and the line of blue larkspur stood up still in the sun against the hawthorn hedge and the pink snapdragon against the dark green beech hedge at the bottom of the garden. After breakfast I went out and walked in the rose garden. The day, the sunshine, the clearness, the expanded feeling (one of those days when the whole lovely summer seems spread out, unrolled for you) and the larkspur made me feel especially festive. "This is a *special* day—a special lovely day," I kept feeling. And I was so glad for Con and all of you that it was so, over here, even. I hope it is there, too. The day and the larkspur, like the winding garden in Maine, made me feel very close to you.

I have sent a cable to Con. I hope it arrives all right. The man wanted to know what state "Maine" was in! I wanted to send all of it—the poem—and keep thinking of it in my mind.

> "There grows the flower of Peace,
> The Rose that cannot wither . . ."

And I wanted first to send a line from Vaughan's poem "Corruption" because it expressed a feeling North Haven has—full of the love and spirit of the people who are not there. I don't mean in a mawkish Arthur Conan Doyle way, but Vaughan's lines best express it. However, they seemed a little sad to send. Most weddings one thinks of as unalloyed joy, young people's joy, but this wedding seems to be that of slightly older people who know about life's being sad and who perhaps will be happier because of this knowledge. I think this analyzes my mixed feelings about this wedding and helps me to think about it. So I write it to you, hoping it may help you.

Here are the lines of Vaughan. You will understand what I mean by saying it applies to North Haven.

> . . . "and still *Paradise* lay
> In some green shade or fountain.
> Angels lay *Leiger* here; Each Bush, and Cell
> Each Oak and highway knew them,
> Walk but the fields, or sit down at some *well*
> And he was sure to view them . . ."

I love "Angels lay *Leiger* here"—*leiger* is similar to the word *liege-lord*—more or less *as ambassadors* I think it means.

I hope this will get to you before Dwight's wedding. I shall think of you then, too. I cannot see Martha's Vineyard. But I can see Dwight, beaming and more like Daddy than ever. I am glad Con and Aubrey will be there.

Yesterday C. went down and registered the baby's name. It still sounds very strange but as we couldn't agree on any first names, we have taken a last one, Land Morrow Lindbergh. (The Land family has a fine old history and I like keeping the name.)

It sounds strange at first, but it is a good name, has a *real* connection, is simple and easy to say. I really think it has a lovely sound, and will not sound so strange at school, as boys often call other boys by last names.

I am glad to have the *Morrow*. His eyes and his mouth look more and more Morrow. And this morning, when I was thinking of all my other birthdays, sitting on the bed, remembering little Charles, he gave me the most beautiful *real* smile—not a "windy" one. A real one that fills his whole face and is, I think, like Daddy's, and the blue eyes trying to talk, too. I was so happy—so happy to have on this birthday my two little boys.

DIARY   *July 10th*

The days go now with seemingly little done. I try to analyze it at night, lying in bed very tired.

Where does my day go—what have I to show for it? It goes into the baby, into Jon and C. I wouldn't change that really a bit and I don't grudge one minute of it, and yet I feel hopelessly inefficient not to do the baby, C., and Jon as a matter of course—"on the side," so to speak—like those women C. is always talking about who cook, take care of the house, a large family, do the sewing, washing, and some of the farm work, etc. It is true I take too much time doing everything, from feeding the baby to writing a letter. All my contacts with people take too long. Bathing and dressing take too long, and getting Jon to bed. Is it because I try to do everything perfectly or because I get distracted and do not concentrate or because I am hesitant and timid and undecided?

What is my criterion for a successful day? The baby should get enough milk, C. should get enough companionship and intellectual sympathy and understanding, and Jon should get . . . a whole education! That is the big lump in my day. Everything for and about Jon seems so vital now. It must be done right, it must be done well. There must be no waste, no mistakes. And the problems are constantly new, constantly changing, and so absorbing.

I feel if Jon interrupts my morning to ask for help in building a house, I should give it. It was a good idea, showed initiative and creativeness, and he should be encouraged. He will get a sense of accomplishment out of it, a sense of confidence in his tools, in his hands, in what he can do. If I say *No, I am too busy,* he will give it up and throw stones for Thor and Skean. Countless things come up: Jon carrying wood, emptying the flower vases . . . Those things must be checked or encouraged *at the time.* It's no good saying, "I will train my child between three and four in the afternoon." It is a constant thing—it is life itself.

Of course he should play alone and do things for himself, which he does, but he should feel he can come to me for help.

It is rewarding, of course. Jon learning arithmetic from carrying wood (so many logs in a basket, so many trips) or from the haying in Mr. Page's field ("He has done one quarter, Jon, in one day. How long will it take him to do the whole field?") etc.

But it isn't just "arithmetic," "stories," "questions" which constitute what I mean by his education. It is the whole *stuff* of the day like weaving a material.

The day is made if I feel I have given him something, like taking him down into Mr. Page's field and having him watch the haying.

Or when we made a map of the garden and Jon put his footsteps onto it—little red dotted line for where he went, down the brick paths, around the tennis court, past his "workplace." "Make a mark there for where I fell off the gate"!

Or if I send him out to watch his father unpack a wooden case, so he can see how to use a hammer well.

Yes, and let him hammer the damask hanging above the dining-room chest, even if it takes longer, and let him empty and fill the flower vases, even if he *may* drop one.

And now I have taken too much time to write in my diary because it is five to ten and time to feed the baby and go to bed!

Today Jon rode on the farm horse in the field pulling the hay cart and on the hay cart too. He was very happy.

Dear Thelma,[1]

I have thought so often of you and have found it this year so difficult to write. I think because I have been absorbed in a purely physical life, a very satisfying one but completely absorbing. Having a baby, going to India, taking care of a house, etc. And only lying flat on one's back in bed (staring up at the marks of old leaks in the ceiling!) does one get a chance to write those letters and say those things one means to say. There have been a great many things I have wanted to talk to you about, and your letter has intensified them. I felt, reading it, very acutely that you were feeling some of the same things I was in my very rural peaceful life in this heavenly house and garden.

It goes back to that book *The Thinking Reed* [by Rebecca West]. Somewhere in the book the woman said that she was perfectly happy—only strangely lacking in friends. She suddenly realized that was the lack in her life. And it was not just a peculiarity of her life but a seemingly inevitable part of marriage —a certain kind of happy and absorbing marriage. She wondered sometimes if it were not a conscious or unconscious conspiracy of the male to keep their women so occupied and absorbed that there wasn't room for anything else. And she had a feeling that all her life that could not be expressed, transmuted, or passed on in some way to the outside world was being wasted. If she died it would all die in her. (Not that that would matter perhaps!) I quote from memory and may enlarge.

I have gone on thinking about it. Because we have been very much like that here. I don't think I have ever been—we have ever been—so happy, peaceful, and absorbed simply in living. And yet at the same time, strangely lonely. I don't think C. has been, because his work and contacts have taken him out more. For me it has been partly the English (who don't intrude or even make advances, a rather welcome relief), and partly shyness, and partly having a baby and being somewhat tied, and not knowing very

[1] Thelma Crawford Lee, a friend of E. R. M. M. and A. M. L.

many people. And although I feel I could go on quite happily living like this forever I think there is a definite kind of scurvy of the mind that sets in after a while—a lack of vitamins somewhere! I have figured out (lying in bed staring at the ceiling) that it is definitely one's friends that keep one alive in a certain sense. Don't you think so? Your husband and your marriage may be *life* itself but you haven't got the spark to live that life without something from the outside. The impersonal part of you doesn't stay alive—or perhaps you might call it the very very personal part, the straight stick inside of you that was there before you got married and goes on existing somehow irrespective of marriage. That is your true self, after all—the person, presumably, your husband fell in love with. And you must keep it going. It gets rather soft and vinelike without outside contacts. And so it is your friends, really, who make life "livable" in a strange sense. Even if one sees them only once in five years, or through letters, or even a very vivid remembrance of a person, like Elisabeth. Just to think about Elisabeth makes one more oneself and conscious of life.

This is only to say that I miss you very much, Thelma—a real homesickness at times, like my homesickness for a Maine day: a clear, crisp blue sky.

Train to London, July 31st

Darling Con,

I am thinking about you starting your Western tour. Heaven knows where this will get to you. Your letters pleased me so—about the wedding. What a beautiful passage in the ceremony. I hadn't remembered it: "not to be entered into lightly." That is just the way I felt about it, only I felt terrified with the responsibility of it.

Your North Haven letter arrived on one of the days here that make me most homesick for Maine, with the wind blowing all the trees white. It would have been a "smoky-sou'wester" in Maine. It's nice to associate Maine with being happy, isn't it? I'm glad C. and I were there on our "honeymoon," too, at least in

Maine waters. He says someday we must get a place in Maine. But probably not in North Haven as it is getting too settled. I should love to get Leadbetter's Island,[1] but I'm sure he thinks it too unprotected. The mail boat goes by the front door twice a day!

I wonder what your trip will be like. I think of it because those Western trips with C. have given something *utterly* new to me—something that our lives before never could have. And I am incredibly grateful for it, especially looking back on it from here—meeting a kind of person one does not meet in the East, or even in college (one meets the younger generation, but they are not typical always, and only a so-called "upper-class" younger generation at that). I think it is a kind of "sense of Americans" I got from the trips. A quality of America that you only get from the casual people you meet on business. It has to be casual, because you can see characteristics more easily in the casual. And it has to be on business because the people you meet socially or through your family or through interest in their personality—those people are not "provincial" enough. I don't mean that snobbishly, I mean simply that the "provincialism" of your own friends eludes you because you are looking at other things. And I mean by provincialism a quality that grows from the place you live—a native plant.

Then there is the fun of meeting "young marrieds" on the plane of "young marriage." I feel that most of the world is "young marrieds"! (But that sounds illogical.) Perhaps because it is the middle of life it lets you into more of life on both sides.

Nearing Charing Cross.

Going home

Didn't you think that the American quality in *They Came Like Swallows*[2] was wonderful? Perhaps it was most vivid to me.

[1] An island near Vinalhaven, Maine, on which one old house stood, and where the Morrows used to picnic.

[2] Novel by William Maxwell, writer, editor on *The New Yorker* magazine.

because I have been away from it now. It made me quite home-sick. All that breakfast-conversation part, and playing baseball in the back lot, and calling up Willie So-and-So's mother to find out how he was, and sisters dropping in for Sunday lunch and discussing clothes and food. "I beat it" and "then I bring it to a boil slowly" and that boy's *songs:* "Just pickle my bones in alkyhol." And all his mother's friends—"aunts" who came in for tea, Aunt Millie, Aunt Gladys, Aunt Ruth, etc.

This is Bank Holiday weekend—crowds and crowds going to the sea. Miss W. has just been off for a week by the sea. But we can't seem to find anything, so we are staying home, which is nicer really for Dwight and Margot, who come on the 16th.

TO E. L. L. L.   Long Barn, Weld, Sevenoaks, August 28th
Dear M.

We have had a very crowded three weeks—or month, almost. First the visit to the Carrels' island. We planned to go by car, taking Jon, Land, cribs, etc. Then there were no accommodations at all. You have to plan weeks ahead in England. Then we decided to go by plane, taking Land in his basket. It meant only a little over three hours in the plane, with a car trip of an hour and a half at each end. But that meant leaving Jon, which was a blow. I hardly wanted to go then, especially as that island with its rocks and fields and beach and farm seemed made for him. And C. and I had talked so much of what we would do with him there (not to him, though). And to miss his birthday *again.* However, it seemed the only thing to do. C. wanted ten days there and felt the change would be good for me (I have hardly left this garden). And I couldn't leave Land. So we decided to go.

Mme Carrel met us at Morlaix and arranged that no one but the airport manager and his daughter should be there, and we got quietly into her car and drove to Saint-Gildas, where Mme Carrel had fixed up a little room for the baby—crib, tub, and all! We had lovely weather and the baby thrived, gaining an ounce a day during the ten days there. Coming back I fed Land just before we left Morlaix and he slept all the way to Saint-Inglevert, not even waking for the plane's stopping and starting. Then I fed him again at Saint-Inglevert (by bottle) and held him in my arms the last half-hour across the Channel to Lympne. Not a cry out of him at all. And no trouble at Lympne. We got into the car and drove quietly home. And nothing has ever come out about our (the baby and I) flying!

It was wonderful to see Jon's face light up as we came through the door. Though he said only (running up to us), "See this very old knife I found. That's all right for me to use, 'cause it's not sharp, I can cut down suckers with it," and then ran off to cut suckers off the rosebushes and fruit trees.

Each evening I have told him a "story" about the island. He loves especially stories about Land on the trip and most of all how his father dove in a plane over the farm and dropped a note in the very center of the garden, to say when he would be arriving and to save some supper for him!

Jon gets so much joy out of Land even now. I wish you could see them. Jon bending over Land talking to him. "You'll see rabbits when you get older . . ." and Land staring up at Jon with wide blue eyes and rather a wobbly head!

Monday, September 13th

Mother darling,

I am up to London for the dentist—a welcome change, really, as I have this morning had to deal with the cook-housemaid problem. There is something eternal about it, like the round faces of pots and pans, the smug self-important expression accompanying the perennial phrase, "I don't want to make any trouble, but . . . (!) . . . if Mrs. S. stays *we* will have to leave." Of course Mrs. S. *must* stay, after that, everyone gets talked to all around—the usual. ". . . doesn't speak to me for days on end." . . . "Never been spoken to like that before." . . . "Never had any trouble before." . . . "more food thrown away than eaten," . . . etc., and the whole thing simmers for another month.

I begin to think sometimes in discouragement that you cannot treat all people the way I always want to—that the more freedom and advantages you give to some people the more they use them to bully other people and make trouble. *Must* I go out in my kitchen every three or four days and say the larder is a disgrace, the icebox is a mess, etc.? *Must* people be forever at each other's necks or do they do it on purpose (unconsciously, perhaps) to get a little drama and excitement and attention in their lives? And would I do it, too, if I had their lives? I suppose perhaps I would. I don't seem to remember as much of it in Englewood—or was it kept at one end of the house?

Seriously, everything is going very well now. Land is just over his vaccination without much trouble—no high fever, and only a rash. I am starting to wean him and expect to be through the first week in October if all goes well. I hate to have this period over. I can remember your saying to me when I was nursing one baby (little Charles, it must have been) something about the "first separation." We were in the guest room in which he was born and you looked down at him and said, "Next week he will be going off to school, and the week after that he will be getting married."

It is so wonderful to be giving a child everything—life itself— and see his contentment. He "talks" now at the end of each feed, as if to say, "There now, I really can't take any more!" The times with him are such pure, simple, and complete happiness. You know you can do no more for him. And it is still a miracle to watch his face and try to pick out the past and the future, inextricably blended there. A smile from whom? Whose eyes turned up that way? That perplexed brow? What will he be like? What will he say when he can talk?

DIARY   *Sunday, October 10th*

We leave Long Barn for Reading and Germany.[1] Get up early, good-bys to *two* children, running back and forth between the rooms. Jon in his bed. "You must take care of Land, Jon, while

[1] C. A. L. was to attend the Lilienthal Aeronautical Society Congress in Munich and planned to continue his investigations of the growth of the German Air Force for U. S. Army Intelligence.

I'm away," and Land looking up from the converted bathtub crib, wide-eyed, smiling. The long drive to Reading, chestnut trees, fog, quite cool.

Fly toward the thick fog, then turn and go around London, to the north. Lovely piled-up clouds, a sea of them. Lympne, clear and sunny, and out across the Channel. Then under a dark sky into rain, then wisps of cloud, some fog. Over the hills it gets thicker. "Can we get to Brussels?" C. turning back to me, "That *may* be where we spend the night."

Then on, turning, wheeling, around the patches of weather. C. opening the cockpit cover and putting on his goggles. Trying first this valley and then that. It is quite cold. I have no idea where we are. I try to figure out. He will probably try for Cologne. I realize it is just the kind of weather he likes—"moseying" around to find a way through. "Going to try for Cologne. If we can't get there, go back to Brussels," he shouts back.

We get through the hills, a low ceiling, sky and land a glowering gray, but not as bad. I see the two spires of Cologne on the horizon, dark points against a slate-gray sky. "Going to try for Frankfurt. We could motor from there (to Munich) if we get bad weather tomorrow." Follow the Rhine, weather is worse, but have the Rhine to follow.

Bonn, Koblenz, and Mainz—I count the towns and the railroad bridges. Pass castles on hills and finally through the cut follow the Main, a tributary of the Rhine, off to the left. It is getting dark. Land in the rain. An officer comes up, signals, and talks a flow of German: *"Platz Militär—verboten!"* We take off again, directed to the Frankfurt commercial field.

The lights spring on as we approach, red lights outlining the field, great runways and hangars.

Land. A long period of stamping our papers and then in to hotel.

Monday, October 11th

Leave Frankfurt for Munich. Fly over beautiful rolling country, cultivated fields, farms in narrow strips, little clusters of tile-roofed houses, grouped higgledy-piggledy around the spire of a church. (Onion-shaped steeple.) The towns have strips of newly constructed houses on their outskirts and new airfields. Land at Munich, shake hands, etc. The inevitable clicking heels and hand-kissing. We get in the car and drive out of Munich. We are going to a "schloss"—Mrs. Truman Smith, Mrs. Vanaman,[1] and I. We drive south on the *Autobahn* from Munich to the mountains. The country becomes more rolling, very green fields, pine forests. Everything is beautifully cared for, the fields, the roads, the gardens, the forests. It looks like a great park. Only the great mountains, a rough wall in the background, are not tamed.

Then down one valley and at the end of it against the mountains, rather grim upon a hill, something that looks enormous with great walls and a tower—the schloss.

We wind through the little village. Painted Bavarian cottages with overhanging eaves, window boxes and gay shutters, clothes hung out on a line under the eaves. We stop in front of a lodge gate and look up, craning our necks, at a scenic railway, a steep green precipice and the walls of the castle rising sheer above us. The little gatehouse has old prints in it, a cushioned seat, and an old and polite notice (in German) saying if the elevator is not there please be patient until it comes. It comes, rattling perpendicularly down the hill. We get in and are shut in by an old gray-mustached watchman. Like an elevator with windows on the sides. A musty smell, rather sweet, of old leather, varnish, and left-over beer. We sit down stiffly on the seats and the thing starts with a jump and then creaks, shaking, up the hill, a grinding noise going on with the shaking. We rise, trembling, between green banks and then enter a tunnel and stop with a jerk. The doors open. There is an old lady in black, with a pompadour of gray hair and a parchment-white saintlike face.[2] She smiles and

[1] Wife of Major, later Colonel, Arthur Vanaman, Military Attaché for Air with the U. S. Embassy in Berlin.

[2] Baroness Cramer-Klett. See note, p. 181.

takes us by the hand. Her hands are lovely, soft and gentle, silken.

Someone stands behind her, her daughter, thin and pale, with a straight medieval headdress and large dark eyes, slanting up. She looks like an early Italian Madonna. She is not beautiful, but one cannot keep one's eyes off her. There is another daughter, fat, nice-looking, not mysterious. There are other people, too, around, and we shake hands.

The old lady takes me by the hand. "Come with me," she says, and then beckons to Truman Smith (the tallest person there): *"You,* Colonel Lindbergh . . . Oh, *this* is Colonel Lindbergh." She bends apologetically and smiles confusedly at her mistake, like a girl. "Oh, *you* come with me." Up the marble stairs to an octagonal room, huge puffs on the bed, lacy and white, paintings on the ceiling. "Lunch in ten minutes." We look out of the window onto a turret—a sheer drop—down the walls to trees and, below, the valley with little alpine houses, fields, cows. Only the mountains are up around us, our equals, shoulder to shoulder.

We look down the marble steps into a court, completely enclosed, like a block of houses, and above its red-tiled roofs you can see only the top of a mountain (the gray-bearded kind) impertinently near, snow-sprinkled and grim-looking. The shutters are painted red and ivy leaves turned red grow on the walls and bronze nasturtiums up an iron well cupola.

We meet more people, or remeet them, in a small room—surprisingly small for such a big castle—the kind of room people live in constantly. It reminds me of those little rooms in the north, in which people crowd around a table, with a stove, their pictures and papers, and shut out the outside world. There is a large table with a lamp on it, a large green-tiled stove, several big pieces of furniture, a desk, a cupboard (stuffed with papers), many too many pictures on the walls, and a small shrine, or picture in metalwork, the center of one wall.

A man sits hunched by the window. He does not get up as we come in but sits reading in the corner. When the old lady calls to him he comes over abruptly and shakes hands, a little grumpily, I think. He is young and nice-looking but evidently unsociable (German, I think, women don't count!). "My son-in-law," she says.

We sit down for lunch in another one of those small rooms. Two large tile stoves, chamois heads over the walls, old beer mugs on the shelves, and an *incredible* chandelier over the table, a painted figure of a hausfrau with wings of antler horns, holding lights. Out of the low windows one looks down dizzying heights onto the sides of mountains. One sees no sky—a very odd feeling.

The table is spread with an enormous white cloth and neatly sprinkled with red ivy leaves and nasturtiums. Conversation is slow. The Smiths go ahead bravely, holding things up. Mrs. Smith conversationally to the person next to her; he, in a big, generous, all-embracing way, as though to draw in the whole table heartily. I feel shy and smiley. I look around the table and try to place the people. The Baroness, opposite me, is next to Charles. She is talking about *"Kraft durch Freude"*.[1] "Very much *Kraft,*" she says, "and not much *Freude,*" with a sigh. Apparently great hordes of people (workmen) from the north are sent down on trips to southern Germany for their holiday and in an attempt for them to know Germany better and be more united.

It is a very good idea, says the Baroness, but it will not work, for no real Bavarian ever likes a real Prussian.

The son-in-law, next to me, is dark-eyed, big, hunched over. I turn to him. He lifts his hands and smiles shyly—he speaks no English. The two girls—one fat and ruddy, the other incredibly pale with a pointed face. She speaks excellent sophisticated English—"Anna has been in England." Which one is married to the son-in-law? Not the fat one and not the thin one, either: she is too sad, and detached. She is not married.

[1] "Strength Through Joy," an institution created by the Nazis to provide the working population with vacations, travel, sports, and training courses.

After lunch we went across the court again into a very hot room—the library of the Baron. The walls were lined with bookshelves and above them hung with pictures, portraits of prelates, etchings of cathedrals. The tops of the bookcases covered with pictures and small statues. It was the room of an old person who had collected things all his life, but the room of a learned person also. The Baron came forward, emaciated and bent—a white-haired man. Very pale, with hawklike features. He shook (or took to his lips in a courtly way) our hands. He spoke with great effort, breathily, a strange bloodless whisper. He had asthma, the Baroness explained. He seemed a courtly and rather feeble old man, past any life or emotion, until he took us down to two small rooms, also lined with books, and showed us, on top of a big chest, a bust of some prelate (of Bamberg), and began telling his history. An ancestor of his wife, a Prince of the Church, he "saved Bavaria for Catholicism"! His eyes flashed.

Then he told of his own life, how he had written articles ("because they know I am versed in such matters") for the cause of Rome when it was not popular at all. How he did not pander to people (he made a courtly dance step, his foot pointing out, his arm bent forward, flatteringly, his whole body the curve of a dancing master) but told what he knew was the truth. His voice became harsh, rose from that pale whisper into a passionate utterance. He straightened like a rod and his arm shot forward, like a fencer's. His body was all angles. Steel—he was pure steel. "A black dog" he called himself—member of the Church party.[1]

[1] In Truman Smith's report, "Air Intelligence Activities," he says: "An interesting sidelight on political conditions in Germany at this time is shown by the Air Ministry's selection of Baron Cramer-Klett to be Lindbergh's host. Although his castle was indescribably picturesque, its location was inconvenient for guests attending the Lilienthal Congress (60 miles away). Baron Cramer-Klett had been and was still a violent anti-Nazi, and was therefore in some personal danger. Yet he had many friends in German government circles and particularly in Göring's entourage. These Luftwaffe friends of the Baron decided that if Cramer-Klett could be induced to act as host to a distinguished foreign guest of Gör-

Then we went through the castle—through innumerable halls, with statues of the former owners (the Preysing family) and old portraits, up and down stairs, through vast kitchens (a large glass tank held a big fish swimming around, to keep him fresh for dinner!) and up onto a tower which faced the mountains. It was like being up in a plane, its isolation was so complete, its height so tremendous. And yet in the middle of walls and turrets one felt not part of the modern world but of an old one read about in fairy tales as a child ("Rapunzel, Rapunzel, let down your hair"). You could almost stand on the walls, flap your arms, and glide off into the sky, as in flying dreams.

The men go off for dinner and we stay and have dinner with the Baroness, the two daughters, the son-in-law, and his "Exzellenz," the General. I do not remember meeting him before. He is small, old, but still erect and ramroddy. He speaks English with effort and some humor. He is not a subtle person, but staunch and kind with a nice humor and much experience packed away in a dry and unromantic fashion in his mind. *"Politique* is not for us military men," he says with a shrug of his shoulders and a little smile.

Some men from the village have come up to play Bavarian folk music at night. They sit in a corner of one of the small, low-ceilinged halls. They have short leather pants on, gaily embroidered, and leather jackets. But evidently they are not "dressed up." They are *not* entertainers. They are peasants in their normal clothes, playing the music they normally play for village dances. Only here, in the castle, they are quite solemn and a little shy. They are very solid, sturdy, ruddy young men. They sit around a table and play zithers, square, rather metallic dances, like the dances of mechanical dolls, or the music boxes one had as a child.

The daughter of the house (the fat one) gets up and does a

ing's, the enmity of the Nazis could be neutralized. This proved to be the case, and after Lindbergh's visit, the Baron was left undisturbed for several years."

dance with one of the men. She has on the national costume (which is *much* more becoming to her than her regular clothes): blouse, tight bodice, big skirt and apron. It is a very intricate dance—the hands interwound in hundreds of different positions while the two dance around each other. The girl goes around twice as fast—with tiny little steps—as the man, who takes the inside of the circle, at half-beat, as though steadying and holding up the girl. Big steins of beer are brought in to the players from time to time.

It amazes me that the peasants should have no self-consciousness at all at dancing with the young Baroness, and yet perfect dignity. The dance becomes more and more complicated and we clap delighted. Outside the small lighted hall, in the dark court, the servants stand at the windows and watch.

Tuesday, October 12th

The men go off to the conference in Munich. We (Mrs. Smith, Mrs. Vanaman, and I) go to Munich, to take a general look at the city. It is cold and damp and rather gray. Then to the "Museum of Degenerate Art" and the New Museum and to lunch with Mr. Merkel.[1] He talks so slowly that I almost lose the train of thought, and yet he is very interesting on the report of the Zeppelin disaster, on the new helicopter he is interested in. He is nice to talk to, because he talks to you as if he believed you were intelligent.

Back to Hohenaschau. The peaceful valley, the river, the little alpine cottages, the great castle on a hill above them all. It is like going back to the Middle Ages.

By comparing notes, Mrs. Smith, Mrs. Vanaman, and I learn that the son-in-law is not married to the thin daughter or the fat daughter but to the elder daughter, who died. Also that the fat daughter studies singing in Berlin, the thin daughter, dancing. That the son-in-law is a gynecologist (who discovered that?).

The Baroness is always there to greet us at the elevator. She

---

[1] Otto Merkel, an officer with Lufthansa Airlines.

always looks pale and sad and patient, as though the cares of the household rested heavily on her.

We (the Smiths, C. and I) go back to Munich for dinner with General von Reichenau[1] and his wife and son and daughter (or governess?).

He is one of those completely rounded, charming, cultured men of wide experience, great strength, and concentrative ability, combined with fineness of perception and breadth of vision, delightful for dinner-table conversation and also impressive talking to Major Smith about technical points on war and army tactics. I do not think I have met more than two or three of his type in my life. Not that he gave you the impression of being a "great" man, or a genius, or of great strength. It was not the feeling one has meeting a Balbo or hearing a Carrel talk or seeing a Chiang Kai-shek. It was something one felt gradually, increasingly through the evening: Here is a civilized man, as balanced and as well educated a man as one is likely to find; training on top of native ability.

We talked about China, which he had just left as military adviser. The feeling that the Chinese stood on their own culture, proud of it, their roots in it, and that on the basis of that one could meet them, whereas the Japanese were always trying to stand on a little borrowed piece of *your* ground.

We also talked about mountains, the feeling of superiority, of peace, but also of arrogance one got from standing on them and looking down, how I felt coming over the mountains in a plane, fighting up through them and then suddenly over the pass, the feeling of a "promised land" spread out below you—all yours. Then he told me never forget that Satan tempted Christ from a mountaintop.

C. talked to him about the war in China. (It has come too soon, he said—a little later and China would have been more prepared.) After supper the men talk war tactics and the

[1] Walther von Reichenau, then commanding general of the troops in the Munich area, later Field Marshal.

women's conversation fritters off idly on the side. We are not content simply to listen to the men (I would be) and are too polite to strike through to what interests us and force the conversation—pin it on that. Or else perhaps we cannot find the lowest common denominator for a three-cornered conversation. I do not remember what we talked about. Frau von Reichenau was charming, though, of the race of charming women (the V. Woolf–Mrs. Dalloway kind of woman). I could not keep my eyes off her, tall and soft and rippling (in lavender blue, fair hair, blue eyes), feminine and yet contrary, yielding but skittish. She had a lovely voice and laugh and something slightly impish in her smile. One felt she had been spoiled, loved, and laughed at lightly always, and liked it.

Finally, at the end of the evening, I found she knew and liked Rilke's poetry. "It is *not* degenerate—who said it was degenerate?" But it was too late and yet I felt I could have talked to her.

Wednesday, October 13th

After the men go to town, Mrs. Vanaman, Mrs. Smith, and I go for a walk with his "Exzellenz," the General. He puts on a greenish loden cape and thick reddish leather walking shoes and a cane, and we start out. It is a delicious morning, clear and crisp, cold and sunny. The fields in the valley are green and glistening and the pine trees sharp and fragrant. It is very quiet, only the sound of rushing water, the river (also neatly banked up with stone banks).

In the afternoon we drive to Berchtesgaden, through a pass in the mountains. It is so strange to be doing it by car. I am always feeling it by plane, thinking instinctively, There, that light patch, that light V of sky in between the mountains, that is where we will go—that will open up for us.

Coming home, Mrs. Smith and C. discuss courage—how much is physical and how much mental, how much inherited and how much trained. I feel in her tremendous courage, beyond her strength. It is the strongest thing I feel and what I admire the most in her.

At night after supper the men come again to play Bavarian music and two girls in peasant costume come to sing and dance. When they sit quietly among the players smiling shyly and fingering their dresses they are quite plain buxom peasant girls, but when they take off their silver-bead choker necklaces and stand up to sing, with clear cool voices, they are beautiful. They glow with youth and beauty and sadness and joy. They sing the songs of the girls who take the cows up into the mountains in the summer. When they sing I realize how old I am! Then they dance those flirting dances, the girls twirling in their skirts, the men doing those wonderful smack-kick-hop steps that ring through the room (and yodeling shouts!).

The Baroness smiles rather sadly at them, relaxed for a moment. The son-in-law stands in the door, in the background, watching inconspicuously, ready to slip away if anyone notices him. We all sit around the walls. The young Baroness is in the ascendancy tonight. She has blossomed out in a beautiful long black velvet *robe de style*—bare shoulders and a little pearl heart strung on a small gold chain falling to the middle of her bodice. She looks suddenly incredibly beautiful, her skin very white and her long dark eyes, slanting up in a heart-shaped face, very dark. She moves with a languid grace and everyone watches her. It is a fairy tale and she is the ugly duckling by day, who is the most beautiful princess of all by night. She sits on a table against the wall and officers surround her. But she is not gay. No one is gay in this house. The General comes the nearest to it, with his dry and crusty remarks. ("Formerly they sent young and beautiful girls up the mountains, but now they send only old women because it is not safe!")

At the end of the evening (some of the guests have gone), one of the peasant dancers comes up to me smiling, *"Bitte?"* Very politely. I feel incredibly shy and young. "But I cannot dance like that." I turn to C. and the dancer does too. *"Ein Valse?"* and off we go—the speediest twirl I have ever had. I am quite breathless and giddy and then I hear a yodeling shout at my ear and it is another dancer "cutting in"! I am twirled from one to another. They dance very well but seem made of iron—you cannot do anything but follow. I only hoped I would not fall in a dizzy heap on the floor. Finally, flushed and panting, I beg for a rest. At last we all shake hands and go to bed.

Thursday, October 14th

The Smiths leave for Berlin. They are both remarkable with people, observant, sympathetic, able to make people at ease. She, more unconsciously, spontaneously; he, more consciously. I feel, too, that he is not so much interested in people's conversation as he is in people themselves, skipping the steps of conversation and jumping ahead with sheer perception. She follows the paths of observation and conversation, but both come to the same end.

The General and I go for another walk, this time up a mountain, following the course of the stream to a waterfall, zigzagging up the hill through brilliant trees all yellow and red and pine trees, looking back every once in a while at a marvelous view of the castle sitting on its hill, like a Grimms' fairy tale or the background of a Dürer painting.

It is very nice. I should like to do it every day as he does (and he is eighty-one!) and should find a nice companionship with him, I think, although a completely wordless one, not based at all on the exchange of thoughts but on some kind of understanding running underground, felt, but not expressed. It is always surprising to me to find such understanding existing because I am apt to judge relationships by what is expressed—which is absurd, of course. Then I remember Uncle Jay and Sir Francis [Younghusband].

In the afternoon C. takes the Baroness, the young Baroness, and the General (in his loden cape and shoes) to the field at Prien for a flight over the castle. The Baroness is done up in a large fur coat, a black turban, and a little veil. I am afraid she will be blown to bits. She is quite calm and unruffled, with her otherworldly look (as if she lived in the past and not in the present or future at all). At the field we meet a nice Frau Braun[1], a young-looking woman, ruddy-faced, with golden hair and a smile that wrinkles her whole face, and a handshake that crushes your fingers.

S.S. President Harding, *November 28th*

Over a month since we got back from Germany and we are on our way to New York, after a rather crowded month. Some seeing of people. But on the whole it has been hard work at my desk, every morning, trying to get off the water at Bathurst before we sail.[2] I have not felt very happy about it—the writing—as it has gone slowly and clumsily, this part that I wanted to have "flow." I wanted it very simple and swift but charged with intensity, so that every tiny thing stood out in relief like a landscape under a flash of lightning. It is so well planned and so badly written. Working at my desk, I felt this discouragement at the lack of ease, of perfection. But then bathing Land and singing to him, or running through the fields holding Jon's hand, I would feel, This is all that matters. Everything smoothed out in my mind—without reason, happily.

The days went very quickly. The alarm clock and Jon fumbling at the door, tumbling in with his heap of tangled clothes in his arms, coming over, tousled, sleepy, and jumping into bed for a moment. "What did you dream about—a mugwump?"—"No, a nice animal"—"A fox?"—"No, because a fox is not nice to a hen" (!)

Then dressing in the bathroom, Jon racing me exercising. I find the part in his hair. Down for breakfast, and off to school, in the frosty air, Jon jumping up and down in his blue jacket in

[1] Wife of Major Braun, an early German flier and World War I pilot, at this time second in command of the Civil Air Corps in Bavaria.

[2] The reference is to *Listen! the Wind,* the book A. M. L. was writing about the 1933 flight over the South Atlantic.

the back seat. "Do you think we'll catch the train!" We went over a railroad bridge and sometimes met a train there—great excitement when we did, Jon clasping his hand to his mouth, all crunched up with excitement: "Did *you* think we'd meet that train?!"

Back to the house, a peek at Land, lying kicking on the bed, his big dark eyes looking over his head for anyone coming in, and then when you spoke to him the quick delighted smile and crows.

Work until lunchtime. After lunch, feed Land, wrapping him up tightly in a shawl and tucking the diaper under his scream-ing (with impatience!) mouth. Sitting on my knee afterward. He will stop everything when you sing, and listen and smile, and when you pause he gurgles back in answer.

Jon in his overalls goes out to gather leaves and sticks and to watch (and tend like a vestal virgin) the bonfire. I back to work. At about 3:30 or 3:45, Thor gets up and stretches and noses me impatiently; Skean stretches and scratches the floor and sneezes. I get up, to go for a walk. C. and Jon and I, Jon in his ragged overalls and boots, set across the field, the dogs bouncing and leaping wildly, Jon and I running sometimes hand in hand, sometimes I chasing him. Across the two right-of-way fields, past the oaks, over the bridge, through the second pasture and over the stile, down the road to the chestnut wood.

There was that wonderful day we found chestnuts under the leaves and filled our pockets to overflowing. Jon was wild with joy, and greedy with the collecting instinct: "Just one more!" The day I lost him (he had gone ahead and was waiting for me). I called and called and got hot and cold through fear and finally heard him answer. (After that he never let me get far away—not that *he* was afraid but that he somehow sensed my fear and unhappiness and did not, for my sake, want it to happen again.)

Then running home, through the thick evening mist, pulling Jon along through the mud, striding along the road, the cold air burning in your throat and chest because we were out of breath. The trees, bleak and dark against the sky, Thor ahead, Skean behind, over the stile through the field—what a long pull it was, that last field. The lights of Long Barn behind the trees, the stile, the leaf-moldy road under the trees, the flagstone walk (shiny and wet). The light from the kitchen, bright around the brick walk to the back; stamping in, warm and tingling.

And we have walked out in the moonlight. One lovely night, clear, we walked miles along the hill. A soft milky light and the fields frosted and crisp. The road dark and shadowed or bright and shiny, Thor running ahead all mixed up with his shadow. Trees lacy against the sky. We sit on a gate and look down over hay-cocks and through a tangled oak tree at the moon. A thin film of milky clouds rolls up little by little over the sky. A plane goes by, a light moving slowly in the dark, a bore of sound in the silence. And we walk home, tingling and warm, with chilled cheeks.

The last days have been very rushed and it is hard to remember them—only bits out of them, and the general excited choky-this-is-the-last-time atmosphere that I always get into before leaving anywhere. Monday and Tuesday were all work at my desk. Wednesday I was still working at my desk. I meant to go to town early but the take-off [in the book] wasn't done. C. said we should leave Thursday evening. Wednesday was my last full day. I just finished in time to catch the 12:48 train—a back-breaking day: lunch at the hairdresser's and rushing to get Christmas things done—what a terrific effort it was.

Thursday I took care of the children. We were to have our Christmas tree because I wanted to have some Christmas with Jon. About a month ago when I told him I must be away for Christmas, Jon said, "Must you go?" "Yes, Jon, I'm afraid so—your father must go and I must go with him." "But why Christmas—because I *like* Christmas."

I told him the story of Christmas as he ate supper in my room, I, sitting by the fire with Land on my knee, staring wide-eyed at

Jon. Jon loved that ("Do this again some night!") and having Land there made it very real ("A beautiful baby like Land"). "And what did they see there in the hay?" *"You* tell *me!"* said Jon, his eyes sparkling. When I told him about the three wise men following a star, he asked, "How fast did the star go?" "Well, it must have gone quite fast because they were riding on camels." "What would have happened if they had been riding in a car—would the star have gone faster?"

After supper C. says the boat has been delayed by fog again and we will not have to leave until the next day.

Friday I go again to see Jon in school. I have been meaning to do it all fall but first went on Thursday to see him "singing." He was out finding "conkers" when we came. He looked up, smiled shyly without moving, and said, "It's break-time." After "break" they ran into their big room. They were only about six, sitting in a circle. Children, I can see, still baffle Jon. He cannot see why they don't behave like adults, thinks them rather silly at times, and doesn't quite know how to deal with them. "John is twisting my hand," "John won't hold my hand" (it wasn't complaining exactly but simply a statement of fact: What shall I do about this silly child?).

On Friday we came to watch the dancing. There were only four little boys. Jon flashed a little smile as we came in, "It's late—it's already started." It was very satisfying to watch them. To see your child among others is peculiarly illuminating, both as to him and as to your feelings about him. That was Jon—that child, taller than the others, slimmer too (what thin legs he had compared to the others). Hair too long, untidy over his forehead. Face not as ruddy as I imagined, compared to the others. It was fair but not ruddy English-fair or Scandinavian-fair. It was more pearly-fair. Face eager, sensitive, absorbed, serious—dark eyes, trying very hard. He was trying so hard that he forgot to be gay, and looked vague with his effort to grasp everything at once.

He seemed, too, not to be a child, not to have the tricks and play of a child—to be quite serious, and adult in what he was doing. But he looked there among the others incredibly dear, not as a child but as a person, as someone familiar and dear to me beyond his few years. The past and the present mingled—Elisabeth or Daddy. And I felt so strongly, Oh, what I could do with him! What I have there! Why should I spend so much time trying to write? I should put everything into him. How much he needs, how much I could give, much better than this school. When I come back, I will.

DIARY   *Englewood [Next Day Hill], December*
Mother, lovely and gay and back in life again; Con, with a world on her shoulders—three worlds (the theater, studying at Columbia, and marriage, not to speak of the Welsh campaign)—and managing it.

The house, appallingly beautiful and luxurious. Sinking back into it, carpets, heat, bath salts, flowers, food, servants, and ease of living. Overwhelming and a little suffocating. But Mother is alive and precious in it.

The confused feeling of not belonging here and trying to find myself. The place is full of ghosts and new people I don't know.

New York and the shock of it: the speed, the luxury shops, the mad keeping-up with things, even in the so-called spiritual things like art and music. It is all smart, fashionable, and biting at your heels, instead of being a still temple to retire to. Perhaps it should not be a "still temple"—that is a dead conception—but it should be a door *out,* not this hothouse atmosphere of possession, as though the arts were jewels to decorate a woman's throat.

The pages and pages of luxury gifts in the magazines and papers: for women, for children; hens that lay eggs and cackle, dolls that you pour water into and they wet their diapers, furs and jewels and gadgets—especially gadgets—of no use whatsoever, and clothes.

And at the theater, the women in ostrich capes and ermine, with their hair curled up perfectly and bits of silver flowers plastered on top, the latest wrinkle. It did not seem to me smart and gay and young as it used to but only crude and ostentatious and childish.

Then the news of two couples breaking up, with all the attendant divorce, remarriage, gossip, boredom, and bitterness connected with it. Their old lives cut from under them. And a whole era of early married friendships and good times ended for us, a whole circle shattered for good.

The unrest and feverishness of Englewood again. Who is taking what car? There is that perpetual, slightly Chekhov atmosphere to the transportation business—those plays in which the old servant comes in periodically and says, "Sire, the horses are not ready," "The horses have gone to Vladivostok," or "There are no horses." What nights are free? Christmas presents. The temptation of being swept along, in just talking, or reading the magazines and newspapers, cutting out shopping advertisements, clothes, plans. And yet, the luxury of having Con and Mother to talk to whenever one wants.

1938

This last month has been such a rushed one, and looking back on it, it is hard to see what has been accomplished. I don't like to think "nothing." It has been a rush of seeing people, trying to see them all, to squeeze in as much as possible. The list is appalling: the Blisses, the Hands, Mary Hand, the Davisons, the Vaillants, the Stevenses, Mrs. Lindbergh in Detroit, Grandma and Aunt Annie in Cleveland. The Carrels, the Flexners, Connie Chilton, Mrs. Curtiss, Mrs. Loomis. The Munroes, Thelma, to count only the ones we have seen on my or our responsibility, to say nothing of the Englewood ones: the aunts at Christmas, the Howes, Hulsts, etc., and one big Englewood party.

And there are lots more. I feel at the end of it as if I had only a list checked off! Not quite that—there is a little more residue and I think the value will come out when I go back to England and can chew the cud of all those contacts. There was something real from many of them, and that is a link, a steppingstone in a sea that would become too wide if you never bridged it at all, or too seldom. That is the way I must look at these contacts—only as a kind of touching hands, to make the next time easier, so I shan't lose them entirely.

And yet even that touching of hands can become deadened too, if you do too much of it. It is only that I have had so little, I think, lately, that I can stand so much now. I have those two "underground" having-a-baby-living-in-an-English-garden years to draw from. A reservoir of peace, family contentment, and family wisdom.

Leadbetter's Island has been sold—another dream gone. I feel as if I couldn't bear to sail by that lovely house again. The hill with the sheep and the afternoon sun on it, and the staunch old house. So lovely and square and New England—such peace.

On the night of the 15th, Saturday, I called up Laura [Stevens].[1] (She had left a message to call.) She said, "Anne, I just wanted to let you know: we finished your book [*Listen! the Wind*] last night and we think it's *grand!*" She said they couldn't put it down and that it was much more mature than the other book, but just as good.

I gave them the book Sunday night and then hadn't thought of it again—too busy. But I dreamed the night before (when they were reading it) that they came to me through a crowd of people and told me they liked the book. When I woke I thought, Dreams go by opposites—they didn't like it!

It wasn't a dead book, then—they liked it! They were excited by it.

There was a full moon on the snow and I ran out and raced in the cold air, ran around like a dog in my excitement, trying to get rid of that force in my chest—that wound-up spring, that giant stretching, and I thought, Oh God, oh God, then maybe I can write [a book about] Elisabeth!

And I thought I would burst waiting for C. to come home so I could tell him.

Monday, January 17th

Most of morning spent trying to telephone and make plans. So many mornings go like that here: Mrs. Norton, Lucia, Anna Fay.[2] The line is busy; call Brentano's. Cars—how to get in. Have to leave by 11:45 for a 12:30 lunch.

Must go out. It is snowing, the full milky kind that makes a big difference on the ground. I cannot walk fast, too stiff from yesterday. (How hard it must be for old people to keep warm when

[1] Laura Brandt, friend and roommate of A. M. L. at college, and her husband, George Stevens, editor.

[2] Mrs. Charles Norton, Lucia Norton Valentine, Anna Fay Prosser Caulkins, old friends of the Morrow family.

they can't walk fast.) Follow yesterday's half-blurred footsteps in the snow and C.'s sharp broken ones of today over the brook and up the slope. A lovely piece of grass with the snow sticking just to the burrs or seed pods, the leaves shining and clear. The precision of snow to paint *just* the seed pods and leave the grass spears bare as a bone.

It is a wonderful thing to see the world transformed by snow, down to the smallest twig and piece of grass. It makes one understand better all the big "conversions" of nature, in oneself, like falling in love, religious conversion, sleep and dying.

Mother just back from a large meeting at Mrs. Lamont's about *Pacifism*. Mother had a cold but went through it nobly. She said a little wearily that she would like so much to have discussed *Assignment in Utopia* with some woman, quietly in a corner, but Mrs. Lamont shooed them into the big room for general discussion. Mrs. Lamont distrusts all informal, feminine discussion, thinking it gossip. Is that because she can't do it very well? And do I dislike formal discussion because I can't do it at all? Maybe.

Get dressed, go in to Bob and Virginia Thayer[1] for dinner; we really enjoyed it. Trubee and Dot Davison[2] and one other couple whose name I never got because I was looking at their faces. I liked the woman very much. Virginia, very beautiful in black velvet and white shoulders. Dot was beautiful but it was difficult for me to talk to her. I felt so strongly that it was a great effort for her, that she was still fighting for that boy who died. That she had gone on with him, all the way, and with great effort met us in this world, speaking from another one. Of course I did not want to show what I felt so I went on lamely talking about Greenvale School and modern education, though it didn't seem important to either of us.

Talking to Bob is like skating with someone, just as you get a good clear stretch to strike out in, he takes a waltz step. Then I

[1] Robert Thayer, a lawyer, had helped the Lindberghs at the time of the kidnapping in Hopewell; see *Hour of Gold, Hour of Lead*.

[2] Trubee Davison, Assistant Secretary of War for Aviation (1926–32), later president of the American Museum of Natural History.

think, Oh dear, I've been too intense again, when I was just interested in what he was saying. Dot and Trubee are not observers; they are clear colors. I love people like that, in fact, worship them. But they are on the other side of the fence from me.

January 20th

I have got too much into this day: lunch with Lucia (she is only down for two crowded days); opera with Thelma, and Thelma's friend. Then Con wants to do something tonight to forget her exam, to celebrate.

In to the Nortons'. Mrs. Norton comfortable and chatty and quieting and delightful. Lucia, late, competent, and a little rushed (what she is doing and managing: home, college, entertaining, and a profession) but so beautiful. Mother comes up and they discuss feverishly college furnishing. I feel very incompetent, ungrown-up, and left behind.

To *Siegfried,* an hour late. Thelma is rapt; her friend, with the score and little book on the *Ring,* couldn't understand our nonchalance. "Yes—*we* got here on time." It took an act or two to sink down into that romantic German world. Then I was smoothed out by it, by the roll of the Rhine and the gigantic heroes and heroines. (Also fascinated by all the claptrap—dragon, smoke, fire, etc.!) Then, in the end, Flagstad as Brünnhilde welcoming life; her gestures, her voice, made opera exciting, real, living. We are all swept by it.

Back to tea with Con. We have sherry and sit around and talk. C. comes for supper and we eat oysters, cheese, and biscuits and have the champagne. It is very pleasant, if not a spree.

Friday

My watch stops (for ten minutes) and I leave the house at twenty of three, when I promised C. I'd be at Brackman's[1] studio

[1] Robert Brackman, American painter, had agreed to do portraits of A. M. L. and C. A. L.

at quarter of. ("That doesn't mean five minutes of.") I got there, sick with rage at myself, just at five minutes of!

A short, stocky man met me at the door, smiling and a little shy, a little gauche—Brackman. But he has a strong face (stubborn, probably)—independence, pride, and a nice kind of honesty and integrity. I should guess that his brush knows more than he does. That is, his perceptiveness is unconscious and only in his painting, because his painting is good. The pastels have great depth, a sculptural quality, and real characterization.

He is evidently quite sure he can do a good portrait of me. No doubt at all about it.

It is beginning to snow, great wet flakes. We see some nice Nebraska farm pictures (Dale Nichols) at the Macbeth Gallery, cold and clear, and then disperse.

I try on dresses at Harper Fraser, a black chiffon with a pink chiffon cape, which I hope will be *the* all-purpose evening dress. Grand occasion: without cape, plus "jools." (The paste necklace of Elisabeth! Must get some earrings and bracelet to match.) Less grand occasion: plus pink cape. Informal occasion: plus lace jacket and old paste pin. Good idea—if *only* it works now!

It is now all black and white with snow. The streets are beginning to be slushy. I have to drive car out [to Englewood] tonight of all nights. It *would* be a blizzard! The snow has frozen over my windshield and back window. I get the wipers going, but can't keep lower portions clear. Can't see much, all lights fuzzy, the wiper going back and forth and the snow coming at me in circular whorls. Up Riverside Drive, a little hard to start after red lights but not bad otherwise until we get to the bridge entrance. There were five cars stopped ahead of me. Then I was panicky (not at the danger—there was none—but only afraid I couldn't get up and would hold traffic up and it would be humiliating). Some man would have to drive me up.

But a nice policeman pushed me and got some sand under my wheels and I got started and kept going without trouble—really less trouble than some of the other cars. Everyone was in the same fix, and the policeman laughed and said I'd make it.

Then everything was all right until I got to our hill. I stopped halfway up, put on the brake and was about to start down again, looking back to watch the road, when I saw C. miraculously pushing at the wheel. Just like a dream, when I get into trouble and call for him. There he was! Con had called up to say I was coming and C. had been sure I'd never make the hill so he came down to meet me. We crawled up the hill inch by inch and then we went out for a walk afterward in boots and ski suit in the still falling snow. It was lovely and I felt very happy—ecstatic—one of those times when I realize how terribly I love C.

Saturday, January 22nd

In Englewood all day. I feel heavy and stupid and in a bad temper with myself. I will be a month more (because of the portrait) without my main business—the children—so I had better get busy on my secondary business, the book. It is difficult (1) because I have no routine here, so it is easy to be thrown off. (2) I am tempted outward by the fun of seeing people—the luxury of my family. (3) The shopping excitement (how easy and gratifying it is here, compared to London!). (4) I dread starting because I dread the discouragement that always goes with it.

Sunday, January 23rd

Grandma has had a slight stroke. It has left her weaker, apparently, but not otherwise incapacitated or changed. Mother says she knows it is the beginning of the end, but she hates seeing Grandma weakened and changed. It is all very well to say you must expect things like that at her age. It does not help much. One expects death and is apt to think of it vaguely and not unpleasantly, as Professor Woodbridge[1] said the other day, in

[1] F. J. E. Woodbridge, professor of philosophy and Dean of Columbia University.

terms of nature taking you back in her arms. But it is not like that in most cases. It is being struck down, blow after blow, until you can't stand any more. It is that cruel law: to him that hath shall be given and from him that hath not shall be taken away.

Mother is so sad. And everything seems sad for her—at least so much—inevitable sadness, now. I wish every day Jon were here, for Mother, and that Grandma had seen him, and yet I know I am doing the best possible thing for him in leaving him in England. I am afraid to uproot him and bring him over here, with the excitement and nervous tension of Englewood, the many people who would want to see him: aunts, friends, etc., just for a month or two. I think it might undo all the good of the last two years. How much are you justified in jeopardizing the health of your child for the happiness of other people you love? Too many people come to this house and the life is too crowded for a little boy. The circle is too big. He should only have what he is able to grasp and what nature intended a small boy to have—his own small family and a life limited by that. But oh, how much I wish I could give that happiness to Mother—a *positive* thing. She has so many negatives now, in spite of all her outside interests.

We go skiing. I watch Mother walking about the house, the enclosed porch, picking up things, and wonder if someday I shall be facing what she is facing. Con reads the book. She is very helpful. She sees what I am trying to do. What a divine luxury understanding is. She makes me feel I can do it better. Talk with Margot on the telephone.

Monday

President and Mrs. Neilson for supper. I am still very shy with him. She is very tired, and so is he. But she has never learned to accept her life. I wonder if that is an asset or a fault?

The wind howls all night and it is very warm. I wake up and think dreamily, "The woman with the long train is out there. The woman with the long dress is still going by," and it does sound like that.

Tuesday

Breakfast with Mrs. Neilson. She is so lovely. The first sitting with Brackman for pastel head. Lunch with Zaidee Bliss, Mother, Mr. Goodyear.[1] Pictures in the afternoon with Con. Charles Demuth[2]—still life, watercolors, fruit. Here is a modern that really satisfies me, moves me, clears me, and excites me—that I could live with.

Unfortunately, Con and I find out that he is dead and his pictures are very expensive.

Tea at Con's. Drive Aubrey and Con out to Englewood for a talk—all of Englewood in the big room. C. home late. What a day!

Thursday, January 27th

Third sitting for pastel head—done. The sittings have been quite interesting. Brackman is so honest and direct that it is nice to talk with him. He has a very American sense of humor and very decided opinions. He has no "manner" at all, no pose, which is a relief. She is sensitive, perceptive, and aware in a feminine way. He says rather awkwardly, "What . . . uh . . . do you think of aviation in Europe?" But I try to get him to talk about painting, which is more interesting and on which he is very perceptive and articulate.

He says, In the old days painters made painters. Today critics make them—or try to. Also that in an argument with some Communist painters he said, You want to give to the masses, to paint for the masses. You can't do that. The masses won't understand what you paint (the abstractions) without the literature that goes with your painting. The painting of the Florentines would survive and move people even if all the books that were written about them should disappear. Much of modern art is dependent on the literature.

[1] Mr. and Mrs. Cornelius Bliss, Conger Goodyear, early supporters of the Museum of Modern Art in New York.

[2] American painter and illustrator, known especially for his watercolors.

The first day C. said he thought the bottom of the face looked pushed over too much. Brackman said, Yes, you have to exaggerate first—to put down the thrust, the movement in a head (not *of, in*). Then afterward you correct it for accuracy. The moderns, he said, never correct it—just leave it like that.

He says, now it is done, that the original "image" is still there, just as he first conceived of it.

Brackman is anxious to do a pastel of C. I am so pleased. C. thinks he will, and maybe an oil too if Brackman can manage them both at the same time. It will be great fun to watch him work at that.

I like his wife very much. She says I am too "chubby" in the pastel. He always listens with much concern to her criticism, wanting her approval. It is very nice, as he doesn't seem to care about other people's approval. They are nice together—she, a little dark wisp of a person, delicate, lovely. And he, stocky, blurting, honest, almost crude-looking, which belies his touch. She absolutely adores him. And he is humble in front of her.

Shopping for colors (sweaters and scarves) for the oil in the afternoon. I am downtown, my list of other shopping in my hand, and I cannot bear to go on. I *must* get out in the country. I cannot bear to go into another shop, even though it is the perfect opportunity.

I miss the children all the time. It isn't that I think about them so much. In fact, I *don't*. I put them out of my head, like something lovely you can't have. But that very putting them out of my head is such an unsatisfying thing—a suspended feeling.

All the restlessness in me that wants to rest on that—Jon and Land—can never rest. So it just goes on driving cars and looking at magazines and cutting out shopping advertisements and calling up people and making appointments.

The only relief from this feeling is when I shop for them or turn out cupboards and find things for them, or buy books for Jon, or cut out pictures for him. That, I feel, is going into the "main flow" of my life.

I realize what a source of strength and repose they are to me. When I am dissatisfied with how other things are going, with my progress in something else, with my mind, eyes, reading, writing, I turn to them as to a rock. It seems strange because I feel as though they were more necessary to me than I to them—and yet I do feel that Jon needs me terribly right now. I dare not think about it.

The most satisfying part of the days now is when C. comes home at night. That is a "rock," too. Here I seem to be living and satisfying (though I really do not know *why!*).

Friday, January 28th

Out in Englewood all morning, clearing out Jon's toys and getting together sweaters and scarves for C. to look at for my portrait. C. comes back after lunch and we go into town to get another sweater and some scarves from Brooks Brothers. There is something absolutely regal about it. Driving in at four just to go to *one* shop for *one* thing—no hurry and scurry and compromise. An elderly gentleman gets out *all* the Brooks "cornflower" sweaters for me to see and *all* the India scarves. I get one sweater and two scarves and C. says—in a lordly masculine way—"You'd better get several now you're here. These are very nice." (I should say they are—the big ones are 7.50 apiece!) He picks out a number. Finally we go out with the sweater and *five* scarves—perfectly unnecessary, but very nice. C. is quite pleased. Such a lordly way of shopping—so extravagant of time, money, etc., on the surface. Actually probably less extravagant on the whole than my hickity-peckity sort of shopping. But *so* unfeminine!

Mother leaves for Cleveland to see Grandma. She is afraid Grandma may get worse and she may miss the chance of speaking to her. She has a cold and feels rather miserable but she is relieved to go.

Con and Aubrey come out for supper. We discuss the hideousness of old age and Con says, Yes, she thinks sometimes all of life is going to be like a weekend home from college. You think, Oh, it's only Friday—and then suddenly it's Sunday night and it's over! It is wonderful to be able to go through life stopping at points along the way with Con and looking at it together. Such a luxury. But if only we had Elisabeth too.

Saturday, January 29th

Into town for the first sitting on the oil of me. Brackman chooses from our sweater selection (the lavender-blue one I like) and scarf (the one C. picked out. He is very pleased) and my navy skirt. And Brackman chooses the pose. Then he starts out with charcoal (?) or crayon and makes great strokes on the canvas, simple lines and angles (I wish I could have seen the canvas while he was doing it) to get the composition, placing, etc., and enough "air" above my head. She says that sometimes the person looks stifled in a portrait when there isn't enough room around them (she was one of Brackman's students).

Then he starts painting. Just the general outlines and then blocking in, in general, the color. I love watching him mix the paints on his palette, taking quickly from those little worms of color squeezed out in coils on the semicircle of the palette, and mixing to get a taupe, or a putty color (five or six colors going into it).

Then I ask questions about Daumier, Cézanne, Degas. I gather he is most excited by Degas (a marvelous draftsman).

Rush out to Englewood for lunch ("Anne will have to be hostess"): Lady G. and Mr. Jack Carter,[1] Con and Aubrey (Con much more fitted to be hostess), Charles and I. I think it goes really very well. The conversation flowing on C. and Aubrey's good-natured baiting of each other on the British Empire, the state of France, democracy, etc. Mr. Carter asking questions and rather steadying the current and enjoying it from the sidelines. Lady G. being the charming woman of the world, hanging on C.'s *every* word, and taking with feminine coquetry his point-

[1] Of Morgan, Grenfell & Co. in London.

blank contradictions to her own theories: "But how then are we going to unite the world, Colonel Lindbergh?" "I don't believe we can—and even if we could, I don't think it would be advisable," etc.

I said very little and yet I was happy about it and felt that I was playing my part by being the reed (or clump of grass!) in the stream, deflecting it gently this way and then that (usually, I fear, toward my own husband). But perhaps I didn't deflect it at all, but just was in the stream and was deflected by it, as a reed is!

To the Lamonts'[1] for dinner. It was much nicer than I expected. I always feel there so strongly "the least intelligent Morrow." But tonight it was easier. Mr. Lamont was delighted by Con, who argued clearly and very well with Corliss. Corliss was really very sweet and gay and trying so hard to be nice to us. We had decided before we got there that we would *not* argue.

Instead, we let the Lamonts argue among themselves. Tommy and Corliss, Mrs. L. and Mr. L., Margaret and Tommy, Margaret and Mr. L., back and forth across the table. Tommy, loudly and platformly; Corliss, lightly, nervously, and humorously. Margaret, of course, dead serious. Mr. L. suavely and Mrs. L. petulantly. We all sat back quite happily (except for Con, who was grand) and listened. It was great fun.

Then afterward I had a nice talk with Mrs. Lamont about children and poetry and (vaguely) about accepting the evil in life. She handed on to me a saying of some religious teacher: "Christ never spoke about *understanding* the world—he spoke only of *overcoming* it."

Then C. being pelted with questions about aviation—Russian, German, Spanish War, English, U. S. A., etc. C. was *strictly*

---

[1] Thomas W. Lamont, American banker of J. P. Morgan & Co., his wife Florence; his sons Thomas Stilwell Lamont, also of J. P. Morgan, and wife Ellie Miner, and Corliss Lamont, teacher of philosophy, writer, and lecturer, and wife Margaret Irish, old friends of the Morrow family.

technical. It was very amusing to watch him (I-will-*not*-be-drawn-into-an-argument attitude).

Tuesday, February 1st

Mother back from Cleveland, much relieved. Grandma is not as changed as she feared, though quite weak.

Connie Chilton,[1] Con, Aubrey, Dwight, Mother, C., and I for supper. A Little School lecture afterward. Con and I sit upstairs. (I would like to hear the lecture but can't bear to shake hands with all Englewood again and get involved with more people.) I read Gerard Manley Hopkins and find a beautiful poem. "The Blessed Virgin Compared to the Air We Breathe." It is one of those poems that does somehow "convert" you. That is, it makes you wake up (as if from a sleep, or after sickness, or from conversion, or as in falling in love, or after sorrow) to a new world. The sense of air . . .

That lovely line, "sweet and scarless sky"—*scarless!* And all that it means, new every morning, spread out fresh, untouched by time, life, sorrow.

C. says maybe we can rent Illiec[2] for the summer! That is a nice thought. The sea and that beautiful island and the Carrels. Mme C. is writing about it. It does not seem to solve anything but is simply nice because it is a place we both love.

Thursday, February 3rd

Breakfast with Mother. In to Brackman's studio. In the afternoon he works on C.'s pastel head. It is, I think, an amazing likeness. He has, I feel, rather thickened C. His features are not quite as chiseled and fine, as delicate as they are in life, and yet the very

[1] Constance Chilton, cofounder with Elisabeth Morrow of The Little School in Englewood for preschool children, later Director of the expanded Elisabeth Morrow School.

[2] A small island off the north coast of Brittany, which at low tide is connected to the mainland and to the island of Saint-Gildas, owned by the Carrels.

lack of delicacy has added to the strength of the picture. If it were more delicate it would not be *him,* his strength and his character.

That is what I meant when I said paradoxically that the picture was more like him than he himself. All the modeling of the head, eyes, etc., are grand and the intensity in the eyes is very good. I look at the head and can hardly believe that I have it at last.

Ninth Symphony, Toscanini. "Only an old man can paint youth," as Brackman said the other day of Degas, Monet, and Manet. I thought, too, of that line of Shakespeare's, "All losses are restored and sorrows end." Hearing music like that makes time nothing—only those seconds. All your life, past and present and future, is caught in that moment. You will never, even at the end of your life, know more, understand more, sense more than this.

"If it were now to die, 'Twere now to be most happy . . ."

I wished C. had been there and hoped he was listening at home.

It was not such a shock of discovery as the first time I heard it. No, it was a sinking back into it, as into some wisdom, some knowledge you had heard of before, had forgotten, but now remembered and knew again. The melting slow movement is like first young love—real love, I mean, not the shy calf-love kind. But the last movement—at first I said *marriage* and then life itself and then religion. But it is not any of those. It is everything man knows, loves, lives, suffers, and learns in life. When one listens to it one can understand, or at least accept, for the moment, the evil in life. The things one has felt unable to understand, to bear, to absorb—all are absorbed, understood, accepted, for one divine moment.

"There shall not remain even one particle of dust that does not enter into Buddhahood," and Father Zossima's discourse [in *The Brothers Karamazov*].

Tuesday, February 8th

Con, Mother, and C., and I for supper. The pastels are here; discussion after supper.

Mother is very disappointed with mine and says it is too heavy and looks like me as a little girl after I'd cried and got a red nose! Con also says it is too thick and the eye is too sleepy. (He took the small-eye side of my face.) Mother says militantly that I have two very bad features, my high forehead and my nose, and he has played them up, and that I have one good feature, my eyes, and he has made nothing of them!

Everyone is crazy about C.'s, including myself.

Wednesday, February 9th

In Englewood all day. Long walk through the wet damp drippy woods, in the rain, the grass and leaves limp with wetness, soggy and dark. It is quite nice, so unpretentious, and helps my mood —unobtrusive. Find some pussy willow to send Jon. Stop in and see Yates boys[1] out of homesickness for Jon.

Zaidee, Neil, and Mr. Goodyear[2] out for supper. Mother has the Mexican pots full of flowers. The house looks lovely. The best Lowestoft on the table, the best shad, and caramel dessert. It is delicious and all goes very well.

We discuss portraits after supper. Mr. Goodyear says they are *beautiful* drawings: "Didn't know he could draw that well." All agree that C.'s is perfect in drawing, characterization, etc. The family and others think mine too heavy, sad, Slavic, and dull. Mr. Bliss: "It just isn't you at all, Anne." Mr. Goodyear: "It'll look more like you when you're forty."

C. at the end of the discussion: "The trouble is, nobody here cares enough about me. If *my* mother were here, then I'd have someone saying it didn't do justice to *me*."

Friday, February 11th

In to the studio. Mrs. Brackman and I talk about certain things in the face [C. A. L.'s] that are "not quite right." She says of my criticism, "No, there isn't too much space there, but if this line

[1] David and Robert Yates, sons of Mrs. Sheldon Yates, sister of E. C. M.
[2] See note p. 204.

were changed you would not feel that." Then she explains to me how baffling it is about painting. You sense something is wrong and you work on it and work on it and then accidentally you find out it is corrected by something else way down there, apparently unrelated.

I get quite interested in that idea and say, "Why, that is true of so many *other* things" (in life).

And she says, "Yes, it's not the thing itself that is wrong but only its relationship to something else."

And we stop for a moment, pleased, thinking about it and that we have understood each other.

Saturday, February 12th

Aubrey, Mother, C., and I for supper. After supper we discuss the future of The Little School. It must have a new building, must be a model school. It cannot operate as a model school, now, without a good building, surroundings, equipment, etc. Where to build? What neighborhood? This one, on this land? The ultimate use for this property and house, which would not otherwise be used (as none of us children would use it). Mother is absorbed by the idea and very happy that the land and house could be used by the school.

Sunday, February 13th

Breakfast with Mother. She is full of the school and eager to go out and walk over the place with us and plan (*so* like Mother—once she has an idea—to leap ahead of the other person, to plan). We discuss sites: the vegetable garden (because of the brook—my pet site), too much traffic on road.

Of course, says Mother, we have planned the grounds to walk *up* to the garden. But we'll make *another* garden (quite pleased with the idea) somewhere else.

"There, Anne, you children go out and walk around. You tell Charles to look at the garden—tell him that's my latest idea."

Marvelous—so like Mother.

C. says we must consider the time when land will have to be split up and sold, when the value and taxes are too high. We must try to keep the most beautiful part of land—the ravine and the lower part of the brook. We walk down the ravine to the entrance. There is flat ground near the public road and near the most beautiful part of the brook for playground space.

Early lunch and in to Brackman's studio. I am very elated. I think, analyzing it as I sit there, it is because C. is happy about these plans for the school and for the property. And because he thinks Mother is so grand about them and that makes me intensely happy.

Wednesday, February 16th

Letter from Jon!

I to lunch with Mother at the Cosmopolitan Club and on to *Snow White,*[1] the much talked of. I am quite interested in the process but get bored with its cheapness. The idea that illustrations can come to life is exciting, but a lovely fairy story has been cheapened, distorted. Hollywood love interest, Wild West chasing films, Broadway comedy, and detective story crime have been rolled into one to make this. And for *children!* It is too exaggerated (nothing left to the imagination—nothing), too literal, too terrifying, too confusing, and too fast.

The animals, however (animated rabbits, squirrels, fawns, etc.), were *charmingly* done. Mother says in a clear voice, "I would rather be at the *dentist's!"*

Wait in the cold for Burke for hours (Mother goes on, very angry at the film, and bored, to the dentist).

I home. The Hands for dinner: Judge Hand,[2] Mrs. Hand, and Mary—lots of fun. For the first time for a moment (talking about Pierre in *War and Peace*) I am not afraid with him, not shy. He tells me of the feeling of Pierre at his uncle's funeral, of

---

[1] Animated cartoon film by Walt Disney.

[2] Learned Hand, distinguished judge, known for his decisions, writings, addresses.

people telling him he must go through with it and do thus and so. He doesn't know why exactly, but he does thus and so. He is carried along on the stream—he does not know why, but there he is.

Judge Hand saying that so much of his life he had felt like that. You—even you, I thought, because so much of life seems like that to me. "But not to Charles," we agree. "Oh no, not to Charles." "And he's right" (Charles). "Yes he's right."

I love Judge Hand. How nice of him to tell me that.

Englewood, Thursday, February 17th

Stay out in Englewood. At night I lie on sofa and play all of Harriet Cohen's records of Bach preludes and fugues (letting the machine repeat them twice) while I close my eyes and think of the Villa d'Este waterfalls.

C. whistles cheerfully as he cleans his old guns!

Sunday, February 20th

Connie Chilton up to talk Little School business with Aubrey. We walk over the property and site for the school. Mother has taken it into her hands. Connie is so happy, like a dream materializing.

Early lunch and in to Brackman's studio. Last sitting for C. The picture does "come together." I am pleased as it is so much Charles. The seriousness, intentness, concentrated thought in the brow and eyes and that dry practical tart humor of common sense (that very American quality) in the mouth.

And in the hands there is decision, directness, and purpose.

But has he got in either portrait that kind of sweetness, that utter beauty? No, I think he has avoided it consciously, a pitfall of "perfection" that so many people have fallen into in portraying C.

Talk with Con. We agree—New York is not the place in which to see your family, and we ask, *Where* will we all live?

I have a feeling we will be on the coast of Brittany this summer, not because it is the solution of our permanent home and life but simply because it is the nicest thing we can think of for the summer.

Monday, February 21st

Hitler's speech, Eden resigns[1]—

Out for walk. It is beautiful, bright, clear, warm, and crisp. I get such joy each morning from the *sun* here in America (after the days of gray sameness in England). Each day I go out and walk and see the sky, and each night I see the stars. I feel so grateful, a positive joy. I have relearned all the trees on this property, too. The ones like flame (tulip), the ones like water (beeches and birches), and the oaks, nervous, irregular, imperfect, scraggy, unpredictable—like man. Those are all seen against the sky. Then there are the little gray beeches seen among the tree trunks and underbrush, like ballet dancers. They are always balanced, poised, spread, arms out. The color of gray beeches against blue sky, lovely soft color, restful, peaceful. Beeches, a benediction, I kept thinking this morning.

Tuesday, February 22nd

Read Eden's resignation speech. Chamberlain is for a new policy of co-operation with Italy and Germany.

All my feelings, instincts, heart, are for Eden and his uncompromising ideals. But all that my mind has learned, painfully, through living, tells me Chamberlain's earth-bound, practical realism is right.

Wednesday, February 23rd

In Englewood all morning, a gentle dull drizzle, no hard rain that falls off. The little drops clung in beads to the buds on the

[1] Anthony Eden, British Secretary of State, resigns in protest against the policy of Prime Minister Chamberlain of further attempts at co-operation with Italy and Germany. Lord Halifax takes his place in the Foreign Office.

trees. The beech trees are invisible today, they step back among the other trees, their wet bark darkened, no longer that soft gray.

Reread my book. It has been hanging over me, like homework on Sunday afternoon. You know you have a colossal amount of work to do and dread it and put off facing it for fear of the discouragement that comes with it.

But facing it was not so terrible. It was a relief. It does not seem such a job. At least I feel I can do it, when I get alone, and the time away from it has helped. It is fresher and I am anxious to get at it.

Thursday, February 24th

Wander down 57th Street into the Renoir exhibit, landscapes—just twelve. I sat and looked at each one. Shady ones and hot sunny ones (the poppy garden) and one lovely one of two women and a boy resting in the grass under some trees by a road in patches of shade and sun, a lush summer feeling about it and stillness and more than that, in the boy's body, relaxed, half hidden in the grass, a feeling of their accepting and being completely accepted by nature, held, warmed, surrounded by it—as in a nest.

The tree trunks are done just like (his) people's limbs. The shimmering quality of the air.

Also a Degas portrait (and one Renoir head)—*very* different. I liked it very much, a crumpled person in a chair (more important and more pitiful than the Renoir head). That is, his people are more important in relation to the rest of life than Renoir's, but also they are more piteous.

Friday, February 25th

C. puts the pictures of Illiec in front of me and a private note: "I have practically agreed to buy Illiec."

The pictures are beautiful. The house really looks quite nice, well built of stone. It has a small tower I don't like much but it isn't bad. And the views from it are lovely. The island looks bigger than I thought—not just a rock with some grass on it, and the house.

I am crazy to know details: How big? How many rooms. Bathroom? Heat? Probably not—certainly not the last. We would get the furniture too, but Mme Carrel says it is horrible.

But he was a musician.[1] I suppose they won't leave the piano.

I am excited and pleased—terribly happy about it. One of those things that lets the spirit escape in joy. I do not know *why*, exactly. It does not seem especially practical or reasonable. Tie ourselves to an island off the French coast? Remote from people and places. Not particularly secure—France, I mean—nor is the French press situation as good as the English. And how about our "farm" land in America I thought we might buy, in the West? And yet it seems somehow *right* and makes my heart leap, as if it offered—as it does—sheer beauty, quiet, and joy of living, regardless of any other considerations.

C. is excited, too. He said, "I can see Jon digging up clams," and that sold me.

Then the Carrels are there, and that means everything to both of us. We are going in to see them in the morning. My mind swims plans!

I am very happy.

Tuesday, March 1st

In to the Institute for lunch. Mme Carrel is leaving for France to try to see her mother, who is ninety-three and has fallen and broken her hip-bone and will probably not recover. She is sad and tired. She is also going to see about getting us the island, and is happy about that. They do want us there—C., of course, but us as a family, also, on that island.

Then to Harcourt, Brace, to see Mr. Brace about the time my book should be done: in general late April (Heavens!) but I can work on it in May—till June?

---

[1] The stone house on Illiec was built by Ambroise Thomas, the musician and composer of the opera *Mignon*.

Mother and I go to the art exhibit (Modern French Portraits—charity opening). *Beautiful* show but full of mink coats posing beside Renoirs and two flashlight cameras. Lots of people come up. It is rather like a reception. I begin to curl up inside and I cannot enjoy the pictures. Very society-page atmosphere and I am afraid of the cameramen. Mr. Goodyear assures me they will not take my picture but I do not trust them. ("They lie like they breathe," to paraphrase Dr. Carrel.)

We cannot leave immediately because it is a kind of social occasion and because we are meeting President Neilson there. I cower from small room to small room. They do snap me after all, going out (pretending to take someone else).

Mother, President Neilson, and I get into the car—what a relief! Then we take him home. We cannot go up and see Mrs. Neilson, which I *long* to do, because we have to be at the Blisses' for tea. I arrive at the Blisses' feeling very cross, flustered, and cheated. I have not shown the pictures to Margot, I have not seen Mrs. Neilson, I have not seen the art show, I have had to meet a lot of people I could otherwise have avoided, and I have probably been photographed into the bargain—today of all days.

Then Betty[1] comes in and the day is saved, because we talk through the teacup chatter, right through the mink coat and the veiled hat she is always impeccably dressed in. She is lovely, *lovely* and real. It is such a relief.

Margot arrives, very late. Out to Englewood—too late to take a bath—very tired and a headache.

Wednesday, March 2nd

In Englewood all day, a warm March wind blowing, sunny, and soft clouds.

The mornings here go in pleasant, leisurely, breakfast-tray-morning-mail and tentative plans, conversations in Mother's little sitting room. A fire, sunshine in the window, Mother's voice

[1] Eliza Bliss Parkinson, daughter of Mr. and Mrs. Cornelius Bliss, active on the Museum of Modern Art.

through the bathroom door, "Is that you, Anne? I'll be out in a minute. Get my breakfast, will you, Isabel?" (urgent and young). That perpetual *eagerness* of Mother, rising fresh each morning.

The day has not yet hardened, the hours not yet compressed into what one must get done. Mother is leisurely and wistful, not efficient and pressed. We chat and go over things in a light casual way, not really talking but with a kind of understanding glinting through the ordinary phrases.

Yes, the realest part of my visit has been these breakfasts.

The house is in its usual pre-departure panic.[1] The end of Mother's hall is crowded with boxes, tissue paper, hats.

After supper Mother sits at her desk. She gives me more and more books, papers, little notebooks, etc., to squeeze into the already overcrowded bookbag. She is still signing things at her desk, her hat on.

Then we gravitate downstairs for good-bys. Mother is quite sad. The time is all gone and so much unsaid.

I sometimes wonder if the whole of life will go like this day and this vacation, in a way, with the illusion of seeing her, and not really seeing her at all.

She goes off in her little black hat with the red crown, and my red scarf around her neck. I know just how she feels. When it comes right down to leaving I just hate to leave *anywhere*.

Thursday, March 3rd

In Englewood all day. Con is packing [for Mexico]. The place is a welter of clothes, tissue paper, hats, and shoes. I sit on the bed in the midst hoping to have a chance to see her but I don't really, because the attention is on finding belts to match, etc. So all I can say is, "Yes, that is a lovely blouse. Yes, that is a very becoming dress. *What* useful culottes!" Finally we go out for a walk. We talk about plans and hold on to the summer—bank on that—seeing each other in Illiec, maybe.

---

[1] Mrs. Morrow is leaving for Cleveland, en route to Mexico.

After lunch I sit at my desk and try to project myself back or the South Atlantic. I sat that way yesterday morning too, and th morning.

It begins to get a little realer, slowly, and I get *one* idea anyway and feel encouraged.

Mother calls [from Cleveland]. She sounds happier. I tell er we have had a good day and she is pleased. It is so nice to talk, o wipe out the mood she left in last night (we were both feeling the same way) and to be able to say it was better today, and feer her relief. The doctor advised her by all means to go to Mexico. Grandma was not as bad as she expected.

Friday, March 4th

Another crowded day. The morning is spent telephoning. Betty Bliss, the Vaillants. And a few walks. It is very cold but sun y and bright, a lovely day, like a frozen apple!

Then in to lunch with Betty Bliss Parkinson. I was so afraic it would be the usual family lunch in the dining room with all the butlers and the best china. But she was alone and had it planned beautifully on a table in the little sitting room. It was full of flowers and sun and we could talk. I was so glad I went —and I almost didn't. From the subject of children's education we discussed almost everything, "Woman's place . . . ," etc. It was lovely and she is rare as some flower.

Then to Mrs. Hand's for tea.

I come in and say, "May I wash my hands?"

"Of *course,* dearie," says Mrs. Hand. "Run *right* up. You'll find Mary in the bathtub and Frances sitting on the edge talking to her."

Which was quite true!

She talks about *Assignment in Utopia,* and *Goliath,* and Frances and Mary, and we toast our toes by the fire and eat English muffins and insert opinions about Russia and Italy.

Get home to find C. rushing up to Aunt Edith's [Yates]. Grandma is much worse, not expected to live. Mother is wired at

Saint Louis to turn back. There is a call coming through from Cleveland.

I think about Mother and Grandma and smell Mother's eau de Cologne or powder as I draw the light string down in her dark dress cupboard. And all her little things on the bureau and shelf. Will I someday be doing what she is now? I hope Grandma can die quickly without pain.

To bed, too tired to sleep. Shall I or shan't I take a pill? Get up and exercise? Eat a cracker? Will I wake C.? For hours.

Saturday, March 5th

I call Cleveland. Aunt Annie talks to me. Grandma the same, under hypodermic. Mother and Aunt Edith arrive at noon. Aubrey and Con are coming back here.

Then Mother calls: no change.

We have got a passage on the *Bremen* sailing Friday night.

Sunday, March 6th

Margot and Con and Aubrey back. We take walks and wait for word from Cleveland. At six Mother calls. Grandma died at five. She never regained consciousness. We discuss our going to Cleveland. If I go will it bring the press?

We call Mother again at nine. Tell her we all may go. "Dwight too?" she says in a very weak voice. She makes no argument. I think she would want us. But she sounds so tired and sad.

Tuesday, March 8th

Breakfast on the train. Taxi through Cleveland to 2160. Gloomy city. Up the hill to Grandma's corner. Aunt Annie, white and tired but very natural. Mother also and so glad to see us. Aunt Edith is very weighed down.

Arranging flowers—such a lot of bustle for Grandma's house.

The service. We sit in Grandma's room, everything is so *her*: the cut-glass bottles on the bureau, the candlesticks, the picture of Grandpa in a silver frame, the framed Christmas card, her books,

God's Minute, the Victorian watercolor of the Trossachs.[1] The little card on her bureau with that rhyme she was fond of:

> "I heard a bird sing in the dark of December,
> 'We're nearer the spring than we were in September.'"

The picture of Elisabeth in braids and me in curls facing each other. The samplers and two small vases.

Aunt Annie at the last minute brought in a green vase of daffodils—wonderful Aunt Annie!

It was so strange and natural to sit in that room of Grandma's, with the bed neatly made up and covered, like a guest bed that is never used.

The service was very beautiful. The quotation from *Pilgrim's Progress,* Christian's wife who is called to heaven, and her preparation for death, calm, assured, reverent, and also triumphant, was very like Grandma.

It was not a sad service really and I felt happy to be there. Grandma had led a wonderful life. She had lived life as it came, enjoyed it, suffered it—but always accepted it. And she had prepared for and accepted death, with dignity, courage, and beauty, as she accepted everything.

The end of her life and this service about it was *right*. It was not, as most of the services in our family, a tragedy, something wrong, cut down, cruel to bear. No, it was life and death as it always had been, as it should be.

It was Biblical: "for he flourisheth as a flower of the field . . . and the place thereof shall know it no more."

Only it was hard to see Mother, Aunt Annie, and Edith missing her, missing her actual presence, and to look into the future at what it will mean not to have Mother.

We go out the back door into the funeral cars. The door of our car got jammed, we try to force it, kick it, etc. It falls right off its hinge—so like a funeral. The young driver is solemnly humiliated. We force it to shut; I hope it will not fall off in the cemetery.

[1] Picturesque valley in Perth, central Scotland.

Back to the house, which is clear of the funeral flowers and has a bright fire. Aunt Annie and Mother are beautiful, natural, and yet in a way triumphant. But Aunt Edith is still upset about the *accidents* of it. Why *didn't* she come with Mother instead of planning her visit a week later? As if one could control the accidents of life. I understand it so well—the feeling. It is hard to learn that life is so completely accidental that everything you get is really just so much "velvet."

Grandma understood that.

We catch the 8:45 train. They were happy to have us come and I am glad and proud I did—that I was part of Grandma and her life.

Thursday, March 10th

Con, Margot, and I have breakfast in Mother's little room, hoping to be there to welcome her back. The train is late.

Just as we disperse the car comes in. I rush to meet Mother in the hall. (Burke has just said, "I don't believe there is anyone at home.") Mother looks so tired and little and wistful.

We go upstairs to her sitting room. Aunt Annie and Edith are going with her to Mexico, but not Con and Aubrey now. Business has come up.

In to see the Hands. Not much conversation until, just as I leave, Mrs. Hand and I stand in the door and talk for almost half an hour—about the Renoir landscape "nested in nature and summer and life." It was worth a great deal more than all the other visits.

How often it is like this. You cannot force contacts, or conversations, and the best ones are always snatched at the doorstep or in the heart of a roaring crowd or on a train. The flash of understanding is the most wayward of all divinities.

Then to Laura's. We talk quietly, and she says such a nice thing, that I feel often. She feels so much of the time that she has only enough to give to George and the children but not anything extra for anyone else, and when she goes out she feels as if she were looking in her purse for small change: "What, *nothing?*

Not even a penny—where is that penny? Turn the purse upside down, shake it—not even a penny!"

Rush back to the Cosmopolitan Club, where Aubrey, Con, and Margot are waiting for me. Not time to get out to Englewood and back for theater.

Dwight meets us at the theater. *Our Town* by Thornton Wilder—must get and read. It is a lovely play. No scenery and almost an allegory. Very American in its language, quality, setting, etc., but classical in its fundamentals.

The rush of the day slows to the quiet tempo of a small town in Vermont. The dross of New York falls off. This bare play is full of spirit, beauty, and all of life. It is really an enlargement of his myth in *The Woman of Andros,* put in a New England setting.

We were first amused (intrigued, curious), then entranced, and then moved. As Margot says, it frees the top of your head.

"Suddenly the hero saw that the living too are dead and that we can only be said to be alive in those moments when our hearts are conscious of our treasure; for our hearts are not strong enough to love every moment.

. . . before he left he fell upon the ground and kissed the soil of the world that is too dear to be realized."[1]

March 11th, on board the Bremen

One of those last days in which you feel too tired to say anything real to the people you want to say things to.

Packing: Con sits on the floor in my room and reads old *Vogues* while I bury small bottles in the underwear in my trunk and try to fit shoes in with books.

We really do not say anything but I do not want her to go away.

C. home, trunks off, no time to take a bath.

I tell Mother I think we will be in Brittany this summer. She is coming over May 8th. We reach forward to that.

[1] From *The Woman of Andros,* by Thornton Wilder.

And Con and I are holding on to the thought of the island (she thinks they definitely will come over).

C. gets us to the door and our good-bys a half-hour early. Cannot say anything to Mother as usual at these times.

It is snowing as we leave.

The Nazis have taken hold of Austria. Chancellor Schuschnigg resigns. German troops march into Austria. Everyone is shocked —does it mean war?

We *would* be on a boat for a week, with no news—and a German boat at that!

To our staterooms and to bed very tired about two, or after. They cannot find my large trunk! I am so tired it does not seem a catastrophe. I just don't care.

Dream about Jon.

We buy the last New York *Times* and read all the news. The Germans are in Austria. There is great confusion, but no one seems to want to do anything. Apparently a great surprise to Rome!

March 12th, Bremen

Trunk found! Late breakfast, out for walk. Quite rough, spray over the decks. I sit in my cabin most of the day. Get out all my notes, diary, papers for the book. Try to soak myself in that trip across and the old radio work.

The ship's paper reports Hitler's speech in Austria. "If Divine Providence called me from Austria to unite Germany . . . then Divine Providence has called me back," etc., etc.!

Go up before supper and walk around the sun deck. The clouds are broken in places and you can see a few stars—Orion and Sirius. They are comforting and familiar, as though they were part of my own familiar world, instead of—as they are—unknown strange other worlds.

Ship's paper reports Hitler's telegram to Mussolini (for not interfering): "Mussolini, I will never forget this of you, Adolf Hitler"!

I work all day on the radio chapter. A few walks, one at night; almost a full moon and great white luminous clouds sailing by the mast, and stars.

> "The heavens declare the glory of God;
> and the firmament showeth his handiwork.
> Day unto day uttereth speech,
> and night unto night showeth knowledge."

I must teach Jon the Bible—how?

Wednesday, March 16th

This has been a strange trip, completely peopleless. We have seen and talked to no one except ourselves, the stewards, and the Captain.

I like privacy and getting work done, but I miss people, not all the time but at meals. Even stupid people are better than none at all, to me (not to C.).

Thursday, March 17th

Southampton water at six. Get off quite quickly onto the baggage tender. No one sees us. Mr. Gregory [from Morgan, Grenfell] is there. Then a long wait. (Talk with Mr. Gregory about conditions in England, etc.) We are *always* doing this. And an hour-and-a-half trip up the river to the docks, where Miss H. is waiting for us. The long drive in the tiny Ford. Stop for a very poor dinner in Winchester—one of those old inns in which the girl, very grumpily, says, "There's no chicken left. . . . There's only prunes left for a sweet," etc. The usual English "We have *nothing* here that you want" attitude. It is *very* slow. We are back!

Finally through the Weald and into our little shed. And stepping down the irregular brick path in the moonlight. (I know every irregularity—my foot meets it. I could do it blindfold!) Just as we get to the kitchen steps the moonlight on the white blossoms of the plum tree! And the smell of earth and spring. Then Thor at the side door, very furry and thumping his tail. The thin clouds and a moon behind the poplars. How little and overhanging and familiar and warm it seems! It is a house that puts its arms around you and draws you in. Upstairs the smell of a wood fire; primroses and violets in a vase.

We go in to see Jon. The room is hung with paper chains—still! His cropped head is buried in a pillow. He turns over but doesn't wake. (Skean comes out, a flurry and scratch of black wool.)

We walk all through the house. Miss W. has outdone herself on the flowers. The rooms shine, white cyclamen near the Madonna,[1] green-budded leaves and pussy-willow flowers in the blue vases on either side of the St. Francis.[1] Pink blossoms on the piano, daffodils in my study.

Then C. and I walk outside; the smell of hyacinth, dim shape of daffodils on the terrace, and frogs chirping—all still and quiet and smelling fresh.

To bed, very tired, in the big soft bed, with Thor thumping his tail occasionally on the floor.

Friday, March 18th

Wake quite early and keep quiet, waiting for Jon "to wake." All the birds are singing around us. Jon knocks on the door before 7:30! Can he come in? He comes, all in a tumble, and climbs up on the bed. "You know the wretched rat got the guinea pigs?" he says in a rush in a *very* English voice. "Rats are *nasty* creatures." He talks on and on, very excited. I just sit and listen to him, overcome by the strangeness of his outside (accent, cropped head, tallness, etc.) and the same Jon underneath.

He talks about tree stumps he has pushed over, and Hammond and Land. The same smile: "He's fine—would you like to see him?" giving me his hand. I get some little presents out for him.

In to see Land and Miss W. Land very big, rosy, and curly hair on top. I speak to him and he smiles and shows two teeth below. I give him the rattle (Jon's old one), which he immediately shakes with glee.

C. and I take Jon to school. We come back and walk around

[1] Wood carvings of Anton Lang, of Oberammergau, bought in London.

the garden. It is deliciously warm and springlike, like May, a soft sky and warm wind and everything green, the grass and the leaves of fruit trees, daffodils out, and hyacinths. The crocus are over, grape hyacinths out by the hedge, and lots of thrushes.

Back to see Jon dance at 11:20. He still looks pale, pearly blond in comparison with the ruddy blond English boys, but he is much gayer than before, feels at home, laughs while he works, and keeps his own place in the games (even pushing, for which I am glad, as he has had so little experience and is likely to get stepped on).

Not self-conscious at all, once flashing me a little smile.

To bed early—very tired.

Saturday, March 19th

Sleep late (still making up sleep from the boat. It is so quiet and relaxed here). Wake to hear a pounding on the door that I dimly feel has gone on for some time and Jon's plaintive voice the other side of it. "I've knocked and knocked and made a terrible noise but nobody seems to hear me." I woke enough to say, "That's because we're *so* sleepy," but it didn't get through the walls.

Jon and I go outside. It is divine spring weather again. First we get his "presents" out of the trunks. The little pasteboard bureau with the ties and hankies. Mrs. Lindbergh's walnut with the dressed fleas inside made a tremendous hit. And then the folding rule—"just like a carpenter's!" He put it in his back pocket and we go out to plant his wild strawberry plant, which Hammond gave him.

Jon is very happy. He says, walking up the hill with me, "It *is* nice to have you back! This *is* a nice day!" in that strange English voice of his.

We go up to the greenhouse to find a watering can. As we leave Hook notices his rule in the back pocket and says, "Jon's a proper carpenter now!" Jon is thrilled!

C. comes back after lunch. We work on titles for my book. Books of quotations, Shakespeare, Vaughan, Traherne, etc. Find nothing as good as *Listen! the Wind*.

I go for a short walk up the wood path and around the field with Jon.

Land on a rug at tea. He will not make any effort to crawl. He is quite happy anywhere you put him, fat, happy, surprised. He experiments with his hands, holding, touching, moving his wrists, and with all kinds of sounds, imitating. But he makes no effort to move himself.

C. says, Is it the complacency of my Uncle Frank or of your Aunt Hilda?

Sunday, March 20th

C. is doing the cover for *Listen! the Wind*. Half stars, half moon and waves at bottom, black and white. Very good, striking and decorative.

Monday, March 21st

Letter from Mme Carrel: the owner of Illiec must consult with his son. C. and I are worried it won't come off.

Get Jon at twelve. He has got *two* stars for his work, which he announces to me: "One for doing sums and one for drawing a straight line." He is very pleased. "Did you think I'd get *two* stars in *one* day?"

C. and I go for a short walk around the field.

After lunch, work until four, but the chapter won't *come*. I make myself write something according to the plan and it comes out all wrong, words crossed out, sentences stiff, the whole thing dead—even the writing is lifeless.

After supper I read the first radio chapter to C. He likes it *very much*, which is encouraging and makes me happy.

Tuesday, March 22nd—lovely day, still fine

Write Mother and Mrs. L. about the children, to catch the *Normandie*.[1] A rather rushed day because of the boat leaving and

---

[1] Before the days of air mail one watched the newspapers for the transatlantic sailings and addressed one's letters "via the S.S. *Normandie*," etc.

trying to get the *take-off* chapter and the cover design and title on it for HarBrace.

I work correcting chapter up to the last minute of mail time, C. also going over it. He takes it up to the post office.

Feel very tired. Since we have got back it has been such a rush—not exactly a "rush," because it has been orderly. But every minute is filled and there is hardly time to sit back and just be happy, or just *be*.

Wednesday, March 23rd

I finish the second radio chapter. It is just *fair*, I think. It should be light and maybe funny, but I think it is just dull and thin.

C., Jon, and I for a walk across the fields in the afternoon. The primroses are bright patches in the brown leaves of last fall, still under the bare trees in the woods. Violets, too, by the brook. The sky is soft and rayed out with faint cloud streaks.

Jon is only interested in stumps. He brings home four, making his father bring two, and me, one. (We look too odd, walking home on a lovely spring evening, carrying old rotten stumps, and hope no one sees us! Crazy Americans!)

Mme Carrel is coming Saturday. I hope for news of Illiec.

After supper I read the second radio chapter to C. He thinks it's all right.

It has been a lovely day.

Thursday, March 24th

Taking care of the children today. Quite warm. I walk around the garden in sandals and no coat, with a flower basket, and look at all the beds and remember what is coming in them and store up the way they're planted in my mind for reference. Tulips around the base of the fruit trees (yellow crocuses in the grass around all trees). Larkspur in the back beds. Must get some aubretia for Illiec—if we get it!

Wallflowers for Illiec! Remember Mont-Saint-Michel in May.

There is quite a coolish wind blowing. The line "Rough winds do shake the darling buds of May" comes to me over and over.

I leave Land sweetly smiling, rosy, tucked into his carriage, and come back a minute later to see him kicking his bare legs in the air and crowing happily—and the wind is cold ("Rough winds do shake the darling buds of May").

C., Jon, and I go for a short walk in the afternoon up the wood path. All books on child education seem to assume that the child is putty in your hands. *Mine* isn't. It's no good taking him for a walk and thinking you can get in a little nature study, point out birds' nests, catkins, violets, etc., when all he is interested in is dead stumps!

Saturday, March 26th

Clear day, sunny but colder, with thundery clouds and then sunshine blowing by at intervals—very March.

C. goes for Mme Carrel. I stay and work on the *dead period* chapter longer than I planned.

Go out and arrange flowers hastily—daffodils for Mme Carrel's room. Also those odds and ends always forgotten in the guest room. The old soap. No Kleenex. The old books—change. An old 1937 calendar. Do the lights turn on? No crackers by the bed. Dirty towels in the downstairs lavatory. Run around and do these first.

Then to the flowers. I am in the middle of the dining-room table centerpiece when she arrives. All in black for her mother and looking very tired. She tells us about Illiec, a very complicated procedure in order to keep our name out of it—which is right. But she has been to a lot of trouble. And *will* they sell it? The mother and one son want to, one other son does *not* want to. A conference Monday night may tell. They (the Carrels) have bought Île-de-Milieu.

Sunday, March 27th

At night we sit around the fire and talk about Illiec. Mme Carrel thinks she may know about it tomorrow evening. If we can get it, and the papers signed, C. and I could go to Saint-Gildas next week and look it over!

The address would be:
Illiec
   Penvenan
      Côtes-du-Nord!

It is well built but has, I gather, no conveniences. No heat (but probably good fireplaces—I see two chimneys in the photograph). No telephone (good!), no light, but kerosene lamps are all right. Perhaps no running water or plumbing?

But it looks very beautiful, so the rest must be overlooked.

Monday, March 28th

Mme Carrel leaves with C. for Croyden. I cannot work any more—stale; decide to go to town. Enjoy getting into my town clothes and getting off. Buy *Vogue* and sit in the train doing nothing!

To the hairdresser's, lunch there, then walking up Grafton Street to the Medici Galleries. Feel exhilarated to be out walking along the street in leisure, like a well-dressed woman shopping (I never *quite* look well dressed. Always just a little off, a slightly baggy look, I think, from being thin and not holding myself well).

I look at the good-looking Englishmen in cars on the street and consider, "Yes, so good-looking and so stupid—only good for mating."

Very much refreshed, I am glad to be back—and to have gone.

Wednesday, March 30th

Letter from Mme Carrel at breakfast. Says she would have great hope *if* it were not that the oldest son has an *idée fixe* not to sell. A gloom settles on us at breakfast. I feel it is hopeless. I did not realize how much I had counted on it. All my thoughts run to the island, planning ahead, and then stop—rebuffed.

I start looking on the back pages of the *Times* and *Telegraph* at "seaside places." C. talks of the Bavarian Alps vaguely. But everything has rather crashed.

It is quite a hot lifeless day. We let Land kick his legs in the sun.

Mrs. Wood, the postmistress of Weald, comes for tea. She is little and wiry and crisp as an apple in a maroon velvet dress, black coat, and black straw hat with a water lily on it. She is very sweet and shy and breaks her cake with thin dry precise fingers (that can't find enough to do). C. talks to her about the history of the house and the Weald. Jon shows her his blackboard and takes her by the hand into the house. And I talk to her about her baby granddaughter and the children in the Weald (for Jon, perhaps). She leaves not shy.

Thursday, March 31st

Wake discouraged, remembering we can't get Illiec. During my bath C. comes up with another letter from Mme Carrel starting dramatically; "We have won—Illiec is yours!" The morning is galvanized: plans, thoughts, etc.

Friday, April 1st

Charles and I go off to East Grinstead, through lovely English country, fields full of lambs, hills gold with new willow leaves, woods with primroses, and daffodils and japonica in everyone's front garden, and aubretia down every wall.

Charles and I discuss the English, going over and back—their slowness. What would happen to them in a war, unprepared? How did they build the English Empire? etc.

I get hurt and upset as I do when I think of the English going under. I take it personally, somehow. Why, I don't know, except that I have always had such passionately high ideals of and for the English, and perhaps that universal feeling of

> "Men are we, and must grieve when even the shade
> Of that which once was great is passed away."

When I think back on it, I had ridiculously high ideals, they were *the* perfect race. The only civilized, completely rounded people, the modern Greeks, in government, living, literature, law, mortality, spirit, etc.

Slowly I have been disillusioned (not entirely so, though). I am incorrigible, I still believe those demigods exist—only I have not found them.

I remember Mrs. Hand saying to me as I left for England, feeling rather lonely and shy; "It doesn't matter, Anne. You will find your own milieu, your own group wherever you are, anywhere."

But I haven't. I haven't found anyone in England—not one single soul. I have been here almost two and a half years and I have not made a single friend.

It is, of course, not entirely the fault of the English. When we first came, there was a fuss in the papers and we could have seen a lot of people and did get invitations, but we were upset, not organized. No house, no nurse, no plans, and much publicity; and we wanted peace and quiet and not to see anyone.

Then we have been away almost half the time—to France, to Germany, to Denmark, to India, to Italy, etc. (I feel I have made a friend in Mme Carrel in France, and the Smiths in Germany— Americans. And of course Sir Francis [Younghusband]. Yes, I think we could count him—that's one. Florrie, though she's a family friend, *she* has been dear. Margaret Morgan—again family —but I like her. Rosamond [Lehmann] Philipps, whom I have seen twice.

In the time here I have had a baby (which makes me feel ill and not like seeing people), and nursed him for five months (which tied me to the house), and I have written a book, which takes a lot of time.

Then C. has been so interested in work or plans or things he was doing that he has not wanted to meet people. He doesn't need them anyway and can quite well get along with no one except his family.

And finally, most important, I am very bad about people because I hate so terribly to push that I make no effort. I am too shy about it. I want other people to make the effort, and when the "other people" are English they don't.

Well, it is rather silly to complain. We have had so much from England—peace and beauty, a lovely house, lovely country, and perfect family happiness. Real living, we have had. And after all that is the most important.

April 2nd

Sunny, but a cold wind—at least, not as balmy as the last weeks.

C. goes off to fly, Jon to paint his house. He looks rather like a French artist, long "velvet" (corduroy) trousers and a hip-length blue smock.

I bathe Land, who turns over by himself on the rug afterward. Then to work on the last long chapter.

Rescue Jon at 12:30 from his house. He has just finished the painting. His hands, neck, and front hair are pretty much covered with creosote and his smock rather spotted, but the house is well painted.

After lunch I back to work and Jon to climb trees. I hear him shouting from the top of the crab-apple tree—a chant, over and over again, very loud, like a battle cry: "Higher than the coal shed!"

When I finish the chapter I go up to him. He goes on shouting exultantly, "I'm higher than the coal shed," and then to me, "I'm so glad you came—I did *so* much want you to come and see me." He is quite hoarse from shouting.

No further word from Mme Carrel. We are worried. Has something gone wrong about Illiec? C. home for supper. I read him the chapter, which he likes very much, but I know it needs rewriting.

Sunday, April 3rd

Work all morning on last chapter. Finish it roughly, not sure about the ending, and it must all be slung together, but C. says,

"Your book is done—your book is done! Wake up, Anne, it's Christmas Day!" I'm not so sure.

Jon, C., and I go for a walk over the fields; blowy but sunny. Jon making a beeline for the woods and stumps and dead trees. I bring a few of the first bluebells and a bunch of violets. The bank by the stream in the next field was blue with them. I can't resist them—like strawberries.

Wire from Mme Carrel. Everything is all right! She expects us at Saint-Gildas and we will leave Wednesday for a few days!

Long Barn, Weald, Sevenoaks, April 5th

Mother, darling,

So much seems to have happened since I last wrote. We have Illiec—at least for the summer—secretly so far. (It is the island next to the Carrels.) There has been much negotiation but I think it is settled now. We wanted so much to arrange everything quietly. I am very happy about it as it is the ideal "wilderness" or "change" place to have. It is wild and beautiful and different and on the sea—and France, which is fun. It will never take the place of Maine for me. It has not the associations and it is not really the same kind of place. Maine is, and will become more and more I think because of easier accessibility, a vacation place, a holiday place, even a weekend country holiday. It will always be home to me more than any other home, I think. But it is not "wilderness," "isolation," and "strangeness" which this is. It is more "peace," "friendliness," and "home"—Maine.

Well, we can talk more about it when I see you, which won't be long. Tomorrow C. and I fly to Brittany to talk over plans with Mme Carrel and look over the house.

We won't move over (Miss W. and Miss H. too), according to plans now, until the end of May. (Our lease expires here the 1st of June.) We will be somewhat in the process of moving out of Long Barn during your visit here but if *you* don't mind, we don't! C. laughed and said, "Well, your mother is used to moving."

The book—first draft—is finished! Now I must start the very

discouraging, painstaking correcting and rewriting, but I feel a load off my mind to have it once written.

DIARY   *Thursday, April 7th*

Up early. A good day. Jon helps me roll up the bundles. Good-by to Land on the floor.

Long drive to Reading. Take off at 12:20. Land Lympne at 1:03. Quickly through the customs and off for the Channel—quite hazy. "The further off from England, the nearer 'tis to France." Sunny and hazy on other side. Land at Saint-Inglevert 1:44. A few slouchy Frenchmen around smoking pipes (last time I was there Land was hidden in the back!). Off and down the coast. Dieppe, Havre, very pleasant weather, a few clouds, then more. I do quite a little flying, fly up through the clouds, clipping a wing through their soft white sizzle. Farms below, trees in bloom, small bouquets.

One has such a *tender* feeling looking down on the earth from above!

Fields of orange gorse and yellow mustard in Brittany.

Morlaix at 4:30. C. hands back the map. We dive, roaring over the hangar; three people run toward the doors. We circle and land and taxi right into the hangar. M. Masson, smiling and cheery, comes up, Mlle Masson[1] translating laboriously. Mme Carrel taking our hands, our baggage, everything.

Then we go off, Mme Carrel telling us about the sale of the island. It was almost sold in three parts by the mother and two brothers. She has been in a state over it, working every minute. Anyway, now all is finished.

Through Lannion, the nearest "big town." (No, I do not think we can get much in the way of American merchandise here!) Into the mist. It gets very cold. Gorse, flowering and golden, lines the roads in hedges. Fruit trees are out, old peasant women hobble along in black skirts and shawls and white caps.

There is no plumbing *whatsoever* in Illiec, but cistern drinking water. There is quite a good man and his wife on the place who

---

[1] The airport manager and his daughter.

can do cooking and take care of the place, perhaps. The furniture is horrible—atrocious, dirty, "all curls," Mme Carrel says.

We unload the car at the dock, drive it back to the garage at Port-Blanc, and then walk down the deserted road to the dock. You cannot see a thing on the hill—neither Saint-Gildas nor Illiec. "There is your island!" said Mme Carrel pointing at the mist.

Pierre [the Carrels' boatman] in the rowboat—as it is low tide—to take us to the motorboat. Very cold. The rocks of Saint-Gildas appear through the mist. We scramble over the loose boulders up to the steps, over the wall into the court. Chérie barking. Antoinette runs out: *"Oui, Madame."*

To bed early. Tomorrow we plan to walk to Illiec by low tide and come back by boat.

Friday, April 8th

Early lunch (I am ravenously hungry here) and into the boat to go to Illiec.

We stop at Île-de-Milieu and climb a hill to get a good view of Illiec's outer islands. There are a great many, and at least two with trees on. The house is hidden from here.

Then back into Illiec's little harbor. The house perched between the trees and the big rock. A kind of bare space runs down in front of the house to an abrupt wall, falling off into the sea (*both* in back and in front).

We climb up the pebbly spit of rocks and toward the house, approaching the grove of pine trees. The house stands up rather gray and square—stone, quite French, with a tower—next to a huge rock which shelters it from the east winds, and there is a grove of pine trees on its other end. On one side it faces a harbor and the coast, and on the other the open sea and rocks. The island itself is quite small—only one real grassy patch which slopes to the sea on both sides, in the middle of which is the house; the rest is rocks. Around the island are lots of other little islands—two semicircles of them. When the tide is high, these are islands; when the tide is low you walk over flats to them from the main island of Illiec. Illiec is connected to the mainland by a long spit of stones thrown up by the sea. Except at high tide you can drive onto it. At high tide you must come by boat. There is a rather shabby wooden garage and a stone cottage.

Quite wisely, Mme Carrel takes us first up the big rock northeast of the house: "Before we go in that horrible house." There are violets and bluebells in the rocks, and heather and gorse. A wonderful view, out to open sea, broken with wild rocks.

Then we climb down and go in the house: all feeling of charm leaves as you walk inside. The walls are dark and covered with matting. The hall is completely darkened with stained-glass windows at the back and over the door. There are cheap plaques, pictures, and chandeliers on the walls. The dining room on the right is very big like a hotel—a second-class hotel. It has an *enormous* table in it (ugly carved oak, sitting on carved greyhounds), covered with oilcloth, matting, and a cloth tablecloth. There is an old carved wood mantel, heavy but quite nice, and next to it two heavy Victorian dressers, all scrolls. The chairs are ugly and upholstered with red. There is a rather nice old carved wood box.

The living room was the worst (Mme C. rushed to the back windows and threw them open so we could look beyond the room to the sea!), the walls hung with dark cheap paper or matting and, over that, dark cheap modern tapestries. A huge white bust of Ambroise Thomas (the musician who built the house and the present owner's uncle) on the mantel (also draped with carpeting). There were three or four bad rugs, all different colors, on the floor, and at least four large carved sofas or day beds lining the walls, all covered with rugs or upholstering. Some elaborate carved upholstered stiff chairs filled the rest of the wall space. No, I have forgotten one large gilt, heavily carved, long side table, one large, heavily carved mahogany or oak table, one spindly Victorian table, one corner cupboard (no top)—not bad—one enormous mirror behind Ambroise, two phenomenally narrow tall mirrors in two corners, framed in plush, one very nice little old narrow desk, carved, French provincial.

I put my hand on this immediately, going over to it, as you might to a friend in a room full of overstuffed, overdressed strangers. "This," I said feebly, "is nice, and that (grasping the cupboard in the corner) is not bad." You looked from one thing to another trying to find something that you could use. That perhaps? No—never. This? No—*couldn't,* etc.

I have forgotten to mention the numerous carpeted stools, the "whatnots" hung on the walls, and the gilt wreath given to Thomas, and various Victorian pictures.

The whole room gave the effect of being heavily carpeted like those "houses" one built as a child out of overturned chairs covered with rugs. Floors, walls, and furnishings were all helter-skelter, odd colors, horribly run-down, dilapidated, and dirty.

The kitchen was simple and nice, the only clean place in the house, the pans shining (which speaks well for the woman who is there).

We went upstairs. The bedrooms were practically empty of furniture except for poor iron bedsteads and cheap chiffoniers. The walls were covered with dirty paper or flowered cloth. One dreadful room, done throughout—curtains and wall—with a red and white stripe, flowered on top.

But they were well arranged and there is plenty of room. I was already planning to put people in them.

The baby here, Miss W. here, Jon here, next to us. Here, the guest room. Five rooms on second floor and three, perhaps four, on the third floor, or attic. No toilets at all; we will have to buy chemical ones. No cupboards; we will have to put them in. (Plenty of storage space in the attic, and there is a good cellar.) Then we walk around the house, the marvelous view out the back, over the sea. There are clumps of narcissus out and bushes of hydrangea all around the house.

I plant cuttings brought from Long Barn in the tiny cramped bed in front of the house, poking them through the wires. I have no hope of their living, as the book said "shade," and there was no shady place protected from the sheep and rabbits and wind!

We go through the garage, which has, besides room for one

car, two small rooms and a storage room, and the little cottage where the man, his wife, and thirteen-year-old son live.

We walk around the island and off it, from little rocky island to rocky island. One with a wall on it, a few trees, and flowering gorse, like a nest. I thought of Jon making a house under the boughs of the pine, sheltered from the wind by the wall. The man has tried to raise potatoes, making pathetic little fields between the rocks on several islands. But the rabbits have eaten most of his work. He was not allowed to kill them because the owners wanted them kept for hunting. Also he was forced to trap the animals which killed the rabbits.

"Now we will do just the opposite," said Mme Carrel.

We walked over the rocky spit and the muddy flats to the middle island and then across the bridge and back here to Saint-Gildas. I was very tired from all that walking over stones, climbing rocks, and the excitement.

Tea, and a rest—my mind swimming with plans.

Saturday, April 9th

Mme Carrel to Tréguier to see lawyers. C. and I, after that delicious breakfast of coffee in a huge bowl, and raisin bread, sit and write in Dr. Carrel's study and then go in a boat around to Illiec and look at it from the sea. There are wonderful rocks on the sea side. It is quite rough, but clear and fine. The cold, the wind, and the put-put of the motor remind me of the North.

C. says he's going to get a Breton fisherboat and sail in and out of the rocks.

Pierre and his uncle—a very nice weathered fisherman—take us. The Sept-Îles show blue on the horizon. (They, I suppose, will take the place of the Camden Hills as weather indicators.) You can see the white lighthouse on Île-aux-Moines, and a red sailboat.

After lunch the man comes who does *réparations*. He looks like a fisherman with blue trousers and cap and has a nice face. His name is François. We go over to Illiec and climb into the house.

Then follows an hour of going over the house with François, Mme Carrel talking all the time:

"*Tiens, François, voyez donc ici—tout ça . . .*" etc., etc.

She tells him to take the coverings off the walls and replaster where necessary, like Saint-Gildas.

François takes a kitchen knife out of his pocket and picks at the walls: "*Pah! C'est mauvais.*" We go over all the rooms for plastering, then for floors, fireplaces, etc.

I water the cuttings and ask the toothless red-cheeked fisherman's wife to give them some water. "*Oui, tous les jours, Madame,*" she says, smiling. Her name is Marie Yvonne, but you are supposed to say "Maryvonne," all in one.

Also we speak to Louis, Maryvonne's husband, about clearing the gorse from the front of the house.

We are still working in the *cave,* or cellar, when Pierre appears tousled-headed. We will have to go, right away. "*La mer!*"—the sea. The tide will soon be too low. We all scramble for shore. How the tide governs your life here.

Sunday, April 10th

Work in the morning. Read all the first part of the book. How will I ever get this book rewritten, corrected, and off, and Illiec fixed up, and Long Barn moved out of, by the first of June. I won't, I suppose (to say nothing of a visit from Mother!).

After lunch we go in the boat to Illiec, a strong wind against us, quite choppy and spray in your face. It takes about fifteen minutes. It looks beautiful today. The sea is a deep blue green and the cypresses, a dark green against them.

We start sorting out furniture. It is such a relief to tear down some of those dreadful things. We take all the pictures and whatnots off the walls and pile the gilt tables in one corner of the living room to be sold immediately. It looks better even now. We keep only one hideous sofa and two hideous tables and quite a few hideous chairs. You have to have chairs.

We take the leaves out of the "hotel table" and shut it up, but we must have it, to eat on. It is dreadful. The dogs holding it up are even more noticeable when it is small, and it has four extra legs! Finally, just before we leave, I run out in back and find a tough simple kitchen table in the ironing room and ask C. if we can't use that instead? He says fine, so we roll the dogs out into the to-be-sold furniture pile. We save the bust and all souvenirs of Ambroise Thomas. As C. says, it somehow seems ungrateful to turn him out.

Then Maryvonne and Louis come around. Mme Carrel tells them not to let anyone on the island and talks to them about plans for employing them, their work, wages, etc. They are to have the whole of the cottage, unless someone else comes to work (they only had one room before—for the three of them!). He is to do the boat work and all work outside, and she to do cooking and housework. The boy (for extra) to do errands.

They are very pleased.

My cuttings are not doing very well—the santolina and viburnum. But the lavender and rosemary look all right.

Mme Carrel thinks she can start a hedge of bushes along the cliff (transplanted from Saint-Gildas) and maybe some trees. She has an extra big bed she can lend us, so we don't have to use the heavy mahogany ultra-carved one of Ambroise Thomas. She also says Antoinette will teach Maryvonne how to cook. And Pierre will show Louis how to garden and set traps for rabbits!

She is marvelous, one of those people who seem to carry life in them, an excess of it, a whole stream on which they sweep along the people they touch (like C., a little).

We go home quite happy, feeling we (Mme Carrel, that is) have accomplished a great deal. I look at the house as we ride back in the wind and think, Yes, deep green-blue shutters will look very nice, and the windows, inside, done a lighter shade.

I have an idea of the house as cream and blue (clean and light) and modern reproductions on the walls, Cézanne blues, Derain blues, Van Gogh blues, and the Brueghel ships. And blue flowers at the doors, lavender, rosemary, and that blue flowering bush at Long Barn.

Monday, April 11th

Warmer today—still and bright. I wake up thinking, What a lovely day it will be at Illiec!

We give a plate to an artist in Tréguier to copy for the color of our shutters and woodwork, a blue green.

There are fishermen on the dock this evening (at Port-Blanc), spreading their nets. They have just come in from the Sept-Îles. They are ruddy and gay with berets on their heads; and one or two women. They all smile and say a word to Mme Carrel, and to us as we go by.

Mme Carrel always calls them *mes enfants!*

Tuesday, April 12th

C. and Mme Carrel off early on a long day. Chantal (de la Motte—Mme Carrel's niece) and I have breakfast together. Then I work all morning. It is quite cold, a wind blowing and overcast. I am cold working and put on my gloves to write and sit on my feet.

After tea I work again, until they come at 8:15. I am so glad to see them. I have been very bored and discouraged—that dreadful chapter. It is smoother but just as long and just as dull. I feel it must all be rewritten, and yet there is no other way to write it.

We are quite gay at supper. C. and Mme Carrel stopped at a china place and brought home a few samples. It will be nice to have Brittany ware at Illiec. Also they saw some nice pieces of old furniture at Saint-Brieuc. We are going to stay over and see them together.

To bed early.

Wednesday, April 13th

Work all morning on chapters. In the afternoon we walk over to Illiec, at low tide. It takes about ten or fifteen minutes. You can go quite easily but you always get your feet muddy going over the flats, just before Illiec.

Louis has cut down almost all the *ajonc* (gorse) in front of the house and has cut the dead wood off the vines on the house and off the santolina plant. He has cleaned the brush around the well and dug a little bed. There are two ladders up against the house. It looks quite active. He has done very well, especially considering he has no tools except a blunt old handleless sickle. We make a list (in French) of the things he needs right away.

I find a lovely place for a rock garden in a hollow high up in the rocks, between the house and the garage.

We plot out where we can have a low hedge of *fusain* bushes (spindle tree) in front of the cliff. (This is Mme Carrel's idea, and a very good one.) It will act as windbreak and hedge and grows quickly. We can put them in right away.

I should like cypress trees—a row—looking through their black trunks at the water and hills on shore behind, for the front of the house. At the back, a low wall, and then right out to sea and rocks—very Tristan and Isolde.

C. is so afraid I will screen away all his rocks and sea!

We ask about water in the summer, in a dry year. Is there enough from the cistern? Maryvonne says there were twenty-eight people in the house last summer and there was always enough—*"même pour laver"*!

Then the man comes and tells us we must go if we want to get back to Saint-Gildas or the tide will cut us off. We hurry back over the flats. Already a stream of water cuts in two the long pebbly bar that links Illiec's nearest island to Saint-Gildas's far one.

Thursday, April 14th

At 9:30 we rush to get on the boat, before the tide is too low to get across to Port-Blanc. There is quite a wind blowing. On the dock a fisherman is trying to make a fire go under a huge black caldron. Every once in a while he takes off the lid and stirs it with an oar. It is a thick red dye to dye the nets (as a preservative). The fire won't burn, as the wind blows it. He tears up old wicker lobster cages and stuffs them underneath. A little barefoot girl hops around watching.

We start off for Tréguier and Saint-Brieuc through gorse-edged fields and gray villages with many steepled churches. We arrive at Saint-Brieuc at 11:30 (in one and a half hours) and rush to a very high-class antique shop (most of the things are Directoire, Empire, etc.). The owner says he will stay open for us after twelve (the shops close from twelve to two). Then we hurry to a big hardware store. Mme Carrel sweeps all before her. They close the doors on us, but we wait for our package so Louis will have something decent to cut gorse with. Then back to the antique shop.

They have a very nice armoire, also an old oak chest, quite beautiful (we *do* run to chests—we have three English ones!), and a small buffet—a low chest with doors that I think would be useful. Also some pretty chairs.

Upstairs I find a little sofa that I love, provincial, with *vieux tapis,* old chintz, on it. Little and low and very pretty. The *antiquaire* says he has some chairs that go with it but he can't find them and can't give us a price on them. He will not say whether he will sell the sofa alone.

It is such a temptation to take things that are *almost* right in order to have your house look nice as quickly as possible.

On the way back we stop at Tréguier at Savina's.[1] He is an artist who copies old furniture.

He is coming to Saint-Gildas tomorrow to see Mme Carrel's chairs. We have decided to have him make six dining-room chairs like hers. Also he will come with us to Illiec, to see if he has "some idea," as Mme Carrel says, of what to do with the tower off the study. She thinks he might panel it, put in bookshelves, *une petite bibliothèque.* He has a nice ruddy face, is sensitive and

[1] Joseph Savina, friend of the Carrels, artist and sculptor who ran a woodwork shop in Tréguier.

quick, and has very good taste. He says he can take us to a little town in the south of Brittany where we can get some old pieces of furniture.

When we get back to Port-Blanc after our long day we see the nets all rust-colored and hung out to dry on big poles. The fisherman must have got the pot to boil!

Good Friday, April 15th

I work all morning on chapters. It is cold, overcast, and very windy. I work with a coat and gloves on. Also after lunch.

After tea, Savina comes to Saint-Gildas. Then we go over in the boat to Illiec. The sea is very gray as are the sky and the rocks. Only the hill of the middle island of Saint-Gildas is a cushion of yellow gorse. Quite choppy, and spray in your face.

Savina is very nice and tells me that he will try his best to do something pretty for the house. We go over the shutters first, deciding on color. Savina is a great help. Then into the house, and gradually, from asking his advice about the tower (he is going to panel it, put bookshelves in, a curved window, a little desk, and a curved door!), we are asking his advice about the woodwork, the floors, the stairs, etc. He says the woodwork, doors, windows, and mantels can be painted wood-color or stained, and they will look very nice. He will supervise the whole thing, *comme un architecte*.

He and Mme Carrel talk so fast, running from one thing to another, that my head (translating French, trying to keep up) spins following them and C. just gives up, as he does when some member of the Morrow family gets started. He leans against a door and waits until they stop.

Savina will have our dining-room chairs done by the time we arrive—the 1st of June—and sell *all* the things we do not want, as he will lend us things until we get them. So we push out the dreadful red chairs from the "save" room into the "sell" room! I am intensely relieved to see them go. I couldn't bear to think of eating on them the first night.

Finally we leave at about seven, but not before Maryvonne comes up with a strange, long, dry pancake, which we tear in four and eat, standing among the discarded furniture.

Then a rough ride home, the wind blowing from the northeast, stormy and wild.

We are very happy about the afternoon and to have a man like Savina in charge. I hope it will not be much more expensive, but Mme Carrel says he is very fair about prices and I am sure he will save us in the end—at least from mistakes. I think he is pleased about doing it, too, which is nice.

Saturday, April 16th

Decide not to fly to England, as it still looks very stormy and low, and it will take half the day to find out whether the weather is worse somewhere else.

Work all morning. In the afternoon it clears up (we could have gone after all!).

Easter Sunday, April 17th

Wake to see it is overcast again and the same wild wind blowing. C. says it is not as bad as yesterday and will clear and we can go.

When we get down for breakfast we find that Mme Carrel and Chantal have gone to *Mass* and Mme Carrel when she was over in Port-Blanc telephoned M. Masson at Morlaix that the weather was too bad for us to go! So we can't go till tomorrow.

I am somewhat dashed, as I hoped to be home by Friday anyway and now we won't be home until Monday. We went away for three or four days and stayed almost two weeks. Work all morning and most of afternoon correcting chapters, both with C. and alone. It is frightful work, so discouraging, looking all the time at your failures, your mistakes and imperfections. C. goes at it like a bulldog. I don't see how he can stand it either.

We go over to Illiec at three at low tide. There is a tearing wind blowing, but it has cleared up, big clouds blowing by, a very blue sky.

I begin to think it is going to be very cold and blowy at Illiec and I plan for *enclosed* gardens, and *small* rooms to sit in, with fires.

[*Long Barn*] *Monday, April 18th*

Leave Saint-Gildas, cold, blowy, and overcast; drive to Morlaix.

Fly over Illiec and then Mont-Saint-Michel—the long hunk of land—up the coast to Saint-Inglevert (through some rain and a little snow!). Across the Channel to Lympne. It is *very* cold. England is overcast; scattered showers, as usual.

Home at 11:30—Thor barking and a pile of mail.

Tuesday, April 19th

A rushed day. Much to do and feeling tired. Jon looks very well and the baby big and rosy.

The garden looks lovely. Jon and I take a walk around it and up the wood path. The fruit blossoms are out on the four trees in the beds, and the pink clematis under my window. Blackbirds and thrushes are singing, and a nightingale.

I go out and tell Hook and Hammond we are leaving (they don't mind nearly as much as I do).

Miss H. is crushed that there is no bathroom at Illiec!

C. going over the proofs of his ms.[1] all day. I correct grammar. It is not nearly as hard work as he puts in on mine but I get quite dizzy doing it. It is so involved and difficult to follow.

Friday, April 22nd

Work all morning. Hear the cuckoo.

Very tired. This week has been such a rush—no time to think, read, or go out for walk. But a lot done.

Saturday, April 23rd

Work all morning. In the afternoon Jon, C., and I go to Maidstone, I, to practice for my driving test on Monday. I go through all the signals, answer questions, etc.

---

[1] *The Culture of Organs,* co-authored with Alexis Carrel.

Miss W. put some fresh stiff tulips in my room. They were incredibly beautiful the first night. Stiff and straight like candles, crisp, unyielding, graceless as youth. They are really heartbreaking in their brittle spun-glass beauty, because you know they will only be like that for a few hours and then they will sway, droop a little in "graceful" more yielding profiles, losing that stiff uncompromising wide-eyed look of youth.

I meant to sit quite still and look at them a long time until I discovered something I felt sure was hidden in them. But I couldn't. I must work, get the chapters done, recorrect, see that the children are fed, write letters, get to bed.

Once in bed, I lay there thinking of them, regretfully, disappointed, as though I had missed something priceless.

And so life seems to go. There is no time or place for revelations.

Monday, April 25th

I work all morning on the book. In the afternoon to Maidstone with Miss H. to take my driving test. I do not drive badly and make no mistakes (except I do not do quite a good enough back turn into a side road the first time). He treats me, with the smug patronage the English use for all Americans, as a nervous child. I answer all the questions correctly and never go over the speed limit.

And am appalled when I drive up to a stop to have him say in that kindly grandmotherly tone, "I am afraid you are not quite up to the grade. You see, we find you drive a little fast," with a patronizing smile. "I suppose you all go very fast in America. And you don't keep enough to the left. You see, over here we keep very strictly to the left. And then at pedestrian crossings it isn't a wise thing, you know, to pull up so abruptly. But I think if you follow my suggestions in another month you may be able to take the test again." He said, of course, he thought I was rather nervous; he had done his best to put me at ease!

I was aghast. I thanked him and said I was afraid I couldn't take the test again as I was leaving England in another month. He said he was sorry and possibly, after a month, they could arrange to have it quite quickly in a day or two.

As he was leaving the car he said kindly that I didn't feel quite sure of myself, I probably hadn't been driving long.

"About fifteen years," I said.

"Well, perhaps you are not quite familiar with the car."

"I have been driving the car for two years."

He then asked me what I thought of English driving. I said I thought on the whole it was very bad.

He also said half apologetically that he supposed I had "all kinds of licenses?"

"Yes," I said, "I have an American license, of course, and an international license."

Then they went off down the street.

I was angry all night about it. It was not exactly the failure. It was that air of kindly patronage—the smugness of the English. He just had a fixed idea in his mind of nervous, fast American driving and he assumed I was it.

It is really very funny, too, because according to English regulations I was allowed to drive a car alone for the first year on my U. S. license (killing heaven knows how many people, for all they cared!). And now after two years I take a test and am termed an "incompetent driver." After fifteen years' record of driving in the United States without an accident, and two years in England. The last test I took was in New York. I am a good enough driver for New York but not for Maidstone!

It falls—a tiny last pinprick—on all the other English humiliations and the sore place they made. My book, not selling here. No friends in two years. And that personal snobbery of the English you meet almost every time you meet an Englishman which always hurts—at least me.

C. and I went for a long walk up the big hill in the mist tonight. I feel quite sad to think of leaving England. How I have loved this place, but what illusions I have lost here.

Long Barn, Weald, Sevenoaks, Tuesday, April 26th

Mother darling—

I have been working hard on the book. (I am *so* glad you like the title! It strengthens me in it. *Listen! the Wind* it is.) After we got back from Illiec there were letters waiting here for us from Harcourt, Brace. They liked the chapter very much. I got such a nice letter from both Mr. Harcourt and Mr. Sloane. It quite set me up. Also they liked the title and I can use it. And they liked very much a perfectly *beautiful* book cover that C. has done for it. I am not trying to get them anything but a first draft by June 1st (that will be hard enough work) and not the finished ms. until July 1st or August. That may bring the book out later. But I cannot go any faster. There is so much to do at the same time—moving out, moving in. I expect we will move out the last of May. C. and I plan to go to Illiec a week early, to install basins, tin tubs, chemical toilets, etc., and to get an extra person to heat and haul water for washing and to do the housework, and all the thousand last-minute things.

DIARY   *Tuesday, April 26th*

Go into Sevenoaks to sign papers. The Commissioner of Oaths asks C. if he passed his driving test—with humor (the last time he was in there he was about to take it, which much amused the C. of O.). We said yes, and told him about yesterday and my not passing, and he got quite upset and said that he never heard anything so preposterous. He said his boy was failed for no reason and that they have to fail half the people in order to get double the money (the six-shilling charge).

Thursday, April 28th

C. goes to Reading early to fly to Southampton; gone all day. I call Mrs. Berkeley [the doctor's wife] and ask Nigel to come for the afternoon and her for tea. It was nice to see her (to see anyone!). The normalness of our sitting there together having tea, discussing schools, babies, and boys while our boys sat and ate currant buns on the sofa was very gratifying to me. It acted as a kind of balm to some place that had been needing it. It wasn't that anything we did or said was interesting, but the fact itself was gratifying. And I like Mrs. Berkeley. She has a difficult time to manage her home, a doctor's house, with two children and no cook and the telephone going all hours of the day and night.

After tea the boys ran away and we continued talking until we heard *bellows* from upstairs. We rushed up. They had been chasing one another and Jon had slammed a door in Nigel's face and Nigel had been badly knocked. He screamed loudly. Jon was whimpering. I reprimanded him and he cried.

Then Nigel discovered a wheelbarrow and was fascinated with it and took it outside. And—just as it was time to leave—they were playing quite well together, Jon gathering sticks for the wheelbarrow which Nigel pushed (each at his favorite occupation, but really co-operating for a purpose!). And each said, *"Must* I go now?" "Must you go now?" and we looked on and were pleased because we each knew our own boy had gotten a little of the companionship and competition he needed badly.

Saturday, April 30th

Work in the morning. In the early afternoon C., Margaret [Morgan], and I motor over to Sissinghurst to see Mrs. Nicolson. It is the nicest visit we have ever had. She was alone and it was much easier to talk. She looked quite lovely in her black corduroy knickers and coat and her black felt hat, with two police dogs straining at the leash. And the place was beautiful: all kinds of wine and pink wallflowers growing up the old walls, and walks of red tulips, and a whole carpet of primroses, primulas, etc., under the flowering apple trees, like a Persian print.

We told her how we hated to leave Long Barn and I asked her what would grow in a garden by the sea. She said that if hydrangeas grew there, lots of other things might, and she gave me some names. I can see I am going to become one of those gardening women, after all!

At tea C. talked politics with her, and "Does Mr. Nicolson think . . . etc." And after tea we walked through the garden and left, she applauding my "Learner's" start in the car (with two large L's on)—"L. for Lindbergh," she said, "not for Learner!"

I could not help thinking how much nicer it was than generally—some real contact. Is it just because we've known her now for two years at very infrequent intervals, or is it because we're leaving, or is it only because it's so much easier to talk to one person at a time? (Unless you know them equally well and have the same things in common.)

Then home, just in time to put Jon to bed before C.'s visitors arrive—Colonel Scanlon and the Burdette Wrights[1]—aviation. The supper was good, though confused with people jumping up and down. Those ham-cheese-sauce things first and duck and applesauce, peas, salad, and Mme Carrel's *chocolat crême*—quite good, really.

After supper the men very quickly disappeared into the study to talk aviation, while Margaret, Mrs. Wright, and I sat around the fire and tried to talk. Mrs. Wright is a nice average American who has not been here very long. She had just spent the day at Knole. She professed a polite interest in the Sackville family, whereupon Margaret and I launched upon the full history, re *Pepita*.[2] This was a mistake. Mrs. Wright was very tired and had a frightful head cold. She got more and more confused, "Who was that—Mrs. Nicolson?" "No, her mother—the second Pepita." "Oh, about when *was* that?" "Oh, well, late Victorian." "And she married . . . ?" "A second Lionel Sackville. . . ." "And how old was she then?" etc.

Sunday, May 1st

This morning Lady Astor called C. and said she wanted him to meet Sir Thomas Inskip, Minister for Co-ordination of Defense,

---

[1] Burdette Wright, vice president and director of Curtiss-Wright Corporation.

[2] *Pepita*, Vita Sackville-West's biography of her grandmother and her mother. Pepita, the grandmother, was a Spanish dancer; her daughter, Victoria, whose father was Lionel, 2nd Lord Sackville, married Lionel, 3rd Lord Sackville.

and would we come over for lunch and dinner and the night. He said, Yes, but we had Margaret Morgan with us, and she said, Bring her along, which I didn't mind doing as they have a huge house and staff and never know how many people are there for lunch. We broke it to Margaret, who was pleased but slightly startled and petrified. I know just how she feels, too. She said, "I have a *very* nice tweed suit in London." She arrived here (knowing we live the most mouselike life, never see anyone, entertain, or go out) with her old tweed suit, one sweater, one tennis dress, and one wool dress. And for the first time in all her visits here she was taken to Sissinghurst, then people came to dinner, and on Sunday we go to Lady Astor's!

It is pouring rain. I get into the checked jacket and new skirt (it is never warm enough to wear nice things in England). Jon sees us as we go. Bedraggled and wet in his old red macintosh and hat, he looks up from behind the woodshed as I run to the garage: "Where are you going?" "I'm going out to lunch, Jon dear." "Why do you have to go?" (It is quite rare for him to mind, but today with the rain and Hammond away he did.)

Drive through the pouring rain (*very* good—for the drought) to Taplow and Cliveden. I drive most of the way while C. navigates. Margaret sings us Noël Coward's "The Stately Homes of England"!

We arrive just before lunch and drive in that perfectly kept and magnificent place. There are about eight cars parked in front of the portico. We draw up the little Ford with the L's on it, at the end. And walk in. Lord Astor meets us at the door. (I think he is *the* nicest man I've met in England, very quick, keen, perceptive, and kind.) He takes us very quickly up a backstairs to Lady Astor's room and calls "Nancy!" knocking at the doors.

She looks lovely in pale blue, and is her usual bantering self. So we are quickly made at home. Then swept downstairs.

She starts to introduce us: Sir Thomas Inskip, an oldish lady, one or two young people, and then gives up and just waves her hand: "There are too many of you!" There were indeed, lined up in front of the enormous fireplace, dozens of young men, as usual, standing stiffly around, and quite a sprinkling of young women, casual and well dressed and coifed.

We go in to lunch. She seats a few people—C. and me—and then lets the others scatter. I sit between Lord Astor and Sir Thomas (who has the nice-looking oldish lady on the other side). Lord Astor is kindness itself. I am afraid I talk too much, out of shyness, partly, but he is such a temptation, because he is both understanding and intelligent. I tell him we (C. and I) admire very much what they are doing now, just lately, both in rearmament and in their new realistic policy of trying to make peace, to meet people on their own grounds.

He says the trouble with getting the nation behind Chamberlain is that he is so little known; speaks of great opposition to Chamberlain.

I am sitting up and on my toes. My whole attitude talking to a man like Lord Astor is: Dear God, let me escape before he finds out that I'm *not* the intelligent daughter of a very intelligent father, or the intelligent wife of a very intelligent husband. This is the wrong attitude, even if it is true, as it makes you breathless and shy or bumptious and stuttering.

I do not feel at ease with Sir Thomas. He looks very British and John-Bullish and un-get-at-able. Though, no doubt, some of it is just British reserve, shyness, and lack of social grace, and my conversation was mostly informational and "My husband says," or "My husband thinks" . . . on Germany, aviation, etc.

He said the great lesson to be learned from both the wars in China and in Spain was that bombing did comparatively little damage. That he should indiscriminately lump the flying in China with the flying in Spain made me feel he did not know much about the subject (flying—*not* damage done by bombs). In fact, I should put him down as one of those typically English bulldogs who will *not* see anything that is unpleasant or detrimental. But perhaps I was wrong. He may see it and just put a British face on it. (Most of my information *was* unpleasant, too, I am afraid: German aviation preparedness, gliding camps, etc.!) I did not contradict him on the bombing (or anything). He made a very uncontradictable point—that no real objectives had been destroyed that way, that the communications had not even been cut, south of Madrid, which led me to ask whether the bombing had been done by German or Italian planes. Answer: Mostly Italian. (I *cannot* understand how modern German bombing could not be more successful. C. says he is able, though I should not have guessed it. But C. talked more with him.)

The lunch was *delicious,* eggs in baked apples in pastry, etc. The plates whisked out under your nose (they have to, to get through with so many people). The table stretched the length of the room. There were twenty or more at it—C. and Lady Astor at the other end, and several extra chairs. I suppose they never know just how many will be there.

We go into the big green room, great masses of white and purple lilacs, beech branches, etc., a flock of young girls wait for me to go out first—*me*—think! There are only three or four older women who go out first! I am startled.

Lady Violet Astor[1] comes and talks to me. She is nice—Mother's sort of person. She lives at Hever Castle. I am sorry we have not met her before. We talk about the Younghusbands. She is lovely-looking too, English and fair, a soft voice and face, in soft blue. She will age nicely. She invites us to Hever Castle next Sunday.

Lady Astor is trying to stuff pillows in some Peer's waistcoat to make him look dignified and portly. He doesn't seem to mind.

Everyone else looks on. The young girls talk about gardens. I draw up to Margaret so we can discuss the strange lilies (but she seems to be getting on quite well, especially at lunch).

Lady Astor is going out to play golf. She instructs the young girls to take us for a walk (the men have disappeared for good). The girls, including Wissie, her daughter, go to get shoes, coats,

[1] Wife of the Honorable John Jacob Astor, youngest son of the 1st Viscount Astor, chairman of the Times Publishing Co., and M. P. Dover Division of Kent.

etc., while Margaret and I are left with two or three women. One, the oldish one, and a gray-haired intelligent or wishes-to-be-considered-intelligent one, talk about spiritualism. The oldish lady in black sits on the bench and puts in very sensible New England tart remarks now and then, bringing it all down to earth. I like her. She is a real person.

Out for a walk with Wissie, who talks loudly the whole time about the gardens, the greenhouses, her herb garden, the "knot garden" she wants to have, and her nurse problems ("always playing tennis with the second footman!"). It is incredibly funny —"the stately homes of England." We see miles of greenhouses, melons in nets, peaches up the sides of roofs, figs, orchids, grapes, etc., and miles and miles of lovely walks; heath gardens and Botticelli gardens and formal gardens and sunken gardens and kitchen gardens and herb gardens. Also the little World War I sunken cemetery with flat stones which has a timeless air of always autumn—still, mossy, and leaves dropping. We talk gardens, mostly, I asking for information, for the island.

Then back to the house for tea. (I have decided we *must* leave after tea. It suddenly comes over me—I *cannot* stay another meal. Lord Astor might discover how unintelligent I am! Margaret seems to agree with me and also, evidently, C. It is best not to outstay your welcome.)

But tea was fun, and before tea I discover that that wonderful oldish woman is Dame Edith Lyttelton.[1] She perches herself upon a table and we talk—*Man, the Unknown,* etc. She is the biggest person (woman) I think I have met in England, and the most interesting.

She gives me names of books. There is a completely natural grandeur about her that I love. I cannot describe it because she was not *grand,* but just rather New England and simple, but you were aware she was a great woman.

C. comes in and I catch his eye halfway across the room. He must meet her. I throw out the rope, rather a long way, to draw him in: "Here is an admirer of Dr. Carrel's book." (There, now

[1] New Zealand writer of novels and short stories.

they are connected, and both pleased to meet each other. But will C. *see* what a great woman she is? How can I tell him!)

Then tea: Lady Astor and C. on Germany, and C. shocking the life out of everyone by describing Germany's strength.

Lady Astor violent on the French and their actions in Germany at the end of the war: "Putting Negro troops in and demanding brothels!"

Then she takes us off into her sitting room to talk.

Someone comes running in: "Queen Mary on the telephone! Quick—Queen Mary!"

It turns out it is the *boat* and not the *Queen*, but even that is exciting enough.

The Kennedys[1] arrive, Mrs. and many tall daughters.

People are always arriving here. Confusion about going.

Finally we are off after signing the guest book with a divine pen which C. asks the name of for me and which Lord Astor in a quick perfect gesture takes out and gives to him.

Long Barn, Thursday, May 5th

To town in morning with C. to have lunch with Lady Astor and George Bernard Shaw! I rush to have my hair fixed (where I read the *Times* from front to back in an effort to be well informed).

To Lady Astor's at 4 St. James's Square. A beautiful old Georgian house. Lord Astor, Ambassador Bullitt,[2] and Ambassador Kennedy are there alone when we come in. Lord Astor always makes you feel at ease at once. So, of course, do the two Americans. (It is strange, after living away from home for two years, one is struck, when one meets Americans again, by a delicious ease in meeting one's own countrymen, hearing one's own language, like suddenly striking a warm patch of water in the swimming pool.) Also, how strange it is that Ambassadors used to be

[1] The family of Joseph P. Kennedy, U. S. Ambassador to Great Britain 1937–40.

[2] William C. Bullitt, U. S. Ambassador to France 1936–41 (to Russia, 1933–36).

rather awesome and revered gentlemen (with long beards and august presences) but now they are "young," and if not exactly "my own age" at least the right age for me, our generation.

Ambassador Bullitt had just come from Paris. He seemed nice, jovial, young. Ambassador Kennedy has a hearty attractive American face, ruddy, clean-cut, humorous, and intelligent. I liked him immediately.

Lady Astor came in and we were swept along through those lovely rooms. Various people came in—men, chiefly. I could not get them all straight. A nice Welshman they called T. J. (Thomas Jones[1]). He was twinkly and gay. He asked me how much of England I knew, and I said I had gone first to Wales, at which he shook my hand again. Also the Editor of the *Times*.

They were all people in or near the Government. They discussed how funny it was that Winston (Churchill) was going to attack the Government on the Irish settlement—the one thing that everyone everywhere agreed on. How like Winston, they said, he has to be on the other side!

George Bernard Shaw came in, erect, white-haired, but rather pale and old and not nearly as *fierce* as I had expected him, and Mrs. Shaw and a youngish cousin of Lady Astor's whose name I don't remember.

We were swept into the dining room. Lady Astor and George Bernard Shaw sat at one end of the table and Lord Astor at the other. I was next to G. B. S. and a man who came in late, an Englishman who had just come from Portugal—officially, I gathered—and was very intelligent.

It was hard talking to G. B. S.—one, because he is famous and you feel you can't just barge right in and say how many of his plays you've read, and because I felt shy at the thought of his brilliance. But also because he is old and used to being the center of things. Things must be turned toward him. Lady Astor did this very well, banging the table and saying in the beginning, "Now be quiet, I want to know why G. B. S. has turned Fascist.

[1] Dr. Thomas Jones, confidant of Lloyd George, Ramsay MacDonald, and Stanley Baldwin, Deputy Secretary to the British Cabinet in 1938.

Is it true?" Laughter. I think he said vaguely there was something to be said for Fascism. She bantered him about Russia, democracy, etc., but it was mostly banter; also about the Queen, whom everyone adores and he also apparently.

Much banter about the "Cliveden Set"[1] propaganda against the Astors—that they are Fascists, etc.

A charge answered by Lord Astor in a long letter to the *Times* this A.M. (What a good thing I read the invaluable *Times* this A.M. at the hairdresser's!)

The most interesting person to talk to was the man from Portugal, though I didn't talk much, because the conversation centered about Lady Astor and G. B. S. across from me. He said, in answer to a question of mine, that the *Anschluss* was a complete surprise and shock to Italy. That, among other things, Mussolini considers himself the Senior Dictator and rather resents the patronizing air of the Upstart Dictator, i.e., the "I will never forget this of you" telegrams, etc.

He also said (in answer to a comment of mine on the announcement in an Italian paper of Italy's approval of the Nazi statement that the unification of the German people was now at an end, read in the *Times* this A.M.) that yes, there certainly were a lot of German people under Italy, and they were among the worst treated minorities.

He also said that he did not think the *Anschluss* would be good for Germany in the end. They had too much to do as it was.

On the whole, though, the conversation was Lady Astor's. It was really too fast and too topical for either the old, like G. B. S., or the feminine, like me. But I loved sitting on the edge of my

---

[1] Reference is to an article on the Astors and their friends by Claud Cockburn in his small newssheet, *The Week* (he was also London correspondent for *Pravda*). It was he who created the term "Cliveden Set," accusing the group of pro-Nazi and pro-Fascist intrigues. Nancy Astor's biographer, Christopher Sykes, although obviously unsympathetic to her politics, dismisses these accusations as fabrications. See *Nancy* by Sykes, pp. 365-409. See also *Nancy Astor and Her Friends,* by Elizabeth Langhorne, p. 159 f.

chair listening to quick intelligent talk. All the people there *were* intelligent, well informed, alive, and vitally in politics, in history. It was exciting and invigorating—even though I didn't talk much.

I talked some, across the table, to Kennedy. We discussed the Jewish question, Lady Astor telling about her getting Judge Frankfurter's uncle out of Germany[1] and Kennedy telling about Lotte Lehmann, who broke down singing in the opera last night because of worry about her children in Austria.

Then out—the ladies. Mrs. Shaw is nice and intelligent. I liked her. I think she has spirit and sense.

Lady Astor says I have a very pretty hat; and I think I must have looked nice, for C. thought so and was pleased and happy about the whole thing.

C. has a good time talking to Kennedy—I cannot tear him away. Lady Astor sticks some false teeth in her mouth, entirely changes her face, and is an Englishwoman—rather a coarse one! C. and I both think someone else has come into the room. She goes up to C., nudges him, and asks him why he didn't marry a Mae West sort of woman instead of that little shrimp? She is screamingly funny.

Just as we go, it appears that she has asked us for dinner on the 23rd to meet the King and Queen! She says it is a dance—her grandest party—and I must have a tiara (*must* I?) and that C. must learn to dance before then and that we have all put up with him for too long!

We go out very gay into the fresh London sunshine, excited by the people and conversation. C. pleased at Kennedy, someone he can really talk to.

[1] Nancy Astor besieged the German Ambassador in London with calls in behalf of Judge Felix Frankfurter's uncle, who had been imprisoned in Vienna at the time of the *Anschluss*. As a result the uncle was released. Lord Astor, "apparently alone among the Englishmen who had met Hitler, had had the courage to mention the mistreatment of the Jews." Quoted from Elizabeth Langhorne, *Nancy Astor and Her Friends*.

We walk almost all the way to Charing Cross. C. says I look pretty but it is only really because I am happy and the day is lovely.

Back to Sevenoaks in time to give orange juice to Land and have tea with both children in the study—a lovely calming antidote to excitement. The wind is my favorite kind, turning the leaves white. The poplars are all bending this way and that.

Sunday, May 8th

A cable from Mother: arriving for teatime! Read the Sunday paper quite thoroughly, foreign-affairs parts, and arrange a small bouquet of flowers for Mother's bureau, like the ones she does—forget-me-nots, one pink tulip, rosemary, candytuft, and pink thrifts.

C. and I drive to Hever Castle for lunch. It is the most perfect castle I have ever seen, small, moated, beautifully set in a park. But this does not convey the warmth, the utter charm of the place, which is I think due to the fact that added to the great age and beauty of the place, there is a freshness and color given by its being lived in and beautifully cared for. Lovely flowers growing around the moat and the lawns outside (a big bed of blue forget-me-nots which were reflected in the moat), flowers at the big portcullis gate and drawbridge, wallflowers, and a purplish shrub (olearia) that looked like Michaelmas daisy, azaleas, and clematis. It gave the place an indescribable charm—this old and evidently very real fortified castle turned gay and young with flowers, like weapons of war used in a parade with ribbons tied on them. (I'm thinking of very *old* weapons—Elizabethan ones, used for show only!)

Lady Violet Astor was not there but he came forward, a rather shy, distinguished man, not as easy as his brother but very nice and intelligent. It was not easy for him as she had been called away to a very ill sister and he had never met us. There was also the son of the house, his American bride, Lady Astor's niece, an elderly man, and another English couple, youngish, named

Anderson. The man, Anderson, got into an argument with C. over the state of aviation in England and Germany (you'd think *anyone* would know better than to do that), and C. got himself deeper and deeper. It was a gloomy prospect that was painted. The man said he didn't think a war with Germany would last three months—they would collapse. C. said he thought it would be truer said the other way around—at least that it was doubtful whether England could win, prepared as she was now, against Germany. Though he thought it would take more than three months for Germany to win. This statement was, to put it mildly, not very well received.

Then we went out in the garden and the men retired to talk more Germany, see the house, and cool off!

Lovely garden, old trees and walks, the "Anne Boleyn walk." This is where Henry VIII came to court her. Up a hill, between aisles of trees, green turf steps. Rather Italianate gardens and lake, but very beautiful, and an old box garden with cut-out box figures.

We leave after the walk.

Home, I arrange more flowers, Jon cutting the tulips for me.

I get through tea and bathing and feeding Land before Mother comes. Jon was in his bath.

I hear the car and go out to the gate to meet them. The limousine is backed into the small gate, bags, baggage, a huge box on top (containing Jon's airplane, and duck for Land). Isabel in hat and veil! The inevitable Mr. Gregory and the chauffeur struggling with bags. And Mother very small, tired, eager, in black and white again.

Jon is very pleased to see her, and Land stares from the blanket with large eyes, but won't really smile.

It is lovely to see the guest room transformed into Mother's room in a few seconds: tissue paper, bags, hatboxes, Isabel unpacking, pictures on the bureau, powder (chamois square and all). Books, pamphlets, letters, and Mother's pink wrapper and slippers by the bed.

We cannot talk much, you never can at first, and I feel baffled by it—by the too much to say and show and catch up. The evening by the fire in the big room goes into plans—*whom* Mother has to see in London, *when* she is going to Paris, Rome. *Can* she stop and see us on Illiec for a night on the way home?

Mother to bed early. She did not sleep last night, from excitement.

I do not sleep very well either, for the same reason.

Monday, May 9th

Mother and I walk slowly around the place. The flowering trees in the lower beds are still slightly pink, the beech hedge a rich green, the grass another yellow green, and all the different greens and gray-greens on the shrubs—santolina, lavender, rosemary—that line the walks and beds.

Mother takes out her scissors and snips as we walk—one of her little bouquets, blue forget-me-not, a pink tulip, and, of course, candytuft.

It is perfect.

There are daisies, little English ones, in the grass. Mother says Grandma loved them and all English things. She says so sadly that you seem only to really understand your mother and father as they go. I know but I can say nothing. It is *Our Town* again.

Mother starts my book.

Wednesday, May 11th

Mother reads the rest of *Listen! the Wind*. She thinks it is much better than *North to the Orient*. Her suggestions on grammar and titles are very helpful. C. and I are quite thrilled at her excitement. She says to C. as she kisses me good night, "She's *your* wife—but she's *my* daughter!" which means a lot from the Puritan in Mother.

Thursday, May 12th—Land's first birthday

Another delicious spring day, soft, and a warm wind blowing. Yes, it *is* spring today—just today. And everything seems to bloom at once before one's eyes: the lilac bush, two big wrinkled pink poppies, the slender salmon tulips, the roses on the house (one large red rose has somehow crept into the big room and is blooming inside against the window).

Tea is a little hit-or-miss as Mother rushes up to change for the birthday picture. Land, oblivious, kicks on the mat. I change him into Mother's present of a light blue sweater-suit in which he looks very masculine and tough (how can we keep him in smocks!). He has a little round cake with one candle, and LAND in silver button candies on it. C. takes his picture sitting in Mother's lap and mine, while I try to make him smile.

It is a divine spring evening. The soft green of the fruit tree leaves, light against the beech hedge. It is like the evening last year just before I went to the hospital when I called C. out and said, "It is spring *right now,* this second is spring—look at it." He remembered it, too.

We walk around the garden in light coats.

Friday, May 13th

Work in morning.

Mother, C., and I to town on the 12:48. We get into the diner and C. asks for "everything we can get between here and London," which consists of soup, cold tongue, bread and butter, cheese and coffee. But it saves time. We are alone in the car.

Then Mother and I start out on a jaunt, by taxi, to Rose Taylor, to look for a BALL dress for me for Lady Astor's dinner. We go to all the places I have been dying to go to but felt I had no excuse. They are not really as expensive or terrifying as you might imagine. Rose Taylor has *lovely* things, but only one evening dress that would do, and that doesn't set me up enough. Besides, I don't want to take the *first* one I see. Mother feels that way, too. She says she'd be terribly disappointed if I took the first one and all our shopping were over! We walk along the Berkeley Street, Bond Street, Dover Street area. It is such fun, and Mother loves it. Then through that funny alleyway, back to Berkeley

Street into a cheap little shop with lots of models. I try on a few. The woman is very pressing: "Isn't this a *lovely* dress—she looks lawvly in that!" etc. I feel like a little girl. The things are not quite right, but the woman is insistent. Anything can be fixed. Too expensive? She'll reduce it. Don't like the lace? She can make it in another material. No time? She'll do it in four days.

I get more and more polite because I know that nothing will induce me to buy a dress from that woman—at least not that afternoon.

Mother and I, rather wilted, get into a taxi and I say "Anne Talbot," vaguely having a nice (and rather grand) impression of it from advertisements.

We are ushered in by a doorman and run up the gray-carpeted stairs of a house on Berkeley Square. A woman in gray at the top looks at us inquiringly. I ask if they have any ready-made evening dresses. She says not usually, but wouldn't we come in, perhaps they could show us something. Two women are sitting in the window going over books and books of samples. Two society women are quietly having tea and chatting casually. There isn't a sign of hurry, salesmanship, or a dress—only mirrors and carpets.

A model comes in, in a blue and silver, then out. More models come in. There is a pretty taffeta, very simple, a bouffant skirt, with shirred pannierlike pockets on the side. I ask Mother how much she thinks it would be. She says "Twenty guineas." (The one at Rose T. was twelve and a half. The most expensive one at the other place seventeen.)

We ask the saleslady about it. She says eighteen guineas, and that it could be done in another color—blue or pink. She has samples.

I decide to try the model on. It is long but very pretty. I say I would like it. We look at colors. They are going to get a big piece of material of a lavender blue. They will have it in an hour.

We will miss the 5:31 and Jon's reading time, but otherwise it will mean another trip to town tomorrow, so we decide to do it. I telephone so Jon won't be too disappointed.

We say we'll come back after tea and go out, very relieved and pleased.

We then go, again in a taxi, to the Berkeley for tea with Margaret and Gerald [Morgan], which is very nice, and then back to Anne Talbot, to see the color, a lovely grayish lavender blue, and then to Fortnum and Mason (an extra half-hour before the train cannot be wasted), where I buy a Coronation mug for Land, some Japanese biscuits for C., and Mother gets some tray cloths.

Then to the station, to sit back in tired contentment and think over our highly successful day.

Mother is as pleased as a girl. Just the kind of successful day she likes. We accomplished our errand with some trials and excitement, managed to see some people, and a little extra shopping you hadn't counted on!

C. meets the train. He is gay and teasing but I can see he is pleased about his day and mine ("Get a *good* dress now, *good* material"). He went (after his shopping) to the Royal Academy show and then to an art store where he bought me a highly special oil-paints box and book on landscape painting! Also a rubber eraser!

Monday, May 16th

I am dizzy with all that is crowding into this last ten days. And underneath it the ache of the beauty and happiness of this place— how I love it and hate to leave it. It is a very personal feeling. I love this house as if it were mine, part of me—as if I had made it and it had recognized and accepted me as belonging to it.

And the precious quality of the happiness we have had here. I feel dimly that I shall look back on this period as the happiest in my life—the two years in this house.

Tuesday, May 17th

Mother and I up by train to London to the Ritz with bags. Then call for appointments. Lunch at the Ritz: omelette and strawberries—delicious.

Out to Anne Talbot for fitting. Then to the Royal Academy show with Mother, crowded with pictures and people and none of them good, except one lovely portrait of a girl in white by Philpot.

Then to Jane Seymour, where I treat myself to the Guinea Treatment—hair, nails, face, and feet!

Then back to rest and tea and dress for dinner at U. S. A. Embassy.

I wear the black bouffant dress with pink chiffon scarf and the lovely pink amethyst earrings and pin Mother gave me. Mother looked enchanting and small in a gray bouffant net.

It was rather fun: lots of long white gloves and jewels. It was exciting going out again and looking nice. Quite a few Americans: Henry Luce (*Life, Time, Fortune,* etc.) and Claire Luce (who wrote *The Women*). I sat way at the other end from C. at the long table, between Herschel[1] and a Mr. Kent. I had a lovely time talking to Herschel. It was fun having that quick understanding again. I thought all the time of Elisabeth and the many times she had sat next to him at Embassy dinners and turned to his understanding sensitivity.

After dinner we were taken in to see a movie—*Test Pilot*. Just before they started Lord Halifax came in and sat down in the empty chair next to me. I felt shy but managed to get out (before the lights went out) that C. and I admired what he was doing, and I think it pleased him. He said how many letters he got from all over the world criticizing and advising and pleading this and that. He has a very fine face, sensitive, kind, perceptive, patient (but perhaps lacking in humor?).

The movie was terrible—very good flying and bloodcurdling, but a very cheap story and I felt embarrassed by it—embarrassed to have it spread out in front of these people who would judge

---

[1] Herschel Johnson, foreign service officer and counselor of the U. S. Embassy in London; he had been a member of Ambassador Dwight W. Morrow's staff in Mexico.

America by it. I wanted to explain that America wasn't like that, cheap and wild and mad. Mostly the cheapness bothered me.

It was funny because the language was so nasal and so slangy that for the first five minutes I couldn't understand it at all. Also I kept thinking that all the English would just take it for granted that that was our life—C.'s and mine—mad and drunk and terrifying! And that was funny. But it did seem a waste of time for people like Lord Halifax.

I like the Kennedys. They are natural and simple and make people feel at home. Truly American—very nice.

But the movie—America has better things to offer than that!

Drive home very late.

Friday, May 20th

Mother goes to see Jon at school. Confusion in the household. I run around getting cars and meals arranged. C. is disturbed by the atmosphere (Morrow atmosphere I am afraid it is) and the feeling of pressure.

I up to town for last fitting on the dress and also get long white gloves and a paste bracelet at Harrods, rush back in time for lunch with Mrs. Morgan and Mrs. Miles.[1] Isabel fixes the flowers and the house looks lovely. Lunch is quite good and goes well.

But it is Mother's day on the whole—completely conversational and family. Not much accomplished but a good-will afternoon. No real contact, for me, except a moment with Mrs. Miles on the sofa. For the rest we talk news, houses and children, and clothes and plans.

Mother's friend Olive Schill came quite early for tea (and night). A perfect stranger to us, but Mother seemed to manage it all right. Rather a confused tea, as C. is working hard over papers, business, checks, and letters for the boat to U. S. A. He keeps running in and asking for me and I go out. Jon and Land on the floor (Land at Miss Schill's shoelaces). Mother goes with

[1] A Welsh friend of Mrs. Morgan, and the mother of a friend of E. R. M. M.

Mrs. Morgan and Mrs. Miles to the station. I take Land, and in desperation ask Jon to take Miss Schill to see the garden. Jon promptly takes her miles and miles down the wood path to get stumps! We shout and shout but cannot make them hear in time for Jon's supper. He is very late and everyone rather upset, and I very tired.

Saturday, May 21st

I work all day on the book with C. It is difficult to work. It isn't quiet anywhere and we are jumpy. Even in the office Hook sticks his head in the window and asks C. a question about the wood!

In between times I walk around the garden, make lists of things I want to remember, and try to judge what will be out before we go—which roses? the white clematis? the larkspur? I am greedy about this garden and underneath is such an ache to have to leave it that I want to keep every moment I can.

Sunday, May 22nd

Headlines—the Czechs and the Germans are massed on the border of Czechoslovakia. It looks very serious. France says it will mean war if Germany attacks and that she will defend to the hilt her obligations with Czechoslovakia. What will England do?

C. and I work all morning. We have got a secretary coming Monday to type the whole book this week.

Tea at Sissinghurst. It is a hot and blowy day, restless. Harold Nicolson, Mrs. Nicolson, Mrs. St. Aubyn, and Ben are there. We walk two by two down the walks. I have Mrs. St. Aubyn, of course. C. gets Harold Nicolson and evidently pummels him hard with gloomy aviation data. Mrs. St. Aubyn is full of "How happy we would be this lovely day if only . . ." Mrs. Nicolson looks gloomy but talks to Mother of other things, and Ben (whose business it is, whose generation the war will take) says nothing.

We all meet at tea and Harold Nicolson talks a little. He really is quite dashed. He evidently thinks the policy of the present Government is quite wrong, just weakness, that Eden was right, that the U.S.A. is right to be idealistic and hopes she holds the torch, etc. If all the idealism dies in the world, what will happen, etc.

I feel rather sad. How it would have thrilled me a year or two ago, this defense of idealism, and yet today it seems out of place—not facing the facts.

A cloud has descended on us. Mother tells Harold Nicolson how fond I am of the house and hate to leave. I'm glad she does that as I hadn't a chance and he is a sweet person.

Back *just* before the Lees[1] and the Scanlons arrive for supper. (*Must* change into a cool dress.) It is hot and thundery. Mrs. Lee is real and sensitive and understanding and lovely to look at too—willowy and Southern and exquisite. I long to talk to her and wish so I had seen her before. *Why* should I meet her just as I'm going? We talk a little of homesickness. She said she was terribly, here. . . .

But most of the conversation is of possible war, and the atmosphere is suspended. Colonel Lee is a very intelligent, keen man. He gets two calls while he is here. There has been a special Cabinet meeting, to discuss the [Czech] situation.

Mother leaves in the middle of the evening. The strange confusion of feelings: ache at Mother's going as always, and that I can't say anything, and my ache underneath about leaving the house, and the tenseness about war, and the stimulus of those people, and the smell of the garden in the thundery heat.

I do not sleep at all at night. C. is sweet about it and we try to analyze what does it. Working hard and very little exercise and trying to cram too much in a day, and not having time to digest life, to think about it, analyze it, and write about it during the days—so it comes out at night. The tension of having guests and

[1] Colonel Raymond L. Lee, Military Attaché for Air in the U. S. Embassy in London, 1935–38.

trying to make it smooth, and holding things in, and feeling bad at leaving this place.

But lack of sleep spoils everything. It is not fair and it must be controlled. I must learn to control my life and my nerves. I will not be a neurotic who cannot see people without going to pieces.

Monday, May 23rd

Rather exhausted and C. says, "I feel as if I had been flying all night," poor man.

Get out in morning and then to town at 12:30 for Lady Astor's ball; lunch on the train and then to the hotel. Accidentally I get a spot of cologne in my eye ("That's what happens when you try to beat the fourth dimension!" says C.), which is very painful. Eye wash, cold water, pads—nothing helps. I am watery-eyed and red-nosed when it is time to go—of all nights! Still I powder over it—we cannot wait. The dress is perfect and fits in every way so that I feel completely *right* in it and unself-conscious—just as a dress should be. C. says loyally that I look fine. But I know I look as if I'd been crying all afternoon and I see everything double on the way to St. James's Square. The fresh air helps. C. is very good-looking in his tails (a new one—the first new one since Paris 1927).

There is quite a crowd and a long awning out in front of 4 St. James's Square and photographers who don't see us. But I am No. 1 in the cloakroom! No one to watch; pull on the long white gloves. Do you wear the bracelets *in* or *out*? And how high up are they to go?

Then someone comes in I know, the nice girl at Cliveden, Helen Mildmay; she is so natural, with a quiet sense of humor.

Then Wissie comes in, blowy and rather imperious, and many "My deahs," her tiara rather incongruously set on her rebellious head. Then more encrusted ladies. Everyone has a tiara, long white gloves, etc. Mrs. Kennedy comes in and I can ask her about the bracelets—whether in or out. She wears them out! Then up the long stairs, footmenned and carpeted (Miss Helen Mildmay insists we go first). "Colonel and Mrs. Lindbergh," I say to the footman who shouts it on, and we enter.

The big ballroom is lined with beautiful women in gold and silver lamé or very bouffant skirts, stiff with jewels and coronets. The younger ones are lovely-looking. The older, regal but ramroddy. One gray-haired, erect lady in lamé, powdered and jeweled, literally looks almost corseted in jewels. It makes her neck very long and stiff.

Lady Astor, in pink, has a high coronet. She is perfectly natural, and yet somehow I think of Alice in Wonderland. Perhaps that I feel like Alice and she is the White Queen, or the Red Queen. "Curtsy while you're thinking," she might say to me kindly. Instead she said, "Look at you in your smart frock. I'm glad you made that Swede spend some money!" And then we were introduced to one or two people.

My eye was normal by now.

Everyone stood stiffly around the edge of the room, like dancing school. A beautiful room, gold scrolling on the ceiling and walls, beautiful long mirrors and old chandeliers. Masses of laburnum dripped gold from huge pots at each end of the room. I found I was talking to Mrs. Winn,[1] a nice hearty person I met at Lady Astor's lunch, and Helen Mildmay. Then an elderly man who turned out to be my partner at supper, who looked nice, and then a young woman about my age came across the floor to me. She had met me and Elisabeth at Nassau. So strange—that note back into the past, that precious time I had with Elisabeth when I was so worried about marrying C. "Were you engaged to him there?" she asked. She was nice, but the kind of English person that is hard to talk to. But I think it's shyness, not unkindness. I had no idea who she was. (Then later discovered she was Viscountess Cranborne.) Then we were introduced to Lord (Viscount) Cranborne,[2] who was nice and easy to talk to. He had been to Russia and had the same profound (and unreasoned) impression of gloom that I had from it.

[1] Mrs. Anthony Winn, a niece of Lady Astor.

[2] Undersecretary of State under Eden.

Then there was a hush—the Duchess of Kent. She did look incredibly beautiful in a black lace Winterhalter dress, flounced all around, a lovely tiara, and long old diamond earrings and a large diamond bow in the front of her dress. She was extremely graceful, with great dignity and style as she walked from person to person putting out her hand, her flounces moving gently as she passed. Everyone, of course, curtsied. The English do not bow their heads: they bob up and down, stiffly erect. She is much more beautiful than her pictures because her face has more color and animation, and the regularity of her perfect features is broken by a charming trick of speaking a little on one side of her mouth. She has a lovely low voice.

The Duke of Kent is small and does not bear himself well. I thought he had rather a weak though good-looking face. (The King's face is far stronger and has more character.) When they had completed the circle and come back to the end of the room, Lady Astor called (stamping her foot, or an impatient gesture like that—quite gracefully—it sounds so awful) across the room, *"Wissie!* Come over here and take care of Her Highness while I . . ." (There—she *is* like the Red Queen. "Look up, speak nicely, and don't twiddle your fingers all the time!") Wissie blew across clumsily and the Duchess of Kent gave a delicious giggle or what might have been a giggle. It was more dignified, a ripple of amusement, but still young and delicious—at Lady Astor.

Then the King and Queen,[1] slowly and with quiet dignity. She came in first. She had on a wide bouffant-skirted evening dress, pink and lacy, with an off-the-shoulder, Victorian neckline. A tiara and necklace. She looked, somehow, very Victorian—the best of it: her short and almost plump figure, her walk, which would have suited a bustle, her dignity, which was not like the stylish foreign dignity of the Duchess of Kent but solid and English. And then that very pretty, surprisingly young, but old-fashioned face.

And yet all this does not exactly give the impression of great charm which her appearance alone gives. She does really remind

[1] King George VI and Queen Elizabeth.

you of an old-fashioned rose, the round, small full ones, not brilliant in coloring but very fragrant. He was smallish with an intelligent and quite strong face with real character and integrity in it. He looks quite like Edward VIII, though slightly homelier and stronger (in character). He looked, I thought, though, quite nervous and sickeningly tired (what a frightful life they must lead—it shows in his face, the dark rings under his eyes, and in the self-contained way she sometimes pressed her lips together).

They came up. She rustled gently but gracefully across the floor (very Victorian) to greet the Duchess of Kent, the Duke of Kent, and a few others—Royalty or near-Royalty, I gathered—and with great dignity (as though it were the most natural greeting in the world) they kissed (shaking hands is too ordinary for Royalty to Royalty). Then they were led around the lined room and we all curtsied as we were introduced, one by one. She really looks at you, too, when she shakes hands. A real person looks out at you. How *can* she do it, when she must go through it so often? I hardly remember him, because I was so astonished and admiring of her.

Then they started out to supper. C. asked me in a stage whisper, "Who is Mrs. Winn?" I was about to turn to the nice hearty niece of Lady Astor's on my right and ask her when I heard Lord Cranborne say to C., "The lady on your wife's right"! Then the elderly man took me in to dinner. He had an open, rather quizzical American face. He said his daughter of nineteen was there. She was very pretty (the only person at the table besides me without a tiara!). There were two large tables with low bowls of flowers on them—just the blossoms, no leaves. I sat at Lady Astor's table, about opposite her and the King (also the Duke of Kent). The elderly man on my left was the Honorable R. H. Brand.[1] On my right was the Honorable David Bowes-Lyon (cousin of the Queen?). I had a lovely time talking with Mr. Brand. He said he knew Daddy and admired him very much

[1] Robert Henry Brand, later 1st Lord Brand, author and authority on finance, married Lady Astor's sister Phyllis.

(during the war, I gathered). It was very easy to talk to him and he was interesting on the problem of conscription in England (he was pro; C., I said, was also). On the Czech problem, on Germany, about air preparedness, about "occupation" being impossible by aviation alone. Daddy's quote about the war: "may start in the air but will end in the mud." But also on books: Whitehead, his quote about the mistake of the Catholic Church in making their God the symbol of conservatism instead of the symbol of progress or revolt. About Liddell Hart's[1] book. He said he violently disagreed with L. H.'s thesis that man was becoming less important, the machine more and more. I agreed. From there on to Carrel's book. All this time I was struggling to take *off* my gloves (and hence my bracelets, watch, etc.) to eat. They are a nuisance. He said he had read my book. It pleased me very much. He said, "I read very few books and I read it several times."

I could have gone on and on (the nice thing about really intelligent people is that when you talk with them they make you feel intelligent too) but I saw that the lady on the other side was impatient—I was monopolizing. So I turned to the Honorable David Bowes-Lyon, who was talking to the American bride of young Lord Astor [of Hever Castle]. She looked lovely in tiara. A three-cornered conversation, rather dilatory. He was charming and teasing and also easy to talk to, but I do not remember a thing we said, except that he informed me that he thought England was better equipped with planes, etc., than anyone knew. I listened but did not believe him.

Then we rose. The Queen was going out ("I missed that one!" said the young American bride behind me). Then we went out, the ladies curtsying to the King as they left ("You go first!" whispered the young bride behind me).

Then a group of ladies went up to powder in Mrs. Winn's bedroom. (Shades of dances as a young girl.) I had a chance to

---

[1] Sir Basil Henry Liddell Hart, English military authority and writer, author of *Europe in Arms* (1937), *The Defense of Britain* (1939), etc.

have a word with Mrs. Kennedy, who is simple and nice. Then the struggle to get the long white gloves *on* again *and* the bracelets on top.

When we come down hordes of people are coming in—tiaras and diamonds, knee breeches, etc. I see Lady Linlithgow,[1] who speaks to me about the baby (I saw her in Delhi just before!).

As we come down and stand in the door Lady Astor goes over to me and gets me to come up and speak to the Queen, who is sitting on a sofa. I come up and curtsy (you curtsy going up and leaving) and she beckoned me to sit in the chair. "Do sit down here." Then she said very sweetly, "I hear you had a baby born on Coronation day." I said, "Yes, Your Majesty," and something about my surprise at her knowing (which is wrong, I think—you must say Your Royal Highness). Then she said quite shyly and sweetly, hesitating a little, "I think it's very nice, when something big is happening to you, to think that something big is happening to someone else, too."

It was so lovely, so completely private and direct of her, I was quite overcome. Then I told her I was sorry to miss the Coronation but that I was happy, too. And I told her, in a rush—in an attempt to meet that rare directness of hers—of waking up in the hospital and hearing the people coming home from the Coronation, cheering in the streets outside the open window, and I feeling very happy and not quite sure what the people were cheering about. "Such a long time ago, that day," she said, smiling. She asked me about the baby and I told her how happy we had been in England—that we had never been so happy before and how good everyone had been to us.

Then she asked about Charles rather shyly, hesitating at the words. "He is busy . . . with his . . . inventions?" and how he got interested in science, and then I talked a little about C., forgetting my shyness then, and the "Your Majestys," speaking of

[1] Wife of Victor Alexander John Hope, Viceroy and Governor General of India (1936–43), whom the Lindberghs had met on their flight to India.

his education and not being able to get into the technical schools. And she said, smiling, something about how strange it was that people found their own calling in the end.

And then I saw Lady Astor was about to lead up someone else and I said, "When my baby grows up I will tell him you asked about him." And she said sweetly, with great dignity and in a rather old-fashioned graciousness but simply, "Give him my blessing, will you?" And then I curtsied and went, quite moved.

For she has made her mold real. She has broken through it—no, that is too violent. The Duke of Windsor "broke through it." She shines through her mold, gently, but very real and intense. She burns through. She must be a very remarkable person to keep perceptive, direct, intuitive, real, and clear through all that encrustation of formality and unreality that surrounds her.

The rest of the evening was a strange medley. The people around me melted away to dance (just like those old parties—only now there was C. out there in the hall I could summon to stay by me) and I was left with Lord Cranborne, who asked me to dance but said he did it so badly and I said I hadn't for years, so he said, "Let's sit and talk," which we did and which was absolutely delightful. We talked for ages. I was a little worried about him and got C. to come over, too, so he wouldn't get bored and so he could feel he could leave. But most of the time I was having such a good time talking that I forgot even to worry about his being bored. He is brilliant, sensitive, understanding. And as he was very kind I felt not shy and stiff but very much at ease and opened up.

It was that exciting kind of conversation where you are sure of the other person's understanding and you run along, opening up new paths here and there, striking out here and there, but always sure that the other person is keeping pace with you.

He started out by saying he'd read the (my) book—which was nice—and then we went on to China, Russia, Germany, the present situation, America and England (democracies), the differences, national characteristics. Of the French and the English being more civilized than the more barbaric Germans but the Germans having a direction that they haven't. He said something marvelous about the French: "I always think that the French see *very* clearly—but not very *far*." Which is really awfully good.

He knew Harold Nicolson of course, and Vita Sackville-West, and we talked about their books. Of the Spanish War—of cruelty and brutality, Southern and Northern. Of India and Rhodes, coming back to Greek civilization.

After a while I felt worried about him not seeing other people (C. was talking to the Queen, then) and being bored. But if he was bored, he is both the kindest and cleverest man at disguising it.

Finally, when C. came back, he went off after a while to see if he could locate Mr. Morrison[1] to introduce to us. And came back somewhat later, saying he couldn't find him. But by that time we were with someone else, thank goodness, the Belgian Chargé d'Affaires.

The rest of the evening was spent wandering about, C. and I, alone, stopping to talk to a few people here and there whom we knew—Grandi[2] and Contessa Grandi. It was really quite strange—we knew so few people. It was like the parties I went to as a girl, shy and afraid, wondering if people were noticing that I wasn't dancing, wondering if I could go home, wondering if I could walk through that room again. Only this time C. and I were together, so we enjoyed it. And it wasn't exactly that we were left out and felt out of place—we didn't. People watched us. We looked well there (C. said, low, to me, the first chance he'd got, "That outfit is *very* good," and I could tell it did look well from the way the women looked at it!), only we were foreigners, strangers, outsiders, looking on. It is a strange feeling with people whose language you know well and in whose country you live. Of course I didn't feel a foreigner with Mr. Brand or

[1] Herbert Stanley Morrison, English labor leader and politician.

[2] Dino Grandi, Italian diplomat and statesman, Ambassador to Great Britain 1932–39.

with Lord Cranborne, but they are both of a small race that has no distinct nationality.

There is, too, the rather disconcerting way that people whom you've met before at the last dinner or somewhere else, and whom in America you would normally just-greet passing by, avoid your glance or return a freezing one to your hopeful look.

It chilled me at first, but I think it is more a code than a definite attempt to cut. It is "Yes, I remember you, but it is not convenient for me to recognize you now. I do not want to be bothered."

Some of it, of course, is snooty, but some of it is sheer awkwardness, fear, and lack of real social ability and a kind of shy laziness. I am getting to know the English.

Then—it was about two—the King and Queen were leaving, downstairs, after "supper." People leaned over the stairs to see them go. A wide, beautiful, queenly staircase, too, and all the women in party clothes strung along it, looking down. And C. and I went down, had a few words with Lady Astor and thanked her. Lady Astor said to C., "Where were you? The King wanted to have a talk with you."

And then we went in to "supper," which we discovered downstairs. The little gray girl I met at Lady Astor's waved to us to come and sit by them (by this time I felt sure they were not waving at us as we had been "not recognized" by a number of people). But she *did* mean it and we sat down. He (Mr. Ronald Tree[1]) I found very interesting. We got started talking immediately on portraits and talked about Brockhurst, John, etc. and the Royal Academy show. He said there was *one* lovely picture in it, by a man who was dead, and then he mentioned the only one I really liked—the girl in white by Philpot!

It was a nice end to the evening—to feel wanted. I was glad we saw them again. I like her—little and frail, gray hair and a young child's face, with dark, sensitive eyes.

Then to get our coats, where we refound Lord and Lady Cranborne and went out with them.

[1] Niece and nephew of Lady Astor.

Then back in the limousine (we'd got for the evening) and to talk it over. C. says the Queen is very tired and showing the strain of that life; he just went on talking because he thought it was the easiest thing for her. He told her a little of the life he had to lead just after he flew across: the pressure and people and formality, how sick he got of it. But added that we go to big parties so seldom now that we rather enjoyed this.

"You rather enjoy them?" she asked quizzically.

"Yes," he said, "we go so seldom that it's rather interesting."

Tuesday, May 24th

Drive down to Long Barn; arrive about noon. Dr. Berkeley sees Land, says he is perfectly fine, splendid condition. He stays for lunch. Man from Harrods in afternoon; we go over all things in the house that are ours.

Herschel comes for supper. We talk about foreign affairs and pro and con Germany. Herschel gives the best, sanest arguments versus (although admitting the points for). How can a government prosper that's built on lies, the people fed on them, the truth kept down. Also, the insanity of the Jewish situation, burning books, etc. C. is very interested and I am pleased. He says Herschel has a better mind than he thought, and I am pleased because I thought so all along. Herschel has such a balanced mind, a thorough one (masculine) and yet a sensitive one (feminine). I felt happy, too, because Elisabeth would have been pleased.

Wednesday, May 25th

Work all day long on the book, checking and rechecking. C. works like a dog checking my (Morrow!) figures.

We get an invitation from Buckingham Palace to attend a ball on June 1st! ("You *enjoy* them, do you?")

All plans upset. We will go, of course. It is the Queen. It was lovely of her. Try to replan our exit from Long Barn.

Walk around the garden after supper. My feeling at leaving this place is like the feeling of leaving someone you are in love with. The last days, the last moments, are a kind of agony. Now I still have it I must learn it by heart—just how the hedges go, just what vines grow where. In a week I will not be able to look back and see those pale blue iris again, I will not be able to remember just which way the uneven brick path goes around the house. And all the different greens of the garden—the beech hedge and the hawthorn, the fruit trees, the grays of the santolina bushes, the different vivid greens of the herbaceous beds. In a week I will not be able to pluck off a snip of sweet-smelling rosemary every time I walk in or out of doors and keep it crushed in my hand for a minute or two.

The luxury of closing your eyes and then opening them—and looking *again* and finding it still there.

Friday, May 27th

C. and I go up to town, chiefly for next week's party affairs—he to get knee breeches measured, and I to get some kind of tiara. Both incongruous enough. The tiara seems to be the most difficult. I had an idea that one could get an old paste one but apparently that is very difficult. We go to an antique shop at the corner of Albemarle and Grafton. They had lovely old things but no paste tiaras—a very expensive diamond one that was not at all becoming, and a rather shoddy-looking pinchbeck and fake amethyst one. Then we went into all the antique shops along Bond. Either they didn't have any or they were very expensive. Then into Leighton's in the Burlington Arcade. They had a very pretty one—quite unusual, with three stars and two motifs, making the crown effect. It was not too heavy and not flashy. The stars unscrew and make pins. And it has an old-fashioned look that feels more at home to me than the modern ones.

Then, very tired, catch the train home. Seen Jon in bed.

Go over papers and diaries.

After lunch C. and I to town. He signs the King and Queen's book for us. Then to Paddington to catch the train for Banbury to visit Mr. Brand. Beautiful hilly country. A lovely formal old Georgian house set among beautiful big trees, lawns, and fields. Charming people and not too many: Mr. and Mrs. Barrington Ward of the *Times,* Mr. Thomas Jones (T. J.) knew Elisabeth. Just the kind of evening I like. Very interesting conversation. C. and the *Times* man and Mr. Brand on foreign affairs, Germany, England.

Back to Long Barn on a very slow train.

But it was worth it. Such nice people. The best of England—matured, intelligent, cultured, charming. When they are like that, there is no race can touch them. C. and I feel warmed, expanded, happy from the contact. I feel almost like saying that it is in expectation of people like that, that one lives. There is nothing so exciting, no homecoming more joyful, no pleasure more intense than the recognition of minds like that and being able to talk or listen to them. This is putting too much emphasis on these individuals, these particular persons. And it is not that—it is the *group* that I mean. It is on the whole the group we have met with or through Lady Astor: the Dame Edith Lytteltons, the T. J.s, the Lord Cranbornes, the Mr. Brands, the Lord Astors.

I am glad—oh, I am so glad we have met them before leaving England. It makes me feel better about England.

The men from Harrods come to pack. What a day! Hauling things into the big room all day, books, papers, china, ornaments, the children's toys, etc. Sorting, picking, choosing, answering questions, and labeling (for storage, for shipping). Again all my personal collection of those indefinable what-make-up-a-home things go into the impersonal jaws of a "storage" house. How many times before—Princeton, Hopewell, Englewood, New York.

You never regain just that same home atmosphere. You make a new collection, new associations, a new combination. The old one is gone forever.

The house begins to be in hectic disorder and unhomelike disruption and excitement. How I hate it like this. Thor skulks about restless and miserable. There are newspapers, shavings, excelsior, boxes, wrappings, etc., strewn over the big room. The packers get out just in time to clear up a little. I push around a few things for C.'s guests, Mr. Martin[1] and his mother.

And tomorrow is the ball!

Wednesday, June 1st

Wake, miserable and stuffy, with a cold. *Can* I go? Stay in bed all morning. If I could stay in bed all day I could cure this. We pack and get on the 2:13 train. I arrive late for my appointment at Émile's. M. Pierre does me and I sit under the drier for ages— full on. It absolutely clears my head of cold. Then run back for the tiara (*must* get there in time!). Then in a taxi to Claridge's (where we are dressing). C. is already there and I feel much more cheerful. My hair looks nice and the cold has disappeared. (The atmosphere of Claridge's is like New York or gay London.) We eat upstairs—sherry and melba toast. C. and I opposite each other, he in his knee breeches and I in my tiara, laughing at each other.

Then downstairs in Elisabeth's coat (and her watch on my arm and her paste necklace on my neck and my paste earrings and bracelet) in a car to Buckingham Palace. "See if anyone is going in—we don't want to get there early!" Lots of cars and taxis, so we drive in and C. presents our cards. Up carpeted steps, past butlers waving us on, telling us where to go. (This part was so well done that it was far less awkward than at many big parties. You were wafted along by the many footmen, etc., so there was no question of going to the wrong place.) There were lots of other people coming in encrusted with tiaras, jewels, etc. I turned

[1] Early aircraft pioneer and president of Glenn L. Martin Co. of Baltimore.

right, away from C., down a long hall lined with portraits, into a cloakroom with *lovely* old portraits, familiar ones, and left my coat. Then out again down the long hall—alone—feeling very shy and foreign, to meet C. Then we went in a general throng up steps and steps and steps stretching ahead of us (seeing *no one* that we knew). Up at the top we were again in portrait-lined halls. There were a great many people. At one point they played "God Save the King" somewhere ahead of us ("Land where our fathers died," I sing in my mind instinctively) and everyone stood still (I suppose the King and Queen were coming in, but I could not see). Everyone was pushing toward the ballroom. We saw Lady Linlithgow, who stopped and spoke to us and the Kennedys, and Herschel [Johnson] and a few other people we knew.

Then we found suddenly we were at the ballroom door and the dancing was starting. It was an enormous room and very Victorian, palatial with pillars and gilt, a balcony at one end where the orchestra played and a kind of dais at the other end where the King and Queen, Queen Mary, etc., sat. The floor was lined with banked seats or steps covered in red, all the way around (like an arena), and here people could sit and watch the dancing. But we didn't dare go in and sit down. The seats near the dais were reserved for near-Royalty and the Diplomatic Corps. There was quite a crowd of people in the door and here we met and talked to a few people: the German Ambassador, Sir Philip Sassoon[1] and his mother, Count Grandi. I had a dance with Herschel— very slowly—for the room was crowded and it was so big it took two dances to get around it (like twirling down two city blocks).

It was nice to be able to go back to C. (so different from the old days when one waited to be cut in on and was in terror lest one dance too long and bore or impose on one's partner). Then we wandered about the halls back of the ballroom. And although this first part of the evening was a solitary one we rather enjoyed it, as we had each other. I had a very good-looking man at my side and the dress and the tiara, I knew, were perfect. (My appearance fits this occasion perfectly, even if I don't, *inside*).

[1] British Undersecretary of State for Air, 1931-37.

But one could not really feel out-of-it because there were so many other couples wandering around like us or sitting down talking quietly or looking at the pictures in the galleries (some beautiful Rembrandts). And it was nice to walk down those regal halls in long skirts; day clothes would have been out of place at any time there, I felt, while that swinging taffeta skirt gently drifting across the floor was right.

We tried, however, to change our position often enough not to be "wallflowers." Sometimes we sat in one room or walked down another or sat on one side of the ballroom or another, or went to get refreshments. There were signs pointing the way—a big room lined with two long buffet tables. The butlers asking, "What will you have, Madame?" had powdered (or rather *plastered,* it looked) white heads! (The little paper sandwich holders had G R—the Royal crest—on them, and of course the plates.) And drank lemonade, and ate a sandwich. (The attention that everyone got was marvelous, considering the numbers of people—800 or 1000.) But it never seemed crowded, only a huge place with the proper number of people in it.

But always alone. It felt so strange, like looking at a play or being a ghost. It is strange because there is no party in America or any other place in the world where people would not surround C. even if they didn't know him. But the English don't—not unless they're introduced, and even then, not. They really, as Harold Nicolson once said, don't like strangers. And we are strangers. I saw the Cranbornes but did not look at them (English fashion—not out of Englishness but only because I didn't want him to feel he must come and talk to us and take care of me again. Also—secretly—I did not want to get that English stare back again from him; I should have been hurt. I was afraid he would—so many people do it—and I wanted both to spare him from having to do it and us from having to get it).

In the middle of the evening there was a roll of drums and all Royalty and Diplomatic people walked down to supper. Everyone stood up and watched them go. The Queen looked so lovely, in a stiff white satin or damask *robe de style,* with loops of satin gathered in a garland fashion on the skirt. Also a wide blue ribbon (the Garter?) across her dress. A tiara that was like an unfinished crown on her dark hair.

There were lots of tiaras—some very heavy, encrusted, some like crowns, some imitation bought at Harrods, others just frankly bandeaux or leaves in the hair. Lots of lovely dresses—big skirts and tight shimmering ones. I loved watching them dance and picking out the beautiful ones (women—not tiaras).

Though actually the size of the rooms rather dwarfed individuals, which was good; one was aware only of color and shimmer, with an occasional figure here and there, as in a painting or old print of Vauxhall, in spite of the modern American dance band in the gallery. (A dreadful American "crooner" sang surprisingly from the gallery, and her nasal voice was taken up by the loud-speakers or reflectors at each corner of the room. That was wrong and grated.)

There was a dignity and grace and lack of haste or pressure or crowds. The men in knee breeches gave it an old-world look, and the big dresses of the women made for space and slowness, and wearing a tiara makes you walk with your head up.

C. and I, to vary things, went in to have supper in a big room off one of the halls. At the back of the room a great deal of gold plate was put up against red backgrounds. We were shown to a table with one other couple. Soup, asparagus, and strawberries. (Think of feeding strawberries the first of June to a thousand people!)

Then suddenly sometime after supper in one of the halls (we were about go home—Herschel said we could any time) Lady Astor found us. "Well," she said with a twinkle, "you must admit I launched you in society!" And suddenly the party came alive, with her, as things do around her, as they did around Elisabeth. She said, "Wait till after the next dance. I want to talk to you," and we felt alive again, not ghosts. Lady G. came running up to us. (She thinks we are in the thick of social glitter because, though we had hardly spoken to anyone all evening, when she

Saint-Gildas

Dr. and Mme Alexis Carrel, Saint-Gildas, summer, 1936

Dr. and Mme Carrel with Charles Lindbergh,
Saint-Gildas, summer, 1936

Anne Lindbergh, Saint-Gildas, summer, 1936

*Dr. and Mme Carrel with Anne Lindbergh,
Saint-Gildas, summer, 1936*

Charles Lindbergh flying his Miles Mohawk, fall, 1936

Anne Lindbergh at her desk at Saint-Gildas, summer, 1936

Charles Lindbergh and Jon, Long Barn, Christmas, 1936

Anne Lindbergh with Jon, Thor, and Skean, Long Barn, January, 1937

Segesta, Sicily, February, 1937

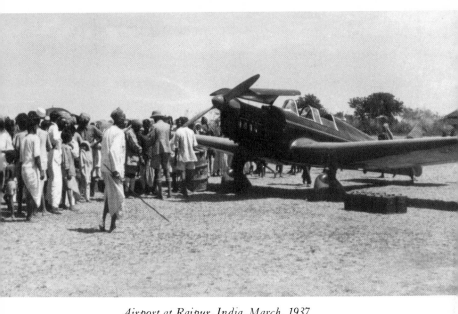

Airport at Raipur, India, March, 1937

Udaipur, India, March, 1937

Charles Lindbergh with Jon, Long Barn, spring, 1937

Anne Lindbergh with Jon and Skean

Long Barn, late spring, 1937

Charles Lindbergh with Jon, spring, 1937

Anne Lindbergh and Land, Long Barn, June, 1937

Anne Lindbergh with Land and Thor, Long Barn, 1937

Long Barn, summer, 1937

Anne Lindbergh with Land and Jon, 1937

Long Barn, summer, 1937

Jon in his peat igloo, June, 1937

Constance Morrow Morgan, June 22, 1937

Charles Lindbergh with Jon, Long Barn, fall, 1937

*The Lindberghs
at Prien airport,
Bavaria, October, 1937*

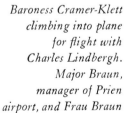

*Baroness Cramer-Klett
climbing into plane
for flight with
Charles Lindbergh.
Major Braun,
manager of Prien
airport, and Frau Braun*

*Charles Lindbergh
with Frau Braun,
Prien,
October, 1937*

came back to introduce her daughter Lady Astor broke in on us.)

Then we sat quite cheerfully in the red-arena seats and watched the dancing. "There's Lord Cranborne," said C. "Yes," I said, not looking, "but I don't want to bother him again." But he was smiling at us, most un-English, from the dance floor. And I felt intensely relieved, somehow, and pleased.

Then the end of the dance, and we joined Lady Astor. She and C. talked, which they both enjoy. And I talk to her son and then dance, after. The floor is quite clear by now; many people have gone home. There are waltzes. I love to waltz. And he is a very good dancer, and we waltz and waltz and I am so happy. I *did* want to waltz in that dress—it was *made* for Strauss waltzes. I can see C. smiling at me from the red seats, so I know he is pleased and that I look well.

And I do not worry about my partner as we are waltzing well (even though I am almost dizzy with it) and most people enjoy dancing if the partner dances and looks well. Besides, I was too happy doing it to worry. The music, the floor, the dress—all made me lose myself in a kind of intoxication. Like those divine dreams when one suddenly finds oneself twirling and twirling in wider and wider sweeps around an enormous ballroom until finally one is not on the floor at all but somehow flying about the ceiling.

I had a strange feeling, seeing C. on the sidelines, smiling at my happiness dancing. I suddenly thought very vividly of Daddy and thought he would be pleased to see me dancing there in my blue dress at Buckingham Palace. Not that he was a snob—he never wanted to bother to get Elisabeth or me presented at court. But this would have amused him. I could see him twinkling at me proudly—proud of C., too.

In between dances we would come back and chat with Lady Astor and C. on the red seats. Her other son came up. It began to seem like quite a gay and intimate party—family jokes, etc. Then as we were standing there with Lady Astor the King and Queen came by and shook us all by the hand and the ladies curtsied. I thanked her (for asking us). She asked how the Coronation baby was and when we were leaving England. She asked me, too, if I had had a good time dancing and spoke with some humor about the "young lady in the balcony" [the crooner]. (She—the Queen —has the most lovely lilting voice.)

It was in between dances, and C., the King and the Queen, and I were standing at a corner of the entrance facing each other, rather awkwardly. She, you could see, was trying to make things unawkward. I said we were leaving in a week and added (for conversation), "It will be a very quiet family time, this summer." She smiled understandingly. "The best kind of time," she said and then turning to him (the King) and with a slight gesture of her hand as if to try to include all of us in the conversation, "*We* also—*we* are going to have a quiet family time this weekend (?)." (Gracious, I thought with a gasp, do they *ever* get a "quiet family time"?) Then again she turned to the King and said rather shyly, with a gesture to us, "Colonel and Mrs. Lindbergh had a baby born on Coronation day." His shy nervous face lit up for a moment with a genuine and very kind smile. C. smiled and nodded a little awkwardly, and I too. Then the Queen, as though explaining to him (the King), "I think it's so nice to think that we . . ."

And then the music started and they went off (I curtsying good-by) to dance together. And the other son of Lady Astor and I danced—or did we talk? We sat and talked, through one dance, about writing. He wants to write and asked *my advice!* Having read my book! I was very startled that anyone should ask my advice. Anyway, it was great fun talking to him. He is sensitive, quick, and observant. And I recognize so much in him—the same language, the same way of looking at things. I am sure I could talk easily to him and we would have much in common. As it was, it was not easy to talk but we danced and I felt happy and at ease. (I remembered what Thelma once said about me: "You, Anne, have a strange protective way of shutting up tight, tight, and then suddenly you open out like a flower when you are in the right atmosphere, with people you feel at ease with.") But of course everyone is like that, really.

But I did open up, the end of the evening. Lady Astor's spontaneous kindness, the joy of dancing, her son's sensitive and understanding mind to talk to . . . I felt happy. And happiness is like a snowball, it brings more as it goes. People came up to us in between dances—Lord Cranborne, Lady Halifax. She talked to me about the book, too (and she was one of the people I thought "did not recognize us," so it wasn't being snooty, at all, it is just a British mannerism!). She was very nice and I liked her. Lady Astor also talked to C. a long time (which I felt pleased about because I know she likes him [and vice versa] and I always feel that C. when he talks to someone *bestows* something upon them).

Then somehow it was time to go. The King and Queen had left and we were going downstairs. And there were the Cranbornes again: "You were so kind to me the other evening . . ." I talked to her going down those endless steps into the cloakrooms. She said we must come and visit them in Dorset. He said so too—in July. But C. said we would probably be going to Germany.

Then into the coatroom. And there were people saying goodby. Lady Astor kissed me and several people came up to me. Happiness lights you like a lamp. When I went into that cloakroom (in the beginning of the evening) I was dull and shy and no one noticed me. But when I went out, happy and alive, everyone was speaking to me and the people who did not know me looked around to see who it was. It is so strange—I was the same person both times.

Then I was walking down that long corridor of portraits again toward C., waiting for me. But not shy now, happy and confident. The taffeta dress, swishing under Elisabeth's long coat of velvet, and I trying to keep my head high. Walking down that long corridor toward the little group at the end: Lord Cranborne, and C., Mr. and Mrs. Winn, and Lady Cranborne standing together talking, turning to smile at me as I came down. I felt, I tasted at that moment, that rare evanescent soap-bubble happiness of youth—a young girl at a dance (I did not ever really taste it as a young girl because I was shy and awkward and not popular and not having found myself), a young girl who feels in the security of that soap-bubble moment, lovely, assured, poised, and wanted.

Then, somehow, the Winns had gone and we were left with the Cranbornes and we were taking them home, he, telling us a dreadful story of some English people caught in Austria.

And then we were back at the hotel, a night watchman letting us into the darkened, bare, swept-of-people hotel lobby. And to bed, C. saying he had never seen me like that, "drunk with happiness." (Though he said it didn't look "drunk" to other people!)

Thursday, June 2nd

A tearing wind flaps the curtains all night. (What is it like in the country!) We sleep late and have a good "bruncheon" in the grill.

Then home. Jon is in bed with a cold—again!

We decide we cannot get off Friday or Saturday as planned.

Friday, June 3rd

Jon in bed. I put him in my bed and light a fire. I carry trays up and down to him, and things to do. He is very good and works at puzzles and drawing games. He has a deep and shaking cough. I pack my trunk all day long, in between doing things for Jon and sometimes sorting papers for C. He has so much to do: the files, letters, last business, planning our get-off, and all the equipment, etc.

I walk in the garden in the evening. There is one large white unearthly clematis out, by the study window.

We sleep in our room in the midst of the half-packed suitcases and tissue paper.

I let Jon sit downstairs in the sun for a half-hour and lunch. But he watches the dogs from the bathroom window and catches more cold. When he sits at lunch he is quite limp and won't eat and then seems almost to wilt under your eyes. He feels miserable and complains of pain in his ear. I put him to bed. His temperature is over 100 and he suffers continually more. I call the doctor.

All afternoon poor Jon lies in bed tossing from side to side, saying, "It hurts—oh, it hurts so much." I sit by his side.

Dr. Berkeley comes at 4:30 (also, C. is back). Jon coughs very badly. Dr. Berkeley thinks it may be whooping cough! He recommends ear drops, medicine, etc., which we give Jon. By suppertime he is much quieted down and drops off to sleep. I feel relieved.

I walk in the garden after supper. All the roses are out on the house. The thrush still sings morning and evening. I shall miss the birds.

Sunday

Another day of packing and Jon in bed. His earache is gone, though he still has a temperature. I give him a paintbox and pictures and he paints quite happily all day. He is very sweet and says occasionally to me, "You're very good to me, aren't you?" "Am I, Jon? Why do you think so?" "Yes, *I* think so—because you let me do what I want to do."

We really finish the packing on this, the third day.

Monday, June 6th

Jon's temperature still up, though he does not feel bad. But he looks so white and his eyes about twice their size (they are so big anyway). I am anxious to get him by the sea, give him some resistance.

After supper I sit on the garden steps. First I walk around the whole garden looking at each bed, trying to learn it all by heart.

Up, first, through the Comtesse de Cayla beds, bounded by box, up the stone path and steps to the upper rose beds above the terrace wall, sweet with pinks.

I walk down the brick paths between the rose beds. Then turn and walk down the steps, past the Comtesse de Cayla beds again, down the second steps, looking up and down the brick walk. Remember: iris and pink valerian together and the rock pinks. Remember the beds bordered by stones on the first terrace. The salmon-pink poppies are out at the end of this lawn. Remember how lovely gray plants look as edging, against taller green ones. There isn't much in these beds on the first lawn. The big rose-bushes, the Michaelmas daisies, a phlox (none in bloom now). Iris, both deep blue and the pale blue kind, are out now.

Down the steps, bushy and sweet-smelling with santolina, rose-mary, and the gray spikes of lavender in bud. Across the little strip of lawn, down more steps, across the second lawn, down the next steps. Thyme here, and more lavender. Along the brick walk past the rose beds—the Château du Clos Vougeot, not out yet. The Frau Karl Druschki, not out. A few of the Caroline Testout are out. Through the beds edged with lavender, catmint, pinks, rock pinks, sea pinks. The anchusa is out, but not the larkspur; there is some blue flax out, and coral flower and iris here and there. The garden is mostly blue, except for a few of those orange poppies and the pinks.

Up again to the first steps. I sit where I have sat so often, looking down over the lawns, past the beds at the bottom, past the beech hedge to the field, just showing, and the curving rounds of treetops and lines of woods and fields alternating beyond—a pleasant, peaceful, English landscape. So peaceful and quiet and there to take—and I am leaving it.

I look back at the house glowing in the evening light—its pinky red bricks, its tawny roof, and the flowers climbing over the walls. The tassels of blue ceanothus are still a mass under our window and the roses everywhere give back the evening light, especially the big red rose vine on the barn glows with a rosy evening light. I try to impress it on my memory. In the years before us we will need this peace we are giving up so lightly. The peace of English gardens may be a rare thing in the near future. I am desperate with the thought that I shall forget it.

And then gradually as I sit there I think it is stupid to "grab at it" so frantically. Of course I must lose this garden, as one has to lose everything in life. Nothing is permanent—nothing stays. It is enough to have had it. And it will always be part of the permanent landscape of the mind and that is enough. And who knows how complete that landscape may be, how deeply engraved it is on my memory—perhaps much deeper than I know, perhaps indelibly marked there, not because of my efforts to keep it but in spite of them. Nothing would be lost. "Not one sparrow shall fall."

I felt convinced of this somehow and comforted and then went back and wrote a note to Mrs. Nicolson to tell her how I loved the house. I wanted really to write him, as he told us about the house first and as he loves it still, but I was afraid it would never get to him through the pressure and busy-ness of his active, brisk, must-see-the-latest-newspaper-or-person-back-from-Spain-or-word-from-Czechoslovakia life. No—even if he read it. And she—she might really hear what I said and be a little pleased because she knows what it is to love houses and places.

Tuesday, June 7th

Leave Long Barn with a sprig of rosemary in the pin in my scarf. Jon's temperature is well down. I am relieved and feel better about going.

Good-bys: to Hammond—I tell him he's been so nice to Jon. He says with difficulty after a little pause; "I'd like to keep him!" To Hook, bending over the east beds, planting out zinnias. To the garden. . . .

We drive away in Maryot's "chariot" with all the plate glass and a trunk strapped on behind. We stop to say good-by to Mrs. Wood [the postmistress]: "Oh, how I'm going to miss you." Then up the hill to Sevenoaks. Leave Reading early afternoon. Fly over Long Barn. Looking down on it was somehow like looking back at it in memory, in time. So little, so neat, so clear, all laid out: the terraces, the garden, the fruit trees. It made altogether an almost perfect square, so small, it could be covered with my hand, a deceptive, fleeting kind of possession. I had said good-by to it, but there it was in my hand.

But so small, now only part of a huge landscape—all of England we were flying over. As it would be now in my life—only a small part of my life, taking its place along with other parts; a small green spot embedded in my memory.

Then Lympne and across the Channel—"the last of England"—to Saint-Inglevert and the trip to Morlaix. The hour along the coast, the hour across land, the last hour of Brittany coastline, Mont-Saint-Michel to Morlaix. Miss H.'s purple coat, Mme Carrel in black, and the Massons. C. does a *chandelle* zooming over the hangar.

We land and taxi in. Thor and Skean are in our car with Miss H., Thor almost bursting with excitement at the sound of the plane. (He remembers it from Maine, bringing us.) We drive to Port-Blanc. It is very dry. They have had no rain since February—a real drought.

It is very low tide. We take the dogs and bundles over the rocks at Port-Blanc to Pierre and the little boat. It is hot driving but cool as we turn the corner to the harbor. Then Saint-Gildas with Thor and Skean and all the big black dogs barking. Thor and Skean are delirious with joy. Antoinette gives them a big pail of water.

Wednesday, June 8th

Over to see Illiec by boat and return the same way. The shutters show from afar, quite a bright (but nice) blue-green. They will fade, however. But the front of the house is in frightful disorder, completely torn up because Louis has been getting the rocks out, and they are scattered about the "lawn." All trace of green has gone, dug up with rocks and gorse and trampled by the workmen (only the santolina bush still grows, staked off by some boards).

To add to the confusion all the furniture is tumbled about in frightful disorder in front of the house (as though it had just been thrown out of the windows). It is pretty much broken up, backs of armoires out, sides gone, etc. The best bureau is out in front of the front door and has sacks of plaster on it! The ground is white and brittle with bits of plaster, wood, and sand.

Inside, the house is full of dust and plaster. The plasterers are still working, scraping and fixing the walls. None of the walls are dry, and the color—my "warm cream"—is a cold cement-gray white! *"Cependant, j'ai mis beaucoup de jaune dedans,"* says little François naïvely to Mme Carrel's complaint. The painting has not even started. I do not see how we can possibly move in this week.

We choose the color for the woodwork and make a fuss about the furniture. Has it been out here all the time? It is broken. The workmen are quite lighthearted about it. They say, *"On arrangera tout ça."* Anyway, we get Louis and a man to move the good pieces in the garage.

Thursday, June 9th

Up early, to get off Saint-Gildas by the high tide. To Tréguier to pick up Savina. We are going to look for old pieces of furniture. Savina knows where to go: to Landivisiau, where a man has two old barns heaped with dusty pieces. There are *lits clos*[1] stacked one on top of another. We climb on top of crates and beds and turn the *lits clos* over one by one. C. finds at the bottom of a pile a very pretty old one with early carving and a crucifix on it. Under the dust and old paint it is difficult to see if they are good enough wood to fix up. They are going to scrub the paint off and we will come back and look at it.

Then we motor on and have lunch in a little inn—a very good lunch, and red wine and cherries.

We go to a little place called Gouezec and stop in front of a café. Two old women, in black, with white caps, come out, also a youngish woman who runs the café. They have, seated on the

[1] Carved Breton bedsteads, that shut like armoires.

floor, a lovely old carved *vaisselier* [dresser for plates] of chestnut. The racks are carved in a flower design. I like it better than Mme Carrel's. Also they have benches, a cradle, and a quite lovely *lit clos*. We say we will take the *vaisselier* and the *lit clos*.

Then on back to Landivisiau to see the washed bed. It is quite late and we must hurry for the tide. The wood is good, Savina says. He will come back and pick up all the pieces with a truck.

Back to Port-Blanc, tired but very happy about our purchases.

Sunday, June 12th

Up at 2:45 to drive to Saint-Malo for the children. We arrive about 7. The boat is just coming in. We are not allowed in the customs house, so we wait at the door—for hours. Finally I see them. Jon, pale, and overwhelmed in a tweed hat too large for him and that dark coat. His eyes very big and his hair over his forehead. Land, fat, rosy, and his hair curly and damp with the heat. I take Land and sit him in the car. He fusses a lot.

We arrive at Buguélès, where the road goes into the water, at about 12:30. Mme Carrel is there with Pierre and a donkey cart, as it is low tide, to take the children to Saint-Gildas. We put the baggage and Miss W. and the children in the cart, and I get up, too, thinking Mme Carrel is coming too. No, she is not—she is walking. So I jump down again and we make her get up—with the greatest difficulty. She wants me to go and we all go off feeling disturbed.

It is so often like that, here. Mme Carrel is generous and strong-minded and used to just pushing everything along ahead of her. It is difficult to spare her any trouble.

Miss W., Mme Carrel, and the children go off in the donkey cart. C. and I and Miss H. come back in our own car alone to Buguélès and drive the car over the sand, mud, stones, and water to Illiec. It is rather hard going. I should not like to do it every day. It will be very bad for the car. Then we walk back to Saint-Gildas and arrive about two. The children are well settled (only I did want to be with Jon when he first saw Saint-Gildas). Miss

W. has everything she wants. Mme Carrel is happy at her approval. All is serene. After lunch we put Jon to bed. Land plays out on a rug in the sun. I feel relieved to have them safely here. Jon really got up out of bed to come.

After his nap C. takes Jon out in front of the house with a net, and they fish for shrimps and crabs. Jon is in ecstasy.

Thursday, June 16th

Work all morning on small corrections on book, repetitions, commas, and "darks," "lights," "side to sides," "listlesslys" that I use too often. The book has now no meaning, no sense of poetry, nothing spontaneous or "mine" about it, to me, because I have read it so often. I am only conscious of its faults. C. goes over it painstakingly by the hour picking out small errors for me to check. Then we go over it together, then I work on them alone.

After lunch we go off by foot to Illiec because Mme Carrel says the painters will be through on the bedroom floor and we can put in the furniture. They are not through but will be by tomorrow afternoon or Saturday morning. However, it is just as well we went over as we got the jolly painter—the ruddy-faced fair one—to paint the upstairs (third-floor) room of Miss H.

Then back to Saint-Gildas to work on the book again.

It is difficult because we are either doing things that are rather hard physically—like the long walk to Illiec—and usually hurrying (or necessities like washing Jon, carrying up water, etc.) or else working on the book, painstakingly, every minute. I am so tired at night, I drop asleep as soon as we stop working. There is no extra time to see Land, play with Jon, write in my dairy, write letters, which are all biting at my heels begging to be done.

The extra time, really, is spent in that odd way when you are visiting, simply "being a guest." You cannot avoid it. It is spent being polite, not rushing away from meals, talking, being around a little, making plans tactfully. And how *much* time is spent this way! Also, it irks me that I cannot help Miss W. more. Land cries a lot, in that tiny room. She does not get enough sleep and I cannot let her get off, as I must spend every second on the book. It should get to them by the 1st of July.

Friday, June 17th

After lunch C. and I walk over to Illiec (it is low tide) carrying our street shoes and bag. Then we take the car and drive across the flats to Buguélès and then, after stopping to change our shoes, on to Tréguier. Stop and see Savina, upstairs to his little *bureau,* which is small and covered with shelves of books and curious stones and sea shells. He has a book about C. there (written I don't know who by) and *Le Monde vu d'en haut.*[1] He is most apologetic for having said yesterday that Americans had not much taste, that they only liked things that astonished them. "I did not mean . . .," going on to say, *"Vous êtes poète, Madame,"* and pointing out the last chapter, which he had marked.

He gave us a little porcelain St. Yves: *"Ça porte bonheur,"* and we left for Saint-Brieuc.

To the hardware store, where we buy milk pails, scales, a lantern, two irons, a saucepan, a playpen for Land, two bathtubs, etc. I struggle with a pocket dictionary. It is terribly funny. The most difficult thing was trying to get a chemical toilet: *"Comme ça, mais avec . . ."* They do not understand, but the obliging young man shows us *everything* in the place, so I guess they just didn't have any.

Then to the *antiquaire,* where we buy the little sofa (C. says it won't last at all—it will fall to pieces) and arrange about transportation.

We rattle back to Port-Blanc with our packages (except for the pails and disinfectant; C. says we can have the toilets *made!*) and fire extinguishers and bathtubs. Arrive Saint-Gildas for supper.

Saturday, June 18th

After lunch, Mme Carrel, Miss H., C., Jon and I and dogs walk over at low tide to Illiec (where we say what beds to go in what

[1] French title of *North to the Orient.*

rooms, etc.) and then to Buguélès to meet Keraudren (a very important person). He keeps a general store, has the telephone, a cart and a truck which carries our luggage, parcels, etc., from Tréguier to Buguélès and Buguélès to Illiec, and he is our baker. Mme Keraudren is Pierre's sister—a nice, fresh-faced, cordial woman. Mme Carrel introduces us and then arranges with the butcher at Tréguier to order our meat for next week. It will come on Tuesday and Saturday from Tréguier. "P'tit Louis"[1] is to go every day to Buguélès to pick up bread, etc., from Keraudren. On Wednesday Keraudren goes to Tréguier and can get us what we want there (if we send a list Wednesday morning by P'tit Louis). Also we arrange about vegetables, eggs, etc. We will get our milk from Mme Carrel. P'tit Louis will go over each morning and get it. It seems to me P'tit Louis has quite a lot to do.

Then we buy the standard things to start with: tea, coffee, lard, eggs, sugar, salt, biscuits, oil for lamps, candles, matches. We see the bread and order a big round loaf. Also *des confitures* and some cans of stewed fruit and some sausage.

In the meantime several old Breton women come in, in black except for their white cotton sunbonnets, and we shake hands all around. Thor and Skean lie in the middle of the floor. Everyone is delighted by them. They bring a tiny puppy in and set it in front of Thor. Everyone oh's and ah's. (Mme Keraudren has heard about Thor from Pierre.) Jon is hopping up and down on one foot. Miss H. and I are trying on espadrilles. There are none big enough for C.

After quite a jolly community afternoon we start back across the mud flats to Saint-Gildas. Jon is very tired, and so am I. I wonder if the housekeeping at Illiec will ever straighten out and be easy. It seems horribly complicated—and all in French!

Work on the book each night.

Monday, June 20th

We move into Illiec. Pack until 10:30 and then pile all our bags, bundles, etc., into the boat. (It is high tide.) Mme Carrel has

---

[1] "P'tit Louis" is the fourteen-year-old son of the Lindberghs' couple.

attached the rowboat, a kind of trailer, to the motorboat, in which are stacked more of our things. It is a lovely day—clear, bright, and quite still. We climb down over the stones, Land's curls blowing in the air. Jon and the dogs get onto the prow of the boat, sitting on the anchor rope. C. takes a picture. We start off and arrive at Illiec before eleven. When we push up to the stones we discover that Louis has gone with P'tit Louis to fetch the provisions from Buguélès, there was so much. However, Pierre and Kerleau[1] and C. and Mme Carrel and I unload. The dogs jump off, Miss W. carries Land, and we start up to the house. It takes almost an hour to unload. Even Jon helps, carrying small bundles (his fishnet that Mme Carrel gave him goes up first).

Meanwhile, Miss W. and I arrange her room and the baby's. We move furniture most of the morning. I pick out the plates that are the least hideous and we have lunch at the small-leaved table under the huge mantel. It is quite good though plain, meat, salad (Mme Carrel sent a huge basket over full of provisions; the dressing is good), stewed fruit (from a can), and quite good coffee.

After lunch I go back to the moving and arranging. Back and forth to the "chalet," bringing mirrors, wicker tables, bottles for drinking water in our rooms, stools, etc.

I get the men to move up the bigger pieces, or show them where they are to go. Also I discover, out in the back yard, a good solid table once used for laundering and ironing in the room off the kitchen. I have them put it in the dining room and cover it with Mother's blue cloth for supper (Mme Carrel is coming). It begins to look orderly. I am pleased.

While I am washing the baby there is a great barking of dogs and commotion, then voices and the rumble of a cart. The trunks have come—over the sand and flats and up the hill in Kerau-dren's wagon.

---

[1] Yves Kerleau, a boatman and watchman for Illiec.

The rooms are now devoid of furniture but full of trunks. I feel a sense of home.

We work at night on the book.

Go to sleep to the sound of waves under our window and stones rolling and grating against each other as they are dragged back by the waves.

June 21st

Breakfast goes smoothly although it is late. Maryvonne works hard, but there is so much to do. Her coffee is good—which is a great deal.

I tell Maryvonne she must get someone to help her and does she know someone in Buguélès? She says *"Ma foi, non,"* but she will ask P'tit Louis to ask Mme Keraudren in the morning.

In the middle of the morning a lot of talk in front of the house. Louis and Kerleau and two of the painters have got the big linen armoire halfway in the front door when the bright ruddy-faced painter tells them it will not go around the curve of the stairs. How did it come out? It was lowered out of the window. But it cannot get back that way because the bars have now been put back in the windows.

There is something about the quick conversation and excitement that reminds me of Alice in Wonderland (Alice, big, caught in the house—Bill, the salamander, etc.). I wait and see what they will do. It is quickly decided. Louis sends P'tit Louis over to Buguélès to get a carpenter to undo the armoire.

Not long after he comes, very deaf and rather bent and old. But Louis shouts at him and he quickly knocks out the wooden pins and undoes the armoire. It is carried upstairs and set up again as quickly.

Mme Carrel finds us there. She must go to Paris before Dr. Carrel arrives. C. offers to take her tomorrow. She will send back word. A great deal of time seems to go in planning here, for the tides, for getting off and on the islands for food, for shopping, etc.

Work on book in the afternoon. At teatime (low tide) there is again the barking of dogs and general commotion which means someone coming over the flats. Keraudren's wagon slowly rumbles up the slope loaded with furniture and two women sitting in the front seat. (It looks like pioneers moving!)

It turns out to be our chairs and a table lent us by Savina, also Mme Keraudren and a girl to help Maryvonne. They all arrive at the same minute. Mme Keraudren, easy and assured, introduces the girl, who is young, shy, but nice-looking . . . except that her two front teeth are out!

It is very difficult to "interview" in French standing in the front hall at the same time telling the men where to put the chairs. Also tea is ready! Mme Keraudren speaks for Marie, saying she is used to work and will do all, all—*"tout, tout."*

She is coming to try on Thursday or Friday.

I ask Maryvonne to give them tea.

In the meantime the painters are slapping on the paint all day long—a funny little rhythmical flick—the last coat, to make it look like the grain of wood. They sing and shout to each other while they work. You never know where they will appear. All doors and windows are open in the house (thank goodness it is fine weather) and ladders against the shutters. I go into my room to change my dress and find a painter at the window.

After supper we *finish* the book. C. will take it to Paris tomorrow. Sitting at Savina's big table in the big bare room, I write Mr. Harcourt by lamplight. All done.

June 22nd

C. leaves about eleven.

After lunch I tell Miss H. and Miss W. to take the afternoon and go to Tréguier. They are pleased. As soon as Miss H. is packed up she is leaving for a week in London—they leave, by foot, across the Sillon,[1] P'tit Louis carrying the bags.

[1] A breakwater of stones that, except for very high tides, links Illiec to the mainland.

Everyone out of the house but the children and me. A beautiful day—I feel very free and happy. I sing as I do the baby. The painters are all singing, too—different tunes—as they slap on the paint. They have been working for two days now on the little entrance which leads to the w.c.s and on the w.c.s themselves. It has been impossible to get near them. They stop and talk to me as we go in and out of rooms and comment on the baby: *"Il est fort,"* *"Beaucoup plus fort que l'autre,"* etc.

As I am putting the baby down in his carriage one of the painters says he hears an *avion*. Yes, there is one. Out of the low clouds comes the plane, diving toward us. The painters, Louis, Kerleau all run out and look at it. I wave a diaper. The noise is terrific. The baby trembles. The painters are much impressed. *"Le Colonel, il a son avion à lui?"* They say it is like the war and ask how fast is it? There are many ah's and oh's. It circles the house once or twice and then goes off. I feel very thrilled—privately—as though (as I'm sure it is) it were a special good-by to me. We were so occupied with plans when they left at Port-Blanc that I hardly looked at C.

Then Jon and I go down on the rocks on the front beach, he with his net and little pail to catch shrimps. It is my birthday and I think I will just drop things and play with Jon for a while. It is nice and absorbing and restful, putting yourself into the world of a small pool with seaweed and a crab or two and shrimps and a few bright stones.

Then I go back and have tea and do the baby. The mail comes (a big mail from America). There is a letter from Harbrace. I tear it open. Mr. Harcourt wrote the same day he received the manuscript of *Listen! the Wind*. He says he sent for it from the Customs and read it all day and had to sit down and write immediately. He said it was one of the days that made publishing worth while—a grand job. I am very pleased, satisfied, and relieved, but not really as excited as by the first praise of Laura and George.

But it makes me happy. Besides, C. will be *so* pleased.

Also there is a fat letter from Mother and one from Con. I sit down in the midst of the confusion and soak myself in them. I feel warmed and happy.

The fog comes in about teatime.

After tea Miss W. and Miss H. come back, blown but contented. They brought with them a huge box of flowers wired from Sue Vaillant[1] for my birthday. As they stopped for gas at Penvenan, the girl said with some excitement, "You come from Illiec. There is a package here for you!" It had come all the way from Saint-Brieuc. Carnations and calla lilies all done up with asparagus ferns. I stick them into two high water pitchers and put them on Savina's big table.

After supper I sit in the big room with two lamps, looking out of the big curtainless windows at the strange rocks swathed in mist, and write Mother.

To bed with a hot-water bottle filled from the stove's tank.

Thor and Whisky [our couple's dog] bark uneasily, wandering around the house until twelve, as Thor always does when C. is away.

June 23rd

Thor gets into the rabbit coop and kills a rabbit. Then hides. I go after him, drag him back to the coop, and spank him with a paper. This—and talking it over with Maryvonne—takes a good part of the morning.

The painters leave at noon. The gay ruddy-faced one comes in while we are at lunch and shakes hands all around in a brisk businesslike way. He tells me it is too bad *le Colonel* cannot land in front of the house, then he could give him a ride.

After tea I go to Saint-Gildas to ask Antoinette about wages for Marie, kitchen matters, and to get my plants. I take Jon on the way to his island (the little nest) which he likes very much. I tell Miss W. to tell Kerleau to watch him, and I set off for Saint-

[1] Susanna Beck Vaillant, A. M. L.'s friend from Mexican years, later Mrs. Robert Hatt.

Gildas over the flats and rocks. Coming back with two of my plants in a basket, I see Kerleau and Jon on the flats, digging for cockles.

And suddenly, behind them—the plane! It dives over us—we run toward it, waving. It goes around, comes down low again. I can see C.'s hand. Jon is very excited. The third time it comes very low and drops something, a map trailing a rope (to weight it). I run to pick it up: a note from C. to say he will be there for supper at 8:15! Then the plane circles again and goes off toward Saint-Gildas.

In the middle of the afternoon the cart comes up the hill again. It is Keraudren with another load of furniture: two armoires and the *vaisselier*. They put it in the dining room. (Louis and Kerleau have been skating over the floor all afternoon with those strange footbrushes that rub wax. And the table and chairs are back in there.)

I am so anxious to have it look nice for C. I find two or three old plates from the chalet to put in the *vaisselier*.

I tell Maryvonne [about supper] and put Jon to bed. Then about 8:15 I go up on the rock to watch. You can see for miles. It is low tide—how will they come? (He said *we* would be there for supper—evidently Mme Carrel.) I can see the road across the flats to Buguélès and the spit of stones that connects our further island to Saint-Gildas, and beyond the harbor and dock at Port-Blanc a white boat—Pierre?

Finally I see the car, a dark form, come out of the gap (where the shore road comes down onto the flats) and start across the mud and sand. I watch it over the sands until it disappears behind the spit of stones. Then I run down and tell Maryvonne and Miss W. waiting in the big room that I've seen the car.

Finally C. comes up. Mme Carrel not there after all.

He goes in to see Jon and asks him if he saw the plane.

"Yes," said Jon, "I saw you, and I caught three cockles and two winkles!"

C. had a good time in Paris talking to people at the U. S. Embassy about the war in Spain.

He says the house looks much cleaned up. And the dining room looks lovely.

Miss W. calls us to say Savina is here. We rush down. Savina in blue trousers, and two of his men, are already working at the doors for the office and at the armoires. He has some coffee with us.

Also Marie has arrived. I must get her room ready, find a few pieces of furniture. She starts right in working and has a nice smiling face (except that the gap of the missing two front teeth shows when she smiles).

We show Savina the various pieces in the house to have fixed and decide where to put the armoires. Then he goes back. About teatime he comes back again with his little girl "Nola" (about five), very small, very pretty, in a navy-blue sunsuit and white hat. She takes off her hat and changes her shoes daintily before tea. Her fair curls are tied up on her head with a little blue ribbon.

I tell Jon to take care of her and show her the rabbits. He is very shy but takes her delicately by the hand out of the door. By teatime they are rushing around quite happily, though not understanding each other at all, and shouting to each other, she in French and he in English.

After tea C., Savina, and I go over the chapel and discuss *réparations*. Which means practically rebuilding the inside; take off the plaster, down to the bare stones, take out the cement floor, repaint or remake the vault. (It is now pale gray.) Savina picked at the walls with a hammer and chisel (I did the translating). Yes, there was stone underneath. Yes, you could take all that out.

By the time we get through it is quite late (for Jon's supper)— 7:30 or so. Nola is flushed and tired but very contented. I take them into the dining room and start Jon's supper and give her some more milk.

I hope she comes again—it is good for Jon.

Savina is here early, taking the measurements of the chapel. We decide to go back to Tréguier with him.

Back late for lunch. All meals are late here. And the beds unmade. They cannot get through all the work—and they work so hard. Is it just the confusion of the beginning or is there too much?

After supper C. and I talk to Louis about the chapel (Louis was worried when he saw Savina hammering at it). I told Louis that Colonel Lindbergh wanted to fix it up so that it looked really nice. He was very pleased. Then C. told him that we would go over the things that should be done in their house, repairs, etc.

The men have worked hard. When they are not moving furniture, clearing the rubbish—old broken bits, dirt, etc.—away from the house, they work with crowbars and pickaxes getting the rocks out.

But Maryvonne works harder. When she is through her work at the house she is down on her knees over at the water trough washing the men's clothes.

We take the car across the flats in the morning so that Miss W. can go off for a while, to church, etc. (How much of the time is spent doing things like this so Miss W. will be more satisfied.)

Then C., Jon, and I go out in the inland-sea flats and fish for shrimps in the little tidal streams. We have a lovely time, and catch enough for lunch.

After lunch, though, Jon comes in from outdoors and says he is cold. His nose is completely stopped up and his head hot: all the signs of a bad cold. I stick him in bed. He can't breathe through his nose. Stuff Vicks and then cotton in his nose and get a hot-water bottle. I pin his pictures up around the walls. Very soon he feels better and by suppertime seems quite clear and happy. But I make him stay in bed. I suppose he got too wet and cold wading in the stream and got a chill.

Miss W. comes back about teatime quite excited. She has had such an adventure. It is a very high tide, and she could not get across by the Sillon and had to go back to Keraudren's store. There they gave her hot coffee and biscuits and got a fisherman to take her over. But as it wasn't proper for her to go alone with the fisherman, big burly, blue bushy-haired Keraudren chaperoned her!

Monday, June 27th

A tearing wind. Dust from the too-dry ground swirls in your eyes and all the doors bang. There is no place to put the baby out of the wind. Jon runs around in a blue toweling pull-over with his bang of hair blown back from his high forehead.

C. and I start out for Malicorne to buy some china. This is the place Mme Carrel told us of. C. said it would only take three hours, but we drove on and on. We arrive at Malicorne after five. C. is not sure of the place. Malicorne seems full of faïence shops, though it is very small.

After walking into one or two others we finally find one not marked that C. remembered. In a big musty barnlike room shelves stacked with things and cups strung up on strings from the ceiling. An old man, portly with a white beard and black skullcap, is in charge. We start rummaging around and soon the floor is untidy with piles of bowls, porringers, cups, plates, little bowls. "Take plenty—we won't get here again for a long time. They're very cheap and probably break easily," C. kept urging me, finding more little bowls. We leave the pile on the floor for the man and a rather disgruntled servant to add up. We will come back in an hour.

We go to another place and buy twelve lovely flower plates

(more expensive) and some pitchers. The first place was short of these. At another place I order a tea set in better ware and a coffee set and a set of *pots* for sweet cream desserts.

Then back to No. 1, where they have scribbled the prices on a dusty sheet of wrapping paper. We add a few more things, almost in the dark—vegetable dishes, more plates, green for salads, serving bowls, soup tureen, etc. The woman is incredulous. She rushes out for the man. He then gives us a present of a large and not very pretty flower pot, which I change for another.

Finally we pay and tell the woman to pack it all right into the back of the car in hay. We plan to eat while she packs, but at this moment the old man finds out who C. is. *"Ah, Leenbairgh! C'est un honneur ... C'est* vous *qui avez ... tout seul—vous ..."* etc. He rushes off for his wife. We meet the whole family. He rushes off for a Curé and then off again, I think, for the Mayor, but I get his wife to stop him. If we get a large crowd around us now, with the packing . . .

We decide not to eat there. It may leak out we're here and be embarrassing. So we wait till we're packed—now after 8:30—near 9 (C. gives the woman a tip; she is very pleased) and off we go, the hay behind us smelling like a meadow.

We won't get home till 2 or 2:30 if we go at this morning's pace, and we'll have to go slower because of the china. It is now dusk. We stop at a hotel at Sable, quite near, and eat under a trellis of grapevines out of doors; a good dinner. But we have so far to go. Very tired but contented.

Then on—miles and miles of dark road. It begins to rain. The china rattles in back and worries us. We get gas enough to go all the way from the last big town open (the towns shut up at 9:30 or 10). We try to figure out the tides. It will be high when we get there (about 3:30 or 4). Then we can't drive across with our load; will have to leave the car, come for it again in the morning, and, worst of all, have to find our way back across the Sillon by dark, without a light.

We decide to spend the night on the road. But where? Not at

Rennes; too big. We try to wake several hotels in small towns—
Lamballe—stopping and knocking, ringing bells. No answer. (I
remember once we drove all night because we couldn't get in
anywhere.) Finally about 3:30 we stop at Saint-Brieuc—a light in
the front hall of quite a big and modern hotel. We ring and
someone comes.

We put our car opposite. We get a room with *bath!* Wonderful. But we cannot get soap at that hour of the night, or water to
drink.

Tuesday, June 28th

A great rumble of carts under the window wakes us. I ring for
soap (two francs) and have a long and delicious bath and feel
civilized and happy again. Then a good breakfast: croissants and
confiture and coffee. Then out shopping, at the hardware store
again, for scrapbaskets, foot-tubs, rope rugs, linoleum, etc. Then
to Grand Bazaar—it is just closing time—for sheets. I get all they
have: two double and four single sheets. We have a hard time
taking them, even saying Mme Carrel sent us and showing the
passport. Finally I explain, "Le Colonel Leenbairgh." The watchman gets it at last (everyone else has now left) and runs to ask
the manager next door. It is all right. We take the sheets!

Arrive at Illiec over the flats at about 2 or 2:30. Dr. and Mme
Carrel have just walked over from Saint-Gildas. There is still that
tearing wind blowing. Jon comes running to me in tears to tell
me he has broken a window (trying to kill flies). Also the window in his room is broken—the wind blew it banging against the
wall.

Dr. Carrel is looking at the baby in his carriage. He says he
should not have so much between his legs and should not be so
much on his back. Miss W. says nothing but is annoyed. At last
we go in to eat—Jon with us.

We climb the rocks and talk about the view. There is no time
to put my things down, wash my hands, or see what the household is doing. Finally they leave. It is too late to take the car back

to Buguélès. The tide is rushing in. Miss W. was told she could take it tomorrow to Lannion to meet Miss H. The next low tide is late tonight—11:30 or 12:00. C. will have to take it over then (after no sleep last night).

The wind is still blowing a gale and slamming doors in your face. Tea is late for Miss W. "Did you ask Maryvonne to have tea for me?"

I did—but Maryvonne had waited because she saw Mademoiselle was busy. "The whole day has been like that," said Miss W.

Over to Saint-Gildas. A tearing wind, spray soaking C. and Pierre in the boat. I get under the hood. It is quieter inside Saint-Gildas. (I must get a place out of the wind at Illiec.)

Dr. Carrel talks with a good deal of understanding and interest of Jon, his sensitivity, his intelligence, his quickness, and of the difference between the two children.

We walk back in dim dusk over the stones to Illiec.

Then C. starts to drive over. I rush out and go with him—so eerie and strange through the mist and dark and no road you can see, but a light on shore guiding us like a lighthouse across the flats and sand and the tidal stream and mud.

Then the long feet-wet walk back—all for Miss W.'s good humor! To bed very tired.

June 29th

Miss W. off early across the long Sillon (it was high tide) to meet Miss H. Marie, Maryvonne, Kerleau, Louis—everyone gets up to help her off. They *are* good people.

There is quite a wild sea dashing on the rocks, though the wind is less. Jon can hardly dress for looking out of our window in the morning.

The Carrels come for lunch. The Breton china looks lovely on the table. It brightens the meals.

C. says Dr. Carrel will hit the ceiling if he sees Land strapped into his carriage (though he can sit up, turn from side to side and completely over in his strap; it only keeps him from falling out). I undo the strap and talk to Miss W. Slight scene. It is more than she can bear to have Dr. Carrel's criticism. She is unhappy and aggrieved. I foresee a dreadful lunch. However, it is not too bad. The meat is good. And when Dr. Carrel asks Jon is he learning to speak French now, Jon answers quite clearly with the confidence of youth, *"Oui!"* About the only word he knows. It pleases Dr. Carrel.

After lunch I do Land. Dr. Carrel wants to see him with all his clothes off on the rug. Land is quite good though does not crawl his best. He (Dr. Carrel) says he is a beautiful baby, and has a magnificent "thorax"!

I put him back in his carriage unstrapped. When I come back he is on all fours peering out the side of the carriage at Dr. and Mme Carrel. I: "I am afraid he will fall out."

"But that is just what we were saying. It is very dangerous."

"Yes, that is why I strap him in."

"Is he supposed to sleep now?"

"Yes."

"Ah well, there is no reason why he should not be strapped in when he sleeps."

I put the straps back on.

C. tries to be nice to Miss W. but she is in a bad state—about everything. Even though I talk to her about the Dr. Carrel incident and try to straighten it out. Everything is wrong. The meals are late. She complains of the food, the lack of service, the way they wash dishes, the way they make beds, they forget to order things. She has no water. Could Marie help to wash the diapers? There is no more Lipton's tea . . . a constant "I can suffer" attitude.

It is very wearing. Especially as I don't want Marie and Maryvonne offended. They work extremely hard, all day and until late at night. If things are a little irregular at first they might be excused.

I try to do all I can to help Miss W. do the baby—carry up

water or get Marie to. But nothing is right. I think it is not the work that upsets her as much as the general lack of order and routine, the unexpectedness of the life here. Never being able to count on anything—tides, meals, weather, laundry, etc. She needs the routine of English life.

Jon and I collect round stones on the beach in the late afternoon, which is nice.

Thursday, June 30th

It rains!

Do Land and write in my diary in the morning. Miss W. still critical of everything. Meals are stiff and dreadful.

After lunch I go to Buguélès by foot at low tide across the flats and take the car to Tréguier (it rains!) and shop for fruit, cereals, a bathtub for Land, an iron and teakettle for Miss W.—quite an outing. Then walk back across the Sillon about six. Tension has eased a little.

Everything looks and smells better after the rain. Also, there is water in the cistern.

C. and I sit on the big rock at night.

Friday, July 1st

Dr. Carrel and Mme Carrel come over right after I have done Land, with M. le Recteur of Port-Blanc. He is a nice perceptive man with taste and such a good kind face. He has some good suggestions about the chapel.

But I can only think how unhappy Miss W. is and how dreadful the summer is going to be on those terms. I ask Miss W. if she doesn't want to take the car and go off in the afternoon. She says can she go with Miss H. C. says yes, so they go off.

C., Jon, and I go crab hunting in the little streams. You knock the stones and lift the seaweed with one end of your pole and then the crabs run out and you catch them in the net. Jon shouts, "Oh—oh—oh—Father," when he gets a big one. Also he finds a "live abalone" on a rock.

Late for tea and Land. I stick him in a high chair while I have tea, which he loves. I do not do his cereal right, in a hurry and everything goes wrong. Cannot bear to have Miss W. find everything wrong. I feed him rusks and milk at last and put him to bed.

They come back much more cheerful. Supper is quite a pleasant meal, with all our crabs! We make Marie show us how to shell them with her deft fingers.

After supper Mme Carrel and Dr. Carrel come over. We go up on the rock and watch the sunset. Dr. Carrel says, "Once in a thousand years you get a sunset like this." After they go we go back to the house. Misses W. and H. are playing that *dreadful* victrola. It resounds through the house, also their voices. We agree something must be done about it but is it worth it at this moment, just before Miss W. goes off on her vacation? Can we put up with it another day or two? You never can speak to Miss W. about anything.

I tell Maryvonne she can send their laundry with ours. They are very pleased. I can get on with her *so* much better.

Saturday, July 2nd

The household still thundery. I try to work out in my mind how to make it better. Let Miss H. and Miss W. take a room at the chalet, have their victrola there, to themselves. Then they'll be out of the house in the evening.

Also get an extra person to do cleaning in the house. Marie to help me, and later Miss W., with the washing, etc.

I do Land in the morning and try to clear out the house. Land sits in a foot tub which he likes very much, holding on to the sides with both hands. He stops crying (he has been screaming so much lately, in anger and impatience for his food, and perhaps teeth—the double ones) and slaps the water.

After lunch C. walks to Saint-Gildas. I ask Jon if he wants to go to Port-Blanc with me to get fishnets and baskets (and a tea set). He says, "I think I'd like to get cockles." "All right," I say, "then maybe I'll stay and watch you—on your island."

"And not go to Port-Blanc?"

"Well, I would go if you wanted to go with me, but I don't think I want to go alone."

"I'll go with you—if you want," said Jon magnanimously and very grownuply. So we set off together across the flats.

"Just you and I," said Jon, "all alone?"

We meet François, on the way, riding a bicycle across the mud! He stops and gives me the estimate for the sea wall (back of house), for buttressing up the cave under the two trees (front), *réparations* on the cottage, etc.—5500 francs.

Jon hops around looking for cockles. It is quite a long pull, though; by the time we get to Buguélès I can see we won't get to Port-Blanc and back in time for tea. I tell Jon.

"I don't mind missing tea," said Jon—again magnanimously and suddenly like his father, encouraging me to go through with my idea.

So I rolled up the garage door and took the car out and we went to Port-Blanc and bought two nets, two salt and peppers (there was no complete tea set), another fish basket, and some chocolate.

Then back to Buguélès, lock up the car, and the long walk back across the flats.

I put Jon to bed with a hot-water bottle; I hope he is not too tired. He has been such a real companion to me today.

Maryvonne makes her first cake. It is dry and rather crumby and needs butter. Tomorrow I shall tell her gently.

After supper, C. and I walk around the island. It is cold but rather fun. We go over rocks I haven't seen before. The big overhanging one, and one out to sea. Thor tries to follow us.

Sunday, July 3rd

Miss W.'s passport has not come back. Can she go? I sometimes wish we had neither a secretary nor a nurse, though I know we need both. I feel as if I could take in my stride the drafty rooms, the late meals, the lack of water and lights, the cold, the sometimes tasteless food, the lack of service, the flies, the general untidiness and disorder—and the extra work—if only I were not trying so hard all the time to protect Miss W. and Miss H. from these, to make things easier for them, because I worry when they are discontented and unhappy. I suppose it's somewhat British homesickness.

But *why* should I make all this effort—only for complaints?

Clean my room, cut papers for shelves and drawers, and put up bars to hang clothes on, etc.

After lunch C., Jon, and I go off to hunt cockles in the flats and *couteau* [razor] clams at Saint-Gildas. When we arrive at Saint-Gildas (with a pailful of cockles got on the way; this was great fun) the tide is not yet low enough and there is a very cold wind blowing. We stay an hour and Mme Carrel comes too, good-naturedly, but it is too windy to get many and very cold. My feet are icy and hands too, and Jon is cold. We start back across the flats—the muddy way—with our catch, which C. and Jon take in to the kitchen for supper.

Jon has *couteau* clams for supper, which he loves. Then a bath, in the tin tub I bought for the baby. Quite successful.

Miss W. (now in quite good spirits) and Miss H. leave after supper.

The house is peaceful again—and ours. I feel much happier. Tomorrow I suppose will be hard work.

Monday, July 4th

A nice day, though hard work. Wake up in the middle of the night to an unaccustomed drip-drop. Rain! It has rained quietly and continuously all night.

The baby is cooing happily next door. I go through and wake Jon. All very cheerful at breakfast, an unaccustomed freedom of speech and feeling.

François was coming today to go over the repairs for the house, but he does not appear. One of his men comes for the afternoon, hammering up rocks in the front yard to use on the sea wall in back. Apparently Monday is a half holiday in France.

I am late, however, with the baby's breakfast (1), because I cook the oatmeal in a double boiler instead of straight on the stove and it takes much longer and (2) because Marie comes in with a strange humorous-faced, freckled girl with kinky light hair, from Buguélès, to help. Her name is Yvonne. (I can't believe it. The cook is Marie-Yvonne and the two girls Marie and Yvonne!) She will come for a week to try and stay in the house—where? Oh, we can sleep in the same room, says Marie. Marie, the shy, the toothless, seems quite assured and a beauty compared to Yvonne. There is a grace about Marie. Yvonne is comical—*Bécassine!* Anyway, they start off working on the rooms.

I do Land. He loves his bath and slaps the ball in the water. After I put him down I do yesterday's diapers and hang them up in the wind by the chalet. Then I clean up the bathroom, put his towels to dry, and then wash his flannel dress and two knit panties in Lux and some underwear for myself.

Then it is time for lunch.

After lunch Land again. The peas to get and mash, the soup to reboil and skim the fat off. The dishes to wash. The milk to boil. Then, with Land down again, I go and lie down for a half-hour. Jon comes and talks to me—about snails. He wants to eat one. I tell him I saw a big one out on the well. He rushes out for it.

At 3:45 I go up and try to plan where Yvonne will sleep. In one of the extra guest rooms? Or in that room I'd meant for storage?

You cannot get into Miss H.'s room, as the doorknob is off. In the other room you cannot see, as the bar that holds the shutters open is broken. Also a window is broken. There is so much to do to this house before it is livable. I make lists all day long. But one is always waiting for "the things from Harrods," for "François's carpenter," for a day in Tréguier, in Saint-Brieuc, for Savina's men, etc.

There is a cold wind blowing now and gusts of rain. I go for the diapers but Marie has already brought them in.

Tea—how pleasant meals are here with only Miss H. and us!

She is young and fun and not in the way. The whole atmosphere is lighter. I put Land on a high chair between us for tea. He bangs on the table with a spoon very happily and loves it. It is gay and untidy. C., oblivious, goes on talking German, English, and French military aviation.

Letter from Margot. They are coming down quite near here—Saint-Efflam, near Lannion.[1]

Land's supper again late, but he is not late to bed and goes down happily. The diapers are back all dried, the bathroom clean for Jon. It has been quite a successful day.

Jon asks for his snail for supper. He took it in to Maryvonne to be cooked but it got lost somewhere—crawled off among the pots and pans in the kitchen!

Jon says every night it's too cold to wash—he wants to jump right into bed. I know just how he feels!

Tuesday, July 5th

The Carrels are here for lunch. The lunch is quite good, though plain. Dr. Carrel asks why should the baby sleep outside in a small carriage when he could sleep inside in a comfortable bed? No special virtue in being outside *all* the time. Is it not another superstition? (In this case it is because he is quieter outside. We work in his room during the day.) Also he does not think the veal broth Land is taking has any particular value.

I am glad Miss W. is not here.

We have quite an interesting lunch, Dr. Carrel discussing the effects of climate on character.

After supper, C. and I go for a walk about the island, out to the farthest point, bare and rocky. Then we cross to "Jon's island," where we sit under the boughs of the pines for a long time. There is a rough rain, and wind blowing, dark clouds and crows overhead, cawing. But we are sheltered in that little "nest" of an island, our backs to the rocks and the pine boughs a low roof

---

[1] Margot and Dwight Morrow were in France on their honeymoon.

over us, looking back to landward and at one big rock at the entrance of Illiec.

Wednesday

After lunch Miss H. and I go to Lannion to buy some essentials for Mrs. Lindbergh's room.[1] Blankets, sheets, pillowcases, towels, two rough sets of tablecloths and napkins, a soup ladle and an egg beater. I ask if they don't have two blankets alike in *any* color?

I walk back very tired and wet over the stones. C. sees me from a long way and sends Thor to meet me. I have a nice coming-home feeling: "This is my home I'm doing all this for."

François is here! I have come just in time to translate, says C. But the baby is screaming on the floor for his supper. "Can't he wait a minute?" He does, while C., François (in his funny cap on one side of his head and that thin scarf tied awry on his neck), and I go over the *réparations* on the house. François said he will bring the itemized account tomorrow and we can go over the new things with him then.

"What time tomorrow?" asks C., hoping to pin him down, the elusive François.

François looks up wistfully, anxious to please. *"Demain matin —demain matin."* (He does not, however, appear until the afternoon!)

Then to the baby, who quiets quickly after cereal and prunes. (Marie skins them for me. She is so willing and helpful. Then goes ahead and gives Jon his supper.)

To bed after supper with a hot-water bottle and *The Thinking Reed* by Rebecca West.

Thursday

The morning goes as usual. There is a gale blowing on the front of the house, where I hoped we could have a garden—what I

[1] C. A. L.'s mother was coming for a visit.

called "the sheltered side of the house." Doors bang all day. You can hardly open the doors on the windy side of the house.

Commotion downstairs. Mme Carrel's voice (quite excited). What has happened? Fisherman's boat turned over in storm? Dr. Carrel ill? or what?

No—four reporters have appeared in a boat in our bay. No one would take them in either at Port-Blanc or Buguélès. So they got a boat and sailed from Lannion—in this wind! Mme Carrel shouted to the men on the place, called Louis and Kerleau from hammering stones, the workman from his wheelbarrow, the mason from the wall, P'tit Louis and all the dogs, and was out with her cane and off down the Sillon to meet them. A warm reception!

They left for Saint-Gildas (where I think Dr. Carrel talked to them, probably to try and persuade them not to bother us).

After lunch François arrives (in his scarf and cap). We go over the house, plan several things for the kitchen, a cupboard, a *garde-manger,* a new door, etc.

Friday, July 8th

Still a tearing wind and gusty rain squalls.

Savina arrives in the morning while I'm doing the baby. After I put Land in the pen, we discuss the shape and dimensions of the dining-room table and go over the house for other things, fittings in the armoires, shelves and bars, also window seats and weather stripping on the windows.

After lunch the afternoon goes into getting Mrs. Lindbergh's room ready. Yvonne and Marie have been on their hands and knees all afternoon polishing the floor with wax.

Finally by suppertime it looks quite nice. The faded blue curtains are up (carefully ironed into wide pleats by Yvonne) and a single one on the tower (bathroom) window. Amey's Italian striped cover on the table, the Quimper inkwell on top, a glass (or old pitcher) of flowers on the bedside table (also covered with a sampler). The kerosene lamp has a lamp shade on it.

I look at the room with pride and then think, But she won't appreciate it because, after all, it's just a *normal* room! It has all the things the rest of the house lacks: curtains, a rug, real wool blankets on the bed, one old armoire, a wash basin and pitcher that match, and a lamp with a lamp shade!

Still, I have the satisfaction of knowing that the heart's blood of the house and its occupants (Marie, Yvonne, Maryvonne, Louis, and I) have gone into its completion.

C. goes to Saint-Gildas at night. I too tired; go to bed.

Saturday, July 9th

In the morning the barking of dogs tells us that the wagon is coming—*la charrette*—with the boxes from Harrods. Keraudren's man, Louis, and Kerleau bring them into the living room and we unpack feverishly: all the linen, Jon's table and chair, our books, but no rubber boots.

I run up and put a pretty homespun bedspread on Mrs. Lindbergh's bed—one of the India ones. In the afternoon, Jon and C. go for Mrs. Lindbergh (Jon is very anxious to go, for the train as well as for "Farmor"). I iron, wash, etc., and Miss H. fixes all the linen in the big linen armoire. It looks very pretty and comforting.

After tea all the household are out looking for C. and Mrs. Lindbergh. They spy the car about seven. Kerleau is over there with his boat but it is too low to sail back. They walk over the Sillon in quite a wind—a lowering day (it has rained off and on). Mrs. Lindbergh in street shoes with heels and holding on to her straw hat with flowers. (She looks very pretty.) Jon is coming behind. Her pockets are already full of stones Jon has made her carry. I keep Land up on the mat to see them. Mrs. Lindbergh can't believe him—says he's very big.

Jon has supper with us. Marie and Yvonne have miraculously cleared up the big room from all the unpacking. It is quite cold but Mrs. Lindbergh goes up on the rock after supper, to see the view.

Sunday, July 10th

The morning goes to the baby, Mrs. Lindbergh watching, then playing with him downstairs on the rug, ten to eleven.

The Carrels come over for tea.

I speak to Miss H. about the phonograph. After supper C. and I walk with Louis over the Sillon to Buguélès to see the little boat that is being made for us. It is that same little deaf man who came the first day to fix the linen armoire (to undo it and take it up the stairs).

C. talks to me in English, I to Louis in French, Louis to him in Breton (shouting). And his wife interposes a little. It is a nice little boat and we are planning to have a small engine in it. Then, Louis says, he can go to Buguélès, Port-Blanc, or even to Plougrescant!

Louis tells us he was almost born on the island (Illiec). His mother was cook there. And his grandfather was *gardien* for Ambroise Thomas. He said Thomas used to come down with his artist friends and play the piano all night!

Monday, July 11th

Mrs. Lindbergh has baby on floor in big room. She dances him up and down and has him kick a ball, which he loves. She thinks, however, that he is cold when he crawls (his top and bottom clothes separate in two). Also that there is too much dust on the rug for him (so he is on her lap a good deal!). She suggests we pasteurize the milk as boiled milk is constipating! C. looks it up in the encyclopedia. It would be easier to start a dairy.

Tuesday, July 12th

After breakfast François arrives *with* his carpenter, at last, to fix the doors and windows.

The morning goes into the baby and then rushing in a few spare minutes to translate for C. with François. The man starts work on the kitchen, tearing out the partition. Maryvonne sweeps up after them. She smiles toothless and good-natured. She says, "It must be dirty before it's clean!" (in French).

I lie down in afternoon for a half-hour (only free time) and wonder why I can't manage the day better. Every day there is something vital that must be done: see the boat, see Savina, translate for C., see François, see Kerleau and Louis, translate, find out what is being done here and there. Shop in Tréguier. The responsibility of a new household is myriad. Everyone comes to you, asks you, waits for you; meals, plans, work; children—all the threads must be held in your hand at the same moment. I like that, only it is difficult to do when you must spend endless time holding a baby on your knees, or washing dishes or baby clothes, or feeding Land, or any of his routine.

Just get Land finished in time to go to Saint-Gildas for supper. It is calm there; the wind is not blowing. The meal is delicious, beautifully laid out, prepared, and served by Antoinette. There are lilies in a vase by the Madonna. There is time to walk about the garden. And there are birds singing.

I wonder, sitting back in it, if our house will ever have such peace.

Dr. Carrel spends much time asking Mrs. Lindbergh what C. was fed on as a child, as he considers it very important to find out the diet of those people who have turned out to be strong (a very sensible theory). There is never, I remark to Mrs. Lindbergh, such interest expended on what *I* was fed when *I* was a baby!

I dream of Long Barn. With a rush of relief at home-coming, I find I am back there and hurry with the joy of anticipation out to the garden in back, to see if it is still the same. Yes, it is there, and lovely. Then, I think, with a practical "there-is-still-time" Morrow mind; "Now that I'm here I'll just take a look and see if I find that Koran stand they say is missing. I feel sure I can put my hand right on it." But I wake first.

Wednesday, July 13th

The carpenter is here all day. The kitchen is much clearer with the partition out. And the shelves give more room. We have run into a snag in our bathroom. The little ridge that I thought was hollow and said to *arracher* is solid stone masonry. So we have had to widen it and make it big enough to put a bathtub on it. But then there is no room for a table. So I said to continue it on two sides. But that puts all the furniture an ankle length higher than us. I shall have to stand on a stool to wash! (It is like *The Peterkin Papers*.)

Thursday, July 14th

The morning goes as usual. (We have moved our bed and when we get up are now in full view of the mason working on the sea wall in back. I must get some curtains from the chalet.) And before I know it, and before the milk is boiled, Savina, Mme Savina in a black tailored suit (so French!), and Nola in a blue sunsuit have appeared. Savina works on the door. Miss H. takes Madame off. C. goes to find Jon and Mrs. Lindbergh (looking for snails). I boil the milk.

Then down to entertain. C., Savina, Mme Savina, and I walk through the pine wood, I translating and talking to Savina. Jon has already got the immaculate little girl picking up pine cones and branches for him.

We wind up by the house for lunch. Such a strange meal. Savina talking to me, I translating, C. asking questions. Mme Savina interposing, Mrs. Lindbergh silent, Nola nudging Jon (she says, "He doesn't speak French but he plays in French") and trying to pass food in two languages: *"Du café—comment?"* "Do you want coffee?" *"Du sucre?"* *"Encore du vin?"* *"Est-ce-que Nola prend . . .?"* etc., etc. Confusion. . . .

It is now a delicious afternoon, still and sunny. I roll up my sleeves. The sea is silken around those wild rocks in front. What peace not to have the wind blowing! I can move and live so much more easily, like a fish gliding through still depths.

July 19, warm day

C. over to Saint-Gildas and brings back the water diviner—a dapper little man in a dark town suit, a tweed hat, shoes, and a dark mustache. Not really "dapper" in a town sense but quite prosperous-looking for these fishermen. He went about his business briskly with a willow "Y," pacing off veins of water (all sixty feet deep); the depth he determined by the swings of his watch chain.

He tells us the well is admirably placed but it should be much deeper!

Went for swim late afternoon after Land is down.

Illiec, Penvenan, Côtes-du-Nord, July 19th

Mother darling—

It seems impossible that it has been almost a month since I've written. The days have flown in this completely absorbing and compelling life. Each night I drop into bed too tired even to write in my diary, and letters, papers, and books drop far behind.

There has been all the business of settling and managing the house and housekeeping.

Even now, after over a month, the meals are *never* on time and they *cannot* remember when to bring up hot water (all heated on the stove) for the baby.

I don't mind much as I like the general gaiety of the household and prefer a happy carelessness to grim order. But it was difficult at first because it got so on Miss W.'s nerves.

After a week she went on a three-weeks' vacation, leaving me the house with the carpenters still in it (and three masons outside on various odd jobs—a sea wall, etc.) and the children to look after.

However, it was such a relief. I would rather do all the work myself, children, diapers, woolens, washing up, scrubbing floors than have her around complaining. In fact, it seems to me that I worked much harder *then,* trying to keep her happy, then I do *now,* doing all her work (and my own).

But it is not as bad as it sounds. I have the routine down to a not too difficult system and have time now to go swimming, take a walk, or a swift shopping tour in the afternoon (for more blankets, coal scuttles, baby cereals, etc.) and my evenings free.

Also Mrs. Lindbergh is here. She does a great deal with Jon. And adores the baby, though she believes he should *never* cry, and if he cries should be immediately distracted from it at any price. Apparently C. was brought up without a single tear! I am afraid that is not true of us nor will it be true of our children.

Life never leaves you with your conquests, does it? I have just gotten so I can swing this with an easy hand when tomorrow (I think) the proofs of the manuscript come, which means all the free time gone, for a while.

Jon looks much better than when he came and he is very happy here, looking for cockles and clams and winkles on the beaches, chasing the chickens out of the kitchen; and, just lately, working in the little woods, where we have cleared out the dead trees. Height of happiness for Jon. "Are we coming back next year?" he said. The first day of cutting he could not find his saw. He really grieved over it. Finally it was found in the kitchen. Maryvonne, in good-natured cheerfulness, was using it to saw the meat bones! Since then Jon has worked with the men, all day, sawing little branches and dragging off small trees.

"He worka lika old man," said Kerleau, the fisherman-guard, watching him with amusement. (He was a sailor and speaks a strange broken English.)

It is 11:15. I cannot go on much longer and there is so much unsaid.

I do not feel so far away from you here as at Long Barn, though descriptions of Leadbetter's Island do make me homesick.

Telegrams are no trouble, but they come by regular mail, on the mailwoman's back. She wades across at low tide, carrying her shoes in one hand.

Miss W. comes back in a week. After that I hope to go to Paris for a short overnight spree of shopping, hot baths, hair-do, and people, maybe.

This letter does not say half the fun of making this place grow, the fun of the people: the painters singing, the deaf boatmaker, the mailwoman, the laundress (she is not used to ironing *any-*

thing and washes all the clothes in the communal washhole in Buguélès). And the wonderful general-store manager, Keraudren (he is baker, garageman, hauler of baggage, keeper of café and telephone for us).

The waves under my window are throwing up little stones and pulling them back with a gentle brushing sound. I must go to bed.

DIARY   *July 20th*

The galleys arrive. C. and I start to work on them in afternoon. Marie knocks on the door to say, *"Madame, votre belle-soeur est là."* I go down to find Margot[1] at the front door—in bare feet, over her ankles in black mud. She has walked across from Buguélès. We get her a foot bath and tea, and then we go off and talk. It is such a joy.

We persuade her to stay for the night.

July 21st

Warm day. Margot goes.

Mrs. Lindbergh helps me with Land and I work on galleys with C. all day, just rushing out to do the essentials for Land.

Everyone is cross at François. Maryvonne's *garde-manger* has not come, or the buffet. The doors and windows are still banging, shutters not fixed, etc. The work on the walls is not going fast enough. C. gets Miss H. to write him a letter telling him to speed things up.

P'tit Louis takes it over. In the evening we get back word that *"François arrive demain."*

July 22nd

Work on galleys all day.

As I am doing Land in the morning, François arrives! With carts, cement, buffets, and men! Before he leaves, though, we

---

[1] Margot and Dwight were staying in a hotel in Saint-Efflam with her friend the translator Elizabeth Hapgood.

discover that the buffet has no top and the *garde-manger* has no wire screening, so neither can be used. Maryvonne is very angry.

I talk to François about the blasting, the work on the walls, etc.

He nods his little head and says, *"Demain—demain."*

Saturday, July 24th

Miss H. and I fix up Miss W.'s room with India print curtains and bedspread. The girls work at cleaning her room, also the baby's bathroom.

I feel we'll never get the other guest rooms done, and Miss Nute[1] and Margot and Dwight arrive tomorrow, besides Miss W.

Dr. and Mme Carrel come over and watch Land crawl on rug after Jon. They say what a great improvement and think it is all due to their suggestions. Mrs. Lindbergh thinks it is all because she has been here. Both are *somewhat* right.

The painter comes just at suppertime to put in the pane of glass in Miss Nute's room. Also puts one in Jon's room (where Land is) and Miss W.'s room (where Jon is), waking up both children! However, he was very nice to come off hours all this way.

Monday, July 25th

Mrs. Lindbergh and Miss H. off early to meet Miss W. Miss W. is back mid-morning (all the work is done!). She looks very well and cheerful (I hope!).

C. and I go off by boat after lunch to meet Miss Nute. We meet Dwight and Margot driving to the garage to Buguélès. We leave them to make their way over with Louis by boat.

Miss Nute is youngish, but definitely the woman scholar, quite interesting on her work. How far removed from my life here of

[1] Grace Lee Nute, historian, author, and curator of manuscripts for the Minnesota Historical Society, was collecting material for a biography of C. A. L.'s father.

babies and pots and meals in French and housekeeping and shopping for ink bottles and cookbooks at Aux Dames de France! Her rarefied excitement at the verification of the birth date of an obscure French explorer of the seventeenth century. And yet, I could have felt that way, too, once.

We arrive back, by boat, to find Mrs. Lindbergh bravely at the stone beach to greet us (she dreads Miss Nute's visit). Mrs. Lindbergh disappears quickly from the dining room when she thinks we are going to have tea there.

Hardly a chance to see Margot and Dwight before supper.

Supper is a long and very bad meal. Maryvonne made such an effort—too much effort. There was lobster—not enough of it—and then chicken (the rooster which Maryvonne killed for us and another hen) which was hideously tough. Then eggplant, fried too thin in too much butter. The courses were all served separately, making the meal interminable. The climax was a *tarte* which was burned on top (the apricots) but the pastry not enough done in the middle!

C. had Miss Nute on one side and Margot on the other. That end of the table went well. Dwight and Miss Nute and C. talking all the time.

I took Miss W. and Mrs. Lindbergh. But they both need looking after and "special attention"; it is difficult to deal with them at once. They were quite silent.

Dwight did not speak to Mrs. Lindbergh at all but was absorbed by Miss Nute and history. (Just the kind of methodical, thorough, dry, competent mind he admires, wishes (God knows why) he had, and will, thank goodness, never have.)

Miss H. twinkled across the table at Mrs. Lindbergh and Margot poured oil on the troubled waters.

After supper, everyone heavy with tough chicken and uncooked pastry, we sat in the big room and tried to make a fire go. C. and Miss Nute are talking openly, and Dwight is reading, and Margot and I talk covertly while holding sheets of the *Times* before the smoldering fire, for draft.

The morning starts badly as the milk gives out at breakfast. I go out to get some more and find every speck is gone—even the goat's milk. "You have already drunk it, Madame," says Maryvonne. Dwight has none for his coffee or cornflakes. Maryvonne says naïvely, "Perhaps while Madame has guests it would be better to order some extra." Yes, but couldn't she have seen to that!

However, it is a beautiful day. I leave Miss Nute to Charles and go off and sit on a rock in the sun with Margot. Such bliss—no work this morning, for Miss W. has the baby. (Only I miss him terribly. It was dreadful not to have to go in to him this morning.)

Swimming. Jon swims way out with his ring—delighted.

Lunch is ordinary and therefore better. Yvonne is ill. Maryvonne and Marie are desperate. I tell them to leave everything and have as simple meals as possible.

Margot and I row to Jon's island and sit for a few minutes in perfect peace and quiet.

Mrs. Lindbergh has been out of sight all day.

Tea is late, and also supper. Everything is late.

Yvonne is ill in bed. Dwight and Margot are leaving. It is one of those days when a wind blows everything, doors, windows, shutters, and you must fight against it. And it howls.

No one feels very well after a late supper last night (and we had cheese last night in my attempt to get something non-meat for Margot, the vegetarian). Dwight is anxious to get off and to work.

They go off with C. by the Sillon.

I go up and see Yvonne. She is quite ill and looks dreadful. I am sure she has a fever. She wants to go home, so we send her back with the water cart after lunch. (Maryvonne wraps her up well.)

Françoise, Yvonne's sister, comes to help.

Go over mail and letters in the morning. All those things I've pushed aside for months while moving and taking care of children. Swim.

After lunch we go looking for abalones; Jon has been looking forward to it for weeks. It is a very low tide. We go down with knives and baskets over the rocks, where great ropes of seaweed wash up and down. The sea is strange here, tropical and a little sinister: those great strangling sea monsters of seaweed milling about in the rocks and tide.

Then you must feel under water, under the edges of rocks, locate your abalone (they like the darkest, most inaccessible spots), and then cut him off. It is very difficult. Jon found one and I found two. Miss H. and Miss N. went up to their armpits. The tide begins to come in and it is too late as the abalone ground is covered. We decide to come tomorrow in bathing suits.

We spend the rest of the afternoon crabbing and shrimping in the shallow streams in the inland sea, paddling in warm water with the sun warm on our arms—very pleasant.

The crabs make another long, late meal. Dr. and Mme Carrel come over while we're still at it and sit and talk in the dining room.

A perfect day. At my desk in the morning. The men try to blast the rocks in front of house. Two false alarms, then it goes off. (After the two alarms they wait a little, then go back and pound the hole deeper, pouring water in between times so the old powder won't go off with the pounding!)

We eat our abalones, fried, for lunch—very good. Miss W. won't eat any.

We go for abalones again, farther off out to sea, walk miles over bare low-tide rocks. C. goes in swimming after them, bringing them back in one hand, the knife in his teeth as he swims, like a pirate!

Jon and I strike a gold mine in a long gully where there are lots of abalones in cracks. They go in colonies. He is very excited.

We get lots of abalones. C. gets twenty-nine, but Kerleau and Louis about sixty each!

Very hot. I go for swim alone with Thor. After lunch I go to Lannion with Miss Nute, Mrs. Lindbergh, and Miss H. We are late in starting, of course.

I leave my family at Lannion to shop and have tea and rush on to Saint-Efflam, an hour later than I'd said. I arrive at 4:30. Margot cool and sweet waving from the balcony of their boardinghouse on the sea. It is calm and peaceful.

There is tea laid out. I meet Mrs. Hapgood. She has a lovely face, youngish. She is so clean, all in white with white silk stockings, and her hair neatly waved and netted. I feel so untidy in my bare legs, espadrilles (muddy from the long walk across the flats), and mussed silk shirt, shorts, and skirt outfit. She talks perfect French to her boy of eleven or twelve. Apparently they always talk in French in their family. She has, I am sure, a *perfectly* ordered life. She has arranged her children's education systematically: a year in France, a summer in the château country, a winter here. "Now we are all going to learn . . ." She is essentially well educated and well informed. And she is calm, as though she held life just where she wanted it, in her cool, efficient fingers.

I felt irritated, coming from my difficult household. I wondered how she would like to do all her shopping across the mud flats (no white stockings), have her immaculate clothes washed in the public wash trough by a laundress who can't iron, and wash her hair in a foot-tub, with water hauled across the flats by cart and heated on a stove.

I have an hour with Margot, rush back to Lannion. I pick up my family, who have had a successful day and are much warmed up, having bought china, striped bags, and had tea together. Drive home late. I worry about Miss Nute's train. C. meets us;

only forty-five minutes for supper. It is ready. Miss Nute must pack. She needs blankets for a French train, and a lunch, and water.

Marie comes to me in tears. Yvonne is very ill. She has a high fever. They have sent for her sister. Can she go with her after supper? Françoise is crying in the kitchen.

After supper C., Miss Nute, the two girls, and I leave by rowboat. We drive the girls partway. No one seems to know what it is with Yvonne. C. says Mme Carrel is also seriously ill.

Plenty of time for the train. We buy a paper. A Pan American plane is lost in the Pacific. I have that sinking, hopeless feeling.

We drive home in gloom and go to sleep thinking, wondering, Yvonne—will she live? Mme Carrel—how bad is it? The Pan Am plane—Dr. Meier and Ted Wyman were on it.

Thursday, August 4th

Louis is ill with a cough. It rains. Maryvonne was up all night and is in tears. I give her some Vicks and hot-water bags which helps him.

Miss W. is cross when I suggest taking off Land's diapers for crawlings.

Finally, I go and talk to her about leaving at the end of the summer. She has been more and more unhappy here and it is impossible to speak to her about *anything*. I say that we had only planned on having her during our stay in England and that we are probably not going back again, and it is better to change at the end of the summer. I tell her how splendid she has been and how grateful I am to her for what she's done for the children and how sorry I am to have to make a change, but our lives are going to be very irregular and difficult and she should have a job with a great deal of responsibility, etc.

She cries, and I almost do, I feel so sorry for her, though I know she is better off now than when she came to us. But it is such a dog's life, taking care of other people's children and then leaving just as you get attached to them.

She is very sweet and grateful. It makes it hard. She keeps saying, "I don't want to make you unhappy—you've been so good to me. You've always been so understanding. I'll always . . ." It is quite harrowing.

C. has mail from England: will he go to Russia on the 10th? To see their aviation, etc.[1]

Will I go?

I am too tired to think about it and blue about Miss W. I hate so to make the break and yet I know we must. I have been dreading it for months. Now, at least, I have told her but I feel bad, for her, and also at the change. Will I ever get as good a nurse again for the children, even though she was sometimes difficult?

Friday, August 5th

I decide to go with C. I hate to leave the children, especially Jon, right now. And I don't want much to go to Russia, but feel I must. It is part of the European picture. C. must know it and I must go so we can talk it over together.

Get things together in the morning.

Saturday, August 6th

Up on the rock after supper, still aching with not wanting to go, with fear—unknown, womanly fears. Should I go and leave Jon? What may happen?

I watch C. until he is a speck of white over the path across flats and islands and the bar of stones to the Carrels'.

Why do I go? Why do I keep my eye on that white speck as far as I can see it? The two questions seem to be related.

I must go, I must be part of C.'s life. I must go even though I

---

[1] C. A. L. received a telegram from Colonel Lee, Air Attaché in London, suggesting that he make a trip to Russia to study their aviation situation. It was part of a larger project to make a comparative study of the air strength of the major European countries for U. S. Intelligence reports.

am afraid to go. "Not to be afraid of this world, said Hari, one must belong to it."[1]

And for your children—perhaps sometimes you must do things that show them that you are not afraid of life, even if you die in doing them. Perhaps it might teach them more than staying at home and trying to protect them.

I look over all the islands and try to learn that I and they and that lost liner in the Pacific are all in "God's hand." It is hard to accept. But sooner or later one must learn it.

Illiec, Penvenan, Côtes-du-Nord, August 6th

Mother darling,

It has been a long time again without a letter and there has been so much on my mind to write you about. Perpetual problems and joys of the island, and now tomorrow we are off for two weeks—a trip to Russia, C. to see Russian aviation. I don't really want at all to go, in one way. I dislike the ballyhoo of the trip— inevitable—especially to Russian "aviation week." And I dislike the unreal kind of life I must lead (in Moscow, on tourist tours, etc.) while C. goes off to see factories. And finally, I hate to tear myself away from this island and house, just getting fixed, and Land, so enchanting now, and Jon, who needs me. And yet I know I should go, to shake me out of this intense housekeeping life I've been leading.

Our Russian clearances are not yet ready but we are flying (if the weather permits) to a place near Lille to spend the night with Détroyat,[2] a French flier. The day after I think we will be back in London again.

After we get back from Russia, I hope Aubrey and Con will spend some time with us. And you, darling Mother, why couldn't you come over? We expect to be on the island all September. In October C. has another trip of two weeks or so in Germany. I

[1] A quotation from *The Root and the Flower* by L. H. Myers.
[2] Michel Détroyat, French test and acrobatic pilot.

don't know whether or not I'll go—probably yes. We are apt to be on the island quite late in the fall, when new problems face us.

Where to go for the winter? And a new nurse!

Europe is so unsettled it seems arrogant to make plans. But then again, that is one reason why I should like to have you see Illiec this summer.

DIARY   *Sunday, August 7th*

Start off about 9:30, Kerleau, P'tit Louis, and C. taking the bags, Mrs. Lindbergh and Miss H. walking across the flats, and C. and I going by the Sillon (in our flying clothes, he in a business suit, I in navy divided skirt, cotton sweater, and check coat). I look back to see Thor sitting nobly by the pen with Land in it, but his head turned wistfully toward us.

A long, hot walk. Jon comes with us as far as the heart-stone I found the other day and propped up on the Sillon. He takes it in his arms, pleased, and starts back with it.

We are dripping by the time we get to the car but cool off on the drive to Morlaix. Very hot at Morlaix airport. Take off just before 2. Low clouds, heat, past Mont-Saint-Michel, past Havre. C. smells something burning, turns, oil spatters on windshield. He lands at Le Havre to see what it is. A Sunday crowd of Aéro-Club members and old planes. People crowd round. I try to translate. There is a fat pompous expert on engines there. He says the engine is too hot. C. says the temperature is normal. Expert says it is very high. I think we will never get away.

C. goes up to try it. Finds nothing seriously wrong. Explain, with the aid of a member of the Aéro-Club who speaks very good English, that since we find nothing serious we are going on to Saint-Inglevert and Reading and will take the plane to the factory there.

Finally take off. Very soon get into low haze, clouds, and then mist. I lose all sense of direction, don't know which way we're pointing, as I can't see compass. I freeze up with the memories of old encounters with fog. It is instinctive. I know C. is careful and we have been in much worse, but I freeze up nevertheless. It is getting late.

Finally he turns around and says we can't get to London (fog all along coast). Will go to Paris, find out weather there for tomorrow.

Weather gets better though stormy and we see smoke and haze from city, and the Eiffel Tower rising out of the evening haze. Thunderstorms. Land Le Bourget about 7—in almost the same direction, C. says, as he landed on his flight. It is very hot and close. We take a taxi into Paris through wet deserted streets. Sunday and August—everyone has left because of the heat. Gradually pass through the squalid section into the elegant section, even more deserted. (Paris is such a mixture of elegance and dishevelment—no, wrong word; I can't think of the right one for the unkemptness, dirt, untidiness, and squalor of the end of Rue Lafayette.)

We stop at the Crillon and get out with our cloth gypsy bundles and in our mussed clothes. I feel very dowdy in my wool stockings, divided skirt, English jacket, and old hat.

I try to call Weather Bureau at Le Bourget for weather tomorrow to London. It does not sound very good; difficult to understand the man.

Then a bath! Cool clothes, and we go out and walk the still wet lit-up streets of Paris and eat at a restaurant. Several Americans and many French recognize us, but no fuss. It is very nice. I feel happy, relieved after the tenseness of the flying, and pleased we can go out and eat together in a restaurant without any trouble. Delicious steak, and raspberries and cream, and a cool, light white wine.

Home through a darkened and deserted Rue Saint-Honoré. The Place Concorde, though, looks unnatural lit up with floodlights. The old buildings which should be left to shadows, night, and dim lights look stagy and cardboard, with a garish light on them.

As C. says, "Why not let night have its own?"
Tomorrow to London—if possible.

Monday, August 8th

Hot. Breakfast downstairs. Leave the Crillon for Le Bourget. Plane refueled. See Bureau Météo: weather not very good. C. says, as usual, we will go anyway as far as we can, come down if it's bad. Back into the fight!

It was not bad, after all. We got into Saint-Inglevert just after the clouds had risen. Talk to a little girl who had a child of two in her arms. Fog over Channel, quite low, just covering the level of steamstacks of boats, a ripple of black smoke showing on top in one place where you could not see the boat. But it clears before we strike the coast. Low clouds and heat mist.

I love flying over a flat and pearly sea. The expanse of it, together with its smoothness and fragility, excites me. The moments of ecstasy in flying for me are almost always over the sea: a coastline, Maine or Illiec or Long Island Sound, rolled out like satin.

For there is still ecstasy in flying—of fear, but also joy.

On to Reading, over Long Barn, and no one to run out and wave. The beds were yellow (with those poppies I didn't like).

Land at Reading about 2, very hot, taxi to station, half-hour to wait, so we go in to eat in a restaurant. The girl begins to tell us what we *can't* have on the menu. Finally end up with a *most* English lunch of mutton, cabbage, plum tart, and custard.

Very hot in London. Taxi to Brown's Hotel to try it. Seems much more cheerful than the Washington. C. goes to talk to Colonel Lee, I to the hairdresser's, where I get hair and nails done; frightfully expensive, but it looks nice. I wanted it well washed, cut, and set because it's been so long since anyone's touched it.

Enjoyed walking back in the evening. The streets are quite empty. It smells like summer in a city after rain; damp, coolish pavements.

To Lympne about 2:30, too early to go to the Détroyats' (should arrive at 5). So we walk around the hangars, have a lemon squash at the Aéro-Club where we meet a slim, sleek woman flier, very smartly dressed in sky blue and a striped blazer and shoes and long, Chinese, dark red fingernails.

Sir Philip Sassoon comes in in his new plane and talks to us for a moment. Very sugary: "My dear Charles," etc. Wants us to stop, but we must go on.

Leave Lympne about 3:40. Clear over Channel except for heat mist; pearly again and lots of boats.

> "The sea being smooth,
> How many shallow bauble boats dare sail
> Upon her patient breast."

Arrive at Lille, Détroyat's private field in the country next to an island of trees. Land almost on the dot of 5. Détroyat is there and a mechanic and his butler. We meet his wife, whom we first met four years ago in America. Very smartly dressed in blue with lacquered toenails peeping out of sandals, and hair, light curls, piled high on her head and held up with a blue bandeau, Greek fashion, like the fantastic models in *Vogue*.

I was introduced to a friend, also very smart, with hair curled high. They both looked immaculate and had bright lipstick. We also meet Mme Détroyat's mother, whose place this is. She is young-looking and wears her hair like ordinary mortals.

"*Je suis* ravie *de vous voir ici,*" etc., etc.

It is a lovely place, very parklike, set in old trees, a circular pond with ducks and swans and gardens running down to it. A low, curving single-storied thatch-roofed house *à l'Anglaise,* with vines all over it, honeysuckle and roses.

We are shown our room and change quickly and come out for tea. We have a delicious tea and make conversation. C. talks to Détroyat about military aviation. I to the women, half in French and half in English, about the island.

Another friend comes, a quite intelligent man who speaks very good English. Also the girl's husband "Albert" flies over us, back from polo at Le Touquet.

She has a nice flicker of pride and pleasure in her grave and charming face as he flies over. I like that—I know how she feels.

After a swim I meet "Albert." He kisses the hand most gallantly but does not look nearly as French as that sounds. He has a tumbled and quizzical face, intelligent and humorous. I like him immediately.

Dinner in the bungalow house. Albert is very interesting on the state of France. He does not agree that it is better—only a temporary lull. He says it is not war he fears but civil war. He says that instigators have told the French workers that wealth is there for them to take—take it. And they grab and they have not yet learned the price. He talks in French and the translation is slow. C. and I are interested but the others are not and rather make fun of him for his seriousness. "Oh, Albert!" they cry down his gloom, *"Tu parles toujours comme ça,"* and will not let him go on, much to my disappointment, so the conversation falls to pieces—unfortunately—as he is the most interesting person there. His wife is charming and also intelligent, but she is young.

Also I like the mother. She has good sense and I can meet her on the everyday grounds of life as I can't meet the young girls, somehow. Why is it? They are separated from it by those fancy hair-do's and their lipstick and Paris clothes, perhaps?

The mother was driven out of La Vallée at the time of the war by the Germans. They fled for miles on foot and with cart horses. She was about to have a child. The Germans destroyed the old château but kept the trees to hide the stables built for their horses.

To sleep in a delicious bed, but the mosquitoes are frightful. C. says, "Wind the sheet around your head—as you breathe you blow them away"!

But the buzzing bothers me even if they're not biting.

Wednesday, August 10th

C. is up for breakfast. I have a delicious French one in my room. Peaches and jam and toast and coffee.

It is raining and quite low. We go (the women) to Lorette, a huge war cemetery and monument on top of a hill, by car. It is a dismal country: ugly brick towns, dirty, no gardens, no trees, and very flat. Of course the trees are gone because of the war. There are still hills badly pitted with craters where nothing grows.

The country is full of cemeteries—English, German, and French. Lorette is very sad, ugly, and gloomy. By the big stone which says "To the memory of thousands of unknown soldiers dead for France," relatives have put up little mementos, plaques and sometimes pictures of their father, husband, or son *disparu* on such and such a date.

At lunch I sit next to Albert and try to talk to him again on France. But the conversation involves the table and then they make fun of him again and he pleads, *"She* started it."

After lunch we leave. The engine begins to spout oil, all over the windshield, now a stream of oil slowly ripples back and covers the whole shield, like a stained-glass window, only you can't see through it. C. wipes it off as it begins to curl over the edges and whip back. He sops up two handkerchiefs and throws them away. Still this flood of oil, slowly spraying out from a central point in the windshield, like a yellow chrysanthemum, creeping nearer and nearer the rim of the shield, and then curling over in ugly brown lips which fly back into the cockpit. I give C. three paper handkerchiefs. They help temporarily but the flood continues. The other covers are all cloudy (with the damp weather?). You can't see through them.

I put on C.'s sou'wester and my helmet and goggles. We should be getting to Saint-Inglevert. C. asks for another cloth to wipe his goggles, which are now spotted with oil. He can't take them off or he will be blinded. He must see to land. There is no more cloth, so I tear off my silk panties and give them to him (sacrifice all!). I still have a slip I can give him, too. But the panties are enough. He clears his goggles, gives another wipe to the windshield, and we land at Saint-Inglevert.

Then everyone comes out to help us with rags and gasoline. They clean off the engine and C. runs it up. The oil is coming out of the propeller shaft. We find out the weather to Croyden. It is better. C. decides the leak is not dangerous and we take off for Reading, armed with lots of rags. We have to keep wiping the windshield, but that keeps the oil from whipping back.

Land at Lympne, then on to Reading, in perpetually worse weather. C. overshoots Reading. I am timing it and I get more and more nervous. The weather is worse, lower all the time, and getting darker. It is almost seven.

I can see he is trying to find his bearings, turning back and circling and looking. Just as I'm very unhappy and I touch C. on the shoulder, he shouts back, "It's Reading." I sit back relieved. He does know where we are. Soon he finds the field and we land.

Very grateful to be down.

Train to London, to Brown's Hotel, where the hotel manager meets us saying, "Your friends have been inquiring for you."

"What friends?"

"Mr. and Mrs. Morgan." Con and Aubrey!

They are on the same floor. The surprise and joy of seeing them—the ease and feeling of homecoming. Con looks very sweet in black with her hair done in curls close to her head.

We have a late and delicious dinner downstairs, talking at ease—what a luxury it is—then go out for a short walk through the London streets. Con and I walking ahead, C. and Aubrey behind. Con and I are almost picked up and don't dare stop on the street corner lest we be mistaken for those highly dressed women who are always standing at street corners in London.

We giggle a lot and feel gay. No flying tomorrow and nothing in the immediate future to worry about.

August 11th, London all day

The Russian permit has not come through. The engine trouble, though, does not seem to be serious.

C. says we can't get off tomorrow. Con and Aubrey plan to come back tomorrow and have supper with us.

Lunch alone at Brown's. (The "Negus"—Haile Selassie[1]—in great black cape and beard, sits tragically in a corner.)

There are new restricted areas all over Germany and the reserves are being called out for "maneuvers." The English Foreign Office is very worried. The Prime Minister is in London for "treatment of his nasal catarrh." The rumor is *der Tag* is August 15th.

August 12th

Con and Aubrey arrive at 11 A.M. Con and I go to look for shoes—the blank wall of British shopping. Finally in exhaustion I buy a pair which are too tight which the girl says "will stretch." "If you get them any larger they'll drop off."

To the German twentieth-century art exhibit and then to the hotel. C. and I set out for Claridge's and lunch with Herschel [Johnson]. Herschel, you can see, has had a lot of people drop in on him and has assembled them all for lunch. The Scanlons (she very smartly dressed), an older couple, Mr. and Mrs. Stabler, who had been ten years in Venezuela—now in the Mellon interests in Belgium.

I sat next to him at lunch and found him very interesting. He had been in Austria at the time of the *Anschluss,* had firsthand information of Spain. I longed for C. to be able to talk to him. (He also had known Daddy and Uncle Jay.) After him I found Mr. W. on my right, nice but rather immature. How strange it is that Americans who have not lived abroad seem immature. And an American who has lived abroad and yet who still keeps his American strength and youth and life is a marvelous mixture, like the Lees, or the Smiths, or this man.

After lunch, C., Con, Aubrey, and I go to Hampton Court by train. It is hot, I am in my white and very tight new shoes (to stretch them). The gardens are lovely, especially the "knot garden," of herbs entwined in patterns.

[1] Emperor of Ethiopia, 1930–36, driven from Ethiopia by Italian conquest and occupation, 1936–41, lived in England, restored to throne 1941, deposed, died 1975.

C. and Aubrey race through the maze, then put Con and me in. We get lost and come out together. Then tea among wasps under an awning in the Tilting Yard. during terrific cloudbursts.

Then home. Con and I discuss war. She says she will take all the Morgan and Miles children to the U. S. A. to rear and save for the New Generation!

No word from the Russians. C. calls up and asks if it would be convenient if we started out and went to Warsaw and waited for word there? They say *No,* it would *not* be convenient—it would be better to wait here!

Saturday, August 13th

Go out to a Boots to get aspirin etc. See instructions for putting on gas masks, for making a shelter in Boots basement. Pamphlets. The sense of "war is near."

C. and I go to a Swedish restaurant for lunch. Then to a news film which is incredibly boring and stupid and cheap and then to the Tate Gallery, to get the taste out of our minds. Then to a Russian film—*The Last Night*—on the revolution, and a sentimental English one, after.

The Russian movie is better than *Potemkin.* It is more coherent, and it does not wring out the emotions as crudely. It is, of course, obvious and childlike propaganda throughout. The types glorified are poor and stupid and brutal.

Even the English laughed at some of the obvious pomposities, as when the crowds asked the hero how were they to believe that Lenin would give back the land. "On the word of a Bolshevik," said the hero. Laughter in the theater.

I feel as if all the things I like best in the world are going to go under for a long time. There will be only war, brutality, and counter-brutality to put it down—only extremes.

A long article in the *Observer* about England taking the lead in transoceanic flying service and waiting for America, who is lagging behind. A completely false report. We have made all our practice flights and are waiting for *them.*

Pan American has been flying the Pacific for over a year, but most of the English don't know it. Our new Boeing can carry fifteen times the payload of the English "pick-a-back" plane, etc. At one moment I feel very sentimental and sorry for the English, in their blindness and unprotectedness. But the next moment they enrage me beyond words.

C. and I go down the river on a Thames boat to Kew. The announcer with a megaphone points out the sights, including the sites for anti-aircraft guns and bombproof roofs on one or two of the factories.

Monday, August 15th

Permits arrive.

At the Russian Embassy Mr. Maisky,[1] an able keen man, pumps C. on aviation in Italy, Japan, and Germany etc. He has several theories why Japanese aviation is not good. He says the eyes of the Japanese are poor because the babies are all tied to the mother's backs and look up at the sun. Also schoolboys have to learn so many characters!

They are obviously not very pleased at C.'s report of German aviation. They say, "How about pilots, Colonel?" C. tries to be tactful and keeps saying, "With the possible exception of Russia, which I don't know . . . ," when he quotes figures.

There are three men there. One (Kahn) is clever, quick, but I should say the unbalanced and fanatic type. Then there is the Ambassador, M. Maisky, who is able, intelligent, and I should say balanced; might fit into any regime. Then a third is good-natured, pleasant, and not very bright—the kind that falls in with anything.

We talk about the splendid flights the Russians have just made over the Pole. Also they tell us about three women pilots who made a record flight across Russia—"three military pilots"! Apparently they have women battalions in Russia and are very proud of it.

[1] Ambassador of the U. S. S. R. in Great Britain 1932–43.

I feel quite out of sympathy with this. They have taken women's work away from women in Russia and given it to the state. I do not believe it can be done as well *en masse* by the state. A woman is just another tool, like a man, to be pressed into mechanization.

Lovely to see the Rublees.[1] Sometimes he seems like Pierre in *War and Peace*.

"I don't seem at all fitted for the job, but somebody in Washington seemed to think so and I didn't feel I could refuse, so here I am. I don't know that I can do anything . . . but here I am," with that gesture of his hands.

August 16th

Get off about 9 (8 G.M.T.).

The Channel is rough but quite good visibility. The corner of France is overcast and hazy. Thunderstorms over Belgium, haze over Holland, and then better over Germany, with occasional storms. An overripe August day, bruised with storm patches.

We land at Hanover. The mechanic tells us that Udet, Hannah Reitsch,[2] and a number of fliers are going to the U. S. A. on a tour, sailing on the *Bremen*. (What--no war?)

Long afternoon. Local storms and rainbows, sweeping the fields. Fly over Germany, south of Berlin, lots of airfields and planes up. We follow the *Autobahn*. The weather gets better. Higher ceiling, still hazy.

C. has to pick and choose his route very carefully to avoid forbidden fortified areas.

Poland is very flat: little farms, lakes and rivers. The day now clear and perfect. Land Warsaw. Reporters and no one who speaks English, except one of the reporters! I gather from him (he does the translating on the field) that Poland is not at all

---

[1] George Rublee, lawyer, adviser to the U. S. Embassy in Mexico under Dwight Morrow. Chairman of the Inter-governmental Refugee Committee with headquarters in London.

[2] German woman pilot.

sympathetic to Russia. He says none of the nations have any communication with Russia except Czechoslovakia and she feels very much in sympathy.

Go to the Embassy and meet U. S. Ambassador [Anthony] Drexel Biddle and his wife. Ambassador Biddle said there was very little communication from Poland to Russia. We are the first plane (for a long time) to be allowed straight through. He said there were good roads up to within a few miles on each side of the border, and then so bad you could hardly get a tank over them.

At our hotel we are shown an elaborate room, all the furniture covered with summer covers. It looks quite cool and pleasant until the chambermaid pulls these off and reveals the red satin underneath. We have supper in our room. Order hors d'oeuvre which turns out to be beet soup and puff pastry. The sound of little carriages and trotting hooves of horses through the quiet streets at night.

August 17th

The hotel man tells me how poor Poland is. It was so long under the domination of Russia and needs a long time to build up. Too bad Pilsudski[1] died so soon. Poland needs a strong man to hold her together. Warsaw seems a completely modern city with some quaint touches: flower baskets on the lampposts and flower boxes on public buildings.

A long wait at airport. It seems the Polish Embassy in London said we didn't need any permission to fly *out* of Poland and these officials say we do. "You came so quick, before telegrams . . ." They telephone, C. apologizes. Said he thought he had obtained permission. Finally we get off.

Good weather, clear sky, and very warm. We fly over flat country scattered with small rivers and some lakes and swamps. The little villages have grass roofs for the most part, with a few modern tile roofs. We cross the border, following the railroad

[1] Polish general and statesman, 1867–1935.

track. It looks as though the roads go right through. Much more activity and life on the Russian side of border. Big town, better roads, a railroad, and a military camp, villages, etc. (This concentration, however, lessens as you get farther on.) The villages look much like Polish ones only the haystacks are all together by one big shed instead of scattered about.

We fly over Minsk.[1] Lots of construction everywhere near the towns and some tall buildings. Why? No need for it way out in country. To copy U. S. A.? C. says the field looks not so good for landing and take-off with all our fuel. We go on to Mogilev. A big field with small Army planes, low wing and retractable gear. We land and officers come up, in khaki belted blouses and caps with sickle and hammer on them. We spend about an hour talking or *trying* to talk to them. C. shows his papers, the Russian note from M. Maisky, etc. They stand in a group and talk quite good-naturedly and say things in Russian to C. and make signs. In the meantime the planes are landing and taking off to signals and there are two cloudbursts.

One young boy speaks a little English. They bring up a truck and start to refuel. Then again conversation: "You go to Moskva —tonight?"

"Yes, right away."

?

"Yes, quickly."

"No—*no* quickly. The commander wishes you eat here, with him."

"All right—but quickly."

(He seems to understand "quickly.")

We go off in a bumpy car to a big hall, wash our hands at the entrance. Pictures of Stalin on the wall, long tables, officers and some girls (nice-looking and better dressed than five years ago in print dresses, socks, and white summer shoes; short, curly hair).

[1] The route to Moscow was laid out by the U. S. S. R. Embassy in London, including the two airports at which landing was allowed, Minsk and Mogilev.

They all look at us with great curiosity. Questions (incredulous):

"It . . . is . . . *your* . . . plane?" and, of my watch,

"Very . . . good . . . watch . . . gold . . . gold watch!"

"No, no—*good,* but not gold," we protest.

The girls look at me with what seemed to me envy (perhaps for flying, perhaps my clothes, which hardly pass in London) and put their hands up to their hair instinctively to arrange it—*not* certainly because mine is well arranged. All mussy from the helmet and matted. A woman in bandanna and apron sets food down in front of us: tomatoes covered with whipped sour cream, and a cold canned fish in vinegar. Then a large plate of hot milky-rice-puddingy soup, then meat covered with onions and tomato sauce! It is evidently real supper. Our watches say 3 P.M. (Greenwich) but theirs say 6.

Finally we ask, "What time dark Moscow?"

"Nine," they say.

"We must go QUICKLY."

"Quickly, yes, you will be in Moskva tonight." (I begin to doubt it. We have been there two hours.)

Finally go out, without the *météo* they are waiting for, and take off.

In the air. The sun is setting behind a pink-edged cloud and the land is gray. C. still says we'll be in before dark. I don't see how.

Land Moscow 17:34. The field lights are on, the city is smoky and dark, lights on the rivers, but there is still enough light to land easily. A small group of people waiting, officials, Alexander Kirk,[1] immaculate and erect in gray, Colonel Faymonville,[2] genial and kind-faced, an official in white uniform, Colonel Slepnev, head inspector of civil airports, and two women, young, pretty, and very nicely dressed, one in a brown suit, the other in a

[1] Acting U. S. Ambassador in U. S. S. R. See also note p. 141.
[2] Lieutenant Colonel Philip R. Faymonville, Military Attaché, U. S. Embassy, Moscow.

print dress, lipstick, red fingernails, with large bunches of flowers to present. General embarrassment of receiving flowers in front of a bright light and cameras, usual discomfort of being asked questions with reporters hanging around to nab up details.

Alexander Kirk drives me to Embassy. The streets are much better than before,[1] wide boulevards, traffic lights, more cars, trolleys, buses, etc.

Alexander Kirk is evidently not at all in sympathy with the U. S. S. R.—"This is *not* my idea of fun"—and talks quite freely. His chauffeur, he says, is Italian and the car is searched every day for microphones. Anyway, he says, for himself he doesn't care. They know how he feels and if they choose to eavesdrop it's their own funeral. He says this (U. S. S. R.) system cannot last. It is based on the denial of two fundamental human instincts—the instinct for worship, the Church, and religion, and the instinct for personal property. And, he says, this [Communism] being the most intellectual, the most purely theoretical of all systems, it particularly needs the emotional outlet of religion. He says thirty million people were killed here, or wiped out.

The Embassy is a colossal palace with huge chandeliers and fake marble columns. It belonged to a private person, a manufacturer, before the revolution, a man who was shot by his illegitimate son in the front hall. It then belonged to the state, used by President Kalinin[2] to entertain diplomatically. Then it was rented by Bullitt.

Supper, very late, with Alexander Kirk and Colonel Faymonville. After supper C. talks to Colonel Faymonville on aviation and I to Alexander Kirk on the general state of the world. He is a true eccentric but brilliant. He says some very perceptive things—things I wish C. could hear and argue about. That "no country keeps for long a government better than it rates." That he does

[1] During the Lindberghs' trip to Russia in September, 1933 (*Locked Rooms and Open Doors,* pp. 116–20).

[2] Mikhail Ivanovich Kalinin, President of the U. S. S. R. 1923–46; Chairman of the Presidium of the Supreme Council.

not believe U. S. A. is immune from the troubles of Europe and will get them in a month or a year or a decade later, just the same. That if there is another war, social upheaval will follow and it will be the Russian kind—bloody and confused and terrible.

We talk about the cheapness of life in America and how it can be changed. He says only by the people having a man of integrity to look at—to lead. He says C. should run for President. I say he never will.

He speaks of the insensibility of the Russians, both the old regime and now. I wonder. Isn't it that we can't read them? Alexander Kirk says he sees no Russians. They are all too afraid. He can't get a barber or a doctor to come to the house.

I cannot get to sleep afterwards—thinking.

August 18th, "rest day"

Lunch at the Embassy with Alexander Kirk. At 1 P.M. first to the Métropole Café, then out to the airfield to watch the Aviation Day civil air show with the officer from the airfield, Slepnev, and his interpreter. We sit on the roof with the Supreme Council of Soviets, representatives from all over Russia. We see Mme Kollontai,[1] the Troyanovskys,[2] and Mme Litvinov[3] and her son Misha. "Tea" at the Embassy.

In the morning C. and I drive out alone to see the people. There is a terrific change from last time: new buildings, wide streets, subways, stores (selling food, hams, canned foods, also women's clothes, hats, tennis rackets, guitars, even toys; the clothes and materials do not look very good but still, they are there). Posters on the streets advertising movies, chocolate, ciga-

---

[1] Aleksandra Mikhailovna Kollontai, Russian Soviet Commissar and diplomat, Ambassador to Mexico 1927, Sweden 1930.

[2] Aleksander Troyanovsky, first Soviet ambassador to the United States.

[3] Ivy Litvinov, British-born writer and wife of Maksim Maksimovich Litvinov, Russian Communist leader and diplomat, People's Commissar for Foreign Affairs 1930–39.

rettes. The people, too, are much better dressed. There is color on the streets, print or cotton dresses, men in European shirts and trousers or Russian blouses and trousers. Women are hatless for the most part with no stockings but cotton socks and summer shoes. The streets are much cleaner and there are uniformed policemen, stop lights, and some order.

However, when you look at the faces of the people they do not look very well fed—pasty, thin, and unhappy. They look as though they had struggled hard, which, of course, they have. It looks as though the material progress were ahead of the physical and spiritual (as it is in all big cities, for that matter. You do not see very healthy crowds on the streets of Paris, London, or New York).

Neither are the faces very intelligent or fine-looking here. (Is that because I am not used to the Slavic type?) They are all the same, too. You do not—as you do in Paris, London, or New York—see *some,* at least, outstanding faces. Here the cream has been taken off (at least one draws that impression). The best types are in uniform—soldiers, or policemen, or officials. Very few old people, and these bent and harrowed-looking. The children look sickly and malnourished and not happy. (Or is that Slavic too, and I can't read through it?) There are some happy and better-looking faces in large trucks evidently taking crowds on sightseeing tours through Moscow.

Lines of people on street corners in front of small stands, evidently for fruit or vegetables. Back streets are still cobbled and quite dirty, but much better than before. Lots of streets with demolished buildings on them. They build a row of new buildings and then blow up the old in front (with dynamite). It looks like the war.

Lots of modern construction but nothing very startling or new or beautiful—no new contribution in architecture but very good workable copies; some good modern subway stations.

Lots of pregnant women on the streets. Two beggars. Very few children—I suppose they have them in nursery schools.

Lunch at the Embassy with Alexander Kirk. Then Colonel Faymonville comes to take us to the Métropole Hotel to meet our hosts. He is an eager, generous man—one of those people, I gather, perpetually for the underdog, which is his attitude on Russia (I suspect). He is pleased we see an improvement and speaks with an undertone of bitterness about the carping critics who did not see what a terrible state Russia *was* in after the war, the revolution, and the famine and how it has built up from that. This may all be true (and seems to be); one certainly has to give them credit for what they have done and yet one can still hold back from such a system.

Go to the Métropole, where we meet Colonel Slepnev in white uniform and gold braid. He looks just like a German officer of the same type—fair, florid, and fat, a kind face, able and quite balanced. Not particularly an intellectual—a good executive, a good officer. Also the same two girls who met us at the airport. The pretty one, quite well dressed, in a print dress and flowered straw hat and beads [glass] at her neck and a turquoise ring on her finger. (I gather she is someone's wife but I don't know whose.) Also the fat one, who is an interpreter, pretty, also nicely dressed in lavender cotton, no hat or stockings, but socks and shoes. Also a stoutish young woman: a face with no breeding, sensitivity, or intelligence, snobbish and brutal (the *nouveau-riche* type). She shakes hands with condescension and looks with ill-concealed envy (and submerged anger) on the good clothes, stockings, beads, and manners of the really quite sweet, finely cast little "wife." (Little "wife" turns out to be Slepnev's mistress.)

I describe this woman because somehow I think there is something both typical and dangerous in her type. It is something I once heard described as the most dangerous thing in the world: blind stupidity (like stampeding cows). Also it makes one credit all those flippant, carping (and extremely clever in this case) things that people like Alexander Kirk say about present-day Russia: "The cream of the skimmed milk will be there."

Is this what happens in a regime where one takes as a motto

"The last shall be first and the first shall be last"—and where, on top of that, one wipes out each succeeding layer of efficient people as they emerge from mediocrity into some kind of enterprise?

What will happen to a nation where only the unenterprising, the ordinary, the mediocre are safe? Or perhaps this is not true, or perhaps it was even more true in the days before the revolution?

Meet at the Métropole one of the three women fliers who are in the Army. (There are many more than three, but these are very good.) She has on trousers (jodhpurs) and boots and a white blouse. She was the navigator on a flight of three women fliers across Russia. I keep asking questions about these "military" fliers. Apparently it is not usual, and there are no regiments of women fliers, but those who want to, *can* join the Army and are treated just like men: go up in the ranks, etc. She instructs at an Army field. She has an extremely nice face—open, intelligent, healthy, and good. One of the best faces I have seen. She wrings our hands cordially.

All three of these women are married and have children!

Then we drive out to the aviation grounds. The streets as we approach (and long before) are lined with marching lines (not in formation) of people going to the field. And the trolleycars jammed and hung with people.

Not many cars, so we get out quickly. The streets are divided in half by lines of police. We go under a new canal (why did they build a tunnel rather than a bridge?). Everywhere large posters are hung up on red drapes: pictures of Lenin and Stalin, side by side, or silhouetted against each other (many more pictures of Stalin than there used to be—before, it was all Lenin).

We are not sitting on the terrace of the Air Club with the Diplomatic Corps but on the roof with the representatives of the Communist republics of all Russia.

However, there is some delay about the tickets and we stand about. Alexander Kirk says, "Again I'm not invited," with mock complaint. He shakes hands with our group, who receive him coldly. I gather they know he's very "anti."

On the roof there are crowds of people, many different types: Mongolian, Caucasian, Oriental and Indian, etc. And a few air people. They have very good faces, on the whole, and the Polar fliers are nice-looking.

We also meet Ambassador and Mme Troyanovsky (he said he'd read my book). Troyanovsky has a round, deceptively guileless child's face which shows humor, ability, and a kind of stubborn courage. She has a sensitive and sympathetic face. Mme Litvinov, an independent Englishwoman, and her son Misha, a nice darkish English boy, and Mme Kollontai—that becloaked, soft-voiced, faded-rose, somewhat untidy but charming oldish woman I remembered meeting in Stockholm, five years ago.

Everyone is eating peaches and spitting out the stones or drinking fruit drinks. A radio announcer blares at our ears.

The air show is long and drawn out and not very spectacular except for the mass parachute jumping at the end ("like sea anemones," said Alexander Kirk) and the formation gliding and some fast pursuit planes stunting (the kind we saw at Mogilev). They also have numbers of "student" fliers going up in formation. These young boys (and girls) have their jobs during the day and only study flying (theory) at night and on "rest days." I think that quite impressive. Misha Litvinov is a teacher. He looks very young and is enthusiastic and thoroughly nice—a little shy, eager, and intelligent-looking. If there is a class of young people like him, it is something to be proud of. But he is the first I've seen. (In Germany you see them everywhere.)

I enjoy talking to Mme Litvinov, who is a flat-shoed, downright Englishwoman with a mind of her own (and a very good one) and much sensitivity and perception. We talk about books. She says she only likes Henry James, of Americans, and I say, "But you must have a very calm, peaceful life to read him."

"Not at all," she says, "*I* read him!"

I also talk a little to Mme Kollontai and tell her how Russia (Moscow) has improved.

She says yes and is pleased and explains again how much they had to do after the war, the revolution. "But now everyone has enough to eat and clothes to wear and a place to sleep." She also says that they are going to let C. see things that no one has been allowed to see before. He can see everything.

They have a sham battle in the air. A sham hangar is bombed and explodes, bombers raid the field, pursuit attack. "Dreadful!" said Mme Litvinov. "I hate war, don't you?"

And all I can think, watching them against a sky piled high with clouds, now thundery, now white and blue, with the tiny specks dogfighting against that gigantic canvas, is Hopkins' line: "With sweet and scarless sky . . ."

Back to the Embassy for tea. The Russians come too—uncomfortable and shy. The two girls sit stiffly on the brocade chairs. "This is a beautiful house. It was a private home before." And I try to talk to them and hand them crackers. Alexander Kirk in his most polished diplomatic manner does not put them at ease, though he tries to.

I meet a lovely person, Mrs. Chipman, half Greek, half French, beautifully dressed—in defiance, I feel, against the mediocrity here—and a Dr. Nelson and his wife (nice sensible American people). He says he thinks the people (in the streets) look pretty well considering what they eat.

Supper alone with Alexander Kirk. When I speak of Mme Kollontai as "very charming," Alexander Kirk says, "Yes, she has a long history of charm." C. talks a good deal to him. We agree in thinking that Alexander Kirk, who is a hothouse product to some degree (very meticulous, believes in "elegance," in a broad sense, but also in a narrow sense—sensitive as a woman, fastidious as a woman), whose wealth has separated him from some of the realities of life, has, on the other hand, gained from that wealth—which so few wealthy people do—tremendously. He has really thought and lived and evolved a character and mind of originality and integrity.

His separation from the world has given him an insight into it, much like a mystic's. For, oddly enough, he has disciplined himself mentally and spiritually to a rare degree in a person who has had everything. It is a delight to talk to him. How refreshing the originals are.

After supper Colonel Faymonville comes for us and we go to the Métropole and meet the usual group again.

"Is that Colonel Slepnev's wife?" Alexander Kirk asks of the pretty young girl with some delicacy.

"As it were," nods Colonel Faymonville genially. I ask about the fat pretty interpreter: is she someone's wife?

"These things are not always clear," says Colonel Faymonville, "but in this case I think she is just his secretary."

We drive in the rain to the Park of Culture and Rest to an open-air theater. The rain stops and we watch a ballet, *The Caucasian Prisoner,* which is simply enchanting. All the grace, the beauty, order, and precision, all the perfection that one does *not* see in life in Moscow. The relief of it was indescribable. Here at last was something not mediocre. Here was something absolutely "top."

I kept feeling: How can people see this perfection, this beauty, and still put up with the squalor and ugliness of life around them (of course they have to—there is nothing else). Perhaps it serves as religion once did—as an escape, a dream, another life. But how can the same people who lap this up also lap equally well the propaganda, the harshness of such films as *Potemkin* and *The Last Night?*

At any rate, it is very impressive that such crowds of people throng to see this, the best music, the best dancing. You would not get such a crowd to a ballet in America or England. It is a rather smart and sophisticated taste. They would flock to see the *Follies* or, at best, *Show Boat.* Would the people here also prefer a cheaper, more mediocre kind of entertainment if it were offered them—and have to take what they can get? Or have they a better innate taste in the arts than Americans? I suspect the last is true but the first also a little; there is not so much choice in entertainment.

After the performance we go behind the scenes and meet the

actors and actresses. They have more intelligent faces than almost anyone else we've met here, except the people in aviation and that woman flier.

Get up rather late and go out to a conference of the Civil Air people on the plans for our visit here, with Colonel Faymonville. He is evidently bitterly afraid we are going to be prejudiced by Alexander Kirk against the U. S. S. R. He keeps saying, "The critics will say . . . You will find people that say . . . Don't let anyone tell you . . ." I begin to feel extremely sorry for him. He has a hard job and is doing it well. His job is to get to know Russia and the Russians, which he, a rare exception to most foreigners here, is evidently able to do. He feels sympathetic to them. He likes them; he feels they have made tremendous strides "considering" the terrific state they were in. (One is always prefacing remarks here with the word "considering.") He feels they have a wonderful spirit and push they never had before, that their projects are splendid. Of course, they are only at the beginning, it will take a long time, but he believes they will succeed and he is *with them*.

Well, I can understand and sympathize with much of this. They *have* made tremendous strides, "considering." The wonderful spirit and push I have not yet seen, except in a young boy like Misha Litvinov, who is half English.

For some strange reason I cannot yet interpret, I felt *more* of their push and spirit the last time in spite of the squalor and poverty of the material conditions then surrounding them. Whether because last time we were surrounded more by Russians, or whether, as some people say, they were much freer then and felt more enthusiastic. That spontaneity and enthusiasm and youth and fervor and gaiety that was there five years ago—in spite of the poor conditions—I have now missed entirely. Perhaps it *is* there, as Colonel Faymonville says. But for some reason we are separated from it. Because of an official trip? But we were official before. Because we are staying with an anti-U. S. S. R.? But even an outsider, staying in a hotel in Berlin or Italy, sees more of the enthusiasm of youth than one does here, in the streets.

As for liking the Russians, I do, too—I really feel more sympathetic to them than to Germans, innately. Of course, you are "for them," but it doesn't mean you are for a system that believes in absolute leveling.

Besides, that system has disappeared, rightly or wrongly. There is definitely an upper class of officers, technical people, officials, etc.

And how does he explain, or include in his support, these terrific trials, murders, espionage system?[1]

We can never ask him because we never see him alone. He has a Russian chauffeur. I sometimes feel he is so busy seeing and finding the good in Russia that he hasn't time to sum up what the shortcomings are—what the price is, or where it is all going.

The people at the Civil Air conference want to know what C. wants to see. There is much talk. They get out maps and point out wonderful trips, through the Caucasus—beautiful scenery. C. tries to explain that our time is short, that he would like to see aviation, factories, laboratories, schools, etc., and then go out perhaps via the South, through Rumania. They say, Yes, they will need a day to make out plans.

There seems to be a good deal of discussion on irrelevant points: how to get out of Russia, which airport to go to in Rumania, how high can our plane go, etc. One has a feeling of confusion and suspense and indecision.

I look around at the faces. In general in groups here one sees three or four types. The stupid, the fanatic, the clever, or one might almost say the criminal, but it is too strong a word. And then, quite rarely—but most obvious in aviation—the able, like Slepnev. He does not look like a very broad type but quick, and intelligent in his field, strong and decisive; not a man of thought

[1] At that date, Stalin's purges were at their height.

but a man of action and ability. But I have seen no one as intelligent as Dieckhoff or von Reichenau, in Germany. No one as able as Milch—no one as great as Balbo.

Around the walls there are pictures of heads of the U. S. S. R. There is Stalin, Voroshilov,[1] Molotov,[2] Kalinin, and Litvinov.[3] There is no picture of Lenin! Last time any office was plastered with pictures of Lenin. The inkwell, too—instead of the invariable Lenin's head inkwells of five years ago was Stalin's head.

Finally we take our leave. Nothing is decided, though it is generally accepted that we will meet at three and from three to six see something. Probably the Red Army Museum and the subways. After this conference we go to another department— Commissar of Defense. And see one man—an officer. There is a great difference. This man has a list of things that Colonel Faymonville asked whether C. could see. He comes to the point immediately and says that it is possible to see all those things and he will let the civil aviation people know. Colonel Faymonville beams. We all shake hands and go out.

After lunch to the Museum of Fine Arts (no, not the Red Army Museum, they have decided) to see a panorama of one of the last struggles of the Red Army against the Whites and the allied forces in the Crimea at Pericop.

This is absolutely dreadful. We are taken through these small theaters where we look out on various scenes of the battle, with a guide pointing out things and telling the history. It is the most infantile propaganda. The tone of voice every time the Red Army is mentioned is enough to draw tears.

Naturally, the Red Army is always victorious in spite of great handicaps. The Whites running away (she never said "retreat,"

[1] Ukrainian commander in the Soviet Army; member of Politburo and People's Commissar for Defense.

[2] President of Council of People's Commissars 1930–41; from 1939, Commissar for Foreign Affairs.

[3] Communist leader and diplomat; People's Commissar for Foreign Affairs 1930–39.

always "running away") even before the Reds shot at them, because they knew it was hopeless. They were either running away (the officers in cars) or else the soldiers, who were only paid capitalist troops, were giving themselves up—joining the Red forces. In one panorama a Red woman was riding a horse into battle—red bandanna on head, healthy face, and pistol in hand.

I asked about her. Yes, I was told, she was "the new woman" helping her country in contrast to the poor officer's wife prostrate in a broken-down cart, her white hands stretched out hopelessly for some overturned milk cans—"the poor helpless housewife," as the guide described her.

At this stage I was getting hot with irritation and suppressed rage. I put my hand to my throat, which felt dry and sore. "Is anything the matter?" said the guide.

We then made a little tour of the museum. The panorama had angered me so that I looked at the early Italian Madonnas with a kind of passionate pity—why should they be in here? They meant nothing to these people. How far away from a world of Christian grace and holiness one was here. The sense of pity and grace and beauty of spirit in the copy of a Nuremberg Madonna —where has it gone to? But then, it is not in Germany either. The Nuremberg Madonnas in Nuremberg look down on a lot of un-Christian things.

Then we go to a subway station, which is excellent. Very beautifully done, very clean—marble (?) floors. It looks much more like a museum or a palace. This is "top" too. But the sculptures in niches in the halls are second-class and the people on the escalators look just as desperate as ever.

Why didn't they put that money into the people's health, I want to ask. But I suppose that is difficult. It is of course impossible to completely separate physical and material benefits. And it is hard to judge what they have done, in the way of physical betterment. Then home to the Embassy in time for a tea for the U. S. A. colony. Colonel Slepnev and the girl interpreter, taking us home, want to get out *outside* of the Embassy gate and let us drive in alone. Finally after some persuasion they remain in the car, drive in the gates, and let us out. They refuse to come in, though, and we do not press them.

All the people from the Embassy are there and also the U. S. A. press. I talk to Mr. Brown, a businessman, who says that outside of Moscow the people haven't changed much; life goes on the same. People still go to church, etc.

I also talk to a Mr. Michaels from the U. S. A. Department of Agriculture, an authority on farm work, who has just made a tour all over Russia. He made the same tours over Russia before the revolution. He says undoubtedly the Russian peasants are better off now than before the revolution. He explains the two kinds of farms—state and collective. On the state farms the state pays wages to the workers. It is a kind of model farm and has equipment, etc. In a collective farm, the peasants own the land, pool together to hire or buy equipment, tractors, used for all. In both types, the farms, which were formerly in small strips and cultivated by hand, are now lumped in big areas and can be cultivated more efficiently by machine.

C. asks about the tractors: are they making their own, what quality and how well are they operated, and how well standing up?

Mr. Michaels (who worked as a laborer in the Ford plant for a while) says they are making tractors of quite good quality and they are handling them well. They also have airplanes—three or four for a small town. Why, we ask—what use? Well, he said, he asked and they said that they wanted to go up for airplane rides on their rest days. However, this sounded rather impractical to him and he believed that they were trying to encourage centers of air forces in the outlying regions.

He also said that the recent things happening in the Government (they always talk in a veiled way here about unpleasant things [the purges] as though they had caught this from the Russians) had not affected the farmer at all. The farmers really have done well and have got quite a little money.

What do they buy with it? I ask him. Well, he says, there isn't really very much they can get—now.

I asked if the peasants looked better than the people in the streets here in Moscow. He said, "I don't quite know what you mean by that—what is in the back of your mind. You no longer see the quivering old man bent over with fear raising his cap to anyone that comes along. These people are beginning to have some self-respect."

I say, "No, I meant simply as physical specimens." (Heavens! how touchy everyone is here—everyone except Alexander Kirk, who is completely untouchable because he has lost the only thing that ever touched him, his mother.)

The smartly dressed and independent Mrs. Chipman carries on my thought and describes the physical specimens you see here, compared with the Russians you see abroad. "One is accustomed to think of Russians as rather good-looking, but here . . ."

"Now, now, Comrade," says Mr. Michaels with a dry but touchy humor, "I'm afraid you're prejudiced. If you want to see some good-looking men you must go to Georgia" (answering only her lipstick and her clothes). And of course she must take the feminine defense and laugh coquettishly.

Also he said—to us women—that it was interesting as you went farther south into the crop areas themselves (where there were less problems of distribution) you saw better specimens, better dressed and more make-up—a sign of prosperity. At which the men all hooted and said it was a bad sign and a return to capitalism, etc.

There is by now quite a group around the table, and, I gather, a good deal of smothered feeling. Everyone feels so intensely here. It is being isolated, I think, and the general feeling of unrest and disturbance in Russia. People lose their nerves, get unbalanced, jumpy. They talk in low tones of the trials and liquidations. They gossip about the G.P.U. men and the spy system and the microphones. The "antis" carp at everything, in irritation and loneliness and as a relief to pent-up feelings. The pros rise fiercely to the defense of insignificant little things. I think, though, it is more than these surface things that make people nervous and irritable. They sense a fundamental challenge to our established modes of thought and feeling and living. They feel the rumblings of the volcano. They feel the need for coming to a decision about things. And yet it is not clearly enough defined for people to know what to oppose. So they oppose superficials. And the other side also urges, and holds up for praise, superficials. They are at variance on fundamentals but they quarrel on superficials.

"Come, come, Comrade," says Mr. Michaels to Dr. Nelson [attached to the U. S. Embassy], "do I catch a slight accent of 'anti' in your statements?"

"You certainly do," comes out the Doctor solidly.

At supper, a young man (Charles Bohlen[1]) from the Embassy, intelligent underneath his blasé Harvard manner. He is—or could be, for we do not get started—interesting on the situation here. He says Troyanovsky is a Menshevik—much safer to be a Menshevik than a Bolshevik, now. It is very tactless, he says, ever to inquire about anyone who is absent or who has disappeared. You are supposed not to notice it.

Colonel Faymonville calls for us and we proceed to the Métropole to find the Russians. I ask Colonel Faymonville what rank Slepnev is. He says his title is "Hero of the Soviet Republic," but he calls him Colonel.

I tell him about my conversation with Mr. Michaels. He is fervently pleased. You can see he feels that we are apt to have our minds poisoned by Alexander Kirk.

Colonel Slepnev, his "wife" and the interpreter, also the other Air officials are all there. We proceed to the park where people are strolling about, eating at cafés, playing chess in a chess-tournament house, sitting on benches, going to movies, the theater, etc. A large fountain plays beneath two neon-red silhouettes of Lenin and Stalin facing each other. There are one or two

[1] Charles E. Bohlen, in the diplomatic service, later Ambassador to Russia and France.

electric signs showing beer flowing from a bottle and a smoking cigar. There are also shooting galleries. The people in the park look better dressed, healthier, and happier than any I've seen so far.

I remark to Colonel Faymonville what nice-looking faces— better faces than on the street—and see immediately I should *not* have said it. I don't know why, exactly—I suppose because it's a reflection on the U. S. S. R. to say there are better faces one place than another.

We see a rather mediocre operetta about a state farm. Some of the dancing is good—Caucasian—and then the Red Army comes to help the state farm and does a dance. I ask, in fun, if all the Red Army dances as well as that, and the interpreter replies quite seriously that many of them dance better!

We walk up and down between the acts. I notice that there is one man in European clothes and hat who keeps his eye on us the whole time, following behind us.

There is absolutely no sense of jollity in these men, especially out in company with us. There is one officer who never looks at us when he shakes hands and never smiles—the coldest of duties.

Saturday, August 20th

C. goes off for the day with Colonel Faymonville on a tour of factories, airports, laboratories, schools, etc. I go off with Mrs. Chipman (very smart in a suit of maroon and blue) and a Mr. Bender (a Russian contact man of the Embassy). He leaves the car at one point, in which I ask; "*Who* is Mr. Bender?"

"Well, we will have to be a leetle care-ful what we say (she speaks with a strong French accent) because he is undoubtedly one of ze boys."

So I am careful. We go to see icons—lovely stained-glass colors; one Madonna with a gesture of infinite pity and understanding and yet dignity and restraint. (The thing one doesn't see here— tone.) Also some modern paintings: one quite good of Lenin and some busts of Lenin.

Then to the Boyar house, a seventeenth-century house of a merchant, early home of the Romanovs. Very lovely things in it.

Mr. Bender says, "You do not want to go upstairs—it is only pictures of Lenin and propaganda" (with a smile).

Then to a walled nunnery—one of those bubbly, onion-steepled churches—with a gorgeous gilded altar back studded with icons. Walking around the grounds, we see a tomb of some noble. The name the same as that of the former head of the Department of Education (now in exile or prison).

Mrs. Chipman asks if he is any relation?

He laughs and says, No, and then goes on to say it is too bad about the former head . . . in a most American fashion. Mrs. C. does not comment and neither do I. Afterward she tells me that was "what we call in French *une pêche.*"

Lunch with Alexander Kirk and Major Haine [Assistant Military Attaché] and Mrs. Chipman at the Embassy. The conversation is chiefly about the G.P.U. men who follow the diplomats about. When Bullitt was leaving, he shook hands with all the people at the station and those two familiar faces at the edge of the crowd (the G.P.U. men). They said quickly and naïvely, "Oh no, we are going with you."

Alexander Kirk's saying, when he knew he was followed, that he must thank his escorts, give them a drink, some cigarettes, in common courtesy—and the Russian disconcertion. "I *beg* you not to . . ."

Also Major Haine's story of his trip to the Caucasus. He said he always made the G.P.U. men ride in a separate taxi if they insisted on following. The only thing that disconcerted them was for him to turn around quickly and try to take their pictures!

I write all afternoon. C. comes back after a very good day; has seen everything he wanted to. He certainly rushed in where angels fear to tread, because he said—at lunch when the white bread was passed—that five years ago they had good black bread and that white bread was a return to capitalism! He got the black bread!

At six to Colonel Faymonville's for cocktails. More Russians than I have seen gathered together since the last visit. They are, though, quite shy and awkward. There are some very good faces, the best I've seen; the General of Pericop, "Hero of the Soviet Republic," with long mustaches; a Soviet polar flier, the first man to set his plane down on the North Pole; our group of civil air officials and the heads of Civil Air; Ambassador Troyanovsky, etc. Some Americans and *all* the reporters.

I talk to Ambassador Troyanovsky about Will Rogers, the ballet, the English, English and American press.

Desultory conversation with Americans.

C. talks to the Russians and gets quite a lot out of it.

I make a bad break, without realizing it, in a purely conversational way. I look at the tray of delicious hors d'oeuvres and say (by way of a compliment), "Look—you say it's difficult to get things, and a tray of delicious food like that . . ."

"Oh no," says Colonel Faymonville quickly. "You never heard that story from me," jovially trying to pass it off.

"No," I said, "you never said that, but you did say you had to plan a week ahead."

I have discomfited him in front of the Russian interpreter and put him in a false position. Oh dear, how touchy people are here.

Home and dress for dinner with the British Ambassador and Lady Chilson, people from the Italian and French Embassies, and the Chipmans. They are all "antis," I gather. Lady Chilson is lovely—oh, very lovely. An English mold, but lit from within with real spirit, thought, and warmth. She has remained cool and in control of herself here while still being perfectly honest and real underneath.

She has also managed to interest herself in the ballet and theater and made herself a specialist (but not a pedantic or arrogant one) on it. A person who gets the most out of her life wherever she is, yet never succumbs to the temporary influences of time and place too much. Still cool, still collected, still in control of her life, and yet compassionate and understanding too.

Sunday, August 21st

C. goes to aviation factories. I stay home and write all day. It is very hot. Lunch with Alexander Kirk alone. He talks about his mother and their relationship with such delicacy and formality that it is not embarrassing as it is when most people talk about personal grief. It is very difficult for him to adjust to life all over again. I think he is more lost than most men who lose their wives, and yet he hasn't even the comfort of the formalized bereavement of a widower.

C. comes home and we have a quiet supper—Alexander Kirk, C., and I. We talk about the abyss the world is facing and what could be done about it. And we talk of Communism (as a solution) and the people it appeals to. It is too bad that conversations like this cannot be preserved verbatim. They are such a frequent part of one's life nowadays, and looking back on it will be so indicative of our times to our grandchildren—if any survive!

Alexander Kirk expressed it when he said that all of us who looked at the world today—at its misery and chaos—longed for a solution. But we want to have *some* proof that the solution we try is the right one. The Communists are those who jump off the springboard and expect to remain in mid-air!

Monday, August 22nd

C. goes to see No. 1 aviation factory in the morning. I go out with Mrs. Chipman to the Museum of Western Art, a very wonderful collection. A beautiful Degas—a single ballet dancer against a window—also a pastel of three or four ballet dancers (just head and shoulders), some Manets (among them two women under a cherry tree), a lovely out-of-doors Renoir, a room full of Gauguins and another of Van Goghs. Some of the famous Cézannes: the aqueduct, Mont-Sainte-Victoire, and a self-portrait. Mary Cassatt's Mother and Child and a Derain. A great joy to see her apartment afterward. The lovely Van Gogh poplar trees framed in parchment-colored wood, with a thin inner paper frame or facing of deep blue—very good.

In the afternoon we go to the Red Army Museum—the twentieth anniversary—showing paintings representing the whole history of the Red Army, its victories and generals, and also their present life. Most of it was such pure propaganda it was not interesting from the point of view of art, though there were some good portraits and drawings. The beginning showed the recruiting for the Army *before* the revolution—men dragged from their families, etc. Also Kerenski fleeing in nurse's clothes. And caricatures of all the invaders of Russia. Lots of pictures of Lenin, Stalin, Voroshilov, Kalinin, ending up with pictures of the Red Army at museums, the Red Army in parks, the Red Army's wives, children, etc.

When we get back, C. and I go over plans with Colonel Faymonville for our trip. We also ask him about the executions, etc. He explains: (1), that there was definite evidence of treason; (2), that there is so much tension in this country striving so hard to build up to success that it shows itself in this brusque throwing out of anyone suspected of error (and many, he says, regretfully, were innocent). He also says they feel they have so much to draw on, from youth, such vast numbers newly educated in the ideals, pushing up, that they can afford to slough off those even tainted with the merest suspicion of doubt. He says the whole country was behind the executions. That (he thinks) the treason was only confined to the leaders and did not have any following in the country. Of course they haven't "democracy" now, but they say they have. They think of it as one of the stages to be passed through on the way to the ideal goal of communism.

I gather that "more power to them" is his general sentiment about it.

Members of the Diplomatic Corps come in at six, Estonian (well informed and intelligent), Danish, and Norwegian. The Norwegian, although not as intelligent a man as the Estonian, was a practical and very honest man of action. He has been Consul here for twenty-five years or so. He was up in Archangel for five years. He said he had been here too long. He could not live here any longer; he was alone, there was no one to talk to.

But the Diplomatic Corps? someone asked. The Diplomatic Corps do not talk about anything serious, he said bluntly. The Russians did: they liked to talk philosophy, life, etc., and he once used to talk to them. But now no one would come to him. He said he would make one circle of friends and they would all be wiped out. And then he would start over again, and that circle was wiped out; and again.

He lived five years in Archangel. When he arrived in his house there was an empty hen-coop opposite him. It was immediately filled with a projector, a beam of light which fell on his front door. For five years it was there, on everyone who came in and out of his door. And for five years no one came in but occasional foreigners (Danes, Swedes, or Norwegians)—no Russians.

There was a period of N.E.P.[1] when things were better "The trouble is," he said, "that I have seen a time when things were better—when one could talk to them. I must say, though, that it is not Bolshevik, that distrust of foreigners, espionage, and terror. It was always so, in the old regime." He put it down to an inferiority complex. "They feel they are inferior, and they are *not* inferior" (with some passion).

Here Colonel Faymonville injected his smiling face and said, "That bears out just what I was saying to you" (with pleasant brotherly love).

The other people went on talking gaily: "Don't tell me any of those awful stories, I won't sleep," cackled an American.

But a sinister crack of light had been thrown in by that big honest and crying-out Norwegian.

We get dressed for dinner (street clothes) and go out with Colonel Faymonville to dinner at the "Hero of the Soviet Repub-

[1] New Economic Policy, adopted in 1921, a new course of domestic policy which allowed the use of private capital for Russian reconstruction.

lic" Vodopyanov.[1] The dinner *starts* at ten! I take a rest before-hand—almost go to sleep. A tight-lipped gray-faced Foreign Office man (Russian) also comes for us. He is the clever type, quick, unhealthy, and vindictive. He has lived in America and England and is always trying to tell jokes and to ingratiate himself that way, to show that he knows your country, your language, your way of living. (I think it is inferiority complex at the bottom.)

I say how much Moscow has improved in five years.

"Not enough," he says briefly, waiting, I suspect, for my answer. But I don't give it. I jump out of the car at our destination, a new apartment building across the river, rather grim and shoddy-looking inside—institutional—and rather dirty "institutional."

Upstairs to a three- or four-room apartment. Vodopyanov and six or eight other fliers, his wife and secretary.

We go into a small office and sit down on an old leather sofa and face a bookcase that has a dozen books in it. Then began a long evening of fliers' tales slowly exchanged by means of translation. Vodopyanov, with his beautiful dreamy disheveled look, would go on and on and then Faymonville or a Foreign Office man would translate, Faymonville with beaming smiles, and the Foreign Office man with slick and cynical proficiency. Neither of them caught the childlike dramaticism of Vodopyanov. C. is tired, or at least tired of this kind of exchange of compliments. So I, who am comparatively fresh, try to carry up my end with questions and counter-stories. We are shown an album of photos. We ask more questions. They laugh a lot and there is good feeling; they are relaxed and free.

We do not start eating until eleven. The table is set with lots of wine glasses and a double cover of plates. There is a huge gilt ornament in the middle of the table (old regime—worst style) and a huge and hideous flowered teapot on top of a dresser

[1] Mikhail Vodopyanov, one of the Russian Arctic fliers, who landed at the North Pole.

against the wall. The furniture and curtains are poor middle-class mediocrity and the atmosphere has that curious air of stuffiness that goes with it.

Mme Vodopyanov is dressed in black, drably, and has an honest but completely devoid of any spark-of-life face, flat, tired, and expressionless. The fliers around the table have good, simple, open faces. They are very much at ease and happy-go-lucky, and it is easy to banter and laugh with them. The humor is a little sophomoric but it is genuine, honest, and healthy.

Example: C. asks Vodopyanov how many children he has.

Vodopyanov starts off with that dreamy expression on a long story.

C. says, with some humor; "Is he counting them?" And then C. goes on to tell of Charlie Brower,[1] in Point Barrow, who, when asked, said he never could remember if it was seventeen or twenty-four. They laughed at this and said he would have been a lucky man in the Soviet Union—he'd get a bonus. Then round pumpkin-faced nice Kakkinaki said his ambition was twelve children.

Then the others said that was the first they'd heard of it. . . .

The only person that had any look of delicacy or keen perception and thought, real thought, was Colonel Slepnev. He was not as uproarious as the others, who as the evening progressed with caviar, smoked salmon, salad, meat, ice cream, a rich cake, fruit, wines, got gayer and more released.

He was rather quiet (and the tight-lipped Foreign Office was bloodlessly sober) but contributed as his story—rather wistfully, and with quiet humor—a fairy tale:

"Once upon a time there was an old woman who had three sons. Two of them were good boys, but the third was an aviator."

It is hot and there are lots of mosquitoes dying on the table-cloth. Vodopyanov has a cough and keeps spitting into his hand-kerchief (malaria—quite a lot in Russia, even in Moscow) and elaborately wiped his brow (not with spit, but with the same

[1] Early pioneer and settler at Point Barrow, Alaska.

handkerchief!). It is after twelve thirty before we are through. Toasts to C., to Mrs. Lindbergh, to American and Soviet friendship, to fliers. . . .

And I propose a toast to Vodopyanov's five children (I find out afterward he only has four), at which I get the first spark of life from Mrs. Vodopyanov. Then we go and sit in the office again. Then the good-bys and the compliments and those crushing handshakes and I telling Vodopyanov that his flights (the first man to land on Pole) are part of history and I shall tell my children that I have met him. And then down into the quiet streets and home.

It was really a very jolly evening and cheered one to see those nice open honest children having a good time. Colonel Faymonville, of course, clucked like a mother hen over it: "Aren't they fine people! Don't let anyone tell you . . . That did more good . . ."

Tuesday, August 23rd

My sore throat and cold has returned to me as a result of last night. Stay in all morning. Write diary and letters to Mme Carrel, Miss W., and Jon. (I am so anxious to get back. I have that superstitious feeling that my time with Jon is short and very precious—terrifyingly precious.)

Lunch with Alexander Kirk at Embassy. He talks about C. He really sees much in him that few people see. It is a relief. He says it is very difficult for him to think of C. as a flier.

C. comes back in the afternoon from a laboratory (he was shown every detail of construction and works, as though they had put him in an airplane and told him; "Now this is the stick; when you pull this back . . ." etc.). He is tired. It is very hot— breathless. Later we walk the streets of Moscow and look into shop windows. The material in the windows—pieces of flowered silk, cotton underwear, dowdy women's felt hats—is all shoddy, third-rate, and looks neglected and dusty. Alexander Kirk says the things are never changed. And you cannot buy anything out of a window. The prices are extremely high (if the ruble is five to a dollar, a dowdy 1.98 hat is about 6 or 7 dollars).

The food in the windows is all plaster of Paris or papier-mâché —hams, sausages, rolls, cakes. We pass several antique shops. Terrible junk in the window, hideously highly priced. The worst rococo style, elaborate, tortured gilt ornaments, beflowered toilet seats, etc. Inside there are some nice things, silver and china, but it is all very expensive. (To do them justice, the foreigners used to "do them in" terribly in the early days, Alexander Kirk says.)

The streets are hot, dusty, crowded with humanity and the smell of humanity. I feel dizzy but am determined to walk home. I do not seem to be as strong as the proletariat! (There is something about it that reminds me of India.)

Dinner at the Embassy in the evening. I am told not to dress, so I literally don't. I wear street dress and Mme Troyanovsky comes in evening dress. I am embarrassed, not for myself but because I feel she may feel insulted. Also Vodopyanov and his drab honest wife in her black dress, Colonel Slepnev and [I. P.] Mazuruk.[1] Also the Foreign Office man who came last night, and the Russian chef de protocol, Barcov.

The Russians are rather stiff and embarrassed, except for the Troyanovskys. She is a sympathetic, quick, and intelligent woman. Also a "lady." One turns almost unconsciously to the old and snobbish-"capitalistic" terms here. I mean by "lady" that she had a true and gracious sense of kindness. She saw that I was trying to make Mrs. Vodopyanov feel at home and talk to her and she helped me with no taint of snobbishness or condescension (as you see in the *nouveau-riche* type here). She showed grace and tact and understanding and sympathy. I liked her for it.

I sit between Troyanovsky and Barcov. Both are interesting. Troyanovsky (that round, simple, impenetrable face) is both quick and intelligent and has a caustic sense of humor. I did not

[1] Pilot of one of the Russian planes that landed at the Pole; at this time chief of the flying service of the Northern Seaways.

see how he could fit many of the things he said into the Soviet theories.

For instance on education. He feels there is something wrong with the educational system in the world—that it kills the inventive spirit. Inventions do not come from technicians. You must give the individuals more play. I agreed with him, but—I did not say this—I feel that Communism does just what he says he disapproves of: it standardizes everyone, levels everything to the mass, to mediocrity; equality for all, mediocrity for all.

He said it was not quite adjusted even in his country but told me about the Stakhanovite system, where individual inventiveness and excellence is rewarded. He talked to me about youth being given more chance in Russia, positions of responsibility.

He listened to my remarks with round pebbly eyes. I could not tell how they registered but knew they did somewhere, deep down. For he is a thoughtful man. I do not feel that I touch him at all (he disapproves of me and my class) except he rather likes laughing at my jokes, while *she* likes me as a woman.

Barcov, the chef de protocol, is an educated man of sensibility, finely attuned and sympathetic. He has lived for a long time in China and is very sympathetic to them and their culture and philosophy. I feel that it is an accident that he is a Communist. He does not fit into any of the usual types: the stupid, the clever, the fanatic, the able but limited men of action. He is a man of culture and thought and sensibility and of sense. Probably he is not very strong.

(He was replaced shortly after our visit—retired or "liquidated," though not apparently due to us.)

After they all leave, Alexander Kirk lets himself go on the manners of most of the people there tonight and how out of place they were and the folly of dealing with them in that way. They sopped their food up with their fingers, they said the cigarettes were bad. They had no sense of form. (I think he feels it is a kind of insult to his mother and her creed to entertain them.)

But he is hard on them. I do not mind the honest and crude

people (though it may not be wise or kind to put them in a setting that is not theirs and where they do not feel at home). I mind the clever and twisted people, the deceptive and the cruel. Those are the people I would mind having in my house, under the guise of friendship. For that is a lie. One does not feel friendship for them, while for the Vodopyanovs one does, one can feel honest respect, moral respect and warmth.

Colonel Faymonville (who did not hear the tirade) felt it was a great success!

Wednesday, August 24th, "rest day"

Leave at 9:30 and drive out to a newly made canal [completed in 1936] and its newly constructed station; very well laid out, beautiful buildings and gardens. It is apparently simply a passenger station. We were shown an illuminated raised map on the wall and given a short explanation of the canal, which connects Moscow with the Volga. Then we were taken upstairs to see a small nursery for children of mothers traveling on the canal. The walls of both the playroom and the nursery are charmingly painted, the playroom with animals, and the nursery, deep blue with stars and a frieze of silver pine trees below. It looked very new, practical, and clean. Also an isolation ward. Apparently the mothers who travel on the line can leave their children here for the day or even for two days. There is no charge for the care but a small charge for food.

There was only one child in the nursery. She very obligingly slid down the slide for us!

Then we got on a very neat river boat, a closed and open deck holding fifty or sixty people. We were a party of fifteen or so—all the Air officers: Colonel Slepnev and his "wife," Kakkinaki and his wife. Also Mazuruk and his wife, a very nice and intelligent girl, joined us by speedboat later.

We sat down at tables in the closed deck. The officers took off their coats, the girls their hats. They were all in nice summer dresses and though stockingless had high-heeled summer shoes.

They were definitely relaxed—off on a holiday. We hardly got started down the canal (almost a lake here) when one of the ship's men started laying the tables and then setting down food (about 10:45). Then proceeded one of those long, delicious, but overwhelming Russian meals. It lasted the whole canal trip of three hours, with spaces in between courses. Caviar, smoked salmon, salad, stuffed tomatoes, cold fish, chicken, ice cream, peaches, melon, grapes, and drinks. I took only Narzan water and a little white wine. But everyone else—men and women—took glass after glass of cognac, vodka, etc., to wash down the meal. Much catching of eyes and raising of glasses (when you toast you are supposed to empty your glass of vodka or cognac). C. only sipped.

A great set-to between C. and Colonel Slepnev's girl, who was bound and determined to make C. drink a glass of cognac. She took two whole ones in the effort and was very disdainful of his sips.

All this time we were going up the canal, the banks lined with stones and the sides of the banks planted with criss-cross grass plots. Also we went through pine-wooded lakes. Everywhere there were people bathing, very scantily dressed and poor-looking, but having a good time on the "rest day." We also passed some camps (factory or office owned) where people can come to rest.

After the ice cream the climax of gaiety was over. It became very hot. We stopped to go through some locks. Everyone felt rather heavy and sleepy. A slightly drunk man gazed at me with sentimental fixity and tried to sit on Mrs. Mazuruk's lap, which he thought was a chair.

Finally we stopped at a station where many people were bathing; several big restaurants and a woods beyond.

We got out and started to walk up blazing cement steps and dusty paths to the woods, which were full of crowds, families sprawled out in the shade, some with accordions and victrolas, and hundreds of lumpy sweating barely dressed people, simply asleep on the ground, faces turned toward each other. *Everywhere*. You get the feeling of swarming humanity here, much as you do in India or China. All badly dressed, all poor, all hot, all tired. A girl selling cider from a can with one glass for everyone to drink out of.

Our group definitely did not want to sit with the other people. We trudged through dusty paths under sparse birch trees looking for shade and isolation. They finally pick on a spot.

Then the men go off to swim and the girls (six of us) sit down exhausted. I had a splitting headache and felt very wilted. Unfortunately, the "drunk" instead of going off with the men decided to stay with us, reclining by a tree and still staring fixedly at me. But I let "Shopova" (the interpreter) deal with him while I talked to the nice Mazuruk wife. She came over to me and said quite simply; "Are you not tired? I am very tired. It is too hot and I have headache." I agreed and felt drawn to her for I was beginning to be depressed again by how much stronger the proletariat is than me—and this is a day of "rest"!

The men come back spruce and cool. Then we trudge through dust, heat, sun, and people to the docks where unfortunately I say, "Yes—I would like a glass of water." We push through a restaurant jammed with people, upstairs. It is breathless and hot and smelly. But I forget the smell after a while and only feel hot. We wait and wait and wait. There is a line in front of the booth and lots of people at tables.

Finally a tray of fruit drinks comes. The Narzan water has given out! We walk to a car. Mrs. Mazuruk and I put our heads back on the seat and let the wind blow us and shut our eyes.

Back to the Embassy, which is dark and cool. Rest until dinner. I do not dress as usual (I can't *not* dress for one group of fliers and dress for the others) and of course the women *are* in evening dress. Great consternation. Colonel Faymonville meets us at the door. *Mrs.* Schmidt[1] has come and apparently no one knew she

[1] Wife of Professor Schmidt, a Polar expert.

existed, or, at least, expected her. Mr. Kirk's table can only hold twelve, comfortably. Also two other people turned up who hadn't replied! Colonel Faymonville tells us to go in and keep them (the guests) occupied while he and Alexander Kirk have a consultation. I sit between the two women—Mrs. Kakkinaki, a big blonde who speaks only Russian, and Mrs. Schmidt, a delicate and birdlike little woman with a charming head who speaks very little French. After appropriate gestures there is nothing to do but look at some reproductions of a modern Russian artist. Professor Schmidt is a tall, distinguished man with a huge gray beard. He speaks English. The fliers stand around and Bohlen tries to engage them in conversation. Also a Mr. and Mrs. Smirnov. Mr. Smirnov is Cultural Relations head (VOKS), tall, compact, good carriage, aggressive (in an American go-getter way), quick and clever. You cannot really get a good look at him because his glasses and his prominent teeth flashing when he smiles take up your attention.

At dinner I sit next to Professor Schmidt, whom I find extremely interesting. He is well educated, gentle, charming, and intelligent. I do not know (until later) what his specialty (Polar study) is, which is just as well. For we talk books—Tolstoy and Dostoevsky, and some of the modern Russians. Kakkinaki on the other side, smiling, good-natured, pumpkin-faced, is not so easy (but I do like him) for we have to get our far neighbor to translate. There are uncomfortable silences. Alexander Kirk holds up the whole table by a continuous Russian lesson he carries on with Mrs. Schmidt and Mrs. Smirnov, mispronouncing all the words, and causing great delight to all the Russians. It is marvelous.

After supper Mrs. Chipman comes over, also Major Haine and Dr. Nelson. (Major Haine was sent back from the door before supper because he made thirteen!) They speak some Russian, which helps. It is hard sledding. I am very tired. My efforts to communicate in French to Mrs. Schmidt are not successful. I say, "Professor Schmidt told me two modern Russian books to read—

Peter the Great and *Quiet Flows the Don*. Have you read them?"

She looks confused, then signals for her husband. He comes over, strokes his beard gently, and asks delicately, "You ask my wife if she has any babies?"

I am glad when the "day of rest" is over.

Thursday, August 25th

Write all morning, waiting for Miss "Shopova," who was to come for me at 11 and take me to the crèche I have been trying to see ever since I got here (Alexander Kirk says they are building one for me!). She arrives at 1:20 (I telephoning in the meantime to find out what had happened). She says, "Mrs. Lindbergh, I am come to take you to the crèche." I explain that I thought she was coming at 11 and that I must stay for lunch at the Embassy and that I will move the appointments I have for the afternoon if I can see the crèche then.

She says they have just got through with C.'s program. He asked for a day or a morning to work on the plane. He was to have the whole morning. Then they wanted him to see the War College but said he'd be through at 10. They finished at 11:30 and then had one of those huge Russian meals. The rest of the time (Miss Shopova's) was spent (I discovered later from Colonel Faymonville) trying to find a crèche for me to see. They called up four or five, and all the children were out in the country! Also the Institute of Mother and Child is closed for repairs. Finally they discovered one.

After lunch I go out with Shopova and one officer to a factory, No. 22, that has a crèche attached to it. We are taken into the office and talk to the matron, a nice-looking woman, a practical-nurse type. The building looks moderately clean and up-to-date. We put on white smock coats, so as not to contaminate the children with our street clothes, I gather. We enter the children's rooms. The first room: tiny babies in cribs. The cribs and bedding are good and clean. The children wear almost nothing but crash panties, which are instantly removed by the nurse-girls when wet or soiled. Most of the children are asleep. They are pale and do not look very well nourished and are covered with flies. Each child had three or four on him—on his lips, eyes, penis. The precaution of putting on immaculate smocks seemed a little unnecessary.

I try to find out what they eat—when they start meat, vegetables, etc., but can get no definite answers. They said I could read the pamphlets of the Institute of Mother and Child. But you could see they did not want to take the responsibility of giving out information.

"And that," said the interpreter, "is all there is to see."

It was very baffling and rather futile, though I have no doubt it is a vast improvement on the state of similar children before the revolution.

At 8:30 we go to a reception given us by VOKS (Cultural Relations) and the Civil Air fleet. For this I dress up—at least put on my long flowered silk hostess gown. This is just as well, as we find it is a real party. Lots of cars outside in the street and people going in and—strangest sight of all in a Communistic country—a small crowd of poor people at the door watching the "grand" people go in.

The house is big and spacious. It is the clubhouse for VOKS, made for receptions—old-regime grandeur. Candelabra, columns, brocade sofas, etc. Mr. and Mrs. Smirnov meet us; she, in a really smart black evening gown, he, flashing smiles and cordiality. We are swept out into a garden. There are lots of people already and more coming. We shake hands. I see Mazuruk's little-girl wife, who comes over to me. I ask her how she feels after yesterday and she says she has been in bed all day! Other people come up. All degrees of elegance (or almost elegance) in dress. The ballerina, with laughing slant-up eyes, in evening dress and red taffeta jacket. Mme Tolstoi, wife of a writer who is a nephew of *the* Tolstoi (very interesting head), in Parisian clothes, long green gloves, and with blasé manner. All the fliers in uniform, and the American press. Also members of the Embassy: Charles Bohlen, the Chipmans, Major Haine, Dr. Nelson, etc.

We go down and walk in the garden, dusty but cool, with lights on the leaves giving it a theatrical cast. I go at Mrs. Mazuruk's suggestion (I never dare suggest anything to Russians lest it should be not allowed and embarrass them). Here Major Haine joins us and Professor Schmidt and a young woman from VOKS, sent, I gather, to take care of me, for she is always around.

Here, in this atmosphere of semidarkness, moving figures, and strangely lit-up trees, I sensed strongly, for the first time really, the thing that hovers over Moscow. Two men are standing together at a slight distance, watching us with half-shut eyes, saying to each other (it was obvious, even though in Russian), "So-and-So is talking a lot to So-and-So." Little groups all over—watching, noticing, gossiping. Till I felt uncomfortable and frightened for Mrs. Mazuruk, for Professor Schmidt talking so kindly to me and Major Haine. He is the most open and frank of Americans, but his contacts with Russians are noted down with suspicion, one can see.

We moved inside for music. A boy playing dramatically on a tinny piano, photographers, flashlight picture. A woman singing a melting folksong. Then a stand-up dinner at a long table heaped with hors d'oeuvres, hot dishes, and wine (all very good). A crowd of men talking to Mme Tolstoi leaning in a corner with a glass of wine in her long green gloves.

Yes, this came as near to elegance as anything I have seen, in a social way, in the U. S. S. R.

Dance music starts. Colonel Slepnev asks for a dance, and others. I am afraid of getting started, but finally after many valentine gestures from Colonel Slepnev (he is very gay and indicates that he will take the dance and tuck it in a pocket next to his heart, etc.), I dance, first with Colonel Slepnev and then with the aviator, leader of the "Red Five" stunt planes. The Russians, I think, are pleased that I am dancing and watch with childlike pleasure.

I am very tired and with the Americans simply give in and cannot talk. For the things I am really thinking—the strangeness of this new elegance, this party—I cannot say. Besides, one must either talk to Russians or to Americans. It is very hard to mix the two. I find I spend my effort talking small talk to the Russians and then have not the effort to talk small talk to Americans. I *could* talk seriously, but one feels one can't. You are always watched.

The lovely Mrs. Chipman and Alexander Kirk make gay conversation in a corner.

But I have lost my mask. Finally C. (who has been talking to the fliers—Papanin, Kakkinaki, Mazuruk, etc.) comes up and says we must go. We shake hands (at 12:30). Alexander Kirk gives a tip to the men at the door (in the U. S. S. R.!) and we go out into the cool night, again through a crowd of peering faces, looking at our clothes, our shoes, our cars, waiting for the grand people to come out on their way home.

Friday, August 26th (written in plane)
Breakfast at the Embassy. Alexander Kirk comes in to say goodby. I think he minds our going. He has given me a tiny old Russian box full of peppermints. Very like him. I really think he is a rare person and I feel sorry for him. I wish he would leave Russia, as it is not good for him.

We drive to the field with Colonel Faymonville. He is very enthusiastic about our visit. Says we see his picture (I feel very hypocritical about this). It is true, I like the Russians, especially the ones we've met—those nice, open, healthy fliers. I feel spontaneously drawn to them and gay with them. But I still do not think we see "his picture." Or rather he does not see ours. And you can't make him. He is hurt when you say that anything is wrong. When I said, about the crêche, that it was not perfect but it had many good things, he was hurt, and I had to talk for half an hour before I got him over it. Of course, he always looks at the "spirit" of the people—their ideals, their aims, their enthusiasm, and not at their materialistic results.

But the Russians themselves have put up materialistic standards for themselves, and therefore you must somewhat judge on these.

Drive to the field: Mrs. Chipman, Alexander Kirk, Major Haine, Dr. Nelson, and the fliers (but not Slepnev—where is he?). No press, so it is not the confused embarrassment take-offs and good-bys usually are for me. Lots of smiles and pictures and good-bys and desultory conversation.

Kakkinaki, nice smiling Kakkinaki, nearly breaks my fingers, shaking hands, and I laugh and tell him so which I have been dying to do each time! He takes my little finger and wiggles it gently to see if it is broken—with great humor.

Off at 11:15. The dusty field, the heat hanging over Moscow in a haze. The curves of the river. It is a relief to be off, though I have enjoyed it. Write in diary all morning. Quite bumpy, and a strong head wind. Russia is very impressive from the air—flat stretches of land as far as you can see, great fields, state or collective farms. The houses line a road with small green patches of gardens behind them. Then the great collective fields are out beyond.

Land in intense heat and dust at Kharkov after four and three quarters hours. The smiling fat Shopova is already there in a red dress. (The Russians sent a plane before us with mechanic and interpreter.) Refuel and start again. It is so hot that all the gray grease on the sliding hatch grooves is melting and coming off on our clothes. It is impossible, I decide for the hundredth time, to wear anything but an overall in a plane.

We start off after three quarters of an hour for Rostov. It is cooler in the air. We fly over a mining area. It looks quite well run: new settlements of houses, lots of trees, parks, gardens, many collective farms, towns. Factories on rivers, and much new construction everywhere. Again, perfectly flat country and very few woods (more south of Moscow).

In the evening haze we see a corner of the Sea of Azov and shortly after, Rostov. Land at seven. There is Colonel Slepnev and of course Shopova and a nicely dressed woman with a bunch of flowers.

Slepnev greets us with open arms and rushes up to kiss my hand. (This left-over elegant gesture of the old days seems particularly inappropriate when you are stepping out of a plane in trousers and grease-stained hands.)

There is no hangar here but C. asks for rope to tie the controls. They say they will do everything. The rope does not come. "Just ordinary rope—just a little bigger than this."

"Yes, yes—*da, da, da*—yes, yes." But it does not come.

"Will it take long to get the rope?" C. asks.

"Oh, you want it?" Men run. Finally C. shows how the stick should be tied, taking some wire to do it, and tells them to do it like that with rope.

Then we go off with Slepnev, who flew down this morning very early, Shopova, and the woman with the flowers. She has twinkly eyes and a sympathetic face. We are told that she was a machine-gunner for six years under Chapayev.[1] She was very young and a peasant girl. After the war she went to school and university and now is married, has a child of seven, and is the head of Intourist in Rostov.

She does not look like a machine-gunner, is quite pretty, about forty, with a quick sympathetic face. She has on a nice printed silk dress and straw hat. Shopova tells us she is famous all over Russia.

Also with us is the mayor of Rostov. He has a good-natured smiling face—a good face. He was a turner.

We drive over rough dusty roads under dust-covered trees, through straying cows and barefoot people into town. A fairly big, modern town; the streets are full of people. They look healthier than in Moscow and happier; quite well dressed, no hats or stockings but cotton or silk dresses and socks and shoes. It is cooler now, evening.

We stop at Bolshaia Hotel and are taken to our rooms: two

[1] Russian military hero; Red Army leader during the Civil War (1918).

small ones elaborately furnished with a marble bust, gilt Empire clock, embroidered-with-gold-thread chairs and sofas. All the objects in the room are ticketed with a metal ticket and marked with a number. Even the curtains. There is an Eastern-looking hanging on the wall. I feel it carefully for microphones but find none.

We wash in a rather dirty bathroom with a minute square of pink soap that smells like candy.

Then downstairs for supper. There is a long table set and various people. The Chapayev heroine, the mayor, Slepnev, Shopova, and pilot and mechanic, a man with a good—if rough—face marked with a deep scar over his eye. He is a delegate from the district to the Supreme Council of Soviets. He runs a horse and pig farm. His wife, a simple peasant woman with a white embroidered cap on, sits beside him and there are one or two other people I can't distinguish.

A huge meal comes on: caviar, smoked salmon, cold salads, fish, chicken, and ice cream—and the usual drinks.

It is very hot. There are a good many toasts. The peasant wife catches my eye and smiles and gets less shy. She giggles embarrassedly into her hand when Shopova explains that her husband wanted to fly to the Council at Moscow but she didn't want to. She took her first train ride a year ago. They discover that the delegate and C. were born in the same year—1902. "Ah, that is a good reason for a drink!" says Slepnev. It seems much gayer than Moscow.

The meal ends at ten. I am very sleepy. We go up to our rooms, look down over the street from our balcony. It is swarming with people. The shuffle of feet, the confusion of voices, the heat, the noise, all remind me of India.

Sunday, August 28th

Breakfast at the hotel, on the porch. Slepnev has left early on the passenger plane for Kiev. But the rest of the crowd are there at the long table.

We all drive out to the airport. Here C. finds the stick was not properly tied and the cowl of the engine opened too high and not closed properly. However, he doesn't want to make any trouble for the people there so he says nothing. Shopova, billowy in her red dress, takes off in the biplane before us. Then we, after all the good-bys.

It is a relief to be out of the dust. Tail wind, and it is cooler in the air. Land at Kiev about two. I see Shopova's red dress, Colonel Slepnev's white uniform, and a small group of other people. Also some cameramen. We get out and meet the various officers. The head of Intourist, the head of VOKS, and two Intourist girls (a much higher-pressure place than Rostov, evidently); one quite pretty girl who looks fairly intelligent and one very stout billowy woman with dyed light hair and very made up. She has a large bunch of flowers for me held against her incredible bosom.

We get into a car and drive to Kiev. It is nice country, pine trees and rivers. I can see the glint on the onion domes of Kiev in the distance. Kiev is on a steep hill which rises abruptly from the wide Dnieper. I remark on the towers on the hill. Yes, that is an old monastery, now an antireligious museum we are going to see this afternoon. We climb up the steep cobblestone road. Trees and shade and people in real peasant skirts and embroidered blouses. We tear through the town (wide streets, new buildings, trees, parks), up and down hill, to the hotel. A quick change into the cotton dress. (Real hot water in the tub and two palatial rooms full of old regime loot.)

Then out sightseeing, in an open car which roars through the town, followed by two other cars. They hoot their horns continually and tear up and down hill. The billowy woman, Shopova, and I sit in the back seat and C. on the little one, Slepnev in front. Our new guide points out all the new buildings in an incredible accent and dreadful propaganda, which she has learned by rote and which sometimes she does not understand herself, such as, "Heah ees de noo Pioneah Palace wheah all de best children of de Soviet Union are demonstrated"!

We are taken to a platform which overlooks the river and beaches far below and the green valley leading down to it. It is very lovely. Our guide waves the proletariat off the platform and sticking out her incredible bosom gives us in a loud nasal voice the history of Kiev, ending up with a dramatic gesture. "And now forevermore, forevermore a part of de Soviet Union." C. mixes her up by asking how long it has been a part of the Soviet Union—eighteen years? (She gave the date of liberation as 1920.) But as she evidently couldn't subtract, she started the whole history over again, all about "de yak (yoke) of de Poles, de rich merchants, de White Army," ending up again with the dramatic "And now forevermore a part of de Soviet Union." "And how long is that?" said C.

We go through an old Cathedral of St. Sophia, built by Yaroslav the Wise or the Good. "Before de revolution dey tell us dis catedral was built by Yaroslav de Wise, but *we* know it was built by de workers."

There was one mosaic of the Last Supper so beautiful, with such harmony, grace, and restraint, such reverence, that it was a relief to look at it, to escape into it from this cheap, flamboyant person with no sense of reverence, or beauty, or restraint.

By now, only C. and I were left walking around. Slepnev and the other two Intourist girls, the mayor, and the rest of the cavalcade had dropped off long ago, in little groups, laughing and joking.

Driving back, again the cavalcade of cars, tearing through the streets, honking horns. We pass a man who has been struck down by a truck. It was not us who did it but it might well have been, the way they tear around. His stiff crouched body—nameless, faceless, speechless, in dark worker's clothes, lying in the street—was somehow typical of the suffering one feels much of the time in Russia. I shall remember him a long time. C. did not think he was killed. A Red Cross truck came to take him away.

Then we go up a hill overlooking a park and into a restaurant. They order drinks, caviar, salad, and a typical Georgian meat dish. There is music and tables of people sitting about, fairly well dressed. I dance with Colonel Slepnev and another officer. Colonel Slepnev dances well but it is slightly embarrassing as we are the only couple and everyone watches us. It is after twelve before we leave, tearing through the empty streets in those cars.

Monday, August 29th

Breakfast in the hotel at the long table. I have "spiked ball" indigestion and struggle to eat no caviar (we have it at *every* meal), no salad, no wine, no fruit, only bread, a soft-boiled egg, and coffee in a glass. We drive out in an open car to see a shoe factory. The shoes look very poor quality and the people sad. Eighty per cent are women in peasant kerchiefs. I ask if they come from farms. Our guide says quickly, "Oh no, our people on our collective farms are so happy they do not wish to come into the city and work." "I should think not," I say.

Then we go tearing down to the river for a ride in the boat. It is very hot and clouds of dust on the road; our faces are black with it. There is an excursion boat tied up to a dock and here we sit for hours. I do not quite know why.

The men go in swimming in their shorts. (Maybe this is why we are waiting.) They come back and again we wait. I see some men running down the dock with baskets, bottles, etc. Ah, I think, *now* I see why we have been waiting—for the food. Presently we go into a closed deck and are served sandwiches, caviar, ham, and cheese, and beer. I take a cheese sandwich, knock off the cheese and eat only the bread and Narzan water (a fizzy salt water that is recommended strongly here for its beneficial effects. C. and I drink quarts of it as it is the only water that is safe). There is much joking and teasing and laughing about the speed our boat is making. Colonel Slepnev is having a very good time with the black-eyed Intourist girl. He has a great deal of dash and charm, a quickness and snap and spontaneous humor that the others lack. He is the center of every group, leading the toasts and the jokes. He likes to flirt and always—no matter how many men and how few women are at the table—*always* has a woman on either side of him!

We go out on deck and wait some more. It appears that there is a speedboat at the end of the dock that is meant to take us for a ride but it won't start and they are trying to fix it.

Finally it is ready and we all get in. It is quite small and crowded. We tear down the river, spray coming up on either side. People get wet and go into the tiny cabin. Only C. and I, Colonel Slepnev and the dark-eyed Intourist girl, and one other man stay outside. Everyone sings and it is very gay. We pass one beautiful picture: six dark horses playing on the cream-white sand. Nothing else beyond—the sand, some wavy grass on the near horizon, and those horses playing. Like a dream, or a Chirico painting.

Going back, it is much wetter and we all crowd inside, soaking wet—I on C.'s lap. C. teases Colonel Slepnev, says he didn't know a Hero of the Soviet Union would be so hesitant. Much singing and laughter.

Back to the hotel for a "light lunch" at which I pick and scatter (there is quite a technique to not-eating politely. There is the "direct-refusal method" and there is the "pick-and-scatter" method). I say *no* to the caviar, wine, and fruit, but pick and scatter the hot dishes.

Then out in an open car again, driving like mad over rough cobblestoned roads to a collective farm. This was very disappointing from the point of view of the farm, which was scattered, messy, and gave the impression of being not well run at all. We walk around kicking up clouds of dust, our guide heaving ahead and giving us her line on collective farms.

She kept telling us how badly off the peasants were before. "Ah, yes," I would say, "I know, because of the rich kulaks!" She also told me how they were being educated at the school—some were becoming engineers. I asked what would happen when they all wanted to be engineers—who would run the farms?

We walked to the little enclosure where the badly built frame schoolhouse stands. A crowd of people met us, women and children and some men. They had bunches of flowers they gave Colonel Slepnev (who is a great hero and very popular in Russia) and to us. The people were dressed chiefly in rather drab peasants clothes, kerchiefs, etc., and had for the most part bare feet.

However, they were *much healthier and happier-looking* than anyone else I had seen in Russia. The people looked carefree and the children well fed and rosy—a great relief. There was a band playing on the bandstand (local talent) and all the children gathered around us and Colonel Slepnev and begged him for a speech.

He got up on a little box and gave them the greetings from all the fliers in Moscow, told them about us coming to see Russian aviation and how we also were interested in the work that was being done on the collective farms. The speech ended with an exhortation to work hard, help the country get strong, and then the Japanese would no longer dare invade their shores (or words to that effect. This is the first reference to outside, or inside, politics we have heard).

Then we walked through the schoolhouse, clubrooms, Young Pioneers Club, etc., all bare rooms, and then through one of the peasant's houses. These are frame houses—one story, with thatched straw roofs and valentine windows. It was very clean and neat, whitewashed walls, sparsely furnished with large photographs of Stalin, Voroshilov, Kalinin over the walls, draped with handworked embroidered linen scarves. In one of the rooms over the brass bed was an old icon—a madonna and child, also draped with a scarf. This interested me as, of course the Church has been wiped out of life here, though I have been told that out in the country worship is going on much the same as before.

We climbed back into our cars heaped with tight bunches of marigolds, asters, and zinnias, and big melons at our feet. A crowd of children, women, and boys around the car.

Drive back and arrive at the hotel at nine. We wash the dust off and sit down for another "light meal," which lasts until eleven. At eleven we are still waiting for something. I cannot find out what. Finally it appears that in about three minutes the orchestra is going to play some Russian music, which I said I liked, including the newest popular song:

> "If tomorrow there is a war
> We must learn to march today."

We, however, go up before they play it; very tired.

Tuesday, August 30th Kiev—Odessa, "rest day"
Eight-thirty breakfast in the hotel. Then the long drive out to the airport, the usual three cars full of people. Good-bys at the airport (which is big, well arranged, with a fine-looking new airport building). Our guide says to C., "I do not cry only because you promise to come back again to Kiev." I tell her that Kiev is a very interesting and charming city and I should certainly tell anyone who was visiting Russia to come there to see it. At this, she beams with self-approval and rushes off and nabs two officers and tells them what I have said.

With her usual tact she almost insists that I go into the new airport building and use the bathroom. When I try to refuse she says, "But you have a long trip before you—you will need to use the toilet!"

Colonel Slepnev kisses her good-by, chiefly, I gather, so he can also kiss the other dark-eyed Intourist girl.

Finally we are off. I write in my diary on the way to Odessa. Land about 1 P.M. Flowers, officers, Intourist girls, hand-kissing. It is hot and damp. We drive into the city. The town is very unprepossessing, low, fairly modern (nothing old or charming), and not well swept or kept. The hotel on the sea front is nicely situated. A promenade park in front and a view of harbor.

We are told to dress quickly as the Young Pioneers at the Pioneer Camp on the shore outside of Odessa are waiting to have "breakfast" with us. We rush into our clothes. It is about two. I feel a little faint with heat and hunger. We tear out in cars to the Pioneer Camp—a lovely situation on the shore with trees, low buildings, a beach. The place is very quiet. The manager, an intelligent man, takes us around.

It seems the Young Pioneers have already eaten and are all fast asleep! We put on white coats and go around and see them in their dormitories. The children look healthy, well cared for, and happy. They have a library, they swim, play games, and dance.

There was a large map of Spain in the front garden. Yes, we were told, the Young Pioneers like to watch the progress of the Republican Army in Spain.

"It is such a shame," the director says, "that you came just now when the children are asleep." It is indeed, I think, feeling fainter by the moment. At about three, when I am resigned to the fact that we will wait now for one of those five o'clock meals, Colonel Slepnev points to his mouth and I gather we are going back to the hotel to eat.

Back to the hotel for a long meal—three to five—at a long table.

A telegram from Faymonville. We must wait for our route through Rumania! Can't leave tomorrow morning? Can we go back to Kiev and go through Poland? We send telegrams. Colonel Slepnev gets down to business; studies maps and routes and sends a wire. I like him like this. He is an able man.

We take a rest, since the mayor, the head of the VOKS, etc., want to give us a last dinner tonight. All right, we say, but it must be a short one, as we are going to fly tomorrow and must get up early.

We are ready at nine. It is after ten when we sit down at a long table in the garden (the longest one yet). I feel sleepy and wonder how I will stay awake through the meal. But the Russian music revives me. We have a long, long dinner from ten to one, and much toasting and drinking. (Colonel Slepnev says half a bottle of wine and six glasses of cognac is his limit. He does not take vodka but champagne also, on top of this.) In Colonel Slepnev's speech I think Stalin, Lenin, and the Lindberghs were all toasted together!

The music was good and everyone very gay. As might be expected, by the end of the evening most of them were drunk or at least had had too much to drink. They have remarkable staying power and do not get objectionable. Only C. and I had not drunk much, always raising the glasses to our lips and the amount of wine in the glass remaining approximately the same. I had that strange feeling looking around the table of being on a desert island in the midst of a sea and looking across at C., another desert island lifting its head above the waters. The Intourist girls were not drunk, nor the old musician, but we were all tired.

Colonel Slepnev got more fluent than ever before and leaning over my chair went off into a long wish for me that I should find happiness according to my wishes, as happiness varied with each person. And my happiness, he said, lay in C., pointing to him across the table.

He said we should come back and bring the children and settle in Russia and we could go off on long trips together to the North and shoot white bears and then when I got old—for I was young now but I must get old sometime—I could sit and think about all the wonderful things we had done.

The orchestra played "Black Eyes" and "If Tomorrow There Is a War" and "Moscow" and the "Young Pioneers March" and a wistful song that Colonel Slepnev said was "I shake your hand and say good-by, for you must go far away"—with appropriate gestures!

Finally, after champagne and coffee, we toast each other in coffee. Colonel Slepnev gives the signal to rise, and we leave, to my great relief.

Wednesday, August 31st

Wake to the usual clamor of factory sirens, people in the street, etc. C. says sleepily, "I never heard any people that liked to make a noise as much as these people do." Half awake, I thought that there were two factories trying to be roosters.

Breakfast is at ten by prearrangement. The Intourist girls are up but not Colonel Slepnev. Finally he appears, looking *terrible* but fairly cheerful. Wire from Faymonville. We have the required route into Rumania and can go. Breakfast at a comparatively small table, only ten or so! The mayor's representative and the head of VOKS give me a Kiev embroidered peasant dress. The mayor sends a press man as his messenger to ask us how we have enjoyed Odessa!

Out to the field, with the cavalcade. Colonel Slepnev says that a pursuit plane will escort us over the border, so not to be alarmed.

Good-bys on the field. The VOKS man has brought a bunch of roses. Colonel Slepnev tears one rose out and gives it to me, meaning I do not have to take the whole bunch, which the VOKS man does not like. Good-by to Shopova, Slepnev, VOKS, Intourist, etc.

Take off about one, cross a lake and border—no pursuit plane! Our good-by to Russia—how typical! Fly over flat, disputed country and then up into wooded mountains. It gets cool; clouds. When we come down over the mountains, it is a different land— green, rolling, little fields, villages, forests, rivers; very pretty, peaceful, and welcoming.

About four we fly over Cluj [Rumania]; a green airport with a scattering of little bright-colored planes like toys in one corner of the field—an air meet. We land away from them but before long there is a crowd of clamoring people and pressing photographers. We go into an office. People jam the windows. The officers speak good French but have no control over the crowd. C. is about to take off again. Finally one officer says he will take us in his car to the military side of the field, which we do.

It is quiet. The office is immaculate and luxurious, after Russia. The officers are very dapper and gallant. A boy stands in a corner holding a tray of lemonade glasses. C. refuels. The officers take pictures; all the little officers inside with me rush out so they can be in the picture. Autographs. Where will we sleep? The chief officer says it is best not to go to a hotel but to a private home—of a doctor.

We drive to town. Carts of hay and peasants in native dresses look happy and easy. The streets of the town are clean. The shops look full of things and are busy. The people on the streets are nicely dressed and there are not those hordes of people that one sees in Russia. I have a feeling of great relief. It is hard to analyze just what gives it, just why this differs so from Russia. For it is not merely the things I mention but a much more all-pervading atmosphere underneath. I want to say "tone" or "health," or "ease." And yet none of those things seem exactly it. It is as though this place were bathed in a different element from Russia, and one can breathe more easily.

We meet the doctor and his wife, who speak French. (Rumanians look and seem quite Latin.) We have a delicious tea and the first water that is plain water and not fizzy. We drive through the sleepy but charming little town. The doctor has started the first sports park in Rumania for young people, in memory of his boy, who died. The wife speaks to me about him. They are both nice cultured people and he is perceptive and kind.

We have supper with the officers and their wives and the doctor and his wife. And, thank goodness, only one kind of wine. The officers here all wear an outsize uniform cap. (That's why King Carol aways looks so funny in his pictures!)

Go to bed early, staring up at the chandelier and thinking, Well, at least there is no microphone in that chandelier!

But the people here have not the strength of the Russians, of a man like Colonel Slepnev. Is that because they are in a sleepy little place or is it their race? Or the system? I gather they are not very sympathetic to Russia (or Germany). I tried to find out news of Czechoslovakia. Rumanian looks a little like French in the paper. I make out only "Great inquietude."

September 1st, Cluj—Cracow—Olomouc

Breakfast in a little room with our host and hostess. Then pack. The officers have arrived to take us to the field, where there are more officers, more pictures taken, embroidery, flowers, and a book given us. Finally we take off. The first part of the trip is quite lovely, scattered clouds down on our shoulders, skimming over tops of hills, checkered with pine forests and farms and shadows of clouds and sun. But we detour the mountains because clouds are too low. Follow a railroad and come out into flatter country; haze is greater. C. says he is landing to find out weather. Land and drive up to hangar. "My God, we're in Poland!" Wait for weather to Prague and set off again through rain storms.

Then one of those long and terrible afternoons of flying through bad weather, following the railroad up and down hills, through narrow passes under clouds in fog and storm. It gets worse instead of better, and a tearing wind shaking us in the passes. I am very cold, wet, and shaking. C. tries to get through to flat country. Finally we turn back (through the passes) to Olomouc. Land at a military field, soaked. To hotel, autographs, dinner with officers, mayor, and press in hotel. The Czech situation better in the last twenty-four hours.[1] They are a very courageous people.

[*Prague*], *September 2nd*

Uncomfortable night under those pillowcase comforters. We wake to find quite a crowd assembling on the street in front of our window; foresee complications. We hope the weather is good enough to go on to Prague. An officer comes with weather which is much better. Also six friends of his who want autographs. Set off through a roaring crowd of people—flowers, pictures, etc. "Eet ees chust because they luf you."

It is very cold—autumn. We start off with three pursuit planes, which leave us at about the point we turned back yesterday. We go over the pass and the place where we turned back. The hills with those lookout chalets on them that I prayed to as I went by yesterday now far below us, in sunshine and blue sky. Easy trip

[1] The crisis between Germany and Czechoslovakia over the cession of that portion of Czechoslovakia which included German-speaking peoples (Sudetenland) was building to a climax.

to Prague; towers and bridges and the river. Land at the airport. The crowd breaks and runs toward us—photographers, etc. C. taxies farther out. Crowd uncontrolled. Very bad. Finally it is held back and a car comes up. Major [Lowell M.] Riley, the U. S. Military Attaché. We meet officers, receive flowers, get into a car and drive to the Legation. Mr. and Mrs. Wilbur Carr[1] in an old palace on the hill. Quiet lunch. In the afternoon we go up the hill and see the cathedral. C. goes to a factory with Riley.

Prague, Saturday, September 3rd

C. goes off with Riley to see factories and to meet President Beneš. I go to see a baroque church and monastery library with baroque ceilings. Lunch in Major Riley's apartment with Ray Cox (Consular Service) and Mr. and Mrs. Carr. They talk Czechoslovakia, tension and the probability of war. The extent of German propaganda versus Czechs is terrific. Carr tells me that the Czechs and Bohemians are homogeneous; Slovaks consider themselves partners with the Czechs, though they are different. There is a fringe of Sudeten Germans. There are Poles around Teschen and Magyars on border of Hungary. The Czechs evidently have a good army, good equipment, good workmanship, and machine guns.

Sunday, September 4th

Bad weather. C. and I and Major Riley motor to Teplice-Šanov in the Sudeten country (toward Dresden) for lunch with Prince and Princess Clary Aldringen in an old palace. They have lived in the Sudetenland and seen that side and are for some measure of autonomy, I gather. A large family dinner. All very Edwardian, as is the atmosphere of the house. The Prince is interesting on former Russia: it was always guarded, always a closed country, always terror, espionage, and always Eastern.

[1] Wilbur John Carr, U. S. Assistant Secretary of State, 1924–1937; with the U. S. Legation in Prague, 1938.

We drive to the border, the road to Dresden; concrete barriers in the fog. Also along German Sudeten towns. There are dirndls and Hitler Jungen (or almost).

Prague, Monday, September 5th

Bad weather; we can't go. C. sees Commander MacDonald, the British Air Attaché. In the afternoon Mrs. Carr takes me to see an old Jewish synagogue and cemetery, also the old town hall and clock (1490).

Tuesday, September 6th

Bad weather.

Wednesday, September 7th

Bad weather again. Get all packed up, but the report says "worse than yesterday." After lunch I go with the Swiss Minister, Carl Bruggmann, and his wife to see the Bohemian primitives in a gallery above the library. They are lovely, full of feeling and reverence, and, as he said, there is not any vanity in them. The artist has not yet pushed himself in. I have a short time to talk to Mary [Wallace] Bruggmann[1] after. I like them.

September 8th, Prague—Stuttgart—Paris

Leave Prague in the morning. Good weather to Stuttgart, clouds and warmer, a nice group of young officers in Stuttgart; all serene. On to Paris, Le Bourget (cross Rhine and Maginot Line). Take taxi to Crillon.

September 9th, Paris—Chantilly

I go out in the morning, along Rue Saint-Honoré. Shops look wonderful. Into three department stores—not so wonderful. Lunch with Détroyat and a friend of his at the Crillon. Their attitude toward the Czech crisis: "But why don't they let the

[1] Sister of Henry A. Wallace, Vice President in the Roosevelt administration.

three million Germans join Germany?" We decide to stay over a night to see Ambassador Bullitt and meet the French Air Minister. We drive out to Chantilly (dodging reporters). Dinner with Bullitt, Guy La Chambre, the Air Minister, Colonel Fuller[1] and Secretary. Very interesting. The French are planning mass suicide for the Czechs—very gallant, but still suicide.[2] Why must they?

September 10th

Ambassador Bullitt, C., and I walk in the park of Chantilly. One of those extremely beautiful but inescapably formal French parks. Discuss present affairs. Bullitt is very American, perceptive, quick, sympathetic, generous, if not (possibly?) entirely accurate or thorough. I should guess that he *might* jump to conclusions and be prejudiced by sentimental considerations. But perhaps not. Americans can be very precise and objective under a loose happy-go-lucky manner.

He is less pessimistic than most people on war. He thinks *if* we can get through the autumn (every day we approach bad flying weather is hopeful) there might be a good chance for European peace; that all thinking people in France and England do not really object to the Sudetens joining Germany as long as it is done tactfully—as long as France feels her honor is not at stake. A readjustment in Czechoslovakia could come about, if only the Germans would be content to have it come slowly. He is most pessimistic about the outcome in Europe if war starts. Once the first soldier puts his foot across the border our whole civilization is wiped out.

[1] Colonel Horace F. Fuller, U. S. Air Attaché in Paris.

[2] See Ambassador Bullitt's letter to Franklin D. Roosevelt, of June 13, 1938: "[General] Réquin, who will command the French troops, looks upon this prospect of a frontal attack on the Siegfried Line with absolute horror. . . . He said that the battle in that area would resemble the Battle of the Somme on a much larger scale. It would be direct frontal attack on fully prepared positions. . . . The casualties of the attacking side, that is to say, the French, would be three to four times the casualties on the German side. 'It means,' he said, 'the death of a race.' " (*For the President,* pp. 267–68)

After lunch we leave for Le Bourget. A tail wind. To Mont-Saint-Michel. Diving through clouds. Over the islands, a tearing wind and whitecaps. Jon waving. Diving at the Carrels on a rock.

Land at Morlaix. Con and Aubrey in their car. They are on their way to England after a week spent waiting for us here. I am so disappointed. We drive together to Tréguier, talking furiously, chiefly the gloom of war. C. delivering fearful pronouncements on the state of unpreparedness of France and England compared to Germany. The possibilities of avoiding war. Is there any hope —this year? Is it too late for a war? It is like discussing the small improvements and depressions in a fatal illness. The sense of impending disaster.

We leave them gloomily at Tréguier and drive to Buguélès. It is high tide. A tearing wind. Louis and P'tit Louis are there. We load the boat. The engine won't start. Lowering skies. The boat is little and splashes badly. Miss W. meets us at the Sillon in flapping waterproof and Thor swims out—very thin. C. goes over to Saint-Gildas. I go upstairs to see Jon. It is almost dark. He sits up in bed, smiling. He shows me his flashlight, his boat, his boy-scout outfit box.

Then Land, big, wide-eyed, curly-haired, looks at me startled from his crib and cries until I sing "Pattycake."

Supper by candlelight. It is dark. The Carrels come over half-way through. We discuss war. "It is as bad as we thought."

I feel confused with so many impressions and emotions today. Happy to be home, disappointed to miss Con and Aubrey. And over all, the threat and talk of war.

Hard to sleep.

Illiec, Sunday, September 11th

Try to unpack, see the house, talk to Miss W. and Maryvonne, and tidy up in the morning. Land is in fine shape. Jon looks better but has had some lice (!) apparently caught from the girls. Poor Jon.

We go down together so I can watch him pry limpets off rocks.

C. and I go swimming. Very cold, but feel better after it. I feel sleepy and rather dazed, here. Partly the damp climate and partly, like Thor, I cannot fully realize I am back or get the happiness I should from it.

In the afternoon, I feed Land, who looks at me with deep grave suspicion but takes his food beautifully. He pulls himself up alone in his pen and walks around it hanging on to the side. He has a crop of fine gold curly hair, a look of great deliberation, is stocky and solid, and wears those old creepers Betty made for little Charles. He looks amazingly like him that last summer in North Haven.

Out to the Carrels' for supper. We take ourselves back in our motorboat, which splashes badly. "Very good engine," Kerleau says, "boat no big enough for engine. Engine fine, boat too small."

Tuesday, September 13th

Morning fog, clearing later. I plant the lavender cuttings I took from Chantilly. Maryvonne has talked to the two girls about washing their hair (the delousing process) and they do not want to stay. They say Maryvonne is not nice to them. They say that they are not worked too hard, they don't want anything in their room, that they are entirely contented with us, but they cannot stay because of Maryvonne.

Mr. Newton[1] comes over from the Carrels'. He is a nice open friendly American, very much involved in the Oxford Movement, [Moral Re-Armament] more intelligent than most. He talks late about the time being ripe in the world for a great spiritual re-awakening. (1) The need for it. (2) The means of spreading it at our disposal. (3) The freedom from old conventions makes men's minds peculiarly open and receptive to a new spiritual force, this time equally balanced with the physical.

Newton is impressive as a genuine person of integrity and

[1] James Newton, close friend of Henry Ford, Firestone, Alexis Carrel, and, later, the Lindberghs.

feeling. He is also impressive as a selfless and spiritual person. Many of the things he says are true, perceptive, and practical. But I somehow feel there is a false simplicity about the Oxford Movement. I am in sympathy with its incentive and many of its beliefs, but the form and expression of it still seems immature and even somehow arrogant in its smugness. (He was *not* arrogant or smug, at all.) His humility and earnestness forces your respect. He has a nice American humor and lightness too.

To bed late. Newton stays the night as there is no sign of Pierre and the boat.

September 14th

Morning fog. See François about the wall and chimney. He looks a bit peaked in his stringy scarf and cap. He asks if there is going to be a war? Half his men are off serving their military service.

Telegram at noon from Aubrey, very gloomy: "Events rapidly moving . . . to worst possible conclusion."

We swim. It is warm and sunny. Jon paddles a bit alone. The mailwoman comes. The news in *L'Ouest-Éclair* is bad. Great disorders in Sudetenland, following Hitler's speech. Martial law declared. The Sudetens give a six-hour ultimatum. Police must be withdrawn or they will not be responsible for what happens. The Czechs do not agree to ultimatum.

At seven C. and I go over to Buguélès in the boat to get the news (from England, through the car's radio). It is not much better. Henlein[1] told one of the English mission that all negotiations were off until the Czech police were recalled. Also that due to the Czech incidents of the past few days the Sudetens would demand (above their old demands) absolute self-determination as a prerequisite to any discussion.

All the Ministers are ominously saying, "There is still hope," "Nothing is desperate," like doctors over a deathbed.

Tomorrow is the 15th—the day forewarned as one on which war might start. However, the statements from Berlin do not

[1] Konrad Henlein, leader of the Sudeten Germans.

sound engineered to incite people to war. They are fairly calm and reasonable. "Surely the democracies of the world will not go to war to prevent the carrying out of one of the principles for which they fought the last war."[1] (Self-determination of peoples.) And a hope that differences may still be settled by reason and negotiation.

We put-put back to Illiec, in the gray, damp, darkening evening. Supper by candlelight.

September 15th

I spend the morning studying books and ways to teach Jon reading or give him some book or drawing work on bad days.

Tea. The news in the paper is heartening. Chamberlain is flying to talk to Hitler.[2] I think it is courageous of Chamberlain, and hopeful.

September 16th

After lunch Miss H. and I go shopping in Tréguier and Lannion. A long afternoon. It is quite hot on the mainland.

Rush back to the car for the news. Start home. On the way, pick up the Irish news on the radio: Chamberlain is back from Germany, says he has had a frank talk with Hitler. Each understands better the other's point of view.

Chamberlain is to discuss all with the Cabinet and Runciman[3] and possibly to fly back for another interview with Hitler in a few days. All that sounds hopeful. Locally, however, the situation seems worse among the Sudetens—more martial law, more riots, etc.

[1] Reference to Woodrow Wilson's Fourteen Points which formulated the U. S. platform for peace (1918).

[2] This refers to the first of the three visits of Prime Minister Neville Chamberlain to Germany in order to solve the Czechoslovakian crisis and avoid war. He and Hitler met at the Berghof in Berchtesgaden.

[3] Lord Runciman was sent to Prague by Chamberlain as mediator and adviser in the Czechoslovakian crisis.

Walk back across the Sillon; lovely still night, silken water, an evening glow, but a mist hanging over it all—autumnal.

Sunday, September 18th

Sheets of rain. Storms alternate with short periods of sunshine all day. I spend a long time, as usual, in the kitchen, planning the day's meals and translating recipes. Maryvonne is anxious to try anything, so willing and sympathetic. I wish she would stop blowing on the milk and keep the chickens out of the kitchen!

Have Land and Jon in the big room. Land crowing, Jon running in and out, or talking to me through the window.

To the Carrels' for dinner. I get dressed in my oilskin trousers and hooded coat. Across the flats in the pouring rain with C. It is great fun and very beautiful, especially as you climb the Carrels' gorse hill and look beyond under a gray curtain of rain to a band of gold sky with the Sept-Îles amethyst in the distance.

The Carrels were rather sad, we thought. I felt, suddenly, that they were old. No, not that they were old, but that they *felt* they were old. Dr. Carrel said C.'s talk with Guy La Chambre[1] in Paris had great effect, and C. was quoted in the French Chamber.

Back in pitch-blackness, wet, across the islands and flats. No light. Strange how you come to see differences in rocks and terrain, even in such darkness. Also the sense that your feet were literally "feeling" the way, like hands, or like those pliant feet of the trapeze walkers in Russia, who seemed to stroke or caress the rope as they walked.

Monday, September 19th

C. has got a telegram from Ambassador Kennedy asking him to go to London to talk to him this week. Of course he is going.

---

[1] Reference is to the conversation C. A. L. had with the French Air Minister, La Chambre, on September 9 on aviation production in France, Germany, England, etc. at the home of Ambassador Bullitt (see Charles A. Lindbergh, *Wartime Journals,* p. 69).

Shall I go or not? I should like to this time, and Kennedy has asked us both. Leave Jon again? But it is only for a few days.

C. talks over plans with the Carrels and tells them he is thinking of Berlin for the winter.[1]

Tuesday, September 20th, Illiec—London

Jon comes in to dress with us. I tell him that his father must go to London. "And are *you* going too?" "Yes, I think I'm going too." His face fell. It was enough to make me stay. "But not for long, Jon—only for a day or two. We'll be back the end of the week."

"When will that be?" said Jon precisely.

He stays around while I pack all morning, very much in the way but very sweet, spinning shells on the floor.

Leave about 2:30. Fly over Illiec and watch that precious flickering speck of white that is Jon's waving handkerchief, far below. Lowering sky. Under the skirts of the rain all the way. Lovely flying: green fields, thundery curtains of rain, and a strip of clear horizon we fly through.

Land at Saint-Inglevert. The landing gear gives way. We roll plane into the hangar and prop it up. The head of the Air Club takes us to Boulogne. We catch the boat for Folkestone. It is cold and drizzly, English weather. I feel too English and dowdy for words in my divided skirt and sack-of-potatoes tweed travel coat and old felt hat. I look fat, too.

We get a paper. Evidently, Chamberlain and the French have laid out a peace plan for Czechoslovakia based on Hitler's demands. Will the Czechs accept it?

Into London at 11 P.M. Brown's Hotel is full up, just one room left.

Wednesday, September 21st

Hair done in the morning. To the U. S. Embassy for lunch. "Only" Mr. and Mrs. Kennedy and their large and nice family!

[1] C. A. L. was considering spending a winter in Berlin, to pursue his investigations of German air strength for U. S. Intelligence.

After lunch C. and Ambassador Kennedy talk, Mrs. Kennedy and I listen. It is profoundly depressing. Ambassador Kennedy gives the diplomatic counterpart to C.'s technical picture of the state of Europe at this juncture. The picture of Hitler (if it is accurate) quite prepared to start a European war at any further interruption of his wishes. The picture of England and France completely unprepared for war, compared to Germany. Chamberlain wishing to avert war but unable, probably, to carry his country behind him if he submits further to Hitler. Hitler possibly contemplating the complete dismemberment of Czechoslovakia, which England and France will not stomach.

The French at least are committing suicide with their eyes open. But the English, who are talking about "the great betrayal," "humble pie," "dishonorable peace," still think they have a big stick with which they can punish the "Fascist aggressors."

Chamberlain flies back tomorrow to Hitler. If the Czechs agree to the plan (which they probably will, forced by France and England) it will immediately encourage Hungary and Poland to ask the same for their minorities. This means the dismemberment of Czechoslovakia. And that will mean war.

They talk about air warfare and how long it would take to "level" a city like London or Paris (Germany is perfectly able to do it). With the first real air raid on one or the other I think America will be shocked into the war, too.

It all rests on the personal equation of one man—Hitler. Is he astute? Is he far-seeing? Or is he a blind fanatic?

If only he could see that plunging into war will only bring about the thing he claims to be destined to prevent—world Communism.

We go out and walk in the drizzle, going down Piccadilly—buses and cars, policemen, bicycles, women with hair "brushed up." The great streams of traffic going on oblivious, between those old buildings. I feel as though I were watching the dead, seeing the doomed. Impossible to think it might all be interrupted with bomb holes and shattered buildings in another week. And yet so possible that I had the feeling I was looking on an old film, showing "the good old days of prewar England," before the destruction.

Sleep badly.

Thursday, September 22nd

Papers very gloomy. Hitler apparently is not content with the Sudetenland and wants to push for complete dismemberment of Czechoslovakia. German troops are ready to march in, whatever way it goes. Any opposition will be ruthlessly put down. Hitler supposedly assumes that France is unwilling and England unable to interfere. Terrific anti-Czech campaign in German papers. Also a truculent "we will not wait" attitude. I feel it is hopeless.

Friday, September 23rd

A kind of trembling "stand-still" in the papers this morning. Chamberlain is in Godesberg. And there are disquieting rumors; sense of pressures and counter-pressures. Are the German troops marching into Sudetenland? If they do—and if they meet resistance—what will happen? This rumor, this pressure, must be real, because Chamberlain is appealing for calm: nothing to start incidents, etc.

C. over to see Herschel [Johnson]; no news yet. All day has been like that. I go out and walk the streets for something to do. Lunch alone. To Harrods by bus. Tea at the hotel. No news yet.

C. and I to the Lees' for dinner. Before dinner the telephone rings. Colonel Lee goes to it. Chamberlain and Hitler have not had another meeting. Chamberlain flies back tomorrow. Negotiations are off.

It sounds desperate. We are all chilled. Go in to dinner. It is very unreal. During dinner Colonel Lee is again called to the telephone. "Negotiations are off" and some German troops marching into Czech territory. I feel it's desperate. And yet we talk, we act as though it were not happening.

Bulletin board reports nothing new, really, all day. Chamberlain back, going to Cabinet meetings. However, the German troops do *not* seem to have moved into Czechoslovakia. Later it seems that Hitler gave Chamberlain his last terms to be given to Czechoslovakia.

Brown's Hotel, London, Sunday, September 24th

Mother darling,

Charles and I are waiting here in London from day to day—as you and Aubrey and Con and Dwight and Margot must also be waiting—to see if there will be a war. We came over from Illiec because of a telegram from Ambassador Kennedy. He (and some of the English technical people) wanted to talk to C. about air preparedness in Europe.

We came fairly cheerfully. Chamberlain had made his un-English gesture of flying to Hitler. An English-French peace plan had been drawn up and apparently the Czechs were going to accept it. There was a lull, at least.

But since then everything has piled up with frightful rapidity and to stupendous proportions. We wait from day to day, watch every scrap of news on the bulletin boards—even bits of news from conversations, newspapers, etc. It is terribly like watching a fatal illness. One clings to superficials: "Chamberlain smiled cheerfully," "The German press has abated its propaganda slightly"—just like saying "He had a slightly better night," "He took a teaspoonful of beef tea."

But one does this partly because all the fundamentals are hidden. None of the terms, threats, countermoves have come to light. One has to guess at these from the slightest gestures, pressures, or relief of pressures in certain spots—seen from the outside.

And all is so confused because the English, U.S.A., and French press is excited and inaccurate, jumping to conclusions, while the German and Italian is of course completely controlled and biased.

On the whole, though, one learns more from the latter because at least it is an accurate barometer of one side's intentions.

One of the most dreadful signs throughout this whole period (of English negotiation) has been the atrocious propaganda against the Czechs in the German newspapers. And since Goebbels has been with Hitler throughout, it does not look accidental. Last night it seemed the propaganda had been called off a little and the Germans were looking forward to a peaceful solution. The "final peace terms" have been handed to Czechoslovakia and they are given six days to comply (this came out through a speech of Mussolini's). But at least that is six days. And time is important. The Germans are not yet (so they say) marching and have given some assurance (this evidently from German papers) that they will not this week.

C. has been hopeful throughout (though he is increasingly less so) because he hoped Hitler was astute enough to see that a European war would exhaust everyone, including any victor. Also because Germany has the trump card and can hold out on that till the last minute. No one is going to start a war until she does. She can afford to stand out for a hard bargain. And it still may not mean she is desirous of starting a world war or intends to.

I am not discussing the right and wrong of it. I only feel desperately that unless war is averted now, there will be no one left who knows the meaning of the words "right" and "wrong." It seems no longer a national affair—to do with national pride and laws of right and wrong. It is a case of our whole civilization going under.

I do not agree at all with the "We must stop the dictators now or never." Unfortunately, it is most doubtful whether they can now be stopped. England and France are so piteously weak, and even with America it would be a long struggle. And practically, I think the only way to stop them is to let them come up against Russia. As a brilliant article I saw the other day said, it is only a new and broader application of the game England has played for so long on a smaller scale—the balance of power. Now, she and the democracies should play it on that broader scale, against the Fascist countries.

C. and I go tomorrow to Cliveden for the night. After that probably to Paris. There is nothing more we can do here. C. will still be in touch in Paris, and we will be nearer the children. Illiec is I think fairly safe at present. It is remote, and even from a question of food one can always get milk, eggs, and possibly fish locally.

If there is no war C. and I will go to the air conference in Berlin from the 12th to 25th of October. (Oh, how much I've been away from Jon this year!) I feel I must go, because if there is no war I think we may spend the winter in or near Berlin. And I could do some groundwork on houses, nurse, household, etc., while C. visits factories and fields.

I have spent the whole afternoon writing you. One of those dreadful Sundays in London. It has drizzled all day. How I hate to be left in London when it shuts up like a coffin on Saturday afternoon. Restaurants, shops, newsstands, and the streets are empty. Today nothing is open but the large gas-mask center on Piccadilly, in the ground floor of one of those huge motorcar showrooms where volunteers sit showing people how to fit and wear gas masks. All children under five are to be evacuated from London.

I wonder what will happen during this next week here in England, when all is disclosed before Parliament. The British people are completely ignorant of what has been happening—and also, unfortunately, of their state of unpreparedness. What will they do when they are told they are unprepared for war? You may have a terrific wave of feeling, and then what? A change of Government? Eden and Churchill? Or Labour? And a demand for an uncompromising attitude and war? Perhaps they cannot now be told, for it would spoil the game of bluff (for outside consumption). And yet I feel they should know, before they rush blindly in. At least it would somewhat justify Chamberlain.

Go down to Lady Astor's at Cliveden in the evening. C. and Lady Astor talk antiwar: that war now is hopeless for the democracies, but that no one will win, not even Hitler; that Communism will follow for the world.

Lady Astor says that she would die for freedom, but it is not freedom we will be fighting for.

Lord Astor and Thomas Jones come in. They are stiff with seriousness and emotion. They say Chamberlain has sent a messenger to Hitler with two notes. The first, a last plea for more negotiations on the Paris-London terms. The second (if he refuses an answer to the first) to say that if he refuses to negotiate and marches in, England will go to war. Hitler is to see them before he addresses his country. It is as though war was already declared. We feel appalled. Lady Astor rails at the madness. Thomas Jones says grimly, "There are some things that are worth more than life."

Lord Astor argues that Germany must be stopped now, before she is any stronger (after feeding on the small Mitteleuropa countries) or after making alliances with Russia (which he thinks there is a possibility of her doing in the future).

His arguments are more practical, whether or not they are true. That this same crisis will be repeated in three weeks or three months on the colonial question or on the Ukraine or on Alsace. That England will be forced to fight sooner or later, and that if she waits and backs down further she will have no friends left when the day comes for her to fight. By then, disillusioned by this policy of giving in to Hitler, all the smaller European states and Russia will have left her and she will be worse off then than now.

C. says to Tom Jones, "What is your line of attack? What are you going to do first?" (If you fight.) He says simply, "That is for our military heads to decide." In other words, "That is out of my realm"—as if the two were separable.

We listen to Hitler's speech—quite a gathering of people by now. Two Germans, young men visiting England, are here. Also the Winns, and another cousin of Lady Astor's, and some of Thomas Jones's sisters and friends. They turn the radio on. You hear the mob shouting in Germany. It is terrifying.

Lord Astor and Thomas Jones are on the floor at the feet of the radio and C. near them listening tensely. They are quite prepared for what is tantamount to a declaration of war from Hitler.

Then Goebbels speaks. Cheers and shouts punctuate his high ranting voice. The German boys lean over the radio with pad and pencil, translating (during the roars of the crowd), "Goebbels says 'The Führer leads; we follow,'" etc.

Then Hitler. His voice is quite measured and calm. He talks slowly but with feeling. His voice is lower and much stronger and less excited than Goebbels'. The German boys are taking down what he says. Lady Astor, the women, and a few of the men go in to dinner. Conversation is almost impossible. It seems past the point of talking, arguing about what should have been done, what will happen if . . . All one can do is wait for each scrap of news—listen, whenever anyone says anything new.

The men come in. There has been no declaration of war. The faces of Lord Astor and the others look slightly relaxed. One gets scraps of the speech. Hitler traced the whole of the postwar history, his attempts toward peace and settling of the European situation. How he was forced to use force, to give up diplomatic means and establish a strong Army, Air Force, etc., which is equal to none, with which Germany can stand up to the world. He says he is still ready for peace, that his peace plan, or offers, are the same as the English-French ones except in the matter of execution—which he will have no delay on. Beneš cannot squeeze out, this time. Saturday they will occupy the Sudetenland. He says melodramatically that there is only one man who understands his difficulties, and that man is Benito Mussolini.

Apparently (though there is some confusion on this point) he speaks of guaranteeing the remainder of Czechoslovakia if there are no minorities left in it. At least, he does say that it is the last territorial demand he will make in Europe. Throughout the speech he rails at Beneš and puts the blame and responsibility for the decision of world war entirely on him. He speaks, however, with gratitude of Chamberlain and his efforts for peace.

On the whole, people are relieved. There is no declaration of war. It was not a speech inciting to war. It referred in kindly terms to the English. It spoke of guarantees, of no more territorial demands, and of a desire for peace.

Around the table people snatch at straws. It is interesting how much confusion there is here—even among well-informed people —as to what actually has been or has not been stated or promised, on one side or another.

Tom Jones saying, "He spoke of guarantees. He has never done that before, has he? He spoke of British being on the commission to watch the plebiscites. That is a step forward."

Then we go out to hear the English news. There is no mention made of guarantees. People are confused. Someone runs out to telephone and check it. We listen to Harold Nicolson on "This Week in Current Affairs." He still speaks in that pleasant, half-humorous, and rather effeminate accent of cynical sideline detachment, but you can feel his emotions. He speaks of Chamberlain as pleading "Do not shoot this bird" (Czechoslovakia) "and in a short time we will bring it to you in a cage." And then of the Germans, having the bird in the cage, not being satisfied—wanting a dead bird.

People begin to break up and talk in little groups. It is interesting how they fall. The older people follow the old line of rather romantic idealism, without really thinking it out. A pattern of chivalry, a game of rules and good sport, rather a splendid one, but applicable to a smaller world which now no longer exists. "There are some things that are worth more than life." Yes—but what are they? The issues are not clear, as they used to be in war. They are fighting because of a series of entanglements, a series of blunders, and because, it seems, they are committed to abide by the blunders, right or wrong.

It is not really to save Czechoslovakia. It is (1) to fulfill a roundabout obligation; (2) fear of Germany and what she may do in the future; and (3) because the cause of Czechoslovakia is the traditional one—of a small nation oppressed by a bigger one; and (4) because war feeling has been whipped up by people's revulsion to the stupid and outrageous press propaganda of the Germans during all the negotiations and by the whole of the Germans' barbarian *method* of getting their ends.

The older generation react emotionally, and the reaction is *war*.

The younger generation see no reason to make a final blunder in order to get out of all the previous blunders. They see quite plainly and face their complete unpreparedness, and probably failure in case of war—mass suicide (the older generation do not *really* face this, or rather they dive at it blindfold). They do not see anything gained for the world after this sacrifice. And much to be gained by staving off the conflict. "Press for time, and then arm like hell so as not to be caught napping again" is their practical and disillusioned policy.

Lady Astor is on the side of youth. Her arguments are not as practical but her instincts are right. It is too bad she has to argue about them, for she argues wildly and it weakens her case.

"Fight for what—Czechoslovakia? For Beneš? For the word of a Frenchman?" she rails. And then she has Germany and the "scrap of paper" and the last war thrown at her.

But her instincts are that the war is not worth fighting at this moment. Her son, Bill, can argue it better and more practically. But none of them have her fire, her spirit, her intuitive quality.

Everyone, however, goes to bed relieved—I do not know why, exactly. Things are not noticeably improved. But we were all so worked up before dinner, really expecting a declaration of war. And like people who have been through a crisis, the letdown has been great. We have swung the other way—a kind of re-embracing of life and hope.

Tuesday, September 27th

Thomas Jones and Lord Astor plan for C. to see leaders of opposition. They go off.

Rumors all day and no alleviation. C. comes back. Saw Lloyd

George.[1] Just before bed we hear dreadful word over the radio. Germany is mobilizing. To bed; very sunk, desperate feeling. Is Hitler *mad*? If he *wants* to fight there is no use. What can be done? I feel war is inevitable and cannot sleep. I must go back to Illiec. What can C. do?

All night long I think of war and what Europe is plunging into—of Florrie and Lady Astor and their sons, of hundreds more like them, wiped out, England going under, air raids, gas, misery year after year.

Wednesday, September 28th

Breakfast with Lord Astor and C. Can President Roosevelt send another appeal, to offer to supervise plebiscites? C. to see Kennedy. Papers gloomy—full of war preparations, gas masks, trenches. Air-raid preparations. Fleet orders, etc. Lord Astor gloomy about Parliament meeting and the effect of Chamberlain's "weak" speech. I pack for C., then walk in the garden (gray and drizzle) to the sunken garden where the soldiers of the last war are buried. I try to pray.

In to town with Lady Astor, who is still courageous.

Billboards say "Second appeal Roosevelt." We buy a paper. The appeal is very good. Also the German mobilization rumor is false. London is full of air-raid preparation signs, some sandbags on sidewalks, and trenches being dug in Hyde Park. We try on gas masks—U. S. Army ones that C. has got. C. to Harrods to move papers.

Lady Astor calls up on Chamberlain's speech. Last peace plea to Hitler and Mussolini. Hitler agrees to a conference in Munich: Hitler, Mussolini, Daladier, and Chamberlain—magnificent! Hope again. C. back. It seems real, a great load lifted. We go out to Thomas Jones's.

After we come home at night—lighthearted, gay, life given back to us again—C. gets out the gas masks and says we must try

[1] For account of conversation, see Charles A. Lindbergh, *Wartime Journals*, p. 77.

them on again. Grimly: "Good practice . . . where most people slip up." So like Charles!

Thursday, September 29th

Papers thrilling this morning. The account of Chamberlain in the House of Commons—that great humble and courageous man—completely justified in his efforts and faith, rewarded, sweeping the house with enthusiasm. I can hardly read it without crying. Also his words on getting into the plane to go back for the third meeting: "I hope when I come back I shall be able to say with Hotspur in *Henry IV,* 'Out of this nettle, danger, we have plucked this flower, safety.' "

After the great tension of the last week, the desperation of night before last, the emotional reverse, the joy and relief of last night, today I am desperately tired and like a fighting animal inside wanting to get back to the children. Each delay seems unbearable. It takes so much energy to be patient that I can do nothing else all day. I am worn out by the struggle.

And yet now, in this breathing spell—if we are given it—now is the time for action. France and England *must* arm. America must see the situation as it really is. We must all face things practically, and I believe C. can help here, and perhaps also in Germany next month.

However, the day goes in waiting, in making mistakes about train times (I did this), so we miss the afternoon train to Paris. (Bullitt has called C. and wants him in Paris. Perhaps C. can help there.) We must take the night ferry service. As we taxi to the station at ten we hear newsboys shouting in the streets. On the train someone comes on and says, "They say they have agreed —the four Powers!" We cannot really believe it.

The train rattles out into the night.

Friday, September 30th

The Paris station. Ambassador Bullitt's secretary meets us. He looks haggard but cheerful. The four Powers have agreed! Drive to Embassy. Bullitt meets us. He looks white and tired. M. Monnet[1] is in the garden. He also looks rather gray. They have all been through an awful time here—worse than London, I expect.

Bullitt wants C. to help in organizing some kind of air rearmament for France, talk to people and maybe help them in U. S. A. He wants M. Monnet to organize it.

Silvia Monnet is charming, as usual. We argue about Europe. She and the French, I gather, are very depressed. They think this is only a temporary reprieve. They do not trust Germany, see no possibility of an understanding with her, and only want to arm like hell in preparation for her next move. I argue that they must come to an understanding, as they have no time to arm.

In the afternoon I walk from the Monnets' flat to the Champs Élysées and down Rue Saint-Honoré. I walk instead of taking a taxi as it makes me feel surer of myself and my surroundings and buttresses me a little. Home. Ambassador Bullitt is still seeing Ambassadors and C. is talking to M. Monnet. M. Guy la Chambre comes in, also very white and tired.

I go up and rest. Dinner at the Monnets'. Ambassador Bullitt, C., and I alone with them. It is very nice, but we are all too tired to talk well. Also there is a slight underground constriction though it hasn't come to light yet. (C., Ambassador Bullitt, M. Monnet, and the plans for air rearmament?)[2] All is not easy, somehow. M. Monnet and C. never seem to agree, and yet I like both their minds so much. I am always surprised and a little hurt (on both sides) to find them disagreeing.

I keep longing to hear the old M. Monnet who used to talk with Daddy: "My dear Monnet . . ." It is worlds away. They are generations apart. A prewar split. It is so strange. The cockles of

[1] Jean Monnet, French political economist; later responsible for European Common Market. Worked with D. W. M. on Allied Maritime Shipping Council.

[2] Bullitt had asked C. A. L. to Paris to confer about a possible establishment of factories in Canada to supply military aircraft to France. See Charles A. Lindbergh, *Wartime Journals*, p. 80.

my heart warm to the conversation of one, and yet I have been converted to the practical, hard facts-of-life of the other. And yet that is not fair either, nor do I mean it exactly. C. is not only "practical hard-facts-of-life." He is idealism too. But it is a new idealism, of another age. M. Monnet, in spite of his youth, belongs to another. My father's.

C. goes off early to see Dr. Carrel, who sails tomorrow. Ambassador Bullitt and I leave soon after. He is really exhausted.

Saturday, Ocotber 1st

I go off in the morning. Ambassador Bullitt takes me to the station. Left there, I feel very much like the freshman left at Northampton so many years ago. Will I ever get to Lannion? How and where do I change? The ticket man says I take an *autorail* from Saint-Brieuc. The *controleur* says I change at Rennes. I assume that is right.

In my compartment an Army officer is holding forth on the inefficiency of the Army's plans. I got off at Rennes and ask an official the way to the train for Plouaret. He says I must go to Saint-Brieuc and change there. I give my bag to a porter for Saint-Brieuc. He rushes me right onto the same train I have just got off. I get back into the same compartment! The officer has left, but the two other men there greet me and explain that the train is split here. (I still don't see why the *controleur* told me to change at Rennes!) At any rate, from now on they take care of me, carrying my bag off the train at Saint-Brieuc, putting me on the train for Morlaix (and Plouaret), and putting me off the train at Plouaret, where I get an *autorail*, jammed with *sous-marin* middies. All the way as I get further from Paris and nearer home I feel progressively calmed and strengthened. The healing power of going "with the grain."

Miss H. meets me. We drive to Buguélès, where Louis meets us, and walk across the Sillon. Thor comes to meet me. It is quite dark. A light on at Illiec and a wind blowing. I climb upstairs and into Jon's room. He turns over in the dark and says, "The hatchet was broken, but it is mended again," and, "I'll see you in the morning."

First copy of *Listen! the Wind*.

Sunday, October 2nd

Tell Miss H. and W. to go off. I take care of the children all day. Land looks at me wide-eyed, but eats his porridge quite contentedly. It is strength flowing into me to hold him on my lap—solid power and strength. Women should not separate themselves from this, for their strength comes from it in some inexplicable way.

Land is very good and happy. Jon plays in the big room with him. I come down, after cleaning up (even this is restful—to *do* something, after days of emotion and nothing one could *do*), to find them both at the toy cupboard, Land standing up, sturdily.

Mme Carrel comes over. We talk excitedly. She came back from Paris with a trainload of women about to have babies. She would, somehow. What strength she has.

Monday, October 3rd

Jon comes into my bed in the morning. "What kind of day is it, Jon?" "The wind has stopped a little" (which is just what I'd say). However, it climbs up again in the morning and blows a gale. It is cold and raw, Land inside all morning.

After lunch Miss H. and I battle across the Sillon in the tearing wind and driving rain to Keraudren's garage, where, wet and blown, we find a collapsed tire on the car. We change it, grubbing in the dirt, and feel exhausted as we start out for Tréguier at 3:30. Then on to Lannion. I talk to Miss H. about Miss W. leaving.

To Dames de France—still pouring rain. Dreadful woolen underwear for Jon (but it is getting so cold, he must have some), rubber boots for me, and raincoats for us both. Then home in the dark across the flats, loaded with boxes, groceries, a stove,[1] etc., the rain and wind behind us.

[1] There was no heat, only fireplaces, at Illiec.

Thor runs out to meet us and Kerleau with his lamp: *"Quel mauvais temps!"*

A nice supper of cheese soufflé and talk. To bed deliciously sleepy. A very restless night as the wind shakes the house all night—doors, windows, and even the bed rattle. I wake to each explosion of noise frightened, not knowing what's the matter.

Tuesday, October 4th

Still a tearing wind. The sea is wild and gray with breakers; much white spray over the rocks. But it is clearer—rain showers alternate with sun. I take care of Land in the morning while Miss W. and H. go shopping. When I put him down at 11:30 Jon and I put on our warmest things and go out on the farthest-out rocks and watch the spray, waves churning white at our feet, and white soap-suddy foam blowing over our heads. Gather driftwood coming back.

Everyone has gone into sabots since I went away—even the two girls. They wear heavy bedroom slippers in the house, then slip on wooden sabots for running back and forth outside. It keeps them very dry and warm.

No word from C.

Wednesday, October 5th

Wind and storms again. C. coming this afternoon, Morlaix at 4:30. Decide to go with Jon. Leave at 2 in our raincoats. Strong wind blowing, strike a heavy squall of rain. P'tit Louis loses his cap and I (at the rudder), going back for it, go over a rock. Decide to leave it! Heavy waves and spray and driving rain going over to Buguélès. We all get soaked. Jon and I, dripping and wilted, trudge to the garage, where I find another collapsed tire. Just as I start to fix it, Louis comes up. He knows nothing about tire changing but he turns the nuts. Completely dirty and messy with handling the jack, tire screws, etc., I start off. In sunshine now. Jon patiently at my side. We feel it is quite an adventure. On to Morlaix. I am afraid we will be late for C. The day is alternately bright and stormy. Arrive in Morlaix at 4:35. But no sign of C. Jon and I go to the little café, into the big kitchen behind, with all the *lits clos,* the *vaisselier,* the open fire, and a big bench and table. The old Breton lady and her daughter greet us. We say we would like cocoa. The girl cooks it over some sticks of wood on a tripod. Jon sits on a little stool by the fire and watches. There is some cured ham hanging over the huge fireplace. A large gray cat rubs herself out from under the table. Jon is delighted. *"Petit chat, petit chat."* We sit on a bench of a *lit clos* by the fire and drink our cocoa from big bowls. Jon says it is very good. The old lady says Jon looks like me. "Why, yes," I say, "he does." "But you are not the mother?" "Why, yes, I am Mrs. Lindbergh." "Oh, I thought you were Colonel Lindbergh's secretary" (all in French)!

Then it is about 6; still no planes. Jon and I go out to walk over the field, simply to pass the time away. We begin to find mushrooms. Jon is very pleased but does not like my looking up at the sky. "Look at the grass all the time," and, "If you want to get mushrooms you have to go slowly." Finally it is almost dark and quite cold. It is late—almost 7. It will be 9 before we're home—so late for Jon. Will C. come still? Was he delayed? Is he down in bad weather? Finally, at 7—it is quite dark—I decide to go, telephoning back from Keraudren's later. I get in the car. Someone calls from the café: it is a message that he is coming by train.

The long drive back. I am glad when we get on the familiar stretch from Lannion. At the garage we are met by Mme Keraudren and her little boy, who tell me that I must go *au bourg* to pick up Louis. Back again to Penvenan. We meet Louis on the road. He helps us shut up the garage and takes Jon's hand as we follow the road and across the flats by bright moonlight. "It's just like sunshine," said Jon. He walks along quite sturdily and insists on carrying the basket of mushrooms himself all the way.

Late supper.

Thursday, October 6th

C. arrives at about 10. He got as far as Le Havre yesterday and had to turn back to Paris. Very bad weather.

Saturday, October 8th

Afternoon packing. I plan to leave Sunday on day train, C. goes tonight.[1] How I hate to go off again. It tugs at me all day long so I can't enjoy anything, not even the time on the ledges with Jon (*"I* want to dig worms, but *you* don't want to!").

Do Land as usual, in semidarkness. Rock him in my lap before putting him down. Wash Jon, feeling very heavyhearted. He watches the lighthouse before he goes into bed.

During supper I decide to go with C. tonight. I feel so miserable that I probably won't sleep at home anyway, so I might as well go with him on the night train. Once you know you must go (condemned), it is better not to delay the awful feeling of just before.

Going through Jon's room, he is awake, and I tell him I am going (I would not have waked him, but as he was awake I could not bear to slip away without telling him). "Right now?" Jon says with some consternation. *"Why?"* (I did not think he would mind—he never has much before.) "Yes, after supper, Jon. I would have had to go anyway early in the morning." "When will I see you again?" (rather plaintively). "In two weeks, Jon." He turns toward the pillow. "That's a long time" (with a quiver of the lip that was quite unexpected). "Oh no, Jon, that won't be long. I'll write you a letter in between and I'll bring you back some chocolate," I said in a rush. (That helped!)

But I went out feeling very miserable. Tie up the bundle and change my clothes. C. is so pleased I am going with him. He is like a small boy about it.

[1] C. A. L. had been invited by the Lilienthal Society, the German Air Ministry, and the U. S. Ambassador, Hugh Wilson, to make another visit to Germany. Ambassador Wilson hoped the visit would help him develop personal contacts with Göring. (See Introduction.)

Speak to the girls and Maryvonne about plans (not staying here the winter) and to Miss W. for a second about the probability of our going to Germany for the winter and getting a German nurse. (She knew we were not keeping her before.) But it is difficult and we are both near tears. (Though I know it is the only thing to do.) She is so sweet, it makes it very difficult. (Why can't she always be that understanding person?)

Louis and Kerleau sling our bundles across their backs (Thor slinks upstairs in the dark, in misery) and we start out into the windy night across the flats, I in my town suit and fur coat but boots on my feet and a wool bandanna on my head, carrying my shoes and hat. It rains before we get started. I fasten the raincoat on top and try to shield my new hat under it.

We arrive at Plouaret to find the billet booth shut and the Paris train arriving any minute—an hour before we expected it! Rush to get on and without tickets. Get into a first-class *couchette*. We lock the door and settle for the night, I staring up at the night light on the ceiling. I feel better, having left, but still dumbly miserable that the motion of the train is taking me farther and farther from home. (How different it was, going down a week ago! I felt rested and strengthened as I got nearer home instead of feeling attenuated and pulled out as you do leaving, and somehow drained of strength.)

Paris, Sunday, October 9th

Arrive Paris 7:15 A.M. after not too bad a night. To the Crillon. Breakfast. C. and I go out and walk—through the Tuileries Gardens and up the Seine, left bank, past the bookstalls to Notre Dame and go in for a few minutes. Lunch with Jean Monnet in his little apartment. He is such a rare person—a true balanced wisdom into life itself. And he has that wonderful French quickness and lightness that makes communicating with him such a joy. He thinks it is much overrated—that children need their mothers all the time. Yes, I say, it is true, neglected children always turn out well. While, says Jean, neglected husbands do *not!*

I enjoy it thoroughly. He, C., and I seem to be really more or less in accord about the things that matter to us in life. I am happy and feel synchronized. The worlds I felt were so separate the other night are united. This was the "my dear Monnet" I used to hear talking with my father—and here was C. talking to him, C. and I, happily.

Détroyat and his wife (very smart in a green tweed suit and curls on top of head!) come for tea. Great effort to talk to her. Nice but like a child: "You lahk to go to Berlin?" etc.

To the Monnets' again for dinner. A man from the French Air Ministry there; nice but slow at English. The evening is slowed to that tempo. A nice talk with Silvia Monnet about women's struggle to choose between husband and children. We are both, however, very tired from train trips.

C. and I walk home happy. There is a moon and a milky sky. Paris looks classical under it. It has that "true elegance" Alexander Kirk was always talking of.

If it is clear tonight, I think, perhaps we will have good weather tomorrow to fly.

Monday, October 10th

Wake early to the steady drip of rain. Go to sleep again, hoping I haven't heard right. But it is a dreadful day at 7:30—the fine rain that lasts all day.

Most of the morning spent telephoning Le Bourget and the weather bureaus, trying to ask for weather in French and translate for C. *"Nuages bas"* . . . *"Hauteur"* . . . *"Plafond"* . . . *"Est-ce-que ça améliora demain?"* *"Quelles sont les prévisions pour demain,"* etc.

It is not as difficult as it was in the beginning of the summer. I can really get all I want, which is a comfort. At 1 we find that the bad zone around Paris extends only to Beauvais and is getting better. It may be passable at 2. We pack up and rush out to Le Bourget. The *météo* man says, *"C'est faisable"* (that's a new word—better remember).

We try to convince the control officers that it isn't necessary to send word ahead or word back or to call the commandant (all to help us). Finally get off at 2:20. It clears soon after leaving Paris, though there are low clouds all the way.

We cannot get to Hanover or Cologne and decide to land at Rotterdam. Clear sky. The last time we came down with the Sirius (in the water) after hours of bad weather, trying to get to Geneva. And I remember sitting in the airport teahouse talking to a nice man who flew with his wife, like C. and me. He spoke beautifully about it. And it made me take heart again after such a dreadful day. He has since been killed.

Take KLM bus to Rotterdam. C. calls Truman Smith. Great fuss in Russia. Some English paper printed something C. said (?) about Russia. Russians are very angry, so the report says.

Tuesday, October 11th. Weather is good!

Leave about 10:30 with a tail wind and a lovely sky of clouds. Haze over Germany. C. said we would be there exactly at 2 Greenwich time, so we slow down and fly back and forth over canals before going in to Berlin. I get very cold. I wish he had told me we were not getting in till 2. I would have packed some lunch.

Colonel Vanaman, Mrs. Vanaman, the Smiths are there to meet us. She looks thin and tired, also he. Quickly drive out from the crowd of officers, press, etc. The streets of Berlin look quite prosperous, full of cars, the shops luxurious.

To Ambassador Hugh Wilson's for tea. He is a nice, quiet, observant man. She is quite striking and charming with white hair and a young face.

Dinner at the Smiths' (C. is out for a stag dinner), all women. Mme Liotta,[1] wife of the Italian Air Attaché, is charming, perceptive, and has a kind of integrity and feeling. A person who, for all her delicacy and femininity, has life courageously in her hands. I should have liked to talk to her alone.

[1] Wife of General Liotta d'Aurelio, Italian Air Attaché in Berlin.

Also Mme Milch and her daughter, who is studying Geopolitik.

Wednesday, October 12th

The papers this morning carry a column about the Moscow affair. Apparently a news sheet in London (not even a newspaper)[1] printed a story that C. had come back from Russia, reported to Beneš, Chamberlain, Lady Astor, at a dinner party that the Russian Air Fleet was "nonexistent" (which of course he never said—in fact, quite the contrary, he has always said it had at least numbers to make itself a sizable factor in any war, something definitely to be reckoned with); that the German Air Fleet was the strongest in the world and could whip France, England, and Russia put together (the first part is true, the second twisted); that he said he was offered a post in Russia (absurd), and more embroidery about C. being in the midst of political intrigue.

The Russians have taken the story down lock, stock, and barrel, given it great publicity, and written a scathing letter criticizing C. personally—which they have published. The letter is childish and spiteful and absurd. "A former airman and political speculator who since his first flight has done nothing that any ordinary worker or peasant could not do in Russia!" That he was a political pawn of the Fascists in England, and the most involved and childish accusations.

I am startled at its crudeness, at the fact that all those jovial nice open fliers should rush to put their name to such abuse, except that of course any rumors coming back about C. having Fascist sympathies (and ten days ago he was supposed to be on a mission for the "democracies" of the world!) would throw suspicion on them and that to save their necks they must deny him vigorously.

But I mind C.'s being misquoted and labeled and I mind the

[1] Claud Cockburn's *The Week,* see note p. 261.

blind stupid hate and fear and jealousy in it. It is the most dangerous thing on earth.

Also I worry about Faymonville. It will kill him and his work up there.

In the evening, we dress up in our best clothes and go to the palatial Fliers' Club—a big dinner for all the people at the air conference. A beautiful big hall, lovely use of marble and wood and gold and modern tapestries. A great many people. At the table Mme Liotta and her husband, the von Gronaus, the son of Admiral Horthy, a young von Falkenhayn (son of a famous German general in World War I), and later General Milch and his wife and daughter. I enjoy talking to von Falkenhayn, who is quick, observing, and intelligent (with a nice gaiety and lightness of touch that seems quite un-German to me). We speak about the dangerous element in this situation, the emotions that can be whipped up by the press on rumors and lies. I was asking how it could be changed. He said it would be changed. It would have its own reaction—"Everything has its own reaction, Mrs. Lindbergh." I danced with him, with von Gronau, and with the Hungarian. It was rather fun, but I thought with a kind of wry humor that the last time I had danced it had been with Slepnev! General Milch came in. I do enjoy talking to him. He is able and quick as the crack of a whip; but he has a kind of pure knifelike directness that knocks the wind out of you. Like the first breath of air walking out of doors on a cold bright winter morning. Pure, clean, bright—and freezing!

We talked a little about where we (C. and I) were living now and where we would be this winter. "You should come here," he said with that blue-eyed directness and seriousness. "Well," I said, "that would be nice. There are many things that my husband is interested in here," etc. He said we would have sympathy and protection here and understanding from the German people.

He said, however, that the American people would not like it if their hero came to live in Germany (smiling). We talked, too, about the past crisis. He said with a kind of brutal frankness and simplicity that the English and the French had nothing to fight with in the air, absolutely nothing, and that they did not know it!

He said also, gazing earnestly at me with those blue eyes, always, "I think you like the German people, you and your husband."

We went home quite early.

Thursday, October 13th

Morning spent writing, reading, and talking to C. (who left the Lilienthal meeting because the speeches were in German) and a walk in the Tiergarten. I wonder more and more whether we can live here this winter.

Lunch at home with the Smiths. In the early afternoon Truman takes me to see the Deutsche Museum. Early wood carvings and Madonnas, lovely, beautifully set in chapels and arches. Also early Gothic paintings. I feel at home and nourished (my heart is nourished) whereas here I feel always overstimulated intellectually and half starved spiritually or emotionally.

Talk to Kay Smith a little after I get home. What are we going to do this winter? She suggests Rome or Paris. I gather they do not think it a good idea for us to be here. Go back in my room and write in the afternoon till C. comes back.

Supper (dinner) at Horchers, with the von Gronaus. They are such good people, and it glows from their faces.

I sit next to Prince Kinsky, a Sudeten German, head of the Austrian Aero Club. He is interesting after we get off of weather and aviation on to the European situation. We went from Russia to the dangers of a European war (the only gainers, Russia and the Communists). He agreed with that but also said he was afraid that the English Empire could not stand another war; it would break to pieces, and that would be a great loss to civilization and to the white race (with the underlying thesis that we must look at the world in terms of races and of civilizations now, not merely in terms of nations). He talked about the English as still playing bridge by the old rules when everyone else had learned Culbertson, and that the average Englishman never looked beyond the shores of France. Some of the things he said of the British were very amusing, such as there being only three classes of people in the English mind: 1, the English, 2, the Foreigner, 3, the Native.

But the last part of the evening was spent in listening to a terrific blast of anti-Jewish propaganda. I had never had it quite so strongly before from an intelligent person. I was depressed. He had no use for them at all. Said they were "creepers," parasites, and could not be *used* even by our civilization and recommended expelling them all to Madagascar. I listened shocked, open-mouthed, offering arguments here and there as best I could.

Also von Falkenhayn, on the other side, gave me an impassioned support of National Socialism from the "Socialism" side. He talked to me about his factory and the workmen in it. As wages are regulated, the workmen, he says, feel secure and work better and are happier. Also all the *Kraft durch Freude* programs for the workman make him feel he is cared for (as he is). He decries the old capitalism as exploiting people for personal aggrandizement, for selfish ends, whereas in Germany personal enterprise is allowed but not simply for personal aggrandizement. It is all for the state. (This sounds rather naïve, written down here, but it was quite impressive as he said it, coming as it did from a member of one of the oldest aristocratic families.)

The picture he gave was really one of a great revolution in Germany. Which is what they have tried to do in Russia. A spirit of self-sacrifice and of selflessness—"for the state"—extending right down from the employer through the employees. You must admire it (and it is self-evident as C. and I noticed the first time we came here) even if you may feel that the end to which it is directed may not be worthy of such a spirit. The costs, however, one suspects are great, as indicated by the nervous tension of the people and the life here.

How can it last and how will it solidify? Even admitting as one man did that there were certain things that must be changed eventually, such as the suppression of public opinion, of freedom of knowledge, free thought, he still said this had been necessary to begin with.

The history of dictators is always to start some measure "to begin with" and then find it has a stranglehold and cannot be dropped but must even be increased, like a drug.

Friday, October 14th

Lunch at Horcher's given by Mr. Merkel. Lots of technical people there. Hanna Reitsch—a little slip of a girl who flies the new helicopter. She has a glowing quality of life that is very appealing. Also Tommy Tomlinson[1] and wife (simple but nice Americans enthusiastic about Germany). Dr. Focke,[2] Gray[3] of the English magazine *Aviation,* etc. I always enjoy talking to Mr. Merkel though it is hard at a big lunch or party, he talks so slowly and deliberately. He says he trusts two things to keep us out of war: (1), aviation (the terror of military aviation) and (2), radio (news broadcasts in foreign languages—the other person's point of view reaching the other country). (This assumes you are going to have accurate and broadminded broadcasters.)

Saturday, October 15th

Lunch (C. and I and Kay) with Sikorsky.[4] A keen-eyed, sensitive, deliberate man, with a great deal of insight. A strange combination (in manner) of old-fashioned sedateness and a frank modern American directness. He is very interesting on old Russia, also hopeful as to some comeback in modern Russia in

[1] Daniel W. "Tommy" Tomlinson, naval officer and test and acrobatic pilot; later vice president in charge of engineering with Trans World Airlines.

[2] Henrich Focke, German aeronautical engineer, who did pioneering work with helicopters.

[3] C. G. Gray, English writer and editor of aviation publications.

[4] Igor Sikorsky, Russian-born scientist, aviation pioneer, and aeronautical engineer; built and flew first multimotor airplane (1913), produced first commercial amphibian airplane (1928); developed practical helicopter (1939).

the form of a military dictatorship to begin with, I gathered. He talked with a kind of restrained and disciplined intensity for about two hours. We listened enthralled.

Large tea at the Ambassador's [Wilson]. C. not very happy about this. "A tea—given for *us!* We haven't had a tea given for us for years. We don't go to teas!" etc. (This was accepted by the Smiths for us before we arrived.)

I had a word or two with him. Such a compact, quiet, and thoughtful man—a conservative man—who says very little and watches very hard and is balanced. He reminded me of Daddy without Daddy's open charm and gaiety.

The rest of it was making conversation, getting stuck with someone in a corner, shaking hands—a helpless feeling of knowing no one, smiling, saying useless things, and refusing food over and over again.

Kay and I have dinner alone and go to a *Kino* afterward. We saw news films of Hitler going into the Sudetenland. The Czech fortifications. Some bridges blown up. The cheering crowds. Göring very fat in a flowing raincoat, patting children on the cheek and feeling in his pocket for cookies which he stuck in their mouths. The movies were crowded. Lots of cars on the streets and brilliant illuminated signs and advertisements.

C. out to a stag dinner of air men at Vanaman's.

Sunday, October 16th

Drive out to Frederick II's palace. Walk through a lovely rundown park with big beech trees, sprays of yellow leaves over the water, and damp moldy leaves underfoot. Back to Berlin for tea at home.

In between all this I am thinking perpetually: Where will we go this winter: London—Paris—Berlin? London is the easiest for me, for the children, nurses, doctors, schools, and friends. But it has gotten on C.'s nerves, and *is* really rather dull.

Paris may present difficulties. Can we get security there? Advantages are the language and the closeness to Illiec.

Berlin the most appealing to C. Disadvantages: language, readjustment, dependence on other people.

Before we go out C. talks to Truman and Kay about next winter. I come in on the end of it. They suggest Brussels: French language, more security, quieter, and central.

Also they talk about Germany. Apparently they are not opposed to it.

To dinner at the British Embassy with Sir Nevile Henderson[1]; quite a lot of people. I, shy, as usual, with the British. He is charming and easy. Other people are the Belgian Ambassador and his wife, the Italian Ambassador, a German Minister of State and wife, another German officer and wife, and various British people.

As we were going, C. and Nevile Henderson begin to talk of the strength of the German Air Force,[2] Sir Nevile Henderson saying that no one has believed him when he has reported it and that C. must tell them so.

Monday, October 17th

C. off all day.

In the afternoon Truman and I go for a walk with the dog. He talks about our problem of where to live for the winter. I gather he feels, on the whole, it would be better for C. not to be here this winter. He feels, I think, that the period of German–U. S. A. agreement and understanding is a year off anyway. America now is completely misinformed about Germany and cannot see the German point of view. The effort to bring America to see it, by intelligent balanced people like the present Ambassador [Wilson],[3] may bring a lot of disagreeableness and he wants C. to stay

[1] British Ambassador to Germany 1937–1939, author of *Failure of a Mission*.

[2] Only Winston Churchill had for some time been alerting the British on German rearmament, but his Cassandra-like warnings were not listened to.

[3] Efforts were being made by the U. S. Government to bring about better U. S.-German understanding in an attempt to avert a European war. See

out of it—not to be labeled in this bitter period. On the other hand, he feels that C. wants to come and that if he does it can be managed quite well. He feels C. is destined eventually for some political life. I wonder. He is so averse to it. But perhaps nowadays one cannot keep out.

Colonel Faymonville has sent another telegram to C. asking him to undo the "incalculable harm done here" (due to the article in an English paper) by sending him or the Moscow paper a direct denial. I feel terribly sorry for Colonel Faymonville. It looks as though his position and influence is gone up there.

But C. cannot start to deny any stupid rumor that any scandalmonger chooses to print. Also, if he denied it, the Moscow press would twist it into some such statements as they printed while he was there: "Greatest aviation in the world," etc.

They can't have it all their own way.

Out to tea at the Henry Mann's[1]. He is a German, brought up in U. S. A. He thinks Germany will push very quickly into Russia. Truman does not believe this; that they are going to be much too occupied consolidating Mitteleuropa.

Henry Mann gave an estimate of a German General on the relative value of soldiers of different nationalities

1 German = 1 Frenchman
1 German = 2 Englishmen
1 German = 4 Russians
1 German = 8 Italians

Supper at home, with the Smiths alone. A Count Rocamora, Military Attaché of Franco's Spain, came in after supper, a slight quick Spaniard with a gray-white face, dark slicked hair, and a pencil-line mustache. He, C., and Truman talked about the war in Spain, especially the effectiveness of aviation. In general he gave the impression that the effectiveness was not as great as one always assumes it to be in a modern war.

correspondence between Franklin D. Roosevelt and William C. Bullitt, *For the President*, p. 242, Dec. 7, 1937.

[1] A long-time resident of Berlin, represented an American bank.

C. asks if it would be possible for him to go down and see the military aviation. He (the Count) is delighted, of course. And Truman urges him on.[1] (Then C. *will* be labeled, more than by any six months in Germany.) They discuss methods of getting into Spain.

Tuesday, October 18th

C. off all day. Kay takes me to see a school (with Jon in mind). We go by bus and streetcar. It is out in the Grunewald and has a lovely big garden, trees and grass and chestnuts fallen down. Black-skirted nuns scurry down the corridors. (The school is run by French Catholic nuns.) It has all nationalities in it, mostly the children of diplomats. The atmosphere is quiet and calm and the schedule not too hard. Reading and writing in French, and arithmetic, also German, a little. The sisters speak English.

Read and write after lunch. Out for walk in rain with C. late afternoon. We talk more about plans for winter. The same old problems. I think we will come here.

Dinner at Mrs. Vanaman's—all ladies (while C. went to the U. S. Embassy—a dinner for General Göring). C. came back late from his dinner, with a German decoration presented him quite unexpectedly by General Göring.[2] Henry Ford is the only other American to get it. The parchment is signed by Hitler.

[1] The Attaché knew that units of the German Luftwaffe were participating in the Spanish Civil War on Franco's side. He was anxious to obtain data on the efficiency of these units and their equipment but was unable to obtain these because of strict German secrecy.

[2] Ambassador Wilson had given a stag dinner at the American Embassy for General Göring (see Introduction, p. xxi). The dinner guests were totally surprised when Göring presented a civilian award to Lindbergh. To quote Colonel Smith's Air Intelligence Report: "But if the men present that evening took the presentation in their stride, the same cannot be said for the women. When Colonel Lindbergh and the Military Attaché reached home . . . Colonel Lindbergh, without comment, drew the medal box from his pocket and handed it to Mrs. Lindbergh. She gave it but a fleeting glance and then . . . remarked, 'The Albatross.' This reaction was shared by the Military Attaché's wife."

A long and rather tiring day of trying to find out about houses, schools, secretaries.

Saturday, October 22nd

To Wannsee to look at houses. The François-Poncets' house we were sent to cannot be heated! We go to an agent in Wannsee. He takes us to the Italian summer Embassy—an enormous house and stone-cold. Then to the English summer house—modern and too small.

Tuesday, October 25th

Cables from Mother and Aubrey asking if they can come over for one week. Where, they ask, will we be?

We have, of course, *no* idea. We talk it over all day. Shall we stay on at Illiec, or shall we postpone visits?

Decide to sleep on it, with a leaning toward staying at Illiec and having them come there.

Wednesday, October 26th

Mother has sent a sheaf of reviews—the first ones on the book! They are very good. C. has been reading them over and over all day, with a broad beam on his face. I feel elated too and light-headed. But the reviews are unreal, as if written about someone else's "book," not those pages of blue scribbled notes I worked on so long or that C. and I corrected night after night. I keep feeling: But how little they know us really! (Though I am pleased at the things that show through—unconsciously—of C. "my husband.") They do not see how much of the book *is* C., how much of it he made. Not that I didn't write it all, struggle over every scrap, but how much of it is *him,* or rather how much the book is a product of our marriage, not in literal content only but in the writing itself, in the substance and spirit of the book. C.'s completely childlike joy and pride at its success is touching beyond words. It is a great reward.

Mother's letter is wonderful, fiercely proud and happy. It is so *her*.

Thursday, October 27th

Send cables back to Mother and Aubrey: "Yes, come if you can brave weather. We must leave Illiec again around 17th."

Go in morning with Kay Smith to see a little house in town. Narrow and high with a tiny garden, like Turtle Bay gardens. It is not at all what we asked for but it is charmingly furnished and has a nice atmosphere. I can see ourselves in it. Though it would mean readjustments. The street is quiet and secluded and yet you are near everything. You can see trees from the garden (there are trees around you though not *in* the garden).

Then we go out to a place in the country on a lake: not a bad-looking house, lovely view. Bedrooms modern and comfortable. But downstairs it was cold and bare. A large oval marble-floored dining room, almost all glass-enclosed, with little summer-furniture chairs around a table, a horrible orange-lighted, wicker-chaired sunporch, and a dark heavy-furnitured den with an electric fireplace.

In spite of the lovely garden and comforts upstairs I was depressed by the place. There was a large *Jews are not wanted here* sign at the entrance of the little village.

There is a report in a German paper that C. has been forbidden by the Russian Government to return to Russian soil!

Saturday, October 29th

I feel very discouraged. The town house I thought would fit us has fallen through. I feel as though we had worked terribly hard this last week for nothing and that we might just as well have been at home.

Now there is nothing more to be done. The weather is foggy and bad and likely to be bad for three or four days. We decide to leave on the night train for Paris.

Dinner out at the Atelier with the Vanamans and Smiths.

They take us to the train. I feel really fond of Kay. She has been such a brick on this trip. She manages her life with great courage and sense and real devotion and selflessness in regard to her husband.

We get onto the train and into our beds (really quite comfortable!) and jiggle out into the misty night towards Paris.

C. says smiling what a woman I am for him, of all people, to have married! I can't sleep just before I start on a trip and I can't sleep in the train. I get upset when I find a house we can rent and I get upset when I *don't* find one!

Sunday, October 30th. Misty and damp

Coming out of the train in the morning I am horrified to see three or four reporters with their black boxes jumping ahead of us. I just get behind a large party to hide when I notice a burly man in a buff raincoat striding along beside me. He motions the photographers to stop—and they vanish! There seem to be several burly men in raincoats. We are swept along through the ticket office and two of the men in raincoats get us a taxi. C. says there are four or five at least and that they are Secret Service men, probably sent by the Government to see there is no trouble.

To the Crillon, where we have baths. (We have not had one for over a week, as the boiler burst in Berlin in the apartment and there was no hot water—just like Illiec!)

Delicious lunch at Fontainebleau with Mr. and Mrs. Jay.[1] Then out for a walk in the forest. C., Mr. Jay, and I. He is very interesting on conditions in France and Europe. He says "the little people" in France were not well treated, and better conditions were needed for them. But the reforms came quickly and with the wrong emphasis. The emphasis on *"take"*—it is your right—instead of on some kind of return loyalty and service to the state.

He says that the problem of the world is the economic one—of labor. Russia has attempted to solve it, unsuccessfully. France has

[1] Dean Jay, head of Morgan & Cie, Paris.

attempted. Even Roosevelt has seen it, but he has *used* it for political ends rather than tried to solve it. In Germany the laboring man has been made to feel that the state is his and that he has a duty of service and loyalty to it. And in return he has security and something to look forward to.

He is very interesting on Spain, which he went to just after the King had left—on the question of a loan. I asked him the question that so many people in U. S. A. asked me. If one believes in democratic government, how can one help but side with the Government in Spain? Franco had a chance to get in by vote and lost it. Now he wants to take it by force.

Mr. Jay said the terms "democratic" or "republican government" take on different meanings in Spain, which was a backward and illiterate country, not able to take the responsibility of that kind of freedom. It became lawlessness. He gave examples of moderate men who were simply murdered for their views. And the kind of lawlessness which wildly set fire to churches, etc. Franco and his group simply felt that there must be some kind of discipline and order and a stop to the lawlessness.

I do not, of course, believe that the whole Government side is Communist. It must have idealists, moderates, etc., in it, but it is backed and used by the Communists, over whom the moderates and idealists have no control.

Monday, October 31st. Damp drizzle

Out on a shopping tour, all day. I set out with misgivings, feeling I don't know my way around Paris, can't make myself understood, don't know where to find things. However, I am quite successful, much to my surprise.

Pass Brentano's on the way, scan the window for *Listen! the Wind:* not there. Very disappointed. Go in, try to get *With Malice Toward Some.* Sold out. See *Listen! the Wind,* in the English edition. As I am looking at it a lady asks for it, a salesman takes it from under my nose and hands it to her! Very funny feeling.

Pack in a terrible rush, for at 9:30, when we think we have an hour for the train, we find it leaves at 10:05 instead of 10:25. Throw our things together and get into a taxi. "Montparnasse—*vite.*" But when we get there we have fifteen minutes to spare (how did we do that!).

A long day to Plouaret. It is rainy and cold but lovely to be going home. C. and I feel quite gay as we get to the wild and gray country of Côtes-du-Nord. A half-hour late into Plouaret. It is rainy and dark (at 5:45). Miss H. is there in a new hat and hair-do from Paris. We hear all the news going home in the Ford (which breaks another brake rod on the way!). Jon has been in bed two days, Land almost walks. Maryvonne has had all her teeth out! Yvonne has eloped! Fat, untidy, dumpy, red-haired Yvonne! She hasn't exactly eloped but she came one day and said she wasn't coming back any more because she was getting married. Françoise (her twin) would come instead. She is marrying secretly because his parents do not approve of her!

Louis, Kerleau, and P'tit Louis meet us at the garage. We change into boots, put on raincoats. Off with the London hat, tie a scarf around the head, and set out (carrying city hat and shoes) across the flats. A half-moon and clouds and occasional drizzles. Thor does not come out to meet us, as he is being fed.

You can open the front door from the outside! François has put a brass knob on it!

Jon is in the dining room eating supper. He is shy and pleased. I put him to bed. He said, "You just missed the surprise. They hardly ever get that big." (A large toadstool this turned out to be.) Also he told me he had caught a fish. "Sometimes you catch them with your hands."

It is clear that things are not going so well with Miss W. Miss H.'s account of the time was full of amusement. Miss W. said it had been very cold and disagreeable. Jon has been sick. Land can't go out at all, it is such bad weather. Land is cutting his eyeteeth and cries a lot at night. Also at supper everything is wrong.

I wonder if she will stay another three weeks. What a problem. There is a stack of letters—congratulations, book reviews, and mail from home. I feel overcome by the variety and mass of emotions. Letters from home about the war; Con having a baby, and the book. But the thing that moved me the most is Emily's[1] death. It is really my whole life: Emily hugging me in the garden when I was unhappy about dances and saying, "Anyvay, ve like you best!" And Emily with little Charles, and then when Jon was born—when everyone was speaking of the new baby—Emily blurting, like a child, with a child's sweetness and regret, "If only *he* could see his little brudder." I can hardly bear to go back to Englewood without her. Only *she* had not changed. She still hugged me. She was still just as simple and blundering, and that broken English.

I go to bed confused with the shock of different things— joys, fears, and sorrows—all at once. And cannot sleep.

Wednesday, November 2nd

Up late. Everything seems somewhat in confusion. The "salon" is terribly untidy, strewn with Land's toys, crowded with chairs, wrongly placed, and Land's sprawling pen. Savina has made two more tables which are very nice, and the oldest bed-front (with carved crucifix) has been made into a lovely low cupboard.

There seems to be a great deal to do. I go out and order meals. Maryvonne does look very old with all her teeth out and her mouth sunken in and a black kerchief tied around her head and under her chin to keep off *les piqûres*. I tell her she will look much younger when she gets her new teeth.

Jon hangs around the kitchen waiting for me to take a walk. It is a nice day—blowy but clear and sunny, patches of sun when the clouds are blown by. We walk around the island, run down the paths. I feel much better. C. and Kerleau discuss trees. Kerleau has seen a man who has them; they are not expensive and now is the time to plant (small quick-growing cypress).

C. and I discuss the immediate future while Jon trails behind;

[1] Finnish maid who had been in the Morrow household for many years.

how long can Jon stay here? How long will Miss W. stay? Could we go to Paris? London? Jon and I? En masse? But Mother and Aubrey?

Lunch comes in no time. We send Miss W. and H. off for the afternoon. I take care of Land. He comes to me very naturally. After lunch I take him out in his carriage (he has not been out for weeks). By the time I get him into his "ski suit" the sun is gone already, behind clouds, and a strong wind blowing. However, I take him anyway.

Kerleau tells me that the tree man has lilacs too and that I could put two by the well and they would smell very sweet in the upstairs windows. It makes me hungry for spring.

In the evening I get out all the garden books and make lists of what I want from the tree man. Everything needs a spot protected from winds, and we have none. I read what to plant as a windbreak—"first line of defense"—but think no English winds are so fierce as these!

Also I read books on how to teach Jon reading.

Thursday, November 3rd

François has arrived. C. and Miss H. rake him over the coals. Everything he has done has gone wrong. The shutters keep breaking, the locks and door handles won't stay on, the plaster cracks and falls, and he forgot a large check we gave him and demanded it over again! Also, his men don't work. They lie around all day and drink cider in the kitchen. He has brought over a new carpenter, a mousy little man, to do over the bad work of the first man.

Quite cold in the evening. C. and I sit in the big room, I huddled over the small coal grate. But the wind blows in the cracks of the front window. I wonder if Mother will freeze.

Friday, November 4th

A lovely day, like a cool April or May day: blowy, sunny and shady, but a warm wind.

Most of the day is spent on trees. In the morning go out with C. and choose where to put them, marking lines with stones. We plan to plant most of the western slopes of the island with trees. There are already three small groves there. This will act as a windbreak and also cover the bleakness of that side of the island, a bleakness not particularly exciting like the other side. Kerleau knocks in stakes after we mark with stones. Louis is digging holes, Jon helping him.

C. and I go over to Saint-Gildas for lunch and get quite hot walking over. We discuss a walled garden in front of the house to take in one tree of the old line and the well. That would be bliss—one place of calm where one could have a garden. I begin planning.

Saturday, November 5th

A misty drizzle and fog, clearing up in the middle of the day and settling down again at twilight.

After lunch we go off by boat to Port-Blanc and meet the Rector by the garage. He directs us by back roads through Port-Blanc, along the coast to Trevou and Trestel and other little places. It is wild and heathery; you look back over Port-Blanc and the islands.

We look for ruins, broken-down deserted farms, with old doors that we can use in the chapel and in the "walled garden." The Rector knows of several. The best ones were in an old mill half hidden by vines and blackberry bushes under the hill in a lovely long valley leading to the sea. When we walked off the main road into the little sunken path down among the trees we were suddenly in another world. Beautiful trees, all turning yellow—still mossy, wet underfoot, a brook, and no wind—absolute quiet; peace, seclusion.

This deserted farmhouse—the walls crumbling, the roof fallen in, overgrown with brambles—had two old stone arches (doors) and a stone fireplace, also a watering trough.

The Rector—a quick, perceptive man—is very nice. He says he

will supervise the redoing of our chapel. He loves old things and knows this country well. He keeps saying, with real affection, of some fallen slab of stone; *"C'est une belle pierre là."*

Back late, in the fog. There is a review in the London *Times* of the book. It is titled "In an Airplane" and does not speak of the writing. It is pleasant in tone and speaks mildly of a very agreeable aviation book. I will *never* impress the English!

Sunday, November 6th

Misty all day. Give Jon a first "lesson" in reading this morning. Very short.

Miss W. and H. out in the afternoon. I take care of Land. I sit on the side of his bed for a minute and the springs fall down and we collapse onto the floor. Land bawls with rage and annoyance (he is angry to begin with, waiting for his lunch). From my constrained position I put him out on the floor gingerly and then climb out of the debris myself.

Jon comes in much excited and rushes off to tell Louis and "Father." C. comes back while I am feeding Land. Says the wood was rotten—much too weak. But he can fix it temporarily. He and Jon saw and hammer on bits of wood, like splints, Land peering at them round the corner and imitating the "he-haw" of the saw with deep breaths!

In the middle of this, Mme Carrel and the Rector arrive! C. finishes the bed quickly, leaving Jon a few nails to hammer in. I put Land in and go down.

The Rector and Mme Carrel stay for tea. It is quite dark. I am very sleepy and no letters written today, either. Where does the time go to?

Monday, November 7th

In the morning I work with Jon on reading material. It goes very well and encourages me. He is interested even with Land in the same room!

After lunch look over the furniture in the guest rooms for Mother and Aubrey's visit.

Miss W. complains of the water: it is never hot and the girls can't remember to heat it or bring it. I go out in the kitchen and find they have to heat six cans of hot water at the time they're cooking supper. One for Land (early), one for Jon, and two each for Miss W. and Miss H., who prefer to wash before supper than after. Miss W. has also complained of the lamps, the lack of good light. Also of the grease in the food!

I am tired of complaints. They all go through me. The house does not run absolutely smoothly. These are completely untrained people in a new and comparatively unfurnished house. I have not given enough time to it, (1) because I dislike driving people, (2) because I have been away a great deal, and when I have been here it has been crowded with things—shopping for the house and countless odd jobs like going after the trees, and also I have been tied down with the children, partly from wish and partly in a vain attempt to make things more pleasant for Miss W.

I am trying to be nurse, mother, teacher, housekeeper, wife, and general odd-jobs-man all at the same time.

Wednesday, November 9th

A beautiful day, mild and sunny. In the morning I teach Jon and arrange the rooms, hammering pictures in Mother's room—the St. Francis over the desk, the little print of a boy catching a butterfly over the chair. I take down the big gray mirror over the mantel (single-handed) and put up my woodblock of spring flowers. The effect is marvelous! Pictures make a great difference.

Jon and I go around the island trying to find flowers for Mother's room—a few sea-pinks and some short-stemmed daisies from the windswept potato field.

After supper—from 7 on—I tell them to watch in the kitchen for lights on shore (I wrote Mother to come to the water's edge and signal with the car lights). But I didn't expect them. After supper I sat by the fire, looking up every few minutes at the window across to the shore. At 10:25 I started for bed but went to the window for a last long look. At that instant a light flashed over the hill—a car. I watch it coming down the Buguélès road and, yes, to the water's edge! The lights go off and on. I whistle for Charles and move the lamps in front, and away from, the window as a signal. (No one else would be awake at Buguélès at that hour of the night. It must be they.)

We rush to get boots and coats. Françoise comes running down to say she has seen the lights. I tell her yes, and to light Mother's fire and to get Louis to follow us over. We set out, flashing the light, but get no answer. I wonder if it is they. It is blowy but mild and a good moon. The stream is quite high and rushing; C. carries me across. We flash again—they answer. It must be they. We go very fast and soon see the car, a large high touring one (so strange to see in Brittany; reminiscent of Daddy and family trips starting at the Ritz in Paris), and Mother, a little figure out in front in a mink coat, and Aubrey, and the chauffeur.

Great excitement and pleasure and confusion getting out Mother's rubber boots, old shoes, tissue paper—so carefully put in by Isabel—blowing about the Buguélès flats! Louis guides the chauffeur to the garage where he leaves the rest of the luggage, he carrying one piece. We start across the puddled flats in the moonlight, Mother and I arm in arm talking furiously.

When we arrive at the house everyone is up in the kitchen— Maryvonne, Marie, Françoise, and P'tit Louis, and coffee going on the stove. I take Mother out to meet them. We sit in the dining room and they have sausages and hot milk. Then I get Mother and Aubrey hot-water bottles, hot water, extra blankets. Mother's room is nice and warm with a fire.

We go in and see Jon—fast asleep. Then to bed, much excited.

So like Mother to come tonight! They drove straight from Cherbourg, not stopping to eat, for five hours.

Thursday, November 10th

A beautiful day, mild and clear, a blue sky and a gentle wind.

Maryvonne, in the excitement of Mother's arrival, has completely forgotten to cook the figs for breakfast that I got especially for Mother and told her to cook yesterday.

Miss W. and H. off early. I take care of Land, order meals, in the morning. It is rather a rush and I am tired (we did not get to bed till 1:30). Jon is in Mother's room most of the morning. Great fun unpacking, tissue paper, presents, and conversation; the luxury of catching up on everything, both the big and the small things of life.

I show Mother the island, up the big rock. She thinks it very beautiful. She is impressed with the blue Sept-Îles which I, for some reason, had never emphasized in the letters. We take Land out in afternoon in his carriage. Mother and I sit under the pines and compare notes, she giving me notes and letters to read.

Meals have been quite good. I am spacing out all Maryvonne's best dishes. Also Aubrey appreciates the wine. We try a new bottle at each meal.

Friday, November 11th

Scattered showers; clearing. "School" with Jon in the morning, very slow and distracted. Land howls and Jon fidgets. Lack of attention due to yesterday's holiday and general excitement.

The meat does not arrive for lunch. Lunch is already late when I go out in the kitchen. Maryvonne is just sitting in the kitchen wringing her hands waiting for it. "Sometimes it is very late," she says. I say to open a can immediately and start lunch on that. We open what I think is chicken fricassee but turns out to be noodles.

The liver turns up halfway through lunch!

Mme Carrel comes for supper. I put on Mother's new gay cloth; the table looks very pretty and the meal is good. Maryvonne makes a perfect cheese soufflé and delicious candied chestnuts (from the Swedish Princess cookbook!).

Clippings have come about the Russian incident and the following German medal. How I dislike C. being labeled.

Saturday, November 12th. Land 18 months

The weather is still miraculously mild.

After lunch we go to Tréguier—Mother, Aubrey, and I. We go into the cathedral and walk around the cloisters. Also look at the beautiful war memorial in the square and the rakish statue of

Renan. Then to Savina's and Mother and Aubrey on to an antique shop, while I, with my marketing basket, shop for oranges, cheese, tomatoes, and chestnuts. We have run out of lemons. Maryvonne simply cannot remember to keep herself supplied with the simplest things.

We go home late, just in time to get across the flats by a few minutes, the tidal stream lapping at the edge of our boots.

Quite a long day for Mother—two trips over the flats—but she was happy over it.

We are very depressed by accounts in the newspaper of German riots on Jews.[1] Apparently there were terrible demonstrations, supposedly "spontaneous"—smashing shops, driving out Jews, harassing them all over Germany in revenge for vom Rath's murder in Paris by an insane Polish Jew.

You just get to feeling you can understand and work with these people when they do something stupid and brutal and undisciplined like that. I am shocked and very upset.

How *can* we go there to live?

Monday, November 14th

C. and I decide to mark time on where to move for the winter.[2]

Letter from Kay Smith. She was in Vienna the day of the anti-Jewish demonstrations. She also is very depressed.

Tuesday, November 15th. Rain and overcast

Miss W. off in morning. Mother takes Jon for "school." "The trees" have arrived, so we let Jon out early to help plant them. He spends the whole day carrying them around and putting them in

---

[1] History has substantiated that this fifteen-hour pogrom on November 7th throughout the Reich had been planned and organized by Himmler's own policemen disguised as hooligans. The murder of vom Rath by a grief-crazed Polish Jew was merely a pretext for the outburst. (Neville Henderson, *Failure of a Mission*, p. 22; John Wheeler-Bennett, *Munich*, pp. 297–98.)

[2] The Lindberghs decide they cannot go to Berlin for the winter and consider Paris, Rome, and Brussels.

the holes. The men are putting in little stakes to tie them, to keep them from being blown over.

Letter by afternoon post from Mme Détroyat giving information about a Swiss nurse recommended by her nurse. The references are all in German, but Mother translates a little. She sounds quite good. Mme Détroyat says she loves the country and would be *ravie* to come to Illiec! I wonder. But it is a godsend. I shall certainly follow her up when I am in Paris.

This afternoon—or evening, when the lamps are lit—the girls discover there is no more petrol!

Miss H. does not feel well so after supper I take C. to Lannion.[1] Louis goes, too, in case we have a blow-out on the way home. At the station C. has me tell Louis he is not to drink too much—to be careful, etc. Louis says sullenly under his breath that he has never been drunk.

He says not a word to me all the way home or on that grinding walk over the Sillon, but when we reach the path of the island he says, "Now I have taken you back to the island and I give you fifteen days in which to get someone else to take my place." Following that blinding circle of the lantern's light on the wet stones swinging ahead of me, I kept thinking "Violence, violence," all the way home, "Louis is a violent man" (though I had never seen him so), feeling that thing in him that finally burst in anger as we reached the island. And then he blows up completely. He has never been drunk. It is an insult. It is Kerleau who has said it, etc., raving wildly. I try to convince him that it was not Kerleau but otherwise do not argue and say as calmly as possible that of course if he wants to leave that is all right.

I go up to Mother shaken and upset by the violence of his temper more than by the consequences which face us if he holds to his word and goes (which is unlikely).

Hard to sleep. It is always this type of thing that makes me deeply angry. When someone takes advantage of your gentleness to try to stamp on you. And there was some of that in Louis's

[1] C. A. L. was going to Paris for a meeting with Jean Monnet.

outburst tonight. He hung his head before C. but he raved at me.
And he had saved it up to do it, all the way home. He is, of
course, like an undisciplined child. I feel sorry for poor wise good
Maryvonne. I do not want her to go. And I dread the atmosphere
of the house tomorrow. Write C. a long letter about it which
calms me, but decide not to send it. It is not important enough,
but did me good to get it out.

Jon comes into my bed in the night after a nightmare, paddling
in with his little flashlight: "Here I am, Mother. I had a bad
dream. You said I could come in."

I *couldn't* send him back!

Jon drops to sleep the minute he gets into my bed. I remember
so well as a child, after a nightmare, screwing up my courage to
get out of bed and walking across the dark corner of my room to
the complete security, comfort, warmth—absolute bliss of getting
into bed with Mother.

About 7 A.M. when I am getting a last snooze Jon sits up in
bed and says sweetly, "This is generally the time I wake up," and
then, "I'd like a glass of water."

Wednesday, November 16th

Mother's room now begins to look just like her: books on the
mantel; the folding picture of all of us; a graduated row of
limpets and a small pitcher of white weedy flowers (all that can
be found on Illiec). Her desk with Grandma's picture, another
tiny bouquet, letters and small leather notebooks, done up in
bright-colored elastic bands, pads, envelopes, pencils and pens—
all in perfect but *used* order.

School with Jon in morning. He does a beautiful page in his
book. He does not mind having school this morning, he says,
because it is raining. It is a heavy cold gray drenching rain. As
Marie says to Mother when she goes in in the morning; *"Il
pleut . . . c'est l'hiver."*

Go out into the kitchen. Maryvonne looks badly (I suppose
Louis gave her no sleep, raving last night) and obviously she has

been crying. I waver between trying to pass over it lightly and having a good talk. Decide on the latter—very glad of it. Maryvonne's face relaxes at once. She is in tears. She is loyal to Louis but explains that he has a weak stomach. He does not drink much, but very little makes him *énervé*. She suggests that I limit the cider (a good idea). I tell her that I do not wish her to go. She has been so loyal, worked well, and we like them so much. She wipes her eyes on the dishcloths hanging over the stove and says valiantly; "I for my part, Madame, I *never* wish to leave you—*never*."

She says Louis did not mean it.

All ends quite happily.

Louis, however, I have not seen all day. He went over to Buguélès early in the morning *pour les commissions* and did not return till mid-afternoon. I have studiously avoided him and he, perhaps, has as studiously avoided me.

The sun comes out in the late afternoon. The sky is pearly and swept feathery. Mother and I go for a short walk around the island before tea.

The mail comes bringing three telegrams for C. from America. Evidently a front-page story about our going to Germany for the winter. Two newspapers want confirmation.

I wish it had not come out just now. It will raise a storm of criticism. What will C. do now?[1] [Ambassador] Wilson has been recalled as a protest on the part of the U. S. A. to the riots. What a day for the papers to wave the flag of our going to Germany to live (for the winter)! Or have the Germans put it out as counter-propaganda? How I hate to have C. *used*.

I wish I could talk to him.

Tonight I read in *The Importance of Living* [Lin Yutang] the following quotation:

"By 'bosom friends' I do not mean necessarily those who have

[1] On November 11, C. A. L. telephoned from Paris to the military attaché in Berlin to say he would not take a house in Berlin, in a country that committed such outrages [diary of Mrs. Truman Smith].

sworn a life-and-death friendship with us. Generally bosom friends are those who, although separated by hundreds or thousands of miles, still have implicit faith in us and refuse to believe rumors against us; those who on hearing a rumor, try every means to explain it away; those who in given moments advise us as to what to do and what not to do; and those who at the critical hour come to our help. . . ."

Thursday, November 17th

A long day. In the morning I teach Jon his lesson. I have him "give me a lesson." I make a big chart for the wall and get him to tell me what to print on it (reading out of his book). He is delighted and watches me very carefully. "If you make a mistake you won't get a star."

In the end he gives me two stars, "two of my best stars!"

The rest of the morning is spent packing, ordering the meals, and collecting papers for Paris.

I run out around the island (it is now foggy) in raincoat and hat, and see what trees have been planted (the west side of the island looks like a young nursery). There are lots of trees left over (after all the holes have been filled), mostly cypress. I talk to Kerleau about putting them on the islands.

Put Land to bed: "Night night."

Early supper. Then off across the flats, Kerleau carrying the bags. All seems serene in the kitchen. I asked Louis to stay and watch the place and he said, Yes, yes, earnestly and offered to help carry the bags over, evidently rather ashamed of the other night and wanting to help.

November 18th
[Paris] the Ritz Hotel—colder, but bright

Mother and I into Paris early, met by Félix [courier for Morgan & Cie] and a large limousine (the old luxury of Ritz days—very strange to me after my vagabond life), to the Ritz—bowing and scraping. Hot bath, breakfast. C. comes over. I call Mme Détroyat. The Swiss nurse can speak French! I plan to see her friend tomorrow. C. has an appointment for me with Despiau (mad idea).[1] We go down. Despiau is a nice little man, sensitive, neurotic, but quite simple and shy. I like him. Lovely heads.

Back to the Ritz. Shopping with Mother. Baby clothes for Con and Margot, and toys, cradles, etc. Lunch at the Ritz— jammed with smart, well-dressed Americans. I feel very shabby and tired, old coat, bad haircut, and suit too long.

After lunch a walk along Rue Saint-Honoré with Mother. I am completely immersed in the atmosphere of Mother's life all day: the sense of hurry, of getting as much as possible into the day, of grand old hotels and grand old shops (Vuitton, Fairyland, Rouff's). And Mother having a wonderful time looking at one exquisite baby dress after another. (I try to dissuade her from the extravagant ones which were all right for the Grand Christenings but not modern or practical.)

November 19th

C. and I take Mother to the train for *Normandie*. Crowds. Marlene Dietrich and photographers—very unpleasant.

Hôtel Crillon, Sunday, November 20th

Mother darling,

It was strange yesterday not to be able to tell you about the day's progress in the evening.

I went in the afternoon to see Mme Détroyat's Swiss nurse. She has a scrubbed shiny brown face, button eyes behind glasses, and a mouth that looked as if she had just broken off a bit of thread for sewing.

Amid the clamors of the children she translated for me the reference letters [of her friend] into French.

"Schwester Lisi" does speak a *very little* English. She once spent three months in England and so knows a little and would pick it up again, I imagine, quite quickly. That is a decided advantage. When I asked Mme Détroyat's nurse if she liked the

[1] C. A. L. had arranged for the sculptor, Charles Despiau, to do a head of A. M. L.

country, she said enthusiastically that "Schwester Lisi" used to go out on long hikes in the mountains by herself and that she was a *véritable enfant de la nature!* That does sound pretty grim. However, we have sent for her, just on the chance that she might do. The letters describe her as efficient, intelligent, *joyeuse,* etc.

Our plans now are to move up to Paris the end of the month to an apartment hotel and stay here while our winter plans are settled.

This afternoon C. and I went to the Salon d'Automne. It was crowded but fun. I do not mind Paris so much on Sunday as London. Everyone seems to be having a good time, not going to a funeral.

Wednesday

The Swiss nurse arrived bright and early Monday morning. Perhaps because I expected something terrible I was quite charmed with her. She is small and dark (Italian-looking) with neatly brushed hair, a gentle voice and charming smile. I talked a long time with her (in French). She seems to have a gentle, understanding sense of humor. I told her all about Illiec and our life, describing the worst, and saying I hoped she did not mind being alone, as that was what we liked. She took it very nicely, and I think she is an easy and pleasant person. I hope she is as competent as she is supposed to be from the letters.

Also—great coup!—I have found through a wonderful agency a small and charming apartment, first floor up, right bang on the Bois, that we can rent for one month, while we make our plans. It is sunny (when there is sun) and quiet and nicely furnished, modern and comfortable and, as far as rooms go, as though made for us. There is even a crib and high chair for Land, an adjoining room for the nurse, and an office for C. And you can *walk* up the first flight, or *down* and across the street to the park.

I am so pleased, as I dreaded a month in an apartment hotel.

Saturday we go home to Illiec to pack up and move up here by December 1st.

Thursday—Thanksgiving Day

Today I have interviewed a cook and man—most French and proper—an entirely new brand to me! Also have spent the day trying to locate a temporary nurse as Miss W. has just wired that she cannot change her plans and stay with us two weeks more (Schwester—or "Soeur Lisi"—cannot come until the 15th). I shall just have to take care of the children for the last days in Illiec and for the trip and have a temporary nurse meet us here.

What a long and tired letter, full of housekeeping details. To add to the confusion, I go each morning to Despiau's studio! But this is calming, even if it does use up precious time.

DIARY   *November 22nd*

Out to the Tour d'Argent for supper; very expensive but nice. Only rather spoiled because a table of Americans behind us talked loudly about us—about C.'s attitude on press and vice versa, on the case, etc. (They said "Dwight Morrow—that was a great man.") It made me curl up inside and feel, Why should we have to be there like dirty newspapers, thumb-marked and turned over by anyone who wants.

Why can't we shrink down into ourselves and live our own little inconspicuous lives like those people? Even those people, who were bandying our names about so loudly and noisily—they are free as air. But we can never become like that—only temporarily, as in England.

Wednesday, November 23rd

To Despiau's studio at 10. We lose the way and are late. He greets us at the door, very polite in a vague old-world manner gone a little hayseed. He looks rather like a scarecrow, thin and in baggy clothes and a battered felt hat over his pale, sensitive, and rather pathetic face (to shade his weak eyes, he tells us). The timidity of a child, with a good deal of intensity and humorous observation. (His face is framed in an unkempt stubble of whitening beard and whitening sparse hair on his small head.)

Timid, apologetic, and weak-appearing, the minute he starts to work he presents an entirely different picture. He becomes intense and works fast, and his hands, small and delicate, become strong and deft, tearing at the lump of gray clay and patting it on a stick.

He sits me up on a stool and works at a high platform beside it, the height of my head, on which there are two spare lumps of gray clay and a perpendicular stick, standing in the flat piece of clay. Then he begins to build up the head on the stick. He says this is the hardest part; there are no limits. All is in the dark. It is only a point of contact, today.

But the head grows very quickly, taking shape, proportion, and even a familiar profile. He works intensely, deftly, and nervously. Then when I rest he stops and looks small and broken again and feels for his cigarettes. He smokes feverishly and talks a good deal of how much he smokes and how nervous and exhausted he is, how the work tires him, etc. But this does not seem affected and you do not mind it.

The studio is not very big and quite untidy—no, not untidy exactly, just neglected. The lower parts of the walls are marked with occasional telephone numbers and scuffed by feet. There are a number of busts around the room on platforms and a dusty cabinet full of them. The walls are hung with modern pictures. Some I like very much.

He works until 11:15 or 11:30 and talks quite easily and jovially in between smoking under his battered hat. I like him.

Out for dinner with the Baron de la Grange and his wife[1]—she charming, very chic and Continental (though American)—at an old and very red-plush and old-leather club. It has a grand musty air and wonderful food. Go later to their house, also charming and old. Have a nice time talking Germany, France, and England. Everyone here seems to expect as inevitable some kind of drastic change in the Government, some kind of strong Govern-

[1] Friends of the Détroyats.

ment akin to dictatorship, to pull France together, "in two months, or three months, or six months."

Can this change happen without a revolution?

Thursday, November 24th

I go alone to Despiau's. He very *épuisé* today, *affaibli;* did not sleep, he says. However, after he starts to work he says he feels better, it calms him. He says he was almost killed yesterday—stepped in front of a truck but someone pulled him back. I can well imagine it!

The head begins to look like me. He says it makes a *beau masque* and seems pleased with it, especially my forehead.

Friday, November 25th

Off to Despiau's in the rain. He feels better today and tells me he slept last night. A gray cat was curled up on one of the stools. He worked very hard putting a tiny piece of clay on the end of my nose, or shaving an infinitesimal crumb off my mouth.

He says he is always afraid when he starts a new piece of work. Nothing he has done before gives him any confidence. He is afraid as though it were the first piece of work he had ever done. He is not afraid of death at all and tells me of a narrow escape he once had driving horses in the snow. But he says he is afraid of himself, of traveling, of new places, sometimes even of going to the tobacco store to get some cigarettes.

I understand well. It would be easy to get like that and I have tendencies that way as it is. But it is also easy to see how just by simple little things he could help himself: if he went out more, if he saw people, if he walked outside every day. But it is easy to plan other people's lives. If he had that much control of himself, he might not be an artist.

I kept thinking all the time this morning while he is working, what a beautiful head he could have done of Elisabeth. So delicate and proud and strong. Finally I tell him about her. *"Elle vous ressemblait?"* he asks. No, I have to say, not much—not at all, really.

He says he has no patience but he has great, intense, minute patience in his work.

> *Hôtel Crillon, Saturday, November 26th*
> *Pouring a cold rain, again*

M. Despiau is very exhausted this morning. He did not sleep last night. He took veronal and poison, he says, everything, and still he did not sleep. He says he read the newspapers last night. (General strike threatened as a protest against M. Reynaud's new finance measures and Daladier's Government in general.) It made him so angry that he couldn't sleep (explaining to me that he was *très, très sensible* and that he got terribly excited by things). He said he believed in the principle of strikes (that is the right of unions) but not for political purposes and talked a lot about the *meneurs* [agitators]. "They have taught laziness to the French workmen," a thing which was unknown before and unnatural to the French. He talked a lot about the French *paysan* and how fine he was. I did not question him too much as he got excited and disturbed, talking.

He is going to a meeting of the Musée Rodin which he says happens about once a year. He does not want to go. But I think to myself, That will be good for you. You will make the effort; you will go out; you will change your routine, talk to people, and you will feel better for it, stimulated, given confidence, shaken up a little. Then you will sleep tonight.

He looked much neater today, though his heavy tweed suit, about two sizes too large, literally *hangs* on him.

After he had worked a little he said he felt better, calmer. He works with great intensity—delight playing over his face as he scans my forehead and then the bust—and then with his small delicate but wiry hands puts a tiny piece of clay on the mouth or pats the cheek with his long, curved scraper-knife. A strange kind of intensity and delight, which of course I know has nothing to do with me, but only his excitement over a line or a curve.

He is very pleased with the bust and says it will be *beau*.

C. comes in to take me back and is also pleased with it. We say we will drop Despiau at his meeting and he is childishly relieved. We take a taxi and drop him at the Musée Rodin, a small, pathetic figure walking vaguely away, in a huge tweed overcoat and a strange plush felt hat on his head.

Back to the hotel. A message to say a temporary Swiss nurse is coming. She is nice-looking, gentle, pleasant, and sympathetic; not very vigorous or young. I don't believe she can manage Jon but she would be easy to live with for two weeks.

Also the cook arrives and I plan out the meals for the day we arrive, give her the Quaker Oats to have ready for Jon and Land, and tell her about milk, oranges, prunes, etc. Then I take her to 11 bis Avenue Maréchal Maunoury and show her the apartment and tell her where the different people will go. She seems both quick and intelligent. However, she thinks there is too much work for two people. I am afraid we will have to have a third person.

I feel quite carefree after a week of plans, telephone calls, etc. I have an apartment, a *ménage,* a nurse coming in two weeks, a temporary nurse, and breakfast ordered for the morning we arrive!

Illiec, Sunday, November 27th

Day spent on the train from Paris. It feels good even to see the country out of the window. Read the papers. General strike is impending for Wednesday. We are met at the train by Miss H. Weather has been dreadful at Illiec. We walk across Sillon in wind and cold. The house looks very desolate.

Jon is sitting up in bed shining-eyed. "I have a *surprise* for you." He has a loose tooth—in front—the big tooth coming in behind. Also he has built a house in the trees with bracken and corrugated iron and slats of wood. He keeps a pot of "baby" pines up there and goes up every day to water them!

We read the mail from home. I feel disturbed especially by a letter to C. saying the feeling at home was very bitter against him because of the story that he was going to Germany to live. I feel badly, deeply, to have C. labeled so unfairly. I do not like to see us linked with the German methods, in this last purge. But also I feel even more deeply a kind of profound foreboding that this is just the beginning of a long period of struggle and hate and jealousy and false names and standards. A period of struggle so terrible that there is no middle way, no reasonable way out, and one will be forced to take sides with something one does not believe in. There will be no moderate party, no moderate state in which to bring up one's children in the beliefs one respects.

Also, thinking about our future plans for the children this winter, I wonder what is the right thing to do. Paris and the general strike; Berlin is out; Italy? Jon should have normal school life, children, peace. Where can he get it?

There is a great deal to be done here. And Miss W. is chafing to go and the household will be tense until she does—and yet I shall miss her very much. It will be hard work packing up and moving the children by myself and without her help.

I wish we were safely established for the winter.

Monday, November 28th

I give Jon his lesson. He is getting ahead quite well and read several pages in the introductory book. Land is almost walking and climbs up against the side of a wall and walks along it.

Jon's tooth comes out. C. wiggles it out with a huge pair of pliers. It looks very fierce but he was gentle and Jon said it didn't hurt at all.

I do the rest of Jon's lessons for the week, as Miss W. is leaving tonight. It was very hard talking to her. She said she had taken a job and that was why she couldn't change her plans—not a job with children but with a friend, which she said pathetically "would help," and then broke down.

I felt so terribly for her. Think of leaving Jon and Land—*for good*. I cannot bear to think of it for her. Especially Jon. She said he had been so sweet with her these last days. She "had that," she said. What *do* they "have"—what is their life? Taking care of other people's children, loving them, and then being torn away. I ached for her.

I tried to tell her we would always be grateful to her. She had been so sweet with Jon, so understanding. She had been part of one of the happiest times in my life, in Long Barn. Oh, she said, "those happy days in Long Barn," as though looking back to a paradise—as though, somehow, all her troubles had started here. And yet she was not really contented even there. There were things that chafed and made friction and just as bad days. No, it is better for all of us that she go, but it is such a wrench.

Sometimes—it is so strange—her sensitivity makes her saintlike and sometimes it sets the whole household by the ear! It has been tense all day, but she has been very brave, saying good night quietly to Jon, putting Land to bed as usual. I sent her a little note and a picture of Jon and told Miss H. to put it in her bag.

Then she kissed me good-by, her head tied up in a scarf, and went out into the night.

How strange it is—as C. said—how people go out of your life. She walks out into the night, and she is gone for good. Someone who was part of our family, our family life, who loved Jon, who saw me nurse Land, the new baby. I may find someone again as competent and I hope more adaptable, but I shall never, in certain ways, meet again such sensitivity and understanding for myself and my children, in a nurse.

Over to see Mme Carrel in afternoon. She looks badly. She has cables from Dr. Carrel about us and our "plans" to go to Germany, and the very disagreeable press about us in America.

Plan out Jon's work for three days.

Tuesday, November 29th

A long day with the children. All goes well, but no time to pack. Savina and Nola come in the afternoon (Nola, like Mrs. Tittlemouse, in a tiny fur coat). That is nice, and I wanted to see Savina before I left about plans for the house.

The day is so beautiful—I must go up on the rock and see it—crystal clear and sharp and rather cold but sunny. You can see the spray on the Sept-Îles. It is like Maine today. And for some reason I do not feel harried or pressed but just happy, as though it were almost the first time all summer I had stopped to enjoy the beauty of the island. Not much wind but a constant roaring of the surf. And the distant points and islands blue as the Camden Hills!

I feel free and happy. Perhaps because there is no one in the house now who does not like the island.

Wednesday, November 30th

A high wind blowing all night and this morning dark and wintry. The day flies, taking care of the children.

Hardly start packing; get out my things and try to plan. How *can* I get it all done and take care of the children too?

Thursday, December 1st. Stormy and gray

A tearing wind, patches of sun, great waves and spray, and sun on the spray against a purple stormy sky.

I take care of the children and pack. Land cries all day. Mme Carrel comes for lunch. Jon's lesson as usual.

I get my trunk packed—or rather just add and subtract from it. I have never unpacked it since Long Barn!

C. and Mme Carrel talk to Louis and Maryvonne. I gather they are staying! The house is untidy with trunks, bags, clothes lying about. We decide we cannot get off till Saturday evening. I am very tired but relieved.

Friday, December 2nd

Stormy and cold. Pack and take care of the children all day. Trunks done at night and down in the hall; a tremendous number of bags. Land's blanket and diapers take up so much room. Only the last odds and ends and the house to put away tomorrow; very tired in the back.

Packing is chiefly *planning*—if it is *planned* in your head the rest is easy.

Saturday, December 3rd

The cart comes for us after supper. I wake Land and dress him, stuff in last things (still drying bedclothes, napkins, etc.). He is bewildered but good, except when I give him to C. while I climb into the high cart. Good-by to Maryvonne, Louis and Kerleau, P'tit Louis, and the girls in the lighted door and poor Thor inside. Jon beside me in his town coat and huge hat. Land clinging to me in his fuzzy Eskimo suit. We start off, rocking over stones and bumps. A still night for once—a mackerel sky with white clouds softly lit by a three-quarter moon shining on the flats. The rumble of the cart, the creak, and Land quite happy and secure now, his head on my chest. Sometimes he half chants in unison to the rhythm. All the rocks show in the half-light and the water gleams: one of our strange exits, our good-by to the island.

We meet Keraudren at the store (nice clip-clop of horses' feet through the quiet street of Buguélès). We get into Keraudren's *camionette,* closed in, dark, narrow seats, and bump to Plouaret, Jon asking lots of questions, in his sleepy, big-eyed tiredness.

Long wait in the car at Plouaret. Onto the train, a rush with the bags. Into our rooms. Land is perfectly happy and quite dry! I tuck him into the lower berth wide-eyed and get in on top. (Jon goes into a *couchette* with Miss H.)

Don't sleep much but rest, satisfied. We got off all right without any great rush or panic. And I am quite encouraged, somehow, that I *could do it!*

Sunday, December 4th

Get Land changed, dressed, and things packed just as we draw into Paris station.

The apartment looks clean and bright. The Swiss nurse is there, but Land won't go to her. I give him some orange juice and a rusk. Jon, Miss H., and I eat a very good breakfast:

brioches, coffee, etc. I feel the house, Germaine and Alfred, the décor etc. are all too refined (for me) after Illiec and even Long Barn. I feel like an explorer gone native, back from Tahiti.

Land is quite good as long as I have him but will not go to the nurse alone, at least when I am there. The worst is at night, when I leave him purposely and he shrieks in anger at the newness of everything.

I take Jon for a walk in the Bois. Jon is not very taken with it. He does not like wearing a town coat or a hat. "A park isn't much fun really, is it?" He is taken aback by the places he is not allowed to go, the fenced-in areas. He says, "There are too many people in this park." However, we work into a slightly wilder part where he finds some dead trees—which there is no hope of our taking home—and some rattly pods. He comes back feeling slightly cheered and saying the park is the nicest place in Paris.

Germaine cooks simple food but very well. Miss H. and I move furniture, taking care that the *distingué* Alfred does not catch us at it.

Dropping with sleep at night. Much to do tomorrow.

Monday, December 5th

C. arrives early, for breakfast. After breakfast I start calling the Bureau about another maid. Then I get Jon and the baby and the nurse started in the carriage for the park.

Tuesday, December 6th

Germaine and Alfred are *exhausted* by the work. I can't see why, exactly. The nurse does her bedroom and Land's. That leaves three bedrooms and three other rooms, all very simply furnished. We have very simple food and there is no valeting or maiding.

They complain terribly of their rooms, which are too hot, and say they have not slept for four nights. Germaine says that she is going mad in the kitchen with all the things to think of and that she could not last out the month as cook (though she came as that). I say I am sorry but I can't help the rooms and I am getting a cook as quickly as possible.

I see two cooks and take one.

The [London] *Times* comes with two pages of Christmas Books. I am childishly hurt when I do not find *Listen! the Wind* in the Travel section (or at *all*), when there are all sorts of books like Byrd's *Alone* and Ellsworth's book, which have not had as good reviews or sold as well in America as *Listen! the Wind*. What a foolish vanity.

After lunch I go to see a school. I like the Directrice very much. The school has a big garden. They have lots of handwork, music, and games, unlike most French schools. There are several English children in Jon's class and the teacher speaks English.

I walk back much satisfied. Tomorrow I take Jon to the doctor, see the school functioning, fit my fur coat, see that Jon has his hair cut (he does look neglected with that mop) and a pair of new shoes for school. Also, tomorrow the cook comes. Germaine and Alfred are calmer tonight, perhaps because of this.

But I am tired of being practical. It will be a relief just to sit in Despiau's quiet studio all morning and do nothing but think.

Wednesday, December 7th

Cold, raw, and damp. The cook arrives as I rush off to see the school and then Despiau. Germaine much shocked that I can't wait to give the orders. The school is nice and quiet, a young girl teaching; calm and intelligent work, not as far advanced as Jon but, of course, in French.

To Despiau. He is rather withered and unhappy and his eyes hurt. He says he feels better after he works a little. I enjoy the calm and sit and think about Elisabeth.

After Despiau, to the fur-coat place, to try on a coat, pretty and deliciously warm.

The Crillon and Place de la Concorde *bristling* with guards for Ribbentrop.[1]

At 2:30 go to Dr. Lestoquoy with Jon—a quick, sharp, young

---

[1] Joachim von Ribbentrop, German diplomat, Ambassador to Great Britain (1936–38), Minister of Foreign Affairs for the Nazi Government (1938–45).

observant doctor. Jon is (by English standards) the height of a child of eight and the weight of one of six and a half. Jon has a thorough examination.

Then to Fouchet's for a chocolate bar and by taxi to the school. (I wanted him to *see* the school before he goes.)

Out to dinner with M. Monnet; his father and sister are there. A wonderful old man—gay, quick, full of love of life and humor. Much joking between him and Jean. Jean is very proud of him. I like him for it. He is always mysterious, though, in a quiet and completely orthodox way. Interrupted by telephone calls, having to leave for England or America on something frightfully important, but no one having the slightest idea what he is doing.

It was a nice evening. He was not the man of the world tonight but only a simple, devoted, charming, admiring son.

Delicious meal and much French talk about it.

Thursday, December 8th

Off early to Despiau. Leave C. with Jon. Feel very tired. Despiau, however, in his battered hat, feels slightly better today, though he says he is in a bad nervous depression. He works on the mouth and chin and is quite satisfied. He had lost something and then found it again. He says philosophically, *"Il faut perdre pour retrouver."* I think this is comforting and true. Also his saying that three minutes of lucid vision in a day is all you can hope for—in fact, is wonderful.

He keeps saying that the likeness, the expression is the last thing to come—you must let it come by itself and be patient.

All this is very true and helpful of writing and of living. A nice quiet time thinking.

Give Jon a reading lesson.

Friday, December 9th

To Despiau in the morning. He did not sleep at all last night, as usual. I stare at my telephone number, which he has scribbled upon the dirty wall along with the enigmatic others. He says my nose is something *très particulier!* I fear it is. He says he has never met a woman yet who didn't say she did not like her nose.

Home for lunch. After lunch Jon and I go off by bus to Jones's department store. Jon is a bit dazed by the new experience: a city, shops, sights in windows. He stops at almost every store window, pointing to hideous but gay polka-dot cocktail glasses and saying, "Look, Mother, isn't that *pretty!*"

Saturday, December 10th

Despiau at 9:30. He again has not slept and looks pretty seedy. He finds my hair difficult, better smoothed back. He works on my mouth and eyes. The eyes are difficult too, he says, because they are *très foncés mais en même temps très clairs*.

He does not want to see me again until Wednesday. Like that, he will have a little repose, he says.

In the afternoon C. and I walk down Avenue Victor Hugo, in the drizzle, and look at scooters for Jon, at Jones's (marvelous place). We get quite a good red one which we bring back by taxi. And then take Jon out with it to try. He smiles his slow shy smile when he sees it. We got out into the wet dark street of the Bois. Jon is very earnest at first but quite typically is not content simply to push the ground with one foot but wants to push the extra pedal as well. In other words, wants to do it all perfectly *at once*. Has some trouble balancing but on the whole does quite well for a start.

Mail from home, including another letter from Dr. Carrel, very much upset by the insidious "campaign" directed against C. in the United States, sending us an article in *The New Yorker* to illustrate this attitude. The story is that we are going to live in Germany in a house of an evicted Jew.[1]

The press have of course used this situation to the best (or

[1] In answer to Dr. Carrel's letter, C. A. L. replied that his decision to take an apartment in Paris was not based on the reaction of the press but he simply did "not want to make a move which would seem to support the German actions in regard to the Jews." (Lindbergh to Carrel, Nov. 28, 1938, Lindbergh papers.)

worst, rather) advantage. I hate to have such unfair labeling going on and have a body of hatred building up against C. for something that is not true. He is not and never has been anti-Semitic. C. is marvelously untouched by all this. Their scorn does not touch him any more than their praise once did.

Only, I think, if he felt he had betrayed his own integrity would he mind.

Femininely, I mind the injustice of it.

Sunday, December 11th

Soeur Lisi arrives, in her black robes, but smiling. We all troop out into the park. Land in his blue ski-suit in the carriage, Soeur Lisi in her black robes, Jon with his new red *trottinette,* and C. and I behind. Soeur Lisi no sooner gets into the park but she meets another long-robed "Sister"!

They go off together, while C. and I go off for a walk. It is a delicious day, sunny and mild. We go through damp woods and watch people ride horseback. What a help to get out. How different from a Sunday in London.

Soeur Lisi has a fine idea—to give Land his high chair (put down so it runs on eight wheels) to walk with. Land, delighted, pushes it up and down the hall, walking firmly behind. Jon steers it.

Jon on God. I try to explain very generally and broadly that the world is so beautiful and wonderful that people think *someone* must have planned it.

"Oh no," said Jon, gravely correcting me, "it is much too big for one person to make."

Land seems happy with Soeur Lisi. He takes his first step alone—to me. He says "Hello" (Hey-oh) delightedly when I come into the room; also "Up! Up!"

11 bis Avenue Maréchal Maunoury, Paris 16ᵉ, December 11th

Mother darling,

We have been one week in Paris today.

Dr. Carrel and Mrs. S. have written us several times about the widespread "campaign" against C. in the United States. C. hissed in the movie theaters, name taken off the *Lindbergh Line,* and Jewish booksellers boycotting my book, etc.

This does distress me as I feel it is unfair labeling due to a series of circumstances, inaccurately reported, with a large amount of malicious gossip on top. The press, I feel, is responsible (the stories that we could easily get a house in Berlin from some evicted Jew) plus, of course, the naturally oversensitive Jews. But it is too bad, all the way round. C. is not and never has been antisemitic.

I am hoping this may somewhat abate when they find we have taken an apartment in Paris. But perhaps not. The ball of rumor and criticism, once it starts rolling, is difficult to stop. I suppose one should (like C.) not weigh much the popularity of press or mob but simply stand by what you've done (and believe is right) and hope your friends understand, somehow.

DIARY   *Monday, December 12th. Gray drizzle*
Jon and I walk to school. Jon is delighted because we pass over a railroad track or open subway just as two cars are going through. Jon does not seem upset by his new environment, though he cannot understand the teacher in French. Smiles good-by at me and another lovely smile, when he sees me come for him, through the window.

I take a bus down Avenue Victor Hugo for a fitting on my blouse (how French! Think of having a *fitting* on a blouse!) and order a little black "tailleur," dressy enough for a tea but simple and smart enough for a lunch.

Lauwick[1] calls. The story is out, we are in Paris.

Tuesday, December 13th
The somewhat disturbed morning is due to headlines in the papers that we are in Paris, and the ensuing sense of no longer

[1] Hervé Lauwick, French writer and translator of *North to the Orient.*

being private. However, they do not give our address and the articles all say they wish to leave us alone, and there have been no reporters at the house and no trouble (which would inevitably have followed in America).

Lunch with M. and Mme La Chambre. Charming house, with an old family air, old furniture, bibelots, portraits, china, etc. Mme La Chambre is Spanish and evidently was a great charmer. I enjoyed talking with her even though it had to be in French.

He is very keen, sensitive, intelligent, and interesting. You must keep on your toes intellectually to talk with him.

C. and I go off much stimulated and walk (partway) to Place Vendôme, where I window-shop for Christmas presents (Rue Saint-Honoré) and arrange to get a muff to go with the tailleur and the coat.

Back to apartment, just in time to pick up C. and go to Mme Blériot's.[1] A lovely big apartment right on the river in grand old style; a house too big for her now. It all reminds me a little of the atmosphere of Englewood—a "ripe" family and life. Mme Blériot strikes me as a courageous, big woman. She has thrown herself into work committees after her husband's death. We meet two daughters and a son.

Back to apartment. Give Jon supper and put Land and Jon to bed. Dress and go to Du Noüys'. They both look better and it is rather fun. He is always delightful. She, although interesting and intelligent, strikes me as restless. All her colors too . . . She had on an Indian costume, black skirt banded with turquoise blue, orange blouse, turquoise jewels (Indian). The house, modern, is done in browns and orange. Tiger lilies are the flowers and there was a glass tiger on the table.

A nice evening. A long and full day, very stimulating and hard work, talking French. At night a half-asleep mind talks French to itself, runs to catch taxis, etc.

[1] Widow of Louis Blériot, French engineer and pioneer aviator, first to fly the English Channel in a heavier-than-air machine 1909.

Jon, Soeur Lisi, Land, and I to school. I to Despiau. He says he does not feel better but he works much better and is pleased with it. The profile somehow reminds me of Elisabeth.

After lunch I go to see pictures with Mrs. Chipman, her husband, and stepfather. It is great fun. We see an exhibit of flower paintings (Rue Matignon) of Utrillo, and Signac. I like some of them very much, also the watercolors of Signac and the smaller canvases of Utrillo.

I love hearing the discussions.

The Détroyats for supper. I have arranged mimosa and Christmas roses (separately). It looks very nice. Alfred is in a grave displeasure. There are not enough knives and forks for a *service américain*. He will have to have half *service américain* and half *service français!* However, it goes well and supper is quite good. Also the wine.

To Despiau. Although he looks as shattered as usual he works well. He says some nice things about his work. The philosophy of it, really. *"Il faut reculer un peu pour aller plus loin."*

And speaks much of the need for patience in work, of those *séances blanches* in which nothing seems to be accomplished but in which something is prepared. Their value comes out only later. He says the difficulty in art is to have the utmost freedom in the middle of the greatest discipline; to balance the two, freedom and discipline.

"But that's all of life!" I say. Yes, he says, *"La vie,"* vaguely, not much interested.

Also he talks much of *les points* [in the planes of the head]— those points that he must fix, that he waits sometimes weeks because he cannot quite find their exact position.

Soeur Lisi is out for afternoon. I take Land and Jon to the Bois. Land climbs all over his carriage (strapped in) and Jon "scoots" ahead. He stops with a beatific smile on his face by a fallen-down dead tree. "What is it, Jon?" "This," says Jon, "makes me think of Illiec."

Friday, 16th

C. leaves for Berlin early.[1]

Saturday, December 17th. Very cold and clear

To Despiau in the morning. He works well and is pleased with the head (though he says again he has lost eight kilos in two months and feels exhausted).

Monday, December 19th. Bitter cold

Depressed all day by rumors and talk about C.'s situation in America: the whole of public opinion against him.

A letter from Mary Scandrett and Mr. Morgan. Ickes[2] strikes out against C. in a speech [before a Zionist meeting in Cleveland] for accepting a decoration from Germany. Anyone who does so forfeits his right to be American, etc. Ickes does not mention the fact that it was at *his* (United States) Embassy that C. was given the medal, at a dinner given by *his* Ambassador [Wilson] for Göring, or that the medal came without warning, or that two other people got one that same week—an Englishman and a Frenchman. (*Their* countries don't seem to have disinherited *them*.)

Tuesday, 20th. Still bitter cold—cutting

Go off to Despiau; talk to him about newspapers. He talks about Germany. He detests the Germans (very French) and talks with tears in his eyes about the Marne and gets very excited. Not a very good séance (after three good ones a *séance blanche*). He says they are necessary and *that no real effort is ever lost* though it does not always pay right away.

[1] C. A. L. went to Berlin on a secret mission for the French Government, which had asked him to negotiate the purchase of much-needed German engines for French planes.

[2] Harold L. Ickes, Secretary of the Interior 1933–46.

Rather a bad night. Jon coughs and talks (or moans in a strange way) in his sleep all night.

Wednesday, 21st. Snow over the ground!
Jon rather worn out. I take his temperature: 101.8. I try to call the doctor; not in until 1:30. Go out to Despiau, leaving Jon with Soeur Lisi and Miss H. to watch him.

Paris is superb under a fresh soft snow. I run through it to find a taxi. The river gray, and the streets white, the trees black—it looks like a Whistler etching. But all the little crooked streets look like Utrillos.

Despiau exhausted as usual. Does not (according to him) work very well.

Rush back to Jon afterwards. He seems a little better—temperature down slightly and coughs less. At 1:30 I call the doctor.

I go out in the park. There are children skiing, the lake is flat and white, frozen waterfalls and a white swan, gray against the spotless snow, huddled in the middle of the lake. Also a black swan who is startlingly beautiful today in contrast to the dirty white gray ones who usually are so beautiful against a green or brown world. Today the black is queen.

A nun in black and white robes running across the snow in her black-slippered feet!

Jon sleeps all afternoon. The doctor arrives at 5. Jon has slight bronchitis. Everything we have done so far for him excellent. I feel relieved.

Look for C. but the blueish haze of a snowy afternoon sets in early. Scan the papers for weather news and watch one plane above my head in the park.

11 bis Avenue Maréchal Maunoury, Paris, December 21st
Dear Mother,
As all possible mails have gone off, a first snow blankets Paris for Christmas, Jon is in bed with a cold (but sleeping peacefully this afternoon) and C. still away in Berlin, I take the chance to write

you about things I never seem to have time to say when I'm writing to catch the boat.

Before C. left he had a good letter from Aubrey about the Little School—also, earlier, one from Connie Chilton. It is quite thrilling to think of their really going ahead on plans.

I hope you are happy about it. I have thought a good deal about it lately (there is much time to think, sitting on the stool in Despiau's studio) whether it is a sound idea—making the school more permanent. And I look at it this way: Elisabeth had a spark of genius in regard to schools and the teaching of children. The test was whether this captured spark of genius could continue as a practical working concern. This, I think, we all feel it has done—in old buildings, crowded space, with not particularly well-paid teachers. This is a great triumph and seems to me due to Elisabeth's practical vision and sound foundations and to Connie Chilton's splendid taking hold of the reins—Connie and the people with and under her who have done a wonderful job.

Now it seems to me quite fair and just that the school should have its proper setting. It should have some new clothes, as in the fairy tales. It should be the best of its kind. That is our only excuse for supporting it. We believe it is enough better to warrant being held up as an example to other schools. And as such it should be given its proper housing and equipment.

I remember Dr. [Abraham] Flexner talking to C. and me about High Fields[1]—that we should not simply have another home or another hospital or clinic but that it should be *the* example of the best cardiac home for children in the United States or the best clinic, etc. And in that way the value of the undertaking would be increased manyfold.

Speaking of Dr. Flexner brings me to the Jewish problem and the letters I get every day—or news, in one form or another—telling of the widespread strong feeling against C. throughout the

[1] The Lindberghs had given their property near Hopewell to be used as a home for children. Abraham Flexner, educator and author, was one of the trustees.

country. It does of course disturb me as I feel C. has been labeled so unfairly due to a malicious campaign of the press who are using the Jewish issue to stir up hatred against him. However, I cannot start on this tonight as I shall be arguing with Mr. Ickes all night in my dreams.

Of course we are relatively free of talk about it here as no one in France or England cares what is happening in America, knows who Mr. Ickes is (or any name, except Roosevelt!), or has the slightest idea that C. is being criticized.

DIARY   *Thursday, December 22nd*
Jon still asleep when I go off to Despiau. He tells me, with rather gloomy satisfaction, that the doctor saw him yesterday and he must go away immediately. He seems really much better today and works very hard and well—changing much. He is pleased with it.

Jon is much better—temperature down a bit and coughs less; making paper chains all over his room.

C. is back! By train. We go out to dinner with the Jays and the Harlan Millers[1] at the Escargot restaurant. Delicious food and red wine. Snow on the ground and in the air—delicious outside, and Christmassy. I very happy, relieved that Jon is better and C. is home.

Sunday—Christmas Day, December 25th
Jon opens his stocking during breakfast sitting up in bed. Then I take Land's small blue sock, bulging with a music box, in to him. He sits on my knee smiling in amazement and pleasure as I turn the handle. When I stop he gives it to me to do again. Then C. gives him his nest of blocks—a marvelous toy.

C. and I go out for a walk and talk about the winter; decide to stay here.

---

[1] Harlan Miller, writer, columnist, and aviator; with U. S. Embassy under Herrick when C. A. L. landed in Paris 1927.

I put a small crêche on the table for lunch. Alfred is most supercilious about it, as he is about everything.

Jon has made calendars for everyone—including himself—with "From Jon" marked gravely on the back.

C. and I go out in the afternoon for a walk from Pont Neuf up to Notre Dame which I hoped to find open. It is stone-cold, shut!

Mme Carrel for supper. I put holly around and the mimosa, Land crawling after me (or pushing the *très moderne* glass and mirror tea table, walking) as I go back and forth.

The wood for the fireplace has not yet come, although ordered, so Alfred goes down and borrows some from the concierge! The concierge is a wonderful institution. You tip her when you come in and then she is an inexhaustible Mother Robinson's bag. The cook runs down to borrow silver and cooking utensils from her. She tells you where to get laundry done. She puts the carriage out for the baby in the morning and when you have run out of wood you can borrow it from her!

Monday, December 26th

Land has a cold and cough. Stays in bed. Temperature 101. C. and I out for walk in the morning in park. When I get back I find the baby's temperature is over 103 and he is very fretful and putting his hand to his ear all the time. I call Dr. Lestoquoy. I sit with Land, play the music box for him: *"Il pleut, il pleut, bergère,"* which puts him to sleep.

The doctor comes, says the baby has not got bronchitis but has tonsillitis and finds right ear "rosy" but not bad. He notices a swelling outside of ear, says it is probably nothing but would like to call an ear specialist. This seems strange to me, but C. says, "Is that what you advise?" And as the doctor says "Yes" we of course agree. In the middle of supper he calls back to say the specialist is coming at 9.

They hurry into Land's room and we wake him up. After the doctor (in fearful eye-piece and mask) has looked at Land's ear, he calls me into the bathroom and says it is not serious but that there is pus in the middle ear and it is best to lance the drum (of both ears). I call C. We are both rather shocked as Dr. L. had minimized it so before supper. They both insist—after our questions—that it will not impair hearing in any way and that mastoid or burst eardrum and impairment of hearing may result if it is left. So we reluctantly agree. They say they have a local anesthetic to give the baby rather than take the chance of a general anesthetic with such a young child.

I stay in the next room and listen to Land's screams and remember how I felt having a baby: pain, terrible pain, imprisoned in it, and nobody understanding and nobody trying (so it seems) to help you, all holding you there in it. And though I cannot bear to hear him scream it is somehow borne deep deep inside, as though in a place estranged from me.

After an age—fifteen minutes—he comes back, his head all bandaged up as the pictures of me as a child with mastoid. But he stops crying very quickly in his crib with one hand around my little finger.

Dr. L. tells me afterward that he knew (before supper) when he saw the swelling that the doctor would have to lance it but that he *did not want to tell me for fear of worrying me!*

In consequence he worried me much more, for with one doctor telling me it was nothing and the other doctor saying it was necessary to lance immediately I felt they were both quacks. I felt, like a primitive mother, that they had taken my perfectly well child and made a sick one out of him. Though of course that is foolish, as a child in pain and with a fever of almost 104 is not well. Only it has been so sudden—yesterday he was all right, just a little cold.

C. said it reminded him (the speed of change) of an airplane crash: everything going along fine and then suddenly there is the plane broken up on the ground.

We go out, after the doctors leave, and walk in the new-fallen snow to calm ourselves—or me, at least.

Land slept well and the fever is less. He looks much better. Dr. S. comes and dresses the ear. Land screams a good deal and struggles as I hold him.

Afterwards I go out for a walk with C. Jon is up today and plays with his toys on floor.

Out to lunch. The Harlan Millers are there. I like them. He is not a conventional person at all and *thinks*. He reminds me of Robert Frost in a strange way. He is an eccentric with humility, vision, humor, and some poetry (I suspect). She is an artist and a kind and seeing woman.

Also Alexander Kirk is there, looking rather seedy. *So* nice to talk to him. It heartens me greatly. There he is—someone who is keeping alive inside of him his own strictly private spark of integrity, with all the odds against him.

I tell him he is like a Chartreuse monk.

"Without the mysticism," he says.

"No . . . I'm not sure."

"Well, without the Chartreuse."

Back to the house. Dr. L. has been there and says the right ear is full of pus but no tendency to mastoid.

Dr. L. comes again after supper. Says progress is normal but temperature will remain high while there is so much pus.

Read *Adventure of Ideas* [A. N. Whitehead] at night.

Mme. Carrel for lunch. She says she knows Dr. S. (the ear specialist) well and he is excellent and that we did quite right in having Land's ears pierced immediately.

Land does not keep anything down today—coughs and then throws up everything.

1939

Dr. L. came tonight to see Land. All going well—only Land pulls the cotton out of his ears and eats it!

Go for Jon and we walk down Avenue Victor Hugo. In one drugstore Jon is given a hydrogen balloon. He carries it carefully home, pulling at the leash in the air above him.

After lunch Jon, C., and I go up the Eiffel Tower. Jon goes to the far corner of the platform and watches the trains going over the bridges, over the sunset-lit Seine far below us.

Sixteen trains!

Tea at home with Land. Land is very fretful, but he has no cold left. I think it is his teeth. I am worn out putting him to bed, by his continuous fretful cry.

Jon goes to bed happy. "What a day!" I say. "Yes," smiles Jon. "Sixteen trains and a balloon!"

To Despiau's this morning at 9:30. He looks better but says he has had *"un voyage assez pénible."* However, he says he has got back his appetite and has determined to stop smoking. I meet his wife (didn't know he had one!), an eagle-eyed woman and rather worn. I feel better about him. I thought there was no one looking after him. But what a man to be married to!

He has a very bad morning of work and cannot get it at all, and is *"désolé";* he says the thing he wants is only a tiny little thing but he cannot find it. C. and I think the face is too tapered (which we don't tell him, of course).

He has not accentuated the point of the jaw which squares my face a little. Also there is something wrong with the nose. I think it isn't *retroussé* enough.

He says he doesn't want a photograph but he wants it *évocateur*.

We go away rather discouraged.

C. and I take a taxi to Rue des Saints-Pères and walk up and down it and Rue Bonaparte looking at shop windows (antiques and pictures). We go into Galerie Zak and look at an exhibit of various moderns. A lovely Vlaminck, a snow scene with lowering purplish blue clouds: 17,000 francs (about $200). An olive grove landscape by Stravinsky (son of the composer), 1200 francs, and a landscape watercolor by Dagoussia which we liked and asked the price of and found to be *250 francs* because the artist is very poor and ill and needs the money badly. We buy it and she says it will give him great pleasure and she will take the money right away to him.

There are several Utrillos upstairs and another large Vlaminck.

We carry off the picture, feeling very pleased, and wander down Rue Bonaparte to the Seine and along the shops there. Then we go home, having had more fun than we've had for a long time. It was discovery—discovery of Paris by ourselves and the kind of thing we never could have done anywhere else in the world. In London there is no such art quarter and in New York we would not be private individuals.

We are much pleased with the picture, which we put in the bare place on C.'s bureau. It has a nice quality of light and shadow—qualities of greens in trees and the movement of trees, too.

To have my hair done in the afternoon. It is a lovely clear sunny afternoon. At 4:30 when I come out it is still beautiful—a deep blue evening, just a slight haze over everything: the trees in the Étoile and down Avenue Kléber, the Arc, the lights. I walk home. It is delicious. The air is slightly thickened as if one had managed to walk into blueness that usually surrounds only distance.

Tea with Jon and C. Play with Land with a bird off the Christmas tree that wiggles on springy feet. Land is delighted. He has a nice sense of humor and enjoyment.

Saturday, January 7th

It comes out in the paper that C. has sent reports on German aviation to the U. S. Government, urging a big rearmament. Some private letters have got out, much garbled.

Everything gets to the press at home.

Now the press has C. on *both* sides of the same fence at once: pro-Nazi—anti-Nazi!

Out to supper with the Harlan Millers. A charming low house in a quiet street, beautifully decorated, and lots of modern paintings. Collecting is their hobby.

We talk and look at all their modern pictures: lots of Vlaminck, an Utrillo, Jean Dufy, Othon Friesz, a Renoir watercolor, a Degas drawing. A lovely little watercolor, in tones of gray (of a Brittany *pardon*), by Boudin, was almost my favorite.

We also talk politics. We come down to the conclusion that eugenics, birth control, etc., is the only thing that can save our civilization—but no one can suggest how it can be brought about.

Miss H. sends a telegram: is not coming tonight as her brother ill and *quarantined for Infantile*.

Sunday, January 8th

The Rublees for tea. What a comfortable person he is. He has a hopeless job.[1] We hear the worst of the Jewish situation. C. and Mr. Rublee will be in Berlin at the same time and C. will introduce him to Truman. Perhaps C. can do something to help.

[1] George Rublee was on his way to Berlin for talks with German government officials seeking moderation of the German attitude to the Jewish population. See note p. 348.

The du Noüys come for supper. Quite an exciting evening. He talks science, or rather putting science into its proper place in life. Some thrilling sentences: "Everything to do with science is *quantitative,* never *qualitative.*" "In science, in matter, one goes on the assumption that everything is equally *probable.* Whereas in life everything goes to show that what happens is highly *improbable.* For two thousand years some people have called this improbability 'God.'"

Also on the breaking down of the Darwinian theory of *progress.* I hope it is all down in his book[1] so I can read it again.

Monday, January 9th

We have got the apartment for three months more!

How will the white-satin sofa hold out? And the green-chartreuse curtains and the white-satin and gold draperies in our bedroom? And the carpet in Jon's room? And the china?

Jon has the papers, paste, boxes, crayons all over the floor as usual. And to my chagrin I find water spilled from the paste jar in the *grooves of the sliding cupboard doors!* I get very angry and scold him about the value of things and this not being our house and that he has spoiled something that is *not ours* and we will have to pay for.

How *does* he do it—how *does* he get chocolate over his lampshade?!

I try to mop up the water with handkerchiefs and scrub the finger marks (pasty and Vicksy) off the white wood doors, but it is caught down under the sliding grooves and will rust there.

Jon is limp and miserable but forgets all about it as soon as I assume a cheerful voice again.

Jon's cold *seems* arrested for the moment, what with the inhalations, drops, pills, and medicine. But he is pale and listless. I give him glucose, which seems to help.

[1] *Human Destiny* by Lecomte du Noüy.

In the afternoon C. and I take Jon to the Jardin d'Acclimatation. Jon is quite impressed by the lions, intrigued by the seals and little monkeys and the bright birds. But the crowning touch was that we rode out of the park on a little train, like a toy train, to Porte Maillot. Jon was so pleased that he didn't even smile. He sat up, bolt-still with excitement, on the front seat with me, looking at everything as we rattled through the park and the man clanged the bell.

C. reading *Aladdin* to Jon at the end of his supper; he gets Jon to rub his lamp (electric lantern) and C. comes as a jinni from behind the bathroom door: "What is your desire?"

Jon: "Bring me my mother!"

Which C. immediately did, picking me up from my desk and setting me down in front of Jon, to his great delight.

Saturday, January 14th

I to Despiau. C. meets me there. He feels the head is completely changed and very lovely—strange, as he has done very little to it lately. Despiau is pleased, says it is *très évocateur*. He is going to put it into plaster Monday.

C. and I go on to the Cluny Museum—musty and medieval. Great charm. Beautiful tapestries on the walls. You walk into the Middle Ages—their lives, their clothes, their flowers, their pets, and even their gestures.

Also some lovely wood carvings, a St. Barbara and an Annunciation.

I read Elisabeth's letters and try to think about how I can write about her. They are gay, lovely, warm, and young and I feel only hopelessly out in the cold after reading them. How far away I am from her, how hopeless to try to recapture her, and how terribly I miss her. That great aching hole there that is my missing her—that deadness in my life.

That is the personal side, but aside from that I have a strange feeling of looking back into youth, into another age and a more golden one. For in spite of personal sorrows and worries, the world was not so heavy then, not so old and worn and tired as it is now, not so overwhelmed by this terrible threat of war, hate, and *despair*.

Is it only because I am older or because I am living in Europe and looking (in the letters) at America, or is the world in the pit that it now seems?

I feel heavy with grief, personal and general, tonight. I wonder if people at the end of the Roman Empire felt like this—not knowing what was coming, waiting for the storm.

Sunday, January 15th

Land never having taken a step alone on his own initiative suddenly stands up and walks alone today—walks right out of his room and down the hall! After that, he staggers around all day, drunk with his new power.

Savina appears at our door, much to Alfred's surprise. It is like a breath of fresh Illiec air in stuffy Paris.

C., Jon, and I out for a walk in the Bois, Jon on his scooter. It is a blowy March day. C. and I talk gloomily about the decisions that have got to be made in the world. What will happen to Europe, to the United States? What to do?

C. packs up and leaves for Berlin after tea.

Wednesday, January 18th

After lunch I go down and try to find a black dress—a very pretty one pictured in *Vogue* at Robert Piguet. After passing the door three times I finally go in and ask about it. Up marble stairs into a room done in cherry satin and blue with blue hyacinths the exact shade in flower pots—terribly swell.

I try not to show how scared I feel.

Several women come in dressed to the teeth. Models come in and parade around. A leisurely air of a sanctuary (a clothes sanctuary), a world in which nothing matters except clothes. All the priestesses of the cult hover about.

I want to know the price of the dress (which is a business—you have to see all the dresses first and then wait a long time while they go out and consult a book and then come back and give it to you from the notebook, as though it had just been decided upon after consultation, which it probably was!) and finally get it.

It is very expensive but not fabulous. It would be if the franc were not so low. How do people get *all* their clothes from a place like this?

I say I will try on the dress Friday (if I have courage enough to go back!).

Go out and walk to Aux Trois Quartiers for dishcloths at the white sale—*torchons de cuisine* (what a comedown!)—and look for sweaters for Jon.

Home for tea.

C. comes in unexpectedly, loaded with coat, brown bundles, the paraphernalia of flying, looking blown and outdoors—lovely surprise. The house comes to life; bustle, excitement, and purpose again. Evidently a very successful visit, though short. Among other things he introduced Mr. Rublee to Merkel, whom he liked (of course he would), and he talked about Mr. Rublee to several people [Udet and Milch]. I do hope it helps. Mr. Rublee has a difficult task. I feel happy and proud of C.

Thursday, January 19th

To Despiau. The head in plaster. Despiau has the radio on—very irritated at Wagner—and says passionately, "I hate him because he is a Prussian and I am a Frenchman!" and "I feel the pointed helmet in everything he does." He gets very worked up and almost cries.

Lovely Beethoven: Fourth Symphony. I must hear more.

C. comes for me, we walk to galleries. Some Vlaminck flowers and a Derain head were the best things we saw. Home for lunch.

Jon has done his homework by himself on his own initiative without Soeur Lisi telling him. It is so easy to let it go until I come home, letting my lateness be an excuse for putting it off. But he just sat down and did it. I am very proud and tell him so.

Jon made a little garden of two pine branches in a box that is very decorative. He put it on the dining-room table as a surprise for me, but Alfred disapproved and put it on the mantel.

C. gets Jon to bed.

Mrs. Hand and Louis Dow[1] for supper. Such a heartening evening.

It is wonderful to talk to people who are still moderates. She talks to me about the archaic Greek things in the Louvre, about things she has been reading. I show her the picture of the Naumburg *Uta*. Very stimulating. I feel as always after talking to her how rich the world is—the world of culture. One must still believe in it and draw from it what joy there is in it.

A nice letter from Lady Astor, who wants us to come to England in February and stay with them.

Friday, January 20th

Talk to Soeur Lisi about leaving the children with her. Call Despiau. Go to have my hair done and try on a black cloth coat at Caroline's with velvet collar and cuffs for winter and spring, very inexpensive—$31.

No one in Paris ever wears rubbers (in the snow they wear high boots). They all look at mine in astonishment. And yet the streets and sidewalks are *always* wet. It rains a lot and the streets never get really dry, as the weather, even if clear, is too damp.

Have they got wet feet all the time?

Nothing is so damaging to the shoes or one's disposition as perpetually wet feet.

After lunch I put on my Paris suit, which is too tight around the hips but the *only* smart thing I have, a blue blouse and hat with the blue feather, and set out for Piguet's. For a while I sit alone in the room with the cerise-satin sofas and the periwinkle-satin chairs (on painted pale green legs) with white walls and valentine trimmings on the doors and windows.

Then a rich woman—fat, powdered, and veiled—comes in with

[1] Friend of the Hands and Morrows, professor of Romance languages at Dartmouth.

her spoiled daughter in an astrakhan suit—gold hair up under a ribboned hat.

They are brought a sketch M. Piguet has just drawn for a dress for the daughter. She looks at it critically and then complains that it is *ordinaire* and has no distinction. Then she shows her mother the wool dress I saw the other day (which I think is about 2700 francs) for ordinary occasions, a simple little dress, and they agree it will do quite well for her, though not of course for anything more than a simple day dress!

Then my dress comes in. From the way everyone recognizes it, I gather it has had a *succès fou,* which means everyone will either have it or a copy of it.

However, I try it on and order it. I gather from the glance the powdered Mama gave me that I do not look too badly (in my suit, hat, etc.), except for my umbrella. No one in their class ever carries an umbrella because of course they never walk in the rain. In rain they travel in limousines, to hotels or grand shops, and the chauffeur or doorman has an umbrella to guide them from car to door!

But going down the carpeted, mirrored stairs I catch a glimpse of myself in the mirror. It is no use; even at my best, I always look like a little girl—a nice little girl sometimes—but I will *never* be smart!

Home for tea with Land and Jon, Land in his rocking horse, Jon on the chair next to me. Land always says *au 'voir* to C. whenever he comes into the room. Whether because he *wants* him to leave, or because C. is always leaving, I don't know.

Telegram from Mother. Margot has a fine boy[1]—both doing well! I feel moved and excited. I pray all goes well. Dear Margot and Mother. Mother must be so relieved and happy.

I think of Elisabeth and wish I could share it with her—how happy she would be. I wonder about the miracle of that new life. Is there some of Elisabeth in that little boy?

Write Mother and pack. C. reads to Jon. Out to post letters after supper.

[1] Stephen Morrow, born to Margot and Dwight Morrow.

To bed early. There is a "deep depression to the west of Ireland" as usual. Will we be able to go tomorrow?[1]

Saturday, January 21st

Up and look out the window to a dark Mitteleuropa sky and drizzle. Dress in all my warm underwear in case we can go. Spend most of the early morning telephoning weather bureaus, "météo," for weather to London. It is very bad, and will be bad all day, and the general conditions are bad! We cannot go. I take off all the woolen underwear and redress, order meals.

Then C. and I go out to see the Conciergerie. It is pouring a dark chill rain by now. What a day to look at a prison and Marie Antoinette's cell. Brrr.

However, there is quite a beautiful old hall (like the Hall of the Knights at Mont-Saint-Michel, although darker) and an old kitchen of St. Louis. And then all the cells and last relics of Marie Antoinette: her chair, napkin, crucifix, and pictures of her saying good-by to her daughter (what happened to her children?). The cell of the Girondists who voted against beheading the King and Queen. The guillotine knife.

It is a good thing, perhaps, to see those things to remind one how terribly savage and cruel people have been—and *can be*.

Then we look into an art gallery or two and buy a small plaque of St. Francis—chiefly I think because we liked the little craftsman and did not like taking his time for nothing.

Read *Can Chamberlain Save Britain?*

Sunday, January 22nd

Slightly better sky. I call the weather man. *"C'est faisable"* between *"deux rubans de pluie"* (or perhaps "regions" was what he said) if we go immediately, getting to London before 1 P.M.

Decide to go. Pack up, dress, start off in twenty minutes.

Motor out to Villacoublay—all quiet. Off at 10 or after. Fly

[1] The Lindberghs were going to England for talks with the U. S. Embassy staff and to renew the Certificate of Airworthiness for their plane.

over Versailles, low clouds but no fog till we hit the coast. Fog on the hills. C. goes around it. We get to Saint-Inglevert about 12:15. Flocks of sea gulls. "We'll herd them!" shouts back C. as we take off over them.

Out across the Channel. It is very beautiful, all overcast and gray, a dark strip of land curving out to sea (Cap Gris-Nez?) behind us. A gray strip—storm, dark, on the gray sea. Gray clouds above. It is one of those times when one seems to feel the beauty and rhythm of nature and feels a part of it. Today I could see like a painter—almost. I saw with my *hands*. I *felt* the roll of the gray clouds, the swirling circles tumbled one on another in the sky, and underneath the answering shadow of the cloud on the gray sea. The color of the shadow was deeper than the color of the underside of the cloud—a wash of stormy blues and grays (Vlaminck blues). The rhythm to it, the sweep of it, was exciting. And we were a part of it.

I suppose this is the way C. feels in a storm and fog (a *real* one). I cannot feel that way when I am afraid. But today I felt it a little.

It is strange that aviation, the newest and most modern of activities, should bring one back into close contact with the elements again. Cradled in them . . .

And then flying over to England I felt I was seeing it more clearly too. The weather was very English—that inside-a-glass-bottle day. The color, too, of the chalk cliffs, grayed by the rain, the curve of the coast, and more than anything the lines of dirty black tankers—little ones, far below us. *That's* England, I felt at that moment, those tubby little tankers, radiating out, chugging back.

I had read about it before, of course, but seeing it was suddenly different, like *seeing* one of those abstract names like *Trade* or *Economics*. You do not get this impression at a big port like Liverpool because you are down in it and only see just around you. But high up from the air it was like seeing a map with the trade routes marked out on it—a map come to life, with the gray-white cliffs of England, the gray shores, the choppy gray sea, and those tiny black freighters far below us, slowly and painfully going out and coming back.

It gets worse as we go on—thick and dark. It always takes longer than I think and I always think we're lost. Land at Reading in the rain. No one there. Taxi to the station. The dingy brick suburban houses, the iron fences, the Bovril signs, the buses—and those dreary, dreary-looking people in mackintoshes.

Train to London. Decrepit old taxis in the station—everything the same. Is that what gives one the *impression* of stability in England? In a world of change, material things that remain the same give one the *illusion* of security. But they do not, of course, mean security.

Going past Hyde Park I am struck again, with whatever I may feel about English people, how I love their country. The trees are so beautiful—the trees and the countryside are the only things in England that give you a feeling of ecstasy.

Start telephoning people. Everyone is away. Here C. and I are again, alone and bored in London on a wet Sunday.

Monday, January 23rd

C. to see Colonel Lee.

A dreadful article in a small American magazine about C. All based on lies, written by a reporter (one of the brand that says the newspapers "made" Lindbergh). It is insidious and vitriolic, speaks of "treasonable" conduct, betraying the trust of America, etc.

Will we ever be able to go back?

And yet, where else can we go?

(C. is at Reading on the plane.)

Tuesday, January 24th

Sunshine—a brief spell—between two troughs of bad weather.

Lunch alone at the hotel. Miss W. comes afterwards to see me. She brings me a bunch of violets and is quite touching, asking about the children. She has a job at the Norland Institute and says she does not think she could ever go into a private post again after leaving us. The average post is so solitary and bereft of the companionship she had with us. I think this life will be more suited to her; I hope so, for I feel sorry for her.

C. and I go afterward to see some galleries and modern paintings: a Brockhurst portrait, some English watercolors, and some nineteenth-century masters.

Back and dress for supper with the Lees.

Mrs. Lee's analysis of the American versus the English woman. The latter, although dull, is nearer to the fundamentals—children and home and husband. While the former has her eye on some half-baked superficial "culture" and is usually much less interesting than her simple and "uncultured" husband, to whom she thinks she is superior.

Colonel Lee on the British upper classes, so repressed emotionally, due in part to the English school system, which he says is really fairly recent (from Victoria). Before them, he says, were the English we understand and read and think about.

We talk about the contradiction that the Russians, who have no—or little—emotional control, could maintain such perfect discipline in the ballet.

He gives me a quotation from an autobiography of a Russian General that I like and that is very profound. The Russian, who now lives in England, said he could not understand the English saying and speaking of going out to "see something of life," to "find some life." We Russians, he said, always felt we *were* life.

Wednesday, January 25th

A dark day with great wet snowflakes coming down heavily and melting as soon as they hit the black streets. To the Athenaeum Club—tea with Thomas Jones and the Madariagas.[1] Madariaga is brilliant and impractical. He suggests France and England

[1] Salvador de Madariaga, scholar, author, diplomat, Spanish delegate to the League of Nations 1931–36.

getting together and laying Africa on the table for an even and fair distribution of the colonies, and then a new League. (No suggestions being made as to what Africa would say to being "laid on the table," or Germany to a new League.)

He believes completely in the League and its return.

C. and I go to the Chinese restaurant for supper (after hearing that the ferryboat train to Paris is full) and then to *The Good Earth*. Very well done. Luise Rainer is a great actress.

Thursday, January 26th

Pack up, and down to Victoria Station. *The Golden Arrow* is very crowded with well-dressed people off to Paris and the Continent. A photographer snaps us through the window. We wish we'd taken the night train. Arrive home about 6 to the misty streets of Paris. Very nice to be back; feel at home.

Jon has gathered mistletoe from fallen branches of trees in the park and put it through the house in vases. Much mail—chiefly "fan" about the book; another dreadful article about C. They are playing up that he is betraying the beliefs of his father.

C. tells me that his father was opposed to war with Germany (the great war) and that he was greatly criticized for it and called a traitor. Now the same thing is happening again, by an odd flick of chance.

A long letter (to C.) from Colonel Henry [Breckinridge][1] is the most depressing thing in the mail. He opposes C. at every point, saying he thinks the press of the U. S. A. is the best and most objective in the world (uncensored), that in general they were accurate, at least that they gave a general impression that is accurate—that the impression gathered from newspapers and from C.'s letter about his views was about the same! He could not say anything more qualified to hurt.

Land staggers into the dining room while we are at breakfast.

[1] Lawyer, Assistant Secretary of War (1913–16), for many years C. A. L.'s legal adviser and friend.

He says *"Bon jou'"* vaguely. His hair wispy and gold and untidy. Sturdy legs under the blue smock he's outgrowing.

Friday, January 27th

Barcelona has fallen. . . .

C. and I out for a walk. Talk about situation in America and where to live.

Sunday, January 29th

The *Times* says Franco has behaved with magnanimity in marching into Barcelona—with order, restraint, and no atrocities.

The *Herald Tribune* says the refugees are being bombed as they are caught north of Barcelona, unable to retreat and unable to get through to France.

It just depends on what paper you read.

Monday, January 30th

C. and I walk in the park and talk about general conditions. He says he thinks we have gained a great deal of wisdom from living in Europe. I say I sometimes feel that it has exiled us forever from either world. It has taught us that we have a youth for which there is no place in Europe, and it has given us a wisdom for which there is no place in America.

In the afternoon Jon and I go to look for a balloon (reward for second tooth out!) and shopping. Jon loves this. We take a bus to the Étoile. Just as we round the corner of the Muette station, near home, Jon stands up and shouts, "There's the balloon man!" There he was standing on the corner, under his swaying cloud of bright-colored balloons, almost on our doorstep. I could not get off the bus just after we'd bought our tickets for the Étoile, so we sailed past him and I told Jon we'd come back.

We went to Jones's and bought some high shoes for Jon—97 francs. "It costs much more than a balloon," said Jon.

Then we walked home, getting Jon some stringing beads and

some groceries. Just at the grocery shop we met the balloon man coming home. Joy!

We came home triumphant.

Read Fisher at night [H. A. L. Fisher's *History of Europe*].

11 bis Avenue Maréchal Maunoury, Paris, January 30th

Dear Mother,

What you say of Margot and Stephen [Morrow] is lovely. I can see her happiness. But I wish I could see her and the baby.

I am *very* touched about the degree from Amherst but I do not know yet about coming home. June is such a difficult time. C. may have to go back to the United States this winter and I am hesitating about going back with him. I want terribly to be with him, with all the criticism that is going around. I would like to be there if he is going to face a hissing mob at the dock.

On the other hand I hate to leave the children in Paris, with the world so troubled and no one knowing what may happen. I certainly cannot make *two* trips home this year, anyway. How hard it is to plan ahead six months.

We see nothing but critical letters although we have had quite a number of the other kind too, lately, defending C. and resenting the critical articles, talking about "treasonable" acts, when C. has always worked directly *with* and *for* the United States reporting to the representatives of the United States over here—the Embassies, etc. He takes the blame and they get the credit, when there is any.

I feel bitter about this sometimes. But C. says he would rather have them get the credit and stay in the background.

I read Jon *Snow White,* the other day. Jon was round-eyed, but asked at the end (a question that always came to my mind, too), "Why did the father marry that bad woman?"

"Well, Jon," I said, "I don't suppose he knew she was bad. I suppose he thought she was good like Snow White's mother, his first wife."

"Oh," said Jon, with a troubled look. "Is it hard to tell the difference?"

Then I laughed and told him, no, it wasn't hard and that he needn't worry, he would *always* know "the difference."

I hope he will, anyway!

DIARY   *January 31st*

To Despiau. He has refound the thing he lost—the rhythm of the cheek! *"Un rien! Quelque chose d'imperceptible!"* It must be subtle, he says, one must not emphasize it or press the point, only suggest it. *"Il ne faut pas insister."*

Hair done (for fitting!). Fitting at Piguet's. All the buyers are there to see the collection. In a kind of terror I go in, but there are no reporters.

To the De Kays'[1] for supper. The Shoemakers were there [U. S. Naval Attaché]. She is very nice; has adapted herself to life here but remained very American. She knew Elisabeth at Smith and said she had a wonderful scholastic mind (this seems odd to me—I had forgotten that). And then added, "She was so lovely-*looking*. I remember she always wore soft blues, blue sweaters and skirts and a little blue felt hat pulled over her fair hair."

It was so vivid. That memory preserved in her mind was like a jewel to me—a jewel from the past, embedded and preserved.

Friday, February 3rd

After lunch I go to Piguet's for my last fitting and stay to see some of the summer collection. Flaring skirts, nipped-in waists, little governessy *broderie anglaise* collars, cuffs . . . *and* petticoats!

The *vendeuse* has quite warmed up by the time I leave—is delighted she has served me and says I must come back.

I smile nicely and say Oh yes, I hope to, walking down the red-carpeted stairs, thinking I shall probably never come in there again. (Not that they were not nice or that the dress is not perfect, but only that spending that much time, attention, and money on clothes is a little stifling. How terrible to be one of

[1] Charles G. de Kay, naval officer and nephew of C. A. L.'s cousin Admiral Emory S. Land.

those women who *must* be perfectly dressed, always. Think what a departure from perfection would do to you—eat your soul out!)

C. meets me to say *four more* are coming for supper: the Rublees, Mrs. Hand, and Louis Dow. I am thrilled to have them, but if *only* we were alone. We will not be able to talk.

The evening does not go well, although the flowers looked well (dwarf hyacinths, blue and white, red and yellow ranunculi in a white bowl I arranged in a great hurry) and the dinner (good for Marie at the last minute) was delicious.

The young American couple come first (I hoped the Rublees would come so I could explain and we could talk a little). He is very nice, sincere, honest, quiet, and intelligent. But she is loud-voiced, without any social sense (the true nice kind) or apparently much intelligence. I could see C. tight-lipped at supper, doing his best. I had George Rublee and Louis Dow which was of course lovely. But after supper somehow that girl dominates and shatters the whole evening. She will not let the conversation go to anyone else. One cannot engage her in a quiet conversation by herself, though Mrs. Hand tried to do this. Mrs. Hand looked so white and frail, I thought, and the Rublees terribly tired. They looked squeezed out and faded from Germany, which depressed them very much, I gathered. I felt so sorry they had to spend another evening making conversation.

Finally—last blow—they all leave together. I call up later to make amends and get Mrs. Rublee, who thinks everything was perfectly lovely, and Mrs. Hand, who understands.

Sunday, February 5th

C. and I go for a long walk in the Bois. It is a lovely day—clear, not cold, and a delicious sun—with the smells of spring. The Bois on Sunday is superb. It is all of Paris. I felt part of something monumental today as I walked through it—a great slice of French life. Children on roller skates, whole families trailing around the lake, men talking politics, girls in high-heeled shoes with their beaux, fathers playing football with their little boys. Boy-scout troops in bright kerchiefs and brown uniforms, shouting and running through the trees. Baby carriages. Couples embracing, or being photographed hand in hand, men selling peanuts, streams of cars, crowds of people at certain points, women in their best clothes, strolling. And all in the mild sunlight and all pleasantly happy and enjoying it. Trailing home in the late afternoon are scooters, dragged children, baby carriages, new hats, high heels, men in overcoats.

Jon and Land play a game of hide-and-go-seek after tea, Jon hiding and calling to Land. Land staggering in, flushed and gay: "Where's Jon?" Much shouting and laughter. It is almost the first time they have really played together. Watching Jon's face is a great satisfaction—what it means to him to have Land. He says several times at supper, smiling, "Land can really play now. He isn't a baby any more."

Monday, February 6th

Out to lunch with the Harlan Millers. Mr. and Mrs. Lin Yutang, Jo Davidson.[1] It was a lovely lunch. Jo Davidson, with his great curly head and round brown child's eyes, his absolute goodness, frankness, and sense of life and vigor, is irresistible.

Lin Yutang is a young man, quiet with twinkling eyes and his nice intelligent wife. (C. and I had expected to meet a hoary philosopher!)

The Millers are kind, genial, and appreciative. I felt warmed by the atmosphere and expanded, a little drunk with the joy of communication.

We went afterward to Jo Davidson's studio and saw his watercolors and busts. They are perfect likenesses and sometimes caricatures, but are they inspired pieces of art? He says he is a historian in clay. I think this is very true and justifies his work.

Tuesday, February 7th

To Despiau. C. meets me there and says he thinks the bust perfectly beautiful. Despiau has worked for days now on the mouth. *"C'est un rien—c'est un soupçon."* He says his busts are

---

[1] American sculptor who lived in Paris.

known for their mouths. He says, *"Ça commence à être vivant—intérieurement."*

When we got back we found a note from MacArthur[1] with the list of the people at the dinner tonight at the American Embassy. It is tremendous and very swell. I am appalled. Will the little black dress do? *How* can I dress it up?

After lunch I rush out to Trois Quartiers and look at small fur capes. They are very cheap-looking. Then to my little fur man where I order one (get a *good* one if you get one, said C.) and borrow one for the evening. Also some black velvet ribbon to tie around the throat—old-lady fashion, which is now smart—and back to Nino's for hair.

Home late for tea. Jon has got butter on the chair. I put Land

---

[1] Douglas MacArthur, Secretary of U. S. Embassy, son of General MacArthur of World War II.

The list:

Dinner in honor of Mr. and Mrs. Anthony J. Drexel Biddle, Jr. (American Ambassador to Poland)

Mr. and Mrs. Biddle
Duke and Duchess of Windsor
Minister for Air and Mme Guy La Chambre
Mme Bonnet
Mrs. Kennedy
Duc and Duchesse de La Rochefoucauld
Marquise de Polignac
M. and Mme Pierre Comert
Senateur Henry-Haye
Colonel and Mrs. Lindbergh
M. Gaston Palewski (Chef du Cabinet of M. Paul Reynaud)
M. and Mme Paul Morand
Mme André Maurois
Mr. and Mrs. MacArthur
Captain Sterling
Mrs. Carmel Snow
M. Yvon Delbos
Mr. Joseph P. Kennedy, Jr.
Mr. Carmel Offie
William C. Bullitt

(Dinner of February 7, 1939)

to bed and read to Jon. Then dress for dinner. My hair looks nice and the black bow around the neck very fetching with a rose clip. But the dress is very plain. However, the cape has come and dresses it up.

We set out, arriving among the first, which is helpful. An oldish lady is pulling on gloves in the ladies' room but seeing me without them pulls them off! I say I started to bring mine but they looked so crushed and dirty I left them at home.

A small crowd of Embassy people about. How well I know the atmosphere—like Mexico before the guests arrive: only the Embassy "family." The MacArthurs, Captain Sterling, Mr. Offie, and a scattering of guests. The Biddles; he is very dapper, she stooping slightly, both affable and American. The La Chambres, she looking like a period piece in gray bouffant stuff (the dress was obscured in the pattern of the "stuff"; very French, that preoccupation with the *material* of the dress). Like a Goya portrait, I thought. No, perhaps not Goya, but one of those Spanish portraits where the dress is so prominent.

There is a quiet gossip going on among the ladies and young secretaries as to "does one or doesn't one?" (curtsy to the Duchess of Windsor). "Last year *he* minded terribly but this year he doesn't care," etc. I said that as the technicality meant nothing to me I thought I would. And just as I was saying it in they swept. She in a purple taffeta *robe de style,* her hair still parted in the middle and swept up in clean rolls on either side. She looked a little like Mary Queen of Scots. Although she is not beautiful, she was easily the most distinguished-looking woman in the room, but most formal, stiffened by dignity (what she must have been through!). He was obviously pleased to see C. and stopped to talk to him; she also went up to C.

I was in a corner talking to some American woman of "a certain age" with a French title, her hair most oddly done in a snood. She looked like Alice in Wonderland—the Red or the White Queen! By now there was quite a crowd in the room. Mrs. Kennedy, young and lovely-looking in white, her son—nice, easy, smiling American face; several stiff-backed French dowagers.

(They may not be dowagers but so they looked.) I am the only woman with a bow around my neck. It is the only thing that saves me and adds distinction to a plain black Madison Avenue dress.

Mme André Maurois in a Mary Queen of Scots black-velvet dress, wandering about a bit vaguely as though looking for some-one—not in a businesslike way though, not in the hopes of find-ing them, but simply wistfully, like a ghost. The last time I saw her, I remember she was tripping in a panic over the grave mounds at Mrs. Hibben's funeral to get out of the way of the procession!

In that same strangely high and trancelike voice (*that* is what she is like—someone in a trance) she cooed at me, "Won't you come to a little dinner with us and the Windsors tomorrow night? My husband would be so *charmed* if you would." I say I am afraid C. has something—not knowing if he will want to go or not. (Now, can I get at him before *she* does, and he gives the same kind of noncommittal answer?)

Then somehow we were going in to dinner, I on young Mac-Arthur's arm. A long table, with a full-length portrait of Wash-ington in a red coat (very ruddy, tight-lipped, and English squireish) on the wall at the end of the room.

I have MacArthur and a M. Palewski ("chef du Cabinet of M. Paul Reynaud"). He was charming, easy to talk to, and seemed very intelligent and interesting. C. is miles away, politely atten-tive to someone, and the Duke of Windsor across the table, look-ing a bit peaked and bored.

We talked of France and its powers of regeneration. I told him how impressed we were with the strength and *health* in France and he was pleased. My impressions in the park on Sunday, the health and happiness of the people and the family life. We com-pared England and France and their regenerative powers and why this is so. He put it to a mixture of races; I, to their closeness to the farms.

It was very easy to talk with him. In fact I now find, after years of shyness, that I can talk with people very easily, almost anyone (except the English), and it is a shock to find this when you have been thinking of yourself as *not* being able to for so long.

I talk to MacArthur, too, a nice, honest, kind and intelligent American. You think *"American"* with pleasure when you talk to him.

Then we are getting up and the procession moves away from the table, arm in arm, as we came in, but gaily, not like an English party (is this Bullitt? or the French?) with much banter about who should go first: *"Après vous, M. le Ministre," "Après vous, Mme l'Ambassadrice."* Much bowing and laughter.

And we are in a smaller room. I seem to be surrounded by ladies. People say they like my book (quite a number of people, both French and American, say this during the evening, which is nice and surprising as I hear very little of the book here). And various people come up, ask to be introduced: M. and Mme Paul Morand,[1] also a M. Comert[2] (he was pointed out to me before dinner by the titled American: "He's the Minister of Propaganda —he's a *Red!*"). He talks to me about Daddy, M. Monnet, the early days of the League. He knew all that group—also Harold Nicolson. He talked quite a bit about the *Life*,[3] which he was most enthusiastic about.

As I talked to him (nice, kind-faced, bright-eyed man) about old times I wondered sadly if my father would be classed "a *Red*" today? How strangely the lines have fallen. Charles is a "Fascist" and Daddy a "Red"! I did not talk politics to M. Comert, but I feel sure he is not a "Red." He is only one of that 1918 group of idealists, League supporters, etc.—Monnet, Harold Nicolson, Attolico, Rublee, Daddy, Madariaga. But Daddy and Mr. Rublee were *practical*. I can remember my father defending to me the American arguments for *not* joining the League. He was for the

[1] Paul Morand, French diplomat and writer.

[2] Pierre Comert, in the French Foreign Service, friend and co-worker of D. W. M. in World War I.

[3] Nicolson's biography of D. W. Morrow.

idea—*ideally,* I think—but saw the difficulties in its practical *immediate* application. It was one of the cases of "All real progress is very, very slow."

Comert talks to me about that vivid bit in Harold Nicolson's book describing Daddy at breakfast. (I am terribly amused, as that is what I wrote and gave Harold Nicolson!)

There is a charming woman who comes up, American, but very Irish, with lovely white hair and a young face. She is beautifully dressed (by Chanel, I am told later) but I did not notice her dress. I was looking at her squizzled-up eyes. She talks about the book but also sweetly and simply about her children and the difficulty of living in New York. There is something about the Irish—they always seem to cut through directly to life. There is an unguarded spot somewhere, where one can touch them. They are closer to their hearts.

I ask hopefully if she lives here? "No," she says, modestly, "I work on a magazine—I'm just over here on a visit." I find out later that she is Mrs. Snow, fashion editor of *Vogue!*

I find I am still in a group of women, one of whom, a stiffish elderly French (dowager type), says that we should go into the other room, which we do. There is a large group of mostly important people—Bullitt, the Duchess of Windsor, C., etc.—around the large center sofa, and smaller groups scattered about the room. The "dowager" sweeps up to the Duke of Windsor sitting on a sofa talking to another man.

I go on past and we make a new little group: MacArthur (who is very kindly looking after me) and a nice plain-faced American woman whom I class as a schoolteacher immediately (pleasant, earnest, idealistic, and sentimental—and, as it turns out, obstinate). I find somewhat to my disconcertion that we are getting into an argument about politics. She is one of those women who talks about *"those two men*—what they have done to the world." Shaking her head fiercely.

Then I found myself arguing rather excitedly that, whereas I hated the unrestricted use of *force* with all my heart and disliked much that was being done, I felt that England, France, and

U. S. A. had *forced* the use of force on Germany (C.'s arguments) and that Germany had got nothing by a policy of nonforce in her League days, her Stresemann days, and therefore had to do it this way.

"Oh, but they never tried the League, they never even gave it a chance," she said, really worked up. "And how about 1914—what excuse was there for *that* war, I'd like to know!"

I could not answer this, feeling too weak on my history to quote Professor Fay on the war guilt.[1]

She went on to talk about the Treaty, which she did not defend, but she said it was a marvel compared to the peace treaty Germany would have imposed or that Clemenceau wanted to impose.

And I argued that if either Clemenceau's peace or the English peace had been allowed—either one, *whole*—we could not have been where we are now. (C.'s arguments again.)

And somehow at the end of the argument I was saying, "Well then, they should have been stopped on the Rhine. Now it will take the lives of thousands and thousands of Frenchmen and Englishmen and maybe Americans, and that I can't bear."

"Oh no," she said, ready to forgive and forget all, "I don't think there's going to be a war."

"I hope not," I said, glad to be agreeing on something.

At this point there seemed to be one of those slight shuffles in the room. Mrs. MacArthur came and crossed to where her husband was by me (very diplomatically leading the conversation into smoother channels and pouring oil on the troubled waters). She had *just* sat down next to me and I had turned to her when the Duke of Windsor opposite got off his couch, between the dowager and the Frenchman, and came over and said in that easy polite and regal manner to young Mrs. MacArthur, "Would you mind giving me your chair so that I may talk with Mrs. Lindbergh awhile?"

It is always a shock, I think, to see that Royal manner—the ease

[1] Sidney B. Fay, *Origins of the World War*.

with which they can make polite a situation which would be rude for anyone else. And yet it was not rude in the least, here, so naturally and with complete lack of embarrassment did he do it.

Everyone else seemed to melt off at that point and I feared the conversation might wither of shyness as he started politely, "You're here in France, are you, now?"

So I simply took the conversation by the horns (you can always make the *attempt* to be real—to touch reality, anyway. The other person does not have to pick it up. But it's better to try) and said, "Yes, we're in Paris. It doesn't seem that we can go home yet. The situation is not really any better for us. Besides (plunge in, Anne) there is such a campaign against my husband at home now."

Then we went on talking quite intensely. He telling me about his experience in Germany and how the press of America had done the same thing with him just because he had visited Germany.

I said that we had been interested in his trip because Germany was, after all, the country which has seen that the laboring classes must be taken in (physically and in loyalty) and had succeeded in doing it in an attempt to give them their own homes, gardens, and something to look forward to, the *Kraft durch Freude* trips etc., and security, and that *he* (the Duke) had realized that. But anyhow, we agreed, however you felt about Germany and what they were doing (and some of the things we agreed we did not like), either way you must *know* what they are and what they are doing, either for peace *or* for war.

He said rather pathetically, I thought, "People say to me you should write your memoirs, you should write about the places you have been to. But I *can't,* you see, now, because it's all *out* of date unless I can visit them now; but when I do, you see what happens. . . ."

I said that we had planned to live in Germany to watch their aviation development but that after their "purge" we had decided we couldn't.

I wished he could talk with C., and he said he'd like to and that we must come over to their new house. It was not finished yet but nevertheless we must come and talk things over. I said we would love to but we knew what their lives were.

"Well," he said, smiling very nicely, "I expect they're very much like *your* life." (That's funny! But they are in some ways alike.) He wanted the address and telephone number.

And then we got up (or he did, I suppose), and I saw the Duchess rustling across the room toward us, smiling, and he said to her, "Yes, I've just been saying, dear, we must get together sometime."

And then she began to talk with me, about the book first. How she envied my being able to write. How she liked *Sayonara* (that is strange, I think). Her voice has changed, become more like his, but as she went on talking I got the impression of a real person. "I think I can stand things," she said, "but I wish I could write about them. I think it would help."

We talked a little about the press situation and how it changed your whole life. She said how difficult it was for her, not accustomed to it, while "the Duke," being born to it, could act naturally. She spoke with some feeling about her not wanting it to *change* her, to get the best of her. "And you find yourself doing strange things, like running out the back door" or "going into a shop for blue ribbon and coming out with black because you were so flustered."

I liked the courage in her as I had the first time I saw her. I like that quality of hers of "holding the head high."

And then somehow we were all four talking together, standing up in the center of the room, oblivious of other people around us, comparing notes like children or like people in a foreign land who suddenly find they speak the same language.

"The *lies* they print about you, the way they set you up on the wrong issues, praise you for the wrong things"—C. just nodding his understanding.

"And one's private life—How would *they* like it, I'd like to know, if I pried into *their* private life, if I said this or that?"

"I was saying I couldn't go into Trois Quartiers to buy a yard of ribbon—I come out with something else."

"Well now, darling, really . . ."

Half laughing, half angry, greedily, we compared notes. She had a good deal of dignity, though, in doing it. He seemed like a boy let out of school.

How strange it was—a pair of unicorns meeting another pair of unicorns!

I had the feeling that they had both gained tremendously from what they had been through and both seemed more interesting people.

Then they left and the party seemed to melt away, with little snatches of conversation as people said good-by. Mrs. Kennedy on the dress collections: "Everyone in London goes to Molyneux, so I go to Patou." But she said it so naturally, in that unsophisticated accent. It always seems strange that she should be in that sophisticated world—a young girl who has learned it but whom it has not touched.

M. Comert, saying he would give me his card and I must call him up and we wouldn't talk politics. He would show us some of the lovely things in Paris, "because I loved your father."

I was suddenly extremely grateful to him, not only because he loved my father but because he had waved aside politics and because, probably, his "politics" differ from C.'s supposed politics (and therefore mine). He is called a "Red" and C. a "Fascist." But he considered us as people—as friends.

My relief at this not labeling was so great that it made me realize how rare it is becoming nowadays, how much rarer it may become in the future. I had not realized how far we had gone from my father's time and world, when men's opinions differed but one was not labeled, branded, hated, and shunned for them.

That light word of easy tolerance—no, not tolerance, human kindness surpassing tolerance—was like a breath of fresh air.

Then the schoolteacher came up. "You did not finish what you were saying about there being no war," I said, to try to make friends. "Oh no, there won't be any war," she said genially as she shook my hand and hurried by. "Ask my husband."

I turned. Alas . . . her husband was M. Comert! Oh, *why* had I argued with her—oh, *why?*

The Mayor of Versailles asking us to come to Versailles. Mme Guy La Chambre sweeping by in her gray taffeta.

People slipped out. C. was talking to Bullitt, so I could not go. When they came back Mme Bonnet (who sat next to C. at supper) asked him to introduce her to me.

She is young, pretty, without pretensions or ceremony; her low evening dress had only one strap and roses climbing up the other side. Impetuous, frank, easy, and a bit startling. Then M. Bonnet came in—gray, beak-nosed (much older than she) but kind and intelligent-looking.

Bullitt takes me by the arm and sits me on the sofa next to Bonnet and they talk in French. Bonnet has come from a meeting where he made a speech, but he has been making speeches all day, on Spain, etc. He is tired but relieved. Everything has gone well: the Government got a big vote. . . . They talk fast—about Spain, about France. I feel they know each other very well, and there are undertones: "My dear colleague, how glad I am to be here. . . ."

"Oh, that has been done very well—enough has been done in that quarter for the moment. . . ."

Bullitt talks beautiful and fluent French and is at ease with them and they with him.

Mme Bonnet keeps interrupting like a child that wants attention: "And *why* did you not *tell* me you were making a speech?"

They have just come back from Spain.

He says it is all over in Spain: the Government is in Perpignan. He tells Bullitt the conditions they demand before surrender—amnesty for prisoners. All foreigners out of Spain and the vote. Bullitt says they won't get the last two. M. Bonnet says that morally the Republicans are defeated—there are planes, still in their boxes, crated, lying about.

"Think of it," says Mme Bonnet, the impulsive child, again,

"they haven't even unpacked the planes we sent them!" . . .
"Ah," she claps her hand over her mouth, " '*We* sent them' "—in
horror, like a naughty child.

"The planes that passed *by way of France* from some unknown
place," says Bullitt, with easy good humor. And Bonnet says
something about dropping by parachutes from heaven.

A little later she again interrupts her husband, "May I tell him
the *truth* about Spain? We have been right there—we have seen
. . . (to Bullitt) May I? May I?"

"No," says M. Bonnet gravely looking at her.

"Ah well, we'll get off together in a corner."

And they start huddling. At this point I think it my cue to talk
in grown-up sedate language with M. Bonnet, which I try to
do.

Mme Maurois comes up with Charles. She has already got hold
of him and he has said *I* make all the engagements! I guess we
will go—which I'd rather like to do.

Soon after this we leave, shaking hands with the Biddles and
the Embassy people—the same group who were there when we
arrived.

Then home to bed.

Wednesday, February 8th

Wake up early thinking sleepily in dismay, "But we asked Poult-
ney Bigelow[1] for dinner! We can't go to the Maurois'. . . ."

Note from Mme Maurois, begging us to come. I write back we
can't because of Mr. Bigelow.

Go out and walk in the park. It is a delicious spring day, warm
and sunny, and makes one feel unbelievably happy ("it's coming
again, then, spring?").

We walk to the Millers' for lunch.

Père Chardin is there: an oldish man, a Jesuit priest interested
in earliest man—found *"Pekin man."* He has a lovely face—intel-

---

[1] American traveler, journalist, and author.

Charles Lindbergh. Portrait in Oil by Robert Brackman, 1938
Photo Macbeth Gallery

Approach to Illiec at low tide

Work on Illiec grounds

Entering Illiec

Illiec, house and chapel; cart delivering furniture

Mrs. Dwight Morrow with Land, Long Barn, May, 1938

Mrs. Dwight Morrow, Anne Lindbergh, Land, with Thor and Skean, May, 1938

Anne Lindbergh and Frau von Gronau

At the Air Club dinner, Berlin, October 12, 1938

Anne Lindbergh with the President of the Royal Hungarian Air Club, Von Horty

Anne Lindbergh with Thor, Illiec, fall, 1938

Land, Paris, 1938

Anne Lindbergh with Land in the Bois de Boulogne, Paris, 1938

Jon in the Bois, Paris, 1938

Bronze head of Anne Lindbergh by Charles Despiau
Photo Richard W. Brown

ligent, perceptive, kind, tolerant, humorous, and understanding. There is also that pure and narrow quality of intellectual zeal, softened by a spiritual quality of human kindness.[1]

Père Chardin talks about China and Japan and his work. Where did man originate? Probably not in Central Asia as people think, for they find very few remains of advanced ape skeletons (I do not use the correct terminology), whereas many of these are found in certain parts of India and Africa. He talks of the difficulty of tracing in the past the *beginnings* of anything. He says, Suppose you draw a straight line on paper and then pass an eraser over it; you may later be able to discern the line in some places but the point where the line starts and stops will be the most difficult to discern. Time, he said, was almost exactly like the eraser.

He says it is better to talk of "a front" of the beginning of civilization, than a "point."

He talked of what one could learn from skulls and skeletons and what not. "But we will never know the color of his face and what his eyes looked like—what was in his mind."

From talking of old races we went on to talk of new, the modern problems of race. And it was marvelous to hear him talk from that point of view, as though it were *all* history we were looking back on. He says *race* is not all physical but a very subtle complicated mixture of physical, mental, moral, cultural elements. Nevertheless it is a very real and precious thing and to be jealously guarded; and that the emphasis must be on race in the modern world. He regretted that Hitler should attack the problem wrongly. He should not go *back,* turn the eyes *backward* to try to find a "pure" race, physically, which is impossible in the first place and undesirable in the second (because that is a purely physical definition). One should rather look forward, keep one's eye on race, yes, but on a broader conception of race, a synthesis

[1] Pierre Teilhard de Chardin, noted French Jesuit paleontologist and explorer, author of the posthumously published *The Phenomenon of Man,* etc.

of the best in many ways, physical, mental, spiritual, cultural. (Only all this was said much more precisely and better.)

I felt so relieved to hear someone argue without passion, clearly, objectively, wisely.

But then C. said, Yes, but how can you define that ideal? We all agree if this man is black or white but we differ greatly on who we think is good or bad, wise or foolish.

And Père Chardin lifted his hands and laughed and said he did not know.

But I felt better for knowing his mind is in the world.

We go out. I walk home, doing a few errands. "One more spring," I keep thinking. How strange that spring is always a shock and surprise. In the winter one is always an unbeliever.

> "When they come back,
> If Blossoms do—"

as Emily Dickinson said.

When I get back, in the delicious soft clear sky, is a small "blimp" in the distance. I take Jon out to see it. He is much excited and wants to know how big it is, how fast it goes, what kind of noise it makes.

Mr. Bigelow arrives for supper. He is the most energetic old man, full of vigor and vitality, full of loves and hates. He is violent on the Jews but also on the Catholic Church—fanatical.

It is interesting, however, to hear him talk about the tremendous scope of his life. He was brought up with the Kaiser. Thackeray dandled him on his knee, etc. He was interesting on Germany. He likes the Germans but says they have always been the same: they like authority.

I am sleepy from last night. I can hardly keep my eyes open after 10 and feel ashamed to be so dopey with such a vigorous old man.

Friday, February 10th

In the afternoon C. and I go down to an art gallery to see some of Eugene Berman's work (for Mother's portrait). It is the gallery that has the Vlaminck flowers in it. Also some lovely Derains. We see one Berman, slightly surrealist (monks in the desert, great rocks—if anything!) but well painted. We asked the price of the Vlaminck flowers: 5500 francs. C. likes them better.

We also see one of his stormy blue landscapes. The flowers have the same colors but are less personal. I prefer them—lovely reds and blues in juxtaposition of color. Thus far I can go with the moderns. I am looking for wedding presents for Con and Dwight.

When we get back C. says if I really think Con would like that painting to get it. But first to telephone Mrs. Miller and ask her if you are supposed to take the first price at an art gallery. She says no, the French never do. So I call the gallery (C. prodding me on) and ask if he would give me the picture for a price slightly less—5000. To my shock he said he would be delighted to! I have never done that before and do not enjoy the sensation of bargaining. But I suppose one must go by the system of the country.

Saturday, February 11th

A warm spring day, blowing clouds. Dress and pack for the night at Senlis with the Carters.[1] A car calls for us.

The Carters have a charming old house, fifteenth or sixteenth century. Sunshine as we come in the court, quiet and old-world. The house is full of lovely old furniture, orange tulips in a paneled room, sherry and a fire. They are both so nice and natural and American, kind and good. I am warmed by the beauty and peace of the house.

After lunch, C. and I go off on bicycles which I haven't been on for ten or twenty years. It is very hard work. After three or four hills we stop and walk up a long ridge through the woods and along a field, looking back across the fields at Senlis and the tower of the cathedral.

The turned, brown fields are a pinky color, the dark forest to the left, purple, some haystacks in the foreground, a tree like a feather to the right, and the tower of the cathedral in the center

[1] Mr. and Mrs. Bernard Carter of Morgan & Cie, friends of the Morrows.

against a strip of gold sky—all that is left of the fine day. A dove-colored overcast curtain has covered the rest of the sky.

C. and I, having looked at a lot of pictures lately, guess at the colors and then look at them upside down. I plan how I would paint it—if I could paint.

Back to the house. Some young people have come for tea—the Harry Woodruffs.

Sunday, February 12th

Delicious to wake up in a new room, and such a pretty one—the angles of the roof, old beams above your head, chintz at the windows, and lovely old furniture. Breakfast in front of the fire, off gay yellow china.

We go for a long walk in the woods. Very French woods—no underbrush, and long allées, the tall thin trees making Gothic arches in the distance. We walk fast and talk all the time. I talk to the young Woodruff about living in France and America, and the American quality. He was brought up in France, went to America as a young man but feels more drawn to it—or at least feels the way we do, I think, loving things in each world. He says he misses the childlike open quality of Americans.

Drive home after lunch.

The picture is there! It is quite lovely—lovely blues. We put it in the dining room where it looks very well. Land and Jon are running about gaily. Jon has painted me a picture and made a tiny balloon out of a broken balloon and is proud of it.

Monday, February 13th

C. and I out after lunch, to the *"hôtel"* of Comtesse de Noailles to see the Berman portrait (for Mother). The dealer from whom we got the Vlaminck is there and his wife. The huge house is full of museum pieces and one small hall hung solid with old masters, with Rouault and Chirico and Dali among them. The dealer thinks this is a fine idea as good things of all ages go together. Maybe so. I thought the old masters made the moderns look pretty tacky. But did not say so.

The portrait of the Comtesse by Berman is not yet hung but we see it against the wall. It is beautifully painted in unhealthy colors—violent pinks and yellows. In a sense it is perfectly conventional and conventionally painted. But at the same time I am struck by a violent lack of health and sanity in the portrait. I feel sure it would not do for Mother.

We see three beautiful Goyas, especially one man in gray (the most beautiful Goya I have ever seen). A Degas boy, a Delacroix portrait of a woman, which are lovely too.

She has a number of Dali, Braque, and Picasso, Dali seeming to be the favorite. A large one over the mantel in a modern salon (which also contains a Rubens covering a whole wall). C. points out a Dali, one of those beautifully painted super-vivid small scenes which has always something so horrible in it that you feel struck in the face—no, not struck in the face but insulted somewhere deeply inside. This one had a man with an elongated head like a huge tumor which hung pendulous on a tripod by his side. It made me ill.

The dealer says he does not like Dali; whether this is to please us or not I don't know. He says we should meet Derain.

We are, however, greatly relieved to get out of the house. I feel oppressed by the sickly abnormal atmosphere of those modern painters. I feel, in a strange way, violently puritan—that there is wickedness there, Sodom and Gomorrah, yet why, I could not say. Picasso seems to me a brilliant genius—overintellectual, spiritual even in his insanity—but these people are physical, superphysical. And their things smell of mortality.

I feel I must see something else to get the taste out of my mouth. So we go to the Orangerie and look at the exhibit of eighteenth-century *gravures,* which is like listening to Mozart.

Then we walk up toward the Louvre—a lovely cold light on the bare trees, an evening light, but cool, almost autumnal.

Tuesday

To Despiau's in the morning. He is still working on the mouth, which he says is *"toute la tête."*

My diaries have come from home. I get absorbed in what I wrote of first meeting C. It is all so thrilling, really. My first picture of him and the revolution it made in my life. It seems to me now, looking back on those diaries, that in that first thunderbolt glance I saw him intuitively very clearly, very well, though I did not trust my own judgment.

Also in those diaries I could see so clearly the evolution of my life. That passion for writing and a *too* literary outlook, suddenly shattered and put to flight by the tremendous shock of C. and all he meant. How it shook me out of my ruts, made my whole world look small, paper-valentiney. And then I can see how there was a long inarticulate period in my life because (so like the young), in my admiration for him and his world, I tossed aside my own as worth nothing and I struggled to lose myself in his, which was after all Life itself. I was plunged into life—active life—loving and living and having children and those terrific trips and the suffering too.

But now it is coming into its own again, that early world of writing and thinking, stronger and realer and richer, and impregnated with C. and with his life and what he has taught me.

And there is no longer that terrific struggle between the two—that divided self—that was there for years. That old self, suppressed, passionate, insisting to come out—pushed down by that other new self, practical, active, outward, and comparatively efficient.

No; somehow they have fused—at least I think so. At last they are one.

And I am closer to C., too, closer than I ever dreamed would be possible when I first fell in love with him. It still seems to me a miracle that I ever married him. And he of course has changed too. Those things I saw are still there, but he has broadened so much, and will still.

My mind is so full of the past it is difficult to come back to the present. As though I were still in the past, still that dreamy passionate girl at college, dreaming her future.

Jon is a dream (I might have dreamed him), but Land, little roly-poly healthy objective animal—who would ever have dreamed I would have a baby like Land! He is like the "horsely horse" of Chaucer I wrote about. He is all the essence of a baby—what a baby ought to be.

C. and I go out and walk, I in a fog. I talk to him about the diaries and my life, also how strangely I was prepared for my life—that Frances Smith[1] ordeal, like a premonition. I can remember that dreadful winter and I appalled, a young girl, that life could be like that, saying in desperation to Mrs. Neilson, "But I do not see how I could stand it, if it were to come to me personally" (after all, this was secondhand). And she said, wise Mrs. Neilson who had lost her only son, "No—it is somehow easier to bear it when it is your own grief." And it is. Whether life helps you in some way . . . But the grief of other people which you cannot do anything to help is somehow the hardest to bear.

Tea with the children. Land is terribly funny with Jon's balloons, and always gets hold of them.

"No! No! Land, those are *mine!"* vehemently insists Jon, leaping after his little brother. Land looks up innocent-eyed ("Have I done anything wrong?") or else staggers off, determinedly hanging on to his prize. He never seems to cry when Jon takes things away from him. He seems to know they are not his, but he is going to get away with as much as he can anyway! He delights C.

Friday, February 17th

Read diaries all morning. Very hard to read them. I get so absorbed. All the period of Hopewell and after. It is still terrible to read them. Less about Elisabeth than I hoped, but here and there a lovely flash. It seems to me I *wrote* better in the old diaries, even in those depressed, nervous, unbalanced times. There is an intensity to it.

[1] A Smith student and friend of A. M. L. who disappeared while both were at Smith College. Her body was discovered months later.

Out for walk with C. around the lake, a strange dream walk, tortuous and complicated, across paths, woods, and streams that C. has discovered. It is always the same.

To Despiau in the morning. Very bored. Today is one of those days when you feel that there is a rat in you, gnawing away. Discontent and dissatisfaction all day, for no real reason. I chafe with impatience at Despiau's (he is still fiddling with the mouth).

In the afternoon C. and I go to the Zak Gallery and look at pictures. All the ones we like are very expensive. C. likes a big snow scene of Vlaminck. I like his blue and white flowers (9000 francs) and a small watercolor (1800) of Marquet (also some oils—these are very expensive), an Utrillo at 8000 and a Boudin at 10,000.

Also into another gallery, where there is a beautiful landscape by Segonzac, very expensive (almost a thousand dollars!), some Utrillos. The one I liked came from the early period and so was also very expensive (45,000 francs), two Vlaminck flower paintings I quite liked, one from the "Fauve" period (4000 francs) and one more of the period of ours—6000 francs. There is an intensity about all the things he does that makes most of the other painters of the same period fade right out, when you look at them together. His things *burn*.

Home late for tea with some white flowers and anemones to freshen up the centerpiece.

The Millers for dinner. They like the Vlaminck. I talk to her about Jo Davidson for a head of C. She tells me a little of her life. After they leave I feel better. Yes, the evening helped after a rather unsatisfactory day. It was quiet and peaceful and we all felt at ease. I felt we had given them something (as well as gotten something from them) and that is the greatest pleasure.

The old tailor who made C. his clothes [after his first flight to Paris in 1927] comes to see us (C. phoned him). He looks peaked and ill—starved. His business had gone to smash, he says, at the time of the depression, but he still makes good clothes. C. picks out four suits (he is completely out). The man is grateful. He has dignity and pride in his work and does not press C., but after we have chosen the suits he says, "You don't know it, Madame, but it was Providence who sent you to us." He says that just before C.'s telephone call came he had gone up to the British Aid Society. . . . He is just out of the hospital and his gas and electricity have been turned off. C. advanced him half the money.

At three we see Jo Davidson about C.'s head. I like him so much and am glad he is going to do it.

Walk in park with C.

Tuesday, February 21st

To Despiau in the morning, C. with me. C. writes in a corner while Despiau works *again* on the mouth. He is exhausted as he did not sleep. C. says the head is beautiful. We take Despiau to his meeting (he seems so lost out in the street in his big overcoat) and then go on to look at pictures, to find a wedding present for Con and Aubrey and Margot and Dwight. Go to the Élysée Gallery to see Vlamincks. There is one large landscape, one small snow scene, one street scene, and one farm. I like the farm, which has a steeple in the back and red roofs and haystacks. But C. says, "No haystack ever looked like that!"

I like it because it reminds me of what I feel about landscapes from the air: the intensity, the spark that always rests on anything touched by man, small specks in the landscape, a steeple, a haystack, tiny figures of men, a red roof—all *burning* with the touch of human life.

C. says I like it because I have never farmed, and that the haystack—a blotch of orange in the center of the canvas— *couldn't* be a haystack. It could be a cliff where a dredge had been at work! Anyway we agree on two pictures: one, a typical Vlaminck snow landscape, nice whites and blues and a stormy sky, and also a street scene with a lovely sky. Finally decide to take the snow scene for Aubrey and Con, have it sent to the apartment.

After lunch all of us go out in the Bois to a dirt road where Jon usually goes. A little boy dressed up in a cowboy suit runs up to me expectantly. He recognizes Land and the carriage—Jon's friend! Then I take Land out and let him walk around the woods, in a smock and rubbers. He loves it and follows Jon, who is looking for maple-seed shoots. Home at 4:30.

I come into my room and nearly fall over. C. has bought the white flowers of Vlaminck and put it on the dresser! (It is the one I said was the loveliest Vlaminck of all, from the Zak Gallery.) It is much more beautiful than I remember—more color. Those white petals, tinged here and there with blue, purple, or red, seem to burn or be blown in a wind against a deep blue background—a picture that makes you catch your breath. There is a wind in it, an intensity, an ecstasy. C. is very happy. "You said it was the loveliest one—that was enough for me!" We call Jon in. Jon says he likes this the best.

The snow scene also arrives. I am afraid to look at it for fear it will look badly next to this beauty. But it stands up very well. We look at all three of them together. C. says we ought to keep all three. They go well together. But I think we ought to keep only the white flowers and give the other two away.

Supper alone, with the white flowers over the mantel.

Wednesday, February 22nd

Pack[1] and do odd jobs all morning.

C. and I to Jo Davidson's for lunch. He is so honest and *big*. I like him very much and so does C. How good it is to be able to talk above politics, to love and understand people right through it—or rather *above* it. (Only I have not told him I have had a

---

[1] The Lindberghs are going to London to visit the Astors.

head done by Despiau. I am afraid it will hurt his feelings, and the longer it goes on, the worse it is and seems like deceit.)

Supper, and off for the train in a taxi (*have* I forgotten anything?). Off into the night, rattling away. Quite comfortable, but no sleep.

Thursday, February 23rd

Arrive at Astors' at 9:30.

That somewhat disconcerting array of hats, coats, canes, and umbrellas strewn over the front hall table that always takes you back a bit when you enter: what, *all* those people here already!

They were evidently not expecting us at that hour and didn't get my letter. Lord Astor runs down—lovely person. Up to breakfast with him and a German (of the old school, not pro-Nazi) who, however, defends the Nazi attitude on religion and Niemöller,[1] etc. Lady Astor argues with him hotly.

I go out in the morning with Lady Astor and her niece, the niece buying a Court dress. Also Wissie, in a mink coat and no hat, with two black ribbons in her loose hair and her careless schoolgirl air of owning all London when she walks down the street. However, I like her. It must be difficult being the daughter of such a famous and incomparable mother. There is something soft and childlike in Wissie, too, in spite of the smart and sophisticated exterior. It is in those large shy brown eyes—lovely like the eyes of a wild creature.

To lunch at "Bill" Astor's[2]—all young people. Someone just back from Spain—Lord Camrose's son. Spasmodic talk at lunch (*wonderful* lunch: strawberries and fresh pineapple!). After lunch the men get together and I find myself alone with a charming girl—fair (pale gold) and rare, too delicate and real. We talk

[1] Martin Niemöller, German Protestant theologian; after 1933 became an opposition leader in the Confessional Church; imprisoned in a concentration camp 1937.

[2] The Honorable William Astor, eldest son of 2nd Viscount Astor. Parliamentary secretary to the Secretary of State for Home Affairs.

children and schools and living in the country—how nice it is but how it unfits you for the city and social life.

Back to the house. C. and I walk down Bond Street and look at [Augustus] John's (early) work in a gallery. Dinner—a scattered group of young people. Wissie looks lovely.

They go off to the movies. I stay home. A stream of that noiseless and invisible army of servants keep coming to the door (expecting me to be out), the girl to make the fire, the chambermaid to take clothes, the valet to find C.'s suit, etc.

Those oddly plain, dark and dingy backstairs up to the bedrooms—areaways and pots and pans and servant girls' gossip—in contrast to the wide royal carpeted front stairs.

Friday, February 24th

Breakfast in my room. Lady Astor comes in afterward, sweet and gay, and runs off to catch a train, tells us *please* to stay the whole week.

C. and I go out and look at galleries: the National (one lovely room of French modern—*Mont-Sainte-Victoire* [Cézanne] and Renoir's *Umbrellas*), the National Portrait Gallery, and the Tate, trying to find portraits by [Augustus] John, Brockhurst, Gerald Kelly, Kennington, Lamb, etc.

Back for lunch. "Jakie,"[1] Lord Astor, the German, and an Englishman there—a *typical* Englishman who says when they talk of the German synthetic rubber, "This comes up every year, this scare about synthetic rubber," with a complacent smile. He exudes the England-is-a-good-little-place-after-all attitude.

Lord Astor is interesting on farms and new farming techniques.

After lunch we pack our bags and are motored out in the Rolls-Royce through the incredibly dreary—no, not dreary, just ugly and mediocre London suburbs, cheap stores, cheap housing districts, to Cliveden, which is suddenly very beautiful, sedate, apart, and perfect (how like England, this contrast). There are snow-

---

[1] Youngest son of Lord and Lady Astor.

drops everywhere by the edge of the woods under the trees. A flowering quince on a wall, doves making a flutter in the dark woods. White heather blooming, and a little plant of primroses by every stone in the sunken World War I graveyard.

The house is empty of people but lovely with great forsythia *trees* and banked spring flowers in the living rooms and fires and a tea table. We have tea and go out and walk in the twilight and serenity.

Supper with Lord Astor and Mr. Brand asking C. about aviation and rearmament. They are both profoundly gloomy.

There are a lot of people coming tomorrow. I feel shy already, as only a group of English people can make me feel.

Saturday, February 25th

Down for breakfast—only Lord Astor and C. and I. C. and I out for a walk in the drizzle, It is cold and blowy. We climb over stiles and down a pasture and up a steep hill. Lovely big beech trees—so English; weathered statues unexpectedly at the end of long allées.

Back in time to walk with Lady Astor (back from Plymouth this morning, early, after a banquet and speech last night, and a six- or seven-hour train trip!) and Lord Astor over to Dropmore, a big place near here being sold. Lady Astor in pull-on hat and old brown raincoat setting off determinedly across the grass in the rain.

Back for lunch. People are beginning to come: Mr. Brand, Thomas Jones, Geoffrey Dawson (head of the *Times*), Mrs. Dawson, a really nice woman. Lord Lothian.[1] But this is still "the family," at least in feeling. Everyone is at ease. Everyone knows everyone else. The jokes are old jokes, the talk is mildly political, full of long understood quips and allusions, most of which I don't understand: "Wait till *Lionel* comes—we'll get him to . . ." After lunch people scatter for naps, golf, "to see the colt,"

[1] Philip Henry Kerr, 11th Marquess of Lothian, active in the Paris Peace Conference 1919. Became British Ambassador to the U. S. 1939.

etc. I, upstairs and read *Three Guineas* [Virginia Woolf] and some poetry of a young girl Mr. Brand gave me.

Policemen are beginning to pace the grounds (for the Prime Minister's benefit).

C. and I go out and walk in the rain before tea (three huge round tables are spread out—silver, cups, plates, cake, bread, jam). But not many people at tea. We gather around the center table. People begin to drive up. "Lionel"—Mr. Curtis[1]—very American face (no, he is very English), mystical, dreamy, and somewhat fanatical—very much the professor, and his nice thin gray English wife.

Mr. Kennedy comes. The men group in the small room. Lady Astor calls us in to listen to young Joseph Kennedy's[2] letter on Spain—very vivid and balanced and yet young too. I am surprised at a young person seeing so clearly and recording so well, in the middle of such moving times.

Lady Astor coming in: "Rise—your betters are coming!" Mr. Chamberlain—straighter, younger, fresher than his photographs, and a young shy and very pretty girl, his niece, who is taking Mrs. Chamberlain's place (home with the flu). There is a stir. He shakes hands gravely and simply all the way round. I am struck with how English he looks—reserved, simple, straightforward, plain.

Soon after I go out but on my way upstairs run into a group of people by the fire, mostly the young or the out-of-the-running. I find the shy girl sitting all alone on a chair, waiting, and talk to her—about being here (her first time) and how I got lost the first time, and about being shy, a little—touched on it, gently. She does not know where her room is, so I wait until Lady Astor comes out and then tell her. (The blind leading the blind; shyness helping shyness!)

Up and dress in a great hurry and *rush* downstairs at C.'s

[1] Oxford professor and British writer.

[2] Joseph Kennedy Jr., eldest son of Ambassador Kennedy, who later died in World War II on a dangerous mission as a Navy pilot, July 1944.

insistence. As usual we are the *first* in the room! Stand by the fire
with Thomas Jones. People come in. But it is not so bad—I find
talking easy. Only the shy girl is in the center of the group
looking lovely in white—frozen in her shyness, with a turned
head, not knowing what to do. I am too far away to reach out a
hand to her. She is in pain and does not know how lovely she is,
even in shyness—or especially in shyness.

In to dinner; a long, long table. I am up near Lady Astor (who
looks lovely in blue and spangles and floating tulle) between
Kennedy and the Duke of Devonshire, a nervous, wizened, little
man who keeps looking at my dress and my earrings in a most
disconcerting way. I say I think "things" seem much better. He
says, yes they are—that the dictators have been scared off by
Britain's rearming and American agitation. (This is a typical
English view.)

Lord Lothian is opposite, watching everything, smiling amused
to himself (all knowing and all laughing and caring for no one,
not worrying; wonderful to be like that).

Mr. Chamberlain is next to Lady Astor. Kennedy can hardly
talk to me from wanting to talk to Lady Astor and Mr. Chamberlain, though when he does I am touched by what he says. He
talks about their life together. How in Boston they had never in
twenty years (before coming to England) given as many as
twenty dinner parties, or been to twenty. They had decided that
the most important thing in their lives were their children and
giving them a family life and they couldn't "go out" and do this
at the same time, so they just took the choice. And when the
appointment came up for England there was much criticism of
them, saying they had no social sense, couldn't give a dinner
party, etc.

He talked beautifully about his wife and the position here. I
was much heartened. If only more people could have that view of
the fundamentals, what strength America could have.

Kennedy and Lady Astor very amusing talking about the
Queen. "I spoke to your girl-friend today. I tried to get her to

come down here." (Kennedy evidently adores the Queen, as everyone does who meets her.)

"Why don't you *really* do something for me? You're no friend!"

"Well, isn't that doing something? I spoke to her and told her you were coming down and tried to get her to come."

Much bantering, ending up with Kennedy saying (rather aptly, I thought), "That's all this country needs now—a romance between the American Ambassador and the Queen. That'd fix you!"

Kennedy, eager and earnest and outspoken and rushing in, perhaps, "where angels fear to tread." Not nearly as subtle or as clever as Bullitt and yet honest and likable. He adores the Prime Minister and is very proud of his contact: "That's how we got to be such good friends, you see."

Then after supper, ladies drift into that long green room full of flowers—white calla lilies, yellow forsythia, spring flower pieces. I talk to the professor's wife about America. Then Lady Astor brings up the Prime Minister: "You know Mrs. Lindbergh. She's much nicer than her husband" (terrible introduction!) and I felt very shy and said something he didn't catch but then he talked about flying: did I enjoy it? To which I said something about liking it for its usefulness, and he said that was his feeling about it the only times he went, and laughed, and told about the way things looked from the air: the huge roads, like ribbons, over Germany and no cars on them, while coming home the roads in England were full of cars. And the squares of fields in Holland— different colors, as though painted. They were flowers!

Such a nice direct simple man with a direct clipped English speech—no undertones (except humor, and quite a lot of that) and no subtleties. A plain man, one wants to say, an ordinary man, and yet that simplicity and goodness and directness is not ordinary.

Then Lady Astor came back, to my relief, and got Mr. Kennedy to read Joe's letter again. Everyone sits around quietly.

Kennedy takes off his glasses afterward and suddenly looks like a small boy, pleased and shy. He looks like an Irish terrier wagging his tail (a *very* nice Irish terrier).

The Prime Minister turns to me as the nearest person and says, "It *must* end soon" or something perfunctory like that and then goes on to say (apropos of Joe's letter and the moral effect of the bombardment of Madrid) that Franco has probably been very clever about his method of dropping bombs—a few every day on Madrid, wearing people's morale down.

I said it was awfully hard for me to look at war technically like that. "My husband can, but I can't." Then very quickly (in case I had misunderstood him and his deeply humanitarian convictions) he went on to say, "But I think that was undoubtedly the most humane method he could take, the most saving of lives," to which I agreed. Then Lady Astor came back and plied the Prime Minister with questions. Daring ones, I thought, about Italy and his visit. But he turned them off, lightly and gaily. (It always amazes me at Cliveden and in England, how frankly people talk about things, with no worry, apparently, of being repeated or misquoted. My long training with C. and the American press makes me gasp at such openness of speech and thought. One could never do it in America. It would go immediately, much garbled, to the press.)

The Prime Minister told the admiring group of an amusing incident in his Italian visit. Before arrival he got a tip in a letter from someone (Italian) that his visit was most important, and to be a success this advice should be followed: "In Europe there is a saying that the destiny of the world is in the hands of a woman. This is still true. Today Italy is swung by a woman. The Countess Ciano."[1] When she went to England she was not nicely treated (according to the letter); people snubbed her, she was not made a fuss of. (One can well imagine this. It is the way the English feel about all foreigners.)

[1] Edda Ciano, Mussolini's daughter, wife of Count Galeazzo Ciano, Minister of Foreign Affairs.

While in Germany she was made a great fuss of, which resulted in the Axis and Göring's daughter being named Edda. Now, the letter advised, if you want to make a success, you, the Prime Minister, must send a large bunch of the most beautiful flowers you can find to the Countess Ciano. It must *not* be sent by Lord Halifax and it must *not* be sent by *Mr. and Mrs.* Chamberlain. It must come from *you.* So the Prime Minister, not neglecting anything, ordered someone at the Embassy to get the largest and finest bunch of flowers possible—not to get it from the little hunchback (?) the Embassy usually got it from but from the swellest place there was. They decided also to send one to "Ma" Mussolini. So when he arrived he found two gigantic bunches, one of red roses and one of white lilacs. The white lilacs went (as considered more appropriate) to "Ma" Mussolini (who was away) but the flaming red roses went with the Prime Minister's "homage" to Comtesse Ciano.

Apparently with *great* success.

Lady Astor then plied the Prime Minister with indiscreet questions (so *obviously* indiscreet that they were simply funny and not embarrassing. She does this kind of thing very well). Such as:

"Did you tell him (Hitler) that we don't like Goebbels?"

"No," said the Prime Minister with a wry smile and dry laugh, "I am not on such intimate terms with Mr. Hitler."

He also said, laughing, that he intended to send Hitler and Mussolini umbrellas on their birthdays.

I don't know how the group split up, but it did eventually. A lovely person—tall and dark, in a big white taffeta *robe de style,* a lovely voice, and rather a charming old-fashioned face—came up and talked to me about the book. I felt I could have had some kind of real contact with her if only it had not been so late and I by that time so tired. And if only she had not turned out to be the Duchess of Devonshire. C.'s face had already "shut up" with that look of "This-is-the-time-all-sensible-people-should-be-in-bed."

And when we did go to bed—around twelve—there were still little groups standing around talking.

Sunday

C. and I up early, no one about, the house all still, lovely with flowers, waiting. We steal out onto the terrace and walk up and down in a delicious sun. It is coldish, though. A bobby appears on a corner of the terrace and looks us over.

Finally into the dining room: only Lord Astor and then Sir Terence O'Connor,[1] an Attorney General. I sit in the middle of the long empty table to leave room for "the great" next to Lord Astor. I am gradually getting used to the system (which I like very much) of wandering about for your food. (Of course we have everything on the table at home for breakfast and at Long Barn, but in this huge room one has to walk *so far* for one's food!) There is a table for fruit, fresh and cooked, a table for coffee and tea, and one with a long array of covered silver dishes: tomatoes stuffed with bread crumbs, fish, bacon, eggs, porridge, etc. And all kinds of bread and toast on the table.

Talk with Sir Terence O'Connor about the Oxford Movement, which now wants to incorporate under that name so it can receive a bequest of money from some old lady. Which makes all Oxford [University] men rise and make speeches from the pulpit, so angry are they at the name being used.

Afterward up to our tower room ("the Oxford room"—one of the boys' evidently) which overlooks the drive. I watch the couples split up and go off. Thomas Jones in an old shepherd's cape-coat. Mr. Curtis and Dr. Dawson setting out, very small and serious, below me across the lawns of Cliveden. That thin-as-a-board Englishwoman striding off by herself; two other people with canes, leisurely; a girl with a golf bag and car, etc.

C. and I write and then go off by ourselves (refusing a ride with Sir Terence O'Connor to show us the country). It is a lovely day—great clouds and a blowy sky, dark purples and blues. C. and I walk over those wide deserted bridle paths deep with beech leaves, our feet in autumn and our heads in March.

There seem to be more people for lunch, the long table even longer. Lord Lothian is on my right and an intensely shy clear-

[1] Irish author and journalist.

eyed young man on my left. I enjoy talking to Lord Lothian on America, which he understands far better than most Englishmen and really seems to like. I tell him about Martin Engstrom[1] and the American quality of that kind of person.

The shy young man on my left with intense blue eyes seems to be a "Mr. Lawrence." From his eyes, the cut of his cheek, and his conversation on Palestine, the Arabs, and archeology I gather he is T. E.'s brother.

I have a nice time talking to him about the place of aviation in archeology and tell him he must talk with C. After lunch people split up to play tennis, golf, etc. Young Lawrence, C., Bill Astor, Mr. Curtis, and I go over to Ipsden to see [Eric] Kennington's[2] memorial to T. E. Lawrence. Bill drives us over and talks of all the pacifists now wanting war—some witty lines repeated in the House:

> "Hark the Norman Angells[3] sing,
> Peace by war to thee I bring."

Kennington is big, bluff, ruddy, very kind and shy, and very independent—sure of himself in a quiet way *in his art.*

The memorial is much more finished than in September.

I am interested in the kind of "scrapbook" he [Kennington] has pinned up in one corner of his barn-studio. Pictures of Crusaders' tombs (Lawrence is done in this style), bits of letters, scraps of poems—*Samson Agonistes,* "Nothing is here for tears . . ." All scraps which have in them a touch of what he has gathered, distilled, and put into the serenely beautiful memorial to Lawrence.

He takes us into the house to see the bust of Lawrence—not as good as the sketch, which I love. He then wants to give us a print

---

[1] An old friend of Charles Lindbergh who owned the hardware store in Little Falls, Minnesota.

[2] English sculptor and friend of T. E. Lawrence, the "Lawrence of Arabia."

[3] British pacifist leader.

of this. We protest, he insists; everyone is embarrassed, especially Mr. Kennington. Finally in a childlike way Mr. Kennington puts it into Mr. Curtis's arms: "Look here (pleading), I *want* them to have it—*you* see that they get it."

Back to the house for tea. Those three big tables spread again; delicious chocolate. I sit at a "young" people's table with Thomas Jones.

Someone is talking with the Prime Minister about Streit's book *Union Now*.[1] They said it was a wonderful idea and especially fortunate in being advanced by an American. They all wanted to push it but it mustn't seem to come from England. "Now if *we* suggested it that would *never* do!" (This has been both the joke and the passion of this weekend. Someone has suggested naming Lord Astor's new colt "Clarence Streit.")

After tea people filter out, including the Prime Minister. Lady Astor thinks the Prime Minister is like Lincoln, a little. But I think he is more like Coolidge, in a strange way—in his plain common sense and his dry humor and in his Englishness. That is, he is just as *English* as Coolidge was *American*.

I talk to Lord Astor's niece, Phyllis Nichols. She says she feels like a veteran, she has outlasted so many guests; new ones appear at each meal and old ones disappear. Apparently she has been painted by John! It was not too successful, for after he did something quite nice, he painted it all out and started on a mammoth head not at all to the family's liking. You have to go down to the country and live near him (which one American girl did for six months!). He is often drunk and a very formidable person—disillusioned and gloomy. It is what the English call an "odd" family. They all play the harp or write or paint, or something. I ask her to feel around and see if he might be disposed to do C.

Although people have left, there is still an enormously long table for dinner. I sit next to Sir Edward Grigg,[2] whom I like

[1] Clarence Streit, American journalist and author of *Union Now* (1939) and *Union Now with Britain* (1941).

[2] Sir Edward Grigg, later Lord Altrincham.

very much. And Mr. Geoffrey Dawson of the *Times,* whom I *cannot* talk to—so don't; always feel very ignorant and ill-informed. He is brusque, piercing-eyed, and has a dry humor: "How do you know they've stopped it?" (German propaganda versus Russia).

He talks to me about a scheme to organize the youth in some kind of labor camps—in England—for training, health, and morale. I think it is an excellent idea. I tell him I can't bear it that the totalitarian states can accomplish things like that and we can't under our system. He says we can and must. (Which is quite true. The English are coming round to realizing that they must organize and adopt, and adapt, some of the German methods in order to survive at all.)

He also spoke of *Union Now.* This little green paperbound book is always in someone's pocket. C. says—from only a glance at it—that it looks impracticable to him.

After supper I talk to Mr. Brand, whom I love, but who is so world-weary. And I also feel exhausted from the excitement of talking and listening to stimulating people this weekend. There never is any letup. Everyone here is vitally interested in politics in the making. Nothing else is discussed. Jakie (who seems non-chalant but who has charm, sense, and sensibility) said to me at tea, "Wouldn't you think it would have been a better idea to give the Prime Minister a *rest* from politics on this weekend? He sees all these people every day of the week"!

We talk poetry and pictures. He, stretched out on the sofa, tells me a story about Hitler (this is typical of the stories going round now): that *his* psychiatrist knows Hitler's psychiatrist, who told him that Hitler hears voices, and when the voices get too loud the doctor tells Hitler he'd better go up for a rest on the mountain!

Monday morning, February 27th

We get down about the same time for breakfast this morning at 9 or 9:05, and almost everyone has left!

Pack (we keep our bags locked here the whole time in a vain attempt to keep the army of maids and butlers from packing and unpacking and *losing* our belongings in obscure bureau drawers all over the room) and leave about 10, in Lord Lothian's car (smiling at the door) with Mr. Curtis. He talks most of the way into town, in that easy and extremely interesting professorial way, about slanders, etc. He is able to look at the slanders of Tacitus and the slanders about "The Cliveden Set" in the same breath, as the same phenomenon. I feel he is not *living* in the modern world. His pace is the scholar's pace.

Shop at Marjorie Castle for a taffeta evening dress (the kind of thing I *should* have had for this past weekend).

To Bill Astor's for lunch. Bill's house always seems to me perfect for the man about town: lovely pictures (conservative and not showy but first-class—expensive and quality), lovely china, delicious food. But all casual and taken for granted. What a rising young man should have. Shows taste, form, and a love of nice living—*all as a matter of course*. He himself has no pose or vanity, is nice, spontaneous, interesting, and young and alive. But the *frame* amuses me.

Back to the house with a splitting headache. Go to bed and take pills. Lady Astor comes and rubs my head and talks about Lord Lothian and Christian Science . . . all a muddle in my splitting head. But it releases my heart, she is so good and I am fond of her. With her I am the person I was with Elisabeth. She then talks to me about my life and the place that Elisabeth took in it. "And you have no one to share it with—when you had Elisabeth . . ." She touched a point so real that I could not speak for tears.

C. out to the U. S. Embassy.

Tuesday, February 28th

Hardly slept at all last night. After the headache left my heart pounds so I can't sleep till morning. What is it from? Overexcitement? tension? or eyes?

Breakfast in bed.

Lord Lothian, C., and I alone for supper. He talks about America's new role in world politics, saying she must bear some of the brunt for the "freedom of the seas" that England has given her for so long.

Wednesday, March 1st

Downstairs to breakfast. "This *is* a pleasant surprise!" says Lord Astor with his charming and kind smile. (There! I think, I've done the wrong thing again. I *never* know what is expected of one in an English household. Evidently the men eat alone downstairs on weekdays—not at Cliveden—and the women in bed upstairs.)

A young German, Von Trott,[1] comes in for breakfast. Talks about China, where he has just been, and Germany, to which he is returning. He is a sensitive, balanced, courageous young person. Talks with a kind of passionate devotion to Germany but not blindly and without that false pride that the unsure have. Such earnestness and yet such sanity and sympathy. The best of the Germans. I wish we could see him again. I should like to talk to him about Rilke.

C. and I take a taxi to the Geoffrey Dawsons'. *Sussex Place.*

Mrs. Dawson is such a nice "plain" person, completely selfless, but not dully saintlike, both feet on the ground. A kind of old garden-gloves and family woman. She makes me feel ashamed of my vanities, self-consciousness, and aspirations. She is what a woman ought to be after all. And she can wear a red dress, too, and paint her front door bright red, and have gay peasant napkins at the table!

The Trenchards[2] are there. He is a grand man of the old days, keen and perceptive still, with a vigor and heartiness that Englishmen seem to lack nowadays.

She is a gallant faded English beauty. I do not mean that *she*

[1] Adam von Trott zu Soltz, a Rhodes scholar, an anti-Nazi working in the German Foreign Ministry. Executed in August 1944 after the July conspiracy against Hitler.

[2] Hugh Trenchard, 1st Viscount of Wolfeton, Marshal of the Royal Air Force.

considers herself or her beauty, as "faded beauties" usually do. No, only one is aware of the fair, tall, perfect type of English beauty she once was. Her dignity and erectness, and a very superb gallantry which I cannot describe. (I learn afterward they lost their only son—flying—in the Air Force.)

After lunch back to Lady Astor's. C. calls up Sir Francis [Younghusband] and we go to see them. They are alone. She is very "down," sitting by the fire, unable to get up, and has had a kind of rheumatism.

I bring her some flowers, freesia, narcissus, and purple tulips—a nice mixture—but that overgrown angular English maid *separates* them and puts them spindly-fashion in three separate vases! I ache to get at them.

Sir Francis says, as always, "What a *fine* time we had on that trip to India!"

"Yes, what a *fine* time!" I say, remembering only the hot dizzy streets of Calcutta and how doped and heavy with child I felt.

C. talks politics to him. I think they are pleased we came. I wish we could do something for them. Inevitable sadness of old age: sickness and being "left behind," derelicts on a beach. Not so bad for him; he still keeps contact with life and people. But she, whose contacts were, I gather, more superficial, social, and gay at one time, is left a tired old woman, still of great charm, alone by the fire, dreaming of the past.

Back to St. James's Square to find that Thomas Jones has been waiting for us to go out to tea with him—at 4:30! (But he said 6 to me.) We rush over to the house of a Mrs. Yates Thompson,[1] an old lady in a wheelchair in a house reeking with associations— pictures, books, whatnots, mementoes; another age. One does not notice the wheelchair or her age. She seems to *come out* to meet you, in the warmest and most heartening way. You feel her life is full—that it was always full but that unlike most elderly widows (and lame also), she does not live entirely in the past but is

[1] Widow of Henry Yates Thompson, a barrister and book collector.

spiritually interested in the present and future too. It makes one not dread old age. I should like to see her again.

A Miss Cazalet, a bright young woman, knows John and is a Member of Parliament. Her mother has a collection, all Johns! We go to see them. They are superb, the best ones I have ever seen—even the women (and I used to think he couldn't do women). The last thing he did was a heavenly little Provençal landscape done during the [Munich] crisis. (Also a lovely white flower picture.) C. and I are stunned by them and completely won over. Miss Cazalet is going to contact him and see if he would do C. (He is most erratic and won't do whom he doesn't want. Thomas Jones tells me that John and his family are the originals for Sanger's family ["The Sanger Circus"] in *The Constant Nymph*.[1] That tells you what to expect.)

(Whenever I talk with anyone about John it is in reference to a portrait of C., but whenever C. talks with anyone it is in reference to me! Confusion in the minds of the listeners!) He would be superb for C., I have always thought, after seeing his Lawrence. He is the only person who could get C.'s "burning-glass" quality.

Off to the Chinese restaurant for a very indigestible meal and then home. The butler meets us at the door:

"Her Ladyship wishes to see you in her boudoir."

We go up. It is not a "boudoir" but a little sitting room. Lord Astor and Lady Astor are there by the fire (Lady Astor went to her Christian Science meeting tonight) and we talk over the day. It is gay and fun. Lady Astor says we'll all be done by John. I'm not sure—his women look so wicked. I don't think he could make me look "wicked," exactly—stupid or mean or selfish, perhaps, or sulky—but nothing so grand as "wicked."

Lady Astor says she's not sure I couldn't be wicked. She teases me like Elisabeth.

[1] Novel by Margaret Kennedy.

An overcast, sullen day. Get up and put on my woolen underwear and flying clothes. They look shabby and hang badly on me and yet they give me confidence.

Breakfast downstairs. Good-by to Lord Astor. His smile is so kind and lovely that I always feel tempted to look at him for it and yet feel sternly that one mustn't. Think how many people he has to smile at! His face has such pure goodness that I don't see how anyone *could* make him out to be the cruel Idle Rich Fascist (Cliveden Set, etc.).

Lady Astor comes upstairs and starts to pack my clothes, talking all the time! She thinks they're *very* pretty, which pleases me.

We leave at 10:15 for the station. C. has a cold and a headache. The weather is fair.

Read the *Times* on train to Reading. C. sits back and does nothing; resting. Wonderful to be dull and relaxed again. It is too stimulating at Lady Astor's.

Reading is full of planes. We leave about 12:30. Over the Channel. Can almost see the "deep depression" moving in on England. But it is clear in France, getting better as we approach Villacoublay, sunny and bright, a summer day and the air swarming with gadflies—planes, blimps, etc.

We meet Détroyat and a friend of his at the airport. They drive us in to Paris. Land and Jon not yet back from the park, still golden and light and full of children and baby carriages.

When the bell rings I run to the door. There is Land, his blue-coated behind in the air, his head and hands on the mat, stooped over. "Hello," I say. "Hello," he crows back joyfully, his head still on the mat. Jon looks much better but has a cough.

C. feels very badly (a cracking headache) and goes to bed. He has a temperature of 103! It is grippe, of course; he should not have flown. Get hot-water bottles, pills, etc.

Jon coughs terribly. Up in the night to give him hot milk and honey and heat some soup for C. He has a bad night.

Saturday, March 4th

The Sloanes[1] come for supper. He beams with warmth and approval on me. He feels responsible (in a very nice way) for launching my "career" as a budding author. I shall never forget how nice he was when I talked—tremulous—to him about the manuscript of *North to the Orient* and how pleased I was by his letter about it. I have it still. It is terribly funny: they consider me an important author! C. talks politics with him and I talk with her about everything—Paris, children, women's lives, etc. I *do* like her, so much.

I think it pleased them to come, and their enthusiasm was very warming after the blank wall (as far as the book goes) in England.

Monday, March 6th

C. still has a temperature; stays in bed all day. He has eaten nothing—doesn't like the vegetable bouillon and doesn't like anyone to come in and fuss around him.

I go out between 12 and 1 with Jon. On the way back I buy a can of meat bouillon for C., also rush into a flower store to get some white violets for Mrs. Miller's birthday "party" tonight.

I go down to Mrs. Miller's car waiting for me. It is raining hard. The violets are soaking wet (because I put them in water). C. said they looked like old crushed white tissue paper!

When I get there Jo [Davidson] and Gertrude Stein and Alice B. Toklas are there. Jo comes up gallantly and makes me feel at home. Mrs. Miller puts on my violets, which drip all over her black velvet sash. Jo has brought her a watercolor. And I see a new flower painting by Vlaminck.

I meet Gertrude Stein. A stocky, solid, middle-aged person with stubbly gray hair cut like a man's; a squarish face, a good chin, aquiline nose, and curious little hard brown eyes, near together. She has on a kind of long-skirted brown crash suit with a white uniform blouse (which looks as if she had made it herself

[1] Samuel Sloane, editor at Harcourt, Brace.

in a fit of independence), clipped at the throat with a very beautiful old paste (no—probably diamond) pendant pin, and old diamond cuff-links. Except for these signs of luxury the dress looks like a costume for a "Mädchen in Uniform" matron. But her face is strong—simple and very American.

Alice B. Toklas (I really never *believed* in her, but there she was!) was more conventionally dressed in black taffeta with a modern Chanel (pink stone) flower necklace around her high-necked dress. This managed to look very old-fashioned and so did she. She had very dark hair combed into a low bang over her forehead, dark sympathetic and intelligent eyes, rather elegant hook nose, altogether a gracious, intelligent, and kind face.

Jo was bantering Gertrude Stein (who talks in a loud, rather harsh mannish voice) on her getting a dog—a new dog after her old one had died. (She got one as much the same as possible, immediately, and named it the same.)

"Oh, how *could* you!" said Jo.

"But it's the only thing to do!" she parried. *"Le Roi est mort—vive le Roi!"*

(She likes to be different, I thought instinctively.)

The Lin Yutangs arrive, he looking around disappointedly for C. I explain about the cold.

We go in to supper, I sit between Gertrude Stein and Lin Yutang.

Gertrude Stein is easy to talk with because she does not want anything from you. She *delivers*—and very well. I found myself pinned down by what she was saying, about Americans (Louis Bromfield in this case) going home and excitedly "discovering" America. "There seems to me something indecent in it, like 'discovering' you love your mother and father or your husband."

I say it's like being afraid you'll "forget" someone who's died.

We got onto memory and she says that when she is asked why there are so few geniuses she always says the same thing. She went into a rather profound definition of genius and its connection to a *time sense*. In other words (I cannot quote her—I was so intent on understanding her that I lost the words) that it was only *the now* which should be written, what you felt and were *now*. The trouble was that many writers looked back or forward. So few could write *the now*. (This is sloppily stated. She said it concisely, and it cut deep; but, as always, abstractions are difficult to quote.) I gathered that it was the same thing, said *philosophically*, that Rilke said *poetically* of writing poetry, "even to have memories is not sufficient. If there are many of them one must be able to forget them, and one must have the great patience to wait till they return. For the memories *themselves are not yet what is required. Only if they become blood within us, sight and gesture, nameless and no longer distinguishable from ourselves*, only then is it possible, in some very rare hour, for the first word of a verse to arise in their midst—to proceed from them" [*Journal of My Other Self*].

After an intense and absorbing conversation with her I turn to the delightful and *not* intense Lin Yutang. We talk about C. chiefly: his life on the farm, his school, his wanting to go into pure science, etc. Lin Yutang is a most sympathetic person. We talked of the soundness one has if one has a basic connection with the land.

After dinner I find (the ladies segregating) that I am again listening to Gertrude Stein, completely absorbed, trying very hard, sitting on the edge of my chair, to memorize those clear chiseled and profound statements.

"Life," she said, with one of her magnificently careless gestures, "is just one thing—just one thing—very simple, that's all it is: we are living here in a finite world, a finite universe, with limits. Even in flying there are limits. One lives in a *finite* world and one is able to *conceive* of the Infinite." (She is sitting down squarely, her legs slightly apart, like a man, her strong firm hands cupping a "finite world" on her lap.) Now—leaving out the disquieting murmur inside me that probably a scientist like du Noüy would dispute the statement that the world is finite—still that is a magnificent statement.

She went on to illustrate what pain, what complexities, what inevitable difficulties arose from this paradox, this lame state of man. "Even Hitler and Mussolini . . . they conceive of the infinite. They want to make the finite (race, nation, etc.) become the infinite. Every world conqueror has dreamed of doing this, but it is doomed to failure . . . carries the seeds of its own death. You are sure to wake up one morning like Alexander brokenhearted because 'there are no more worlds to conquer.' "

She goes on and gives other examples. I am reminded of Christ's "Render unto Caesar the things that are Caesar's." I tell her this and she agrees. *"He* only tried to do it *here."* She tapped the brain. (The Kingdom of God.)

I am quite excited by this idea and am well off down the road it has opened up in my mind. But she goes right on—about *humanitarianism:* "I know. It's the fashion in America." Much overrated, she felt, in industrial and other fields. "Mankind on the whole is pretty contented with life, otherwise it wouldn't live."

"But," I said, "that doesn't mean one shouldn't try to *better* conditions?"

"Who is to say what is *better?"* she said.

A long discussion of "dull" lives. "Everyone's life is dull looked at from the outside."

How did we get onto Munich and Louis Bromfield again? "Louis got excited in September because Europe didn't go to war and he wanted it to go to war. Well, Europe didn't *want* to go to war, that's all. Czechoslovakia—yes, that was too bad, but Europe didn't *want* to go to war for it."

She went on to tell me a beautiful story about a peasant in the south of France, a simple uneducated man. She asked him if there were going to be a war.

"No," he said, "there isn't going to be a war."

"Why not?" she asked.

"Ce n'est pas logique," he said simply (very French, she pointed out).

"Why not?" she asked again.

"Well," he said, "you see, Mademoiselle, I am forty-two. And I fought in the last war and here I am about to fight in another war. And my son is eighteen and he would fight in this war. *Ce n'est pas logique.* If I were *sixty* and it was my *grandson* who was eighteen, *then* there might be a war. But now, *ce n'est pas logique.*"

I do think this is superb. We were still talking when the men came back. About Munich and Chamberlain, whom she was for, oddly enough (since most artistic, literary, and "intellectuals" are against him). She said that he was arranging things in a common-sense way, as a housewife arranges squabbles in her kitchen.

We go into the studio and I talk with Mrs. Lin Yutang, a vigorous, earnest woman who teaches her children Chinese in the morning, works at a China Relief office all afternoon, and takes French lessons besides! She is a little hard to understand and I spend so much time concentrating on the words as they rush out, bubble out over each other, that I sometimes miss the meaning.

Gertrude Stein and Lin Yutang—or rather Gertrude Stein— had a conversation on Catholicism and the young French Catholic Party that I wanted to hear. She said no one could understand France without understanding Catholicism.

And then suddenly we were going. Alice B. Toklas standing up—stooped and small and black—looked like the frail little old maid she is. And Gertrude Stein put a small round felt cap on her head (of no particular shape or size; it stuck on the top of her head and did not fit, having the same impetuous homemade look as the brown crash suit) and suddenly looked absurd. They both seemed to me pathetic at that moment—sad old women going home. Though I suppose this isn't true. I think they are probably very happy and contented with life.

And I go home to C. in bed. I get him some cornflakes and milk and myself some too and sit on the bed and try to describe Gertrude Stein to him. I have the feeling that she is quite a big person of this age—*not* for her literary "pioneering," her own "daring" experiments in writing, as she no doubt thinks, but as a great personality nurturing, encouraging, and stimulating a whole body of writers. The Dr. Johnson of this age. The Mme de Staël. I kept thinking of the Yeats' poem:

> "They came like swallows and like swallows went,
> And yet a woman's powerful character
> Could keep a swallow to its first intent;
> And half a dozen in formation there,
> That seemed to whirl upon a compass-point,
> Found certainty upon the dreaming air. . . ."

Wednesday, March 8th

C. goes for a first sitting to Jo Davidson. I go to the Détroyats' for lunch. (The children—Jon washed and brushed and nails scrubbed, Land with his curls peeping from under his new blue hat—go off with Soeur Lisi and Soeur Dora and baby carriages from the park at noon. At such a pace, too, those black head-scarves flying behind!)

I have on my last year's suit, which does not fit. "Fanny" has on Chanel's faultless navy dress with short sleeves, a cyclamen scarf at her throat and a modern jeweled pin. He is there and his flying friend.

I schooled Jon beforehand on how to shake hands with Mme Détroyat, looking *right at her* and saying *"Bonjour, Madame."* He apparently does this so well that Soeur Lisi is quite astonished. However, two-year-old lisping Jean-Michel nearly bowls me over, when introduced (*"Qu'est-ce-qu'on fait aux dames, Jean-Michel?"*), by kissing my hand!

The children eat upstairs, Land on Soeur Lisi's lap, round-eyed with the newness, and Jon, shy and saying *loudly* as I enter (he is eating carrots), "Does anything come after this?" And Land cries, being put to bed.

I go home soon after lunch. I miss C. awfully. Only *his* technical ability (and the children) fit me into this world.

"What do you do all day?" asks Fanny. What *do* I do?

I walk home. Blowy and sunny. C. telephones me to come to the studio. The head is all slapped up (one feels it *must* have been "slapped up") already! The brow, intensity of gaze, and squizzled eyes (a little *too* squizzled) are very good. I am glad he has got that. But the nose is wrong, or something between the mouth and the nose.

It is amazing how much he has done in one day and there is much of C. in it. He is enthusiastic about it and asks me to come for lunch tomorrow.

The children come home late (the house was tomblike without them at teatime) and slightly flushed and tired.

Thursday, March 9th

To Despiau. I am getting terribly bored with this long, long contact that is *not* a contact. However, he seems in good spirits and looks much better. I cannot see *any* change in the head. He touches a little spot here and a little spot there with a paintbrush.

Afterward I go to Galerie Le Niveau where I see a lovely Vlaminck landscape (a street and bluish snow and sky) which is very expensive (7000 francs). I say, "No, don't take it to the light; it is too much," and they say they might make a *"petit prix"* on it. I also ask about a tiny but nice Utrillo—which is 10,000 francs!

To Jo's, where C. has been all morning. The head is very vivid from the front but the side is not right yet. We talk about it. Jo says, "And think that some people take forty sittings!" And I (we are just about to go for lunch) jump at the chance to tell him about Despiau. (C. says I grabbed at it with both hands!) It has been hanging over me for days and I am so afraid he will find out about it *not* from us, or much later by accident, and feel hurt that we kept it from him.

He is a bit taken aback. But now the ice is broken. "Did *Despiau* do *you? When?*" And I go on to tell him as easily as possible that it was started a long time ago but it isn't done yet. It *looks* done to me, etc. Also it was my half of the bargain—that C. was to have a bust done if I did.

"So he made you sit forty times, and he sits four!"

We go up to lunch with his son and daughter-in-law (very slim and French—dark, gay, and with finesse and charm. She talks English with an enchanting French lilt and accent). Lunch goes quite well, though Jo keeps coming back to Despiau. What is it like, how long did he take on the clay, what does he talk about? And we spill the salt: "Oh dear, we're going to quarrel," says Jo ("Despiau!" I think). And we both throw salt over our shoulders.

We tell him it's very beautiful but that I have been smoothed out a good deal—made into a Despiau. That we don't talk at all.

After lunch I go back to the children. I tell Jo I think he has given C. "too good" a nose. He says with bravado humor he is trying to outdo Despiau.

"Oh no," I say, "*don't* smooth him all out."

"I *couldn't!*" he promises, serious again.

I go out much relieved. It is such a little thing. But I knew it would bother Jo, and I couldn't bear to have our friendship blossoming on that unsteady stone. The friendship is not quite so blossomy now, but it is surer.

Home to the children and take them out in the park. Land insists on walking in all the rough dirty places—ditches and drains, and the rough turf of the bridle paths. He is an adventurer in the art of walking and gets a tremendous thrill out of conquering those mountainous slopes.

Friday, March 10th

A letter at breakfast from Miss Cazalet. "I have heard from Augustus John, who says he will be delighted to paint you or your husband or both of you, when he is finished with a few jobs he has started here.

"He suggests painting you in France as he is under the impression that you have a house in Brittany. . . ."

I give a shout, which startles Jon ("What is the matter,

Mother?") and run in to tell C. I am really terribly excited—but *will* he come to Illiec, and what *would* happen?

"It is not considered advisable to have him come and live with you" (drunk, moody, etc.).

C. pictures him staggering across the Sillon arm in arm with Louis!

However, I am already thinking out how to give him the "chalet" (that's Mother in me!). That big room will be the studio, only it will have to have a rug and some comfortable chairs; and the small room full of Ambroise Thomas's horrors will be the bedroom, and the little room with the odds and ends of china will be a dressing room. We might even get a bathtub in it. . . .

But it must be cleaned out and painted (is it worth it?) and I shall have to go down and fix it up. So my mind goes all morning, taking Jon to school and back.

The Millers here for supper. Much talk and admiration for the new Vlamincks, especially the white flowers. ("I can tell you you never would have got it if I'd seen it first!")

Mrs. Miller trying to explain why the table does not meet around the back of the pot of flowers. She turns the picture upside down and points to lines and talks about "thrusts" and "this side of the picture would be exactly the same as that, and that you must *never* have in a painting." I am quite convinced until C. says drily after all is finished, from the back of the room:

"It's too bad *God* slipped up on that."

The centerpiece looks lovely. The white daisies light up the anemones.

Saturday, March 11th

To Despiau's. He is quite happy about the head—says it gives him pleasure to do it, his friends all like it, it begins to approach the general, to leave the particular. *"C'est la plastique qui m'in-téresse."* He did not mean to *"supprimer les oreilles"*—it just happened that way.

He says he has gained five kilos since he started to work on my head. (I tell him I have lost!)

He works with a brush on a tiny spot where the hair leaves the forehead and on one ear. The other ear is not nearly as much done but he is not going to do any more to it. *"Ça ne compte pas."*

Back to the house and over to Jo's. The head is much better. I am very happy about it. The conversation again gets onto Despiau. I think he feels an unconscious disappointment that though he (Jo) has had great success, great fame, he has never quite got the thing Despiau has—the acclaim of artists. It torments him and he wants to know just how Despiau does it—is his (Jo's) method lacking? This takes itself out in a passionate defense to me of his own methods of working. "I could go on and on, on this, but I think I'd lose something—I think that kind of perfection is death."

I agree in principle, though Despiau is not "death." He manages it. But Jo couldn't. Each one *must* work his own way. I feel sorry for Jo and wish I could comfort him. How insecure he is under that good-natured full-blooded exterior! After all, weak, temperamental, neurotic Despiau is much more *secure,* really, in himself.

Sunday, March 12th

Before breakfast (even!) Germaine comes to me with that self-important air and asks if she can have a word with me. After breakfast she breaks it to me that she and Alfred cannot stay any longer. They cannot put up with Marie. It is impossible; long bursts of invectives in French of the indignities they have suffered. Alfred cannot even open a window. She heats the dishes so hot in order to burn his hands. She says dreadful, unrepeatable things to them. So that finally she (Germaine) was obliged to say to Alfred, *"N'écoute plus cette ordure!"* She also says, *"Elle est Juive. Elle est divorcée. Personne sait d'où elle vient."*

My sympathies are with Marie.

I talk to Marie. She does not fling invectives but says she has had a great deal to put up with, but if I wish, she will leave. But I do not want her to.

She says it started when she "passed the time of day" with Alfred, just to be polite, and Germaine kept running in and asking what they had been talking about.

"I do not know if it was a little jealousy or not," she went on to say in a typically French way, "but you can see for yourself, Madame, that old man is too old for me!"

We also get a note from Miss H. She says she will not be back until the end of the month.

Monday, March 13th

Out to Jo Davidson's at night for dinner. The Lin Yutangs, the Millers, and Jo.

C.'s head is all done in plaster. I am really very happy about it. Not only is it C., but it is C. as you like best to think of him—the brows and eyes concentrated with that cool intensity that is very typical. The man of vision and the man of practical common sense united. And the mouth is good too, almost smiling, with dry humor—*very* C.

But it is the forehead that attracts one—as it should—that he has played up even as to texture, leaving it smoother than the lower part of the face, so that it is lighter, somehow, like a highlight in a painting.

Yes, I am very happy about it, and yet—though I wouldn't breathe this to anyone—a little disappointed. It *is* C., yes—but nothing more. Shouldn't a work of art be something more? Shouldn't you have that extra thrill of surprise, shouldn't something come out that you never saw before—the mystery that is in every human being, the divinity?

The Despiau head, though it is much *less like me* than this of C., has that extra quality.

I am happy to see (and sometimes help) C. and Lin Yutang meeting in conversation, on Dr. Carrel, on Chinese medicine, on "luck." "Everything being infinitely improbable, nothing is surprising." I also enjoy talking to Mme Lin Yutang. She tells us about her child being cured by a Chinese doctor. An astounding story bare with anguish, even through her broken cataracting English and in that small after-dinner parlor of women almost Biblical in its intensity (the woman taking her child to Christ). How her child, in the care of a Western specialist, was wasting away under her eyes and finally she snatched her up and ran with her to the Chinese doctor, who gave her all sorts of odd things in the prescription: a piece of iron, a sea-shell, an old tooth, etc. (forty or fifty ingredients). She had to wait and take her place with hundreds of patients. But the child lived, began to get better, and was cured.

And Jo—big, bearded, jolly—his rich voice filling the rooms with his stories, his philosophies, warm, poetic, full of life and understanding. Saying as we are about to leave, of me, "I want to do *her*. I'm jealous of Despiau, I can get something of you that Despiau can't get."

"I *know* that," I say, "you got it in the head of Charles."

"Oh, I'm *good,*" says he, tapping his chest with bravado, "I've not got any inferiority complex. I *know* I'm good!"

"Oh," I laugh, "I wasn't trying to buck you up when I said that—I really meant it."

And yet . . . that was *just* what I *was* trying to do, now I analyze it. I *do* want to buck him up and *do* feel sorry for him, in a strange way. And he *has* got an inferiority complex, even if he doesn't know it or show it.

Tuesday, March 14th

To Despiau in the morning. He says he didn't sleep well and feels tired but after working for a while he feels better. *"Je me sens en train."* He says he enjoys working on the head (he pats at an ear, today). He stands back from it, his eyes squizzled and twinkling, his face aglow with pleasure. *"Ça commence!"* he says to himself ecstatically (after four months!). Each day near the end of the session he says, *"Ah, maintenant je vois ce qu'il faut faire la prochaine fois!"* He says I am a very good model.

I, however, am tired, and cannot help thinking of the *hours* spent in that studio, what I might have done with them—or should I? I feel I have wasted the winter, not learned French, not written anything, not started a child (which is the cause of my real gloom). The "winter" of course has only been three months and much of it has gone into getting settled in a new place, the business of living, settling, finding what you want to do. Schools, doctors, exercise, shops.

At least Jon is better—much better. I think my vigilance is partly responsible for that. Soeur Lisi, the doctor, the school, the park, the diet have all been good for him. He is in a position to profit from Illiec and the summer now—to start "even." And that makes the winter worth while.

And I have enjoyed the sense and feel of Paris—the look of it—and the fun C. and I have had getting the pictures, and people—Jo, the Millers, and meeting the Lin Yutangs and Gertrude Stein.

And perhaps the book, so painful and vague, is ripening inside, although nothing is written but notes and plans.

In the afternoon, I call the Benedict Bureau to find out if we can keep the apartment till June. It seems very unlikely, which is a blow. I hoped to retrieve the winter in the last two months.

I also try to get someone to take Germaine and Alfred's place.

To bed early. I feel very limp, and C. still has not got back his strength after the flu.

Wednesday, March 15th

Something is breaking in Europe. Slovakia splits from the Czechs. The Slovakian Minister goes to Berlin. The Czechs declare all will be settled peaceably and as before (no break-up of state). But there are disquieting rumors. The papers contradict themselves. What part is Germany playing in this? *Supposedly* none, but one can't help sitting on the edge of one's chair again.

People are talking with a kind of glum and cynical acceptance of "the news": "Of course one knew it was coming, but still . . ."

We go out to supper with the du Noüys to see their films.

Much French spoken. A delicious dinner and I get into a conversation with a French surgeon on Van Gogh—in French! (Which I find is not so difficult as I imagined. The du Noüys say my French has improved tremendously and people say the accent is good, which gives me confidence!) He is apparently a specialist on the Impressionists and argues passionately for Van Gogh. He reminds me of the painting Van Gogh did of a pair of shoes—an old dirty worn pair of shoes—which he has painted with the passion and intensity of his whole life. (This clicks in my mind and I think, That pair of shoes . . . I had forgotten. That is one of those "points of light" that are the center of a whole field of vision. This is the kernel that I shall carry away from this dinner. It is worth while going for that.)

Then we see a color film the du Noüys took of the [American] West—the Grand Canyon, Taos, the Painted Desert, etc. It is very well done, with appropriate music ("Give me my boots and saddle," cowboy songs). It was fun hearing du Noüy describe, in French, the beauties and rarities of the West, like an initiate explaining Picasso to a group of society art-smarts. The West as a "discovery," as a *"pièce de résistance."* It does not fit well into that role—gets cramped.

The film is beautiful—those unreal blues and amethysts of the canyon—the reds and pinks of the desert, and the plains . . .

Everyone around me is saying, *"Épatant!" "Éblouissant!" "Formidable!"* in an astonished way, as though it were the moon.

And I (and C. too, I think) am only feeling—although the West is not my home—homesickness, and recognition: This is mine—yes, even though it is fantastic, even though it looks like the moon, still, it is part of me, it is natural to me. I am native to it, much more native than I am to the last and familiar shot of the Dôme des Invalides in the falling snow. C. has flown over every inch of that country and I have flown over much of it with him. Those early-married T.A.T. trips.

Refreshments afterward. The Van Gogh man is going to take us to the Louvre on Sunday to see the Impressionists.

But we get home late—at twelve—and C. is cross about it. It

does seem stupid. And yet I got something from it: the shoes of Van Gogh and the sense of America. I think of what Gertrude Stein said of her scorn for Americans who get excited about "discovering" America, like discovering you love your father or mother, or your husband. I understand now what she meant.

Thursday, March 16th

Germany has annexed Bohemia and Moravia. They have "put themselves" under her "protection"—how "willingly" is self-evident. German soldiers are at Prague. Hitler is in that castle on the hill we looked at so often and the swastika floats on top of the city. I am glad there is no war and Prague has not been destroyed, but there is something terrifically sad about the accounts of those German soldiers filing grimly into the streets of Prague with the snow falling. The silent crowds of Czechs, and that heartbreaking and spontaneous last singing of the Czech national anthem bursting from the crowd in the square.

I feel fiercely and instinctively angry inside. This time you have gone too far. You are *wrong*. You are standing on a wrong and you (Germany) will ultimately fail because of it. And yet there seems to be no reason why she should fail. She has straightened her frontier, gained arms, men, money, industries, and food—without a struggle.

The papers are full of Hitler's broken promises: "I have no further territorial ambitions in Europe." The Race principle: his only wanting to defend, unite, and protect *Germans*.

Of course all treaties are broken. All nations break their word eventually, but the Germans break their word the moment it leaves their lips. The ink not yet dry on the paper.

And all the Edens and Hulls are right. I can't bear it. Poor Chamberlain. I still feel he was right to do what he did—right to go ahead on the faith, on the assumption, that the Germans were honest, meant what they said. And, besides, it was the *only* thing he could do, really. Their hands were tied—and are still. But do they realize it (the Edens) or will we have war?

France is very excited. England is stunned.

Off to Despiau. Do not speak of the news. He is far away from it all and works well (so he says). In the end he says, "You have been very good"—*"très sage"*—in that rather gentle humorous way he has, as though talking to a child. "Because you have been so *very* good, I will show you that (a head he has worked at in a corner, for a big statue). He puts it up on a high pedestal for me to see. It is lovely, with great feeling in it, a kind of yearning.

I come back to the house to see a couple who seem very nice and willing; I engage them.

In the afternoon I take the children out in the park. As usual, all the little boys who are Jon's friends come up and shake my hand.

Friday, March 17th

Slovakia is also under the "protection" of Germany. Hungary gets Ruthenia and a common border with Poland. The boundary of Germany now looks terrifying on the map—like a finger pointing to the Ukraine (the point of Slovakia).

Go to Mrs. Carter's for tea, where I meet three or four carelessly well-dressed charming French and American (married to French) young women. Intelligent, sympathetic, but enclosed—enclosed in a safe world, a closed corporation. I feel as if they were doomed. (I *mind* their being doomed, too, much more than I mind the usual stupid social people being doomed. These were intelligent aristocrats—a pleasant, tasteful, sophisticated world.) They talk politics (international) with a kind of gloomy acceptance of the situation.

Dinner at the Millers'. Chamberlain is speaking on the radio as we come in—a *bitterly* disillusioned speech. We cannot hear the end as people come in talking and do not want to hear. "What *is* the use," some woman says, "saying the same thing over and over?"

(There is a disquieting *après nous le déluge* attitude here in France.)

England has "come to" with a blast of protests. Rumors that the German troops are going right on through Czechoslovakia, of ultimatums to Rumania. Daladier asks for dictatorial powers in the crisis. Conferences of France and England.

But what *are* they going to do?

C. and I go down to Despiau. Not a very good morning. Despiau fiddles on the mouth, in despair, because he says he tried to do something better and he has lost something; works the whole time to recover it. Finally says, *"C'est fait—j'ai gagné."*

"What?" I say. "Have you really got it, have you got what you were trying to get?"

"Oui (he smiles), *presque!"* We laugh.

A friend of his, a sculptor, comes in to see it. He thinks it very beautiful and *"très évocateur."*

Despiau smiles and is pleased. He says to C. (in French, which C. doesn't understand), "Your wife has been a very good model—very good. I have really enjoyed doing it, really had my heart in it."

I think he has, in that vague way of his, and rather likes me.

Jon is in bed with swollen glands and a red eye and a temperature. His ear aches, he says. It looks like mumps. I thought he was getting on so well. . . .

Call the doctor. Go out to get flowers for tonight, cookies and peppermints.

The doctor comes at 6:30: Jon *has* mumps! He played with Land this morning so Land will probably get it in fifteen days!

Jon is quite good and we laugh about it.

The papers are still full of protestations, meetings, and speeches. Daladier has been given full powers. The Rumanian rumors of an ultimatum denied. Still, things are pretty upset.

It is very cold and gray—winter again. We go to the Tour d'Argent for lunch with the Van Gogh man. We sit on the enclosed roof and look at the Seine below in the gray half-mist and the back of Notre Dame. It looks, as he says, like a Marquet painting. One of those superb French meals. Quenelles of fish with cheese sauce, white wine; duck with sauce, red wine; salad; crème brûlée with pears in the cream.

Then, stuffed, we go on to the Louvre, which is crowded and rather gloomy.

Through the medieval rooms (newly arranged) and up into the nineteenth century. I kept thinking, They could *never* move out all these in case of war. There are *miles* of priceless pictures, to say nothing of sculpture, ceramics, glass, tapestries, furniture. It could all be destroyed overnight.

It was like being in the sun to be in the rooms of the Impressionists, and going "indoors" to move on to other rooms.

Out into the snow and cold.

The Du Noüys for tea. He talks to C. about his work and new laboratory. But he is very tired at night and says, "I am two nights sleepier than I usually am." Land comes in. He is like the Soviet guides: he *asserts* everything in a loud voice. He never just "speaks."

Jon's temperature is down to 100 and he has drawn pictures happily all day.

Monday, March 20th

Alfred and Germaine leave, still with protestations that it was too much to *supporter*. The new couple arrive. They are willing and painstaking. Marie tells me that the old couple had a long conversation with the new couple and have undoubtedly poisoned their minds (the suspicion of the French!). I talk to the new couple and hope all will go well. They find the house *badly* in need of cleaning! The whole morning goes into telling them what to do, arranging accounts, seeing that Jon has something to do in bed. . . .

Out for a walk between 12 and 1. C. and I discuss plans. What are we going to do? What is going to happen in Europe? Mother has sent me a letter suggesting she come over for a short visit. Shall I tell her to come? It is very difficult with everything in the air. Is C. going home? Shall I go too? I can't leave the children. Move them to Illiec? Now? Later? With Mother's trip and the trip to England and Augustus John all extra factors. It is too difficult and the international situation too uncertain. Decide to cable Mother not to come, although I *hate* to do it.

In the evening to the Lin Yutangs' for a wonderful dinner of Chinese food. (Jo Davidson, Mrs. Miller, and another American woman there.) But we can hardly enjoy it. The talk is on war.

Mrs. Lin is preoccupied with the food and the party going well, but deeply disturbed by war talk and agitation. He is serious and disturbed, more than I have ever seen him.

After dinner the women again talk war and the practical things we should prepare for: get passports ready . . . money . . . car . . . petrol.

I feel depressed—not so much frightened—about war, for I still feel it is some paces off and many things can happen. But I feel angry at the waste of time, strength, and mind of a man like Lin Yutang and hundreds of people like him. The waste of such an evening, made for conversation, philosophy, meeting of minds, learning to live and understand and enjoy life, all going into fruitless (but irresistible) fear . . . war . . . talk.

It is not just that evening but that it symbolizes the world—unable to live, think, work, because of this sword of Damocles. It is dangerous, too, because man cannot live in suspense; after a while he rebels—anything is preferable, even the blind stupid terrible chaos of war.

I am oppressed by the ghost of what the evening might have been and the ghosts of all evenings that are disappearing from the world.

Tuesday, March 21st

To Despiau in the morning. He is quite calm and himself. We talk a little of war. He says he went through the last and does not want another. I say the Germans do not do well on success. He says, *"C'est la chose la plus difficile du monde, de supporter la gloire*—to remain oneself in success." I say I think *he* has done it, and also C. He says, *"Ah, votre mari—il est magnifique!"*

Then he works intently and calmly all morning—something to the nose. It is quiet and he is absorbed in work and we forget war. He says he worked all through the September crisis and never moved. I like that—in contrast to last night.

There is a sublime indifference about Despiau that is very impressive. I really believe he would just as soon do my head as C.'s—in fact, even rather, and he does not care *who* we are.

Then to Jo's for lunch. Frida Rivera[1] is there, enchanting in a Tehuantepec costume: big skirt (black or brown) with bands of gold and red embroidery and a deep stiff pleated white lace ruffle at the bottom. Her dark hair around her head with a band of yellow wool (braided into it) and some little yellow orchids caught in the braid in front, like a tiara of flowers.

She looked enchanting, not artificial at all, but natural as a child—as she is.

When she spoke it was in a terrific New York slang and accent. "Gee, Jo, it's *swell!*" she says of C.'s head, and "I'm skinny as hell, yes?"

Then when I ask her what kind of things she paints (she has a show here), she lifts her hands and smiles and says lightly, "Oh, cuckoo things!" (Which I gather they are—Surrealist!)

We go up to lunch—delicious. Frida sits at the head of the table with the sun behind her shining on the gold orchids in her black hair. A very good lunch: *quiche Lorraine* and *poulet rôti,* and red wine and cheese and salad. Jo and Frida laugh and tease each other through the meal. I can't keep my eyes off her. She is not pretty, really, but she *acts* like a pretty woman, like a beautiful woman—no, like a child who is used to being spoiled.

After lunch she curls up in Jo's yellow sitting room against a

[1] Artist and wife of Diego Rivera, the Mexican mural painter.

brown satin chair, her head crooked, her big skirt slantwise across the chair: "I am so slee-e-epy." She curls up, like a kitten.

When I say I must go Frida says she must go too, to sleep. She puts both hands on my shoulders gently, like a child, and bends forward gently and kisses me on both cheeks—naturally, more naturally than most people shake hands. She also kisses Jo. Then when she came to shake hands with C., he says, teasing, "I am the only one you leave out?"

"Oh, is it?" says Frida, wide-eyed, and then just as easily puts her arms up to him and kisses him on both cheeks. She is a little embarrassed afterwards, and he a little surprised!

Then I walk home in a tearing umbrellas-inside-out wind and rain.

Wednesday, March 22nd

Walk "around the lake" with C. This walk hardly touches the lake but is like a dream landscape. Several familiar and associated spots, strung together like a dream, but no real connection. Across the open space, a road to the "pink-sidewalk woods," across another road to the "mistletoe woods," through these and across a stream through another woods; head for the Van Gogh poplars, a winding stream which we cross eventually, C. tightrope walking across a narrow iron railing (while I take the bridge of stones).

During or just after supper Mrs. Miller calls up and says, "Have you heard the news?" "No," I say, "what is it?" "They've just given it out on British Broadcasting that Hitler is on a battleship going to Memel and that ultimatums have been sent to Lithuania, Estonia, Latvia, Poland, and Denmark. They must join the Reich." C. and I just don't believe it. We turn on the radio to get news but hear only Ravel's "Bolero" and announcers describing the Ballet at Sadlers Wells to which the King and Queen are taking M. and Mme Lebrun.[1]

---

[1] The French President.

Look for news in the paper. Find, of last night's rumor, the only true one is that Hitler is on a battleship going to Memel.

Sunday, March 26th

Around the lake with C. talking intently plans for the summer: to go home? Get our feet in America again, see what is going on, I and the children in Maine, C. going about more. *Maine itself* appeals to me very much. But I hate to give up Illiec and our summer there, making it *our own* place. Also I wanted Augustus John to paint C.

But on the other hand we do not want to lose touch with America. I feel that quite strongly, and also for the children. I'd love Jon to have a summer in Maine.

I feel that C. especially should get back.

During lunch the secretary of the Duke of Windsor calls up to get our address! After lunch a note appears from the Duchess asking us to dine at 8:45 (what an hour!) on Thursday.

We will go, but *how* do you address a Duchess? "Peers" says "Her Grace" and "Madam," but I *can't* quite do that.

Monday

To the Cézanne show at the Rosenberg Gallery. The best one I have ever seen. Some beautiful still lifes and landscapes. A vase of tulips that made one catch one's breath. They stood up in the clear blue air. I felt if only I could stand in front of it long enough I would learn something.

I arrange the flowers after tea: red ranunculi with yellow daisies look well in the yellow vase.

Maryse Hilz, the flier, Fanny and Michel Détroyat, "Michel" Witzig, and Mr. and Mrs. Paul Claudel (the younger) for supper. All went well and supper was good and yet, somehow, after we discuss war, the latest news, and late aviation talk, we come to a blank wall with those nice gay, open, but simple flying people. The Claudels have more depth and interest me. She is Greek.

Michel Détroyat wants C. to fly with him to "greet" the [Pan American] "Clipper" which is making its maiden flight (first regular flight—the experimental one was last summer) across the ocean to Marseilles (from the Azores) tomorrow. C. doesn't want to go. It will be a lot of ballyhoo and there will be nothing he can *do* when he gets there. "It'll land all right without us!" says C., laughing. Michel laughs, too, but he can't understand C.'s not wanting to go. He really can't make out C. at all. I catch him looking at C. a little bewildered at times. He is dimly curious and admiring of C. What does he do in Paris? Why doesn't he go off on flights and more flights? Why doesn't he see a lot of aviation people? And yet he likes C. so much and seems to understand him so well on some subjects. Fanny does not wonder—she never has.

Détroyat and the others seem to think there will be no war . . . with good-natured assurance. Paul Claudel is not so optimistic.

They go home early.

Tuesday, March 28th

Not a scrap of news about the "Clipper" in the London *Times* though it is all over the front page of the French and American papers. There's the English for you!

To Jo's "party" to see his huge bronze Walt Whitman. We go early, before the rest of the people arrive. I like the Walt Whitman: it is very American and Big.

Wednesday, March 29th

After lunch I go downtown to the bank (full of short-skirted, long-legged, slim, beautiful, but slightly hoydenish smart American girls. What a race it is!). I get some cyclamen shoes, a clip, and ear bows for the dinner tomorrow night [with the Windsors].

To the Lin Yutangs' for tea. They have all their trunks packed. They are leaving for America on the 8th. Also the Millers are going on the 12th. They have moved the sailing up because of the war scare.

If C. goes too on the 8th, I shall be all alone in Paris the last month—not that I think there will be a war but I shall miss Mrs. Miller and the fun I've had with them.

Thursday, March 30th

Daladier has made a speech. It is what is called a "strong speech," very French and full of *"Jamais! Jamais!"* (Never will they yield an inch of French soil, though they are still open to peaceable negotiation with Italy[1].)

To Despiau—C. with me. I am quite startled when he says quite calmly that there is nothing more he can do to it to make it better and if it cannot get better it will get worse, so he will stop. *"Merci,"* he says with a little smile and suggestion of a bow, as always when he has finished a sitting. But now it is all finished! Though I may have to come back for a few touches someday, on the wax or the second plaster.

He asks C. whether he will allow several copies to be made for national museums—in London, Paris, New York? C. says yes, of course, anything is all right for museums. Despiau is pleased. He is very happy about the bust. He is not happy about his *bonhomme*—the Apollo he has been working on for three years! He says it needs so little but he can't find it. Only the touch of a wand and it will come to life.

Finally we leave after his gentle smile and handshake.

Home to lunch with Madariaga. He is very brilliant and interesting. A quick birdlike little man with his head cocked on one side and his humorous twinkling eyes. He makes some remarkable statements, including one that universal suffrage is not necessarily an adjunct to democracy. He says that Hitler is the evil genius of Europe—the desire for unity through brute force, the conqueror. But this *devil* cannot be exorcised except by the complementary *god*—the good genius, unity through peaceful means, peaceful organization. But as yet there is no god, no leader. Of the chances for war now: "Who knows—it is all in the mind of

[1] This in reply to Italian demands for such territories as Tunis, Corsica, and Nice.

one man, and (with a gesture and twinkle) I sometimes even doubt whether it is in his mind or whether it is not somewhere else—in his solar plexus." He is not pessimistic about the ultimate future of Europe, only about the near future.

It is intensely stimulating to hear C. and him talking together.

He notices our pictures and likes them. He is on some committee to make sure that the painters are using good colors and canvas, as many paintings are going to pieces. They talk also of the poor ink people use, even for documents. In Washington (C. says) an official used "washable ink."

"Ah," said Madariaga, "that would be the ink for Mr. Hitler!"

Dress for dinner [at the Duke and Duchess of Windsor's] in a hurry, as usual (I never seem to leave quite enough time), in my new deep lavender blue with the big skirt and bustle-bows behind. I put on cyclamen shoes with it and a cyclamen velvet ribbon around my neck in a grandmother's bow. It looks very pretty. We get a taxi and have at least ten minutes to spare, as usual, because they live just around the block from us. Even after coasting up and down Boulevard Suchet we are the first to arrive.

The house is rather formal and French: lots of footmen in uniform. We go up the stairs. The Duke and Duchess are in a little room, paneled in gold and white, with yellow tulips and dusty black iris arranged beautifully on the mantel. They come forward very cordially. She looks very thin and rather tired (though incredibly young—smooth skin, lovely complexion, hair beautifully done in waves away from her face), and dressed in a black dress with a gay striped paillette bolero.

Her rather elaborate attempts at making the ball roll make me ill at ease. I become baffled, as I always do by those people. I have no mask. (And yet she *can* be real, I feel, she has it underneath. This is a mask, a front she is forced to put up.)

Someone immediately comes in—"Kitty"—a tall and rather majestic woman of middle age, quite good-looking, with pride and courage in her face. She is Baroness Rothschild. Then a Prince and Princess. I never got the name. She, simple, with a charming childlike quality. He is very good-looking and charming. Then more people: the Duke and Duchess de Polignac, Ambassador Bullitt.

I feel out of my depth. The women talk that sophisticated ripple of the initiated, a kind of light small talk of a special smart tone, of how much weight they'd lost or gained. "My masseuse died, and since then . . ." How charming the room is, and the Duchess protesting that it wasn't done *at all* (she talks with a strange exaggerated drawl). How they had had the flu, or hadn't . . .

I cannot join in this. The only person I can talk to is the (American-born) Baroness de Rothschild, who has lived, suffered, known almost everything (at least one feels this from her tone talking). She is bitter, tired, and disillusioned, but with real force and a great deal of intelligence. "I no longer hate—or love."

Then in to dinner. A lovely room, formal, with red and gold curtains and mirrors.

I am at the end of the long table between the Duke de Polignac and the Prince. Both French, but they speak beautiful English. They are both intelligent and interesting. I do not find it at all difficult to talk to them—contrary to the women before dinner.

The Duke de Polignac was a strong advocate of a German-French rapprochement but says he does not see what can be done at the moment. He knows Ribbentrop well—says he's very nice, loyal, good friend. He did not get on in England chiefly because of lack of manners, etc. He has just come back from America, which he also knows quite well. We talk chiefly of the foreign situation.

The Prince is very charming, knows Brittany well and loves it—enough to love it gray better than sunny. We talk about Brittany and the French: characteristics, nearness to the fundamentals of living, wisdom and sanity. He is one of those appreciative, intelligent, and sensitive people who win you quickly (at least me, always) and yet I feel a kind of fatalism in him and his kind that is *fatal* to that race of beings. He is completely resigned to war—sure of it—though he says with a kind of half-sad, half-amused detachment, "And yet, you know, the French and the Germans are the only two races . . . they were *made* to get on with each other."

The dinner is very good, though I do not notice what I am eating for I am having a good time. C. does not look as if he were having a very good time. He looks stiff in front, as though his stiff shirt were uncomfortable and he and it were one. The Duchess of Windsor seems to be working quite hard too. She is not next to C. but next to the Prince and someone else, at my end of the table.

The dinner seems to last forever. Finally we get up and the ladies go out into the little gold room. Then the Duchess makes a great to-do about our having to go upstairs and sit in a tiny sitting room, the only one ready. "Now *cree-ee-p* upstairs," etc. It turns out to be an enchanting little room paneled in a pale blue-gray and white with gay chintz and white lilac and white calla lilies in vases and a pale pink and pale blue spray of orchids on the mantel. We also saw the Duke's bathroom and bedroom—quite small—with many pictures of her on the bureau, books on the floor, and a tiny table with a typewriter and special standard lamp where the Duke works on a book he is writing ("from six to eight and from twelve to four," she said. This sounds so very odd I think I must have got it wrong).

Conversation in the room with the ladies is not easy—again about getting thin and the decorations of the room, etc. "I don't care what you say about this house when you leave," the Duchess announces (from which I gather that she *does* care). I talk some politics with the Baroness de Rothschild, who is, naturally, quite bitter. They had to leave Germany for Austria, Austria for Czechoslovakia, and now in France.

The Duchess of Windsor catches me looking at her books, evidently pleased. "I see you are looking at my books!" (Mme de Caillavet's *Salon* and the *Letters* of Proust—this surprises me—also *Edward VII* by Maurois.) "Just to brush up my French . . ."

When the men come in they are all laughing about a bet they made as to how much higher the Étoile is than the Place de la Concorde. Someone had called up a marvelous service called "S'Il Vous Plaît" in Paris which does anything and everything for you—answers any questions, runs errands, etc. The question has been asked but not yet answered. S.V.P. promises to call back. The men stand around, like boys, laughing. It all seems a little infantile to me and C. looks as though he thought so too.

The rest of the evening fritters by in not very good conversation. The Duke comes up and sits next to me and also the Prince but conversation is not as good as it would have been had I talked only to one or the other or if they had been talking together. It is a confused and jumping conversation, with the Duke doing most of the talking. He and I, before the other man comes up, talk a little about our lives: Paris, this spot, hating cities, writing, and C. going back home sometime. He talks to me about the article in some paper about us—both being exiles etc. (very nice he thought it; he didn't mind it at all). I think it is a sentimental and ridiculous article and completely inaccurate—as usual. The modicum of truth in it, or what might have been a truth (of mutual sympathy because of somewhat similar positions), is so cheapened that one recoils from it.

I am amused, however, by their (the press) efforts to find mutual interests: aviation, of course, is all right for the men. But she and I are supposed to talk "fashions, writing, and children"!

He talked about having to watch the outward effect of one's actions a little, even though you didn't like it. (How different to C. I couldn't tell him!) We talked about the press, too, with whom he says they on the whole are on good terms (which he evidently, contrary again to C., thinks is very important). He said, rather out of the blue, that he thought that he preferred an absolutely free press like America (bad as it was) or a controlled press like Germany or Italy (much as he hated it) to the in-between thing the English press was—*supposedly* free but really controlled.

After the Prince came up he talked politics: how he disliked and distrusted this embracing of Russia that was going on now. "We'll find it's a stranglehold." Also about the dreadful conditions of the squatters' ring around Paris, of the French not wanting to pay *direct* taxes, though they didn't mind paying indirect taxes, and why. He went from one subject to another in a rather jumpy and nervous way. We listened and agreed here and there, but any exchange was impossible.

He seemed to me under a strain, like a man struggling with some problem, distractedly talking, from habit—genuinely nice feelings and sometimes *extremely* apt perceptive comments flashing out of this confusion and disorder. Hamlet, I kept thinking. Sometimes flashing out brilliantly, but disturbed underneath, unable to break through to reality—unable to solve life.

How difficult it must be for them!

Later, after the Prince and Princess had gone, the Duchess came over and talked to us a little (C. and I). He is more natural than she is and therefore easier to talk to (for me) in spite of his nervousness. He hides less. It is a curious thing that one feels with her: that she is building up a face that she thinks is appropriate. I have the feeling all the time of immediately thinking the opposite when she says something. She told C. they came to Paris because so many of the Duke's friends had to go so far to see him (in the South of France), that so many people were coming over from London all the time to see him. (C. said he immediately thought maybe nobody *was* coming to see them!)

And yet though this baffles me, it does not make me dislike her. I like her through it, for some reason, partly I think because she is doing it out of defense and because I feel a real person underneath, a person who looks to me (in spite of that lacquered surface) almost tortured underneath in a terrific and rather heroic struggle. But it is such an unnecessary struggle. If they are happy together, as they decidedly seem to be, why make this struggle for a brilliant front? Why try to keep up in this utterly futile world of show? I think both of them have so much more than most of the occupants of that world (though there were interesting people there tonight).

We went down the elevator all laughing and gay. But my predominant feeling, coming home, was relief from the tension, and an immense pity.

Friday, March 31st

A delicious warm spring day, soft with a full sun that seemed to make the world and everyone expand. The kind of day when you open all the windows, lean out, watch people walking on the street, and expect to have something romantic occur. You feel you *must* be outside—you hunger for it, you swim in it, you make excuses to go out, you linger outside, and come in only to go out again. First daffodils and flowering fruit trees.

C. and I go out early for our regular walk. We run across Jon and Land and Soeur Lisi in the Bois, under the green budding chestnut trees. Jon is gathering sticks and Land trotting after him. Soeur Lisi is in her white uniform, no coat (and I have just a suit on—delicious luxury). Land is delighted to see us and tries to run after me.

I cannot think or talk war. The mist of green on the trees is so lovely, and the songs of the birds above our heads. Come back, open the windows, and sit in the sun. Can't work; the sun and softness of the air calls one like sleep—intoxicating. Out again.

C. asks the Allards[1] and Captain Sterling for dinner. The conversation is chiefly technical between Jack Allard and C., though quiet Captain Sterling drops a bombshell by saying, during dinner, that tonight's news was that Chamberlain had announced in the House of Commons that England would support Poland in case of aggression.

"She's said she *would?*" I almost shout. "Yes," he said, "and we have word to the effect that Poland has already been given an ultimatum by Germany. Some people think it may mean war in two or three days."

It is a terribly momentous step. I can't help feeling that I wish they hadn't done it. It means war—and such a frightful war, with nothing gained. Chamberlain (according to the papers) has been

---

[1] With the Curtiss-Wright Corporation.

against this step while Halifax was for it. I suppose Chamberlain was forced to give in, with so many people against him, though I'm sure he does not want war. They have persuaded him that Germany is only bluffing and that all England has to do is to take a firm stand and aggression will be stopped.

I wish I thought so.

The discussion goes on—on technical subjects in aviation. I can't see how they can go on talking so calmly about engines. It is because Allard is an American and fundamentally not so vitally affected by war as a European. And how can Mrs. Allard go on talking about the Windsors?

Saturday, April 1st

Headlines about Chamberlain's pledge to support Poland. Chamberlain says this is only an "interim pact," part of a larger scheme of peaceful organization to resist aggression; Rumania next, etc. Everyone (France, U. S. A., Poland, and Britain) seems very pleased about this. Deep growlings from Germany about an "unnecessary and dangerous policy of encirclement." The situation is very tense.

C. and I out for our walk. It is close and overcast. He feels that if we go on like this (keeping Germany from expanding) it will mean war sooner or later. We discuss our own plans—what to do if there is war. Go to Brittany as soon as possible.

The cook says to me with tears in her eyes that her son will go (in two years) if it is war. They said at the last war it would be over in six months and it lasted four years.

I cannot work. I make lists of what to do and start to sort things and pack in three piles: things to be left in Paris (to go to Brittany), to be shipped to New York, and to go with me (including Brittany).

Sunday, April 2nd

Still good weather, though slightly overcast. Hitler's reply not violent, though warning (Germany will not stand encirclement).

But his lack of violence is taken for weakness by the foreign press.

Dress up in the Piguet dress, black coat, and new straw hat with veil for lunch at the Ritz with Agnes Herrick[1]—quite a small group of people, chiefly social, though I sat next to an intelligent American in politics *who does not want war!* This is so surprising that I underline. He is young and vigorous, too, but he sees the dangers of war, as we do, and also the wisdom of waiting and letting Germany (if that is what she is after) hang herself in the rope of her own conquests.

About suppertime Miss H. comes back, subdued but fairly well and natural. She says the feeling in England is completely changed. They all want war and are quite cheerful and resigned. She brings a rag-cheap paper with headlines on Hitler's speech: "Hitler Jittery," "Backing down." Where do they get it from—incredible wishful thinking.

Also the radio news (British) tells of complete support and approval of Chamberlain's statement, quoting U. S. A. as saying, "While it is a little early yet to say the crisis is over . . . tension eased." I may be quite wrong but I feel that they are all walking ahead blindfold and due for a terrible shock, though perhaps not imminent. I feel deeply and profoundly pessimistic—the moment one gives up hope or sees for the first time that a person that is ill will not pull through. I feel that war is coming. And I see France and England, and everything over here I love, going under. Pack and write.

Monday, April 3rd

The newspaper comments are still cheerful on the stop-aggression front. I do not feel cheerful at all.

C. gives Land a cigarette and some sherry at tea (hoping to break him early of a tendency!). He liked both!

[1] Mrs. Parmely Herrick, daughter-in-law of Ambassador Myron T. Herrick.

Tuesday, April 4th

Still wet but clearing. C. goes to England (weather improving) to take the plane back.[1]

In the evening to the Millers' for dinner. The Lin Yutangs are there. We talk politics. They are all less gloomy than I. No one really thinks Germany would win if there were a war. I quote Lloyd George's speech in the Commons yesterday. The only pessimistic note in a day of fine courageous speeches ("not an inch farther" etc!). Lloyd George is very practical. He approves of the government's move (to support Poland) but he wants to know what the government is planning to do, and then outlines the position the British are in. They cannot send one battalion to Poland. Russia is the only power that can do anything in that area in case of German attack. And the Times editorial describes it as "an inconsolable outburst of pessimism" and goes on to say that Lloyd George seems to live now in a "remote and odd world of his own."

I am not encouraged by the evening. They all take for granted that America should and would come into war.

Wednesday, April 5th

C. comes back at night (by train) and cheers me up. He has talked to Colonel Lee in London, who does not see imminent war.

Thursday, April 6th

To lunch at the Embassy at 1. Lots of people there. Odd Americans and a scattering of French. I sit between MacArthur and Mr. Wilson (of the Embassy). Mr. Wilson is, if anything, gloomier than I on the international situation. He feels, though does not say it out and out, that war is inevitable. He agrees with me that Poland is a poor issue because it is such an appealing one

---

[1] C. A. L., before leaving for the United States, returned the Mohawk plane to the manufacturer at Reading for storage. At the start of the war the Lindberghs gave the plane outright to the British government.

for the German people (they have rightful claims to the Corridor). One of the only things to count on in this coming breach is that perhaps the German people might rebel. But they will never do this on the issue of Danzig, the Corridor, and that excellent piece of propaganda(so neatly put into the Germans' hands by the English) "English encirclement." He agrees that Hitler grew out of England's and chiefly France's nonsupport of the postwar German governments. He talks of the Weimar Republic's trying to make an economic pact with Austria after the war which was stamped on by the French.

Next to Mr. Wilson is a social Frenchwoman of the kind that has no conception of what is going on at all. She says, "But surely the French will not fight for Poland. The English may . . ." Mr. Wilson just looks at her tongue-tied and I say simply, "Well, you're *pledged* to."

C. is talking with Mr. Howard[1]—a small, round, bright-eyed, checked-suited, exuberant little man of great native wit and ability.

Good Friday, April 7th

C. is packing[2] and arranging papers, plans, etc. We walk in the Bois. Just before lunch Harriet Miller calls up and tells us Italy has bombarded Durazzo (Albania). We call Information 10 (news agency constantly repeating news on telephone) and find that Italy has invaded five ports. King Zog is calling on his people to resist to the last man. The Italians say it is nothing and they are defending their nationals. . . .

C. is very worried. We call Information four or five times all afternoon.

At tea we get the English radio news. Very upset but appar-

---

[1] Roy Howard, American journalist, director of Scripps-Howard newspapers; Editor (1931–60) and President (1931–62) of the New York *World-Telegram and Sun.*

[2] C. A. L. was planning a trip back to America. A. M. L. was to follow later.

ently no immediate action will be taken. Everyone is saying, "And on Good Friday!" I think of the Queen with a three-day-old baby, bumping over those dreadful roads to Greece!

C. and I talk about developments. Germany said she would not wait until the net encircled her and she means it. They will surely strike when and where we least expect it. C. and I talk about moves in case of war: Brittany immediately.

Supper alone. C. and the Vlaminck blue and white flowers behind him on the mantel. We have had such a happy winter here. I hate to have it over.

Saturday, April 8th

C. is packing. I also. Awful atmosphere—so awful to think of his going that I wish it were over. Out for a short turn in the woods. He leaves about 12. Jon and I go out in the park until lunch and look at the flowering trees.

After lunch I take Jon to get his hair cut and also get some flowers and some Easter eggs for Jon and Land. It is a delicious day, warm and springlike. The chestnut trees on Avenue Henri-Martin are out enough to throw a shadow.

I feel, however, sunk, with C. gone. It is not just the ocean and all the heave and push I must go through before seeing him again, but the sense of war separating us.

Dinner at night at the Café de Paris with Harriet and Harlan Miller. There is music and lights and pretty hats and I feel cheered up.

(The reporters are ringing the house about C.)

Sunday, Easter, April 9th

Albania seems to be conquered. London and Paris are moving up on pacts with Greece and Turkey.

Germany is massing troops near Poland (so the papers say) and a violent press campaign against Poland is under way. It sounds ominously like September and Czechoslovakia.

Delicious day. I give Jon and Land their Easter eggs. Go out and get Jon at 11:30, scrub knees, face, comb hair, and change him into little gray trousers and sweater for the day at Mrs. Carter's. Finally start out in Mrs. Carter's car. Jon is excited by all the trains on the way—also Le Bourget airport "where Father landed."

Senlis is warm and delicious in the sunshine. Jon says, "The first time I've been out in the country since Illiec," and "Isn't it lovely!" He runs to pick dandelions on the lawn and to explore the garden.

. Jon sits next to me at a delicious meal, looks out of the window through a beautiful blue cineraria (cinerarias are very fashionable just now—strange to have fashions in flowers) and says, "Isn't it lovely outside!" He helps himself and eats nicely and his frank but quiet enjoyment and pleasure is very attractive. People like him and I am proud of him.

After lunch we lie in chairs in the sun. It is quiet and peaceful and I feel far from war, though we talk of it. They have seen Ambassador Bullitt and the Polish Ambassador that morning and report that both seem pessimistic.

We leave quite late at 7. The woods are yellow with daffodils and full of people coming home in cars, bicycles, festooned with the yellow bunches they have picked.

Jon is tired but happy. It has been great fun to go this first time visiting with him. He is a winning little boy. Old Mr. Carter said he reminded him of Daddy.

Monday, April 10th

Margaret, Trevil, and Janet Morgan come for dinner. They are quite jovial and gay, even about the international situation. Worried about coming over? Oh no, they couldn't wait around for Hitler any longer. Trevil has a surprising sense of humor for such a solid person, with a nice twist to it. He is quite keen too, only he is rather apt to say on some point, "Surely *they* must have thought of that (Chamberlain and Halifax) and they must have some reason. . . ." Rather apt to trust the powers that be to know and handle things better than he. Very British, that.

Tuesday, April 11th

A busy day. I start out by calling Mr. Wynn and Mr. MacArthur at the Embassy on Soeur Lisi's going to U. S. A. Go down to see about passage on the *Paris*.

Talk with Soeur Lisi about going to U. S. A.

After lunch Harriet Miller and I sit outside at a café on the Champs Élysées under an umbrella looking up at the pale green chestnut leaves against the pale blue spring sky and sip orangeade and discuss plans and living in Europe and America. The moment is full of leisure and happiness—one of those lovely unexpected ones.

Then I go and meet Margaret and Janet and Trevil [Morgan] at Rebattet's and we eat piles of soft ice cream under new hats (pale blue and pink birds on Margaret's) and feel like children and discuss with Anglo-Saxon humor the French taxi drivers, storekeepers, clothes, and habits in general (all of which are more understandable and natural to me than the English ones but nevertheless I laugh with them).

Then home. The seeds of the morning calls have borne fruit. Mr. Wynn has called on staterooms on the *Paris*. Mr. MacArthur and Miss H. have been discussing best methods of getting Soeur Lisi into U. S. The quota is really the safest, in case there is war and she's caught over there. We decide to try for this. Soeur Lisi wants to come but weeps and says she must go home first. We make plans for this.

Wednesday, April 12th

Soeur Lisi goes off for her passport and application for entering the U. S. A. with permission to work there.

I take the children to the park. It is really quite hot. We sit under the trees. I take pads and diary and letters but can only read the papers. One reads the papers each day with the minutest care because it is never the headlines that are really significant, one knows them already, or they are an empty form and mean nothing. One looks for straws, to guess at what next. It is the little item on the second page on the Polish Ambassador in Berlin making a trip to Warsaw to see Colonel Beck, on his arrival back from England (the Ambassador bearing Germany's terms, suggestions for negotiations, on Danzig, the Corridor, etc.?).

Or that note on the members of the Hungarian Cabinet who are going to visit Mussolini and then Hitler.

Tomorrow Chamberlain speaks to the House on his decision on guarantees to Greece and Turkey. What stand will he take? And what will be Hitler's answer—and how quickly?

Thursday, April 13th

Supper alone. (Soeur Lisi leaves for Switzerland. I feel so apprehensive that she will not come back.) Afterward hear the news. Chamberlain has announced that England will guarantee Greece and Rumania against aggression or threats of aggression. He speaks gravely of Italy's move in Albania but does not denounce the Italo-Anglo pact.

Friday, April 14th

Supper alone; read the papers. Germany's reaction angry but no particular surprise or hint of retaliation though the German fleet leaves home ports for its spring "games" off Spain on the 18th. (The Russian fleet starts its maneuvers on the 20th in the Baltic. Hitler's birthday is the 20th!)

Sunday, April 16th. Wire from C. telling me to come! Roosevelt has addressed another appeal to Hitler for peace and a pledge not to attack thirty nations in return for economic understanding. This offers something construcive but I fear it will do no good, though it may *delay* the next *Putsch.* I don't think they *can* walk into Poland on top of the appeal.

Home for tea with Mme Claudel, who is in mourning for her father. I like her so much. She is "my kind" of person and we talk easily.

Monday, April 17th

Soeur Lisi arrives! Great relief. She is happy and content, now she has seen her mother, to go to America.

We start getting ahead in earnest: telephone calls, the school, hair, suits for C., etc. I go off to Despiau as he wants to see me once again.

I sit thinking of all I could do in that hour, this last day or next to last. Near the end of the hour I can see he is getting nervous and pressed so I say I can come tomorow too. He is much relieved and pleased.

Back to lunch. The pictures stacked up to go. The apartment looks cold and bare.

Pack trunk and bags all evening. Trunks must go in the morning.

April 18th. A windy blustery day

Off for Despiau at 9:15. He not pressed and finishes early. He says he has enjoyed working on it very much, that I have been *"très sage"* as a model, that he *"garde un souvenir très spécial"* of me.

I try to say (lightly) that he has taught me a great deal. (Patience in working, and patience with those dull days, and patience that it *will* come. Patience and persistence—though I don't say all this.)

Shopping until 12; back to the house. The trunks are leaving. Pack bags. Out to lunch with Mme Claudel's brother-in-law. Our host is charming and we talk portraits and portrait painters, and I discover his wife is "La Grecque" whose head Despiau has in his studio and that I have looked at so often. I enjoy it but in spite of my protestations yesterday that I could only go to a short lunch, as I had an appointment at 2:20, they don't sit down until 1:30 or leave the table till 2:30. I leave immediately, much annoyed and flustered inside and rush to the dentist. A patient has canceled her time, so it is not so bad. Another siege.

Write notes in evening; listen on radio for any sudden developments to keep us from going.

At 7:15 Angèle knocks on my door (I am dead with sleep), with that scared-rabbit look she has, to say that "the boat that Madame was to sail on has burned up with all the pictures on it." I am stunned and think it is a dream ("My pictures!" I think in a dull panic. No—the pictures for the Fair. However, it seems they were not burnt up, but all rescued.) She says she heard it on the radio at 6:30 and she thought right away she had better wake Madame early and tell her (Why, of all stupid things!). She opens the blinds. "Well," I say, *"il n'y a rien à faire,"* and turn over again and think it out: (1) Is it true? (2) Where are our trunks? (3) If true, what next boat can we take? Don't want to waste that money. Will they refund it or only give you passage on next French boat? Which is the *Normandie* on the 26th. When does Hitler make his speech? The 28th. Is it safe to stay in Paris? Then get up, read the papers. It seems true. Mr. Wynn calls and like a wizard gets to work on a new passage. The French line are putting on the *Champlain* to take the passengers of the *Paris*. We get cabins on that.

Up early and wake Jon. Apparently nothing has happened to the *Champlain* and we are really leaving. Jon in his new gray hat. Good-bys, much wringing of hands. They all take it very dramatically—very French. Pile into the taxis and set off; a nice day. "Look, Jon! Look back at the chestnut trees!" I say in the taxi as we enter Avenue Henri-Martin. "You must remember the chestnut trees." (The big full ones in the Bois are just out.)

"I think I'll remember them," said Jon gravely smiling.

And as I think of it, all of Paris is linked with the chestnut trees. When we first came it was the chestnuts themselves that Jon collected. Then the sprouting chestnuts (wormlike, red and white curling sprouts) and the chestnut buds brown, sticky, cracking white, on broken branches. Then watching the trees bloom, walking to school. Buds opening, green sprouting, and the buds of flowers and then the unbelievable green shade from leaves. Jon's "street of marronniers" in the Bois where I wheeled the carriage so often. Eating under the fresh green chestnut leaves at Armenonville in the Bois. Sitting on the Champs Élysées with Mrs. Miller under chestnut leaves against a pale blue sky, on that first delirious day of spring.

And then suddenly the whole of Paris seemed full of chestnut blossoms—candles on the trees (the perfect pattern of them), white dust of broken flowers on the pavements, gutters, streets, torn by the wind (picked up by Jon and taken home wilted to be put in a tooth-brush glass). Chestnut trees everywhere suddenly come to life—one was startlingly aware of them. They pervaded the place like a song you can't forget or a perfume all-pervading, like being in love, like spring.

We get to the station in plenty of time, change money, buy magazines, and get Land a net bag for the ball.

Félix is there. We get on the train compartment with all the bags. A very easy walk past cameramen on the platform. They don't spot us until we are inside. They ask for pictures. I refuse, of course, but dread Le Havre. Miss H. leaves. She has been so nice and understanding. It has been an unspoken kind of relationship. Casually she came, was, and left. I am so sorry to lose her. It is the last of England that goes with her. She is a person of sensitivity and real quality.

We leave. Jon is entranced looking out of the window. The suburbs of Paris are overflowing with lilac, fruit blossom, and green. It is very beautiful. We watch the Seine. Land gets tired and fusses near the end. He wants to sit on my lap (and does!).

At Le Havre there are *no* photographers! Only two or three local reporters who had seen C. and me at the airfield. They are quite nice and don't press me at all.

Onto the boat and to our cabins with no trouble—much relieved. Down to lunch with the children in the "children's dining room." Land to bed in a crib put up for him—quite peaceful, though very tired.

Jon and I (as all seems quiet) go up on deck and walk around;

very few people. We see the *Paris* lying over on its side in the water. A really shocking sight (that anything so big and secure as a liner could collapse like that). Coming back an elderly gentleman stops us, politely raises his hat, and offers the "greetings" of the International News Service. I say I have nothing to say. He says he isn't going to bother us, but just one question: "How long are we going to stay?" I say I have nothing to say and pull off. Then he says conversationally, "Have you seen the *Paris?*" I say, "I have nothing to say" again, but poor Jon leaps out: "But *I* have. *I* saw it. *I* . . ." "Oh, *you* have, have you, my little man!"

But I pull him away as gracefully as I can, still talking, down to the cabin. I then explain to Jon as best I can about reporters and not speaking to *anyone* unless I say it is all right. Always, if he is not sure, to ask me; "Is he a reporter?" But I feel flustered and annoyed at the incident, at having to restrict Jon, at myself for not having foreseen the incident. What will C. think?

We don't come up again until after teatime at 6. The gongs have rung and I think it safe. Even then a fluttery old lady comes up to me from the Paris *Herald,* but I say nothing and she scurries off. Jon says, "Who was that?" "That was a reporter too." Astonishment: "I thought there were only men reporters!"

I arrange for chairs. Land runs up and down the deck in his little blue linen coat. He is so manly and independent, everyone looks at him and watches him with admiration. But there is no fulsome attention.

I sit with the children as they eat supper. Jon, standing at the portholes, watching the boats: "I am very happy," he says, "seeing the boats and everything!"

I eat dinner alone in the big *salle à manger*. The food is good. I sit alone and feel content but only wish C. were there. Looking at the menus with pictures of Normandy lanes and Brittany rocks and hearing the French around me I feel suddenly with a pang at leaving it: How I love France, I love its country, and I love its people. The people one can talk to at dinner tables but also the simple people. Despiau in his studio the other day talking about the French rallying calmly and heroically to this crisis. The fathers in the park playing ball with their children on Sundays. The innkeepers. The Brittany fishermen.

I really love it all very deeply. I never felt this way about England. I love and feel close to certain people in England. I admire a small class (an intellectual, not a social, class). I loved Long Barn and the country around it like my own flesh and blood. But "England and the English" I do not love the way I love "France and the French." It is like falling in love, and this discovery of it—on leaving it—is like being in love, too, but not realizing it until suddenly, with a pang, you find you are without the person.

INDEX

Index